Lecture Notes in Computer Scie

Edited by G. Goos, J. Hartmanis, and J. van

T0250838

Springer

Berlin
Heidelberg
New York
Barcelona
Hong Kong
London
Milan
Paris
Tokyo

Grzegorz Rozenberg

Wilfried Brauer   Hartmut Ehrig
Juhani Karhumäki   Arto Salomaa (Eds.)

Formal and
Natural Computing

Essays Dedicated to Grzegorz Rozenberg

 Springer

Volume Editors

Wilfried Brauer
Technical University of Munich, Computer Science Department
Arcisstraße 21, 80333 Munich, Germany
E-mail: brauer@informatik.tu-muenchen.de

Hartmut Ehrig
Technical University of Berlin, Computer Science Department
Franklinstraße 28/29, 10587 Berlin, Germany
E-mail: ehrig@cs.tu-berlin.de

Juhani Karhumäki
University of Turku, Department of Mathematics
20014 Turku, Finland
E-mail: karhumak@cs.utu.fi

Arto Salomaa
Turku Centre for Computer Science
Lemminkäisenkatu 14A, 20520 Turku, Finland
E-mail: asalomaa@cs.utu.fi

The illustration appearing on the cover of this book is the work of Daniel Rozenberg (DADARA).

Cataloging-in-Publication Data applied for

Die Deutsche Bibliothek - CIP-Einheitsaufnahme

Formal and natural computing : essays dedicated to Grzegorz Rozenberg /
Wilfried Brauer ... (ed.). - Berlin ; Heidelberg ; New York ; Barcelona ;
Hong Kong ; London ; Milan ; Paris ; Tokyo : Springer, 2002
    (Lecture notes in computer science ; Vol. 2300)
    ISBN 3-540-43190-X

CR Subject Classification (1998): F.1-3, F.4.2, E.1, G.2

ISSN 0302-9743
ISBN 3-540-43190-X Springer-Verlag Berlin Heidelberg New York

Springer-Verlag Berlin Heidelberg New York
a member of BertelsmannSpringer Science+Business Media GmbH

http://www.springer.de

© Springer-Verlag Berlin Heidelberg 2002
Printed in Germany

Typesetting: Camera-ready by author, data conversion by Boller Mediendesign
Printed on acid-free paper   SPIN: 10846466   06/3142   5 4 3 2 1 0

Preface

This book presents state of the art research in theoretical computer science and related fields. In particular, the following areas are discussed: automata theory, formal languages and combinatorics of words, graph transformations, Petri nets, concurrency, as well as natural and molecular computing. The articles are written by leading researchers in these areas. The writers were originally invited to contribute to this book but then the normal refereeing procedure was applied as well. All of the articles deal with some issue that has been under vigorous study during recent years. Still, the topics range from very classical ones to issues raised only two or three years ago. Both survey articles and papers attacking specific research problems are included.

The book highlights some key issues of theoretical computer science, as they seem to us now at the beginning of the new millennium. Being a comprehensive overview of some of the most active current research in theoretical computer science, it should be of definite interest for all researchers in the areas covered. The topics range from basic decidability and the notion of information to graph grammars and graph transformations, and from trees and traces to aqueous algorithms, DNA encoding and self-assembly. Special effort has been given to lucid presentation. Therefore, the book should be of interest also for advanced students.

The feature common to all writers in this book is that they want to dedicate their work to *Grzegorz Rozenberg* on the occasion of his 60th birthday, March 14, 2002. In addition the topics belong to areas of his central interests, either currently or in the past. The broad spectrum of the topics is an indication of the width and diversity of the research of this great scientist. We have included in this book the bibliography of Grzegorz Rozenberg but we have not undertaken here the challenging task of describing or even outlining his scientific work. Instead, at the end of this Preface, each of the four editors presents his personal gratulatory greeting to Grzegorz. It is also very well known that Grzegorz Rozenberg occupies a central role in the theoretical computer science community in Europe. He was the President of EATCS for nine years and is still the Editor of the *EATCS Bulletin*, after being in this position already for more than twenty years. More about these matters can be read, for instance, in the book *People and Ideas in Theoretical Computer Science* (C. Calude, Ed.), Springer-Verlag, 1999, ISBN 981-4021-13-X, or in the *EATCS Bulletin* 46, 1992, 391–413.

The articles in this book are divided into five parts, according to their topics. A brief description of the individual parts now follows.

As its title *Words, Languages, Automata* indicates, the first part is concerned with the oldest issues in theoretical computer science. However, the papers reflect some currently active aspects of research. Classical context-free languages are considered in connection with the currently popular XML-documentation. Another old topic studies how simpler languages (for example regular languages) can be used via trees to define more complicated ones (namely, context-free languages). Models of concurrency are discussed in two papers, using structural and logical approaches, respectively. The other four papers are connected to words. In two of those, old fundamental problems are addressed, namely, the celebrated Post Correspondence Problem and the commutation problem of Conway. Patterns occurring in infinite words is a challenging new topic. Finally, recent fundamental results on the structure of finite words are related to the notion of information.

Part two on graph transformations starts with a sightseeing tour of the computational landscape of this interesting field. The relationship between local action systems and algebraic graph grammars and bisimulation equivalences for graph grammars are discussed in two other contributions.

The concept of processes is addressed in part three on Petri nets from the high-level net point of view. Moreover, it is shown how Petri nets can be used as a control mechanism for grammar systems. Finally an interesting conjecture is presented relating regular event structures and finite Petri nets.

In addition to graph transformations and Petri nets, in part four, other models for concurrent computing are discussed. It is shown how object-oriented collaborative work can be supported by the concept of team automata. Other interesting topics are temporal concurrent constraint programming and how to use grammars as processes.

The final part deals with natural computing. Computation gleaned from nature is at its best in the article describing the amazing capabilities of ciliates. Studies about aqueous algorithms and self-assembly computations are also close to practical laboratory work. P systems have turned out to be a very useful model for natural computing. Some of the early aspects of DNA computing, namely splicing and DNA encoding, are addressed in two papers.

Acknowledgements. We thank all the authors and referees for their cooperation and timely work. We express our gratitude to Dadara for the cover, and to Hendrik Jan Hoogeboom and Marloes Boon–van der Nat for their help in various "local" matters. Special thanks are due to Arto Lepistö for unifying the files for print, and in many cases preparing parts of the script in the format required. Finally, thanks are due to Springer-Verlag, especially Mrs. Ingeborg Mayer.

Munich, Berlin and   Wilfried Brauer, Hartmut Ehrig

Turku, December 2001   Juhani Karhumäki, Arto Salomaa

Wilfried Brauer, personal greeting

Dear Nonpareil Amiable Grzegorz,

Sure, there are many more attributes fitting to you – but these are not suited to denote the area of your current scientific interest. Nevertheless, I cannot resist mentioning some more of your characteristics. Cooperative, multi-interested and witty: these features became evident to me when we first met (in the early 1970s) at Oberwolfach where you demonstrated how to squeeze languages out of Lindenmayer systems. Already then you did fruitful interdisciplinary research with biologists – as you do now in DNA computing. Quick to comprehend and speedy in entering new fields of research: so you conquered the area of Petri nets and concurrency after I invited you in 1979 to the first Advanced Course on Petri Nets in Hamburg. Determined, influential and winning: I got to know these traits of yours especially when you came onto the board of EATCS and (with many new ideas and activities) pushed EATCS forward on its way to becoming a large well-organized international scientific society. You are a good friend: this became obvious to all the many persons who listened to the excellent and cordial laudatio you presented at the festive colloquium in Munich on the occasion of my 60th birthday. And now it is your turn to celebrate this special birthday. I hope you will have a similar experience as I (and many others) have had: from this age on one looks at disorders and troubles from a more distant point of view and develops a more serene and calm attitude of mind. My congratulations and all my best wishes to you.

Wilfried

Hartmut Ehrig, personal greeting

Dear Grzegorz,

When I visited you for the first time in Utrecht you invited me to one of the famous pancake houses to investigate stacks of pancakes. In this way I learned by eating about the relationship between stacks in different areas, like computer science, biology and real life. Consequently we established a link between our favorite topics at that time, L-systems and graph grammars, leading not only to the new topic of parallel graph grammars, but also to the first international workshop on graph grammars with applications in computer science and biology. This first international workshop in 1978 was continued by five other ones in Europe and the USA until the last one in 1998. This, however, was not the end of graph grammars and graph transformations, but the starting point of a series of international conferences on graph transformations.

The special present from the entire graph transformation community and especially myself on your 60th birthday is the first International Conference on Graph Transformations, to be held in Barcelona, October 7–12, 2002. Let me thank you for your continuous support and cooperation concerning scientific as well as real-life topics, and I wish you all the best for the future in science and real life and the continuation of our friendship for further decades.

Hartmut

Juhani Karhumäki, personal greeting

Dear Grzegorz:

I met you for the first time in 1974 at the Workshop on Unusual Automata Theory in Aarhus. Two years later I was lucky to have you on the committee that heard the defence of my dissertation, and after that even luckier to work with you on scientific problems. In those years, and later, I learnt a lot from you not only about the spirit of science, but also about life itself. One teaching was: what ever you do, do it as well as you can – or even better! In all of your activities, whether it is writing papers, organizing conferences or collecting owls, this principle is strictly followed. After saying this I should not say anything about your unmatched scientific achievements. However, I will take a risk. You have written just one article on the theory of codes. This, written jointly with Andrzej, solved one of the main problems of the field. It provided a method, subsequently known as the Ehrenfeucht-Rozenberg method, for how to embed a rational code into a rational maximal one. This result amazed the French School and others who had worked for years on the problem. Still, it is only one of the jewels you have created.

I wish you all the best in all areas of your activities, including collecting owls.

Juhani

Arto Salomaa, personal greeting

Dear Bolgani:

Another scientist with his birthday on March 14, Albert Einstein, once said: *It would be possible to describe everything scientifically, but it would make no sense; it would be without meaning, as if you described a Beethoven symphony as a variation of wave pressure.* Let us look at your bibliography in this book. No matter how impressive it is and no matter how many landmark papers it contains, still much of Bolgani's magical impact in opening new vistas lies elsewhere than in numbered papers. I have experienced this personally already for over three decades. Cooperation with Bolgani, be it about L systems or ciliates, about decidability or finite automata, has been for me an inexhaustible source of ideas and inspiration. Our discussions about science also went on to considerations about important matters in life. Many questions remained unanswered, perhaps we will find an answer in Jerusalem. But we always had great fun.

On your birthday, I wish you all the best for the years to come, both in life and in science.

Tarzan

Table of Contents

III   Petri Nets

IV   Concurrent Computing

V   Molecular Computing

Bibliography of Grzegorz Rozenberg

A. Books

5. A. Ehrenfeucht, T. Harju, G. Rozenberg: *The Theory of 2-structures – A Framework for Decomposition and Transformation of Graphs*, World Scientific, 1999.

4. G. Paun, G. Rozenberg, A. Salomaa: *DNA Computing - New Computing Paradigms*, Texts in Theoretical Computer Science - An EATCS Series, Springer-Verlag, 1998.

3. G. Rozenberg, A. Salomaa: *Cornerstones of Undecidability*, International Series in Computer Science, Prentice Hall, 1994.

2. G. Rozenberg, A. Salomaa: *The Mathematical Theory of L Systems*, Academic Press, 1980.

1. G.T. Herman, G. Rozenberg: *Developmental Systems and Languages*, North-Holland/American Elsevier, Amsterdam, 1975.

B. Edited Books

51. G.A. Agha, F. De Cindio, G. Rozenberg (Eds.): *Concurrent Object-Oriented Programming and Petri Nets (Advances in Petri Nets)*, Lecture Notes in Computer Science **2001**, Springer-Verlag, 2001.

50. A. Condon, G. Rozenberg (Eds.): *DNA Computing - 6th International Workshop on DNA-based Computers, DNA 2000, Leiden, The Netherlands*, Lecture Notes in Computer Science **2054**, Springer-Verlag, 2001.

49. G. Paun, G. Rozenberg, A. Salomaa (Eds.): *Current Trends in Theoretical Computer Science – Entering the 21st Century*, World Scientific, 2001.

48. H. Ehrig, G. Engels, H.-J. Kreowski, G. Rozenberg (Eds.): *Theory and Applications of Graph Transformations, 6th International Workshop, TAGT'98*, Lecture Notes in Computer Science **1764**, Springer-Verlag, 2000.

47. G. Rozenberg, W. Thomas (Eds.): *Developments in Language Theory, Foundations, Applications, and Perspectives*, World Scientific, 2000.

46. J. Billington, M. Diaz, G. Rozenberg (Eds.): *Application of Petri Nets to Communication Networks (Advances in Petri Nets)*, Lecture Notes in Computer Science **1605**, Springer-Verlag, 1999.

45. H. Ehrig, H.-J. Kreowski, U. Montanari, G. Rozenberg (Eds.): *Handbook of Graph Grammars and Computing by Graph Transformation, Volume 3: Concurrency, Parallelism, and Distribution*, World Scientific, 1999.

44. J. Karhumäki, H. Maurer, G. Paun, G. Rozenberg (Eds.): *Jewels Are Forever, Contributions to Theoretical Computer Science in Honor of Arto Salomaa*, Springer-Verlag, 1999.

43. J. Karhumäki, A. Mateescu, G. Rozenberg (Eds.) Special Issue of Fundamenta Informaticae Dedicated to Arto Salomaa, 38, 1999.

42. W. Reisig, G. Rozenberg (Eds.): *Lectures on Petri Nets, I: Basic Models (Advances in Petri Nets)*, Lecture Notes in Computer Science **1491**, Springer-Verlag, 1998.

41. W. Reisig, G. Rozenberg (Eds.): *Lectures on Petri Nets, II: Applications (Advances in Petri Nets)*, Lecture Notes in Computer Science **1492**, Springer-Verlag, 1998.

40. G. Rozenberg, F. Vaandrager (Eds.): *Lectures on Embedded Systems*, Lecture Notes in Computer Science **1494**, Springer-Verlag, 1998.

39. J. Mycielski, G. Rozenberg, A. Salomaa (Eds.): *Structures in Logic and Computer Science - A Selection of Essays in Honor of A. Ehrenfeucht*, Lecture Notes in Computer Science **1261**, Springer-Verlag, 1997.

38. G. Rozenberg (Ed.): *Handbook of Graph Grammars and Computing by Graph Transformation, Volume 1: Foundations*, World Scientific, 1997.

37. G. Rozenberg, A. Salomaa (Eds.): *Handbook of Formal Languages, Volume 1: Word, Language, Grammar*, Springer-Verlag, 1997.

36. G. Rozenberg, A. Salomaa (Eds.): *Handbook of Formal Languages, Volume 2: Linear Modelling: Background and Application*, Springer-Verlag, 1997.

35. G. Rozenberg, A. Salomaa (Eds.): *Handbook of Formal Languages, Volume 3: Beyond Words*, Springer-Verlag, 1997.

34. G. Rozenberg, A. Salomaa (Eds.): *Special Issue on Formal Language Theory*, Theoretical Computer Science **183**, 1997.

33. J. Cuny, H. Ehrig, G. Engels, G. Rozenberg (Eds.): *Graph Grammars and Their Application to Computer Science*, Lecture Notes in Computer Science **1073**, Springer-Verlag, 1996.

32. G. Rozenberg (Ed.): *Special Issue on Petri Nets*, Theoretical Computer Science **153**, Springer-Verlag, 1996.

31. G. Rozenberg (Ed.): *Special Issue on Formal Language Theory*, Fundamenta Informaticae **25**(3,4), 1996.

30. J. Dassow, G. Rozenberg, A. Salomaa (Eds.): *Developments in Language Theory II - At the Crossroads of Mathematics, Computer Science and Biology*, World Scientific, 1995.

29. V. Diekert, G. Rozenberg (Eds.): *The Book of Traces*, World Scientific, 1995.

28. J.W. de Bakker, W.-P. de Roever, G. Rozenberg (Eds.): *A Decade of Concurrency, Reflections and Perspectives*, Lecture Notes in Computer Science **803**, Springer-Verlag, 1994.

27. J. Karhumäki, H. Maurer, G. Rozenberg (Eds.): *Results and Trends in Theoretical Computer Science, Colloquium in Honor of Arto Salomaa, Graz, Austria*, Lecture Notes in Computer Science **812**, Springer-Verlag, 1994.

26. E. Best, G. Rozenberg (Eds.): *Special Issue of Selected Papers of the Third Workshop on Concurrency and Compositionality, Goslar, Germany, March 1991*, Theoretical Computer Science **114** (1), June 1993.

25. B. Courcelle, G. Rozenberg (Eds.): *Special Issue of Selected Papers of the International Workshop on Computing by Graph Transformation, Bordeaux, France, 1991*, Theoretical Computer Science **109** (1-2), March 1993.

24. G. Rozenberg (Ed.): *Advances in Petri Nets 1992*, Lecture Notes in Computer Science **609**, Springer-Verlag, Berlin, 1993.

23. G. Rozenberg, A. Salomaa (Eds.): *Current Trends in Theoretical Computer Science, Essays and Tutorials*, Series in Computer Science **40**, World Scientific Publishing, Singapore, 1993.

22. A. Salomaa, G. Rozenberg (Eds.): *Developments in Language Theory - At the Crossroads of Mathematics, Computer Science and Biology*, World Scientific, 1993.

21. G. Rozenberg, A. Salomaa (Eds.): *Lindenmayer Systems*, Springer-Verlag, 1992.

20. J.W. de Bakker, W.P. de Roever, G. Rozenberg (Eds.): *Foundations of Object-Oriented Languages (REX School/Workshop, Noordwijkerhout)*, Lecture Notes in Computer Science **489**, Springer-Verlag, Berlin, 1991.

19. H. Ehrig, H.-J. Kreowski, G. Rozenberg (Eds.): *Graph Grammars and Their Application to Computer Science (4th International Workshop, Bremen, Germany)*, Lecture Notes in Computer Science **532**, Springer-Verlag, Berlin, 1991.

18. K. Jensen, G. Rozenberg (Eds.): *High-Level Petri Nets, Theory and Applications*, Springer-Verlag, Berlin, 1991.

17. G. Rozenberg (Ed.): *Advances in Petri Nets 1991*, Lecture Notes in Computer Science **524**, Springer-Verlag, Berlin, 1991.

16. G. Rozenberg (Ed.): *Advances in Petri Nets 1990*, Lecture Notes in Computer Science **483**, Springer-Verlag, Berlin, 1991.

15. J.W. de Bakker, W.-P. de Roever, G. Rozenberg (Eds.): *Stepwise Refinement of Distributed Systems; Models, Formalisms, Correctness, REX Workshop, May/June 1989*, Lecture Notes in Computer Science **430**, Springer-Verlag, Berlin, 1990.

14. G. Rozenberg (Ed.): *Advances in Petri Nets 1989*, Lecture Notes in Computer Science **424**, Springer-Verlag, Berlin, 1990.

13. W. Brauer, W. Reisig, G. Rozenberg (Eds.): *Petri Nets: Central Models and Their Properties - Advances in Petri Nets 1986, Part I*, Lecture Notes in Computer Science **254**, Springer-Verlag, 1987.

12. W. Brauer, W. Reisig, G. Rozenberg (Eds.): *Petri Nets: Applications and Relationships to Other Models of Concurrency - Advances in Petri Nets 1986, Part II*, Lecture Notes in Computer Science **255**, Springer-Verlag, 1987.

11. H. Ehrig, M. Nagl, G. Rozenberg, A. Rosenfeld (Eds.): *Graph-Grammars and Their Application to Computer Science*, Lecture Notes in Computer Science **291**, Springer-Verlag, 1987.

10. G. Rozenberg (Ed.):*Advances in Petri Nets 1987*, Lecture Notes in Computer Science **266**, Springer-Verlag, 1987.

9.   K. Voss, H.J. Genrich, G. Rozenberg (Eds.): *Concurrency and Nets*, Springer-Verlag, 1987.

8.   J.W. de Bakker, W.P. de Roever, G. Rozenberg (Eds.): *Current Trends in Concurrency*, Lecture Notes in Computer Science **224**, Springer-Verlag, 1986.

7.   G. Rozenberg (Ed.): *Advances in Petri Nets 1985*, Lecture Notes in Computer Science, Springer-Verlag, 1986.

6.   A. Salomaa, G. Rozenberg (Eds.): *The Book of L*, Springer-Verlag, 1986.

5.   H. Ehrig, M. Nagl, G. Rozenberg (Eds.): *Graph-Grammars and Their Application to Computer Science*, Lecture Notes in Computer Science **153**, Springer-Verlag, 1983.

4.   A. Pagnoni, G. Rozenberg (Eds.): *Applications and Theory of Petri Nets*, Informatik Fachberichte **66**, Springer-Verlag, 1983.

3.   V. Claus, H. Ehrig, G. Rozenberg (Eds.): *Proceedings of the International Workshop on Graph Grammars and Their Application to Computer Science and Biology*, Lecture Notes in Computer Science **73**, Springer-Verlag, 1978.

2.   A. Lindenmayer, G. Rozenberg (Eds.): *Automata, Languages, Development*, North-Holland, Amsterdam, 1976.

1.   G. Rozenberg, A. Salomaa (Eds.): *L Systems*, Lecture Notes in Computer Science **15**, 1974.

C. Papers

349. Team Automata for CSCW, in: Proceedings of the 2nd International Colloquium on Petri Net Technologies for Modelling Communication Based Systems (H. Weber, H. Ehrig, W. Reisig, Eds.), Fraunhofer Institute for Software and Systems Engineering, Berlin, Germany, 1–20 (with M.H. ter Beek, C.A. Ellis, J. Kleijn), 2001.

348. Team Automata for Spatial Access Control, in: Proceedings of the 7th European Conference on Computer-Supported Cooperative Work (ECSCW 2001), Bonn, Germany, 2001 (W. Prinz, M. Jarke, Y. Rogers, K. Schmidt, V. Wulf, Eds.), Kluwer Academic Publishers, Dordrecht, 59–77 (with M.H. ter Beek, C.A. Ellis, J. Kleijn), 2001.

347. Synchronizations in Team Automata for Groupware Systems, Computer Supported Cooperative Work, (with M.H. ter Beek, C.A. Ellis, J. Kleijn), 2001.

346. Sequences of Languages in Forbidding-Enforcing Families, Soft Computing **5**, 121–125 (with A. Ehrenfeucht, H.J. Hoogeboom, N. van Vugt), 2001.

345. Formal Properties of PA-matching, Theoretical Computer Science **262**, 117–131 (with S. Kobayashi, V. Mitrana, G. Paun), 2001.

344. String Tile Models for DNA Computing by Self-assembly, Lecture Notes in Computer Science **2054**, 63–88, Springer-Verlag (with E. Winfree, T. Eng), 2001.

343. Pancyclicity of Switching Classes, Information Processing Letters **73**, 153–156 (with A. Ehrenfeucht, J. Hage, T. Harju), 2000.

342. Complexity Issues in Switching of Graphs, Lecture Notes in Computer Science **1764**, 59–70, Springer-Verlag (with A. Ehrenfeucht, J. Hage, T. Harju), 2000.

341. Forbidding and Enforcing, in: *DNA Based Computers V* (E. Winfree, D. Gifford, Eds.), DIMACS Series in Discrete Mathematics and Theoretical Computer Science **54**, 195–206 (with A. Ehrenfeucht, H.J. Hoogeboom, N. van Vugt), 2000.

340. Universal and Simple Operations for Gene Assembly in Ciliates, in: Where Mathematics, Computer Science and Biology Meet (C. Martín-Vide, V. Mitrana, Eds.), Kluwer Academic Publishers, 329–342 (with A. Ehrenfeucht, I. Petre, D.M. Prescott), 2000.

339. Double-Pullback Graph Transitions: A Rule-Based Framework with Incomplete Information, Lecture Notes in Computer Science **1764**, 85–102, Springer-Verlag (with H. Ehrig, R. Heckel, M. Llabrés, F. Orejas, J. Padberg), 2000.

338. Computing with DNA by Operating on Plasmids, Biosystems **57**, 87–93 (with T. Head, R.S. Bladergroen, C.K.D. Breek, P.H.M. Lommerse, H.P. Spaink), 2000.

337. On Strongly Context-Free Languages, Discrete Applied Mathematics **103**, 153–165 (with L. Ilie, G. Paun, A. Salomaa), 2000.

336. A Characterization of Poly-slender Context-Free Languages, R.A.I.R.O. – Informatique Théorique et Applications **34**, 77–86 (with L. Ilie, I. Petre), 2000.

335. Uniformly Scattered Factors, in: Finite VS Infinite, Contributions to an Eternal Dilemma (C. Calude, G. Paun, Eds.), Discrete Mathematics and Theoretical Computer Science **243**, Springer-Verlag, London UK, 187–198 (with L. Ilie, I. Petre), 2000.

334. Membrane Computing with External Output, Fundamenta Informaticae **41**, 313–340 (with G. Paun, A. Salomaa), 2000.

333. Cross-Fertilization between Evolutionary Computing and DNA-based Computing, in: Proceedings of the 1999 Congress on Evolutionary Computing, 980–987 (with T. Bäck, J.N. Kok), 1999.

332. Watson-Crick Finite Automata, in: 3rd DIMACS Workshop on DNA Based Computers (H. Rubin, D.H. Wood, Eds.), DIMACS Series in Discrete Mathematics **48**, 297–327 (with R. Freund, G. Paun, A. Salomaa), 1999.

331. Contexts on Trajectories, International Journal of Computer Mathematics **73**, 15–36 (with C. Martín-Vide, A. Mateescu, A. Salomaa), 1999.

330. X-Families: An Approach to the Study of Families of Syntactically Similar Languages, in: Issues in Mathematical Linguistics (C. Martín-Vide, Ed.), Studies in Functional and Structural Linguistics **47**, John Benjamins, Amsterdam, 145–163 (with C. Martín-Vide, G. Paun, A. Salomaa), 1999.

329. Some Properties of Duplication Grammars, Acta Cybernetica **14**, 165–177 (with V. Mitrana), 1999.

328. DNA Computing: New Ideas and Paradigms, Lecture Notes in Computer Science **1644**, 106–118, Springer-Verlag (with A. Salomaa), 1999.

327. Permutations, Parenthesis Words, and Schroeder Numbers, Discrete Mathematics **190**, 259–264 (with A. Ehrenfeucht, T. Harju, P. ten Pas), 1998.

326. On Representing Recursively Enumerable Languages by Internal Contextual Languages, Theoretical Computer Science **205**, 61–83 (with A. Ehrenfeucht, G. Paun), 1998.

325. Bidirectional Sticker Systems, in: Pacific Symposium on Biocomputing (R.B. Altman, A.K. Dunker, L. Hunter, T.E. Klein, Eds.), v. 3, World Scientific, Singapore, 535–546 (with R. Freund, G. Paun, A. Salomaa), 1998.

324. DNA Computing, Sticker Systems, and Universality, Acta Informatica **35**, 401–420 (with L. Kari, G. Paun, A. Salomaa, S. Yu), 1998.

323. Universality Results for Finite H Systems and Watson-Crick Finite Automata, in: Computing with Bio-Molecules, Theory and Experiments (G. Paun, Ed.), Springer-Verlag, Singapore, 200–220 (with C. Martín-Vide, G. Paun, A. Salomaa), 1998.

322. Simple Splicing Systems, Discrete Applied Mathematics **84**, 145–163 (with A. Mateescu, G. Paun, A. Salomaa), 1998.

321. Characterizations of RE Languages Starting from Internal Contextual Languages, International Journal of Computer Mathematics **66**, 179–197 (with A. Mateescu, G. Paun, A. Salomaa), 1998.

320. Shuffle on Trajectories: Syntactic Constraints (Fundamental Study), Theoretical Computer Science **197**, 1–56 (with A. Mateescu, A. Salomaa), 1998.

319. Sticker Systems, Theoretical Computer Science **204**, 183–203 (with G. Paun), 1998.

318. Complementarity versus Universality: Keynotes of DNA Computing, Complexity **4**, 14–19 (with G. Paun, A. Salomaa), 1998.

317. Elementary Net Systems, Lecture Notes in Computer Science **1491**, 12–121, Springer-Verlag (with J. Engelfriet), 1998.

316. Grammar Systems, in: Handbook of Formal Languages, Volume 2: Linear Modelling: Background and Application (G. Rozenberg, A. Salomaa, Eds.), Springer-Verlag, 155–213 (with J. Dassow, G. Paun), 1997.

315. 2-structures – A Framework for Decomposition and Transformation of Graphs, in: Handbook of Graph Grammars and Computing by Graph

Transformation, Volume 1: Foundations (G. Rozenberg, Ed.), World Scientific, 401–478 (with A. Ehrenfeucht, T. Harju), 1997.

314. Invariants of Inversive 2-structures on Groups of Labels, Mathematical Structures in Computer Science **7**, 303–327 (with A. Ehrenfeucht, T. Harju), 1997.

313. Semantics of Nonsequential Tree-Based Computation Schemes, Fundamenta Informaticae **29**, 305–324 (with A. Ehrenfeucht, K. Salomaa), 1997.

312. Node Replacement Graph Grammars, in: Handbook of Graph Grammars and Computing by Graph Transformation, Volume 1: Foundations (G. Rozenberg, Ed.), World Scientific, 1–94 (with J. Engelfriet), 1997.

311. L Systems, in: Handbook of Formal Languages, Volume 1: Word, Language, Grammar (G. Rozenberg, A. Salomaa, Eds.), Springer-Verlag, 253–328 (with L. Kari, A. Salomaa), 1997.

310. Shuffle-like Operations on Omega-Words, Lecture Notes in Computer Science **1218**, 395–411, Springer-Verlag (with A. Mateescu, G.R. Mateescu, A. Salomaa), 1997.

309. Geometric Transformations of Language Families: The Power of Symmetry, International Journal of Foundations of Computer Science **8**, 1–14 (with A. Mateescu, A. Salomaa), 1997.

308. Syntactic and Semantic Aspects of Parallellism, Lecture Notes in Computer Science **1337**, 79–105, Springer-Verlag (with A. Mateescu, A. Salomaa), 1997.

307. Contextual Grammars and Formal Languages, in: Handbook of Formal Languages, Volume 2: Linear Modelling: Background and Application (G. Rozenberg, A. Salomaa, Eds.), Springer-Verlag, 237–293 (with G. Paun), 1997.

306. Computing by Splicing: Programmed and Evolving Splicing Systems, in: Proceedings of the 1997 IEEE International Conference on Evolutionary Computation (ICEC'97), 273–278 (with G. Paun, A. Salomaa), 1997.

305. Finite Languages for the Representation of Finite Graphs, Journal of Computer and System Sciences **52**, 170–184 (with A. Ehrenfeucht, J. Engelfriet), 1996.

304. Group Based Graph Transformations and Hierarchical Representations of Graphs, Lecture Notes in Computer Science **1073**, 502–520, Springer-Verlag (with A. Ehrenfeucht, T. Harju), 1996.

303. On Representing RE Languages by One-Sided Internal Contextual Languages, Acta Cybernetica **12**, 217–233 (with A. Ehrenfeucht, A. Mateescu, Gh. Paun, A. Salomaa), 1996.

302. A Note on Binary Grammatical Codes of Trees, Theoretical Computer Science **155**, 425–438 (with A. Ehrenfeucht, P. ten Pas), 1996.

301. Linear Landscape of External Contextual Languages, Acta Informatica **33**, 571–594 (with A. Ehrenfeucht, G. Paun), 1996.

300. Characterization and Complexity of Uniformly Nonprimitive Labeled 2-structures, Theoretical Computer Science **154**, 247–282 (with J. Engelfriet, T. Harju, A. Proskurowski), 1996.

299. Pattern Systems, Theoretical Computer Science **154**, 183–201 (with V. Mitrana, Gh. Paun, A. Salomaa), 1996.

298. Computing by Splicing, Theoretical Computer Science **168**, 321–336 (with G. Paun, A. Salomaa), 1996.

297. Pattern Grammars, Journal of Automata, Languages and Combinatorics **1**, 219–235 (with G. Paun, A. Salomaa), 1996.

296. Restricted Use of the Splicing Operation, International Journal of Computer Mathematics **60**, 17–32 (with G. Paun, A. Salomaa), 1996.

295. Contextual Grammars: Parallellism and Blocking of Derivation, Fundamenta Informaticae **25**, 381–398 (with G. Paun, A. Salomaa), 1996.

294. Contextual Grammars: Deterministic Derivations and Growth Functions, Revue Roumaine de Mathématiques Pures et Appliquées **41**, 83–108 (with G. Paun, A. Salomaa), 1996.

293. Grammatical Codes of Trees and Terminally Coded Grammars, Fundamenta Informaticae **23**, 1–33 (with A. Ehrenfeucht, J. Engelfriet, P. ten Pas), 1995.

292. On the Generative Capacity of Certain Classes of Contextual Grammars, in: Mathematical Linguistics and Related Topics (G. Paun, Ed.), Editura Academiei, 105–118 (with A. Ehrenfeucht, L. Ilie, G. Paun, A. Salomaa), 1995.

291. Dynamic Change within Workflow Systems, in: Proceedings of the ACM Conference on Organisational Computing Systems, 10–21 (with C.A. Ellis, K. Keddara), 1995.

290. Dependence Graphs, in: The Book of Traces, World Scientific, 43–68 (with H.J. Hoogeboom), 1995.

289. Generalised DOL Trees, Acta Cybernetica **12**, 1–9 (with L. Kari, A. Salomaa), 1995.

288. Parikh Prime Words and GO-like Territories, Journal of Universal Computer Science **1**, 790–810 (with A. Mateescu, G. Paun, A. Salomaa), 1995.

287. Transition Systems, Event Structures and Unfoldings, Information and Computation **118**, 191–207 (with M. Nielsen, P.S. Thiagarajan), 1995.

286. Grammars Based on the Shuffle Operation, Journal of Universal Computer Science **1**, 67–82 (with G. Paun, A. Salomaa), 1995.

285. Clans and Regions in 2-structures, Theoretical Computer Science **129**, 207–262 (with A.H. Deutz, A. Ehrenfeucht), 1994.

284. Hyperedge Channels Are Abelian, Theoretical Computer Science **127**, 387–393 (with A.H. Deutz, A. Ehrenfeucht), 1994.

283. Quotients and Plane Trees of Group Labeled 2-structures, in: GRAGRA'94 Proceedings, 247–251 (with A. Ehrenfeucht, T. Harju), 1994.

282. Incremental Construction of 2-structures, Discrete Mathematics **128**, 113–141 (with A. Ehrenfeucht, T. Harju), 1994.

281. An Introduction to Context-Free Text Grammars, in: Developments in Language Theory, World Scientific, 357–369 (with A. Ehrenfeucht, H.J. Hoogeboom, P. ten Pas), 1994.

280. Combinatorial Properties of Dependence Graphs, Information and Computation **114**, 315–328 (with A. Ehrenfeucht, H.J. Hoogeboom), 1994.

279. On the Generative Capacity of Certain Classes of Contextual Grammars, in: Mathematical Linguistics and Related Topics, The Publishing House of the Romanian Academy of Sciences, Bucharest, 105–118 (with A. Ehrenfeucht, L. Ilie, G. Paun, A. Salomaa), 1994.

278. Properties of Grammatical Codes of Trees, Theoretical Computer Science **125**, 259–293 (with A. Ehrenfeucht, P. ten Pas), 1994.

277. Context-Free Text Grammars, Acta Informatica **31**, 161–206 (with A. Ehrenfeucht, P. ten Pas), 1994.

276. Normal Forms for Contextual Grammars, in: Mathematical Aspects of Natural and Formal Languages (G. Paun, Ed.), World Scientific Series in Computer Science, v. 43, World Scientific Publishing, 79–95 (with A. Ehrenfeucht, G. Paun), 1994.

275. Dynamic Labeled 2-structures, Mathematical Structures in Computer Science **4**, 433–455 (with A. Ehrenfeucht), 1994.

274. Dynamic Labeled 2-structures with Variable Domains, Lecture Notes in Computer Science **812**, 97–123, Springer-Verlag (with A. Ehrenfeucht), 1994.

273. Square Systems, Fundamenta Informaticae **20**, 75–111 (with A. Ehrenfeucht), 1994.

272. Semantics of Trees, Mathematical Systems Theory **27**, 159–181 (with A. Ehrenfeucht, K. Salomaa), 1994.

271. Reductions for Primitive 2-structures, Fundamenta Informaticae **20**, 133–144 (with T. Harju), 1994.

270. Decomposition of Infinite Labeled 2-structures, Lecture Notes in Computer Science **812**, 145–158, Springer-Verlag (with T. Harju), 1994.

269. Structuring Grammar Systems by Priorities and Hierarchies, Acta Cybernetica **11**, 189–204 (with V. Mitrana, G. Paun), 1994.

268. Prescribed Teams of Grammars, Acta Informatica **31**, 525–537 (with G. Paun), 1994.

267. Marcus Contextual Grammars: Modularity and Leftmost Derivations, in: Mathematical Aspects of Natural and Formal Languages (G. Paun, Ed.), World Scientific Publishing, 375–392 (with G. Paun, A. Salomaa), 1994.

266. Contextual Grammars: Erasing Determinism, One-Sided Contexts, in: Developments in Language Theory, World Scientific, 370–388 (with G. Paun, A. Salomaa), 1994.

265. Handle-Rewriting Hypergraph Grammars, Journal of Computer and System Sciences **46**, 218–270 (with B. Courcelle, J. Engelfriet), 1993.

264. On the Structure of Recognizable Languages of Dependence Graphs, R.A.I.R.O. – Informatique Théorique et Applications **27**, 7–22 (with A. Ehrenfeucht, H.J. Hoogeboom), 1993.

263. Combinatorial Properties of Texts, R.A.I.R.O. – Informatique Théorique et Applications **27**, 433–464 (with A. Ehrenfeucht, P. ten Pas), 1993.

262. T-structures, T-functions and Texts, Theoretical Computer Science **116**, 227–290 (with A. Ehrenfeucht), 1993.

261. An Introduction to Dynamic Labeled 2-structures, Lecture Notes in Computer Science **711**, 156–173, Springer-Verlag (with A. Ehrenfeucht), 1993.

260. Permutable Transformation Semigroups, Semigroup Forum **47**, 123–125 (with T. Harju), 1993.

259. Computation Graphs for Actor Grammars, Journal of Computer and System Sciences **46**, 60–90 (with D. Janssens, M. Lens), 1993.

258. Angular 2-structures, Theoretical Computer Science **92**, 227–248 (with A. Ehrenfeucht), 1992.

257. Elementary Transition Systems and Refinement, Acta Informatica **29**, 555–578 (with M. Nielsen, P.S. Thiagarajan), 1992.

256. Elementary Transition Systems, Theoretical Computer Science **96**, 3–33 (with M. Nielsen, P.S. Thiagarajan), 1992.

255. A Survey of Equivalence Notions for Net Based Systems, Lecture Notes in Computer Science **609**, 410–472, Springer-Verlag (with L. Pomello, C. Simone), 1992.

254. Context-Free Handle-Rewriting Hypergraph Grammars, Lecture Notes in Computer Science **532**, 253–268, Springer-Verlag (with B. Courcelle, J. Engelfriet), 1991.

253. Grammatical Codes of Trees, Discrete Applied Mathematics **32**, 103–129 (with A. Ehrenfeucht), 1991.

252. Net-Based Description of Parallel Object-Based Systems, or POTs and POPs, Lecture Notes in Computer Science **489**, 229–273, Springer-Verlag (with J. Engelfriet, G. Leih), 1991.

251. Nonterminal Separation in Graph Grammars, Theoretical Computer Science **82**, 95–111 (with J. Engelfriet, G. Leih), 1991.

250. Graph Grammars Based on Node Rewriting: An Introduction to NLC Graph Grammars, Lecture Notes in Computer Science **532**, 12–23, Springer-Verlag (with J. Engelfriet), 1991.

249. Diamond Properties of Elementary Net Systems, Fundamenta Informaticae XIV, 287–300 (with H.J. Hoogeboom), 1991.

248. Structured Transformations and Computation Graphs for Actor Grammars, Lecture Notes in Computer Science **532**, 446–460, Springer-Verlag (with D. Janssens), 1991.

247. Vector Controlled Concurrent Systems, Part II: Comparisons, Fundamenta Informaticae XIV, 1–38 (with N.W. Keesmaat, H.C.M. Kleijn), 1991.

246. Labeled 2-structures, Lecture Notes in Computer Science **555**, 268–282, Springer-Verlag , 1991.

245. Post Correspondence Problem, in: Encyclopedia of Mathematics, v. 7, Kluwer Academic Publishers, 252–253 (with A. Salomaa), 1991.

244. The Complexity of Regular DNLC Graph Languages, Journal of Computer and System Sciences **40**, 376–404 (with IJ.J. Aalbersberg, J. Engelfriet), 1990.

243. A Characterization of Set Representable Labeled Partial 2-structures through Decompositions, Acta Informatica **28**, 83–94 (with A. Ehrenfeucht), 1990.

242. A Theory of 2-structures, Part I: Clans, Basic Subclasses, and Morphisms (Fundamental Study), Theoretical Computer Science **70**, 277–303 (with A. Ehrenfeucht), 1990.

241. Theory of 2-structures, Part II: Representation through Labeled Tree Families (Fundamental Study), Theoretical Computer Science **70**, 305–342 (with A. Ehrenfeucht), 1990.

240. Primitivity Is Hereditary for 2-structures (Fundamental Study), Theoretical Computer Science **70**, 343–358 (with A. Ehrenfeucht), 1990.

239. Partial (Set) 2-structures, Part I: Basic Notions and the Representation Problem, Acta Informatica **27**, 315–342 (with A. Ehrenfeucht), 1990.

238. Partial (Set) 2-structures, Part II: State Spaces of Concurrent Systems, Acta Informatica **27**, 343–368 (with A. Ehrenfeucht), 1990.

237. Formalizing the Behaviour of Parallel Object-Based Systems by Petri Nets, in: Semantics for Concurrency (M.Z. Kwiatkowska, M.W. Shields, R.M. Thomas, Eds.), Workshops on Computing, Springer-Verlag, Berlin, 204–221 (with J. Engelfriet, G. Leih), 1990.

236. A Comparison of Boundary Graph Grammars and Context-Free Hypergraph Grammars, Information and Computation **84**, 163–206 (with J. Engelfriet), 1990.

235. Vector Controlled Concurrent Systems; Part I: Basic Classes, Fundamenta Informaticae XIII, 275–316 (with N.W. Keesmaat, H.C.M. Kleijn), 1990.

234. On Structured Graph Grammars; I, Information Sciences **52**, 185–210 (with H.-J. Kreowski), 1990.

233. On Structured Graph Grammars; II, Information Sciences **52**, 221–246 (with H.-J. Kreowski), 1990.

232. Edge-Label Controlled Graph Grammars, Journal of Computer and System Sciences **40**, 188–228 (with M.G. Main), 1990.

231. Behavioural Notions for Elementary Net Systems, Distributed Computing **4**, 45–57 (with M. Nielsen, P.S. Thiagarajan), 1990.

230. Mathematical Theory of Computation, in: Encyclopedia of Mathematics, v. 6, Kluwer Academic Publishers, 146–148 (with A. Salomaa), 1990.

229. L-systems, in: Encyclopedia of Mathematics, v. 5, Kluwer Academic Publishers, 325–327 (with A. Salomaa), 1990.

228. Cryptography, in: Encyclopedia of Mathematics, v. 2, Kluwer Academic Publishers, 466–468 (with A. Salomaa), 1990.

227. Complexity Theory, in: Encyclopedia of Mathematics, v. 2, Kluwer Academic Publishers, 280–283 (with A. Salomaa), 1990.

226. Clans and the Complexity of Dependence Graphs, in: A Perspective in Computer Science (R. Narasimhan, Ed.), World Scientific Publishing, 33–37 (with A. Ehrenfeucht), 1989.

225. A Characterization of State Spaces of Elementary Net Systems, in: J.W. de Bakker, 25 jaar semantiek, Liber Amicorum, C.W.I. Amsterdam, 193–201 (with A. Ehrenfeucht), april 1989.

224. Actor Grammars, Mathematical Systems Theory **22**, 75–107 (with D. Janssens), 1989.

223. Theory of Traces, Theoretical Computer Science **60**, 1–82 (with IJ.J. Aalbersberg), 1988.

222. Recording the Use of Memory in Right-Boundary Grammars and Push-Down Automata, Acta Informatica **25**, 203–23 (with A. Ehrenfeucht, H.J. Hoogeboom), 1988.

221. Apex Graph Grammars and Attribute Grammars, Acta Informatica **25**, 537–571 (with J. Engelfriet, G. Leih), 1988.

220. Restricting the Complexity of Regular DNLC Languages, Lecture Notes in Computer Science **291**, 147–166, Springer-Verlag (with IJ.J. Aalbersberg, J. Engelfriet), 1987.

219. On the Structure of Dependency Graphs, in: Concurrency and Nets (K. Voss, H.J. Genrich, G. Rozenberg, Eds.), Springer-Verlag, 141–170 (with A. Ehrenfeucht), 1987.

218. Apex Graph Grammars, Lecture Notes in Computer Science **291**, 167–185, Springer-Verlag (with J. Engelfriet, G. Leih), 1987.

217. Basic Notions of Actor Grammars, Lecture Notes in Computer Science **291**, 280–298, Springer-Verlag (with D. Janssens), 1987.

216. Handle NLC-grammars and RE Languages, Journal of Computer and System Sciences **35**, 192–205 (with M.G. Main), 1987.

215. Fundamentals of Edge-Label Controlled Graph Grammars, Lecture Notes in Computer Science **291**, 411–426, Springer-Verlag (with M.G. Main), 1987.

214. Behaviour of Elementary Net Systems, Lecture Notes in Computer Science **254**, 60–95, Springer-Verlag , 1987.

213. An Introduction to the NLC Way of Rewriting G raphs, Lecture Notes in Computer Science **291**, 55–66, Springer-Verlag , 1987.

212. Combinatorial Properties of Boundary NLC Grammars, Discrete Applied Mathematics **16**, 59–73 (with E. Welzl), 1987.

211. On the Membership Problem for Regular DNLC Grammars, Discrete Applied Mathematics **13**, 79–85 (with IJ.J. Aalbersberg, A. Ehrenfeucht), 1986.

210. Coordinated Pair Systems; Part I: Dyck Words and Classical Pumping, R.A.I.R.O. – Informatique Théorique et Applications **20**, 405–424 (with A. Ehrenfeucht, H.J. Hoogeboom), 1986.

209. Coordinated Pair Systems; Part II: Sparse Structure of Dyck Words and Ogden's Lemma, R.A.I.R.O. – Informatique Théorique et Applications **20**, 425–439 (with A. Ehrenfeucht, H.J. Hoogeboom), 1986.

208. On the Active and Full Use of Memory in Right-Boundary Grammars and Push-Down Automata, Theoretical Computer Science **48**, 201–228 (with A. Ehrenfeucht, H.J. Hoogeboom), 1986.

207. Computations in Coordinated Pair Systems, Fundamenta Informaticae IX, 445–480 (with A. Ehrenfeucht, H.J. Hoogeboom), 1986.

206. Infinitary Languages: Basic Theory and Applications to Concurrent Systems, Lecture Notes in Computer Science **224**, Springer-Verlag (with H.J. Hoogeboom), 1986.

205. Neighbourhood-Uniform NLC Grammars, Computer Vision, Graphics and Image Processing **35**, 131–151 (with D. Janssens), 1986.

204. The Bounded Degree Problem for NLC Grammars Is Decidable, Journal of Computer and System Sciences **33**, 415–422 (with D. Janssens, E. Welzl), 1986.

203. Petri Nets: Basic Notions, Structures, Behaviour, Lecture Notes in Computer Science **224**, 585–668, Springer-Verlag (with P.S. Thiagarajan), 1986.

202. Graph Theoretic Closure Properties of the Family of Boundary NLC Graph Languages, Acta Informatica **23**, 289–309 (with E. Welzl), 1986.

201. Boundary NLC Graph Grammars - Basic Definitions, Normal Forms, and Complexity, Information and Control **69**, 136–167 (with E. Welzl), 1986.

200. CTS Systems and Petri Nets, Theoretical Computer Science **40**, 149–162 (with IJ.J. Aalbersberg), 1985.

199. Traces, Dependency Graphs and DNLC Grammars, Discrete Applied Mathematics **11**, 299–306 (with IJ.J. Aalbersberg), 1985.

198. On Coordinated Rewriting, Lecture Notes in Computer Science **199**, 100–111, Springer-Verlag (with A. Ehrenfeucht, H.J. Hoogeboom), 1985.

197. Adding Global Forbidding Context to Context-Free Grammars, Theoretical Computer Science **37**(3), 337–360 (with A. Ehrenfeucht, H.C.M. Kleijn), 1985.

196. Each Regular Code Is Included in a Maximal Regular Code, R.A.I.R.O. – Informatique Théorique et Applications **20**, 89–96 (with A. Ehrenfeucht), 1985.

195. Strong Iterative Pairs and the Regularity of Context-Free Languages, R.A.I.R.O. – Informatique Théorique et Applications **19**, 43–56 (with A. Ehrenfeucht), 1985.

194. A Morphic Representation of E0L Languages and Other ET0L Languages, Discrete Applied Mathematics **12**, 115–122 (with A. Ehrenfeucht, K. Ruohonen), 1985.

193. On Coordinated Selective Substitutions: Towards a Unified Theory of Grammars and Machines, Theoretical Computer Science **37**(1), 31–50, 1985.

192. On Erasing in E0L Forms, Discrete Applied Mathematics **12**, 175–190 (with R. Verraedt), 1985.

191. On Ambiguity in D0S Systems, R.A.I.R.O. – Informatique Théorique et Applications **18**, 279–295 (with A. Ehrenfeucht, D. Haussler), 1984.

190. On D0S Languages and D0S Mappings, Semigroup Forum **29**, 123–148 (with A. Ehrenfeucht, D. Haussler, P. Zeiger), 1984.

189. Restrictions on NLC Graph Grammars, Theoretical Computer Science **31**(1-2), 211–223 (with A. Ehrenfeucht, M.G. Main), 1984.

188. On Regularity of Languages Generated by Copying Systems, Discrete Applied Mathematics **8**, 313–317 (with A. Ehrenfeucht), 1984.

187. An Easy Proof of Greibach Normal Form, Information and Control **63**, 190–199 (with A. Ehrenfeucht), 1984.

186. On Inherently Ambiguous E0L Languages, Theoretical Computer Science **28**(1-2), 197–214 (with A. Ehrenfeucht, R. Verraedt), 1984.

185. Generalized Handle Grammars and Their Relation to Petri Nets, Journal of Information Processing and Cybernetics EIK **20**, 179–206 (with H.J. Genrich, D. Janssens, P.S. Thiagarajan), 1984.

184. Direction Independent Context-Sensitive Grammars, Information and Control **63**(1/2), 113–117 (with H.C.M. Kleijn, M. Penttonen, K. Salomaa), 1984.

183. Note on Node-Rewriting Graph Grammars, Information Processing Letters **18**, 21–24 (with H.-J. Kreowski), 1984.

182. Commutative One-Counter Languages Are Regular, Journal of Computer and System Sciences **29**(1), 54–57 (with M. Latteux), 1984.

181. Restricting the In-Out Structure of Petri Nets. A Language Theoretic Point of View, Fundamenta Informaticae VII, 151–190 (with R. Verraedt), 1984.

180. On Simulation and Propagating E0L Forms, Theoretical Computer Science **29**(1-2), 41–48 (with R. Verraedt), 1984.

179. Boundary NLC Grammars, in: Ninth Colloquium on Trees in Algebra and Programming (B. Courcelle, Ed.), Cambridge University Press, 257–270 (with E. Welzl), 1984.

178. Context-Free Normal Systems and ET0L Systems, Journal of Computer and System Sciences **26**, 34–46 (with A. Ehrenfeucht, J. Engelfriet), 1983.

177. On Regularity of Context-Free Languages, Theoretical Computer Science **27**, 311–332 (with A. Ehrenfeucht, D. Haussler), 1983.

176. On Binary Equality Sets and a Solutionn to the Test Conjecture in the Binary Case, Journal of Algorithms **85**, 76–85 (with A. Ehrenfeucht, J. Karhumäki), 1983.

175. On the Subword Complexity of Locally Catenative D0L Languages, Information Processing Letters **16**(1), 7–9 (with A. Ehrenfeucht), 1983.

174. Repetition of Subwords in D0L Languages, Information and Control **59**, 13–35 (with A. Ehrenfeucht), 1983.

173. On the Subword Complexity of m-free D0L Languages, Information Processing Letters **17**, 121–124 (with A. Ehrenfeucht), 1983.

172. On the Separating Power of E0L Systems, R.A.I.R.O. – Informatique Théorique et Applications **17**, 13–22 (with A. Ehrenfeucht), 1983.

171. P.S. Thiagarajan Petri Nets and Their Relation to Graph Grammars, LNCS **153**, 115–129, Springer-Verlag (with H.J. Genrich, D. Janssens), 1983.

170. Constrained Petri Nets, Fundamenta Informaticae VI, 81–125 (with H.J.M. Goeman, L.P.J. Groenewegen, H.C.M. Kleijn), 1983.

169. Constrained Petri Nets Part II: Generalizations and Extensions, Fundamenta Informaticae VI, 333–374 (with H.J.M. Goeman, L.P.J. Groenewegen, H.C.M. Kleijn), 1983.

168. Closure Properties of Selective Substitution Grammars Part II, International Journal of Computer Mathematics **14**, 109–135 (with J. Gonczarowski, H.C.M. Kleijn), 1983.

167. Grammatical Constructions in Selective Substitution Grammars, Acta Cybernetica **6**, 239–269 (with J. Gonczarowski, H.C.M. Kleijn), 1983.

166. Closure Properties of Selective Substitution Grammars Part I, International Journal of Computer Mathematics **14**, 19–42 (with J. Gonczarowski, H.C.M. Kleijn), 1983.

165. Graph Grammars with Node Label Controlled Rewriting, Lecture Notes in Computer Science**153**, 186–205, Springer-Verlag (with D. Janssens), 1983.

164. Hypergraph Systems Generating Graph Languages, Lecture Notes in Computer Science**153**, 172–185, Springer-Verlag (with D. Janssens), 1983.

163. Neighbourhood-Uniform NLC Grammars, in: Proceedings WG'83 (M. Nagl, J. Perl, Eds.), 114–124 (with D. Janssens), 1983.

162. Hypergraph Systems and Their Extensions, R.A.I.R.O. – Informatique Théorique et Applications **17**, 163–196 (with D. Janssens), 1983.

161. On the Generative Power of Regular Pattern Grammars, Acta Informatica **20**, 391–411 (with H.C.M. Kleijn), 1983.

160. Multigrammars, International Journal of Computer Mathematics **12**, 177–201 (with H.C.M. Kleijn), 1983.

159. Chain Code Picture Languages, Lecture Notes in Computer Science**153**, 232–244, Springer-Verlag (with H.A. Maurer, E. Welzl), 1983.

158. Subset Languages of Petri Nets. Part II: Closure Properties, Theoretical Computer Science **27**, 85–108 (with R. Verraedt), 1983.

157. Subset Languages of Petri Nets. Part I: The Relationship to String Languages and Normal Forms, Theoretical Computer Science **26**, 301–326 (with R. Verraedt), 1983.

156. Subset Languages of Petri Nets, in: Applications and Theory of Petri Nets (A. Pagnoni, G. Rozenberg, Eds.), Informatik Fachberichte **66**, 250–263 (with R. Verraedt), 1983.

155. The Goodness of {S,a}-EOL Forms Is Decidable, Discrete Applied Mathematics **6**, 263–300 (with R. Verraedt), 1983.

154. Conditions Enforcing Regularity of Context-Free Languages, Lecture Notes in Computer Science **140**, 187–191, Springer-Verlag (with A. Ehrenfeucht, D. Haussler), July 1982.

153. The (generalized) Post Correspondence Problem with Lists Consisting of Two Words Is Decidable, Theoretical Computer Science **21**(2), 119–144 (with A. Ehrenfeucht, J. Karhumäki), November 1982.

152. Representation Theorems Using D0S Languages, Theoretical Computer Science **21**(1), 75–90 (with A. Ehrenfeucht), October 1982.

151. On the Subword Complexity of Homomorphic Images of Languages, R.A.I.R.O. – Informatique Théorique et Applications **16**, 303–316 (with A. Ehrenfeucht), 1982.

150. Repetitions in Homomorphisms and Languages, Lecture Notes in Computer Science**140**, 192–211, Springer-Verlag (with A. Ehrenfeucht), July 1982.

149. Basic Formulas and Languages, Part II: Applications to EOL Systems and Forms, Discrete Applied Mathematics **4**, 11–22 (with A. Ehrenfeucht, R. Verraedt), 1982.

148. Controlled Graph Transformations, in: Proceedings of the 8th Conference on Graph Theoretic Concepts in Computer Science (H.J. Schneider, H. Göttler, Eds.), Hanser Verlag, München-Wien, (with H. Ehrig, D. Janssens, H.-J. Kreowski), 1982.

147. Graph Grammars with Neighbourhood-Controlled Embedding, Theoretical Computer Science **21**(1), 55–74 (with D. Janssens), October 1982.

146. On Sequential and Parallel Noderewriting Graph Grammars, Computer Graphics and Image Processing **18**, 279–304 (with D. Janssens, R. Verraedt), 1982.

145. Corrigendum: Sequential, Continuous and Parallel Grammars, Information and Control **52**(3), 364 (with H.C.M. Kleijn), March 1982.

144. On the Role of Blocking in Rewriting Systems, Acta Cybernetica **5**, 389–408 (with H.C.M. Kleijn, R. Verraedt), 1982.

143. Using String Languages to Describe Picture Languages, Information and Control **54**(3), 155–185 (with H.A. Maurer, E. Welzl), September 1982.

142. Completeness of EOL Forms Is Decidable, Acta Informatica **17**, 69–87 (with R. Verraedt), 1982.

141. Subset Languages of Petri Nets, in: Proceeedings of the Third Workshop on Applications and Theory of Petri Nets, 407–420 (with R. Verraedt), 1982.

140. Studies in Uniformity, Information Sciences **26**, 69–87 (with R. Verraedt), 1982.

139. A Note on the Similarity Depth, Discrete Applied Mathematics **4**, 237–241 (with R. Verraedt), 1982 1982.

138. Pumping Lemmas for Regular Sets, SIAM Journal on Computing **10**(3), 536–541 (with A. Ehrenfeucht, R. Parikh), August 1981.

137. On the Subword Complexity of Square-Free D0L Languages, Theoretical Computer Science **16**, 25–32 (with A. Ehrenfeucht), October 1981.

136. On the Subword Complexity of D0L Languages with a Constant Distribution, Information Processing Letters **13**, 108–113 (with A. Ehrenfeucht), December 1981.

135. FP0L Systems Generating Counting Languages, R.A.I.R.O. – Informatique Théorique et Applications **15**, 161–173 (with A. Ehrenfeucht), 1981.

134. On the Subword Complexity and Square Freeness of Formal Languages, LNCS **104**, 1–4, Springer-Verlag (with A. Ehrenfeucht), 1981.

133. On the (Generalized) Post Correspondence Problem with Lists of Length 2, Lecture Notes in Computer Science **115**, 408–416, Springer-Verlag (with A. Ehrenfeucht), July 1981.

132. A Morphic Representation of Complements of Recursively Enumerable Sets, Journal of the ACM **28**(4), 706–714 (with A. Ehrenfeucht, K. Ruohonen), October 1981.

131. On ET0L Systems with Finite Tree-Rank, SIAM Journal on Computing **10**(1), 40–58 (with A. Ehrenfeucht, D. Vermeir), February 1981.

130. Basic Formulas and Languages, Part I: The Theory, Discrete Applied Mathematics **3**, 235–255 (with A. Ehrenfeucht, R. Verraedt), 1981.

129. A Translational Theorem for the Class of EOL Languages, Information and Control **50**, 175–183 (with J. Engelfriet), 1981.

128. A Characterization of Context-Free String Languages by Directed Node-Label Controlled Graph Grammars, Acta Informatica **16**, 63–85 (with D. Janssens), 1981.

127. Decision Problems for Node Label Controlled Graph Grammars, Journal of Computer and System Sciences **22**(2), 144–177 (with D. Janssens), April 1981.

126. On the Role of Selectors in Selective Substitition Grammars, Lecture Notes in Computer Science **117**, 190–198, Springer-Verlag (with H.C.M. Kleijn), 1981.

125. Sequential, Continuous and Parallel Grammars, Information and Control **48**, 221–260 (with H.C.M. Kleijn), 1981.

124. A General Framework for Comparing Sequential and Parallel Rewriting, Lecture Notes in Computer Science **118**, 360–368, Springer-Verlag (with H.C.M. Kleijn), 1981.

123. Context-Free like Restrictions on Selective Rewriting, Theoretical Computer Science **16**(3), 237–269 (with H.C.M. Kleijn), December 1981.

122. On the Constructive Description of Graph Languages Accepted by Finite Automata., Lecture Notes in Computer Science **118**, 398–409, Springer-Verlag (with H.-J. Kreowski), 1981.

121. Sub Context-Free L Forms, International Journal of Computer Mathematics **9**, 25–41 (with H.A. Maurer), 1981.

120. On Subwords of Formal Languages, Lecture Notes in Computer Science **117**, 328–333, Springer Verlag , 1981.

119. Table Systems with Unconditional Transfer, Discrete Applied Mathematics **3**, 319–322 (with A. Salomaa), 1981.

118. A Hierarchy of ET0L Languages with Rank, Fundamenta Informaticae IV, 197–205 (with D. Vermeir), 1981.

117. E0L Forms and Finite Substitutions of 0L Forms, International Journal of Computer Mathematics **10**, 17–34 (with R. Verraedt), 1981.

116. Recursion and Pumping in L Forms, Information Sciences **25**, 43–72 (with R. Verraedt), 1981.

115. On Fixed, Terminal Fixed and Nonterminal Fixed Interpretations of E0L Forms, Information and Control **48**(2), 119–146 (with R. Verraedt), February 1981.

114. On Pure, Terminal Invariant and Nonterminal Invariant Interpretations of EOL Forms, Theoretical Computer Science **14**(3), 267–288 (with R. Verraedt), June 1981.

113. Simple E0L Forms under Uniform Interpretation Generating CF Languages, Fundamenta Informaticae **3**, 141–156 (with J. Albert, H. Maurer, Th. Ottmann), 1980.

112. Continuous Grammars, Information and Control **46**, 71–91 (with A. Ehrenfeucht, H. Maurer), 1980.

111. On a Bound for the DOL Sequence Equivalence Problem, Theoretical Computer Science **12**, 339–342 (with A. Ehrenfeucht), 1980.

110. Every Two Equivalent DOL Systems Have a Regular Envelope, Theoretical Computer Science **10**, 45–52 (with A. Ehrenfeucht), 1980.

109. DOS Systems and Languages: A Missing Block in the Systematic Theory of Contextfree Languages, Lecture Notes in Computer Science **85**, 134–141, Springer-Verlag (with A. Ehrenfeucht), 1980.

108. On Ambiguity in EOL Systems, Theoretical Computer Science **12**, 127–134 (with A. Ehrenfeucht), 1980.

107. On the Emptiness of the Intersection of Two DOS Languages Problem, Information Processing Letters **10**, 223–225 (with A. Ehrenfeucht), 1980.

106. On Basic Propertis of DOS Systems and Languages, Information and Control **47**, 138–153 (with A. Ehrenfeucht), 1980.

105. The Sequence Equivalence Problem Is Decidable for OS Systems, Journal of the ACM **27**, 656–663 (with A. Ehrenfeucht), 1980.

104. Synchronized and Desynchronized EOL Forms, Discrete Applied Mathematics **2**, 73–76 (with A. Ehrenfeucht, R. Verraedt), 1980.

103. Fixed Point Languages, Equality Languages and Representation of Recursively Enumerable Languages, Journal of the ACM **27**, 499–518 (with J. Engelfriet), 1980.

102. Tree Transducers, L Systems and Two-Way Machines, Journal of Computer and System Sciences **20**, 150–202 (with J. Engelfriet, G. Slutzki), 1980.

101. Restrictions, Extensions and Variations of NLC Grammars, Information Sciences **20**, 217–244 (with D. Janssens), 1980.

100. On the Structure of Node-Label Controlled Graph Languages, Information Sciences **20**, 191–216 (with D. Janssens), 1980.

99. A Study in Parallel Rewriting Systems, Information and Control **44**, 134–163 (with H.C.M. Kleijn), 1980.

98. On Metalinear ETOL Systems, Fundamenta Informaticae **3**, 15–36 (with D. Vermeir), 1980.

97. A Note on the M-growth Functions of FTOL Systems with Rank, Fundamenta Informaticae **3**, 295–302 (with D. Vermeir), 1980.

96. Synchronization and Related Phenomena in the Theory of EOL Systems and EOL Forms, Bulletin de la Société Mathématique de Belgique **32**, 189–208 (with R. Verraedt), 1980.

95. Synchronized and Desynchronized EOL Systems, Information and Control **46**, (with R. Verraedt), 1980.

94. Many-to-One Simulation in EOL Forms Is Decidable, Applied Mathematics **2**, 233–247 (with R. Verraedt), 1980.

93. Context-Free Grammars with Selective Rewriting, Acta Informatica **13**, 257–268 (with D. Wood), 1980.

92. On Arithmic Substitutions of EDTOL Languages, Foundations of Control Engineering **4**, (with A. Ehrenfeucht), 1979.

91. On the Structure of Polynomially Bounded DOL Systems, Fundamenta Informaticae **2**, 187–197 (with A. Ehrenfeucht), 1979.

90. An Observation on Scattered Grammars, Information Processing Letters **9**, 84–85 (with A. Ehrenfeucht), 1979.

89. Finding a Homomorphism between Two Words Is NP Complete, Information Processing Letters **9**, 86–88 (with A. Ehrenfeucht), 1979.

88. A Result on the Structure of ETOL Languages, Foundations of Control Engineering **4**, 165–171 (with A. Ehrenfeucht), 1979.

87. On ETOL Systems with Rank, Journal of Computer and System Sciences **19**, 237–255 (with A. Ehrenfeucht, D. Vermeir), 1979.

86. Equality Languages and Fixed Point Languages, Information and Control **43**, 20–49 (with J. Engelfriet), 1979.

85. Parallel Generation of Maps: Developmental Systems for Cell Layers, Lecture Notes in Computer Science **73**, 301–316, Springer-Verlag (with A. Lindenmayer), 1979.

84. Pure Interpretations of EOL Forms, R.A.I.R.O. – Informatique Théorique et Applications **13**, 347–362 (with H. Maurer, A. Salomaa, D. Wood), 1979.

83. Parallelism and Synchronization in Two-Level Meta-controlled Substitution Grammars, Information and Control **18**, 67–82 (with R. Meersman), 1979.

82. Persistent ETOL Systems, Information Sciences **18**, 189–212 (with R. Meersman, D. Vermeir), 1979.

81. Programs for Instruction Machines, Information and Control **41**, 9–28 (with Z. Pawlak, W. Savitch), 1979.

80. A Systematic Approach to Formal Language Theory through Parallel Rewriting, Lecture Notes in Computer Science **71**, 471–478, Springer-Verlag, 1979.

79. On Acceptors of Iteration Languages, International Journal of Computer Mathematics **7**, 3–19 (with D. Vermeir), 1979.

78. On Recursion in ETOL Systems, Journal of Computer and System Sciences **19**, 179–196 (with D. Vermeir), 1979.

77. Extending the Notion of Finite Index, Lecture Notes in Computer Science **71**, 479–488, Springer-Verlag (with D. Vermeir), 1979.

76. Simple EOL Forms under Uniform Interpretation Generating CF Languages, Lecture Notes in Computer Science **62**, 1–14, Springer-Verlag (with J. Albert, H. Maurer), 1978.

75. A Note on DOL Length Sets, Discrete Mathematics **22**, 233–242 (with A. Ehrenfeucht, J. Karhumäki), 1978.

74. E0L Languages Are Not Codings of FPOL Languages, Theoretical Computer Science **6**, 327–342 (with A. Ehrenfeucht), 1978.

73. Elementary Homomorphisms and a Solution of the DOL Equivalence Problem, Theoretical Computer Science **7**, 169–184 (with A. Ehrenfeucht), 1978.

72. On the Relationship between Context Free Programmed Grammars and ETOL Systems, Fundamenta Informaticae **1**, 325–345 (with A. Ehrenfeucht), 1978.

71. Simplifications of Homomorphisms, Information and Control **38**, 298–309 (with A. Ehrenfeucht), 1978.

70. Increasing the Similarity of EOL Form Interpretations, Information and Control **38**, 330–342 (with H. Maurer), 1978.

69. A Note on Generalized Context-Independent Rewriting, Communication and Cognition **11**, 181–196 (with R. Meersman), 1978.

68. On Cooperating Grammars, Lecture Notes in Computer Science **64**, 364–373, Springer-Verlag (with R. Meersman), 1978.

67. Two-Level Meta-controlled Substitution Grammars, Acta Informatica **10**, 323–339 (with R. Meersman), 1978.

66. Priorities on Context Conditions in Rewriting Systems, Information Sciences **14**, 15–50 (with V. Solms), 1978.

65. On the Effect of the Finite Index Restriction on Several Families of Grammars, Information and Control **39**, 284–301 (with D. Vermeir), 1978.

64. On the Effect of the Finite Index Restriction on Several Families of Grammars, Part II: Context-Dependent Systems, Foundations of Control Engineering **3**, 125–142 (with D. Vermeir), 1978.

63. On ETOL Systems of Finite Index, Information and Control **38**, 103–133 (with D. Vermeir), 1978.

62. On Some Context-Free Languages That Are Not Deterministic ETOL Languages, R.A.I.R.O. – Informatique Théorique et Applications **11**, 273–292 (with A. Ehrenfeucht), 1977.

61. TIL Systems and Languages, Information Sciences **12**, 203–277 (with K.P. Lee), 1977.

60. Two-Level Meta-controlled Substitution Grammars, Lecture Notes in Computer Science**53**, 390–397, Springer-Verlag (with R. Meersman), 1977.

59. Bibliography of L Systems, Theoretical Computer Science **5**, 339–354 (with M. Penttonen, A. Salomaa), 1977.

58. A Note on Universal Grammars, Information and Control **34**, 172–175, 1977.

57. Selective Substitution Grammars, Part I: Definitions and Examles, Journal of Information Processing and Cybernetics EIK **13**, 455–463, 1977.

56. New Squeezing Mechanism for L Systems, Information Sciences **2**, 187–203 (with A. Salomaa), 1977.

55. L-systems of Finite Index, Lecture Notes in Computer Science **52**, 430–439, Springer-Verlag (with D. Vermeir), 1977.

54. Acceptors for Iteration Languages, Lecture Notes in Computer Science **53**, 460–464, Springer-Verlag (with D. Vermeir), 1977.

53. On the Number of Subwords of Everywhere Growing and Uniform DTOL Languages, Discrete Mathematics **15**, 223–234 (with A. Ehrenfeucht, K.P. Lee), 1976.

52. On Proving That Certain Languages Are Not ETOL, Acta Informatica **6**, 407–415 (with A. Ehrenfeucht), 1976.

51. A Relationship between ETOL and EDTOL Languages, Theoretical Computer Science **1**, 325–330 (with A. Ehrenfeucht, S. Skyum), 1976.

50. On Slicing of K-iteration Grammars, Information Processing Letters **4**, 127–131, 1976.

49. More on ETOL Systems versus Random Context Grammars, Information Processing Letters **5**, 102–106, 1976.

48. Context-Free Grammars with Graph Controlled Tables, Journal of Computer and System Sciences **13**, 90–99, 1976.

47. Developmental Systems with Fragmentation, International Journal of Computer Mathematics **5**, 177–191 (with K. Ruohonen, A. Salomaa), 1976.

46. A Note on Family of Acceptors for Some Families of Developmental Languages, International Journal of Computer Mathematics **5**, 261–266 (with D. Wood), 1976.

45. A Note on K-iteration Grammars, Information Processing Letters **4**, 162–168 (with D. Wood), 1976.

44. Subword Complexities of Various Classes of Deterministic Developmental Languages with Interactions, International Journal of Computer Mathematics **4**, 219–236 (with A. Ehrenfeucht, K.P. Lee), 1975.

43. Subword Complexities of Various Deterministic Developmental Languages without Interactions, Theoretical Computer Science **1**, 59–76 (with A. Ehrenfeucht, K.P. Lee), 1975.

42. A Pumping Theorem for Deterministic EOL Languages, R.A.I.R.O. – Informatique Théorique et Applications **9**, 13–23 (with A. Ehrenfeucht), 1975.

41. Description of Developmental Languages, Using Recurrence Systems, Mathematical Systems Theory **8**, 316–341 (with G.T. Herman, A. Lindenmayer), 1975.

40. Some Properties of the Class of L-languages with Interactions, Journal of Computer and System Sciences **11**, 129–147 (with K.P. Lee), 1975.

39. TOL Schemes and Control Sets, Information and Control **27**, 109–125, 1975.

38. L Systems, Sequences and Languages, Lecture Notes in Computer Science **34**, 71–84, Springer-Verlag, 1975.

37. The Equality of EOL Languages and Codings of OL Languages, International Journal of Computer Mathematics **4**, 85–104 (with A. Ehrenfeucht), 1974.

36. Three Useful Results Concerning L Languages without Interaction, LNCS **15**, 72–77, Springer-Verlag (with A. Ehrenfeucht), 1974.

35. DOL Systems with Rank, Lecture Notes in Computer Science **15**, 136–141, Springer-Verlag (with A. Ehrenfeucht), 1974.

34. Generatively Deterministic L Languages, Subword Point of View, LNCS **15**, 93–103, Springer-Verlag (with A. Ehrenfeucht), 1974.

33. Nonterminals versus Homomorphisms in Defining Languages from Some Classes of Rewriting Systems, Acta Informatica **4**, 87–106 (with A. Ehrenfeucht), 1974.

32. The Number of Occurrences of Letters versus Their Distribution in Some EOL Languages, Information and Control **26**, 256–271 (with A. Ehrenfeucht), 1974.

31. The Length of DOL Languages Are Uniformly Bounded, Information Processing Letters **2**, 185–188 (with K.P. Lee), 1974.

30. Bibliography on L Systems, Lecture Notes in Computer Science **15**, 327–338, Springer-Verlag (with K.P. Lee), 1974.

29. Developmental Systems with Finite Axiom Sets, Part I: Systems without Interactions, International Journal of Computer Mathematics **4**, 43–68 (with K.P. Lee), 1974.

28. Developmental Systems with Finite Axiom Sets, Part II: Systems with Interaction, International Journal of Computer Mathematics **4**, 281–304 (with K.P. Lee), 1974.

27. Nonterminals, Homomorphisms and Codings in Different Variations of OL Systems, Part II: Nondeterministic Systems, Acta Informatica **3**, 357–364 (with M. Nielsen, A. Salomaa, S. Skyum), 1974.

26. Theory of L Systems from the Point of View of Formal Language Theory, Lecture Notes in Computer Science **14**, 1–23, Springer-Verlag , 1974.

25. Trade-Off between the Use of Nonterminals, Codings and Homomorphisms in Defining Languages for Some Classes of Rewriting Systems, Lecture Notes in Computer Science **14**, 473–580, Springer-Verlag , 1974.

24. Circularities in DOL Sequences, Revue Roumaine de Mathématiques Pures et Appliquées **9**, 1131–1152, 1974.

23. DOL Sequences, Discrete Mathematics **7**, 323–347, 1974.

22. Generative Models for Parallel Processes, Computer Journal **17**, 344–348 (with D. Wood), 1974.

21. A Limit Theorem for Sets of Subwords in Deterministic TOL Languages, Information Processing Letters **2**, 70–73 (with A. Ehrenfeucht), 1973.

20. TOL Systems and Control Sets, Information and Control **23**, 357–381 (with S. Ginsburg), 1973.

19. Developmental Systems with Locally Catenative Formulas, Acta Informatica **2**, 214–248 (with A. Lindenmayer), 1973.

18. TOL Systems and Languages, Information and Control **23**, 357–381, 1973.

17. Extension of Tabled OL Systems and Languages, International Journal of Computer and Information Sciences **2**, 311–333, 1973.

16. Characterization of Unary Developmental Languages, Discrete Mathematics **6**, 235–247 (with G.T. Herman, K.P. Lee, J. van Leeuwen), 1972.

15. Direction Controlled Context-Free Programmed Grammars, Acta Informatica **2**, 214–248, 1972.

14. Direction Controlled Programmed Grammars, Acta Informatica **1**, 242–252, 1972.

13. Direct Proof of the Undecidability of the Equivalence Problem for Sentential Forms of Linear Context-Free Languages, Information Processing Letters **1**, 233–235, 1972.

12. Constant-Program Address Machines Are Universal, Revue Roumaine de Mathématiques Pures et Appliquées **17**, 417–424, 1972.

11. The Equivalence Problem for Deterministic TOL Systems Is Undecidable, Information Processing Letters **1**, 201–204, 1972.

10. On OL Languages, Information and Control **13**, 302–318 (with P. Doucet), 1971.

9. The Unsolvability of the Isomorphism Problem for Address Machines, Revue Roumaine de Mathématiques Pures et Appliquées **16**, 1553–1558, 1971.

8. P-automata and P-events, Bulletin de l'Académie Polonaise des Sciences **17**, 565–570, 1969.

7. Finite Memory Address Machines Are Universal, Bulletin de l'Académie Polonaise des Sciences **17**, 401–403, 1969.

6. On the Introduction of Orderings into the Grammars of Chomsky's Hierarchy, Bulletin de l'Académie Polonaise des Sciences **17**, 559–563, 1969.

5. Some Remarks on Rabin and Scott's Notion of Multi-tape Automaton, Bulletin de l'Académie Polonaise des Sciences **16**, 215–218, 1968.

4. Languages of Derivations, Bulletin de l'Académie Polonaise des Sciences **15**, 753–758, 1967.

3. Decision Problems for Quasi-Uniform Events, Bulletin de l'Académie Polonaise des Sciences **15**, 745–752, 1967.

2. About Some Properties of Quasi-Uniform Chain Automata with r>0, Bulletin de l'Académie Polonaise des Sciences **15**, 543–546, 1967.

1. Axioms for the Category of Relations with Composition, Bulletin de l'Académie Polonaise des Sciences **15**, 5–9, 1967.

Part I

Words, Languages, Automata

Balanced Grammars and Their Languages

Jean Berstel[1] and Luc Boasson[2]

[1] Institut Gaspard Monge (IGM), Université Marne-la-Vallée,
77454 Marne-la-Vallée Cedex 2
berstel@univ-mlv.fr
[2] Laboratoire d'informatique algorithmique: fondements et applications (LIAFA),
Université Denis-Diderot,
75251 Paris Cedex 05
boasson@liafa.jussieu.fr

Abstract. Balanced grammars are a generalization of parenthesis grammars in two directions. First, several kind of parentheses are allowed. Next, the set of right-hand sides of productions may be an infinite regular language. XML-grammars are a special kind of balanced grammars. This paper studies balanced grammars and their languages. It is shown that there exists a unique minimal balanced grammar equivalent to a given one. Next, balanced languages are characterized through a property of their syntactic congruence. Finally, we show how this characterization is related to previous work of McNaughton and Knuth on parenthesis languages.

1 Introduction

Balanced grammars are extended context-free grammars of a special kind. They generate words over a set of parenthesis that are well-formed (i.e. Dyck words). The right-hand side of any production of a balanced grammar is well-formed in a sense to be described. Moreover, for each nonterminal, the set of right-hand sides of productions for this nonterminal is a regular set.

The motivation for studying balanced grammars is twofold. First, it appears that grammars describing XML-documents are special cases of balanced grammars. The syntactic properties of these grammars have been considered in [1]. Next, parenthesis grammars, as developed by McNaughton [8] and Knuth [6], also appear to be balanced grammars, but with finitely many productions and only one pair of parentheses.. Parenthesis grammars have many interesting syntactic and decision properties, and it is interesting to investigate whether these properties carry over to grammars with regular sets of productions and several pairs of parentheses. As we shall see, many constructs carry over, although the proofs are sometimes more involved. In the course of this investigation, we will consider how several well-known constructions for standard context-free grammars behave when the sets of productions is regular.

A context-free grammar will be called *regular* if, for each nonterminal, the set of right-hand sides of productions for this nonterminal is regular. If these

W. Brauer et al. (Eds.): Formal and Natural Computing, LNCS 2300, pp. 3–25, 2002.

sets are finite (the case of usual context-free grammars) the grammar is called finite context-free. A well-known exercise on context-free grammars shows that the language generated by a regular context-free grammar is context-free. Thus, extending the set of productions does not change the family of languages that is generated. On the contrary, questions about grammars may turn out to be more difficult in the case of regular context-free grammars. One example is given in Section 4 below, where it is shown that every grammar can be converted to a codeterministic grammar. This was proved by McNaughton in the case of parenthesis grammars, but appears to hold for general regular context-free grammars.

The paper is organized as follows. Section 2 and 3 introduce regular context-free grammars and balanced grammars. Section 4 is about codeterministic grammars. Section 5 groups elementary results, examples and undecidability results for balanced languages. In Section 6, it is shown that every codeterministic balanced grammar can be reduced to a minimal balanced grammar, and that this grammar is unique (Theorem 6.3 and 6.5). In Section 7, we show that balanced languages are closed under complement. This is a result that holds only within regular balanced grammars, and does not hold within the framework of parenthesis grammars. Section 8 presents a syntactic characterization of balanced language. These are well-formed languages such that the set of Dyck words intersects only a finite number of congruence classes for the syntactic congruence of the language. Although this property is undecidable, it is closely related to the decision procedure in Section 9 where balanced languages with bounded width are considered. Indeed, we show that this property always holds in the case of bounded width.

2   Regular Context-Free Grammars

A *regular context-free grammar* $G = (V, A, \mathcal{P})$ is defined as follows. The set V is the *finite* set of variables or non-terminals. The alphabet A is the terminal alphabet. The set $\mathcal{P}$ is the set of productions. For each variable X, the set

$$R_X = \{m \in (V \cup A)^* \mid (X \to m) \in \mathcal{P}\}$$

is a regular subset of $(V \cup A)^*$. It follows that the set $\mathcal{P}$ itself is regular. A convenient shorthand is to write

$$X \to R_X$$

The set R_X is the set of X-handles. The language generated by a variable is defined in the usual way. We consider grammars that may have several axioms.

Regular context-free grammars have been considered in particular by Conway. In his book [2], the theory of context-free languages is developed in this framework.

Example 2.1. Consider the regular grammar $G = (\{X\}, \{a, \bar{a}\}, \mathcal{P})$ where $\mathcal{P}$ is the set

$$X \to aX^*\bar{a}$$

It generates the set of *Dyck primes* over $\{a, \bar{a}\}$.

In the sequel, we simply say *context-free grammar* for a regular context-free grammar, and we say that a grammar is *finite* if it has a finite set of productions. For every (regular) context-free grammar, there exists a finite context-free grammar generating the same language. In particular, all these languages are context-free.

3 Balanced Grammars

The main purpose of this paper is to study balanced grammars, as defined below. As we shall see, these grammars are a natural extension of McNaughton's parenthesis grammars.

A context-free grammar $G = (V, T, \mathcal{P})$ is *balanced* if the two following restrictions hold. First, the terminal alphabet T has a decomposition $T = A \cup \bar{A} \cup B$, where $\bar{A} = \{\bar{a} \mid a \in A\}$ is a disjoint copy of A, and B is disjoint from A and from $\bar{A}$. Next, productions are of the form $X \longrightarrow am\bar{a}$, with $m \in (V \cup B)^*$. It follows that the regular sets R_X of X-handles admit a decomposition

$$R_X = \bigcup_{a \in A} a R_{X,a} \bar{a}$$

where

$$R_{X,a} = \{m \in (V \cup B)^* \mid X \to am\bar{a}\}$$

Of course, the sets $R_{X,a}$ are regular subsets of $(V \cup B)^*$. We write for short:

$$X \to \bigcup_{a \in A} a R_{X,a} \bar{a}$$

It appears useful to call letters in A *colors*, and to call the initial letter of the right-hand side of a production the color of the production.

If $B = \emptyset$, a balanced grammar is called *pure*. A language L is (pure) *balanced* if

$$L = \bigcup_{X \in W} L_G(X)$$

for some subset W of V.

A language over $A \cup \bar{A}$ is *well-formed* if it is a subset of the Dyck language over A. Clearly, any pure balanced language is well-formed, and the converse does not hold (see Example 5.8 below).

The set D_A of *Dyck primes* over $A \cup \bar{A}$ will play an important role. Let us recall that it is a prefix and a suffix code, and that every word $x \in D_A$ admits a unique factorization of the form $x = az_1 \cdots z_n \bar{a}$, where $a \in A$, $n \geq 0$ and $z_1, \ldots, z_n$ are Dyck primes. A *Dyck factor* of a word w is any factor x of w that is a Dyck prime.

The set D_A has strong synchronization properties. We state them in a lemma.

Lemma 3.1. (*i*) *If a Dyck prime z is a factor of a product $z_1 \cdots z_n$ of Dyck primes, then z is a factor of one of the z_i.*
(*ii*) *If a Dyck word $w \in D^*$ is a factor of a Dyck prime z, then $w = z$ or there exist Dyck words $x, y \in D^*$ and a letter $a \in A$ such that the Dyck prime $axwy\bar{a}$ is a factor of z.*   □

Let us start with two simple examples of balanced languages.

Example 3.2. The language of *Dyck primes* over $\{a, \bar{a}\}$ is a pure balanced language, generated by

$$X \rightarrow aX^*\bar{a}$$

Example 3.3. The language D_A of *Dyck primes* over $T = A \cup \bar{A}$ is generated by the grammar

$$X \rightarrow \sum_{a \in A} X_a$$
$$X_a \rightarrow aX^*\bar{a}, \qquad a \in A$$

The variable X generates the language D_A which is well-formed. Although the present grammar is not balanced, the language D_A *is* a pure balanced language. Indeed, it suffices to replace X by $\sum_{a \in A} X_a$ in the second part, and to consider that every X_a is an axiom.

There exist several families of context-free grammars $G = (V, T, \mathcal{P})$ related to balanced grammars that have been studied in the past.

Parenthesis grammars have been studied in particular by McNaughton [8] and by Knuth [6]. Such a grammar is a balanced grammar where the alphabet A is a singleton (just one color), so $T = B \cup \{a, \bar{a}\}$, and with finitely many productions.

Bracketed grammars were investigated by Ginsburg and Harrison in [4]. The terminal alphabet T is the disjoint union of three alphabets A, $\bar{B}$ and C, and productions are of the form $X \longrightarrow am\bar{b}$, with $m \in (V \cup C)^*$. Moreover, there is a bijection between the set A of colors and the set of productions. Thus, in a bracketed grammar, every derivation step is marked.

Chomsky-Schützenberger grammars are used in the proof of the Chomsky-Schützenberger theorem (see e. g. [5]), even if they were never studied for their own. Here the terminal alphabet is of the form $T = A \cup \bar{A} \cup B$, and the productions are of the form $X \longrightarrow am\bar{a}$. Again, there is only one production for each color $a \in A$. So it is a special kind of balanced grammar with finite number of productions.

XML-grammars have been considered in [1]. They differ from all previous grammars by the fact that the set of productions is not necessarily finite, but regular. XML-grammars are balanced grammars. They are pure if all text elements are ignored. XML-grammars have the property that for each color $a \in A$, there is only one variable X such that the set $R_{X,a}$ is not empty. Expressed with colors, this means that all variables are monochromatic and all have different colors.

4   Codeterministic Grammars

A context-free grammar is called *codeterministic* if $X \to m$, $X' \to m$ implies $X = X'$. Codeterministic grammars are called backwards deterministic in [8]. In the next proposition, we show that codeterministic grammars can always be constructed. The main interest and use is for balanced grammars. In this case, the codeterministic grammar obtained is still balanced (Corollary 4.2). This also holds if the grammar one starts with is e.g. in Greibach Normal Form.

Proposition 4.1. *For every context-free grammar, there exists an equivalent codeterministic grammar context-free grammar that is effectively computable.*

The proof is adapted from the proof given in [8] for the case of finite context-free grammars. We give it here because it is an example of how an algorithm on finite grammars carries over to regular grammars.

Proof. Let $G = (V, A, \mathcal{P})$ be a context-free grammar. It will be convenient to denote here variables by small Greek letters such as α, β, σ because we will also deal with sets of variables. For each variable $\alpha \in V$, let R_α be the regular set of α-handles. Let $\mathcal{A}_\alpha$ be a deterministic automaton recognizing R_α. We first describe a transformation of the automaton $\mathcal{A}_\alpha$.

For any finite deterministic automaton $\mathcal{A} = (Q, q_0, F)$ over the alphabet $V \cup A$ with set of states Q, initial state q_0 and set of final states F, we define a *power automaton* $\mathcal{A}'$ recognizing words over the "big" alphabet $W = A \cup (2^V \setminus \emptyset)$ as follows. Each "big letter" B is either a nonempty subset of V, or a singleton $\{b\}$ composed of a terminal letter $b \in A$. The set of states of $\mathcal{A}'$ is 2^Q, its initial state is $\{q_0\}$, its final states are the sets $P \subset Q$ such that $P \cap Q \neq \emptyset$. The transition function is defined, for $P \subset Q$ and $B \in W$, by

$$P \cdot B = \{p \cdot b \mid p \in P, b \in B\}$$

This is quite similar to the well-known power set construction. A word $M = B_1 B_2 \cdots B_n$ over W is composed of "big letters" $B_1, \ldots B_n$. Given a word $M = B_1 B_2 \cdots B_n$ over W, we write $m \in M$ for $m \in (V \cup A)^*$ whenever $m = b_1 b_2 \cdots b_n$ with $b_i \in B_i$ for $i = 1, \ldots, n$. Observe that $B_i = \{b_i\}$ if $b_i \in A$. In other words, each $w \in A^*$ is can also be viewed as a "big" word.

For each $\alpha \in V$, let $\mathcal{A}_\alpha$ be a deterministic automaton recognizing R_α, let $\mathcal{A}'_\alpha$ be its power automaton, and let R'_α be the language (over W) recognized by $\mathcal{A}'_\alpha$. Then the following claims obviously hold.

   (a) If $m \in R_\alpha$ and $m \in M$, then $M \in R'_\alpha$.

   (b) Conversely, if $M \in R'_\alpha$, then there exists a word $m \in M$ such that $m \in R_\alpha$.

It follows from these claims that $M \in R'_\alpha$ if and only if there exists $m \in M$ with $m \in R_\alpha$. In other words, $M \in R'_\alpha$ if and only if $M \cap R_\alpha \neq \emptyset$.

For each word M over W, let $V(M)$ be the subset of V composed of the variables α such that M is recognized in the power automaton $\mathcal{A}'_\alpha$. Thus

$$V(M) = \{\alpha \in V \mid M \cap R_\alpha \neq \emptyset\}$$

For each subset $U \subset V$, define the set

$$S_U = \{M \in W^* \mid U = V(M)\}$$

of words M such that $U = V(M)$. This means that $M \in S_U$ iff U is precisely the set of variable α such that $M \in R'_\alpha$ (or equivalently $M \cap R_\alpha \neq \emptyset$). The set S_U is regular, because it is indeed

$$S_U = \bigcap_{\alpha \in U} R'_\alpha \setminus \left(\bigcup_{\alpha \notin U} R'_\alpha \right) \tag{1}$$

We define now a new grammar G' as follows. Its set of variables is $\mathcal{V} = 2^V \setminus \emptyset$. The productions are

$$U \to S_U$$

The grammar is codeterministic because in a production $X \to M$, the handle M determines $V(M)$. It remains to prove that G' is equivalent to G. We prove that

$$L(G, \alpha) = \bigcup_{\alpha \in U} L(G', U) \tag{2}$$

The proof is in two parts. We first show that for $\alpha \in U$, one has

$$L(G', U) \subset L(G, \alpha)$$

Consider a word $w \in L(G', U)$ and a derivation $U \xrightarrow{k} w$ of length k.

If $k = 1$ then $w \in A^*$ and $U \longrightarrow w$. Thus w is in S_U. By Eq. 1, and because $\alpha \in U$, one has $w \in R_\alpha$. It follows that $w \in L(G, \alpha)$.

If $k > 1$, then $U \longrightarrow M \xrightarrow{k-1} t$ for some $M \in S_U$ and some terminal word t. Set $M = U_1 \cdots U_n$. Then $t = t_1 \cdots t_n$ and $U_i \xrightarrow{*} t_i$ for $i = 1, \ldots n$. By induction, one has $\alpha_i \xrightarrow{*} t_i$ for each i and for all $\alpha_i \in U_i$. Next, since $M \in S_U$, one has $M \in R'_\alpha$. Consequently there is some $m \in M \cap R_\alpha$. Setting $m = \alpha_1 \cdots \alpha_n$, one has $\alpha_i \in U_i$ and $\alpha \longrightarrow \alpha_1 \cdots \alpha_n$. It follows that $\alpha \xrightarrow{*} t$. This proves the inclusion.

Consider now the converse inclusion

$$L(G, \alpha) \subset \bigcup_{\alpha \in U} L(G', U)$$

This means that, for each word $w \in L(G, \alpha)$, there exists a set U containing α such that $w \in L(G', U)$.

We shall in fact prove the following, slightly more general property. Let $m \in (V \cup A)^*$. If $\alpha \xrightarrow{*} m$, then for every set M containing m, there exists a set U containing α such that $U \xrightarrow{*} m$.

Assume indeed that $\alpha \xrightarrow{\ell} m$. If $\ell = 1$, choose any "big word" M containing m and let $U = \{\gamma \mid M \in R'_\gamma\}$. Then $U \longrightarrow M$. Moreover α is in U because $m \in R_\alpha$. This proves the claim in this case.

Assume $\ell > 1$. Consider the last step of the derivation $\alpha \xrightarrow{\ell-1} x\beta y \longrightarrow m = xhy$, with $\beta \to h$ a production in G. Choose any "big word" M containing m.

Then $M = XHY$, where $|X| = |x|$, $|H| = |h|$, $Y| = |y|$. Then $x \in X$, $h \in H$, $y \in Y$. By the first part of the proof, there exists a set N containing β such that $N \longrightarrow H$. Consider now $Z = XNY$. This set contains $x\beta y$. By induction, there exists a set U such that $\alpha \in U$ and $U \xrightarrow{*} Z$ in the grammar G'. Consequently, $U \xrightarrow{*} M$. This finishes the proof. $\qquad \square$

Corollary 4.2. *If a context-free grammar is balanced (pure balanced, in Greibach normal form, in two-sided Greibach normal form, is finite), there exists an equivalent codeterministic grammar that is of the same type.*

Proof. It suffices to observe that, in a "big word" constructed from a word, terminal letters remain unchanged, only variables are replaced by (finite) sets of variables. $\qquad \square$

5 Elementary Properties and Examples

Balanced context-free grammars have some elementary features that are basic steps in proving properties of this family of grammars. Given an alphabet $A \cup \bar{A}$, we denote by D_A or by D the set of *Dyck primes* over this alphabet. Given an alphabet $A \cup \bar{A} \cup B$, where B is disjoint from $A \cup \bar{A}$, a *Motzkin word* is a word in the shuffle $D_A^* \sqcup B^*$. It is not difficult to see that every Motzkin word has a unique factorization as a product of *Motzkin primes*. Motzkin primes are the words in the set

$$M = B \cup \bigcup_{a \in A} a(D_A^* \sqcup B^*)\bar{a}$$

We are interested in the set

$$N = \bigcup_{a \in A} a(D_A^* \sqcup B^*)\bar{a}$$

of *Motzkin-Dyck primes*

Lemma 5.1. *Let $G = (V, A \cup \bar{A} \cup B, \mathcal{P})$ be a balanced grammar. For each variable $X \in V$, the language $L(G, X)$ is a subset of N, and if G is pure, then $L(G, X)$ is a subset of D.*

Proof. The proof is straightforward by induction. $\qquad \square$

There are only tiny differences between balanced and pure balanced grammars. Moreover, every balanced language is a homomorphic image of a pure balanced language. To get the pure language, it suffices to introduce a barred alphabet $\bar{B}$ and to replace each occurrence of a letter b by a word $b\bar{b}$. The grammar is modified by adding a new variable X_b for each b, with only the production $X_b \to b\bar{b}$. Finally, in all other productions, each b is replaced by X_b. The original language is obtained by erasing all letters in $\bar{B}$.

For this reason, we assume from now on that all balanced grammars are pure.

Lemma 5.2. *Let $G = (V, A \cup \bar{A}, \mathcal{P})$ be a balanced grammar. Assume that*

$$X \xrightarrow{*} az_1 \cdots z_n \bar{a}$$

for some letter $a \in A$ and Dyck primes $z_1, \ldots, z_n$. Then there exists a production $X \to aX_1 \cdots X_n \bar{a}$ in G such that $X_i \xrightarrow{*} z_i$ for $i = 1, \ldots, n$.

Proof. Assume $X \xrightarrow{*} az_1 \cdots z_n \bar{a}$. Then there is a production $X \to aY_1 \cdots Y_m \bar{a}$ such that $X \to aY_1 \cdots Y_m \bar{a} \xrightarrow{*} az_1 \cdots z_n \bar{a}$. Since $Y_1 \cdots Y_m \xrightarrow{*} z_1 \cdots z_n$, there exist words $y_1, \ldots, y_m$ such that $Y_i \xrightarrow{*} y_i$ and $y_1 \cdots y_m = z_1 \cdots z_n$. By Lemma 5.1, the words y_i are Dyck primes. Thus $m = n$ and $y_i = z_i$.   □

Lemma 5.3. *Let L be the language generated by a balanced grammar $G = (V, A \cup \bar{A}, \mathcal{P})$. If $gud \in L$ for some words $g, d \in (A \cup \bar{A})^*$ and some Dyck prime $u \in D$, then there exists a variable X and an axiom S such that*

$$S \xrightarrow{*} gXd, \qquad X \xrightarrow{*} u$$

Moreover, if G is codeterministic, then the variable X with this property is unique.

Proof. The second part of the lemma is straightforward. If $gud \in L$, there is a left derivation $S \xrightarrow{*} gud$ for some axiom S. Let a denote the initial letter of u. Since letters in A appear only as initial letters in handles of productions, the step in the derivation where this letter is produced has the form

$$S \xrightarrow{*} gX\delta \longrightarrow gam\bar{a}\delta \xrightarrow{*} gud$$

for some $m \in R_{X,a}$. Since $am\bar{a}\delta \xrightarrow{*} ud$, there is a factorization $ud = u'd'$ with $am\bar{a} \xrightarrow{*} u'$ and $\delta \xrightarrow{*} d'$. By Lemma 5.1, the word u' is a Dyck prime, and since $ud = u'd'$, and the set of Dyck primes is a prefix code, it follows that $u = u'$ and consequently $d = d'$.   □

Lemma 5.4. *Let L be the language generated by a balanced grammar $G = (V, A \cup \bar{A}, \mathcal{P})$. If $gu_1 \cdots u_n d \in L$ for some words $g, d \in (A \cup \bar{A})^*$ and some Dyck primes $u_1, \ldots, u_n \in D$, then there exist variables $X_1, \ldots, X_n$ and an axiom S such that $S \xrightarrow{*} gX_1 \cdots X_n d$ and $X_i \xrightarrow{*} u_i$ for $i = 1, \ldots, n$.*   □

Lemma 5.5. *Let $G = (V, A \cup \bar{A}, \mathcal{P})$ be a codeterministic balanced grammar. If X, Y are distinct variables, then $L(G, X)$ and $L(G, Y)$ are disjoint.*

Proof. Assume there are derivations

$$X \longrightarrow aX_1 \cdots X_n \bar{a} \xrightarrow{*} u, \quad Y \longrightarrow a'Y_1 \cdots Y_{n'} \bar{a}' \xrightarrow{*} u$$

for some word $u \in D$. The proof is by induction on the sum of the lengths of these two derivation. If $n + n' = 2$, then $n = n' = 1$, and $a = a'$. Thus $X \longrightarrow a\bar{a}$

and $Y \longrightarrow a\bar{a}$, and since G is codeterministic, $X = Y$. If $n + n' > 2$, then u has factorizations

$$u = ax_1 \cdots x_n \bar{a} = a'y_1 \cdots y_{n'} \bar{a}'$$

where $X_i \xrightarrow{*} x_i$, $Y_j \xrightarrow{*} y_j$. Clearly, $a = a'$, and because D is a prefix code, one has $n = n'$, $x_i = y_i$. By induction, if follows that $X_i = Y_i$, and by codeterminism one gets $X = Y$. □

5.1 More Examples

Example 5.6. Consider the grammars

$$\begin{matrix} X \to aY^*\bar{a} \\ Y \to b\bar{b} \end{matrix} \quad \text{and} \quad \begin{matrix} X \to aY \\ Y \to b\bar{b}Y \mid \bar{a} \end{matrix}$$

They clearly generate the same language $a(b\bar{b})^*\bar{a}$. The left grammar is infinite and balanced. Thus the language is balanced. The right grammar is finite and not balanced. It follows from a result of Knuth [6] that we will discuss later that there is no balanced grammar with a finite number of production generating this language.

Example 5.7. The language

$$L = \{b(a\bar{a})^n aa\bar{a}\bar{a}(a\bar{a})^n\bar{b} \mid n > 0\}$$

is well-formed but not balanced. Assume the contrary. Then, for each $n > 0$, there is a word $m_n \in V^*$ such that

$$S \to bm_n\bar{b} \xrightarrow{*} b(a\bar{a})^n aa\bar{a}\bar{a}(a\bar{a})^n\bar{b}$$

Moreover, the word m_n has the form

$$m_n = X_1 \cdots X_n ZY_1 \cdots Y_n$$

where $X_i \to a\bar{a}$, $Y_i \to a\bar{a}$, $Z \xrightarrow{*} aa\bar{a}\bar{a}$. Each word m_n is in the regular language $R_{S,a}$, and a pumping argument gives the contradiction.

Example 5.8. Consider the grammar

$$\begin{matrix} X \to aY^*\bar{a} \\ Y \to b\bar{b}Yc\bar{c} \mid \varepsilon \end{matrix}$$

The language is balanced if and only if $b = c$. Indeed, if $b = c$, then the language is generated by the grammar

$$\begin{matrix} X \to a(ZZ)^*\bar{a} \\ Z \to b\bar{b} \end{matrix}$$

If $b \neq c$, the language is $\{a(b\bar{b})^n(c\bar{c})^n\bar{a} \mid n \geq 0\}$, and an argument similar to Example 5.7 shows that it is not balanced.

Example 5.9. The grammar

$$X_0 \to Ya\bar{a}$$
$$X \to aY\bar{a} \mid aa$$
$$Y \to aX\bar{a}\bar{a}aa\bar{a} \mid aY\bar{a}\bar{a}\bar{a}aX\bar{a}$$

generates a balanced language. It was used by Knuth ([6]) to demonstrate how his algorithm for the effective construction of a balanced grammar works.

5.2   Decision Problems

In this section, we state two decidability results. There are other decision problems that will be considered later. The following result was proved in [1]. It will be used later.

Theorem 5.10. *Given a context-free language L over an alphabet $A \cup \bar{A}$, it is decidable whether L is a subset of the set D_A of Dyck primes over $A \cup \bar{A}$.*

The following result is quite similar to a proposition in [1]. The proof differs slightly, and is included here for sake of completeness.

Theorem 5.11. *It is undecidable whether a language L is balanced.*

Proof. Consider the Post Correspondence Problem (PCP) for two sets of words $U = \{u_1, \ldots, u_n\}$ and $V = \{v_1, \ldots, v_n\}$ over the alphabet $C = \{a, b\}$. Consider a new alphabet $B = \{a_1, \ldots, a_n\}$ and define the sets L_U and L_V by

$$L_U = \{a_{i_1} \cdots a_{i_k} h \mid h \neq u_{i_k} \cdots u_{i_1}\} \quad L_V = \{a_{i_1} \cdots a_{i_k} h \mid h \neq v_{i_k} \cdots v_{i_1}\}$$

Recall that these are context-free, and that the set $L = L_U \cup L_V$ is regular iff $L = B^*C^*$. This holds iff the PCP has no solution.

Set $A = \{a_1, \ldots, a_n, a, b, c\}$, and define a mapping $\hat{w}$ from A^* to $(A \cup \bar{A})$ by mapping each letter d to $d\bar{d}$.

Consider words $\hat{u}_1, \ldots, \hat{u}_n, \hat{v}_1, \ldots, \hat{v}_n$ in $\{a\bar{a}, b\bar{b}\}^+$ and consider the languages

$$\hat{L}_U = \{a_{i_1}\bar{a}_{i_1} \cdots a_{i_k}\bar{a}_{i_k} h \mid h \neq \hat{u}_{i_k} \cdots \hat{u}_{i_1}\}$$

and

$$\hat{L}_V = \{a_{i_1}\bar{a}_{i_1} \cdots a_{i_k}\bar{a}_{i_k} h \mid h \neq \hat{v}_{i_k} \cdots \hat{v}_{i_1}\}$$

Set $\hat{L} = c(\hat{L}_U \cup \hat{L}_V)\bar{c}$. Assume $\hat{L}$ is a balanced language, generated by some balanced grammar with set of axioms W, and consider the set $R = \bigcup_{X \in W} R_{X,c}$. Since each word in $\hat{L}_U \cup \hat{L}_V$ is a product of two-letter Dyck primes, the set R is equal to $L_U \cup L_V$, up to a straightforward identification. Thus $L_U \cup L_V$ is regular which in turn implies that the PCP has no solution. Conversely, if the PCP has no solution, $L_U \cup L_V$ is regular which implies that $L_U \cup L_V = B^*C^*$, which implies that $\hat{L} = c\hat{B}^*\hat{C}^*\hat{c}$, showing that $\hat{L}$ is balanced.   □

6   Minimal Balanced Grammars

The aim of this section is to prove the existence of a minimal balanced code-terministic grammar for every balanced context-free grammar, and moreover that this grammar is unique up to renaming. This is the extension, to regular grammars with several types of parentheses, of a theorem of McNaughton [8].

Let G be a balanced codeterministic grammar generating a language $L = L(G)$, and let H be the set of axioms, i.e. $L = \cup_{S \in H} L(G, S)$.

A *context* for the variable X is a pair (g, d) of terminal words such that $S \xrightarrow{*} gXd$ for some axiom $S \in H$. The set of contexts for X is denoted by $C_G(X)$, or $C(X)$ if the grammar is understood. The *length* of a context (g, d) is the integer $|gd|$. Two variables X and Y are *equivalent*, and we write $X \sim Y$ if and only if they have same contexts, that is if and only if $C(X) = C(Y)$.

Proposition 6.1. *Given a balanced codeterministic grammar G, there exists an integer N such that $X \sim Y$ if and only if they have same contexts of length at most N.*

The proof will be an easy consequence of the following construction.

For any pair (g, d) of terminal words, we consider the set $W = W(g, d)$ of the variables that admit (g, d) as a context. Thus $X \in W$ if and only if $(g, d) \in C(X)$.

Lemma 6.2. *Let G be a balanced codeterministic grammar G. There exists an integer N with the following property. For any pair (g, d) of terminal words, there exists a pair (g', d') of length at most N such that $W(g, d) = W(g', d')$.*

Proof of Proposition 6.1. Assume that X and Y have the same contexts of length N. Let (g, d) be any context for X, and set $W = W(g, d)$. By definition, X is in W. Next, there exists a pair (g', d') with $|g'd'| \le N$ such that $W = W(g', d')$. Since X and Y have the same contexts of length N, and since (g', d') is a context for X, it is also a context for Y, and consequently Y is in W. This shows that every context for X is also a context for Y.   □

Proof of the lemma. Consider the set $W = W(g, d)$. The construction is in three steps.

For every X in W, there is a derivation $S \xrightarrow{*} gXd$ for some axiom $S \in H$. Clearly, gd is well-formed. Moreover, since the grammar is balanced, the words g and d have the form $g = a_1 g_1 \cdots a_n g_n$, $d = d_n \bar{a}_n \cdots d_1 \bar{a}_1$, where $g_1, \ldots, g_n$, $d_1, \ldots d_n$ are (products of) Dyck words. Thus every g_i is a product of Dyck primes, and similarly for every d_j. Because G is codeterministic, there is a factorization of the derivation into $S \xrightarrow{*} a_1 M_1 \cdots a_n M_n X M'_n \bar{a}_n \cdots M'_1 a_1$ where each M_i and M'_j is a product of variables, and $M_i \xrightarrow{*} g_i$, $M'_j \xrightarrow{*} d_j$. For each of the variables appearing in these products, we choose a Dyck prime of minimal length that is generated by this variable, and we replace the corresponding factor in g and d by this word of minimal length. Denote by N_0 the greatest of these minimal lengths. Then (g, d) is replaced by pair (g', d') of the form $g' = a_1 g'_1 \cdots a_n g'_n$, $d = d'_n \bar{a}_n \cdots d'_1 \bar{a}_1$ with the property that each g'_i, d'_j, is a product of Dyck primes of length at most N_0. There may be many such Dyck primes, but they are all small. Thus $W(g, d) = W(g', d')$, and we may assume that the initial (g, d) satisfies the property of having only small Dyck primes.

In the second step, we compute an upper bound for n. Observe that this integer is independent of the variable X chosen in W and also independent of the actual axiom. Fore each X in W, there is a path in the derivation tree from the axiom S to X. This path has $n + 2$ nodes (S and X included), and each of the internal nodes of the path produces one pair $(a_i, \bar{a}_i)$ in the factorizations of g and d. Assume that there are h variables in W. Then there are h different paths. Considering all these paths, one get h-tuples of variables, which are the labels of the internal nodes at depth $1, 2, \ldots, n$ for these paths. If n is greater than $h^{\|V\|+1}$ then two of these tuples are componentwise identical, and all derivation trees can be pruned simultaneously, without changing W. Thus, one may replace (g, d) by a pair such that $n \leq \|V\|^{\|V\|}$.

After these two steps, we know that $g = a_1 g_1 \cdots a_n g_n$, $d = d_n \bar{a}_n \cdots d_1 \bar{a}_1$, with n not too big and each g_i, d_j product of small Dyck primes. The number of primes in say $g_i d_i$ is exactly the number of variables minus 1 in the right-hand side of the i-th production on the path from the axiom S to the variable X. More precisely, assume that a production is $Z \to a_i \gamma Y \delta \bar{a}$, with $\gamma \xrightarrow{*} g_i$, $\delta \xrightarrow{*} d_i$. Then the number of Dyck primes in g_i is $|\gamma|$, and similarly for d_i. There may be several of these productions at level i, but for each of these productions, the handle $a_i \gamma Y \delta \bar{a}$ is the same up to possibly the variable Y. Each of these handles in in some fixed regular set, determined by the variable Z which also may change. Since there are only finitely many regular sets, it is clear that γ and δ may be chosen of small length. It follows that in each g_i, d_j the number Dyck primes they factor into may be bounded by a constant depending only on the grammar. This finishes the proof. $\qquad\square$

A balanced codeterministic grammar is *reduced* if two equivalent variables are equal.

Theorem 6.3. *A balanced codeterministic grammar is equivalent to a balanced codeterministic reduced grammar.*

We start with a lemma of independent interest.

Lemma 6.4. *Let $X \to aX_1 \cdots X_n \bar{a}$ be a production of a balanced codeterministic grammar G. For all variables $Y_1 \sim X_1$, $\ldots$, $Y_n \sim X_n$, there exists a variable $Y \sim X$ such that $Y \to aY_1 \cdots Y_n \bar{a}$ is a production of G.*

Proof. Consider indeed a derivation

$$S \xrightarrow{*} gXd \longrightarrow gaX_1 \cdots X_n \bar{a}d \xrightarrow{*} gax_1 \cdots x_n \bar{a}d$$

where $X_i \xrightarrow{*} x_i$ for $i = 1, \ldots, n$. The pair $(ga, x_2 \cdots x_n \bar{a}d)$ is a context for X_1, thus also for Y_1. Consequently, there is a derivation

$$S_1 \xrightarrow{*} gaY_1 x_2 \cdots x_n \bar{a}d \xrightarrow{*} gay_1 x_2 \cdots x_n \bar{a}d$$

for some axiom S_1 and some word y_1 with $Y_1 \xrightarrow{*} y_1$. Since the grammar is codeterministic, it follows that $S_1 \xrightarrow{*} gay_1 X_2 x_3 \cdots x_n \bar{a}d$. Thus $(gay_1, x_3 \cdots x_n \bar{a}d)$ is a context for X_2 (and for Y_2), and as before, there is a word y_2 with $Y_2 \xrightarrow{*} y_2$ such that, for some axiom S_2, one has

$$S_1 \xrightarrow{*} gay_1 Y_2 \cdots x_n \bar{a} d \xrightarrow{*} gay_1 y_2 x_3 \cdots x_n \bar{a} d$$

Continuing in this way, we get a derivation

$$S' \xrightarrow{*} gay_1 \cdots y_n \bar{a} d$$

where $Y_i \xrightarrow{*} y_i$ for $i = 1, \ldots, n$. Since the grammar is codeterministic, it follows that

$$S' \xrightarrow{*} gaY_1 \cdots Y_n \bar{a} d$$

and since the grammar is balanced, this derivation decomposes into

$$S' \xrightarrow{*} gYd \longrightarrow gaY_1 \cdots Y_n \bar{a} d$$

for some production $Y \rightarrow aY_1 \cdots Y_n \bar{a}$. Observe that (g, d) is a context for Y. It follows easily that $X \sim Y$. $\qquad\square$

Proof of Theorem 6.3. Let G be a balanced codeterministic grammar, and define a quotient grammar $G/\sim$ by identifying equivalent variables in G. More precisely, the variables in the quotient grammar are the equivalence classes of variables in G. Denote the equivalence class of X by $[X]$. The productions of $G/\sim$ are all productions $[X] \rightarrow a[X_1] \cdots [X_n]\bar{a}$, where $X \rightarrow aX_1 \cdots X_n\bar{a}$ is a production in G. Observe that the sets of productions of $G/\sim$ are still regular.

Note that if $X \sim Y$ in G and X is an axiom, then Y also is an axiom, because X is an axiom iff $(\varepsilon, \varepsilon)$ is a context for X. Thus the axioms in $G/\sim$ are equivalence classes of axioms in G.

Set $L = L(G, H)$ and $L' = L(G/\sim, H/\sim)$. It is easily seen that $L \subset L'$. Indeed, whenever $X \xrightarrow{*} u$ in G, then $[X] \xrightarrow{*} u$ in $G/\sim$. Conversely, suppose $[X] \xrightarrow{k} u$ in $G/\sim$. We show that there exists Y in $[X]$ such that $Y \xrightarrow{*} u$. This clearly holds if $k = 1$. If $k > 1$, then $[X] \longrightarrow a[X_1] \cdots [X_n]\bar{a} \xrightarrow{k-1} ax_1 \cdots x_n bara$ with $[X_i] \xrightarrow{*} x_i$. By induction, there exist variables Y_i in $[X_i]$ such that $Y_i \xrightarrow{*} x_i$ in G. Moreover, by the previous lemma, there exists a production

$$Y \rightarrow aY_1 \cdots Y_n\bar{a}$$

in G for some Y in $[X]$. Thus $Y \xrightarrow{*} u$. This proves the claim. It follows that if $u \in L'$, then $u \in L$. $\qquad\square$

Before stating the next result, it is convenient to recall the syntactic congruence of a language. Given a language L, the context of a terminal word u is the set $C_L(u) = \{(g, d) \mid gud \in L\}$. Observe that this is independent of the device generating L. The syntactic congruence $\equiv_L$ is defined by $x \equiv_L y$ iff $C_L(x) = C_L(y)$. This congruence will be considered later.

Theorem 6.5. *Two equivalent reduced grammars are the same up to renaming of the variables.*

Proof. Let G be a reduced grammar generating the language L. If X is a variable of X and $X \xrightarrow{*} u$, then $C_G(X) = C_L(u)$. Indeed, if $gud \in L$, there is a derivation $S \xrightarrow{*} gud$ for some axiom. This can be factorized into $S \xrightarrow{*} gYd \xrightarrow{*} gud$ for some variable Y because G is balanced, and $Y = X$ because G is codeterministic. Thus (g, d) is a context for X. The converse inclusion is clear.

Consider another reduced grammar G' also generating the language L. Let X be a variable in G, let $u \in L(G, X)$ and let (g, d) be a context for X. Then $gud \in L$. Thus, there exists a derivation $S' \xrightarrow{*} gud$ in G'. Since u is a Dyck prime and G' is balanced, there is a variable X' in G' such that $u \in L(G', X')$. Moreover, (g, d) is also a context X' (in G'). By the previous remark, $C_G(X) = C_L(u) = C_{G'}(X')$. Consider another word v in $L(G, X)$. Then there is a variable Y' such that $v \in L(G', Y')$. However $C_{G'}(X') = C_{G'}(Y')$ and, since G' is reduced, $X' = Y'$. Thus, to each variable X in G there corresponds a unique variable X' in G' that has same contexts. It follows easily that $L(G, X) = L(G', X')$.

It remains to show that the productions are the same. For this, consider a production $X \to aY_1 \cdots Y_n \bar{a}$ in G. Then there are words $u_1, \ldots, u_n$ such that $X \xrightarrow{*} au_1 \cdots u_n \bar{a}$, $Y_i \xrightarrow{*} u_i$ in G. In the grammar G', there is a variable X' such that $X' \xrightarrow{*} au_1 \cdots u_n \bar{a}$. Since G' is balanced and codeterministic there are variables Y_i' such that $X' \to aY_1' \cdots Y_n' \bar{a}$ and $Y_i' \xrightarrow{*} u_i$ in G'. This finishes the proof. $\square$

Observe that a reduced grammar is minimal in the sense that it has a minimal number of variables.

7   Complete Balanced Grammars

In this section, we consider complementation. Any balanced language is a subset of the language D of Dyck primes. Thus, complementation of a balanced language makes only sense only with respect to the set D.

Proposition 7.1. *The complement of a balanced language with respect to the set of Dyck primes is balanced.*

It is straightforward that balanced languages are closed under union. They are therefore also closed under intersection.

Proof. Let L be a balanced language and let G be a balanced codeterministic grammar generating it, so that $L = L(G, W)$ for some subset W of the set of variables V. Set also $M = L(G, V)$. Then M is precisely the set of Dyck factors of words in L. Hence, $D \setminus M$ is the possibly empty set of Dyck primes that are not Dyck factors of words in L. We show that $D \setminus M$ is balanced.

Consider first the subset N of $D \setminus M$ composed of words x such that any proper Dyck factor y of x is in M. Thus

$$N = (D \setminus M) \setminus (A \cup \bar{A})^+ (D \setminus M)(A \cup \bar{A})^+$$

A word is in $D \setminus M$ if and only if it has a Dyck factor in N.

A word $x \in N$ has the form $x = ay_1 \cdots y_n \bar{a}$, where $y_1, \ldots, y_n \in M$. Thus, there is a derivation

$$aX_1 \cdots X_n \bar{a} \xrightarrow{*} x$$

and the word $aX_1 \cdots X_n \bar{a}$ is not a handle in G. Conversely, if $aX_1 \cdots X_n \bar{a}$ is not a handle, then any word it generates is not in M because the grammar is codeterministic. Set $U_a = \bigcup_{X \in V} R_{X,a}$, consider the grammar G' obtained by adding a variable Φ and the productions

$$\Phi \to \bigcup_{a \in A} a(V^* \setminus U_a)\bar{a}$$

Then $N = L(G', \Phi)$.

Consider the grammar G'' obtained form G' by adding the productions

$$\Phi \to \bigcup_{a \in A} a(V + \Phi)^* \Phi (V + \Phi)^* \bar{a}$$

Since a word is in $D \setminus M$ if and only if it has a Dyck factor in N, one has $D \setminus M = L(G'', \Phi)$.

Observe finally that, in view of codeterminism,

$$D \setminus L = D \setminus M \cup \bigcup_{X \in V \setminus W} L(G, X)$$

This finishes the proof. □

A balanced grammar G with set of variables V is *complete* if

$$D = \bigcup_{X \in V} L(G, X)$$

Proposition 7.2. *For each balanced codeterministic grammar G, there exists a balanced complete codeterministic grammar G' with at most one additional variable Φ such that $L(G, X) = L(G', X)$ for all variables $X \neq \Phi$.*

Proof. This is an immediate consequence of the proof of the previous proposition, since the grammar G'' constructed in that proof is indeed complete. □

As a consequence, if G is a minimal grammar for a language L and G' is minimal for $D \setminus L$ than G and G' have the same number of variables, up to at most one.

8 A Characterization

We have recalled (Theorem 5.10) that it is decidable whether a context-free language L is well-formed, that is whether L is a subset of a set of Dyck primes. We also have seen (Theorem 5.11) that it is undecidable whether L is balanced, that is whether there exists a (regular) balanced grammar generating L. In the case of a single pair of parentheses, a remarkable result of Knuth [6] shows on the contrary that, given a finite context-free grammar generating L, it is decidable whether there exists an equivalent finite balanced grammar generating the context-free language L. Moreover, Knuth gives an algorithm for constructing a finite balanced grammar from a given finite context-free grammar, if such a grammar exists.

The purpose of this section is investigate this relationship. More precisely, we shall prove a property that is equivalent for a language to be balanced. This property is of course undecidable. However, it trivially holds for languages generated by finite balanced grammars. In this way, we have a characterization that in some sense explains why Knuth's algorithm works, and why it cannot work in the general case.

Recall that the syntactic congruence $\equiv_L$ of a language L is defined by $x \equiv_L y$ iff $C_L(x) = C_L(y)$. Here $C_L(u) = \{(g, d) \mid gud \in L\}$ is the set of *contexts* of u in L. The equivalence class of u is denoted $[u]_L$ or $[u]$ if L is understood. Any language is a union of congruence classes for its syntactic congruence. It is well known that a language is regular if and only if its syntactic congruence has a finite number of equivalence classes.

A language L will be called *M-finite*, where M is a language if the number of equivalence classes of $\equiv_L$ intersecting M is finite. We will be concerned with languages that are D-finite or D^*-finite. Since D is a subset of D^*, any D^*-finite language is also D-finite. We will see that in some special cases, the converse also holds.

Observe that for a given (balanced) language L, the set of Dyck primes needs not to be a union of equivalence classes of $\equiv_L$. Consider indeed the language

$$L = \{aab\bar{b}\bar{a}ab\bar{b}\bar{a}\bar{a}, aab\bar{b}\bar{a}\bar{a}b\bar{b}\bar{a}\bar{a}\}$$

The pair $(aab\bar{b}, b\bar{b}\bar{a}\bar{a})$ is the only context of both words $a\bar{a}$ and $\bar{a}a$. So they are equivalent for $\equiv_L$. However, $a\bar{a}$ is a Dyck word and $\bar{a}a$ is not.

Theorem 8.1. *A language L over $A \cup \bar{A}$ is balanced if and only if it is well-formed and D^*-finite.*

Proof. Assume first that L is well-formed and D^*-finite. We construct a balanced grammar generating L. Since D is a subset of D^*, the language L is also D-finite. Let V be a finite set of variables in bijection with the equivalence classes intersecting D. For $u \in D$, denote by $X_{[u]}$ the variable associated to the equivalence class $[u]$. Conversely, let $[X]$ be the equivalence class of $\equiv_L$ associated to X. For $X \in V$ there is a word $u \in D$ such that $X = X_{[u]}$ and $[X] = [u]$.

Each word w in D^* has a unique factorization $w = u_1 \cdots u_n$ with $u_i \in D$. We define a word $\phi(w)$ over V associated to w by $\phi(w) = X_{[u_1]} \cdots X_{[u_n]}$. The mapping ϕ is an isomorphism from D^* onto V^*. We consider the grammar defined by the productions $X \to a R_{X,a} \bar{a}$, where

$$R_{X,a} = \{\phi(w) \mid aw\bar{a} \in D \cap [X]\}$$

and with axioms $\{X_{[u]} \mid u \in L\}$. This grammar generates L. Indeed, it is easily checked that variable X generates $[X] \cap D$. Thus $X_{[u]}$ generates the class $[u] \cap D$, for $u \in D$. Thus if the sets $R_{X,a}$ are regular, the grammar is balanced.

Consider a fixed $X \in V$ and a letter $a \in A$. Denote by $\approx$ the syntactic congruence of $R_{X,a}$. Thus for $p, q \in V^*$, one has $p \approx q$ iff $rps \in R_{X,a} \Leftrightarrow rqs \in R_{X,a}$.

Let p, q be words in V^* and let y, z be words in D^* such that $\phi(y) = p$, $\phi(z) = q$. Assume $y \equiv_L z$. Let $r, s \in V^*$ be such that $rps \in R_{X,a}$. Choose g, d such that $\phi(g) = r$, $\phi(d) = s$. Then $agyd\bar{a} \in [X]$. Consequently $agzd\bar{a} \in [X]$, showing that $rqs \in R_{X,a}$, and therefore $p \approx q$. This shows that to each equivalence class of $\equiv_L$ intersecting D^* corresponds one equivalence class of $R_{X,a}$. Since there are finitely many of the former, there are finitely may of the second, and $R_{X,a}$ is regular.

Conversely, assume now that L is balanced. Then it is of course well-formed. Consider a codeterministic balanced grammar G generating L. Let $u \in D^*$ be a Dyck word that is a factor of some word in L, and set $u = v_1 \cdots v_n$, with $v_1, \ldots, v_n \in D$. There exists a unique word $X_1 \cdots X_n \in V^*$ such that $S \xrightarrow{*} gX_1 \cdots X_n d$ for some words g, d and some axiom S, and $X_i \xrightarrow{*} v_i$. We denote this word $X_1 \cdots X_n$ by $X(u)$. Define an equivalence relation on words in D^* by $u \sim v$ if and only if $X(u) \equiv_{R_{X,a}} X(v)$ for all $X \in V$ and $a \in A$. Here $\equiv_{R_{X,a}}$ is the syntactic congruence of the language $R_{X,a}$. Since the sets $R_{X,a}$ are regular, there are only finitely many equivalence class for $\sim$. We show that $u \sim v$ implies $u \equiv_L v$. This shows that the set of Dyck words that are factors of words in L are contained in a finite number of classes for $\equiv_L$. The other Dyck words all have empty set of contexts for L, and therefore are in the same class. This proves the proposition.

Assume $gud \in L$. Then there exists a unique derivation of the form

$$S \xrightarrow{*} g_1 X d_1, \qquad X \to aZ_1 \cdots Z_p X(u) Y_1 \cdots Y_q \bar{a}$$

such that $Z_1 \cdots Z_p \xrightarrow{*} g_2$, $Y_1 \cdots Y_q \xrightarrow{*} d_2$, and $g = g_1 a g_2$, $d = d_2 \bar{a} d_1$. Observe that $(Z_1 \cdots Z_p, Y_1 \cdots Y_q)$ is a context for the word $X(u)$ in the language $R_{X,a}$. Since $u \sim v$, it is also a context for $X(v)$. Thus $X \to aZ_1 \cdots Z_p X(v) Y_1 \cdots Y_q \bar{a}$ whence $S \xrightarrow{*} gvd$, showing that $gvd \in L$. $\qquad \square$

Observe that it is undecidable, whether a well-formed (even context-free) language L, is D^*-finite. Indeed, by the theorem, this is equivalent for L to be balanced, and this latter property is undecidable (Theorem 5.11).

9   Bounded Width

In the sequel, we describe a condition, the bounded width property, that implies the existence of a balanced grammar.

Let L be a well-formed language over $A \cup \bar{A}$. We denote by $F(L)$ the set of factors of words in L. Given $N \geq 0$, we denote by $D^{(N)} = \{\varepsilon\} \cup D \cup \cdots \cup D^N$ the set of product of at most N Dyck primes. The language L has *bounded width* if there exist $N \geq 0$ such that

$$F(L) \cap D^* \subset D^{(N)}$$

This means that every Dyck word that is a factor of a word in L is a product of at most N Dyck primes. The smallest N with this property is the width of L.

Example 9.1. The language $L = \{ab^n\bar{b}^n\bar{a} \mid n > 0\}$ has width 1.

Example 9.2. The language $L = \{a(b\bar{b})^n(c\bar{c})^n\bar{a} \mid n > 0\}$ has unbounded width.

We recall without proof a result from [1] (Theorem 6.1).

Proposition 9.3. *Given a well-formed context-free language L, it is decidable whether L has bounded width.*

Bounded width has many implications. As already mentioned, if a well-formed language L is D^*-finite, then it is D-finite. Bounded width implies the converse.

Proposition 9.4. *Let L be a well-formed language with bounded width. If L is D-finite, then it is D^*-finite.*

Proof. Let q be the number of equivalence classes of L intersecting D. Let N be the width of L. Let $u = u_1 \cdots u_n \in D^*$, with $u_1, \ldots, u_n \in D$. By a general result on congruences,

$$[u_1] \cdots [u_n] \subset [u]$$

If $n > N$, then u is the equivalence class of words that are not factors of L. Otherwise, $[u]$ contains at least one of the $q + q^2 + \cdots q^N$ products of equivalence classes. Thus the number of equivalence classes of L intersecting D^* is bounded by this number.   □

The proposition is false if the width is unbounded.

Example 9.5. Consider the language $L = \{a(b\bar{b})^n(c\bar{c})^n\bar{a} \mid n > 0\}$ of the preceding example. There are just for classes of the syntactic congruence of L intersecting D. Their intersections with D are L, $\{b\bar{b}\}$, $\{c\bar{c}\}$, and the set $D \setminus F(L)$ of Dyck primes which are not factors of words of L. On the contrary, there are infinitely many equivalence classes intersecting D^*. For instance, each of the $(b\bar{b})^n$ is in a separate class, with $(a, (c\bar{c})^n\bar{a})$ as a context.

Another property resulting from bounded width is the following.

Proposition 9.6. *Le G be a balanced grammar generating a language L with bounded width. Then G is finite.*

Proof. Let $G = (V, A \cup \bar{A}, \mathcal{P})$ be a balanced grammar with productions

$$X \to \bigcup_{a \in A} a R_{X,a} \bar{a}$$

Assume that a language $R_{X,a}$ is infinite. Then, for arbitrarily great n, there are derivations $X \xrightarrow{*} a z_1 \cdots z_n \bar{a}$, and since these words are factors of L, the language L has unbounded width. Thus all $R_{X,a}$ are finite. □

We shall prove the following proposition.

Proposition 9.7. *A well-formed context-free language with bounded width is D-finite.*

In view of Theorem 8.1 and Proposition 9.4, we get

Corollary 9.8. *A well-formed context-free language with bounded width is balanced.*

In fact, we have

Theorem 9.9. *Let L be a well-formed context-free language. Then L has bounded width if and only if L is generated by a finite balanced grammar. Moreover, the construction of the grammar is effective.*

The rest of the paper is concerned with the proof of Proposition 9.7.

We need some notation. The *Dyck reduction* is the semi-Thue reduction defined by the rules $a\bar{a} \to \varepsilon$ for $a \in A$. A word is *reduced* or *irreducible* if it cannot be further reduced, that means if it has no factor of the form $a\bar{a}$. Every word w reduces to a unique irreducible word denoted $\rho(w)$. We also write $w \equiv w'$ when $\rho(w) = \rho(w')$. If w is a factor of some Dyck prime, then $\rho(w)$ has no factor of the form $a\bar{b}$, for $a, b \in A$. Thus $\rho(w) \in \bar{A}^* A^*$.

In the sequel, G denotes a reduced finite context-free grammar over $T = A \cup \bar{A}$, generating a language L. For each variable X, we set

$$\mathrm{Irr}(X) = \{\rho(w) \mid X \xrightarrow{*} w, w \in T^*\}$$

This is the set of reduced words of all words generated by X. If L is well-formed, then $\mathrm{Irr}(S) = \{\varepsilon\}$ for every axiom S. Moreover, $\mathrm{Irr}(X)$ is finite for each variable X. Indeed, consider any derivation $S \xrightarrow{*} gXd$ with $g, d \in T^*$. Any $u \in \mathrm{Irr}(X)$ is of the form $u = \bar{x}y$, for $x, y \in A^*$. Since $\rho(gud) = \rho(\rho(g)u\rho(d)) = \varepsilon$, the word x is a suffix of $\rho(g)$, and $\bar{y}$ is a prefix of $\rho(d)$. Thus $|u| \leq |\rho(g)| + |\rho(d)|$, showing that the length of the words in $\mathrm{Irr}(X)$ is bounded.

A grammar is *qualified* if $\mathrm{Irr}(X)$ is a singleton for every variable X. It is easy to qualify a grammar. For this, every variable X is replaced by variables X_u, one for each $u \in \mathrm{Irr}(X)$. In each production $Y \to m$, each variable X in the handle is replaced by all possible X_u. For each new handle m' obtained in this way, substitute u for X_u for all variables, and then compute the reduced word r of the resulting word. The word r is in $\mathrm{Irr}(Y)$. Add the production $Y_r \to m'$. When this is done for all possible choices, the resulting grammar is qualified.

We recall the following two lemmas from [1].

Lemma 9.10. *If $X \xrightarrow{+} gXd$ for some words in $g, d \in (A \cup \bar{A})^*$, then there exist words $x, y, p, q \in A^*$ such that*

$$\rho(g) = \bar{x}px, \quad \rho(d) = \bar{y}\bar{q}y$$

and moreover p and q are conjugate words.

A pair (g, d) such that $X \xrightarrow{+} gXd$ is a *lifting* pair if the word p in Lemma 9.10 is nonempty, it is a *flat* pair if $p = \varepsilon$.

Lemma 9.11. *The language L has bounded width iff G has no flat pair.*

We are now ready for the proof of Proposition 9.7. Consider a finite context-free grammar G, with axiom S, generating the well-formed language L with bounded width. Consider a word Dyck prime u that is a factor of a word in L. We define, for each word u, a set of tuples called *borders* of u. We shall see that if two Dyck primes u, u' have the same set of borders, then they are equivalent in the syntactic equivalence of L. The main argument to show that L will be D-finite will be to prove that the set of all borders is finite. This relies on the fact that L has bounded width.

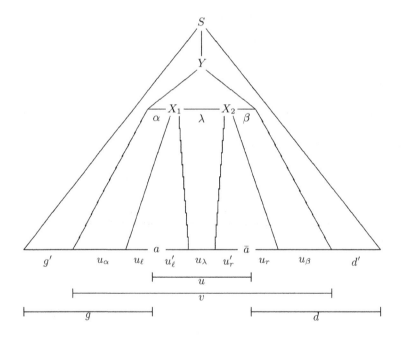

Fig. 1. The derivation tree.

Let (g, d) be any context for u. Consider a derivation $S \xrightarrow{*} gud$. In the derivation tree associated to this derivation (Figure 1), we consider the smallest subtree that generates a word v that has as factor the Dyck prime u. Let Y be the root of this tree. Then $S \xrightarrow{*} g'Yd'$, $Y \xrightarrow{*} v$, and u is a factor of v. The minimality condition on the subtree implies that the derivation factorizes into $Y \longrightarrow \alpha X_1 \lambda X_2 \beta \xrightarrow{*} v$ where $\alpha \xrightarrow{*} u_\alpha$, $X_1 \xrightarrow{*} u_\ell a u'_\ell$, $\lambda \xrightarrow{*} u_\lambda$, $X_2 \xrightarrow{*} u'_r \bar{a} u_r$, $\beta \xrightarrow{*} u_\beta$ and

$$v = u_\alpha u_\ell a u'_\ell u_\lambda u'_r \bar{a} u_r u_\beta$$

with $v = u_\alpha u_\ell u u_r u_\beta$ and $u = a u'_\ell u_\lambda u'_r \bar{a}$. Observe that $g = g' u_\alpha u_\ell$ and $d = u_r u_\beta d'$. Notice that there might be the special case $X_1 = a$ and similarly $X_2 = \bar{a}$. Also, u_λ may be the empty word.

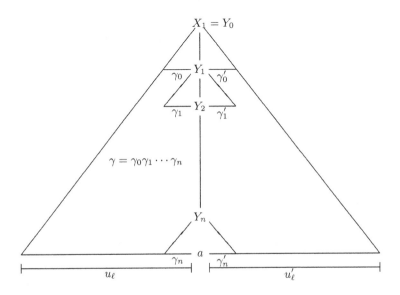

Fig. 2. The path from X_1 to the distinguished letter a.

Consider now the variables $Y_0 = X_1, Y_1, \ldots, Y_n$ on the path from X_1 to the initial letter a of u (Figure 2). Denote the productions used on this path $Y_i \rightarrow \gamma_i Y_{i+1} \gamma'_i$ for $i = 0, \ldots, n-1$, and $Y_n \rightarrow \gamma_n a \gamma'_n$. It follows that $\gamma_0 \gamma_1 \cdots \gamma_n \xrightarrow{*} u_\ell$. Similarly, there are words $\delta_0, \ldots, \delta_m$ such that $\delta_m \cdots \delta_0 \xrightarrow{*} u_r$. A *border* of u is the tuple $(Y, \alpha, \gamma, \delta, \beta)$, with $\gamma = \gamma_0 \gamma_1 \cdots \gamma_n$ and $\delta = \delta_m \cdots \delta_0$. If $(Y, \alpha, \gamma, \delta, \beta)$ is a border of u, then by construction, there are words $g', d', u_\alpha, u_\ell, u_r, u_\beta$ with $S \xrightarrow{*} g'Yd'$, $\alpha \xrightarrow{*} u_\alpha$, $\gamma \xrightarrow{*} u_\ell$, $\delta \xrightarrow{*} u_r$, $\beta \xrightarrow{*} u_\beta$ such that $(g'u_\alpha u_\ell, u_r u_\beta d')$ is a context for u in L. It follows that if u' has the same borders that u has, then u' has the same contexts as u.

In order to complete the proof, we show that if L has bounded width, then the lengths of the components γ and δ in any border are uniformly bounded. This shows that the set of all borders of all Dyck primes is finite.

We carry out the proof for γ. As described above, $\gamma = \gamma_0\gamma_1\cdots\gamma_n$, where n is the length of the path from variable X_1 to the initial letter a. If this length is not bounded, then there is a variable, say X that appears arbitrarily often on this path. Consider all consecutive occurrences of this variable on the path. Assume there are $k + 1$ of them. Each of the first k yields an iterative pair $X \xrightarrow{+} g_i X d_i$, and by Lemma 9.10, there exist words $x_i, y_i \in A^*$, $p_i, q_i \in A^+$ such that $\rho(g_i) = \bar{x}_i p_i x_i$, $\rho(d_i) = \bar{y}_i \bar{q}_i y_i$. Consider the derivation obtained by composing these iterating pairs:

$$X \xrightarrow{*} g_1 g_2 \cdots g_k X d_k d_{k-1} \cdots d_1, \quad X \xrightarrow{*} w$$

The resulting word $g_1 g_2 \cdots g_k w d_k d_{k-1} \cdots d_1$ is a factor of $u_\ell a u'_\ell$. Moreover, the occurrence of the letter a is an occurrence in the factor w, that is $w = w' a w''$, and the letter a cannot be reduced, in the Dyck reduction, with any letter in $w'' d_k d_{k-1} \cdots d_1$ since it reduces with the letter $\bar{a}$ in $u'_r \bar{a} u_r$. Hence this occurrence of a remains in $\rho(w)$. The word $g_1 g_2 \cdots g_k w d_k d_{k-1} \cdots d_1$ simplifies into $\bar{x}_1 p_1 x_1 \cdots \bar{x}_k p_k x_k \rho(w) \bar{y}_k \bar{q}_k y_k \cdots \bar{y}_1 \bar{q}_1 y_1$.

Observe that in the suffix $\bar{y}_k \bar{q}_k y_k \cdots \bar{y}_1 \bar{q}_1 y_1$, the number of barred letters exceeds by $|\bar{q}_k \cdots \bar{q}_1|$ the number of unbarred letters. All these letters must reduce to the empty word with letters in w''. Since $\rho(w)$ is fixed, this cannot happen. Thus k is uniformly bounded.

The set of all borders of all Dyck primes is finite. If $(Y, \alpha, \gamma, \delta, \beta)$ is a border, there are words $g', d', u_\alpha, u_\ell, u_r, u_\beta$ with $S \xrightarrow{*} g' Y d'$, $\alpha \xrightarrow{*} u_\alpha$, $\gamma \xrightarrow{*} u_\ell$, $\delta \xrightarrow{*} u_r$, $\beta \xrightarrow{*} u_\beta$ and a word z such that $u_\ell z u_r$ is a Dyck prime. Wee have seen that the lengths of γ and δ are bounded. The existence of z is easy to check for a given pair (u_ℓ, u_r). Thus the construction is effective. $\qquad\square$

Acknowledgment. We thank Isabelle Fagnot for helpful discussions.

References

1. J. Berstel and L. Boasson. XML-grammars. In *MFCS 2000 Mathematical Foundations of Computer Science* (M. Nielsen and B. Rovan, Eds.), Springer-Verlag, Lect. Notes Comput. Sci. **1893**, pages 182–191, 2000.
2. J.H. Conway. *Regular Algebra and Finite Machines.* Chapman and Hall, London, 1971.
3. N. Chomsky and M.P. Schützenberger. The Algebraic Theory of Context-Free Languages. In *Computer Programming and Formal Systems* (P. Braffort and D. Hirschberg, Eds.), North-Holland, Amsterdam, pages 118–161, 1963.
4. S. Ginsburg and M.A. Harrison. Bracketed Context-Free Languages. *J. Comput. Syst. Sci.*, 1:1–23, 1967.
5. Michael A. Harrison. *Introduction to Formal Language Theory.* Addison-Wesley, Reading, Mass., 1978.
6. D.E. Knuth. A Characterization of Parenthesis Languages. *Inform. Control*, 11:269–289, 1967.
7. A.J. Korenjak and J.E. Hopcroft. Simple Deterministic Grammars. In *7th Switching and Automata Theory*, pages 36–46, 1966.

8. R. McNaughton. Parenthesis Grammars. *J. Assoc. Mach. Comput.*, 14:490–500, 1967.

9. W3C Recommendation REC-xml-19980210. *Extensible Markup Language (XML) 1.0*, 10 February 1998. `http://www.w3.org/TR/REC-XML`.

10. W3C Working Draft. *XML Schema Part 0,1 and 2*, 22 September 2000. `http://www.w3.org/TR/xmlschema-0,1,2`.

Safety and Liveness Properties for Real Traces and a Direct Translation from LTL to Monoids

Volker Diekert[1] and Paul Gastin[2][*]

[1] Inst. für Informatik, Universität Stuttgart, Breitwiesenstr. 20-22, 70565 Stuttgart
`diekert@informatik.uni-stuttgart.de`
[2] LIAFA, Université Paris 7, 2, place Jussieu, 75251 Paris Cedex 05
`Paul.Gastin@liafa.jussieu.fr`

Abstract. For infinite words there are well-known characterizations of safety and liveness properties. We extend these results to real Mazurkiewicz traces. This is possible due to a result, which has been established recently: Every first-order definable real trace language is definable in linear temporal logic using future tense operators, only. We show that the canonical choice for a topological characterization of safety and liveness properties is given by the Scott topology. In this paper we use an algebraic approach where we work with aperiodic monoids. Therefore we also give a direct translation from temporal logic to aperiodic monoids which is of independent interest.

Keywords Mazurkiewicz traces, temporal logics, safety and liveness properties, concurrency, aperiodic monoids.

1 Introduction

Trace theory has been initiated in computer science by Antoni Mazurkiewicz [21] and early works of Robert Keller [19]. Since then many researchers have made important contributions to trace theory, in particular let us mention the work of Grzegorz Rozenberg, see e.g. [1,11,12,26,27]. Nowadays, it is one of the most popular settings to study concurrency. The richness of trace theory led to the monograph [8], which contains more than 250 bibliographical entries related to trace theory. One of the basic ideas is that the behavior of a concurrent process is not represented by a string, but more accurately by some labeled partial order, which, in the setting of trace theory, means by its dependence graph. We refer to [18] for a systematic study about dependence graphs and to [14] for a systematic study about real traces.

A suitable way for formal specifications of concurrent systems is given by temporal logic formulae which in turn have a direct interpretation for dependence graphs. It is therefore no surprise that temporal logics for traces have received quite an attention, see [4,7,22,23,24,25,28,29,30,31,32].

In [30] it was shown that the basic linear temporal logic with future tense operators and only past tense constants is expressively complete with respect

---

[*] Support of ADVANCE, CEFIPRA, and PROCOPE is gratefully acknowledged.

W. Brauer et al. (Eds.): Formal and Natural Computing, LNCS 2300, pp. 26–38, 2002.
© Springer-Verlag Berlin Heidelberg 2002

to the first order theory of finite and infinite traces (*real traces*). Finally, in [7] we were able to show (by a quite different approach) that the fragment with future tense operators only is expressively complete. This has answered positively a long standing open question [9,30]. The present paper shows how to use our result [7] in order to establish the very same characterizations for safety and liveness properties of real traces, which are well-known for infinite words. The characterizations are related to some topological concepts. But as soon as we have independent letters a and b, $a \neq b$, we should not use any topology being Hausdorff. This is perhaps a surprise, because in the case of infinite words one might also use the Cantor topology on Σ^ω which can be defined by the usual prefix metric. The single infinite string $(ab)^\omega$ defines a safety property over infinite words, but if a and b are independent, then every safety property containing $(ab)^\omega$ should also contain a^*b^ω and b^*a^ω. This is exactly captured by the Scott topology, which turns out be the appropriate choice. Safety means Scott-closed and liveness means Scott-dense. Of course, in the special case of infinite words, we obtain the classical result [2].

For the syntactic (or nearly) syntactic characterizations of safety and liveness formulae we prefer an algebraic approach using aperiodic monoids. Therefore, we give first a direct translation from temporal logic to aperiodic monoids. In the setting of trace theory these constructions are more involved than in the word case, and the translation seems to be new. But in any case, this direct translation from temporal logic to aperiodic monoids is still much simpler than converting first to first-order logic and then passing from first-order logic to aperiodic monoids. Since we give the translation for formulae having simultaneously future tense and past tense operators, we introduce the new notion of a homomorphism recognizing a formula. Once we are in the framework of aperiodic monoids, a separation theorem (in the spirit of Gabbay [13]) is a direct consequence of our result in [7], and the syntactic descriptions follow.

2   Real Traces

By (Σ, I) we mean an *independence alphabet* where Σ denotes a finite alphabet and $I \subseteq \Sigma \times \Sigma$ is an irreflexive and symmetric relation called the *independence relation*. The complementary relation $D = (\Sigma \times \Sigma) \setminus I$ is called the *dependence relation*. It is reflexive and symmetric. A dependence graph is (an isomorphism class of) a node–labeled, acyclic, directed graph $[V, E, \lambda]$, where V is a set of nodes, each node $i \in V$ is labeled by $\lambda(i) \in \Sigma$, and we have $(\lambda(i), \lambda(j)) \in D$ if and only if $(i, j) \in E \cup E^{-1} \cup \mathrm{id}_V$. A *real trace* is a dependence graph $[V, E, \lambda]$ such that for all $j \in V$ the set $\{i \in V \mid iE^*j\}$ of elements below j is finite. In the following we consider real traces, only. A *real trace* can be finite or infinite. The *empty trace* is denoted by ε, it corresponds to the empty graph. The alphabet of a real trace $x = [V, E, \lambda]$ is $\mathrm{alph}(x) = \lambda(V)$. The set of real traces is denoted by $\mathbb{R}$ and the set of finite traces is denoted by $\mathbb{M}$. We also write $(x, y) \in I$, if in fact $\mathrm{alph}(x) \times \mathrm{alph}(y) \subseteq I$, so I becomes a relation between real traces.

The concatenation of a finite trace $[V_1, E_1, \lambda_1]$ with a real trace $[V_2, E_2, \lambda_2]$ yields the real trace $[V, E, \lambda]$, which is defined by the disjoint union of the labeled graphs together with additional arcs from all vertices $v_1 \in V_1$ to $v_2 \in V_2$ where $(\lambda(v_1), \lambda(v_2)) \in D$. By this the set of finite traces becomes a monoid with the empty trace ε as unit. It is also clear how to define the infinite product $x = x_0 x_1 x_2 \cdots$ of a sequence $(x_i)_{i \geq 0}$ of finite traces. This infinite product is a finite trace if and only if $x_i = \varepsilon$ for almost all $i \geq 0$. As usual, we denote by x^ω the ω-product of a finite trace x. A *language* L is a subset of $\mathbb{R}$, it is called *finitary*, if it is a subset of $\mathbb{M}$.

For a graphical representation it is useful to draw the Hasse diagram. For instance, let $\Sigma = \{a, b, c\}$ and $I = \{(a, c), (c, a)\}$. Then $x = (abc)^3$ is given by the following picture.

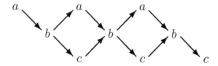

We get the reverse of a finite trace by reading it from right to left. Formally, let $x = [V, E, \lambda]$ be a finite trace. The *reverse* $\widetilde{x}$ is defined by $\widetilde{x} = [V, E^{-1}, \lambda]$, thus is the dependence graph where the direction of arcs has been reversed. The operation is extended to finitary languages by $\widetilde{K} = \{x \in \mathbb{M} \mid \widetilde{x} \in K\}$. The reverse of the trace $(abc)^3$ above is $(cba)^3$ and given by:

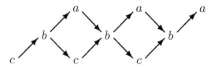

A finite trace $x \in \mathbb{M}$ is a prefix of a real trace $z \in \mathbb{R}$, denoted by $x \leq z$, if $z = xy$ for some (unique) $y \in \mathbb{R}$. The prefix relation is generally defined for two real traces $x, z \in \mathbb{R}$ but here we use it only when the first trace x is finite.

The set $\mathbb{R}$ comes with natural topologies. For our purposes (in the framework of temporal logic) the topology of interest is the Scott topology. A language $L \subseteq \mathbb{R}$ is called *Scott-open*, if for all $z \in L$ there is some finite prefix $x \leq z$ such that $x\mathbb{R} \subseteq L$. The intersection $L_1 \cap L_2$ of two Scott-open sets is Scott-open, because $x_1 \leq z$ and $x_2 \leq z$ with $x_1, x_2 \in \mathbb{M}$ implies that $x_1 \leq x$ and $x_2 \leq x$ for some finite prefix $x \leq z$ (we can take for x the least upper bound of x_1, x_2 which is finite). Moreover, an arbitrary union of Scott-open sets is also clearly a Scott-open set. So, the Scott-open sets form indeed a topology. As usual, a language is called *Scott-closed*, if its complement $\mathbb{R} \setminus L$ is Scott-open. The *Scott-closure* $\overline{L}^\sigma$ of a language $L \subseteq \mathbb{R}$ is the smallest Scott-closed set containing L. It is given by

$$\overline{L}^\sigma = \{z \in \mathbb{R} \mid \forall x \in \mathbb{M}, x \leq z \text{ implies } x \leq y \text{ for some } y \in L\}.$$

Remark 1. The Scott topology (as well as the Lawson topology mentioned below) can be defined in more general settings, see [16] for a standard reference.

For an algebraic dcpo (directed complete partial order), the upper sets of compact elements form a basis of open sets for the Scott topology. Since the set of real traces with the prefix order is an algebraic dcpo with the finite traces as the compact elements [14], these upper sets are exactly the sets $x\mathbb{R}$ with $x \in \mathbb{M}$.

The Lawson topology uses the upper sets of compact elements as a sub-basis of open and closed sets. For the set of real traces this topology is also defined by the prefix metric. Intuitively two words or traces are close if they have the same prefixes up to some length. This prefix metric has many good properties: The metric space of real traces is compact (whence complete) and the set of finite traces is both dense and discrete. Probably, it is also the most frequently used topology on finite and infinite words. Restricted to Σ^ω this topology becomes the Cantor topology, i.e., it is the product topology over the discrete space Σ. However, the topology defined by the prefix metric is not appropriate for us as soon as we have independent letters (see the next remark) or as soon as we wish to deal with finite and infinite words simultaneously (see Remark 4 at the end of the paper).

Remark 2. We are looking for a topology on real traces for which the safe properties define closed sets. We show here that such a topology cannot be Hausdorff (hence cannot be defined by any metric) as soon as there are two independent letters.

Let $\Sigma = \{a, b\}$ with $(a, b) \in I$ and assume (on an informal level) that $(ab)^\omega$ defines a safe execution, then indeed all prefixes of $(ab)^\omega$ should be safe as well. Since $(a, b) \in I$, all finite traces are prefixes of $(ab)^\omega$ and the closure of the singleton set $L = \{(ab)^\omega\}$ should contain $\mathbb{M}$. This is not the case for an Hausdorff topology since then L itself is closed. On the other hand, the Scott-closure of L is $\mathbb{R}$ entirely, which is indeed safe.

We also see that the Scott topology restricted to infinite traces $\mathbb{R} \setminus \mathbb{M}$ is Hausdorff if and only if $I = \emptyset$.

3   Temporal Logic for Traces

The syntax of linear temporal logic $TL(\Sigma)$, as we shall use it here, is defined as follows. There are a constant symbol $\bot$ representing *false*, the logical connectives $\neg$ (not) and $\vee$ (or), for each $a \in \Sigma$ a unary operator $\langle a \rangle$, called *next-a*, a unary operator $\langle a \rangle^{-1}$, called *yesterday-a*, and binary operators **U** and **S**, called *until* and *since* respectively. Formally, the syntax for $TL(\Sigma)$ is given by

$$\varphi ::= \bot \mid \neg \varphi \mid \varphi \vee \varphi \mid \langle a \rangle \varphi \mid \varphi \, \mathbf{U} \, \varphi, \mid \langle a \rangle^{-1} \varphi \mid \varphi \, \mathbf{S} \, \varphi.$$

The semantics is defined by saying when some formula φ is satisfied by some real trace $z \in \mathbb{R}$ at some configuration (i.e., at some finite prefix) $x \in \mathbb{M}$; hence by defining $z, x \models \varphi$. This is done inductively:

$$z, x \not\models \bot,$$
$$z, x \models \neg\varphi \quad \text{if } z, x \not\models \varphi,$$
$$z, x \models \varphi \vee \psi \quad \text{if } z, x \models \varphi \text{ or } z, x \models \psi,$$
$$z, x \models \langle a \rangle \varphi \quad \text{if } xa \leq z \text{ and } z, xa \models \varphi,$$
$$z, x \models \varphi \, \mathbf{U} \, \psi \quad \text{if } \exists y \in \mathbb{M} \text{ such that } xy \leq z, z, xy \models \psi, \text{ and}$$
$$y = y'y'', y'' \neq 1 \text{ implies } z, xy' \models \varphi.$$
$$z, x \models \langle a \rangle^{-1} \varphi \text{ if } x = x'a \text{ and } z, x' \models \varphi,$$
$$z, x \models \varphi \, \mathbf{S} \, \psi \quad \text{if } \exists y \in \mathbb{M} \text{ such that } x = x'y, z, x' \models \psi, \text{ and}$$
$$y = y'y'', y' \neq 1 \text{ implies } z, xy' \models \varphi.$$

As usual, we define $L_{\mathbb{R}}(\varphi)$ by the set of all real traces $z \in \mathbb{R}$ satisfying $z, \varepsilon \models \varphi$. Two formulae are *equivalent*, if they define the same language.

A formula φ not using any past modality $\langle a \rangle^{-1}$ or $\mathbf{S}$ is called a *pure future* formula. If it is not using any future modality $\langle a \rangle$ or $\mathbf{U}$, then it is called a *pure past* formula. We shall also use macros: $\top = \neg\bot$ (true), $\mathbf{F}\,\varphi = \top \, \mathbf{U} \, \varphi$ (eventually φ or future φ) and $\mathbf{G}\,\varphi = \neg\,\mathbf{F}\,\neg\varphi$ (always φ or globally φ). The operators $\mathbf{F}$ and $\mathbf{G}$ belong both to future tense.

Remark 3. Let $L \subseteq \mathbb{M}$ be a finitary language such that $L = L_{\mathbb{R}}(\varphi)$ for some pure future formula φ. Then there is a pure past formula $\widetilde{\varphi}$ such that the reverse language $\widetilde{L}$ satisfies $\widetilde{L} = \{x \in \mathbb{M} \mid x, x \models \widetilde{\varphi}\}$. The formula $\widetilde{\varphi}$ is obtained by replacing in φ the future tense modalities by their corresponding past modalities.

4   Recognizing Homomorphisms

Every language $L \subseteq \mathbb{R}$ which can be specified by a formula φ in temporal logic, can also be specified by some first-order formula over dependence graphs. Using well-known results in trace theory [17,10] these languages are aperiodic.

Proposition 1 ([17,10]). *Let $L = L_{\mathbb{R}}(\varphi)$ for some temporal logic formula φ. Then L is aperiodic.*

However, the results of [17,10] are far from being trivial. Therefore a direct proof of Proposition 1 is of interest. In this section we provide a direct translation from temporal logic formulae to aperiodic monoids. Recall that a finite monoid S is called *aperiodic*, if for some (threshold value) $n \geq 0$ we have $s^{n+1} = s^n$ for all $s \in S$. An example is the power set $\mathcal{P}(\Sigma)$ where the monoid operation is union. It is commutative and aperiodic with $n = 1$.

A language $L \subseteq \mathbb{R}$ is *recognized by a homomorphism* h from $\mathbb{M}$ to some finite monoid S if for all $y = y_0 y_1 y_2 \cdots \in L$ and $z = z_0 z_1 z_2 \cdots \in \mathbb{R}$ with $h(y_i) = h(z_i)$ for all $i \geq 0$, we have $z \in L$, too. The language $L \subseteq \mathbb{R}$ is called *aperiodic* if it is recognized by a homomorphism to some finite aperiodic monoid.

For $A \subseteq \Sigma$, we let $D(A) = \{b \in \Sigma \mid (a, b) \in D \text{ for some } a \in A\}$ and for $x \in \mathbb{M}$, we let $D(x) = D(\text{alph}(x))$. For $x, y \in \mathbb{M}$, we have $D(xy) = D(x) \cup D(y)$ and $D(x) = \emptyset$ if and only if $x = \varepsilon$. Also, if $D(x) = D(x')$ and $D(y) = D(y')$ then $\text{alph}(x) \times \text{alph}(y) \subseteq I$ if and only if $\text{alph}(x') \times \text{alph}(y') \subseteq I$. Indeed, assume that

$(a', b') \in D$ for some $a' \in \mathrm{alph}(x')$ and $b' \in \mathrm{alph}(y')$. Then, $b' \in D(x') = D(x)$ and we find $a \in \mathrm{alph}(x)$ with $(a, b') \in D$. Next, $a \in D(y') = D(y)$ and we find $b \in \mathrm{alph}(y)$ with $(a, b) \in D$.

A homomorphism $h : \mathbb{M} \to S$ is called a *D-morphism* if for all $x, y \in \mathbb{M}$, $h(x) = h(y)$ implies $D(x) = D(y)$. It is worth noting that if a real trace language $L \subseteq \mathbb{R}$ is recognized by some homomorphism $h : \mathbb{M} \to S$, it is also recognized by the *D*-morphism $h' : \mathbb{M} \to S' = S \times \mathcal{P}(\Sigma)$ defined by $h'(x) = (h(x), D(x))$. If S is aperiodic, then the monoid S' is aperiodic with the same threshold value as S (in case S was non trivial). Thus, whenever convenient, we may assume that an aperiodic language is recognized by some (surjective) *D*-morphism.

Let $h : \mathbb{M} \to S$ be a surjective *D*-morphism. For $s \in S$, we let $D(s) = D(x)$ if $h(x) = s$. This is well-defined since h is a surjective *D*-morphism. Hence we may define the relation I on S. For $s, t \in S$ with $s = h(x)$ and $t = h(y)$ we set $(s, t) \in I$ if $\mathrm{alph}(x) \times \mathrm{alph}(y) \subseteq I$. Again, this is well-defined since h is a surjective *D*-morphism. Note that if $s, t \in S$ with $(s, t) \in I$ then $st = ts$. In fact, we are even more liberal, let $f : \mathbb{M} \to S$ and $g : \mathbb{M} \to T$ be two surjective *D*-morphisms, then $(s, t) \in I$ for $(s, t) \in S \times T$ means $\mathrm{alph}(f^{-1}(s)) \times \mathrm{alph}(g^{-1}(t)) \subseteq I$.

There is also a reverse operation $\tilde{\ }$ for monoids: $\tilde{S}$ is the same set as S, but the new multiplication is defined by $s \circ t = t \cdot s$. If S is aperiodic, then $\tilde{S}$ has the same property. If a homomorphism $h : \mathbb{M} \to S$ recognizes some finitary language $L \subseteq \mathbb{M}$, then the homomorphism $\tilde{h} : \mathbb{M} \to \tilde{S}$ defined by $\tilde{h}(a) = h(a)$ recognizes $\tilde{L}$. Note also that if h is a *D*-morphism then so is $\tilde{h}$.

In the proof of the main proposition, we use twice the *I*-diamond product introduced in [15] and which generalizes the Schützenberger product. We modify the version of the *I*-diamond product as given in [14, page 459] to accommodate *D*-morphisms. Originally, the definition was given for *alphabetic* homomorphisms, but the precise alphabetic information is actually not needed. Considering *D*-morphisms allows to use smaller monoids, and our construction does not introduce unnecessary information in the case where the independence relation is empty.

Let $f : \mathbb{M} \to S$ and $g : \mathbb{M} \to T$ be two surjective *D*-morphisms. Consider the power set $\mathcal{P}(S \times T)$ and equip this set with the following multiplication:

$$P \cdot Q = \{(rs, tu) \mid (r, t) \in P, (s, u) \in Q \text{ with } (s, t) \in I\}.$$

It was shown in [14] that this multiplication is associative with $\{(1, 1)\}$ as unit and that the mapping h from $\mathbb{M}$ to $\mathcal{P}(S \times T)$ defined by $h(x) = \{(f(x'), g(x'')) \mid x = x'x''\}$ is a homomorphism. The mapping h is also a *D*-morphism. Note that $h(x) = h(y)$ implies both $f(x) = f(y)$ and $g(x) = g(y)$. Indeed, $(f(x), f(\varepsilon)) \in h(x) = h(y)$ and therefore $y = y'y''$ with $f(y') = f(x)$ and $f(y'') = f(\varepsilon)$. Since f is a *D*-morphism, we deduce that $y'' = \varepsilon$ and $y' = y$. The argument is similar for g.

We define the *I*-diamond product $\Diamond_I(f, g)$ to be the homomorphism from $\mathbb{M}$ to the submonoid $h(\mathbb{M})$ of $\mathcal{P}(S \times T)$ defined by $\Diamond_I(f, g)(x) = h(x)$.

Lemma 1. *If $f : \mathbb{M} \to S$ and $g : \mathbb{M} \to T$ are two surjective D-morphisms onto aperiodic monoids, then the image $\Diamond_I(f, g)(\mathbb{M})$ is an aperiodic monoid and $\Diamond_I(f, g)$ is a surjective D-morphism.*

Proof. We use the notation introduced above. Assume that S and T are aperiodic, let $m, n \geq 0$ such that $s^{m+1} = s^m$ and $t^{n+1} = t^n$ for all $s \in S$ and $t \in T$. We claim that $\Diamond_I(f, g)(\mathbb{M}) = h(\mathbb{M})$ is aperiodic with threshold value $k = m+n+|\Sigma|$. Thus, we have to show $P^{k+1} = P^k$ for $P = h(x)$. We use some standard reasoning from trace theory. First of all it is enough to consider the case where x is connected, this means that the dependence graph of x is connected in the usual graph theoretical sense. Indeed, if x is not connected, then $x = x_1 x_2 = x_2 x_1$ with $x_1 \neq \varepsilon$ and $x_2 \neq \varepsilon$. Hence by induction on the size of the alphabet $h(x_i)^{k+1} = h(x_i)^k$ for $i = 1, 2$ and then $h(x)^{k+1} = h(x_1)^{k+1} h(x_2)^{k+1} = h(x_1)^k h(x_2)^k = h(x)^k$. Hence let x be connected and consider some factorization $yz = x^{k+1}$. We assume that $(f(y), g(z)) \in P^{k+1}$ and we show that $(f(y), g(z)) \in P^k$.

Using the generalization of Levi's Lemma (see e.g. [6, Prop. 3.2.3]) we have $y = y_1 \cdots y_{k+1}$, $z = z_1 \cdots z_{k+1}$ with $x = y_i z_i$ for all $1 \leq i \leq k+1$ and $(y_j, z_i) \in I$ for all $1 \leq i < j \leq k + 1$. If x^{m+1} is not a prefix of y then $z_p \neq \varepsilon$ for some $p \leq m + 1$ and using the fact that x is connected, we deduce that

$$\emptyset \neq \mathrm{alph}(z_p) \subsetneq \cdots \subsetneq \mathrm{alph}(z_{p+q}) = \mathrm{alph}(x)$$

for some $0 \leq q < |\Sigma|$. Then, we have $z_\ell = x$ for all $\ell > p + q$ and x^{n+1} is a suffix of z. Therefore, either x^{m+1} appears as a prefix of y or x^{n+1} appears as a suffix of z. In both cases, the pair $(f(y), g(z))$ appears in P^k, too. This shows $P^{k+1} \subseteq P^k$. The same argument applied to a factorization $yz = x^k$ shows $P^k \subseteq P^{k+1}$. Hence $P^{k+1} = P^k$, and $h(\mathbb{M})$ is aperiodic. □

We turn now to the direct proof for Proposition 1. Since φ may involve simultaneously past and future modalities it is not enough to recognize languages. Therefore, we define that a homomorphism $h : \mathbb{M} \to S$ recognizes a formula φ, if for all $y = y_0 y_1 y_2 \cdots \in \mathbb{R}$ and $z = z_0 z_1 z_2 \cdots \in \mathbb{R}$ with $h(y_i) = h(z_i)$ for all $i \geq 0$, we have $y, y_0 \models \varphi$ if and only if $z, z_0 \models \varphi$. If h recognizes φ, then h recognizes $L_\mathbb{R}(\varphi)$. Therefore Proposition 1 follows from the next lemma.

Lemma 2. *If φ is a temporal logic formula, then there is a D-morphism h from $\mathbb{M}$ to some finite aperiodic monoid S which recognizes φ.*

Proof. The proof is by structural induction on φ. The formula $\varphi = \bot$ is recognized by the D-morphism $D : \mathbb{M} \to \mathcal{P}(\Sigma)$. Next, if a homomorphism recognizes some formula φ, then it recognizes its negation as well. Also, assume that φ_1 and φ_2 are recognized by the D-morphisms $h_1 : \mathbb{M} \to S_1$ and $h_2 : \mathbb{M} \to S_2$ with S_1, S_2 aperiodic. Let $h : \mathbb{M} \to S = S_1 \times S_2$ be the homomorphism defined by $h(x) = (h_1(x), h_2(x))$. Then, S is aperiodic, h is a D-morphism and recognizes simultaneously φ_1, φ_2, and all Boolean combinations of φ_1 and φ_2.

In order to emphasize that we include past tense modalities let us begin with $\varphi = \langle a \rangle^{-1} \psi$. By induction, there is some surjective D-morphism $h : \mathbb{M} \to S$ with S aperiodic which recognizes ψ.

Let $\mathcal{C} \subseteq \mathcal{P}(\Sigma)$ be the family of subsets $A \subseteq \Sigma$ such that A consists of pair-wise independent letters. The meaning for sets in $\mathcal{C}$ is to remember the labels of maximal elements of finite traces. Note that for $A \in \mathcal{C}$ the product $\prod_{a \in A} h(a) \in S$ is well-defined, because $(a, b) \in I$ implies $h(a)h(b) = h(b)h(a)$ in S. For simplicity, we denote this product by $h(A)$.

We define an operation on $S' = S \times \mathcal{C}$ by:

$$(r, A) \cdot (s, B) := (r \cdot h(A \cap (D(s) \cup D(B)))) \cdot s, (A \setminus (D(s) \cup D(B))) \cup B).$$

It can be verified that this operation is associative and that $(1, \emptyset)$ is a unit. Therefore, $(S', \cdot)$ is a monoid. To see that S' is aperiodic let n be the threshold for the monoid S. Hence $s^{n+1} = s^n$ for all $s \in S$. Consider an element $(s, B) \in S'$. Then, we have $(s, B)^{n+2} = ((sh(B))^{n+1}s, B) = ((sh(B))^n s, B) = (s, B)^{n+1}$.

We define a homomorphism $h' : \mathbb{M} \to S'$ by $h'(a) = (1, \{a\})$. The invariant is that if $x = x' \prod_{a \in A} a$ and A is the set of labels of maximal elements of $x \in \mathbb{M}$, then we have $h'(x) = (h(x'), A)$. From this, it follows that h' is a D-morphism. We show that h' recognizes $\varphi = \langle a \rangle^{-1}\psi$.

Let $y = y_0 y_1 y_2 \cdots \in \mathbb{R}$ and $z = z_0 z_1 z_2 \cdots \in \mathbb{R}$ with $h'(y_i) = h'(z_i) = (r_i, A_i)$ for all $i \geq 0$. Assume that $y, y_0 \models \langle a \rangle^{-1}\psi$. We have $y_0 = y'_0 a$ and $y, y'_0 \models \psi$. Since $h'(y_0) = h'(z_0) = (r_0, A_0)$ we deduce from the invariant that $a \in A_0$, $z_0 = z'_0 a$ and $h(y'_0) = r_0 h(A_0 \setminus \{a\}) = h(z'_0)$. Also, $h(y_i) = r_i h(A_i) = h(z_i)$ for all $i \geq 1$. Since h recognizes ψ, we obtain $z, z'_0 \models \psi$ and therefore $z, z_0 \models \langle a \rangle^{-1}\psi$.

The situation for $\varphi = \langle a \rangle \psi$ is symmetric and therefore omitted.

We give now the construction for a formula of type $\varphi \, \mathbf{U} \, \psi$. We may assume that φ and ψ are both recognized by the same surjective D-morphism f from $\mathbb{M}$ onto some finite aperiodic monoid S. We use a nested construction of the $\Diamond_I$-product, and we consider

$$g = \Diamond_I(f, f) \qquad \text{and} \qquad h = \Diamond_I(g, f).$$

By Lemma 1, h is a surjective D-morphism onto some finite aperiodic monoid. We claim that h recognizes the formula $\varphi \, \mathbf{U} \, \psi$. Let $y = y_0 y_1 y_2 \cdots \in \mathbb{R}$ and $z = z_0 z_1 z_2 \cdots \in \mathbb{R}$ such that $h(y_i) = h(z_i)$ for all $i \geq 0$. Assume that $y, y_0 \models \varphi \, \mathbf{U} \, \psi$. Let us show that $z, z_0 \models \varphi \, \mathbf{U} \, \psi$. For some finite prefix $y_{1,1} \leq y_1 y_2 \cdots$ we have $y, y_0 y_{1,1} \models \psi$. Grouping factors together we may assume that $y_{1,1} \leq y_1$ and therefore $y_1 = y_{1,1} y_{1,2}$. Using $h(y_1) = h(z_1)$ we find a factorization $z_1 = z_{1,1} z_{1,2}$ with $g(y_{1,1}) = g(z_{1,1})$ and $f(y_{1,2}) = f(z_{1,2})$. Therefore we have $f(y_0 y_{1,1}) = f(z_0 z_{1,1})$ and $f(y_i) = f(z_i)$ for all $i > 1$. Since $y, y_0 y_{1,1} \models \psi$ and f recognizes ψ, we deduce that $z, z_0 z_{1,1} \models \psi$. Now, let $z_{1,1} = z'z''$ with $z'' \neq \varepsilon$. Using $g(y_{1,1}) = g(z_{1,1})$, we find a factorization $y_{1,1} = y'y''$ with $y'' \neq \varepsilon$ such that $f(y') = f(z')$ and $f(y'') = f(z'')$. Since $y, y_0 y' \models \varphi$ and f recognizes φ we obtain $z, z_0 z' \models \varphi$. Hence the claim.

The construction for $\varphi \, \mathbf{S} \, \psi$ is symmetric. This proves Lemma 2 and Proposition 1. $\square$

5   Safety and Liveness

According to [20] a formula φ is called a *safety formula*, if φ can be written as $\varphi = \mathbf{G}\,p$ where p is a pure past formula. A *safety property* is a language $L \subseteq \mathbb{R}$ which can be specified by some safety formula. Assume that $z, \varepsilon \not\models \mathbf{G}\,p$, then $z, x \not\models p$ for some finite prefix $x \leq z$. Since p is a pure past formula, $y, x \not\models p$ for all y in the Scott-open set $x\mathbb{R}$. Therefore, a safety property is Scott-closed.

For infinite words liveness properties have been widely studied, let us mention e.g. the work of Alpern and Schneider [2,3]. The situation is more complicated. We use the formulation due to [5] and we say that φ is a *liveness formula*, if it is equivalent to a formula of the form $\mathbf{F}(q \vee \bigvee_{t\in T}(p_t \wedge f_t))$ where T is a finite index set, $q = \bigwedge_{t\in T} \neg p_t$, and moreover for all t we have that p_t is a pure past formula and that f_t is a satisfiable pure future formula. Note that this is not really a syntactic description of a liveness formula. The essential non-syntactic part is that we demand f_t to be satisfiable. We may suppress the q for an even less syntactical description. A formula φ is a liveness formula if and only if it is equivalent to a formula of type $\mathbf{F}(\bigvee_{t\in T}(p_t \wedge f_t))$, where T is a finite index set, $\mathbf{G}(\bigvee_{t\in T} p_t)$ is valid, and for all t the formula p_t is a pure past formula and f_t is a satisfiable pure future formula. A formula of the type above is called canonical liveness formula in [5]. The translation between the two variants for liveness formulae is obvious.

If $L = \mathrm{L}_\mathbb{R}(\varphi)$ for some liveness formula, then L is called a *liveness property*. Every liveness property is dense in the Scott topology: Indeed, let U be a Scott-open set and let $x \in \mathbb{M}$ with $x\mathbb{R} \subseteq U$. Then for some $t \in T$ we have $x, x \models p_t$, since $\mathbf{G}(\bigvee_{t\in T} p_t)$ is valid (using the canonical form). Since f_t is satisfiable, we find some $z \in \mathbb{R}$ with $z, \varepsilon \models f_t$. Hence $xz, x \models \varphi$ and $x\mathbb{R} \cap \mathrm{L}_\mathbb{R}(\varphi) \neq \emptyset$.

The following statement is well-known for infinite words, see [5, Thm. 10]. We have now the necessary tools in order to extend this result to the set of real traces.

Theorem 1.

1. *A language $L \subseteq \mathbb{R}$ is a safety property if and only if it is aperiodic and Scott-closed.*
2. *A language $L \subseteq \mathbb{R}$ is a liveness property if and only if it is aperiodic and Scott-dense.*
3. *Every aperiodic language is the intersection of some safety property and some liveness property.*

We will see that in some sense Theorem 1 is a corollary of the following result (which is the extension of Kamp's Theorem to real traces).

Theorem 2 ([7]). *Let $L \subseteq \mathbb{R}$ be an aperiodic language. Then there is a pure future formula φ such that $L = \mathrm{L}_\mathbb{R}(\varphi)$.*

Due to the reverse operation, Theorem 2 and Remark 3 imply:

Corollary 1. *Let $L \subseteq \mathbb{M}$ be a finitary aperiodic language. Then there is a pure past formula φ such that $L = \{x \in \mathbb{M} \mid x, x \models \varphi\}$.*

Using Proposition 1 and the remarks above, we already know that a safety property is an aperiodic language that is Scott-closed and a liveness property is an aperiodic language that is Scott-dense. To get the other claims of Theorem 1 we start with a general observation. Consider an arbitrary aperiodic language $L \subseteq \mathbb{R}$. Let us fix a surjective homomorphism h from $\mathbb{M}$ onto some finite aperiodic monoid S which recognizes L and such that $h^{-1}(1) = \{\varepsilon\}$. We first show in Equation 1 below that L can be expressed by two special formulae of $\mathrm{TL}(\Sigma)$.

For each $t \in S$ let $L(t) = \{z \in \mathbb{R} \mid h^{-1}(t)z \cap L \neq \emptyset\}$ and we let $T = \{t \in S \mid L(t) \neq \emptyset\}$. Since $h^{-1}(1) = \{\varepsilon\}$, we can verify that the homomorphism h recognizes $h^{-1}(t) \subseteq \mathbb{M}$ and $L(t) \subseteq \mathbb{R}$ for all $t \in T$. Moreover, a simple reflection shows $L = \bigcup_{t \in T} h^{-1}(t)L(t)$.

By Corollary 1 and Theorem 2, for each $t \in T$ we may choose a pure past formula p_t and a satisfiable pure future formula f_t such that $h^{-1}(t) = \{x \in \mathbb{M} \mid x, x \models p_t\}$ and $L(t) = \mathrm{L}_{\mathbb{R}}(f_t)$. Hence, from the equality $L = \bigcup_{t \in T} h^{-1}(t)L(t)$, we can derive the following description:

$$L = \mathrm{L}_{\mathbb{R}}\left(\mathbf{G}\left(\bigvee_{t \in T}(p_t \wedge f_t)\right)\right) = \mathrm{L}_{\mathbb{R}}\left(\mathbf{F}\left(\bigvee_{t \in T}(p_t \wedge f_t)\right)\right). \tag{1}$$

We are now looking more closely at safety and liveness properties. We know that if L is a liveness property, then it is Scott-dense. Let us show that if L is Scott-dense, then $T = S$. By contradiction, assume that $T \neq S$ and consider $s \in S$ with $L(s) = \emptyset$. Since h is surjective, we find some $x \in h^{-1}(s)$ and $L(s) = \emptyset$ implies that L does not intersect the Scott-open set $x\mathbb{R}$ which is not possible since L is dense. Hence, we have shown that if L is Scott-dense, then $T = S$. Finally, if $T = S$, then $\mathbf{G}(\bigvee_{t \in T} p_t)$ is valid, so the description $\mathbf{F}(\bigvee_{t \in T}(p_t \wedge f_t))$ is a canonical liveness formula since, by definition of T, all f_t are satisfiable. Therefore, L is a liveness property. Hence, we already have the proof of Theorem 1 (ii).

Note that every liveness property has a description $\mathbf{G}(\bigvee_{t \in T}(p_t \wedge f_t))$, but we have to be careful, in general $\mathbf{G}(\bigvee_{t \in T}(p_t \wedge f_t))$ does not necessarily specify any dense set.

Example 1. Let $\Sigma = \{a, b\}$ with $(a, b) \in D$. Consider the formula

$$\varphi = \mathbf{G}\left(\left(\neg\langle a\rangle^{-1}\top \wedge \neg\langle b\rangle^{-1}\top\right) \vee \left(\langle a\rangle^{-1}\top \wedge \langle a\rangle\langle b\rangle\top\right) \vee \left(\langle b\rangle^{-1}\top \wedge \langle a\rangle\top\right)\right).$$

This formula is of type $\mathbf{G}(\bigvee_{t \in T}(p_t \wedge f_t))$, where $\mathbf{G}(\bigvee_{t \in T} p_t)$ is valid, and all f_t are satisfiable. However $\mathrm{L}_{\mathbb{R}}(\varphi) = \{\varepsilon\}$ which is not dense.

On the other hand, if $\Sigma = \{a, b\}$ with $(a, b) \in I$, then $\mathrm{L}_{\mathbb{R}}(\varphi) = \{\varepsilon, (ab)^{\omega}\}$, which is a liveness property in this case.

Once, we have Equation 1, we can derive the Scott-closure $\overline{L}^{\sigma}$ of L. Recall that $\overline{L}^{\sigma} = \{z \in \mathbb{R} \mid \forall x \in \mathbb{M}, x \leq z \text{ implies } x \leq y \text{ for some } y \in L\}$. We may assume that all f_t are satisfiable (if not, replace T by $\{t \in T \mid \mathrm{L}_\mathbb{R}(f_t) \neq \emptyset\}$). We claim that $\overline{L}^\sigma = \mathrm{L}_\mathbb{R}(\mathbf{G}(\bigvee_{t \in T} p_t))$. Indeed, let $z \in \overline{L}^\sigma$. For each finite prefix $x \leq z$, we find $y \in L$ with $x \leq y$. Using $L = \mathrm{L}_\mathbb{R}(\mathbf{G}(\bigvee_{t \in T}(p_t \wedge f_t)))$ we deduce that $y, x \models p_t \wedge f_t$ for some $t \in T$. Since p is a pure past formula, we get $z, x \models p_t$ and $z, \varepsilon \models \mathbf{G}(\bigvee_{t \in T} p_t)$. Conversely, assume that $z, \varepsilon \models \mathbf{G}(\bigvee_{t \in T} p_t)$. For each finite prefix $x \leq z$, we find $t \in T$ with $z, x \models p_t$. Now, since f_t is satisfiable, there exists x' with $x', \varepsilon \models f_t$. Using that f_t is pure future, we get $y, x \models (p_t \wedge f_t)$ with $y = xx'$ and therefore $y \in \mathrm{L}_\mathbb{R}(\mathbf{F}(\bigvee_{t \in T}(p_t \wedge f_t))) = L$ concluding the proof of the claim.

The claim implies that the Scott-closure of the aperiodic language L is a safety property (hence is still aperiodic) that is expressed by the safety formula $\mathbf{G}(\bigvee_{t \in T} p_t)$. As a corollary, we also get that if L is aperiodic and Scott-closed then L is a safety property, completing the proof of Theorem 1 (ii).

Finally, for Theorem 1 (ii), we want to see how to write L as an intersection of a safety and a liveness property. To do so, we define $q = \bigwedge_{t \in T} \neg p_t$. This is a pure past formula and by the very definition, $\mathbf{F}(q \vee \bigvee_{t \in T}(p_t \wedge f_t))$ is a liveness formula. Of course, $\mathbf{G}(\bigvee_{t \in T} p_t)$ is a safety formula and

$$\mathrm{L}_\mathbb{R}\left(\mathbf{G}\left(\bigvee_{t \in T} p_t\right)\right) \cap \mathrm{L}_\mathbb{R}\left(\mathbf{F}\left(q \vee \bigvee_{t \in T}(p_t \wedge f_t)\right)\right) = \mathrm{L}_\mathbb{R}\left(\mathbf{F}\left(\bigvee_{t \in T}(p_t \wedge f_t)\right)\right) = L.$$

Summarizing what we have done so far, we may restate Theorem 1 in a more precise version.

Theorem 3. *Let $L \subseteq \mathbb{R}$ be recognizable by some aperiodic monoid S. Then for some subset $T \subseteq S$ there are for all $t \in T$ a satisfiable pure past formula p_t and a satisfiable pure future formula f_t such that the following conditions hold:*

$$L = \mathrm{L}_\mathbb{R}\left(\mathbf{F}\left(\bigvee_{t \in T}(p_t \wedge f_t)\right)\right) = \mathrm{L}_\mathbb{R}\left(\mathbf{G}\left(\bigvee_{t \in T}(p_t \wedge f_t)\right)\right),$$

$$\mathrm{L}_\mathbb{R}\left(\mathbf{G}\left(\bigvee_{t \in T} p_t\right)\right) \text{ is the Scott-closure of } L.$$

Moreover, let $q = \bigwedge_{t \in T} \neg p_t$. Then $\widehat{L} = \mathrm{L}_\mathbb{R}(\mathbf{F}(q \vee \bigvee_{t \in T}(p_t \wedge f_t)))$ is a liveness property. The language L is the intersection of the liveness property $\widehat{L}$ and the Scott-closure $\overline{L}^\sigma$ of L (which is a safety property). If L is a liveness property, then $\mathbf{F}(\bigvee_{t \in T}(p_t \wedge f_t))$ is a liveness formula in canonical form.

Remark 4. As a final remark let us comment again on the role of the Scott topology for safety and liveness. A safety property should be prefix closed which is usually not the case for closed sets in a metric space. In the topology defined by the prefix metric every finite subset of finite traces is both open and closed. So, for characterizing safety properties with the prefix metric we need in addition to the topological closure also the prefix closure. But this means we speak about the Scott-closure. Moreover, in the metric space $\mathbb{R}$ a subset is dense if and only if it contains all finite traces, which is again not useful for a characterization of liveness properties.

If however one restricts to the space of infinite words Σ^ω, then the prefix relation is just equality and the difference between the Cantor topology defined by the prefix metric and the Scott topology vanishes. This explains why on ω-words (and on ω-words, only) safety and liveness properties can be characterized using a metric space.

References

1. IJ. J. Aalbersberg and G. Rozenberg. Theory of Traces. *Theoretical Computer Science*, 60:1–82, 1988.
2. B. Alpern and F.B. Schneider. Defining Liveness. *Information Processing Letters*, 21:181–185, 1985.
3. B. Alpern and F.B. Schneider. Recognizing Safety and Liveness. *Distributed Computing*, 2:117–126, 1987.
4. R. Alur, D. Peled, and W. Penczek. Model-Checking of Causality Properties. In *Proceedings of LICS'95*, pages 90–100, 1995.
5. E. Chang, Z. Manna, and A. Pnueli. Characterization of Temporal Property Classes. In W. Kuich, Editor, *Proceedings of the 19th International Colloquium on Automata, Languages and Programming (ICALP'92), Vienna*, volume 623 of *Lecture Notes in Computer Science*, pages 474–486, Berlin-Heidelberg-New York, 1992. Springer.
6. C. Choffrut. Combinatorics in Trace Monoids I. In V. Diekert and G. Rozenberg, Editors, *The Book of Traces*, chapter 3, pages 71–82. World Scientific, Singapore, 1995.
7. V. Diekert and P. Gastin. LTL Is Expressively Complete for Mazurkiewicz Traces. In U. M. et al., Editor, *Proceedings of the 27th International Colloquium on Automata, Languages and Programming (ICALP'00), Geneva*, number 1853 in Lecture Notes in Computer Science, pages 211–222. Springer, 2000.
8. V. Diekert and G. Rozenberg, Editors. *The Book of Traces*. World Scientific, Singapore, 1995.
9. W. Ebinger. *Charakterisierung von Sprachklassen unendlicher Spuren durch Logiken*. Dissertation, Institut für Informatik, Universität Stuttgart, 1994.
10. W. Ebinger and A. Muscholl. Logical Definability on Infinite Traces. *Theoretical Computer Science*, 154:67–84, 1996. A preliminary version appeared in Proceedings of the 20th International Colloquium on Automata, Languages and Programming (ICALP'93), Lund (Sweden) 1993, Lecture Notes in Computer Science 700, 1993.
11. A. Ehrenfeucht, H.J. Hoogeboom, and G. Rozenberg. Combinatorial Properties of Dependence Graphs. *Information and Computation*, 114(2):315–328, 1994.
12. A. Ehrenfeucht and G. Rozenberg. On the Structure of Dependence Graphs. In K. Voss, H.J. Genrich, and G. Rozenberg, Editors, *Concurrency and Nets*, pages 141–170, Berlin-Heidelberg-New York, 1987. Springer.
13. D. Gabbay, A. Pnueli, S. Shelah, and J. Stavi. On the Temporal Analysis of Fairness. In *Conference Record of the 12th ACM Symposium on Principles of Programming Languages*, pages 163–173, Las Vegas, Nev., 1980.
14. P. Gastin and A. Petit. Infinite Traces. In V. Diekert and G. Rozenberg, Editors, *The Book of Traces*, chapter 11, pages 393–486. World Scientific, Singapore, 1995.

15. P. Gastin, A. Petit, and W. Zielonka. An Extension of Kleene's and Ochmański's Theorems to Infinite Traces. *Theoretical Computer Science*, 125:167–204, 1994. A preliminary version was presented at ICALP'91, Lecture Notes in Computer Science 510 (1991).

16. G. Gierz, K.H. Hofmann, K. Keimel, J.D. Lawson, M.W. Mislove, and D.S. Scott. *A Compendium of Continuous Lattices*. Springer, Berlin-Heidelberg-New York, 1980.

17. G. Guaiana, A. Restivo, and S. Salemi. Star-Free Trace Languages. *Theoretical Computer Science*, 97:301–311, 1992. A preliminary version was presented at STACS'91, Lecture Notes in Computer Science 480 (1991).

18. H.J. Hoogeboom and G. Rozenberg. Dependence Graphs. In V. Diekert and G. Rozenberg, Editors, *The Book of Traces*, chapter 2, pages 43–67. World Scientific, Singapore, 1995.

19. R.M. Keller. Parallel Program Schemata and Maximal Parallelism I. Fundamental Results. *Journal of the Association for Computing Machinery*, 20(3):514–537, 1973.

20. Z. Manna and A. Pnueli. *The Temporal Logic of Reactive and Concurrent Systems, Specification*. Springer, 1991.

21. A. Mazurkiewicz. Concurrent Program Schemes and Their Interpretations. DAIMI Rep. PB 78, Aarhus University, Aarhus, 1977.

22. M. Mukund and P.S. Thiagarajan. Linear Time Temporal Logics over Mazurkiewicz Traces. In *Proceedings of the 21th MFCS, 1996*, number 1113 in Lecture Notes in Computer Science, pages 62–92. Springer, 1996.

23. P. Niebert. A ν-calculus with Local Views for Sequential Agents. In *Proceedings of the 20th MFCS, 1995*, number 969 in Lecture Notes in Computer Science, pages 563–573. Springer, 1995.

24. W. Penczek. Temporal Logics for Trace Systems: On Automated Verification. *International Journal of Foundations of Computer Science*, 4:31–67, 1993.

25. R. Ramanujam. Locally Linear Time Temporal Logic. In *Proceedings of LICS'96*, Lecture Notes in Computer Science, pages 118–128, 1996.

26. G. Rozenberg. Behaviour of Elementary Net Systems. In W. Brauer, Editor, *Petri Nets: Central Models and Their Properties; Advances in Petri Nets; Proceedings of an Advanced Course, Bad Honnef, 8.-19. Sept. 1986, Vol. 1*, number 254 in Lecture Notes in Computer Science, pages 60–94, Berlin-Heidelberg-New York, 1986. Springer.

27. G. Rozenberg and P.S. Thiagarajan. Petri Nets: Basic Notions, Structure and Behaviour. Number 224 in Lecture Notes in Computer Science, pages 585–668, Berlin-Heidelberg-New York, 1986. Springer.

28. P.S. Thiagarajan. A Trace Based Extension of Linear Time Temporal Logic. In *Proceedings of LICS'94*, pages 438–447, 1994.

29. P.S. Thiagarajan. A Trace Consistent Subset of PTL. In *Proceedings of CONCUR'95*, number 962 in Lecture Notes in Computer Science, pages 438–452, 1995.

30. P.S. Thiagarajan and I. Walukiewicz. An Expressively Complete Linear Time Temporal Logic for Mazurkiewicz Traces. In *Proceedings of LICS'97*, 1997.

31. I. Walukiewicz. Difficult Configurations – on the Complexity of LTrL. In K. G. Larsen et al., Editors, *Proceedings of the 25th International Colloquium on Automata, Languages and Programming (ICALP'98), Aalborg*, number 1443 in Lecture Notes in Computer Science, pages 140–151, Berlin-Heidelberg-New York, 1998. Springer.

32. I. Walukiewicz. Local Logics for Traces. *Journal of Automata, Languages and Combinatorics*, 2001. To appear.

The Delta Operation:
From Strings to Trees to Strings[*]

Joost Engelfriet[**]

LIACS, Leiden University
P.O.Box 9512, 2300 RA Leiden, The Netherlands

Abstract. The delta of a language L consists of the yields of trees of which all paths are in L. The context-free languages are the deltas of the regular languages. The indexed languages are the deltas of the deterministic context-free languages. In general, the nondeterministic $(n+1)$-iterated pushdown languages are the deltas of the deterministic n-iterated pushdown languages. The recursively enumerable languages are the deltas of the context-free languages. The delta of a string relation R consists of the yields of trees of which all paths are in the R-image of one string. The ET0L languages are the deltas of the relations recognized by deterministic two-tape finite automata. The recursively enumerable languages are the deltas of the finite state transductions.

1 Introduction

There are two elementary ways of associating strings to trees. First, every tree has a yield, which is the string of labels of its leaves. Second, every tree has a set of paths, from its root to its leaves, and each such path is a string of node labels indexed with child information. As an example, the tree $\sigma(a, \sigma(\tau(b, a, a), b))$ has yield $abaab$, and its paths are $\sigma_1 a$, $\sigma_2 \sigma_1 \tau_1 b$, $\sigma_2 \sigma_1 \tau_2 a$, $\sigma_2 \sigma_1 \tau_3 a$, and $\sigma_2 \sigma_2 b$. Note that, intuitively, the subscript 1 in a path means 'go to the first child', and similarly for the subscripts 2 and 3. Let us denote the yield of a tree t by $\mathrm{yield}(t)$, and its set of paths by $\mathrm{path}(t)$. It was discovered in the late sixties, when tree language theory was developed, that these two operations provide a very simple relationship between the regular languages and the context-free languages, as follows. For a language L, let the *delta* of L, denoted by $\delta(L)$, be the language of all yields of trees that have all their paths in L: $\delta(L) = \{\mathrm{yield}(t) \mid \mathrm{path}(t) \subseteq L\}$. Intuitively, this delta operation views the strings of L as a construction kit for assembling trees: if all paths of a tree t are in L, then these paths can be glued together to build the tree t; the yields of all assembled trees form the resulting language. Viewing a tree as a river delta, its paths correspond to the branches of the river, and its yield to the resulting pattern of river mouths at the coast line. The relationship mentioned above is that the context-free languages are exactly the deltas of the regular languages:

---

[*] Dedicated to Prof. G. Rozenberg on the occasion of his 60th birthday.
[**] Gefeliciteerd, Grzegorz!

W. Brauer et al. (Eds.): Formal and Natural Computing, LNCS 2300, pp. 39–56, 2002.
© Springer-Verlag Berlin Heidelberg 2002

CF $= \{\delta(L) \mid L \in \text{REG}\}$. This result was proved in two steps, using finite tree automata as an intermediate. Let $\text{tree}(L) = \{t \mid \text{path}(t) \subseteq L\}$. Thus, $\text{tree}(L)$ is the set of all trees that can be assembled from L, and $\delta(L) = \text{yield}(\text{tree}(L))$. Let REGT denote the class of regular tree languages (recognized by nondeterministic top-down finite tree automata) and let DREGT denote the class of tree languages recognized by deterministic top-down finite tree automata. It was shown by Magidor and Moran ([MMor69], see also Theorem 1 in [Tha73]) that $\text{DREGT} = \{\text{tree}(L) \mid L \in \text{REG}\}$. It was shown by Thatcher [Tha67] that the context-free languages are exactly the yields of the regular tree languages, i.e., $\text{CF} = \{\text{yield}(L) \mid L \in \text{REGT}\}$, and it is not difficult to slightly improve this to $\text{CF} = \{\text{yield}(L) \mid L \in \text{DREGT}\}$, cf. [Eng75]. Combining these two results gives that $\text{CF} = \text{yield}(\text{DREGT}) = \text{yield}(\text{tree}(\text{REG})) = \delta(\text{REG})$.

In this paper we show that the same relationship holds between the context-free languages and the indexed languages. The indexed languages are generated by the indexed grammars, which were introduced by Aho in [Aho68] as a natural generalization of the context-free grammars, and which were subsequently studied in many papers (see, e.g., [Gre70, ERozS76, Eng85]). An indexed grammar can be viewed as a context-free grammar in which a pushdown is attached (as an "index") to each nonterminal that occurs in a sentential form. A rule of an indexed grammar is of the form $X \to if\ \gamma\ then\ w_0(Y_1, \xi_1)w_1 \cdots (Y_n, \xi_n)w_n$, where X and Y_i are nonterminals, w_i is a terminal string (and so, $X \to w_0 Y_1 w_1 \cdots Y_n w_n$ is an ordinary context-free grammar rule), γ is a pushdown symbol, and ξ_i is a string of pushdown symbols. The rule can only be applied to a nonterminal X in a sentential form if the pushdown attached to X has γ on top, i.e., is of the form $\gamma\xi$. After the (usual context-free) application of the rule, pushdown $\xi_i\xi$ is attached to nonterminal Y_i. Derivations start with the initial nonterminal, to which the initial pushdown symbol γ_0 is attached. Thus, the indexed grammar is a beautiful combination and generalization of both the context-free grammar and the pushdown automaton. The former is re-obtained as the special case that in every rule both γ and every ξ_i are equal to γ_0, and the latter is re-obtained as the special case that the context-free grammar is right-linear, i.e., every rule is of the form $X \to if\ \gamma\ then\ w(Y, \xi)$ or of the form $X \to if\ \gamma\ then\ w$, viewing the nonterminals of the grammar as states of the automaton.

As observed above, we will show that the delta operation relates the context-free and the indexed languages in the same way as it relates the regular and the context-free languages. The same way? Well, only if one realizes that the proof of Magidor and Moran is based on a straightforward relationship between deterministic top-down finite tree automata (recognizing DREGT) and *deterministic* finite automata (recognizing REG). To be precise, we show that the indexed languages are exactly the deltas of the *deterministic* context-free languages (recognized by deterministic pushdown automata). We also show that the determinism is essential here: the deltas of the context-free languages turn out to be all recursively enumerable languages.

The proof of Indexed $= \delta(\text{DCF})$, where DCF denotes the deterministic context-free languages, is easy because it can be obtained as a simple generalization of the proof of CF $= \delta$(REG): Generalizing the result of Magidor and Moran one obtains that deterministic pushdown automata on paths correspond to deterministic pushdown automata on trees, and so tree(DCF) is the class of tree languages recognized by deterministic top-down pushdown tree automata (introduced in [Gue83], where it is shown that the nondeterministic pushdown tree automata recognize the context-free tree languages of [Rou70, ESch77]). Since indexed grammars are context-free grammars with pushdowns, the generalization of Thatcher's result shows that they generate the yields of the tree languages recognized by deterministic pushdown tree automata. From these proofs it should then be clear that they hold for any storage type instead of the pushdown. So, we will in fact show that for any storage type S, the context-free grammars with storage S (which generalize the indexed grammars and are defined in the same way as above for pushdowns) generate exactly the deltas of the languages recognized by deterministic S-automata.

The classes of regular, context-free, and indexed languages form the beginning of a well-known hierarchy of language classes: the *OI hierarchy*, which is a more natural extension of the regular and context-free languages than the classical Chomsky hierarchy (see, e.g., [Wan75, ESch77, Dam82, DGoe86, Vog88, Eng91]). It was shown in [DGoe86] that the languages in the class OI(n), the n-th level of the OI hierarchy, $n \geq 0$, are recognized by the (nondeterministic) n-iterated pushdown automata (see also [EVog88]). An iterated pushdown is a pushdown of pushdowns of ... of pushdowns. In general, for a given storage type S, we define the storage type $P(S)$ of pushdowns of S-storages, in such a way that the n-iterated pushdown automata are (a notational variation of) the $P^n(S_0)$-automata, where S_0 denotes the trivial storage type of the finite automaton. As a second, easy, result we generalize the well-known equivalence of context-free grammars and pushdown automata, and show that the context-free grammars with storage S generate exactly the languages recognized by nondeterministic $P(S)$-automata. And hence, the nondeterministic $P(S)$-automaton languages are exactly the deltas of the deterministic S-automaton languages. For the storage type $P^n(S_0)$ this shows that for every $n \geq 0$, OI($n+1$) = δ(DOI(n)), where DOI(n) denotes the deterministic OI(n) languages, i.e., the languages recognized by deterministic n-iterated pushdown automata.

One of the most interesting classes of languages between the context-free and the indexed languages, is the class of ET0L languages, introduced by Rozenberg in [Roz73] and studied in many papers (see, e.g., [ERozS80, RozS80, KRozS97]). Inclusion of ET0L in Indexed was shown in [Cul74], and proper inclusion in [ERozS76]. The ET0L systems (that generate the ET0L languages) can be viewed as a special type of indexed grammars in which symbols can only be popped from the pushdown, not pushed. Derivations start with the initial nonterminal to which an arbitrary pushdown can be associated. In fact, the pushdown corresponds to the sequence of tables that will be applied during the derivation. Since this restricted type of pushdown can easily be defined as a storage type S, ET0L systems can also be viewed as context-free grammars with storage. Thus, it would seem that the results above also apply to ET0L systems. Unfortunately, these results only hold for context-free S-grammars in which the derivations start with a fixed storage element. In fact, we do not know whether there exists a natural class of languages $\mathcal{L}$ such that the ET0L languages are exactly the deltas of the languages in $\mathcal{L}$. For this reason we generalize the delta operation to apply also to binary relations on strings. For such a relation R, the delta of R is the language of all yields of trees that have all their paths in the R-image of one string: $\delta(R) = \{\mathrm{yield}(t) \mid \mathrm{path}(t) \subseteq R(v) \text{ for some string } v\}$. Using the above results we then show that the ET0L languages are obtained by applying the delta operation to the class of binary relations that are recognized by deterministic two-tape finite automata (introduced in [RSco59][1]; see also, e.g., [HKar91, PSak99]). Again, the determinism is essential: the deltas of the relations recognized by nondeterministic two-tape finite automata (i.e., the finite state transductions [Ber79]) are the recursively enumerable languages.

The results of this paper, apart from the last section, were first presented at a so-called "wild-cat" session during the 9-th ICALP conference (Aarhus, 1982), and then written down in detail in the unpublished technical report [Eng86].

2 The Delta Operation

Before defining the delta operation we need some terminology on trees. We assume the reader to be familiar with elementary tree language theory (see, e.g., [Eng75, GSte84, GSte97]; see also [Roz70b, Roz70c, Roz71b, Roz71c]).

A ranked alphabet is an alphabet Σ of which every symbol has a rank in $\mathbb{N}$. For $k \geq 0$, Σ_k denotes the set of symbols in Σ of rank k. The set of trees over Σ, denoted T_Σ, is the smallest subset of Σ^* such that for all $k \geq 0$, if $\sigma \in \Sigma_k$ and $t_1, \ldots, t_k \in T_\Sigma$, then $\sigma t_1 \cdots t_k \in T_\Sigma$. Note that we write trees in prefix notation, without parentheses or commas; however, for the sake of readability, we will also write $\sigma(t_1, \ldots, t_k)$ for $\sigma t_1 \cdots t_k$. A subset of T_Σ is called a tree language.

To allow the empty string ε to be the yield of a tree, we will use the designated symbol e of rank 0. Then, $\mathrm{yield}(\sigma) = \sigma$ for every $\sigma \in \Sigma_0$ with $\sigma \neq e$, $\mathrm{yield}(e) = \varepsilon$, and for $k \geq 1$, $\mathrm{yield}(\sigma t_1 \cdots t_k) = \mathrm{yield}(t_1) \cdots \mathrm{yield}(t_k)$. Note that $\mathrm{yield}(t) \in (\Sigma_0 - \{e\})^*$ for every $t \in T_\Sigma$. For a tree language L, $\mathrm{yield}(L) = \{\mathrm{yield}(t) \mid t \in L\}$, and for a class K of tree languages, $\mathrm{yield}(K) = \{\mathrm{yield}(L) \mid L \in K\}$.

For a ranked alphabet Σ, the path alphabet $\mathrm{path}(\Sigma)$ is the (nonranked) alphabet consisting of all $\sigma \in \Sigma$ of rank 0, and all pairs (σ, i) with $\sigma \in \Sigma$ of rank $k \geq 1$ and $1 \leq i \leq k$. In examples we will write σ_i for (σ, i). Intuitively, (σ, i) (or σ_i) denotes the fact that the path goes to the i-th child of a node labeled σ. For every $t \in T_\Sigma$, the set of paths through t, denoted $\mathrm{path}(t)$, is the finite subset of $\mathrm{path}(\Sigma)^*$ defined as follows: $\mathrm{path}(\sigma) = \{\sigma\}$ for every $\sigma \in \Sigma_0$, and for $k \geq 1$, $\mathrm{path}(\sigma t_1 \cdots t_k) = \{(\sigma, i)w \mid 1 \leq i \leq k, w \in \mathrm{path}(t_i)\}$. Thus, $\mathrm{path}(t)$ contains all paths from the root of t to its leaves, coded as strings.

---

[1] This was one of the fundamental papers studied by the participants of the Seminar on Automata Theory and Mathematical Linguistics at the University of Utrecht, organized by G. Rozenberg (at the age of 27), in the fall of 1969; see also the Abstracts [Roz70a]–[Roz71c]

As an example, let $\Sigma_3 = \{\sigma\}$, $\Sigma_2 = \{\tau\}$, and $\Sigma_0 = \{a, b, e\}$. Consider the tree $t = \sigma\tau ab\tau eae = \sigma(\tau(a, b), \tau(e, a), e)$. Then yield$(t) = aba$ and path$(t) = \{\sigma_1\tau_1 a, \sigma_1\tau_2 b, \sigma_2\tau_1 e, \sigma_2\tau_2 a, \sigma_3 e\}$.

We now define the *delta operation* on languages formally. In the Introduction we have disregarded the ranking of the labels of the tree nodes. Formally, there is a delta operation for every ranked alphabet Σ. For a (string) language L, tree$_\Sigma(L) = \{t \in T_\Sigma \mid \text{path}(t) \subseteq L\}$ and $\delta_\Sigma(L) = \text{yield}(\text{tree}_\Sigma(L)) = \{\text{yield}(t) \mid t \in T_\Sigma, \text{path}(t) \subseteq L\}$. For a class K of languages, tree(K) denotes the class of tree languages $\{\text{tree}_\Sigma(L) \mid L \in K, \Sigma \text{ is a ranked alphabet}\}$, and $\delta(K)$ denotes the class of languages yield$(\text{tree}(K)) = \{\delta_\Sigma(L) \mid L \in K, \Sigma \text{ is a ranked alphabet}\}$.

Let us give some examples of the delta operation.

Example 1. (1) Let $\Sigma_3 = \{c\}$ and $\Sigma_0 = \{a, b, e\}$. Consider the regular language $L = c_2^*\{c_1 a, c_2 e, c_3 b\}$ over path(Σ). A simple argument shows that the trees that can be assembled from the paths in L, are those that have a "spine" of c's, ending in an e, with one a and b sticking out of each c. Thus tree$_\Sigma(L) = \{t_n \mid n \geq 1\}$, where $t_1 = c(a, e, b)$ and $t_{n+1} = c(a, t_n, b)$. Hence $\delta_\Sigma(L) = \text{yield}(\text{tree}(L)) = \{a^n b^n \mid n \geq 1\}$ (recall that the yield of e is the empty string ε). Thus δ_Σ transforms a regular language into a nonregular context-free language.

(2) Let $\Sigma_2 = \{b\}$, $\Sigma_1 = \{c\}$, and $\Sigma_0 = \{a\}$. Consider the (deterministic) context-free language $L = \{c_1^n w a \mid w \in \{b_1, b_2\}^n, n \geq 0\}$. The trees in tree$_\Sigma(L)$ consist of a "handle" of, say, n c's, connected with a full binary tree of b's of depth n, with a at the leaves. Formally, tree$_\Sigma(L) = \{t_{n,n} \mid n \geq 0\}$, where $t_{n+1,m} = c(t_{n,m})$, $t_{0,m+1} = b(t_{0,m}, t_{0,m})$, and $t_{0,0} = a$. Hence $\delta_\Sigma(L)$ is the noncontext-free indexed language $\{a^{2^n} \mid n \geq 0\}$.   □

The first result is that the recursively enumerable languages are exactly the deltas of the context-free languages, and even of the linear context-free languages. Let RE denote the class of recursively enumerable languages, CF the class of context-free languages, and LIN the class of linear context-free languages.

Theorem 1. RE $= \delta(\text{CF}) = \delta(\text{LIN})$.

Proof. Obviously $\delta(\text{LIN}) \subseteq \delta(\text{CF})$ and $\delta(\text{CF}) \subseteq \text{RE}$. It remains to prove that RE $\subseteq \delta(\text{LIN})$. It is well known that every recursively enumerable language is the homomorphic image of the intersection of two linear context-free languages, see, e.g., [ERoz80]. Thus, consider the language $h(L \cap M)$, where L and M are linear context-free languages over some alphabet A, and h is a homomorphism from A^* to B^*. We will construct a linear context-free language K and a ranked alphabet Σ such that $\delta_\Sigma(K) = h(L \cap M)$.

The ranked alphabet Σ consists of the following symbols. It contains the symbol \$ of rank 2, and it contains the symbol $\#_k$ of rank k, for every k not larger than the maximal length of $h(a)$, $a \in A$. It contains every $a \in A$, with rank 2, and every $b \in B$, with rank 0. Finally, it contains the symbol e.

Before defining K we describe the trees that will be in tree$_\Sigma(K)$. For every $a \in A$, define the tree s_a as follows: if $h(a) = b_1 b_2 \cdots b_k$ with $k \geq 1$ (and $b_i \in B$), then $s_a = \#_k(b_1, b_2, \ldots, b_k)$; if $h(a) = \varepsilon$, then $s_a = \#_1(e)$. Thus, s_a is a tree with yield $h(a)$. Now, for every $w \in A^*$, define the tree t_w as follows: $t_\varepsilon = \$(e, e)$ and $t_{aw} = a(s_a, t_w)$. Clearly, yield$(t_w) = h(w)$. We will define K in such a way that tree$_\Sigma(K) = \{t_w \mid w \in L \cap M\}$. Intuitively, the trick is that the tree t_w has a "spine" (when always taking the second child) that consists of the word w and ends on the tree $t_\varepsilon = \$(e, e)$. We force w to be in $L \cap M$ by requiring that the path that ends on the first e is in L whereas the path that ends on the second e is in M.

We now define $K = L_2(\$, 1)e \cup M_2(\$, 2)e \cup R$, such that $L_2 = g(L)$ and $M_2 = g(M)$, where g is the homomorphism from A^* to path$(\Sigma)^*$ with $g(a) = (a, 2)$ for every $a \in A$, and R is the union of all languages $A_2^*(a, 1)F_a$, $a \in A$, with $A_2 = g(A)$ and F_a is defined as follows. If $h(a) = b_1 b_2 \cdots b_k$ with $k \geq 1$, then $F_a = \{(\#_k, 1)b_1, (\#_k, 2)b_2, \ldots, (\#_k, k)b_k\}$; if $h(a) = \varepsilon$, then $F_a = \{(\#_1, 1)e\}$. Obviously, R is regular and L_2 and M_2 are linear context-free, and so K is linear context-free. It should also be clear that tree$_\Sigma(K)$ indeed equals $\{t_w \mid w \in L \cap M\}$ (note that tree$_\Sigma(F_a) = \{s_a\}$), and hence $\delta_\Sigma(K) = h(L \cap M)$.   □

Let DLIN denote the class of deterministic linear context-free languages, i.e., the languages recognized by deterministic one-turn pushdown automata, and let UDLIN denote the class of all finite unions of languages in DLIN. Note that the inclusions DLIN $\subset$ UDLIN $\subset$ LIN are proper. It was shown in Theorem 11 of [ERoz80] that every recursively enumerable language is of the form $h(L \cap M)$, where L and M are even in DLIN. Hence, the proof above shows that the theorem even holds for UDLIN instead of LIN, i.e., RE $= \delta$(UDLIN).

Recently, representations of the recursively enumerable languages have become of interest in the area of DNA-based computation, see, e.g., [PRozS98]. This leads to the question whether the delta operation can be computed in a natural way using any of the proposed Turing-complete DNA-based computation models.

The reader who is interested in representations of the recursively enumerable languages only, can immediately read Theorem 8 (after having read the text between Examples 3 and 4, including the last example).

3   Storage Types, Automata, and Grammars

The notion of a storage type, as an approach to a general theory of automata, was first proposed by Scott [Sco67]. The theory was developed by Ginsburg, Greibach, and many others [Gin75] (see also [Roz70a, Roz71a, Roz71b]). We use a variant of the formalism of Scott, as in [EVog86, Vog86, EVog87, Eng91, EHoo93].

A *storage type* is a tuple $S = (C, \Pi, \Phi, C_0)$, where C is the set of configurations, $C_0 \subseteq C$ is the set of initial configurations, Π is the set of predicates, which are (total) boolean functions $\pi : C \to \{\text{true}, \text{false}\}$, and Φ is the set of instructions, which are partial functions $\varphi : C \to C$; Φ contains the identity on C, denoted by id$_C$ or just by id.

For a storage type S, $\widehat{\Pi}$ denotes the set of all boolean functions $C \to \{\text{true}, \text{false}\}$ that are of the form π_1 *and* π_2 *and* $\cdots$ *and* π_n with $n \geq 0$ and

$\pi_i \in \Pi$, where *and* is the usual boolean operator. In particular, for $n = 0$, $\hat{\Pi}$ contains the boolean function *true*, which is always true. The elements of $\hat{\Pi}$ are called *tests*. Two tests β_1, β_2 are *nonexclusive* if there exists $c \in C$ such that $\beta_1(c) = \beta_2(c) = \text{true}$.

A (one-way, nondeterministic) *S-automaton* is a tuple $M = (Q, A, \tau, q_0, c_0, Q_H)$, where Q is the finite set of states, A is the input alphabet, $q_0 \in Q$ is the initial state, $c_0 \in C_0$ is the initial configuration, $Q_H \subseteq Q$ is the set of final (or halting) states, and the transition relation τ is a finite subset of $Q \times \hat{\Pi} \times (A \cup \{\varepsilon\}) \times Q \times \Phi$. An element of τ is called a *transition*. The set of *total configurations* of M is $Q \times C \times A^*$. The computation relation of M, denoted by $\vdash_M$, is the binary relation on total configurations defined as follows: if $(q_1, \beta, a, q_2, \varphi) \in \tau$, $\beta(c) = \text{true}$, and φ is defined on c, then $(q_1, c, aw) \vdash_M (q_2, \varphi(c), w)$ for every $w \in A^*$. As usual, $\vdash_M^*$ is the transitive, reflexive closure of $\vdash_M$, and the *language recognized by M*, denoted $L(M)$, is $\{w \in A^* \mid (q_0, c_0, w) \vdash_M^* (q, c, \varepsilon) \text{ for some } q \in Q_H \text{ and } c \in C\}$. The class of languages recognized by S-automata is denoted by $\mathcal{L}(S)$.

M is *deterministic* if there do not exist two different transitions $(q_i, \beta_i, a_i, q_i', \varphi_i)$ in τ $(i = 1, 2)$ such that $q_1 = q_2$, β_1, β_2 are nonexclusive, and $a_1 = a_2$ or $a_1 = \varepsilon$ or $a_2 = \varepsilon$. The class of languages recognized by deterministic S-automata is denoted by $\mathcal{L}_d(S)$.

The *trivial storage type S_0* is the storage type with one configuration, no predicates, and one instruction, i.e., $S_0 = (\{c_0\}, \emptyset, \{\text{id}\}, \{c_0\})$. Thus, an S_0-automaton is just a finite automaton (with ε-transitions). Hence, $\mathcal{L}(S_0) = \mathcal{L}_d(S_0) = \text{REG}$, the class of regular languages.

For every storage type $S = (C, \Pi, \Phi, C_0)$, we define the storage type of pushdowns of S-configurations as follows. Let Γ be a fixed infinite set of pushdown symbols. The *pushdown of S*, denoted $P(S)$, has configurations that are pushdowns of which each cell contains a pair (γ, c), where γ is a pushdown symbol and c is an S-configuration. Formally, $P(S)$ is the storage type (C', Π', Φ', C_0'), where $C' = (\Gamma \times C)^+$, $C_0' = \Gamma \times C_0$, $\Pi' = \{\text{top} = \gamma \mid \gamma \in \Gamma\} \cup \{\text{test } \pi \mid \pi \in \Pi\}$, $\Phi' = \{\text{put } \xi \mid \xi \in (\Gamma \times \Phi)^*\} \cup \{\text{id}_{C'}\}$, where the predicates and instructions are defined as follows: for every $c' = (\mu, c)\beta$ with $\mu \in \Gamma$, $c \in C$, and $\beta \in (\Gamma \times C)^*$, $(\text{top} = \gamma)(c') = \text{true}$ iff $\mu = \gamma$, $(\text{test } \pi)(c') = \pi(c)$, and $(\text{put } \xi)(c') = \xi_c \beta$, where ξ_c is obtained from ξ by replacing every (γ, φ) by $(\gamma, \varphi(c))$. Note that $(\text{put } \xi)(c')$ is defined only if φ is defined on c for every φ that occurs in ξ, and $\xi\beta \neq \varepsilon$. For a test $\beta = \pi_1 \text{ and } \cdots \text{ and } \pi_n$ in $\hat{\Pi}$, we denote by '$\text{test } \beta$' the test '$\text{test } \pi_1 \text{ and } \cdots \text{ and test } \pi_n$' in $\hat{\Pi}'$.

The storage type operator can be iterated by defining $P^0(S) = S$ and $P^{n+1}(S) = P(P^n(S))$ for every $n \geq 0$. We denote $P^n(S_0)$ by P^n, and P^n-automata will be called *iterated pushdown automata*. Clearly, P-automata are ordinary pushdown automata, and so $\mathcal{L}(P) = \text{CF}$ is the class of context-free languages, and $\mathcal{L}_d(P)$ is the class DCF of deterministic context-free languages. It is easy to see that the inclusions $\mathcal{L}(S) \subseteq \mathcal{L}(P(S))$ and $\mathcal{L}_d(S) \subseteq \mathcal{L}_d(P(S))$ hold: replace c_0 by (γ, c_0) and replace every transition $(q_1, \beta, a, q_2, \varphi)$ by the transition $(q_1, \text{top} = \gamma \text{ and test } \beta, a, q_2, \text{put } (\gamma, \varphi))$, where γ is a fixed pushdown symbol. Hence, for every n, $\mathcal{L}(P^n) \subseteq \mathcal{L}(P^{n+1})$ and $\mathcal{L}_d(P^n) \subseteq \mathcal{L}_d(P^{n+1})$. The classes $\mathcal{L}(P^n)$ of languages accepted by n-iterated pushdown automata form the well-known *OI-hierarchy*, see [DGoe86].

A *context-free S-grammar* is a tuple $G = (N, A, R, X_0, c_0)$, where N and A are the (disjoint) nonterminal and terminal alphabet, respectively, $X_0 \in N$ is the initial nonterminal, $c_0 \in C_0$ is the initial configuration, and R is the finite set of rules; every rule is of the form $X \to if\ \beta\ then\ \xi$, with $X \in N$, $\beta \in \hat{\Pi}$, and $\xi \in ((N \times \Phi) \cup A)^*$. The set of sentential forms is $((N \times C) \cup A)^*$. The derivation relation of G, denoted by $\Rightarrow_G$, is the binary relation on sentential forms defined as follows: if $X \to if\ \beta\ then\ \xi$ is in R, $\beta(c) = $ true, and φ is defined on c for every φ that occurs in ξ, then $\zeta_1(X, c)\zeta_2 \Rightarrow_G \zeta_1 \xi_c \zeta_2$ for all sentential forms ζ_1, ζ_2, where ξ_c is obtained from ξ by replacing every (Y, φ) by $(Y, \varphi(c))$. The *language generated by* G is $L(G) = \{w \in A^* \mid (X_0, c_0) \Rightarrow_G^* w\}$. The class of languages generated by context-free S-grammars is denoted by $\mathrm{CF}(S)$.

Clearly, a context-free S_0-grammar is just an ordinary context-free grammar, and so $\mathrm{CF}(S_0) = \mathrm{CF}$. Also, as explained in the Introduction, a context-free P-grammar is an indexed grammar, and so $\mathrm{CF}(P) = \mathrm{Indexed}$, the class of indexed languages.

Example 2. For the storage type $P = P(S_0)$ we drop the configuration of S_0 everywhere. Thus, the set of configurations of P is Γ^+, and the put instructions are of the form $put\ \xi$, with $\xi \in \Gamma^*$. Consider the context-free P-grammar $G = (N, A, R, X_0, c_0)$, where $N = \{X, Y, Z\}$, $A = \{a, b, c\}$, $X_0 = X$, $c_0 = \Box$, and R consists of the following rules:

$$X \to if\ top = \Box\ \ then\ a(X, put\ \gamma\Box),$$
$$X \to if\ top = \gamma\ \ then\ a(X, put\ \gamma\gamma),$$
$$X \to if\ true\ \ \ \ \ \ \ then\ (Y, id)(Z, id),$$
$$Y \to if\ top = \gamma\ \ then\ b(Y, put\ \varepsilon),$$
$$Y \to if\ top = \Box\ \ then\ \varepsilon,$$
$$Z \to if\ top = \gamma\ \ then\ c(Z, put\ \varepsilon),\ and$$
$$Z \to if\ top = \Box\ \ then\ \varepsilon.$$

Clearly $L(G) = \{a^n b^n c^n \mid n \geq 0\}$. $\Box$

Note that we may always assume for a context-free S-grammar G that each of its rules is either of the form $X \to if\ \beta\ then\ \xi$ with $\xi \in (N \times \Phi)^*$ or of the form $X \to if\ true\ then\ a$ with $a \in A$. Moreover, in the latter case we may assume that $X \to if\ true\ then\ a$ is the only rule with left-hand side X. We will say that G is in *normal form*. To obtain this normal form, just change every terminal a in the right-hand side of a rule into (X_a, id), where X_a is a new nonterminal with rule $X_a \to if\ true\ then\ a$.

A *(top-down) tree S-automaton* is a context-free S-grammar $M = (Q_1 \cup Q_2, \Sigma, R, q_0, c_0)$, of which the terminal alphabet Σ is ranked, the nonterminal alphabet is divided into two disjoint sets Q_1 and Q_2, with $q_0 \in Q_1$, and the rules are of one of the following types:

1. $q \to$ *if* β *then* (q', φ), with either $q, q' \in Q_1$ or $q, q' \in Q_2$,
2. $q \to$ *if* β *then* $\sigma(q_1, \varphi_1)(q_2, \varphi_2) \cdots (q_k, \varphi_k)$ with $\sigma \in \Sigma_k$, $k \geq 1$, and

$$q, q_1, \ldots, q_k \in Q_1,$$

3. $q \to$ *if* β *then* $\sigma(q', \varphi)$ with $\sigma \in \Sigma_0$, $q \in Q_1$, and $q' \in Q_2$, or
4. $q \to$ *if* $true$ *then* ε, with $q \in Q_2$.

The terminal alphabet of M is also called its input alphabet, and the nonterminals of M are also called its states (and are denoted accordingly). Intuitively, M starts its computation at the root of an input tree, and moves down the tree, splitting itself in parallel copies whenever it processes an internal node, until it arrives at the leaves of the tree, which it should also process and then halt. The automaton is in a state of Q_1 as long as it has not processed a leaf, and is in a state of Q_2 after it has done so. A rule of type (1) corresponds to an ε-transition of an S-automaton: it allows M to operate on its storage without inspecting the input tree. With the rules of type (2) and (3), M processes an internal node and a leaf, respectively, and with a rule of type (4) it halts (which is possible only after a leaf has been processed).

The derivation relation $\Rightarrow_M$ is also called the computation relation of M, and the language $L(M)$ generated by M is also said to be the *language recognized by* M. It is easy to see that $L(M) \subseteq T_\Sigma$, i.e., M recognizes a tree language.

M is *deterministic* if there do not exist two different rules $q_i \to$ *if* β_i *then* $a_i \xi_i$ in R ($i = 1, 2$, with $a_i \in \Sigma \cup \{\varepsilon\}$ and $\xi_i \in (N \times \Phi)^*$) such that $q_1 = q_2$, β_1, β_2 are nonexclusive, and $a_1 = a_2$ or $a_1 = \varepsilon$ or $a_2 = \varepsilon$. The class of languages recognized by deterministic tree S-automata is denoted by $\mathcal{T}_d(S)$.

A tree S_0-automaton is very close to an ordinary top-down finite tree automaton (with ε-transitions), and thus it recognizes the regular tree languages, and $\mathcal{T}_d(S_0)$ is the class DREGT of tree languages recognized by deterministic top-down finite tree automata (which, as shown in [MMor69], does not contain all regular tree languages). A tree P-automaton is a pushdown tree automaton, see [Gue83], which recognizes the (OI) context-free tree languages.

4   The Power of Delta

We have already seen in Section 2 that the recursively enumerable languages are exactly the deltas of the context-free languages.

The first result of this section is that the context-free S-grammars generate exactly the deltas of the languages recognized by deterministic S-automata. As explained in the Introduction, the result is shown in two steps, with the deterministic tree S-automaton as an intermediate.

Lemma 1. *For every storage type S, $\mathcal{T}_d(S) = \text{tree}(\mathcal{L}_d(S))$.*

Proof. ($\supseteq$) Let $M = (Q, A, \tau, q_0, c_0, Q_H)$ be a deterministic S-automaton, and let Σ be a ranked alphabet. We want to construct a deterministic tree S-automaton M' such that $L(M') = \text{tree}_\Sigma(L(M))$. Since all paths of trees in T_Σ are in the regular language $(A - \Sigma_0)^* \Sigma_0$, we may assume, by a standard product construction, that $L(M) \subseteq (A - \Sigma_0)^* \Sigma_0$. Similarly, we may assume that Q is partitioned into Q_1 and Q_2 such that M is in a state of Q_1 before reading a symbol from Σ_0 and in a state of Q_2 after reading such a symbol. In particular, $q_0 \in Q_1$ and $Q_H \subseteq Q_2$. Finally, we may assume that there are no transitions $(q, \ldots)$ in τ with $q \in Q_H$.

We now construct $M' = (Q_1 \cup Q_2, \Sigma, R, q_0, c_0)$ in such a way that it simulates M on all paths of the input tree. The rules of M' are defined as follows.

- If the transition $(q, \beta, \varepsilon, q', \varphi)$ is in τ, then the rule $q \rightarrow$ *if β then* (q', φ) is in R.
- If, for $\sigma \in \Sigma_k$, with $k \geq 1$, the transitions $(q, \beta_i, (\sigma, i), q_i, \varphi_i)$ are in τ, for all $1 \leq i \leq k$, then the rule $q \rightarrow$ *if β_1 and $\cdots$ and β_k then* $\sigma(q_1, \varphi_1) \cdots (q_k, \varphi_k)$ is in R.
- If, for $\sigma \in \Sigma_0$, the transition $(q, \beta, \sigma, q', \varphi)$ is in τ, then the rule $q \rightarrow$ *if β then* $\sigma(q', \varphi)$ is in R.
- For every $q \in Q_H$, the rule $q \rightarrow$ *if true then* ε is in R.

It is straightforward to check that M' is deterministic. It should also be clear that, for every $t \in T_\Sigma$, t is recognized by M' if and only if all its paths are recognized by M. Formally, it can be shown for every $q \in Q$, $c \in C$, and $t \in T_\Sigma \cup \{\varepsilon\}$, that $q(c) \Rightarrow_{M'}^* t$ if and only if for every $w \in \text{path}(t)$ there exist $q' \in Q_H$ and $c' \in C$ such that $(q, c, w) \vdash_M^* (q', c', \varepsilon)$, where we define $\text{path}(\varepsilon) = \{\varepsilon\}$. The proof is by induction on the lengths of the computations involved.

($\subseteq$) Let $M = (Q_1 \cup Q_2, \Sigma, R, q_0, c_0)$ be a deterministic tree S-automaton. We construct a deterministic S-automaton M' such that $\text{tree}_\Sigma(L(M')) = L(M)$. The automaton M' just imitates the behaviour of M, on the paths of trees in T_Σ. Thus, $M' = (Q_1 \cup Q_2, \text{path}(\Sigma), \tau, q_0, c_0, Q_H)$ with $Q_H = \{q \in Q_2 \mid$ the rule $q \rightarrow$ *if true then* ε is in $R\}$, and the transitions of M' are determined as follows. Consider the rules of type (1)-(3) of M as described in the definition of a tree S-automaton in Section 3. Corresponding to these rules, τ contains the following transitions:

1. $(q, \beta, \varepsilon, q', \varphi)$,
2. $(q, \beta, (\sigma, i), q_i, \varphi_i)$, for $1 \leq i \leq k$, and
3. $(q, \beta, \sigma, q', \varphi)$.

Again, it is straightforward to check that M' is deterministic. If the construction of the first part of this proof is applied to M', then a tree S-automaton M'' is obtained that has the same rules as M and some additional rules of which the test is always false (note that β *and* $\beta = \beta$, and that β_1 *and* β_2 is always false if β_1, β_2 are exclusive). Hence $L(M) = L(M'')$, and $L(M'') = \text{tree}_\Sigma(L(M'))$ by the first part of the proof. $\qquad\Box$

Lemma 2. *For every storage type S, $\text{CF}(S) = \text{yield}(\mathcal{T}_d(S))$.*

Proof. ($\supseteq$) Since every tree S-automaton is a special context-free S-grammar, $\mathcal{T}_d(S) \subseteq \text{CF}(S)$. For a ranked alphabet Σ, let h be the homomorphism from Σ^* to $(\Sigma_0 - \{e\})^*$ such that $h(\sigma) = \sigma$ if $\sigma \in \Sigma_0 - \{e\}$ and $h(\sigma) = \varepsilon$ otherwise.

Obviously, $h(t) = \text{yield}(t)$ for every tree $t \in T_\Sigma$. Thus, it suffices to prove that $CF(S)$ is closed under homomorphisms, which can be done in exactly the same way as for context-free languages.

($\subseteq$) Let $G = (N, A, R, X_0, c_0)$ be a context-free S-grammar in normal form (see Section 3). Since the yield mapping turns e into ε, we may assume additionally that R does not contain ε-rules, i.e., rules of the form $X \to$ if β then ε: change such a rule into $X \to$ if β then e, and add e to A.

We construct a tree S-automaton M that, intuitively, recognizes the derivation trees of G: since we want M to be deterministic, we assume that each internal node of a derivation tree is labeled with the rule applied at that node; leaves are labeled with terminals as usual.

Formally, $M = (Q_1 \cup Q_2, \Sigma, R_M, q_0, c_0)$ with $Q_1 = N$, $Q_2 = \{h\}$, $q_0 = X_0$, and Σ and R_M are defined as follows. First of all, $\Sigma_0 = A$ and R_M contains the rule $h \to$ if true then ε. With every rule of G we associate a rule of M, considering the following two cases. (i) Let $\rho : X \to$ if β then ξ be a rule in R, with $\xi = (X_1, \varphi_1) \cdots (X_k, \varphi_k)$, $k \geq 1$. Then ρ is in Σ_k, and R_M contains the rule $X \to$ if β then $\rho\xi$. (ii) Let $X \to$ if true then a be a rule in R. Then R_M contains the rule $X \to$ if true then $a(h, \text{id})$.

It should be clear that the yield of $L(M)$ is $L(G)$. It is also easy to see that M is deterministic, because each symbol of Σ occurs in exactly one rule of R_M (for a terminal a this is true by the definition of normal form). $\square$

Theorem 2. *For every storage type S,* $CF(S) = \delta(\mathcal{L}_d(S))$.

Taking $S = S_0$ we obtain the old result that $CF = \delta(\text{REG})$, and taking $S = P$ we obtain the promised result that Indexed $= \delta(\text{DCF})$, because $CF(P) =$ Indexed and $\mathcal{L}_d(P) = \text{DCF}$.

Theorem 3. $CF = \delta(\text{REG})$ *and* Indexed $= \delta(\text{DCF})$.

In view of Theorem 1 the reader may wonder what can be said about the class $\delta(\text{DLIN})$. It is not difficult to define the storage type of the one-turn pushdown, denoted P_1, such that $\text{DLIN} = \mathcal{L}_d(P_1)$. Thus, taking $S = P_1$ in Theorem 2, we obtain that $\delta(\text{DLIN}) = CF(P_1)$, which is the class of so-called restricted indexed languages of [Aho68]. This is a class of languages properly between the ET0L languages and the indexed languages, see [ESvL80] where it is denoted EB or S-PD.

The second result of this section is that the context-free S-grammar has the same power as the (nondeterministic) $P(S)$-automaton. This has already been shown in Theorem 6.3 (and Corollary 5.21) of [EVog86], as a special case of a more general result. Here we give a direct proof, with a different (but equivalent) definition of $P(S)$.

Theorem 4. *For every storage type S,* $CF(S) = \mathcal{L}(P(S))$.

Proof. ($\subseteq$) Let $G = (N, A, R, X_0, c_0)$ be a context-free S-grammar in normal form (see Section 3). A $P(S)$-automaton M that recognizes $L(G)$ is constructed in the same way as in the classical case; M simulates the left-most derivations of G. As pushdown symbols it uses the nonterminals in N and the symbol $\square$ (which is needed because $P(S)$ has no empty pushdown). Formally, $M = (Q, A, \tau, q_0, c_0', Q_H)$, where $Q = \{q_0, q, h\}$, $Q_H = \{h\}$, $c_0' = (\square, c_0)$, and the transitions in τ are defined as follows.

- $(q_0, \text{top} = \square, \varepsilon, q, \text{put}\,(X_0, \text{id})(\square, \text{id}))$ is in τ.
- If $X \to$ *if* β *then* ξ is in R with $\xi \in (N \times \Phi)^*$,
  then $(q, \text{top} = X$ *and test* $\beta, \varepsilon, q, \text{put}\,\xi)$ is in τ.
- If $X \to$ *if true then* a is in R with $a \in A$,
  then $(q, \text{top} = X, a, q, \text{put}\,\varepsilon)$ is in τ.
- $(q, \text{top} = \square, \varepsilon, h, \text{put}\,(\square, \text{id}))$ is in τ.

It should be clear that $L(M) = L(G)$.

($\supseteq$) Let $M = (Q, A, \tau, q_0, c_0', Q_H)$, with $c_0' = (\square, c_0)$, be a $P(S)$-automaton. We construct a context-free S-grammar G that generates $L(M)$, with the classical triple construction. To this aim we make the following assumptions on M (and leave it to the reader to check that these assumptions can always be realized).

- At each moment of time the symbol $\square$ is at the bottom of the pushdown, and nowhere else in the pushdown.
- $Q_H = \{h\}$ and M always halts with a transition $(q, \text{top} = \square, \varepsilon, h, \text{put}\,(\square, \text{id}))$, for some $q \in Q$; there are no transitions $(h, \ldots)$.
- Every test in a transition is of the form $\text{top} = \gamma$ *and test* β.
- There are no transitions $(\ldots, \text{id})$; note that id can always be changed into $\text{put}\,(\gamma, \text{id})$, where γ occurs in the test of the transition.

We now define $G = (N, A, R, X_0, c_0)$ such that N consists of all triples $[p, \gamma, q]$ where $p, q \in Q$ and γ occurs in τ, $X_0 = [q_0, \square, h]$, and R contains the following rules.

- If the transition $(p, \text{top} = \gamma$ *and test* $\beta, a, q, \text{put}\,\varepsilon)$ is in τ, then the rule $[p, \gamma, q] \to$ *if* β *then* a is in R.
- If the transition $(p, \text{top} = \gamma$ *and test* $\beta, a, q, \text{put}\,(\gamma_1, \varphi_1) \cdots (\gamma_n, \varphi_n))$ is in τ, with $n \geq 1$, then, for all states $q_1, \ldots, q_n$, the rule
  $[p, \gamma, q_n] \to$ *if* β *then* $a([q, \gamma_1, q_1], \varphi_1)([q_1, \gamma_2, q_2], \varphi_2) \cdots ([q_{n-1}, \gamma_n, q_n], \varphi_n)$
  is in R.

It should be clear that $L(G) = L(M)$. Formally it can be shown that for $\gamma \neq \square$ and $q \neq h$, $[p, \gamma, q](c) \Rightarrow_G^* w$ if and only if $(p, (\gamma, c), w) \vdash_M^* (q, \varepsilon, \varepsilon)$, and that $[p, \square, h](c) \Rightarrow_G^* w$ if and only if $(p, (\square, c), w) \vdash_M^* (h, (\square, c'), \varepsilon)$ for some $c' \in C$. $\qquad\square$

Corollary 1. *For every storage type* S, $\mathcal{L}(P(S)) = \delta(\mathcal{L}_d(S))$.

Taking $S = P^n$ we obtain that the languages recognized by nondeterministic $(n + 1)$-iterated pushdown automata are exactly the deltas of the languages recognized by deterministic n-iterated pushdown automata. Let us denote these classes by $\text{OI}(n+1)$ and $\text{DOI}(n)$, because of their relationship to the OI-hierarchy, see the Introduction.

Theorem 5. *For every $n \geq 0$, $\text{OI}(n + 1) = \delta(\text{DOI}(n))$.*

This implies that not all linear context-free languages (and even not all languages in UDLIN) can be recognized by deterministic iterated pushdown automata, i.e., LIN is not included in $\text{DOI}(*) = \bigcup\{\text{DOI}(n) \mid n \geq 0\}$, as shown in a different way in [EVog87]. In fact, if LIN $\subseteq \text{DOI}(*)$, then RE $= \delta(\text{LIN}) \subseteq \delta(\text{DOI}(*)) = \text{OI}(*) = \bigcup\{\text{OI}(n) \mid n \geq 0\}$ by Theorems 1 and 5. However, the languages in $\text{OI}(*)$ are known to be recursive [Dam82, Eng91].

5   ET0L and Two-Tape Automata

As observed in the Introduction, ET0L systems can be viewed as context-free S-grammars where S is the storage type of pushdowns that can only be popped. We now define this storage type and call it OneWay, because it can also be viewed as the storage type of the input tape of one-way automata. We will again use the infinite set Γ of pushdown symbols, which are now also called input symbols or, in view of the correspondence with ET0L, table symbols.

The storage type *OneWay* is (C, Π, Φ, C_0), where $C = \Gamma^*$, $C_0 = \Gamma^*$, $\Pi = \{\text{first} = \gamma \mid \gamma \in \Gamma\}$, and $\Phi = \{\text{read}, \text{id}\}$, where the predicates and instructions are defined as follows: for every $c = \mu v$ with $\mu \in \Gamma$ and $v \in \Gamma^*$, $(\text{first} = \gamma)(c) = \text{true}$ iff $\mu = \gamma$, and $\text{read}(c) = v$; for $c = \varepsilon$, $(\text{first} = \gamma)(c) = \text{false}$ and $\text{read}(c)$ is undefined.

To model ET0L systems as context-free OneWay-grammars, we should allow these grammars to start their derivations with an arbitrary initial configuration, rather than with a fixed one (note that it is easy to see that $\text{CF}(\text{OneWay}) = \text{CF}$). Let $S = (C, \Pi, \Phi, C_0)$ be a storage type. For a context-free S-grammar $G = (N, A, R, X_0, c_0)$ and a configuration $c \in C_0$ we denote by G_c the context-free S-grammar $G_c = (N, A, R, X_0, c)$, and we define the language *fully* generated by G to be $L_f(G) = \bigcup\{L(G_c) \mid c \in C_0\}$. The class of languages fully generated by context-free S-grammars is denoted $\text{CF}_f(S)$.

Lemma 3. ET0L $= \text{CF}_f(\text{OneWay})$.

Proof. If OneWay would not have the identity instruction, this would be immediate: obviously, a rule $X \rightarrow \textit{if}\ \text{first} = \gamma\ \textit{then}\ w_0(Y_1, \text{read})w_1 \cdots (Y_n, \text{read})w_n$ of a context-free OneWay-grammar corresponds to a rule $X \rightarrow w_0 Y_1 w_1 \cdots Y_n w_n$ in the table γ of an ET0L system (cf. also the way in which ET0L systems are defined in [ERozS80]). However, because of the presence of the identity (which we need in order to apply the results of Section 4), a context-free OneWay-grammar actually corresponds to an ET0L system in which the right-hand sides of the rules are context-free languages. Since it has been shown in [Chr74] that such systems (even if the right-hand sides are ET0L languages) still generate ET0L languages (see also [Eng85]), it follows that indeed ET0L = CF_f(OneWay).   □

Example 3. Consider the context-free OneWay-grammar $G = (N, A, R, X_0, c_0)$ with $N = \{X\}$, $X_0 = X$, $A = \{a\}$, and R consists of the following two rules: $X \to$ *if* first $= c$ *then* $(X, \text{read})(X, \text{read})$ and $X \to$ *if* first $= d$ *then* a. Note that c_0 is irrelevant, and that c and d are assumed to be in Γ. Then, for every string $c^n dw$ with $w \in \{c, d\}^*$, $(X, c^n dw) \Rightarrow_G^* a^{2^n}$, and hence $L_f(G) = \{a^{2^n} \mid n \geq 0\}$.   □

We now define *the delta operation for relations.* Let C_0 be a set and A an alphabet. For a relation $R \subseteq C_0 \times A^*$ and a ranked alphabet Σ, $\delta_\Sigma(R)$ is the language $\bigcup\{\delta_\Sigma(R(c)) \mid c \in C_0\} = \{\text{yield}(t) \mid t \in T_\Sigma, \exists c \in C_0 : (c, w) \in R$ for every $w \in \text{path}(t)\}$. For a class K of such relations, $\delta(K)$ denotes the class of languages $\{\delta_\Sigma(R) \mid R \in K, \Sigma$ is a ranked alphabet$\}$.

Let DREGR denote the class of string relations recognized by deterministic (one-way) two-tape finite automata [RSco59], and let REGR denote the class of relations recognized by nondeterministic two-tape finite automata. Note that REGR is the class of finite state transductions (or rational transductions [Ber79]), realized by nondeterministic finite state transducers (or a-transducers). It is shown in Theorem 17 of [RSco59] that DREGR is not closed under union, and hence is a proper subset of REGR.

Note that if $L \subseteq A^*$ is any language, and $C_0 = \{c\}$, then $\delta_\Sigma(L) = \delta_\Sigma(R)$, where $R = \{(c, w) \mid w \in L\}$. Vice versa, if $C_0 = B^*$ for some alphabet B disjoint with A, and $R \subseteq B^* \times A^*$ is any string relation, then $\delta_\Sigma(R) = \delta_{\Sigma'}(L)$, where $L = \{v_1 w \mid (v, w) \in R\}$ with v_1 obtained from v by changing every symbol $b \in B$ into $(b, 1)$, and Σ' obtained from Σ by adding all symbols of B, with rank 1. Instead of v_1, one can as well take v_1^r, the reverse of v_1, in the definition of L. In the latter case it is easy to see that if $R \in$ DREGR then $L \in$ DLIN (the one-turn pushdown automaton first reads v_1^r and stores v_1 on its pushdown, and then simulates the two-tape finite automaton, treating the pushdown as a second input tape). This shows that $\delta(\text{DREGR}) \subseteq \delta(\text{DLIN})$.

Example 4. Let $\Sigma_2 = \{b\}$ and $\Sigma_0 = \{a\}$. Let $C_0 = \{c, d\}^*$ (where c and d are symbols) and let $A = \text{path}(\Sigma)$. Consider the relation $R \subseteq C_0 \times A^*$ defined by $R = \{(c^n d, wa) \mid w \in \{b_1, b_2\}^n, n \geq 0\}$. Clearly $R \in$ DREGR. It should also be clear, cf. Example 1(2), that $\delta_\Sigma(R)$ consists of all yields of full binary trees, and so $\delta_\Sigma(R) = \{a^{2^n} \mid n \geq 0\}$.   □

In order to prove the analogue of Theorem 2 for fully generated languages, we need the *relation* recognized by an S-automaton. Let $S = (C, \Pi, \Phi, C_0)$ be a storage type. For an S-automaton $M = (Q, A, \tau, q_0, c_0, Q_H)$ and a configuration $c \in C_0$, let $M_c = (Q, A, \tau, q_0, c, Q_H)$. The *relation recognized by* M is $R(M) = \{(c, w) \mid c \in C_0, w \in L(M_c)\}$. Note that $R(M) \subseteq C_0 \times A^*$ and hence $\delta_\Sigma(R(M))$ is well defined for every Σ. The class of relations recognized by deterministic S-automata is denoted by $\mathcal{R}_d(S)$.

Theorem 6. *For every storage type S, $\mathrm{CF}_f(S) = \delta(\mathcal{R}_d(S))$.*

Proof. It can easily be checked that the constructions in the proofs of Lemmas 1 and 2 did not depend on the initial configuration of the automaton or grammar. Thus, instead of Theorem 2 we have even proved that for every context-free S-grammar G there exist a deterministic S-automaton M and a ranked alphabet Σ such that for every $c \in C_0$: $L(G_c) = \delta_\Sigma(L(M_c))$, and vice versa. And so, $L_f(G) = \bigcup\{L(G_c) \mid c \in C_0\} = \bigcup\{\delta_\Sigma(L(M_c)) \mid c \in C_0\} = \delta_\Sigma(R(M))$. □

As a particular case we obtain that ET0L is the class of deltas of the relations recognized by deterministic two-tape automata.

Theorem 7. ET0L $= \delta(\mathrm{DREGR})$.

Proof. Taking $S =$ OneWay in Theorem 6 and using Lemma 3, we have shown that ET0L $= \delta(\mathcal{R}_d(\mathrm{OneWay}))$. Clearly, a OneWay-automaton M has two input tapes: the usual one and the one in its storage. In fact, the total configurations of M are of the form (q, v, w) where v is the input string in storage and w is the usual input string. Both input strings are handled in the same way (except that M can test the first symbol of v, but not that of w, which is a detail that is insignificant in this context). Thus, the OneWay-automaton is the two-tape finite automaton, and $\mathcal{R}_d(\mathrm{OneWay}) = \mathrm{DREGR}$. Hence ET0L $= \delta(\mathrm{DREGR})$. □

The "full version" of Theorem 4 is also valid. For an S-automaton M, let $L_f(M) = \bigcup\{L(M_c) \mid c \in C_0\}$; let $\mathcal{L}_f(S) = \{L_f(M) \mid M \text{ is an } S\text{-automaton}\}$. It can easily be checked that the proof of Theorem 4 also shows that $\mathrm{CF}_f(S) = \mathcal{L}_f(P(S))$ for every storage type S. Taking $S =$ OneWay we obtain that ET0L $= \mathcal{L}_f(P(\mathrm{OneWay}))$. The $P(\mathrm{OneWay})$-automaton is closely related to the well-known checking-stack pushdown (cspd) automaton, introduced by van Leeuwen, which recognizes the ET0L languages (see, e.g., [ESvL80, RozS80, ERozS80]).

We finally show that the deltas of the finite state transductions are the recursively enumerable languages.

Theorem 8. RE $= \delta(\mathrm{REGR})$.

Proof. The proof is a variation of the one of Theorem 1. It is shown in Theorem 8 of [ERoz80] that every recursively enumerable language is the homomorphic image of the fixed point language of a dgsm mapping. Here, a dgsm mapping is a finite state transduction that can be realized by a deterministic finite state transducer, and the fixed point language of a partial function $\varphi : A^* \to A^*$ is $\mathrm{Fp}(\varphi) = \{v \in A^* \mid \varphi(v) = v\}$. Thus, consider the language $h(\mathrm{Fp}(\varphi))$, where $\varphi : A^* \to A^*$ is a dgsm mapping, and h is a homomorphism from A^* to B^*. We construct a finite state transduction $\psi \in \mathrm{REGR}$ such that $\delta_\Sigma(\psi) = h(\mathrm{Fp}(\varphi))$, where the ranked alphabet Σ is defined as in the proof of Theorem 1. The definition of ψ is similar to the definition of the language K in that proof. For every $v \in A^*$, $\psi(v) = \{\varphi(v)_2(\$, 1)e, v_2(\$, 2)e\} \cup R$, such that $\varphi(v)_2 = g(\varphi(v))$ and $v_2 = g(v)$, where, again, g is the homomorphism that changes every a into $(a, 2)$, and R is as in the proof of Theorem 1. It should be clear that ψ can indeed be realized by a finite state transducer, which on input v nondeterministically decides to simulate the dgsm or to copy v to the output (in both cases applying g) or to disregard v and generate an element of the regular language R. Using the same terminology as in the proof of Theorem 1, it should also be clear that for every $v \in A^*$, $\text{tree}_\Sigma(\psi(v)) = \{t_v\}$ if $\varphi(v) = v$, and $\text{tree}_\Sigma(\psi(v)) = \emptyset$ otherwise. Hence $\delta_\Sigma(\psi) = \{\text{yield}(t_v) \mid v \in \text{Fp}(\varphi)\} = h(\text{Fp}(\varphi))$. □

References

[Aho68]   A.V. Aho; Indexed Grammars, an Extension of Context-Free Grammars, J. of the ACM 15 (1968), 647–671

[Ber79]   J. Berstel; *Transductions and Context-Free Languages*, Teubner, Stuttgart, 1979

[Chr74]   P. Christensen; Hyper-AFL's and ET0L Systems, in *L Systems* (G. Rozenberg, A. Salomaa, Eds.), Lecture Notes in Computer Science 15, Springer-Verlag, Berlin, 1974, pp.254–257

[Cul74]   K. Culik II; On Some Families of Languages Related to Developmental Systems, Internat. J. Comput. Math. 4 (1974), 31–42

[Dam82]   W. Damm; The IO- and OI-hierarchies, Theoret. Comput. Sci. 20 (1982), 95–206

[DGoe86]   W. Damm, A. Goerdt; An Automata-Theoretical Characterization of the OI-hierarchy, Inform. and Control 71 (1986), 1–32

[EHoo93]   J. Engelfriet, H.J. Hoogeboom; X-automata on ω-words, Theoret. Comput. Sci. 110 (1993), 1–51

[Eng75]   J. Engelfriet; *Tree Automata and Tree Grammars*, Lecture Notes, DAIMI FN-10, Aarhus, 1975

[Eng80]   J. Engelfriet; Some Open Questions and Recent Results on Tree Transducers and Tree Languages, in *Formal Language Theory; Perspectives and Open Problems* (R.V. Book, Ed.), Academic Press, New York, 1980

[Eng85]   J. Engelfriet; Hierarchies of Hyper-AFLs, J. of Comput. Syst. Sci. 30 (1985), 86–115

[Eng86]   J. Engelfriet; Context-Free Grammars with Storage, Leiden University, Technical Report 86-11, 1986

[Eng91]   J. Engelfriet; Iterated Stack Automata and Complexity Classes, Inform. and Comput. 95 (1991), 21–75

[ERoz80]   J. Engelfriet, G. Rozenberg; Fixed Point Languages, Equality Languages, and Representation of Recursively Enumerable Languages, J. of the ACM 27 (1980), 499–518

[ERozS76]   A. Ehrenfeucht, G. Rozenberg, S. Skyum; A Relationship between the ET0L and EDT0L Languages, Theoret. Comput. Sci. 1 (1976), 325–330

[ERozS80]   J. Engelfriet, G. Rozenberg, G. Slutzki; Tree Transducers, L Systems, and Two-Way Machines, J. of Comput. Syst. Sci. 20 (1980), 150–202

[ESch77]   J. Engelfriet, E.M. Schmidt; IO and OI, J. of Comput. Syst. Sci. 15 (1977), 328–353, and J. of Comput. Syst. Sci. 16 (1978), 67–99

[ESvL80]   J. Engelfriet, E.M. Schmidt, J. van Leeuwen; Stack Machines and Classes of Nonnested Macro Languages, J. of the ACM 27 (1980), 96–117

[EVog86]   J. Engelfriet, H. Vogler; Pushdown Machines for the Macro Tree Transducer, Theoret. Comput. Sci. 42 (1986), 251–369

[EVog87]   J. Engelfriet, H. Vogler; Look-Ahead on Pushdowns, Inform. and Comput. 73 (1987), 245–279

[EVog88]   J. Engelfriet, H. Vogler; High Level Tree Transducers and Iterated Pushdown Tree Transducers, Acta Informatica 26 (1988), 131–192

[Gin75]   S. Ginsburg; *Algebraic and Automata-Theoretic Properties of Formal Languages*, North-Holland/American Elsevier, Amsterdam/New York, 1975

[Gre70]   S.A. Greibach; Chains of Full AFL's, Math. Syst. Theory 4 (1970), 231–242

[GSte84]   F. Gécseg, M. Steinby; *Tree Automata*, Akadémiai Kiadó, Budapest, 1984

[GSte97]   F. Gécseg, M. Steinby; Tree Languages, in *Handbook of Formal Languages*, Volume 3: *Beyond Words* (G. Rozenberg, A. Salomaa, Eds.), Springer-Verlag, Berlin, 1997

[Gue83]   I. Guessarian; Pushdown Tree Automata, Math. Syst. Theory 16 (1983), 237–263

[HKar91]   T. Harju, J. Karhumäki; The Equivalence Problem of Multitape Finite Automata, Theoret. Comput. Sci. 78 (1991), 347–355

[KRozS97] L. Kari, G. Rozenberg, A. Salomaa; L Systems, in *Handbook of Formal Languages*, Volume 1: *Word, Language, Grammar* (G. Rozenberg, A. Salomaa, Eds.), Springer-Verlag, Berlin, 1997

[MMor69]   M. Magidor, G. Moran; Finite Automata over Finite Trees, Techn. Report No. 30, Hebrew University, Jerusalem, 1969

[PRozS98] G. Păun, G. Rozenberg, A. Salomaa; *DNA Computing; New Computing Paradigms*, Springer-Verlag, Berlin, 1998

[PSak99]   M. Pelletier, J. Sakarovitch; On the Representation of Finite Deterministic 2-tape Automata, Theoret. Comput. Sci. 225 (1999), 1–63

[Rou70]   W.C. Rounds; Mappings and Grammars on Trees, Math. Syst. Theory 4 (1970), 257–287

[Roz70a]   C. Gordon; Abstract Families of Languages, Seminar on Automata Theory and Mathematical Linguistics (organized by G. Rozenberg), Abstract 4, Utrecht, March 1970

[Roz70b]   J. Engelfriet; Tree Automata, Seminar on Automata Theory and Mathematical Linguistics (organized by G. Rozenberg), Abstract 5, Utrecht, March 1970

[Roz70c]   J. van Leeuwen; Brackets and Parentheses in the Theory of Context-Free Languages, Seminar on Automata Theory and Mathematical Linguistics (organized by G. Rozenberg), Abstract 6, Utrecht, December 1970

[Roz71a]   M. Nivat; Sur la fermeture rationnelle des cônes rationnels, Seminar on Automata Theory and Mathematical Linguistics (organized by G. Rozenberg), Abstract 4, Utrecht, March 1971

[Roz71b]   J. van Leeuwen; The General Theory of Translation, Seminar on Automata Theory and Mathematical Linguistics (organized by G. Rozenberg), Abstract 6, Utrecht, April 1971

[Roz71c]   J. Engelfriet; Tree Automata and Tree Transducers, Seminar on Automata Theory and Mathematical Linguistics (organized by G. Rozenberg), Abstract 8, Utrecht, May 1971

[Roz73]   G. Rozenberg; Extension of Tabled 0L-systems and Languages, Internat. J. Comp. Inform. Sci. 2 (1973), 311–336

[RozS80]   G. Rozenberg, A. Salomaa; *The Mathematical Theory of L Systems*, Academic Press, New York, 1980

[RSco59]   M.O. Rabin, D. Scott; Finite Automata and Their Decision Problems, IBM J. Res. 3 (1959), 115–125

[Sco67]   D. Scott; Some Definitional Suggestions for Automata Theory, J. of Comput. Syst. Sci. 1 (1967), 187–212

[Tha67]   J.W. Thatcher; Characterizing Derivation Trees of Context-Free Grammars through a Generalization of Finite Automata Theory, J. of Comput. Syst. Sci. 1 (1967), 317–322

[Tha73]   J.W. Thatcher; Tree Automata: An Informal Survey, in *Currents in the Theory of Computing* (A.V. Aho, Ed.), Prentice-Hall, Englewood Cliffs, 1973, pp.143–172

[Vog86]   H. Vogler; Iterated Linear Control and Iterated One-Turn Pushdowns, Math. Syst. Theory 19 (1986), 117–133

[Vog88]   H. Vogler; The OI-hierarchy Is Closed under Control, Inform. and Comput. 78 (1988), 187–204

[Wan75]   M. Wand; An Algebraic Formulation of the Chomsky-Hierarchy, in *Category Theory Applied to Computation and Control* (E.G. Manes, Ed.), Lecture Notes in Computer Science 25, Springer-Verlag, Berlin, 1975, pp. 209–213

Infinite Solutions of Marked Post Correspondence Problem

Vesa Halava and Tero Harju

Department of Mathematics
University of Turku
20014 Turku
Finland
{vehalava,harju}@utu.fi
and
TUCS - Turku Centre for Computer Science
Lemminkäisenkatu 14 A, 4th floor
20520, Turku
Finland

Abstract In an instance of the Post Correspondence Problem we are given two morphisms $h, g \colon A^* \to B^*$. Here we prove that if the morphisms are marked, then it is decidable whether the instance has an infinite solution, i.e., whether or not there exists an infinite word ω such that h and g are comparable for all prefixes of ω. This problem is known to be undecidable in general for Post Correspondence Problem.

1 Introduction

Let A and B be two finite alphabets. In the *Post Correspondence Problem*, PCP for short, we are given two morphims $h, g \colon A^* \to B^*$ and we are asked to determine whether or not there exists a nonempty word $w \in A^*$ such that $h(w) = g(w)$. The pair (h, g) is called an *instance* of the PCP and a word $w \in A^+$ a *solution* of the instance (h, g) if $h(w) = g(w)$. The set of all solutions,

$$E(h, g) = \{w \in A^+ \mid h(w) = g(w)\},$$

is called the *equality set* of the instance (h, g).

The PCP is undecidable in this general form, see [6]. Also the restrictions of the PCP have received much attention. For example, if $|A| \le 2$ then the problem is decidable, see [1] or [3] for a somewhat shorter proof. On the other hand, if $|A| \ge 7$, then the PCP is undecidable, see [5].

Here we consider infinite solutions of an instance (h, g) of the PCP. We say that the morphisms h and g *agree* on an *infinite word* $\omega = a_1 a_2 \cdots$ if $g(w)$ and $h(w)$ are comparable for all prefixes w of ω. Recall that two words are comparable if one is a prefix of another. We call such an infinite word an *infinite solution* of the instance (h, g). The following theorem was proved in [7].

W. Brauer et al. (Eds.): Formal and Natural Computing, LNCS 2300, pp. 57–68, 2002.
© Springer-Verlag Berlin Heidelberg 2002

Theorem 1. *It is undecidable, whether there exists an infinite solution to a given instance (h, g) of the PCP.*

Here we shall prove that the existence of infinite solution is decidable, if the morphisms are marked. We say that a morphisms $h\colon A^* \to B^*$ is *marked* if the images $h(a)$ and $h(b)$ of the letters $a, b \in A$ begin with different letters whenever $a \neq b$. Note that marked morphisms are a subclass of the injective morphims or, to be more precise, the marked morphisms form a subclass of the *prefix* morphims, that is, the morphisms such that no image of a letter is a prefix of an image of another letter. Actually, by [7], it can be assumed in Theorem 1 that the morphisms are prefix morphisms (or even biprefix).

It is known that the PCP is decidable for marked morphisms, see [4]. Our proof for the infinite solutions follows the lines of the algorithm for the marked PCP, and therefore we shall outline the proof of decidability for the marked PCP in the next section.

We shall first fix some notations. The *empty word* is denoted by ε. A word $x \in A^*$ is said to be a *prefix* of $y \in A^*$, if there exists $z \in A^*$ such that $y = xz$. This will be denoted by $x \leq y$. A prefix of length k of y is denoted by $\mathrm{pref}_k(y)$. Also, if $x \neq \varepsilon$ and $z \neq \varepsilon$ in $y = xz$, then x is a *proper* prefix of y, and, this is denoted by $x < y$. Recall that x and y are *comparable* if $x \leq y$ or $y \leq x$.

A word $x \in A^*$ is said to be a *suffix* of $y \in A^*$, if there exists $z \in A^*$ such that $y = zx$. This will be denoted by $x \preccurlyeq y$ and, if $x \neq \varepsilon$ and $z \neq \varepsilon$, then x is called a *proper* suffix of y, denoted by $x \prec y$.

If $x = yz$ then we also denote $y = xz^{-1}$ and $z = y^{-1}x$.

2   Marked PCP

In this section we consider the proof of the decidability of the marked PCP. We shall only outline the proofs, the detailed proof can be found from [4] or [2].

The marked morphisms are deterministic in the following sense:

Lemma 1. *Let $g\colon A^* \to B^*$ be a marked morphism and $w \in B^*$ a nonempty word. There exists at most one word $u \in A^*$ such that*

$$w \leq h(u)$$

and $h(u') < w$ for all $u' < u$.

We shall call such a u in Lemma 1 a *g-cover of w.*

Corollary 1. *Let $h, g\colon A^* \to B^*$ be a marked morphisms. For a nonempty word $w \in B^+$, there exists at most one pair (u, v) of words $u, v \in A^*$ such that*

$$wh(u) = g(v)$$

and $wh(u') \neq g(v')$ for all $u' < u$ and $v' < v$.

2.1   Blocks

We shall descripe a decision method for the marked PCP. We begin with the following simpler problem with a simple solution:

> Given an instance $I = (h, g)$ of the PCP, where $h, g: A^* \to B^*$, and $a \in B$. Does there exist $x, y \in A^+$ such that $h(x) = g(y)$ and $h(x)$ begins with a?

Here we do not look for $h(x) = g(x)$, but only for $h(x) = g(y)$, and we additionally require that $g(x)$ starts with a specific letter a. This problem is known to be decidable for PCP in general, the reasoning being that the languages $h(A^*) \cap aB^*$ and $g(A^*) \cap aB^*$ are regular and there exist such x and y if and only if

$$(h(A^*) \cap aB^*) \cap (g(A^*) \cap aB^*) = \emptyset, \tag{1}$$

and the emptiness problem is decidable for regular languages.

If $h(u) = g(v)$ and $h(u') \neq g(v')$ for all $u' \leq u$ and $v' \leq v$, then the pair (u, v) is called a *minimal solution* to the equation $h(x) = g(y)$. From Lemma 1, we easily obtain

Lemma 2. *Let h and g be marked morphisms, where $h, g: A^* \to B^*$. There exists at most one minimal solution (u, v) such that $a \leq h(u)$ and $a \leq g(v)$. Moreover, such a minimal solution for a given letter a can be effectively found.*

For marked h and g, the minimal solution (u, v) of the equation $h(x) = g(y)$ under the constrain $a \leq h(x), g(y)$ is called a *block for the letter* a. We shall denote by $\beta(a) = (u, v)$ if the block (i.e., the minimal solution) exists. Otherwise $\beta(a)$ is not defined. Furthermore, if $\beta(a)$ is defined, the a is called a *block letter*.

We shall give a procedure to construct the block for a letter a: We define a sequence $(x_i, y_i) \in A^* \times A^*$ in the following way: first check if there are letters $b, c \in A$ such that $a \leq h(b), g(c)$. These letters are unique if they exists, since the morphisms are marked. Set $x_1 = b$ and $y_1 = c$. If a solution exists exists, then necessarily $h(x_1)$ and $g(y_1)$ are comparable, i.e., there exists a word $s \in B^*$ such that $h(x_1)s = g(y_1)$ or $g(y_1)s = h(x_1)$, depending on which of the words $h(x_1)$ or $g(y_1)$ is longer. We shall call such a word s an *overflow of h or g*, respectively. If $s = \varepsilon$, then $\beta(a) = (x_1, y_1)$. Otherwise, if $h(x_1)s = g(x_1)$, then there is at most one letter $x' \in A$ such that s and $h(x')$ are comparable, since h is marked. Define $x_2 = x_1 x'$ and $y_2 = y_1$. Similarly, if $g(y_1)s = h(x_1)$, then there is at most one letter $y' \in A$ such that s and $g(y')$ are comparable and we define $x_2 = x_i$ and $y_2 = y_1 y'$. Now again, if a block exists, $h(x_2)$ and $g(y_2)$ are comparable and we have an overflow s. We continue to construct the sequence (x_i, y_i) in a similar fashion. Since the morphisms are marked and the sequence (x_i, y_i) is constructed letter by letter, there are only finitely many different possible overflows. Therefore we shall reach one of the following three cases is reached:

(i) There is no suitable x' or y' or $h(x_i)$ and $g(y_i)$ are not comparable.
(ii) We have the same overflow s of h (resp. g) twice.
(iii) The overflow equals $s = \varepsilon$. Then $\beta(a) = (x_i, y_i)$.

Note that the case (ii) implies that the overflows start to cycle. In this case we have $h(x_i)$ and $g(y_i)$ comparable for all $i \geq 1$, and the overflows are always nonempty. Although the case (ii) is not important in the marked PCP, this case needs to be studied when we consider the infinite solutions of the marked PCP in Section 3.

Assume that $w \in A^+$ is a solution of the instance (h, g) of the marked PCP. Then there exists a unique *block decomposition* of w,

$$w = u_1 u_2 \cdots u_k = v_1 v_2 \cdots v_k, \tag{2}$$

where $(u_i, v_i) = \beta(a_i)$ for $a_i \in A$ for all $i = 1, \ldots, k$. This means that each solution is a concatenation of blocks, see Figure 1.

$h(w)$	$h(u_1)$	$h(u_2)$	$\cdots$	$h(u_k)$
$g(w)$	$g(v_1)$	$g(v_2)$	$\cdots$	$g(v_k)$

Fig. 1. Block decomposition of a solution w

2.2   Successor

Let (h, g) be an instance of the marked PCP and $h, g \colon A^* \to B^*$. We make first two assumptions: $A \subset B$ and

$$a \leq h(a) \quad \text{for all } a \in A. \tag{3}$$

The first assumption is achieved by replacing B with $A \cup B$ and the second one is achieved by applying a permutation to B.

By using blocks we shall define for an instance (h, g) its *successor* (h', g'). Let

$$A' = \{a \mid \beta(a) \text{ exists } \} (\subseteq B).$$

We define the morphisms $h', g' \colon (A')^* \to A^*$ by

$$h'(a) = u \quad \text{and} \quad g'(a) = v,$$

if $\beta(a) = (u, v)$. Note that these new morphisms are marked, since the morphisms h and g are marked and for each letter in B, there is at most one block. Therefore the successor (h', g') is also an instance of the marked PCP. We shall next show a connection between an instance and its successor.

Lemma 3. *Let $I = (h, g)$ be an instance of the marked PCP and $I' = (h', g')$ be its successor. Then*

(i) $hh'(x) = gg'(x)$ *for all* $x \in (A')^*$.
(ii) I *has a solution if and only if* I' *has.*
(iii) *if* w' *is a solution of* I', *then* $w = h'(w') = g'(w')$ *is a solution of* I.
(iv) *since* $a \leq h'(a)$ *for each* $a \in A'$.

Proof. The first claim follows from the definition of a block: for a letter $a \in A'$, let $\beta(a) = (u, v)$. Then $h'(a) = u$ and $g'(a) = v$, and therefore $h(h'(a)) = h(u) = g(v) = g(g'(a))$. Since h and g are morphisms, the claim follows.

For (ii), assume first that I has a solution $w = u_1 \cdots u_k = v_1 \cdots v_k$, where $(u_i, v_i) = \beta(a_i)$ for the letters $a_i \in A'$, $1 \leq i \leq k$. By the definition of h' and g',

$$h'(a_1 \cdots a_k) = u_1 \cdots u_k = w = v_1 \cdots v_k = g'(a_1 \cdots a_k),$$

and so $a_1 \cdots a_k$ is a solution of I'.

Assume that $w' = a_1 \cdots a_k$ is a solution of I', that is, $h'(w') = g'(w')$. By the case (i), $w = h'(w') = g'(w')$ is a solution of I. This also proves the case (iii).

Finally, the case (iv) follows by the fact that $a \leq h(a)$ and therefore if $\beta(a) = (u, v)$, then $a \leq u = h'(a)$.

Note that, by the proof of Lemma 3, there is a one-to-one correspondence between the solutions of I and I'.

2.3   Suffix Complexity

We shall prove that the successor I' is simpler than the original instance I and then use the construction of the successors inductively until we obtain an instance, where the decision can be easily done. We use two measures for the hardness of an instance. The first measure is the size of the domain alphabet. It is immediate that $|A'| \leq |A|$, since at most $|A|$ letters can begin an image and be a block letter.

The second measure is the *suffix complexity*. For a morphism $h\colon A^* \to B^*$ we first define the *set of suffixes*

$$S_h = \bigcup_{a \in A} \{x \mid x \prec h(a)\},$$

and the suffix complexity of h is defined to be the integer

$$\sigma(h) = |S_h|.$$

In other words, the suffix complexity is the number of the proper suffixes of the images of the morphism. Note that $\varepsilon \notin S_h$, since ε is not a proper suffix according to our defition. For an instance $I = (h, g)$ of the marked PCP, the suffix complexity is defined as

$$\sigma(I) = \sigma(h) + \sigma(g).$$

The next lemma was proved in [4].

Lemma 4. *Let $I = (h, g)$ be an instance of the marked PCP and $I' = (h', g')$ be its successor. Then $\sigma(I') \leq \sigma(I)$*

Proof. We define an injective function $p : S_{g'} \to S_h$. Let $w \in S_{g'}$, say $w \prec g'(a) = v = v_1 w$, where $\beta(a) = (u, v)$. Consider the factorization $u = u_1 b u_2$ such that $h(u_1) < g(v_1) < h(u_1 b)$, and let $s = g(v_1)^{-1} h(v_1 b)$. Clearly $s \prec h(b)$ and $s < g(w)$. Note that w may be a suffix of many different images $g'(a)$ and there can be several such suffixes s defined above. Let s_1 be the shortest of these suffixes s. It is unique, since for all suffixes s in the above $s < g(w)$. Define $p(w) = s_1$. It cam be proved that p is injective and therefore $\sigma(g') \leq \sigma(h)$.

Similarly we can define an injective function from $S_{h'}$ to S_g, which proves that $\sigma(h') \leq \sigma(g)$. It now follows that $\sigma(I') = \sigma(h') + \sigma(g') \leq \sigma(g) + \sigma(h)$

Actually, the suffix complexity was already used in [1], where it was proved that Lemma 4 holds in the binary case. Here we stated that the suffix complexity in any instance of the marked PCP cannot decrease. This is a crucial part of our proof for the decidability of the marked PCP.

2.4   The Marked PCP Is Decidable

The decision procedure for the marked PCP uses the successors iteratively, i.e., it generates the successors as long as we obtain an instance where the decision is easy to make. Therefore we define the *successor sequence* as follows:. let $I_0 = (h, g)$ be an instance of the marked PCP, where $h, g : A_0^* \to B^*$. We define the successor sequence $I_i = (h_i, g_i)$ by $I_{i+1} = I_i'$. Moreover, we assume that, for all $i \geq 1$, $h_i, g_i : A_i^* \to A_{i-1}^*$. Recall that we can assume that $A \subseteq B$ and therefore the domain alphabet $A_i \subseteq B$ for all $i \geq 0$.

We begin with a simple lemma.

Lemma 5. *Let A and B be alphabets with $A \subseteq B$ and z be a positive natural number. There exist only finitely many distinct instances $I = (h, g)$, where $h, g : A^* \to B^*$, of the PCP that satisfy $\sigma(I) \leq z$.*

Now since the size of the alphabet and the suffix complexity do not increase, one of the following three cases occurs in the successor sequence I_i by Lemma 5:

(i) $|A_j| = 1$ for some $j \geq 0$,
(ii) $\sigma(I_j) = 0$ for some $j \geq 0$,
(iii) the sequence starts to cycle, i.e., there exists n_0 and $d \geq 1$ such that, for all $j \geq n_0$, $I_j = I_{j+d}$. The cycle is *ultimately periodic*.

In the case (i), we have an instance of the unary PCP. Since there is only one letter in the domain alphabet, the possible solutions are powers of this letter and it is easy to see that if there is a solution, then also the letter itself is a solution. In the case (ii) we have suffix complexity zero, i.e., all the images are of length one, and therefore if there is a solution for this instance, then the first letter of such solution is necessarily a solution. It is now clear that the case (i) and (ii) are decidable. We need to prove that the case (iii), the case of a *cycling sequence*, is also decidable.

Consider now the cycling case. In order to simplify the notations we assume that the cycling starts already at I_0, i.e., the sequence is of the form

$$I_0, \ldots, I_{d-1}, I_d = I_0, \ldots . \tag{4}$$

This assumption can be made, since we know that the original instance and the first instance in the sequence are equivalent.

Lemma 6. *The case (iii), a cycling sequence, is decidable. Moreover, the length of a minimal solution in the case (iii) is one.*

Proof. Let I_0 be as in (4) and $I_i = (h_i, g_i)$. By Lemma 3, for every solution x_i to some I_i, there is a solution x_{i+1} to I_{i+1} such that $x_i = h_{i+1}(x_{i+1}) = g_{i+1}(x_{i+1})$. Suppose x_0 is a solution to I_0 of minimal length. Inductively we obtain that there is a solution x_d to I_d such that

$$x_0 = h_1(x_1) = h_1 h_2(x_2) = \ldots = h_1 h_2 \cdots h_d(x_d)$$
$$x_0 = g_1(x_1) = g_1 g_2(x_2) = \ldots = g_1 g_2 \cdots g_d(x_d).$$

Since the morphisms are marked and hence h_i and g_i cannot be length-decreasing, we have $|x_0| \geq |x_d|$. But since x_0 was chosen to be a minimal length solution to I_0 and x_d is also a solution to $I_d = I_0$, $|x_0| = |x_d|$. This implies that g_0 and h_0 map the letters in x_d to letters. But then the first letter of x_d is already a solution, and hence $|x_0| = |x_d| = 1$. Thus I_0 has a solution if and only if I_0 has a 1-letter solution.

We have proved the following theorem.

Theorem 2. *The marked PCP is decidable.*

3 Infinite Solutions

We shall consider now the infinite solutions of the marked PCP. Recall that an instance (h, g) of the PCP has an infinite solution $w = a_1 a_2 \cdots$ if $g(w)$ and $h(w)$ are comparable for all $w \leq \omega$.

We shall prove that the existence of an infinite solution is decidable for the marked PCP. Actually, our construction for the marked PCP turns out to be useful also in this occasion. We begin with a simple lemma.

Lemma 7. *Let $I = (h, g)$ be an instance of the marked PCP and $I' = (h', g')$ be its successor. For all comparable words x and y, also $h(h'(x))$ and $g(g'(y))$ are comparable.*

Proof. Assume, by symmetry, that $x \leq y$, say $y = xz$ for some word z. By Lemma 3, $h(h'(x)) = g(g'(x))$, and therefore $h(h'(x)) \leq g(g'(xz))$ as required.

Assume that w is an infinite solution of an instance $I = (h, g)$ of the marked PCP. There are three possibilities cases for w:

(i) $w = w_1 w_2 \cdots$, where $w_i \in E(h, g)$ for each i,
(ii) w has a block decomposition, but it is not as in (i),
(iii) w does not have a block decomposition.

Note that we say that an infinite word w has a block decomposition, if

$$w = u_1 u_2 \cdots = v_1 v_2 \cdots ,$$

where $(u_i, v_i) = \beta(a_i)$ for the letters a_i for $i \geq 1$.

First of all, the solutions of type (i) can be effectively found by Theorem 2. Note that if there exists a solution to the marked PCP, then there exists an infinite solution. Therefore we assume in the following that $E(h, g) = \emptyset$ and consider only solutions of the other two types.

Again, the cases where the suffix complexity is zero or the domain alphabet is unary are easy to decide.

Lemma 8. *Let I be an instance of the marked PCP. If $\sigma(I) = 0$ or the domain alphabet is unary, then the infinite solutions of I can be effectively found.*

Proof. Assume first that $\sigma(I) = 0$. Then for all letters, the lengths of the images are one. In this case it is obvious that I has an infinite solution if and only if it has a finite solution.

Assume then that I is unary and let a be its single letter. Then $I = (h, g)$ has an infinite solution if and only if $h(a)^k = g(a)^\ell$ for some k and ℓ. This follows from the fact that $h(a)^t$ and $g(a)^t$ have to be comparable for all $t \geq 0$, and therefore, for some k and ℓ,

$$k \cdot |h(a)| = \ell \cdot |g(a)|.$$

If $h(a)^k = g(a)^\ell$, then $w = aa \cdots$ is an infinite solution of I.

Next we shall prove that a solution of the type (ii) of an instance I reduces to an infinite solution in the successor instance I'.

Lemma 9. *Let $I = (h, g)$ be an instance of the marked PCP. There is an infinite solution w with a block decomposition if and only if the successor $I' = (h', g')$ has an infinite solution w', that begins with the same letter as w.*

Proof. Assume first that there exists an infinite solution w of the type (ii) of I. Then w has two factorizations,

$$w = u_1 u_2 \cdots = v_1 v_2 \cdots , \tag{5}$$

where $(u_i, v_i) = \beta(a_i)$ for the letters a_i. Clearly, $h(a_1)$ and $g(a_1)$ are comparable and $h'(a_1) = u_1$ and $g'(a_1) = v_1$ are comparable. By the assumption (3) on h, they both begin with a_1. Define now $w' = a_1 a_2 \cdots$ By (5) it is obvious that w' is an infinite solution of I'.

Similarly, if the successor $I' = (h', g')$ has an infinite solution, say $\omega' = a_1 a_2 \cdots$, then, by the definition, for each i, $\beta(a_i) = (u_i, v_i)$ for words u_i and v_i. Clearly,

$$\omega = u_1 u_2 \cdots = v_1 v_2 \cdots$$

is an infinite solution with a block decomposition of I.

By Lemma 9, for the solutions of the type (ii), instead of searching an infinite solution of I, we can turn to the simpler instance I'. The difficulty here is that we do not know in advance, whether the possible solution of the successor is of type (ii) or (iii).

We shall first prove a simple case, where all instance of the entire successor sequence have an infinite solution of the type (ii).

By Lemma 9, we obtain that in the cycling successor sequence also the infinite solutions can be found. Actually, these are the infinite solutions for which there is a block decomposition.

Consider now the successor sequence I_i, where $I = I_0$ and $I_i = (h_i, g_i)$. Assume that n_0 and $d \geq 1$ are such that, for all $j \geq n_0$, $I_j = I_{j+d}$.

Lemma 10. *Let I_i , $i = 0, 1, \ldots$, be the successor sequence for an instance (h_0, g_0) of the marked PCP, where $h_i, g_i \colon A_i \to A_{i-1}$. There exists an infinite solution of type (ii) for all I_i if and only if there exists $b \in A_0$ such that $h_i(b)$ and $g_i(b)$ are comparable for all $i \geq 0$.*

Proof. Assume first that there is an infinite solution ω_i of I_i and assume that ω_i is achieved from ω_{i-1} as in the proof of Lemma 9. Let b be that first letter of ω_0. Then, by the assumption $b \leq h_0(b)$ b, we obtain that $b \leq g_0(b)$ and $h_0(b)$ and $g_0(b)$ are comparable. Furthermore, there is a block for the letter b, and therefore by the construction in the proof of Lemma 9, $b \leq \omega_1$. Continuing this way we achieve that b is the first letter of ω_i for all $i \geq 0$. Therefore there is a block in each I_i and $h_i(b)$ and $g_i(b)$ are comparable for all i.

In the other direction, assume that there exists a letter b for which $h_i(b)$ and $g_i(b)$ are comparable for all i. We shall first prove that there is an infinite solution of type (ii) for I_0. By Lemma 7, the words

$$x_i = h_1(\cdots h_{i-1}(h_i(b))\cdots) \quad \text{and} \quad y_i = g_1(\cdots g_{i-1}(g_i(b))\cdots)$$

are comparable and they begin with b for all i by the assumption for all i. Let z_i be the longest common prefix of x_i and y_i. Clearly, z_i is either x_i or y_i depending on the case. Since the morphisms in the successor sequence are nonerasing and h_1 and g_1 are marked, we obtain that $z_i \leq z_{i+1}$. Now the word $\omega = \lim_{i \to \infty} z_i$ is an infinite solution to I_0, since, by Lemma 7, $h_0(h_1(\cdots h_{i-1}(h_i(b))\cdots))$ and $g_0(g_1(\cdots g_{i-1}(g_i(b))\cdots))$ are comparable. The claim follows inductively by setting originally $I_i = I_0$.

We have considered the two simple cases of our problem. These two are the cases where an infinite solution can be detected simply by the algorithm for the marked PCP.

We shall next prove that the infinite solutions of type (iii) can be detected.

Lemma 11. *It is decidable, whether an instance $I = (h, g)$ of the marked PCP has an infinite solution without a block decomposition.*

Proof. Let $I = I_0$ and I_i, $i = 1, 2, \ldots$, be the successor sequence of I, where $I_i = (h_i, g_i)$. Assume that ω is an infinite solution of I without a block decomposition, that is,

$$\omega = u_1 u_2 \cdots u_n \omega_1 = v_1 v_2 \cdots v_n \omega_2, \tag{6}$$

where $(u_i, v_i) = \beta(a_i)$ for some letters a_i, $1 \leq i \leq n$, ω_1 and ω_2 are infinite words, which do not have a block as a prefix. Note that also $n = 0$ is possible.

We shall first prove that a_1 is a disappearing letter in the successor sequence. Assume to the contrary that there is a block for a_1 in all instances I_i. Now $h(a_1)$ and $g(a_1)$ are necessarily comparable and $a_1 \leq h(a_1), g(a_1)$. Therefore for all instances, $a_1 \leq h_i(a_1), g_i(a_1)$. In order to have a block for a_1 in every instance I_i, necessarily $h_i(a_1)$ and $g_i(a_1)$ are comparable for all $i \geq 0$. By Lemma 10, there is an infinite solution for I with a block decomposition beginning with a_1. On the other hand, an infinite solution beginning a_1 is unique by the fact that the morphisms are marked, which is a contradiction, since ω has no block decomposition.

We now know that such solutions ω without a block decomposition can exist only for the letters which disappear in the successor sequence. These letters can be effectively found while constructing the successor sequence.

On the other hand, the prefixes $u_1 \cdots u_n$ and $v_1 \cdots v_n$ in (6) can be effectively found. Indeed, we construct a sequence (x_i, y_i) of the blocks of the instance I as follows: $(x_1, y_1) = (u_1, v_1)$, where (u_1, v_1) is the block for a_1, and $(x_{i+1}, y_{i+1}) = (x_i u_{i+1}, y_i v_{i+1})$, where (u_{i+1}, v_{i+1}) is the unique block satisfying the conditions

- $h(x_i u_{i+1})$ and $g(y_i v_{i+1})$ are comparable, and
- $x_i u_{i+1}$ and $y_i v_{i+1}$ are comparable.

Since a_1 is disappearing, there cannot be a solution or an infinite solution with a block decomposition beginning with a_1, and hence this process ends. Denote by (x, y) the final pair of this process.

Next we shall consider the words ω_1 and ω_2. It is clear that $h(\omega_1) = g(\omega_2)$, since $h(u_i) = g(v_i)$ for all $i = 1, 2, \ldots, n$. Let $b \leq h(\omega_1)$. Thus, b is a letter for which there is no block in I and, furthermore, in the process of constructing the block for b, after some step an overflow appears cyclically. Hence

$$\omega_1 = u u' u' \cdots \quad \text{and} \quad \omega_2 = v v' v' \cdots \tag{7}$$

for some words u, u', v and v' with $|h(u')| = |g(v')|$. There are only finitely many letters b such that there are blocks for b in I, and therefore all possible pairs ω_1 and ω_2 can be effectively found.

Let (x, y) be as defined in the above, and let ω_1 and ω_2 be two infinite words of the form in (7). Clearly, $h(x\omega_1) = h(x)h(\omega_1) = g(y)g(\omega_2) = g(y\omega_2)$, and therefore to decide whether this is an infinite solution, we need to prove that $x\omega_1 = y\omega_2$. Let $k = \max\{|xu|, |yv|\}$. We check first whether the prefixes of length

k of $x\omega_1$ and $y\omega_2$ are equal. If not then $x\omega_1$ is not a solution. Otherwise, let x' be the equal prefix of length k of $x\omega_1$ and $y\omega_2$. Now

$$x\omega_1 = x' z_1 z_2 z_1 z_2 z_1 \cdots \text{ and } y\omega_2 = x' r_1 r_2 r_1 r_2 r_1 \cdots ,$$

where $z_2 z_1 = u'$ and $r_2 r_1 = v'$ (actually, either z_1 or r_1 is ε). It is clear that $x\omega_1 = y\omega_2$ if and only if $(z_1 z_2)^k = (r_1 r_2)^\ell$ for some k and ℓ. Such k and ℓ are unique, if they exist, since

$$|z_1 z_2| \cdot k = |r_1 r_2| \cdot \ell,$$

and clearly they can be effectively found.

Since the pair (x, y) is unique for a_1 and there are only finitely many possible ω_1 and ω_2, we can check all possible words $x\omega_1$ and $y\omega_2$, whether they are infinite solutions of I. Finally, note that we also have to check whether the words ω_1 and ω_2 are solutions themselves. This is the case where $n = 0$.

Corollary 2. *It is decidable, whether an instance of the marked PCP has an infinite solution of type (ii).*

Proof. We have proved that it is decidable, whether there is a solution that reduces to an infinite solution with a block decomposition for all successors in the sequence. If this is not the case, then an infinite solution reduces to an infinite solution without a block decomposition, by Lemma 10, in some reduction step of the successor sequence. Therefore by checking the for the infinite solutions without a block decomposition for all instances in the successor sequence we can detect also these solutions. By Lemma 9, these can be transformed to infinite solutions of the original instance.

We have proved the following theorem.

Theorem 3. *It is decidable whether an instance of the marked PCP has an infinite solution.*

References

1. A. Ehrenfeucht, J. Karhumäki, and G. Rozenberg. The (Generalized) Post Correspondence Problem with Lists Consisting of Two Words Is Decidable. *Theoret. Comput. Sci.*, 21:119–144, 1982.
2. V. Halava. *Post Correspondence Problem and Its Modifications for Marked Morphisms.* PhD thesis, University of Turku, (Manuscript).
3. V. Halava, T. Harju, and M. Hirvensalo. Binary (Generalized) Post Correspondence Problem. Technical Report 357, Turku Centre for Computer Science, August 2000. to appear in Theoret. Comput. Sci.
4. V. Halava, M. Hirvensalo, and R. de Wolf. Marked PCP Is Decidable. *Theoret. Comput. Sci.*, 255(1-2):193–204, 2001.

5. Y. Matiyasevich and G. Sénizergues. Decision Problems for Semi-Thue Systems with a Few Rules. In *Proceedings, 11*[th] *Annual IEEE Symposium on Logic in Computer Science*, pages 523–531, New Brunswick, New Jersey, 27–30 July 1996. IEEE Computer Society Press.

6. E. Post. A Variant of a Recursively Unsolvable Problem. *Bull. of Amer. Math. Soc.*, 52:264–268, 1946.

7. K. Ruohonen. Reversible Machines and Post's Correspondence Problem for Biprefix Morphisms. *Elektron. Informationsverarb. Kybernet. (EIK)*, 21(12):579–595, 1985.

The Branching Point Approach to Conway's Problem[*]

Juhani Karhumäki and Ion Petre

Department of Mathematics, University of Turku and
Turku Centre for Computer Science (TUCS)
Turku 20014, Finland
{karhumak,ipetre}@cs.utu.fi

Abstract. A word u is a branching point for a set of words X if there are two different letters a and b such that both ua and ub can be extended to words in X^+. A branching point u is critical for X if $u \notin X^+$. Using these notions, we give an elementary solution for Conway's Problem in the case of finite biprefixes. We also discuss a possible extension of this approach towards a complete solution for Conway's Problem.

1 Introduction

The *centralizer* of a set of words X is the maximal set with respect to union, commuting with X. As it can be readily seen, the notion of centralizer is well defined for all sets of words; we denote in this paper the centralizer of X by $\mathcal{C}(X)$. For any X, $\mathcal{C}(X)$ is a monoid. As a matter of fact, one can also define a notion of semigroup centralizer and it is an open problem whether or not the two types of centralizers always coincide modulo a finite (or at least rational) set of words. We refer to [8] for more details. In this paper, we actually consider semigroup centralizers.

The best known problem connected to the notion of centralizer is the one proposed by Conway ([6], 1971), asking whether or not the centralizer of a rational language is always rational. Surprisingly enough, very little is known about the answer to Conway's Problem. E.g., it is not even known whether the centralizer of any finite set is recursively enumerable. We know however, that Conway's Problem has an affirmative answer for periodic, binary, and ternary sets, as well as for rational ω-codes, see [4], [7], [9], and [13], as well as [10] for a recent survey. We recall that a set of words X is called *periodic* if there is a word u such that $X \subseteq u^*$. A set of words X is called *binary* (*ternary*, resp.) if X consists of two (three, resp.) words. These results have been generally obtained as consequences of characterizing some special cases of the commutation of two sets of words. Interestingly, the above results were obtained using very different approaches: combinatorial properties of finite and infinite words, equations on languages, and algebraic results on the commutation of formal power series. Still another one

---

[*] Supported by the Academy of Finland under grant 44087

W. Brauer et al. (Eds.): Formal and Natural Computing, LNCS 2300, pp. 69–76, 2002.
© Springer-Verlag Berlin Heidelberg 2002

- the so called fixed point approach - is presented in [8]. We interpret this as an evidence of the challenging nature of the problem.

Following ideas of [8], we propose here still another approach to Conway's Problem. We define the notions of *branching* and *critical* points and prove that Conway's problem can be reduced to those sets of words having at least two words starting with different letters. In turn, for these sets of words, one only has to establish the rationality of the set of critical points to obtain a solution to Conway's Problem. As an illustration of the approach, we give a simple, elementary solution to this problem for binary sets and for finite biprefixes. For binary sets, this gives a simpler solution than that presented in [4]. The result for finite biprefixes is obtained also in [15], through some involved combinatorial arguments, as well as in [7], using some algebraic result on the commutation of two formal power series.

We conclude the paper with a discussion about a possible extension of this approach towards a complete solution for Conway's Problem.

2   Branching Points

For elementary definitions and results on Combinatorics on Words, we refer to [3], [11], and [12]. For definitions and results on Theory of Codes, we refer to [2].

We say that a word u is a prefix of a word v if $v = ut$, for some word t, and we denote $u \leq v$. For a set of words L we denote by $\mathrm{Pref}(L)$ the set of all prefixes of words from L: $\mathrm{Pref}(L) = \{x \mid \exists u \in L$ such that $x \leq u\}$. We say that u is a suffix of v if $v = tu$, for some word t, and we denote $u \leq_s v$. For a set of words L we denote by $\mathrm{Suf}(L)$ the set of all suffixes of words from L.

Let X be a set of words and u a word. We say that u is a *branching point* of X if there are two distinct letters a and b such that both ua and ub are prefixes of some words in X^+. In other words, u can be extended in two different ways to words of X^+. We denote by $\mathcal{B}(X)$ the set of branching points of X. A branching point u of X is called *critical* if $u \notin X^+$.

Example 1.   (i) Let $F = \{a, aba, bb\}$. Then a is a branching point of F: $aa, aba \in F^+$, while b is not a branching point. Indeed, ba is not a prefix of any word in F^+. Also, ab is a critical point: $aba, abb \in F^+$ and $ab \notin F^+$. Note that ab is not in $\mathcal{C}(F)$ since, as it is easy to see, $\mathcal{C}(F) = F^+$.
   (ii) Let $F = \{aa, ab, ba, bb\}$. Then both a and b are critical points of F. Moreover, a and b are both in $\mathcal{C}(F)$. Indeed, $\mathcal{C}(F) = \{a, b\}^+$.

We say that a set of words L is *branching* if L has words starting with different letters. We say that L is *marked* if no two words of L start with the same letter.

For a branching set L the critical points are the only potential nontrivial elements of the centralizer $\mathcal{C}(L)$, e.g., elements outside L^+. This follows from the following simple lemma, cf. [8].

Lemma 1. *For any language L, $1 \notin L$, we have the following:*

(i) $\mathcal{C}(L)$ is a semigroup.
(ii) $L^+ \subseteq \mathcal{C}(L) \subseteq \mathrm{Pref}(L^+) \cap \mathrm{Suf}(L^+)$.
(iii) If L is branching, then $\mathcal{C}(L) \subseteq \mathcal{B}(L)$.

By Lemma 1(iii), if L is a branching set of words, then all words in $\mathcal{C}(L)$ are branching points of L. We prove in the next result that for any rational language L, $\mathcal{B}(L)$ is rational, thus supporting a possible affirmative answer to Conway's Problem.

Theorem 1. *For any rational language R, the set of its branching points $\mathcal{B}(R)$ is rational.*

Proof. If R is rational, then R^* is rational and so is $\mathrm{Pref}(R^*)$. Let $\mathcal{A}$ be a complete deterministic finite automaton accepting $\mathrm{Pref}(R^*)$, with δ its transition mapping, Q the set of states, F the set of final states, and q_0 its initial state. For each $q \in Q$ and each letter a, let $q_a = \delta(q, a)$.

We construct an automaton $\mathcal{A}'$ accepting $\mathcal{B}(A)$. Intuitively, to accept a word u, we walk in $\mathcal{A}$ with u and then we check whether or not both letters a and b lead to final states. Formally, let Q' be a set isomorphic to Q: $Q' = \{q' \mid q \in Q\}$ and let r, s be two new states, $r, s \notin Q \cup Q'$. The set of states of $\mathcal{A}'$ is $Q \times (Q' \cup \{r, s\}) \times (Q' \times \{r, s\})$, the initial state is (q_0, r, r) and the transition mapping is defined as follows:

(i) $\delta'((q, r, r), x) = (\delta(q, x), r, r)$, for all letters x;
(ii) $\delta'((q, r, r), 1) = (q, s, s)$;
(iii) $\delta'((q, s, s), 1) = (q, q'_a, q'_b)$, for all letters $a \neq b$.

The set of final states of $\mathcal{A}'$ is $Q \times F' \times F'$, where $F = \{q' \mid q \in F\}$. Consequently, $\mathcal{A}'$ is a so called generalized finite automaton and hence, it accepts a rational language. As it is easy to see, the language accepted by $\mathcal{A}'$ is $\mathcal{B}(R)$. Indeed, a word $u \in \mathcal{B}(R)$ if and only if $ua, ub \in \mathrm{Pref}(R^+)$.

We prove in the next result that Conway's Problem can be reduced to the special case of branching sets.

Theorem 2. *For any non-periodic set of words L, $1 \notin L$, there is a branching set of words L' such that $\mathcal{C}(L)$ is rational if and only if $\mathcal{C}(L')$ is rational. Moreover, $\mathcal{C}(L) = L^+$ if and only if $\mathcal{C}(L') = L'^+$.*

Proof. If L is branching, then the claim is trivially true, with $L' = L$. Thus, let us assume that $L = aL_1$, for some letter a and some set of words L_1. Then, as $\mathcal{C}(L)L = L\mathcal{C}(L)$, it follows that $\mathcal{C}(L) = aX$, for some set of words X, and so $aXaL_1 = aL_1aX$. Thus, $XaL_1a = L_1aXa$, i.e., $Xa \subseteq \mathcal{C}(L_1a)$. The other inclusion can be proved similarly, and so $\mathcal{C}(aL_1) = a(\mathcal{C}(L_1a)a^{-1})$. Note that $\mathcal{C}(aL_1)$ is rational if and only if $\mathcal{C}(L_1a)$ is rational and moreover, $\mathcal{C}(aL_1) = (aL_1)^+$ if and only if $\mathcal{C}(L_1a) = (L_1a)^+$.

If L_1a is not branching, then we repeat the reasoning with L_1a instead of L. Since L is not periodic, we find in a finite number of steps a branching set L' such that $\mathcal{C}(L)$ is rational if and only if $\mathcal{C}(L')$ is rational. Moreover, $\mathcal{C}(L) = L^+$ if and only if $\mathcal{C}(L') = L'^+$.

Consequently, Conway's Problem can be reduced to two types of sets: periodic sets and branching sets of words. The case of periodic sets is, however, easy to settle.

Theorem 3 ([13]). *Let u be a primitive word and $L \subseteq u^+$. Then $\mathcal{C}(L) = u^+$.*

Proof. Sine $L\mathcal{C}(L) = \mathcal{C}(L)L$, for any word $x \in \mathcal{C}(L)$ and any $\alpha \in L$, $x\alpha^\omega \in L^\omega$. Thus, $xu^\omega = u^\omega$, and so $x = u^n$, for some $n \geq 0$. Due to the maximality of the centralizer, it follows that $\mathcal{C}(L) = u^+$.

From now on, we consider branching sets of words only. Based on this reduction, we give a simple proof for Conway's Problem in the case of binary sets. This result has been originally proved in [4] using somewhat more involved combinatorial arguments.

Theorem 4. *The centralizer of any binary set F over the alphabet Σ is rational. Moreover,*

(i) *If $1 \in F$, then $\mathcal{C}(F) = \Sigma^+$.*
(ii) *If F is periodic, $F \subseteq u^+$, for some primitive word u, then $\mathcal{C}(F) = u^+$.*
(iii) *If F is not periodic and $1 \notin F$, then $\mathcal{C}(F) = F^+$.*

Proof. The first case is trivial and it holds more generally for any set of words F. Also, Case (ii) is concluded in Theorem 3. For Case (iii), note that by Theorem 2, we can assume without loss of generality that F is a branching set of words. Let $F = \{au, bv\}$, where a and b are distinct letters and u, v some words.

Assume that $F^+ \neq \mathcal{C}(F)$ and let $x \in \mathcal{C}(F) \setminus F^+$. Since F is a prefix and $x \in \text{Pref}(F^+)$, it follows that there are unique words $u_1, \ldots, u_m \in F$, $m \geq 0$ such that $x = u_1 \ldots u_m t$, for a word $t \in \text{Pref}(F)$.

Observe now that x is a branching point. Indeed, since F is a branching set of words, all words of $\mathcal{C}(F)$ are branching points of F. Thus, t is also a branching point of F, and so, as $t \in \text{Pref}(F)$, there are $\alpha, \beta \in \text{Pref}(F)$ such that $ta \leq \alpha$ and $tb \leq \beta$. If $t \neq 1$ then, since F is marked, it follows that $\alpha = \beta$ and $a = b$, a contradiction. Thus, $t = 1$ and $x \in F^+$, again impossible. Consequently, $\mathcal{C}(F) = F^+$.

3   A Simple Solution to Conway's Problem for Finite Biprefixes

It is well known, see [14], that the set of prefixes is a free monoid. In particular, this implies that any prefix has a unique primitive root, similarly as words have. It is a consequence of a result of [15] characterizing the commutation with a prefix code that, for any prefix code X, we have $\mathcal{C}(X) = \rho(X)^+$, where $\rho(X)$ denotes the primitive root of X. This result was extended in [7] to ω-codes: any ω-code X has a unique primitive root $\rho(X)$ and $\mathcal{C}(X) = \rho(X)^+$. However, both these results of [7] and [15] rely on some complex arguments. For prefix codes ([15]), one uses some involved combinatorial arguments, while for ω-codes, [7], one relies on some results of Bergman and Cohn, [1], [5], characterizing the commutation of two polynomials and of two formal power series, respectively. Using the notion of branching point, we give a simple, elementary solution for Conway's Problem in the case of finite biprefixes. We begin by proving that the centralizer of any biprefix set of words is necessarily of a very special form.

Theorem 5. *For any biprefix L, there is a set T of nonempty branching points of $\rho(L)$ such that $\mathcal{C}(L) = \rho(L)^+(1 + \sum_{t \in T} \rho(L)^{k_t} t)$, where $\rho(L)$ denotes the primitive root of L and $k_t \geq 0$, for all $t \in T$.*

Proof. As in Theorem 2, we can assume without loss of generality that L is a branching set of words.

Let $x \in \mathcal{C}(L) \setminus \rho(L)^+$. By Lemma 1, $x \in \mathrm{Pref}(L^+)$ and thus, since L is a prefix, there are unique words $u_1, \ldots, u_k, t$, such that $x = u_1 \ldots u_k t$, with $u_i \in L$ and $t \in \mathrm{Pref}(L) \setminus \rho(L)^*$. Moreover, since L is branching, t is a branching point of L, i.e., $ta, tb \in \mathrm{Pref}(L)$, for distinct letters a and b. Because L is a prefix code and $\mathcal{C}(L)L^k = L^k\mathcal{C}(L)$, it follows that $xL^k \subseteq L^k\mathcal{C}(L)$, and so $tL^k \subseteq \mathcal{C}(L)$. Similarly, since L is also a suffix, it follows that $L^k t \subseteq \mathcal{C}(L)$. Thus, there is $k' \geq 1$ and $t' \in \mathrm{Pref}(\rho(L)) \setminus \rho(L)^*$ such that $\rho(L)^{k'} t' \subseteq \mathcal{C}(L)$.

Let T be the set of all words t' defined above, or more formally

$$T = \{t \in (\rho(L)^+)^{-1}\mathcal{C}(L) \mid u \not\leq t,\ \forall u \in \rho(L)\}.$$

For any $t \in T$, let $k_t = \min\{k \geq 0 \mid \rho(L)^k t \subseteq \mathcal{C}(L)\}$. We claim that

$$\mathcal{C}(L) = \rho(L)^+ \left(1 + \sum_{t \in T} \rho(L)^{k_t} t\right).$$

Clearly, by construction, $\rho(L)^{k_t} t \subseteq \mathcal{C}(L)$, and so $\rho(L)^+ \left(1 + \sum_{t \in T} \rho(L)^{k_t} t\right) \subseteq \mathcal{C}(L)$, since $\mathcal{C}(L)$ is closed under union and under multiplication by $\rho(L)$.

For the reverse inclusion, let $x \in \mathcal{C}(L) \setminus \rho(L)^+$. Then, as shown above, there is $l \geq 1$ such that $x \in \rho(L)^l t$, with $t \in T$. Since F is a biprefix, it follows as above that $\rho(L)^l t \subseteq \mathcal{C}(L)$. Consequently, $l \geq k_t$ and the claim follows.

As a matter of fact, based on some involved considerations of [15], we know that $T = \emptyset$. Unfortunately, we do not have a simple argument for this.

Corollary 1. *The centralizer of any finite biprefix is rational.*

Proof. Let L be a finite biprefix. Since T is a set of branching points, $T \subseteq \mathrm{Pref}(L)$. Thus, T is finite and $\mathcal{C}(L)$ is rational.

4   Biprefixes with at Most One Critical Point

We consider in the following some simple cases of finite biprefixes to further illustrate the branching point approach. Namely, we consider the case of finite biprefixes with at most one critical point.

Theorem 6. *Let L be a biprefix code. Then L has no critical points if and only if L is marked. Moreover, in this case, $\mathcal{C}(L) = L^+$.*

Proof. Let L be a biprefix code and assume that L has no critical points. If L is not marked, then there are two words u and v starting with the same letter. Thus, as L is a prefix, the longest common prefix of u and v is a critical point of L, a contradiction.

If L is marked, let us assume that L has a critical point x. Thus, $xa, xb \in \text{Pref}(L^+)$, for distinct letters a and b, and $x \notin L^+$. Since L is a biprefix code, it follows that there are unique words $u_1, \ldots, u_m \in L$ and $t \in \text{Pref}(L) \setminus L^*$ such that $x = u_1 \ldots u_m t$. Since $ta, tb \in \text{Pref}(L^+)$, there are $\alpha, \beta \in L$ such that $ta \leq \alpha$ and $tb \leq \beta$. However, $t \neq 1$, and so, as L is marked, it follows that $\alpha = \beta$ and $a = b$, a contradiction.

If L is marked, then all points of $\mathcal{C}(L)$ are branching points. Since L has no critical points, it follows that $\mathcal{C}(L) = L^+$.

Observe that for any critical point u of a prefix code L, all words in $\rho(L)^* u$ are also critical points of L. We say that v is a *minimal* critical point of a code L if there is no critical point u of L such that $v \in \rho(L)^* u$.

Example 2. Let $F = \{aa, ab\}$. Then the set of critical points of F is $F^* a$. However, the only minimal critical point of F is a.

Theorem 7. *Let L be a biprefix with at most one minimal critical point. Then $\mathcal{C}(L) = \rho(L)^+$.*

Proof. By Theorem 2, we can assume without loss of generality that L is a branching set of words. If L has no critical point, then the claim follows by Theorem 6.

Assume that L has one minimal critical point. By Theorem 5, $\mathcal{C}(L) = \rho(L)^+ (1 + \sum_{t \in T} \rho(L)^{k_t} t)$, for a set T of critical points of $\rho(L)$. Since L has only one minimal critical point, $T \subseteq \{t\}$, with $t \in \text{Pref}(\rho(L)) \setminus \{1\}$. If $T = \emptyset$, then the claim follows. Assuming that $T = \{t\}$, we obtain $\mathcal{C}(L) = \rho(L)^+ (1 + \rho(L)^k t)$, and so

$$\rho(L)^+ (1 + \rho(L)^k t) L = L \rho(L)^+ (1 + \rho(L)^k t). \tag{1}$$

We prove that $\rho(L)^+ t$ commutes with L.

If $\rho(L)^+ \rho(L)^k t L \cap L \rho(L)^+ \neq \emptyset$ then, as L and $\rho(L)$ are prefixes, it follows that $t L \cap \rho(L)^+ \neq \emptyset$. Since L and $\rho(L)$ are also suffixes, it follows that $t \in \rho(L)^+$, a contradiction.

If $\rho(L)^+L \cap L\rho(L)^+\rho(L)^kt \neq \emptyset$ then, as L and $\rho(L)$ are prefixes, it follows that $t \in \rho(L)^+$, again a contradiction.

Consequently, it follows from (1) that $\rho(L)^+\rho(L)^ktL = L\rho(L)^+\rho(L)^kt$. Moreover, since $\rho(L)$ is a prefix, it follows that

$$\rho(L)^+tL = L\rho(L)^+t. \tag{2}$$

Since L has only one minimal critical point, $\rho(L)$ is marked, with just one exception: there are $u, v \in \rho(L)$ such that the common prefix of u and v is t. Let $L = \rho(L)^n$. Clearly, since L is branching, there is a word $w \in \rho(L) \setminus \{u, v\}$.

From (2), we obtain that $Lt \subseteq \rho(L)^+tL$. In particular, $w^nt \in \rho(L)^+tL$. Since $t \not\leq w$ and $w \not\leq t$, we obtain that $t \in \rho(L)^+tL$, a contradiction.

5 Conclusions

Based on the simple notions of branching and critical points, we have proposed a new approach - the branching point approach - to attack Conway's Problem. We have demonstrated its usefulness by giving very simple solutions of the problem in the case of binary sets and finite biprefix sets. As a matter of fact, our result for biprefix sets can be easily extended to codes with bounded decoding delay in both directions, proving that also in this case, the centralizer has a simple, rational form.

We believe that the branching point approach can be used to derive also other results on Conway's problem, maybe even an affirmative answer for the case of all finite sets. To support this idea, let us denote by $T_{\mathcal{B}(L)}$ the tree of all words in $\mathcal{B}(L)$, for a rational language L. By Theorem 1, $\mathcal{B}(L)$ is rational, and so this tree - let us call it the *branching tree* of L - is of a regular type: it contains only a finite number of different (maximal) subtrees. For branching sets of words L, to which Conway's Problem can be reduced, all words in $\mathcal{C}(L)$ are branching and thus, nodes in $T_{\mathcal{B}(L)}$. Let $Z = \mathcal{C}(L) \setminus L^+$. As it is easy to see, for any $z \in Z$, $L^+z \cup z^+ \cup zL^+ \subseteq \mathcal{C}(L)$. Consequently, a single node of $T_{\mathcal{B}(L)}$ from Z determines many other nodes of $T_{\mathcal{B}(L)}$ to be in $\mathcal{C}(L)$. Thus, for a solution to Conway's Problem, an important question is: can one "saturate" $\mathcal{C}(L)$ within the nodes of $T_{\mathcal{B}(L)}$ in a finite number of steps of this type, at least for some types of (finite) sets X ? Intuitively, the regularity of $T_{\mathcal{B}(L)}$ supports this view.

References

1. G. Bergman, Centralizers in Free Associative Algebras, *Transactions of the American Mathematical Society* 137: 327–344, 1969.
2. J. Berstel, D. Perrin, *Theory of Codes*, Academic Press, New York, 1985.
3. C. Choffrut, J. Karhumäki, Combinatorics on Words. In G. Rozenberg, A. Salomaa (Eds.), *Handbook of Formal Languages*, vol. 1: 329-438, Springer-Verlag, 1997.
4. C. Choffrut, J. Karhumäki, N. Ollinger, The Commutation of Finite Sets: A Challenging Problem, *Theoret. Comput. Sci.*, to appear.

5. P.M. Cohn, Centralisateurs dans les corps libres, in J.Berstel (Ed.), *Séries formelles*: 45–54, Paris, 1978.
6. J.H. Conway, *Regular Algebra and Finite Machines*, Chapman Hall, 1971.
7. T. Harju, I. Petre, On Commutation and Primitive Roots of Codes, Submitted.
8. J. Karhumäki, Challenges of Commutation: An Advertisement, in *Proc. of FCT 2001*, LNCS 2138, 15–23, Springer, 2001.
9. J. Karhumäki, I. Petre, Conway's Problem for Three Word Sets, *Theoret. Comput. Sci.*, to appear; preliminary version in *Proc. ICALP 2000*, LNCS 1853 536–546, Springer, 2000.
10. J. Karhumäki, I. Petre, Conway's Problem and the Commutation of Languages, *Bulletin of EATCS* 74, 171–177, 2001.
11. M. Lothaire, *Combinatorics on Words*, Addison-Wesley, Reading, MA., 1983.
12. M. Lothaire, *Algebraic Combinatorics on Words*, Cambridge University Press, to appear.
13. A. Mateescu, A. Salomaa, S. Yu, On the Decomposition of Finite Languages, TUCS Technical Report 222, http://www.tucs.fi/, 1998.
14. D. Perrin, Codes Conjugués, Information and Control 20: 222–231, 1972.
15. B. Ratoandromanana, Codes et Motifs, *RAIRO Inform. Theor.*, 23(4): 425–444, 1989.

A Survey of Some Quantitative Approaches to the Notion of Information

Aldo de Luca[1,2]

[1] Dipartimento di Matematica dell'Università di Roma "La Sapienza"
Piazzale A. Moro 2, 00185 Roma, Italy
[2] Centro Interdisciplinare 'B. Segre', Accademia dei Lincei
via della Lungara 10, 00100 Roma, Italy

Abstract. We survey some formalizations of the intuitive notion of information which have been formulated in different mathematical and conceptual frames. The existence of different formalizations reflects the different aspects of the notion of information which are strongly related to the mechanisms of information processing of the receiver. Finally, some considerations and remarks on information in Physics and Biology are made.

1 Introduction

The concept of 'information' appeared first in Physics related to the physical entropy. It was observed by L. Boltzmann in 1896 [5] in the framework of Thermodynamics that physical entropy is a measure of the 'missing' information about a physical system knowing all the macroscopic information about it.

This concept of entropy was used subsequently by L. Szilard (1929) [49] for information in Physics and H. Nyquist (1924) [42] and R. V. L. Hartley (1928) [33] for problems of communication. A very fundamental contribution in this direction was due to C. E. Shannon (1948) [45] and N. Wiener (1949) [52].

However, 'information' and its measurement are intuitive concepts, or *explicanda*, which have a wide 'semantic halo' so that several formalizations, or *explicata*, are possible. Moreover, the formalization of the notion of information is related to the 'context'. Here, the term context is used in a wide sense. It depends on the 'receiver' and its characteristic features.

Intuitively, information means *minimum amount of 'data' which are required to 'determine' an 'object' into a given class.*

Several approaches have been proposed in order to formalize and quantify the notion of information. Any definition of information requires a suitable specification of the terms 'data', 'determine' and class of 'objects' used in the intuitive definition. These approaches, called *semantic, pragmatic, descriptive, algorithmic, logic, structural, etc.*, are conceptually very different in spite of some analogies, even though often only formal, between the considered quantities. Often some formalizations of the concept of information, even though meaningful and interesting, lack a solid mathematical frame in which one can evaluate the actual implications of these concepts or find deep theorems.

W. Brauer et al. (Eds.): Formal and Natural Computing, LNCS 2300, pp. 77–95, 2002.

In this paper we shall give a brief general view of the conceptual more than formal aspects of the different approaches to a quantitative definition of the notion of information. For the sake of brevity, the presentation is necessarily incomplete and some important approaches, such as, for instance, the *semantic approach* of R. Carnap and Y. Bar-Hillel [8], have not been considered.

As we shall see in more details in the next sections there exist two main conceptions about the notion of information. The first, that we call 'entropic', is based on a global 'measure of ignorance' about the state of a system. This measure is called 'entropy' in analogy to the physical entropy. Any determination of the state of a system yields an information proportional to the entropy.

The second, that we call 'logic', is essentially based on 'formal logic'. In this case information is related to the minimal 'complexity', static or dynamic, required to compute or generate an object of a given class.

Finally, in the last section some considerations and remarks on information in Physics and Biology will be made.

2   Shannon Information Theory

C. E. Shannon in his fundamental paper 'The mathematical theory of communication' of 1948, gives a basic block-diagram describing every process of transmission of information [45].

In the diagram there is a *source S*, which is a system (man or machine) emitting sequences of symbols (or source messages), a *codifier C* which transforms the source-messages in coded-messages, a *channel* which physically transmits the messages, a *decoder D* which from the coded-messages recovers the initial source-messages, and the *receiver R*. Moreover, there is another block, called *noise*, which represents the effects of disturbances on the communication channel which may occur during the transmission of the messages.

This is a very general schema to represent the information transmission. Moreover, *codification* plays an essential role for several reasons such as to 'adapt' the source messages to the channel, to 'compress' the source messages, to keep 'secret' the transmitted messages, and, by making use of 'redundancy', to protect the undesired effects of the noise.

As is well known in Shannon's theory the source S emits symbols according to some probability rules. More precisely S is described by an ergodic Markov chain [34]. The simplest case is that of a 0-*memory* source. In such a case a Bernoulli distribution is given, i.e., a map

$$p : A \to \mathbb{R}_+ \ ,$$

where A is a finite set (set of mutually exclusive events) and $\mathbb{R}_+$ the set of non-negative real numbers, such that:

$$\sum_{a \in A} p(a) = 1 \ .$$

For each event $a \in A$, $p(a)$ gives the probability of this event. With the realization of each event $a \in A$ is associated the emission of one symbol of the source alphabet.

Let S be a 0-memory source. One can introduce the *entropy* of S defined, up to an inessential arbitrary constant, as:

$$H(S) = - \sum_{a \in A} p(a) \log p(a) \ .$$

The entropy $H(S)$ can be interpreted as the *average amount of uncertainty in making a prevision about the result of a random experiment* (i.e. the realization of the event $a \in A$). Equivalently, one can associate with the realization of an event $a \in A$ an *amount of information* given by:

$$I(a) = - \log p(a)$$

(the more improbable is an event the more is the information that one receives from its realization). In such a way $H(S)$ measures the *average amount of information* that one receives from the realization of an event in a random experiment.

We shall not enter into the details of the mathematical theory of information as developed by Shannon [45] and many other authors (see, for instance, [34]). We limit ourselves only to stress the following general aspects of Shannon's information theory.

a). The mathematical expression for the entropy $H(S)$ of an information source S is *unique*, up to an inessential constant, if one wishes that the entropy has to satisfy general properties which are necessary in view of the meaning of the concept of entropy as a measure of uncertainty or as amount of information.

b). The importance of Shannon's theory is due, without doubt, to the possibility of proving, by making use of the theory of 'ergodic processes', some fundamental theorems (*coding theorems*) on communication and information transmission.

c). The validity of Shannon's theory, or better the meaningful application of it, is confined to statistical communication theory which is based on probability theory. Many questions which have a great intuitive appeal from the information point of view, do not make sense in the frame of Shannon's theory.

d). As stressed by W. Weaver [46], in Shannon's theory only the 'technical problems' of communication are considered while the 'semantic' and 'pragmatic' aspects are not taken into account.

e). There is a relation with Thermodynamics. The Shannon entropy is formally similar to the physical entropy. However, there is no an equivalent of physical energy.

3   Fuzzy Sets and Entropy

In 1972, S. Termini and the author proposed a definition of a non-probabilistic entropy in the setting of the theory of *fuzzy sets* [26].

Fuzzy sets were introduced by L. Zadeh in 1965 [53] in order to describe 'classes' of objects which are not well-defined, in the sense that there do not exist crisp criteria of classification, i.e., to decide whether an object of a given universe belongs or not to the class. Most of 'classes' that we consider in our language are of this kind: the 'clever' students, the 'tall' men, the 'nice' women, etc. The *entropy of a fuzzy set* can be regarded as the *total amount of uncertainty in making decisions* in order to classify ensembles of objects described by means of fuzzy sets.

The theory of 'making decisions', that plays a fundamental role in many scientific branches, has been mainly developed in the setting of probability theory. Although probabilistic decision-methods often work very well in many fields, such as *pattern recognition*, there exist cases in which these methods are *ineffective*. This occurs whenever the standard probabilistic formalism is not appropriate for the description of the considered situations; for instance, when the latter are not really *random* so that the introduction of probabilities as measures of empirical frequencies in a large number of identical experiments may become meaningless.

Often the 'source' of uncertainty that arises in decision-making can be in part or even completely 'deterministic'. This occurs, for instance, when in the classification of the objects of a certain universe into two or more classes, the objects may enjoy to a different degree the properties which characterize the classes themselves.

The theory of the entropy of fuzzy sets was very much developed in subsequent papers by S. Termini, the author and many other researchers [27, 28, 29, 30, 31, 7, 23]. More than 200 papers have been written on this and related subjects. Some of these papers concerned with problems of theoretical and mathematical relevance, other papers were of more applicative nature (see, for instance, [1, 2, 51, 32, 3, 35, 36, 43, 50, 47]).

a) Fuzzy Sets

Let X be a set and I the unit interval $[0,1]$. A *fuzzy set* in X is any map

$$f : X \to I .$$

The map f is called also *membership function* to the fuzzy set and for any $x \in X$, $f(x)$ is called *degree of membership*. The name fuzzy sets given to these maps arises from the possibility of interpreting them as a generalization of the characteristic functions of classic set theory [53]. A fuzzy set f is called *classic*, or *Boolean*, if for any $x \in X$, $f(x) = 1$ or $f(x) = 0$.

Let us denote by $\mathcal{L}(X)$ (resp. $\mathcal{B}(X)$) the set of all fuzzy (resp. Boolean) sets defined in X. It is possible to give to $\mathcal{L}(X)$ the structure of a distributive lattice with respect to the operations $\vee$ and $\wedge$ defined point-wise as: for all $f, g \in \mathcal{L}(X)$ and $x \in X$:

$$(f \vee g)(x) = \max\{f(x), g(x)\} ,$$

$$(f \wedge g)(x) = \min\{f(x), g(x)\} .$$

Moreover, with each $f \in \mathcal{L}(X)$ one can associate the fuzzy set f', that we call the *negate* of f, defined as:

$$f'(x) = 1 - f(x), \text{ for all } x \in X .$$

The operation of negation $(')$ satisfies the following properties: for all $f, g \in \mathcal{L}(X)$

$$(f')' = f ,$$

$$(f \vee g)' = f' \wedge g', \quad (f \wedge g)' = f' \vee g' .$$

The operations $(\vee)$, $(\wedge)$, and $(')$ extend to the case of fuzzy sets the operations of *union, intersection,* and *complement* of classic sets theory expressed in terms of characteristic functions. Let us stress that the operation $(')$ is not the *Boolean complement* since it does not satisfy, in general, the *excluded-middle* and *contradiction* laws. Hence, the lattice $\mathcal{L}(X)$ is not complemented. The only elements which admit a complement are the Boolean characteristic functions; in this case the complement of f coincides with the negate f' [27].

In $\mathcal{L}(X)$ one can introduce the following order relations:

i. *Inclusion order.*

We can partially order $\mathcal{L}(X)$ by the relation $\leq$, that we call *inclusion*, defined as:

$$f \leq g \Longleftrightarrow \forall x \in X \ [f(x) \leq g(x)] .$$

It is clear that this ordering of $\mathcal{L}(X)$ generalizes the classic inclusion relation expressed in terms of characteristic functions. If $f \leq g$, then we say that f is *included* in g.

ii. *Sharpening order.*

We introduce in $\mathcal{L}(X)$ the order $\preceq$, that we call *sharpening order*, defined as:

$$f \preceq g \Longleftrightarrow \forall x \in X \ [f(x) \leq g(x) \leq 1/2 \text{ or } f(x) \geq g(x) \geq 1/2] .$$

If $f \preceq g$, then we say that f is 'sharper' than g.

b) Entropy Measures

In the following we suppose, for the sake of simplicity, that the support X is a finite set even though almost all theory can be extended, with some slight change, to the case of infinite supports [36].

Following [26], an *entropy measure* h in $\mathcal{L}(X)$ is any map

$$h : \mathcal{L}(X) \to \mathbb{R}_+ ,$$

which satisfies the following three basic axioms:

A1. $h(f) = 0$ if and only if f is Boolean.
A2. If $f \preceq g$, then $h(f) \leq h(g)$.
A3. $h(f)$ takes its maximum value if and only if $f(x) = 1/2$, for all $x \in X$.

In other words an entropy measure is any map $h : \mathcal{L}(X) \rightarrow \mathbb{R}_+$ which is isotone with the sharpening order, takes its minimum value, equal to 0, if and only if the fuzzy set is classic and reaches its maximum value if and only if the fuzzy set takes the value $1/2$ in all the points of X. This last requirement is quite obvious since this fuzzy set is the more 'distant' from a classic one.

Two further axioms can be added which can be reasonable in some special cases:

A4. The entropy is invariant under the negation operation, i.e., $h(f) = h(f')$, for all $f \in \mathcal{L}(X)$.

A5. The entropy is a *valuation* in the lattice $\mathcal{L}(X)$, i.e., for all $f, g \in \mathcal{L}(X)$,

$$h(f \vee g) + h(f \wedge g) = h(f) + h(g) \ .$$

Typical examples of entropy measures satisfying all the axioms A1–A5 are the following:

a. $d(f) = \sum_{x \in X}(-f(x) \log f(x) - (1 - f(x)) \log(1 - f(x)))$,
b. $\sigma(f) = \sum_{x \in X} f(x)(1 - f(x))$,
c. $\mu(f) = \sum_{x \in X} \min\{f(x), 1 - f(x)\}$.

The entropy measures d and σ have been also called *logarithmic entropy* and *quadratic entropy*, respectively.

An *entropy norm function* is any map $T : I \rightarrow \mathbb{R}_+$ such that $T(0) = T(1) = 0$, T is strictly increasing in the interval $[0, 1/2]$ and strictly decreasing in the interval $[1/2, 1]$. By means of norm functions we can yield entropy measures as follows. Let ρ be the map $\rho : \mathcal{L}(X) \rightarrow \mathbb{R}_+$ defined for all $f \in \mathcal{L}(X)$ as:

$$\rho(f) = \sum_{x \in X} T_x(f(x)) \ ,$$

where for any $x \in X$, T_x is a given norm function. One can easily verify that ρ is an entropy measure since it satisfies axioms A1–A3. Moreover, also the axiom A5 is satisfied. These kind of entropies have been called *additive entropies*. The entropies d, σ, and μ are examples of additive entropies.

An interesting theorem due to C. Alsina and E. Trillas [1] shows that *the class of additive entropies coincides with the class of entropies which are valuations on the lattice $\mathcal{L}(X)$*, i.e., satisfy axiom A5.

An entropy measure satisfying axiom A4 is called *symmetric*. One can easily derive that an additive entropy ρ is symmetric if and only if for all $x \in X$ and $y \in [0, 1]$, $T_x(y) = T_x(1 - y)$.

Let us now suppose that for all $x \in X$ and $y \in [0, 1]$ one has:

$$T_x(y) = w(x)T(y) \ ,$$

where T is a norm function and $w : X \rightarrow \mathbb{R}_+$ is a given weight function. In this case $\rho(f)$ simply becomes

$$\rho(f) = \sum_{x \in X} w(x)T(f(x)) \ .$$

A subclass of particular interest of additive entropies (*additive concave entropies*) is obtained when T is a continuous and concave function in $[0, 1]$. If, moreover, one supposes that T is symmetric and $T(1/2) = 1$, then the corresponding entropies are called *standard entropies*. For instance, the entropies $d(f), 2\mu(f)$, and $4\sigma(f)$ are standard entropies.

The meaning of the entropy of a fuzzy set and its interpretation as a measure of information was widely discussed in [26] and [28]. We summarize here some basic ideas. The entropy $h(f)$ of a fuzzy set f is a measure of the *total amount of fuzziness* of f. The more f is 'near' to a classic set, the smaller is its entropy. The entropy becomes 0 if and only if f is a classic set, i.e., there is no fuzziness. In the additive case the entropy can be interpreted as the *total amount of uncertainty* arising in taking decisions 'yes' or 'not' on the elements of a given universe of objects on which f is defined. We stress that the ambiguity and the related information are 'structural' that is linked to the fuzzy description, while in the classic information theory it is due to the uncertainty in making previsions on the results of random experiments. Moreover, if $\pi : X \to [0, 1]$ is a probability distribution on X describing a random experiment, then there exist two different kind of uncertainty. The first is measured by the probabilistic entropy:

$$-\sum_{x \in X} \pi(x) \log \pi(x) \ .$$

It represents the average uncertainty in making a prevision on the result of the random experiment described by π. The second of 'fuzzy nature' measurable in correspondence to the occurrence of the event x, by $T_x(f(x))$, where T_x is a fixed norm function. It represents the uncertainty in taking a decision 1 or 0 on the observed value $f(x)$ of the membership function. The statistical average:

$$\sum_{x \in X} \pi(x) T_x(f(x)) \ ,$$

is an additive entropy measure of the fuzzy set f. It represents the average fuzzy uncertainty in taking decisions 1 or 0 on the results of the random experiment.

c) Energy Measures

An *energy measure* in $\mathcal{L}(X)$ is any map $e : \mathcal{L}(X) \to \mathbb{R}_+$ satisfying the following axioms [7, 29]:

B1. $e(f) = 0$ if and only if f is equal to 0 in all points of X.
B2. If $f \le g$, then $e(f) \le e(g)$.
B3. $e(f)$ takes its maximum value if and only if f is equal to 1 in all points of X.

In other words an energy measure is any map from $\mathcal{L}(X)$ to $\mathbb{R}_+$ which is isotone with inclusion ordering, takes its minimum if and only if the fuzzy set is constantly equal to 0 and takes its maximum value if and only if the fuzzy set is constantly equal to 1. An energy measure of great interest is the so called *power* of a fuzzy set [26] defined for all $f \in \mathcal{L}(X)$ as:

$$P(f) = \sum_{x \in X} f(x) .$$

The term 'power' is due to the fact that if f is a classic set, then $P(f)$ reduces itself to the power or cardinality of the set. Further examples of energy measures are:

a. $u(f) = \sum_{x \in X} (f(x))^2$,
b. $e(f) = \sum_{x \in X} w(x)f(x)$, where $w : X \to \mathbb{R}_+$ is a given weight function.

An *energy norm function* is any map $E : I \to \mathbb{R}_+$ such that $E(0) = 0$, E is strictly increasing in the interval $[0, 1]$. A class of energy measures, that we call *additive*, can be defined as: for all $f \in \mathcal{L}(X)$,

$$E(f) = \sum_{x \in X} E_x(f(x)) ,$$

where for any $x \in X$, E_x is a given energy norm function.

Intuitively, an energy is a measure of the 'amount of membership' to a fuzzy set. This measure can concern the total amount of membership as in the case of the power. However, the energy is a more general and useful concept when the elements of X can be differently weighted, for instance, when in X is defined a probability distribution π. In this case a natural energy measure is $\sum_{x \in X} \pi(x)f(x)$ giving the average amount of membership to the fuzzy set. We emphasize that energy is both formally and conceptually a quantity independent of the entropy.

Let $\rho(f) = \sum_{x \in X} T(f(x))$ be a standard entropy, where T is a given norm function. From Jansen's inequality on concave functions, it follows that

$$\rho(f) \leq NT(P(f)/N) ,$$

where $N = \text{card}(X)$. From this relation one has that if one keeps the power $P(f)$ equal to a given constant P, then the entropy ρ reaches its maximum value on the fuzzy set taking the constant value P/N; in other words ρ is maximal when the power is 'equidistributed' on X.

Let us now refer, in particular, to the logarithmic entropy $d(f)$ and suppose that a weight map $w : X \to \mathbb{R}_+$ is defined in X. We can consider the power $P(f)$ and the energy $e(f) = \sum_{x \in X} w(x)f(x)$. Let us keep the power and the energy equal to two constants P and E, respectively. The maximum of $d(f)$ is reached for f equal to the fuzzy set

$$f(x) = 1/(1 + e^{\lambda w(x) - \mu}) ,$$

λ and μ being constants whose values depend on P and E [7]. This formula is formally identical to the *Fermi-Dirac distribution law* for a system of non-interacting particles when the spin is half odd-integral, in which case $f(x)$ is the 'probability' that a state of energy $w(x)$ is occupied, μ/λ is the so called *chemical potential*, and λ is proportional to the inverse of the absolute temperature. In the case $w(x) = w = const.$ for all $x \in X$, then $E = wP$ and $f(x) = P/N = E/wN$ for all $x \in X$, so that the maximum of d is reached when the energy E is equidistributed on the N elements of X.

Let us summarize the following general aspects of the previous theory of a non-probabilistic entropy.

a). The 'entropy' can be considered as a measure of the global 'distance' of a non-Boolean universe (described by fuzzy sets) from a Boolean one. Several entropy measures can be introduced. They have to satisfy some basic axioms. The choice of a particular measure depends on the 'context', i.e., the class of considered problems.

b). The uncertainty described by the entropy is different from probabilistic uncertainty. Probability can be superimposed to fuzziness. In such a case the total uncertainty will be the sum of probabilistic and fuzzy uncertainty.

c). There exists a theory of uncertainty based on these ideas which is well developed from the mathematical point of view (theory of concave functions, measure theory). From the applied point of view this theory has a natural application in 'decision theory'. The entropy can be regarded as the total amount of uncertainty in taking decisions. A decision can be viewed as an operator which transforms a non-Boolean object in a Boolean one.

d). There are analogies with Thermodynamics stronger than in Shannon's theory. Indeed, the functionals, which we called 'energies', play a role similar to the energy in the case of a physical system.

4 Information and Complexity

As we said in the Introduction the concept of 'information' can be based on the notion of 'complexity' of a certain 'mechanical system' able to 'produce' an object belonging to a given fixed universe.

A formalization of this concept requires a formal specification of the terms 'mechanical system', 'complexity', and 'produce'. By mechanical system one can mean an 'algorithm', that is a finite list of instructions (or *program*) for an (abstract) machine, or a set of derivation rules of a *formal system*. In the first case the mechanical system makes a 'computation', i.e., if it stops, then produces a unique object after a finite number of steps. In the second case, by using the rules of the system, one can generate at each step more objects. In other terms there is a sort of a 'non-deterministic computation' usually called 'derivation'.

As regards the notion of 'complexity' one can refer to a 'static' or a 'dynamical' measure. A static measure of the complexity is related to the 'size' of the program or of the input in the case of an algorithm and to the 'size' of the set of axioms in the case of a formal system. A dynamical measure of the complexity is related to the 'length' of computation or derivation.

a) Algorithmic Approach to Information Theory

We shall briefly consider, at a level more intuitive than formal, the Kolmogorov minimal program complexity and its information interpretation. A recent formal presentation of this subject is in [38] (see also [20, 21]). Historically, this quantity was first introduced by R. J. Solomonov (1964) [48], and, independently, by A. N. Kolmogorov (1965) [37]. Further G. J. Chaitin (1966) [16] defined relative to a particular class of machines, a complexity measure for binary strings similar to that of Kolmogorov.

In the Kolmogorov approach 'information' is defined in terms of the algorithmic static complexity (*program complexity*). Moreover, the concept of 'randomness' appears related to the concept of complexity of algorithms. Actually, 'random objects' are those having the maximal program complexity. In fact, the intention of Kolmogorov was to give a 'logical' basis to information theory as well as to probability theory. The trade-off between 'information' and 'complexity' requires that one specifies exactly what 'algorithm' and 'complexity' of algorithms mean.

The theory of algorithms is a well developed mathematical theory. We recall that in the same year 1936 different researchers A. M. Turing, A. Church, and E. Post gave, independently, different formalizations of the intuitive notion of algorithm that have been proved equivalent in the sense that they yield the same class of 'effectively computable' functions (*partial recursive functions*) (see [19]). Moreover, a solid mathematical theory of algorithmic complexity was developed by M. Blum [4] in the frame of the theory of algorithms (see also [44]).

In the algorithmic approach the objects are identified with strings (or words) on a finite alphabet. The algorithms may be identified with Turing machines.

The *program-complexity* of an object y given the object (input) x is the minimal size (length) of a program of a universal Turing machine U able to compute y starting with the input x. This quantity is denoted by

$$K_U(y/x) \; ,$$

where the subscript U denotes the dependence on the universal machine U. However, it is possible to prove that if U_1 and U_2 are two universal Turing machines, then

$$|K_{U_1}(y/x) - K_{U_2}(y/x)| < c_{U_1 U_2} \; ,$$

where $c_{U_1 U_2}$ is a constant which does not depend on x and y. Hence, for sufficiently large values of the complexity $K_{U_1}(y/x) \approx K_{U_2}(y/x)$, i.e., the values of the complexities are approximately equal. We shall drop in the following the subscript U.

Let us now consider for each natural number n the set A^n of all sequences (strings) of length n of elements of A. For simplicity we shall take A equal to a binary set $A = \{a, b\}$. For any $w \in A^n$ we can introduce the complexity $K(w/n)$, i.e., the minimal program complexity of w conditioned by the knowledge of its length.

It was proved in [37] that there exists a constant c such that for all n and $w \in A^n$

$$K(w/n) \leq n + c .$$

Moreover, for any d such that $0 < d \leq n$, the number of strings w of A^n for which

$$K(w/n) \geq n - d$$

is greater than $2^n(1 - 2^{-d})$. Thus the fraction of strings of A^n satisfying both previous inequalities is greater than $1 - 2^{-d}$. For large n, increasing the value of d, the value of the previous fraction goes to 1 so that the great majority of the sequences of A^n has a complexity which differs from the length n only by a constant which may be neglected for high values of the complexity. In other words

$$K(w/n) \approx n .$$

These sequences of maximal program complexity are defined by Kolmogorov to be the 'random' elements of the population, i.e., of A^n.

We shall not enter into the details of Kolmogorov theory. We stress here only the following facts.

a). The algorithmic approach is based on the theory of recursive functions which is a very solid and well developed mathematical theory.

b). There is the possibility of defining 'random' objects as those for which program complexity is approximately equal to the size of the object. Random objects pass all conceivable statistical tests (see [41]).

c). There are many analogies often only at the formal level, with Shannon information theory.

d). The theory is an asymptotic theory. The complexity $K_U(x/y)$ is defined for a single object up to a constant.

e). The dynamical aspects of the computation (length of the computation) are not considered.

f). There is no algorithm by means of which one can compute for each n a random string of length n.

g). Even though it is very important from a conceptual point of view (trade-off between information and complexity) the program complexity is not much utilizable in practice.

b) A Logical Approach to Information Theory

As we have previously seen the Kolmogorov measure of information is a 'static' complexity measure, not related to the computation behavior. For this reason it can occur that for some object one can keep 'low' the amount of program (information) required to produce it only by increasing the computation resources (time, space, etc.) beyond any realistic limitation.

We shall give now the general ideas of a logical approach to Information theory based on 'dynamic' complexity measures in the framework of the theory of formal systems [25, 20].

Let us recall that a *formal system* is a pair $L = (A, R)$, where A is a finite set of words (set of axioms) and R is a finite set of recursive transformation rules (inference rules) [19]. A *derivation* (or *proof*) is a sequence

$$w_1, w_2, \ldots, w_n$$

of words such that w_1 is an axiom and each w_i, $i = 2, \ldots, n$, either is an axiom or can be derived from the preceding elements of the sequence by using one of the rules. A word w is called a *theorem* of L if there exists a proof whose last word is w.

For any word w one can introduce the *(absolute) complexity* $K_L(w)$ defined as the *minimal length of a derivation* (or proof)*of w in L if w is a theorem of L, $K_L(w) = \infty$, otherwise.

Another meaningful quantity is the *conditional complexity* $K_L(w/u)$ defined as the complexity of w in the formal system $(A \cup \{u\}, R)$, i.e., in the formal system which has the same set of rules of L but with the word u added to the set of axioms. The conditional complexity satisfies the following inequalities: for all words w, u, and v

$$K_L(w/u) \leq K_L(w) \ ,$$

$$K_L(w/u) \leq K_L(w/v) + K_L(v/u) \ .$$

The first inequality is due to the fact that any proof in L is also a proof in the formal system $(A \cup \{u\}, R)$. The second inequality (triangular inequality) is due to the fact that if we have a proof of v in $(A \cup \{u\}, R)$ and a proof of w in $(A \cup \{v\}, R)$, then one can certainly construct a proof of w in $(A \cup \{u\}, R)$.

Let us now introduce the quantity, called *conditional information*, defined for any pair of words w and u :

$$I_L(w/u) =_{def} K_L(w) - K_L(w/u) \ .$$

This quantity can be interpreted as the amount of information, relative to the formal system L, that the object u conveys on the object w. The conditional information satisfies the following properties: for all words w and u

1. $0 \leq I_L(w/u) \leq K_L(w)$,
2. $I_L(w/w) = K_L(w)$,
3. $I_L(w/u) = K_L(w)$ if and only if $w \in (A \cup \{u\})$.

By using the conditional information one can easily give the notion of 'independence' relative to the formal system L. One says that w is *independent* from u if $I_L(w/u) = 0$. In other terms to add the word u to the set A of the axioms of L does not give any gain in the sense of reducing the minimal length of a proof of w, or, equivalently, if w is a theorem of L, then there exists a proof of w of minimal complexity in $A \cup \{u\}$ in which u does not appear.

Let us now make the following general remarks:

a). There is a formal analogy between the conditional information and the *mutual information* of Shannon's information theory.

b). In the frame of the above logical approach one can consider questions as 'what information a theorem gives about another theorem' which are meaningless in the classic information theory.

In conclusion of this section we remark [20, 21] that an important problem that naturally arises is whether in the previous approach to 'information', based on static and dynamic complexity, one can face problems of 'transmission of information', and possibly to prove some general theorems by means of which one can evaluate the actual implications and the relevance of the introduced concepts of information.

How can a communication system in the context of this theory be envisaged? One can think of transmitting over a channel a computer program for a message instead of the message itself. In making a 'balance' of the advantage of this transmission one has to take into account both the 'length of program' and the 'time of computation'. The 'structure' of the message and of the computer play, then, a relevant role in this transmission. For many purposes, when one wants to have the freedom of transmitting any message, the 'receiver' can be a universal algorithm.

Even though the theory is only at a preliminary stage, we think that the foregoing approach is a good frame for an analysis of the 'semantic-pragmatic' levels of communication. In other words if the receiver is a 'decision-maker' that follows a fixed set of rules, it can be represented just as a formal system (in particular an algorithm) and the possible decisions of it depend on the set of theorems which can be derived. In this way there is the possibility, in principle, of facing the problem of how the transmitted message affects the conduct of the receiver in the desired way.

5 Structure and Information

The notion of information may be related to the 'structure' of an object belonging to a given class. In general, when one studies a given class of objects one tries to analyze each complex object in terms of simpler components of the same type. For instance, in group theory one analyzes the groups in terms of subgroups or by 'simple groups' which are the basic components of groups. Therefore, one can ask the following general question: what information one has about a complex structure by the knowledge of smaller substructures? For instance, what information one has about a word, a tree or a graph by knowing a certain set of subwords, subtrees or subgraphs?

Moreover, an important related question is what is the minimal 'size' of these substructures capable to determine uniquely the structure itself? We shall refer to this kind of information as to 'structural information'.

Let us observe that this approach is similar to the Kolmogorov's approach. The main difference concerns the set of 'data'. In fact, in this structural approach the 'data' about the given structure belong to a class of a certain kind, namely substructures. In the case of a word the substructures are subwords. This kind of problems is of great interest in some applications such as the problem of 'sequencing' DNA macromolecules or the transmission of a long message on several and possibly different channels of communication (cf.[15]).

We shall now give some general ideas about this structural information (see [24, 9, 10, 13]) limiting ourselves to the case of 'words' even though this approach can be followed for several combinatorial structures such as *trees* or *two-dimensional arrays* (see [11, 14]).

Let us recall that a *word*, in the abstract sense, is any finite sequence (string) of symbols, called *letters* belonging to a given finite set A, called *alphabet*. One, usually, represents a word w as:

$$w = a_1 a_2 \cdots a_n \ ,$$

with $a_i \in A$, $1 \le i \le n$. The integer n is called the *length* of the word w and it is denoted by $|w|$. If $w = a_1 a_2 \cdots a_n$ and $v = b_1 b_2 \cdots b_m$ are two words on the alphabet A, then the *concatenation* or *product* of w and v is the word wv defined as:

$$wv = a_1 a_2 \cdots a_n b_1 b_2 \cdots b_m \ .$$

The operation of concatenation is associative but not commutative. For some technical reasons it is also convenient to introduced the *empty word*, denoted by ϵ, which is a sequence of length 0, i.e., without letters.

A *subword* or *factor* of the word w is any 'block' of consecutive letters occurring in w. More precisely the word u is a factor of w if there exist words p and q such that $w = puq$. If $p = \epsilon$ (resp. $q = \epsilon$), then u is called *prefix* (resp. *suffix*) of w.

In this combinatorial approach an essential role is played by the notion of *extendable* and *special factor* of a given word. A factor u of w is called *right extendable* if there exists a letter $x \in A$ such that ux is a factor of w.

A factor u of w is called *right special* if there exist two distinct letters x and y such that ux and uy are factors of w. In a similar way one can define *left extendable* and *left special* factors of w. A factor of w is called *bispecial* if it is right and left special. A factor of w of the kind asb, with a and b letters and s bispecial, is called a *proper box*. A proper box is called *maximal* if it is not factor of another proper box.

The shortest prefix (resp. suffix) of w which is not left (resp. right) extendable in w is denoted by h_w (resp. k_w) and called the *initial* (resp. *terminal*) *box*. We set $H_w = |h_w|$ and $K_w = |k_w|$. Moreover, we shall denote by R_w (resp. L_w) the minimal natural number such that there are no right (resp. left) special factors of w of length R_w (resp. L_w).

Let us give the following example. Let w be the word $w = abccbabcab$. One has: $h_w = abcc$ and $k_w = cab$. Thus, $H_w = 4$ and $K_w = 3$. Moreover, the set of right special factors is $\{\epsilon, b, c, bc, abc\}$. The set of left special factor is $\{\epsilon, a, b, c, ba\}$. Hence, $R_w = 4$ and $L_w = 3$. The maximal proper boxes are:

$$abc, cba, bcc, ccb, bca \ .$$

A basic theorem proved in [9, 10] shows that *any word is uniquely determined by the initial box, the terminal box, and the set of maximal proper boxes.*

The parameters K_w, H_w, R_w, and L_w give much information on the structure of the word w. For instance, the maximal length G_w of a repeated factor of a non-empty word w is equal to

$$G_w = \max\{R_w, K_w\} - 1 = \max\{L_w, H_w\} - 1$$

and the minimal period of a word is not smaller that $\max\{R_w, L_w\}+1$. Moreover, the following important result holds: *Any word w is uniquely determined by the set of its factors up to length $1 + \max\{R_w, K_w\}$*. Moreover, the value $n = 1 + \max\{R_w, K_w\}$ is *optimal*. Indeed, one can prove [9] that for any word w there exists a word $u \neq w$ which has the same set of factors of w up to length $n - 1$.

It is worth noting that in the case of very long DNA sequences the values of R_w and K_w are usually very small with respect to the length of the sequences. For instance, for several genes w of length < 20.000, R_w and K_w are less than 20 (see [18]).

As shown in [9] there exist simple algorithms by means of which one can find the initial, the terminal, and the maximal proper boxes of a very long text and, subsequently, reconstruct the initial message.

Let us now make the following comments and remarks:

a). The preceding approach to information is a 'structural' approach in a non-probabilistic frame.

b). In the case of words the underlying mathematical theory is the 'Algebraic combinatorics on words' which is a recent and very well developed mathematical theory [39, 40].

c). There is some similarity with the algorithmic approach. Indeed, the preceding theory deals with a certain kind of complexity of single objects (words). However, differently from Kolmogorov theory, it is not an asymptotic theory.

d). The use of the results of the theory is simple and there exist very efficient algorithms for 'sequencing' a text and, conversely, for 'recovering' the initial text.

e). The formalism based on the notions of extendable and special factors of a word can be generalized to more general combinatorial structures of interest in computer science such as trees and 2-D arrays.

6   Information in Physics and Biology

As we said in the Introduction the notion of 'information' appeared first in Physics in connection with 'physical entropy' in the frame of statistical thermodynamics.

One can ask the question whether information is a 'physical entity' always related to and measurable by the physical entropy. This connection 'information' 'physical entropy' is certainly true only in some cases, i.e., in some special contexts (cf. [6]). In fact, as we have seen in the previous sections, 'information' is a notion having several different facets so that there is no a unique definition of it. Moreover, it seems that the notion of information cannot be independent from its utilization, i.e., from the characteristic aspects of the receiver.

For instance, in Biology there exist 'sophisticated mechanisms' which are essential to the information processing. These mechanisms are sometimes 'coding processes'. The most typical and famous mechanism of this kind is the DNA, RNA coding mechanism by means of which a sequence of bases (gene) written in the alphabet $\{A, T, C, G\}$ is transformed in a protein, i.e., a sequence of amino-acids written in a 20 letter alphabet (amino-acids alphabet). As is well known the genome contains all 'genetic information' about a living organism and, moreover, it is able to control by this coding mechanism the activity of different genes.

Also the 'brain' and especially the 'cortical areas' have complex and special-ized mechanisms in order to analyze and process information. Indeed, a typical aspect of the brain, seen as a computer, is that it has quite limited physical capabilities (limited volume, power of its elements, etc.) but extraordinary, and no well known, mechanisms for what concerns information processing. In other terms, despite its physical limitations, the brain possesses sophisticated mecha-nisms to process information which increase considerably its efficiency.

As stressed in [22] in this type of information processing the 'coding mech-anisms' play a crucial role. In the brain 'coding' is useful to 'compress' and adapt incoming information to the communication channels, namely to neurons. However, it plays a crucial role for the inner representation of 'metalinguistic predicates' by means of which the 'brain-machine' can 'see' itself in relation within a certain representation that it has of external world. Hence, the opinion of the author is that 'coding mechanisms' are essential in order to explain the 'consciousness' and the 'unconscious' present in the mechanism of human brain and, in a certain measure, of the major part of living organisms.

It seems that 'Life' is the only known case, in the great variety of phenomena of physical world, in which there exist some 'natural' coding mechanisms such as 'genetic code'. The natural origin of these mechanisms is very surprising and extraordinary since the codified objects are very different from the uncoded objects (for instance, genes and proteins) and codification is an operation which, in general, implies the existence of an 'intelligent' mechanism or an entity which makes the coding map.

In conclusion, 'information' is a concept which is not uniquely definable. Moreover, Biology seems to show that any definition cannot be independent from the 'semantic' and 'pragmatic' aspects of the information, which are strongly related with its utilization, i.e., with the characteristics of the mechanisms of information processing of the receiver.

References

[1] Alsina, C. , Trillas, E.: Sur les mesures du degré de flou. Stocastica **3** (1979) 81–84
[2] Backer, E.: A Non Statistical Type of Uncertainty in Fuzzy Events, in: *Topics in Information Theory*, Colloquia Mathematica Societatis Janos Bolyai, vol. 16, pp. 53–73. Amsterdam: North-Holland 1977

[3] Bedrosian, S.D., Xie, W.X.: An Information Measure for Fuzzy Sets. IEEE Transactions on Systems, Man, and Cybernetics **14** (1984) 151–156

[4] Blum, M.: A Machine Independent Theory of the Complexity of Recursive Functions. J. of ACM **14** (1967) 322–336

[5] Boltzmann, L.: *Vorlesungen über Gas Theorie*, vol.1. J. A. Barth Leipzig, 1896, English Transl. *Lectures on Gas Theory*. Berkeley Calif. 1964

[6] Brillouin, L.: *La Science et La Théorie de l'Information*. Paris: Masson 1959

[7] Capocelli, R., de Luca, A.: Fuzzy Sets and Decision Theory. Information and Control **23** (1973) 446–473

[8] Carnap, R., Bar-Hillel, Y.: An Outline of a Theory of Semantic Information. Tech. Rep. 247, M.I.T., Research Laboratory of Electronics, 1952, Reprinted in Bar-Hillel, Y.: *Language and Information*. Reading, MA: Addison Wesley 1962

[9] Carpi, A., de Luca, A.: Words and Special Factors. Theoretical Computer Science **259** (2001) 145–182

[10] Carpi, A., de Luca, A.: Words and Repeated Factors. Séminaire Lotharingien de Combinatoire **B421** (1998) 24 pp. and in: Foata, D., Han, G. (Eds.) *Andrews Festschrift*, pp. 231–251. Berlin: Springer 2001

[11] Carpi, A., de Luca, A.: Repetitions and Boxes in Words and Pictures, in: Karhumäki, J., Maurer, H., Păun, G., Rozenberg, G. (Eds.) *Jewels Are Forever*, pp. 295–306. Berlin: Springer 1999

[12] Carpi, A. , de Luca, A.: Special Factors, Periodicity, and an Application to Sturmian Words. Acta Informatica **36** (2000) 983–1006

[13] Carpi, A. , de Luca, A.: Periodic-like Words, Periodicity, and Boxes. Acta Informatica **37** (2001) 597–618

[14] Carpi, A., de Luca, A., Varricchio, S.: Special Factors and Uniqueness Conditions in Rational Trees. Theory of Computing Systems (to appear)

[15] Carpi, A., de Luca, A., Varricchio, S.: Words, Univalent Factors, and Boxes. Preprint 41/2000, Dipartimento di Matematica dell'Università di Roma 'La Sapienza', 2000

[16] Chaitin, G.J.: On the Length of Programs for Computing Finite Binary Sequences. J. of ACM **13** (1966) 547–569

[17] Chaitin, G.J.: Information-Theoretic Computational Complexity. IEEE Trans. on Information Theory **20** (1974) 10–15

[18] Colosimo, A., de Luca, A.: Special Factors in Biological Strings. J. Theor. Biol. **204** (2000) 29–46

[19] Davis, M.: *Computability and Unsolvability*. New York: McGraw Hill 1958

[20] de Luca, A.: Complexity and Information Theory, in: Longo, G. (Ed.) *Coding and Complexity*, CISM Courses and Lectures No. 216, pp. 207–270. Wien: Springer 1975

[21] de Luca, A.: On the Entropy of a Formal Languages, Lecture Notes in Computer Science, vol. 33, pp. 103–109. Berlin: Springer 1975

[22] de Luca, A.: The Mind as a Mechanism of the Brain. (1982) (manuscript)

[23] de Luca, A.: Dispersion Measures of Fuzzy Sets, in: Gupta, M.M., Kandel, A., Bandler, W., Kiszka, J.B. (Eds.) *Approximate Reasoning in Expert Systems*, pp. 199–216. Amsterdam: North-Holland 1985

[24] de Luca, A.: On the Combinatorics of Finite Words. Theoretical Computer Science **218** (1999) 13–39

[25] de Luca, A., Fischetti, E.: Outline of a New Logical Approach to Information Theory, in Caianiello, E.R. (Ed.) *New Concepts and Technologies in Parallel Processing*, Nato Advanced Study Institutes Series, Series E: Applied Sciences-No.9, pp. 359–380. Leyden: Noordhoff International Publ. 1975

[26] de Luca, A., Termini, S.: A Definition of a Non-probabilistic Entropy in the Setting of Fuzzy Sets Theory. *Information and Control* **20** (1972) 301–312

[27] de Luca, A., Termini, S. : Algebraic Properties of Fuzzy Sets. *J. Math. Anal. Appl.* **40** (1972) 373–386

[28] de Luca, A., Termini, S.: Entropy of L-fuzzy Sets. *Information and Control* **24** (1974) 55–73

[29] de Luca, A., Termini, S.: Entropy and Energy Measures of a Fuzzy Set, in: Gupta, M.M., Ragade, R.K., Yager, R.R. (Eds.) *Advances in Fuzzy Set Theory and Applications*, pp. 321–338. Amsterdam: North-Holland 1979

[30] de Luca, A., Termini, S.: Superposition Sets and Their Entropies, *Proc.s IEEE Int. Conf. on Systems, Man and Cybernetics, Delhi/Bombay, India*, pp. 493–497. New York: IEEE 1983

[31] de Luca, A., Termini, S.: Entropy Measures in the Theory of Fuzzy Sets, in Singh, M.G. (Ed.) *Encyclopedia of Systems and Control*, pp. 1467–1473. Oxford: Pergamon-Press 1983

[32] Ebanks, B.R.: On Measures of Fuzziness and Their Representations. *J. Math. Anal. Appl.* **94** (1983) 24–37

[33] Hartley, R.V.L.: Transmission of Information. *Bell Syst. Tech. J.* **7** (1928) 535–563

[34] Khinchin, A.I.: *Mathematical Foundations of Information Theory.* New York: Dover Publ. 1957

[35] Klir, G.J. (Ed.): Measures of Uncertainty. Fuzzy Sets and Systems (Special Issue) **24** (1987) n.2

[36] Knopfmacher, J.: On Measures of Fuzziness. *J. Math. Anal. Appl.* **49** (1975) 529–534

[37] Kolmogorov, A.N.: Three Approaches to the Quantitative Definition of Information. *Problemi Peredachi Informatsii* **1** (1965) 3–11

[38] Li, M., Vitanyi, P.: *An Introduction to Kolmogorov Complexity and Its Applications.* Berlin: Springer 1993

[39] Lothaire, M.: *Combinatorics on Words.* Reading, MA: Addison-Wesley 1983

[40] Lothaire, M.: *Algebraic Combinatorics on Words.* Cambridge: Cambridge University Press (to appear)

[41] Martin-Löf, P.: The Definition of Random Sequences. *Information and Control* **9** (1966) 602–619

[42] Nyquist, H.: Certain Factors Affecting Telegraph Speed. *Bell Syst. Tech. J.* **3** (1924) 324

[43] Pal, S.K.: A Note on the Quantitative Measure of Image Enhancement Through Fuzziness. *IEEE Trans. on Pattern Analysis and Machine Intelligence* **4** (1982) 204–208

[44] Papadimitriou, C.H.: *Computational Complexity.* Reading MA: Addison-Wesley 1994

[45] Shannon, C.E.: A Mathematical Theory of Communication. *Bell Syst. Tech. J.* **27** (1948) 379-423, 623–656

[46] Shannon C.E., Weaver, W.: *The Mathematical Theory of Communication.* Urbana ILL: University of Illinois Press 1949

[47] Shimizu, A.: Approximate Reasoning Based on Fuzzy Entropy's Theory, in: Piera Carreté, N., Singh, M.G. (Eds.) *Qualitative Reasoning and Decision Technologies*, pp. 662–671. Barcelona: CIMNE 1983

[48] Solomonov, R.J.: A Formal Theory of Inductive Inference. Part I. *Information and Control* **7** (1964) 1–22

[49] Szilard, L.: Über die Entropieverminderung in einem thermodynamischen System bei Eingriffen intelligenter Wesen. *Zeitschrift f. Physik* **53** (1929) 840–856, Reprinted: On Decrease of Entropy in Thermodynamic System by the Intervention of Intelligent Beings. *Behavioral Science* **9** (1964) 301–310

[50] Taneja, I.J.: On Generalized Entropies with Applications, in Ricciardi, L.M. (Ed.) *Lectures in Applied Mathematics and Informatics*, pp. 107–169. Manchester: Manchester University Press 1990

[51] Trillas, E., Riera, T.: Entropies in Finite Fuzzy Sets. *Information Sciences* **15** (1978) 159–168

[52] Wiener, N.: *The Extrapolation, Interpolation and Smoothing of Stationary Time Series.* New York: J. Wiley and Sons 1949

[53] Zadeh, L.A.: Fuzzy Sets. *Information and Control* **8** (1965) 338–353

Nondeterministic Trajectories*

Alexandru Mateescu[1] and Arto Salomaa[2]

[1] Faculty of Mathematics, University of Bucharest
Academiei, 14, Bucharest, Romania
alexmate@pcnet.pcnet.ro
[2] Turku Centre for Computer Science (TUCS)
Lemminkäisenkatu 14A, 20520 Turku, Finland
asalomaa@utu.fi

Abstract. *Trajectories* have been introduced as mechanisms to control the *shuffle* operation, traditionally important in the study of parallelism and concurrency. A variant, *nondeterministic trajectory* will be introduced in this paper. It provides more leeway in the control of the shuffle operation. Ordinary trajectories will be obtained as a special case of nondeterministic ones. The paper investigates basic properties of nondeterministic trajectories, emphasizing algebraic aspects, interconnections with language theory and the property of fairness.

1 Introduction

Methods to define parallel composition of words and languages as well as of ω-words and ω-languages are of a great importance both in theory and practice. The operation of parallel composition is naturally described by new shuffle-like operations obtained by using trajectories. *Trajectories* in this sense were introduced in [5], and the concept was further investigated in many follow-up papers.

In this paper we introduce and investigate a new class of trajectories, the so-called *nondeterministic trajectories*. The trajectories of [5] are obtained as a special case of nondeterministic trajectories. Let us now briefly recall the notion of a trajectory and its use in the control of the shuffle operator.

Consider the alphabet $V = \{r, u\}$ whose letters are called *versors*. Here r stands for the *right* direction, whereas u stands for the *up* direction. A *(deterministic) trajectory* is simply a word $t \in V^*$. A trajectory can be illustrated geometrically as a sequence of line segments, each of unit length, starting from the origin and progressing parallel with one of the axes, depending on the occurrence of r or u. If two words are written letter by letter starting from the origin on the two axes, then a trajectory t determines uniquely their shuffle.

For a *nondeterministic* trajectory, the alphabet V is extended to a set of three versors, $V = \{r, u, n\}$, where r and u are as above but n stands for *nondeterminism*: both directions are possible. Also now a *nondeterministic trajectory* is a

---

* The first author was partially supported by Direcció General de Recerca, Generalitat de Catalunya (programme PIV)

W. Brauer et al. (Eds.): Formal and Natural Computing, LNCS 2300, pp. 96–106, 2002.

word over the alphabet $V = \{r, u, n\}$. The geometric interpretation is as before but now the versor n corresponds to an oblique line segment. (See Figures 1 and 2 below!) In the control of the shuffle operation, n has the same effect as the disjunction of ru and ur. Thus, the shuffle of two words on a nondeterministic trajectory is not any more a unique word but rather a finite set of words.

A brief outline of the contents of this paper follows. The notions needed from the theory of formal languages are defined in Section 2, whereas Section 3 contains the basic definitions involving nondeterministic trajectories. Interconnections between determinism and nondeterminism, as well as some algebraic issues, are studied in Section 4. Section 5 investigates the shuffle of languages under a set of nondeterministic trajectories, assuming that one or more of the sets involved are regular or context-free. A basic property of parallel composition of processes, *fairness*, is studied in Section 6.

The paper is largely self-contained. If need arises, the reader may consult [7] or [6] for language theory, and [1] or [2] for semirings.

2   Language-Theoretic Basics

Let Σ be an alphabet. The empty word is denoted by λ. In connection with processes, the letters can also be viewed as *atomic actions* and words in Σ^* also *finite sequential processes*.

For $w \in \Sigma^*$, $|w|$ denotes the *length* of w. By definition, $|\lambda| = 0$. If $a \in \Sigma$ and $w \in \Sigma^*$, then $|w|_a$ denotes the number of occurrences of the symbol a in w. If $\Delta \subseteq \Sigma$, then $|w|_\Delta = \sum_{a \in \Delta} |w|_a$.

The *anti-catenation* operation, denoted by "$\circ$", is defined as: $u \circ v = vu$, for any $u, v \in \Sigma^*$.

The *shuffle* operation, denoted by $\sqcup\!\sqcup$, is defined recursively by :

$$(a\alpha \sqcup\!\sqcup b\beta) = a(\alpha \sqcup\!\sqcup b\beta) \cup b(a\alpha \sqcup\!\sqcup \beta) \text{ and } \alpha \sqcup\!\sqcup \lambda = \lambda \sqcup\!\sqcup \alpha = \{\alpha\},$$

where $\alpha, \beta \in \Sigma^*$ and $a, b \in \Sigma$.

The shuffle operation is extended in a natural way to languages :

$$L_1 \sqcup\!\sqcup L_2 = \bigcup_{\alpha \in L_1, \beta \in L_2} \alpha \sqcup\!\sqcup \beta.$$

The *literal shuffle*, denoted by $\sqcup\!\sqcup_l$, is defined as:

$$a_1 a_2 \dots a_n \sqcup\!\sqcup_l b_1 b_2 \dots b_m = \begin{cases} a_1 b_1 a_2 b_2 \dots a_n b_n b_{n+1} \dots b_m, & \text{if } n \leq m, \\ a_1 b_1 a_2 b_2 \dots a_m b_m a_{m+1} \dots a_n, & \text{if } m < n, \end{cases}$$

where $a_i, b_j \in \Sigma$ and $w \sqcup\!\sqcup_l \lambda = \lambda \sqcup\!\sqcup_l w = \{w\}$, where $w \in \Sigma^*$.

The *co-literal shuffle*, denoted by $\sqcup\!\sqcup_{cl}$, is defined as:

$$a_1 \dots a_n \sqcup\!\sqcup_{cl} b_1 \dots b_m = \begin{cases} (a_1 \sqcup\!\sqcup b_1) \dots (a_n \sqcup\!\sqcup b_n) b_{n+1} \dots b_m, & \text{if } n \leq m, \\ (a_1 \sqcup\!\sqcup b_1) \dots (a_m \sqcup\!\sqcup b_m) a_{m+1} \dots a_n, & \text{if } m < n, \end{cases}$$

where $a_i, b_j \in \Sigma$ and $w \sqcup\!\sqcup_{cl} \lambda = \lambda \sqcup\!\sqcup_{cl} w = \{w\}$, where $w \in \Sigma^*$.

The *insertion* operation, denoted by $\longleftarrow$, is defined as:

$$u \longleftarrow v = \{u'vu'' \mid u'u'' = u, u', u'' \in \Sigma^*\}.$$

The *bi-catenation*, denoted by $\odot$, is defined as:

$$\alpha \odot \beta = \{\alpha\beta, \beta\alpha\}.$$

All the above operations can be extended additively to concern languages.

3   Shuffle on Nondeterministic Trajectories

In this section we introduce our fundamental operation of the *shuffle on nondeterministic trajectories*. Consider the alphabet $V = \{r, u, n\}$. Let t be a nondeterministic trajectory, $t \in V^*$. We will consider also sets T of nondeterministic trajectories, $T \subseteq V^*$.

Let Σ be an alphabet, t a nondeterministic trajectory, d a versor, $d \in V$, and let α, β be two words over Σ, possibly empty.

Definition 3.1. *The* shuffle *of α with β on the* nondeterministic *trajectory dt, denoted $\alpha \sqcup_{dt} \beta$, is defined recursively as follows.*

If $\alpha = ax$ and $\beta = by$, where $a, b \in \Sigma$ and $x, y \in \Sigma^*$, then

$$ax \sqcup_{dt} by = \begin{cases} a(x \sqcup_t by), & \text{if } d = r, \\ b(ax \sqcup_t y), & \text{if } d = u, \\ (a \sqcup b)(x \sqcup_t y), & \text{if } d = n. \end{cases}$$

If $\alpha = ax$ where $a \in \Sigma$ and $x \in \Sigma^*$, then

$$ax \sqcup_{dt} \lambda = \begin{cases} a(x \sqcup_t \lambda), & \text{if } d = r, \\ \emptyset, & \text{otherwise.} \end{cases}$$

If $\beta = by$, where $b \in \Sigma$ and $y \in \Sigma^*$, then

$$\lambda \sqcup_{dt} by = \begin{cases} b(\lambda \sqcup_t y), & \text{if } d = u, \\ \emptyset, & \text{otherwise.} \end{cases}$$

Finally,

$$\lambda \sqcup_t \lambda = \begin{cases} \lambda, & \text{if } t = \lambda, \\ \emptyset, & \text{otherwise.} \end{cases}$$

Comment. It follows from the definition that if either $|\alpha| \neq |t|_r + |t|_n$ or $|\beta| \neq |t|_u + |t|_n$, then $\alpha \sqcup_t \beta = \emptyset$. Thus, we must have both $|\alpha| = |t|_r + |t|_n$ and $|\beta| = |t|_u + |t|_n$, in order to have some words in the shuffle. Whenever n occurs in the trajectory, we must be able to use both r and u, that is, both of the words α and β should be nonempty. Another natural way would be to require that

$$a \sqcup_n \lambda = \lambda \sqcup_n a = a.$$

(The reader might want to modify the above definition to this effect!) This would mean that, even if one of the words runs out, we could still apply letters n in the trajectory. Our definition above could be referred to as *strict*, whereas the modification could be called *liberal*. Because of many formal reasons, we have preferred the strict definition. But we feel that also the liberal version is worth studying.

If T is a set of trajectories, the *shuffle of α with β on the set T of nondeterministic trajectories*, denoted $\alpha \sqcup_T \beta$, is:

$$\alpha \sqcup_T \beta = \bigcup_{t \in T} \alpha \sqcup_t \beta.$$

If $L_1, L_2 \subseteq \Sigma^*$, then

$$L_1 \sqcup_T L_2 = \bigcup_{\alpha \in L_1, \beta \in L_2} \alpha \sqcup_T \beta.$$

We now consider an *example*. Let α and β be the words $\alpha = a_1 a_2 a_3 a_4 a_5 a_6 a_7 a_8$, $\beta = b_1 b_2 b_3 b_4 b_5$ and assume that $t = r^3 u^2 r^3 n^2 u$. The shuffle of α with β on the trajectory t is:

$$\alpha \sqcup_t \beta = a_1 a_2 a_3 b_1 b_2 a_4 a_5 a_6 \{a_7 b_3, b_3 a_7\}(a_8 \sqcup_{nu} b_4 b_5) =$$

$$= a_1 a_2 a_3 b_1 b_2 a_4 a_5 a_6 a_7 b_3 \{a_8 b_4, b_4 a_8\}(\lambda \sqcup_u b_5) \cup$$

$$\cup a_1 a_2 a_3 b_1 b_2 a_4 a_5 a_6 b_3 a_7 \{a_8 b_4, b_4 a_8\}(\lambda \sqcup_u b_5) =$$

$$= \{a_1 a_2 a_3 b_1 b_2 a_4 a_5 a_6 a_7 b_3 a_8 b_4 b_5, a_1 a_2 a_3 b_1 b_2 a_4 a_5 a_6 a_7 b_3 b_4 a_8 b_5,$$

$$a_1 a_2 a_3 b_1 b_2 a_4 a_5 a_6 b_3 a_7 a_8 b_4 b_5, a_1 a_2 a_3 b_1 b_2 a_4 a_5 a_6 b_3 a_7 b_4 a_8 b_5\}.$$

The geometrical interpretation is given in Figure 1. The trajectory t defines a line starting in the origin and continuing one unit to the right, one unit up or along the diagonal of a unit square, depending of the definition of t. In our case, first there are three units right, then two units up, then three units right, then two diagonals and, finally, one unit up. Assign α on the Ox axis and β on the Oy axis. The trajectory ends in the point with coordinates $(8, 5)$ (denoted by E in Figure 1) that is exactly the upper right corner of the rectangle defined by α and β, that is, the rectangle $OAEB$ in Figure 1. Hence, the result of the shuffle of α with β on the trajectory t is nonempty. The result can be read following the line defined by the trajectory t. When being in a lattice point of the trajectory, with the trajectory going right, one should pick up the corresponding letter from α. If the trajectory is going up, then one should add to the result the corresponding letter from β. If the trajectory is going on the diagonal of a unit square then the result is the union between the set obtained by adding the corresponding letter from α catenated with the corresponding letter from β with the set obtained by adding the corresponding letter from β catenated with the corresponding letter from α. Suppose that the trajectory is going on the diagonal of a unit square. Let

a (resp. b) be the letter from α (resp. β) under scan. Then the shuffle continues by adding both of the words ab and ba.

Assume now that t' is another trajectory, say:

$$t' = nr^4u^3nr^2.$$

In Figure 1, the trajectory t' is depicted by a bolder line than the one used for the trajectory t. We now obtain

$$\alpha \, \sqcup\!\sqcup_{t'} \, \beta = \{a_1b_1, b_1a_1\}a_2a_3a_4a_5b_2b_3b_4\{a_6b_5, b_5a_6\}a_7a_8 =$$

$$= \{a_1b_1a_2a_3a_4a_5b_2b_3b_4a_6b_5a_7a_8, a_1b_1a_2a_3a_4a_5b_2b_3b_4b_5a_6a_7a_8,$$

$$b_1a_1a_2a_3a_4a_5b_2b_3b_4a_6b_5a_7a_8, b_1a_1a_2a_3a_4a_5b_2b_3b_4b_5a_6a_7a_8\}.$$

Consider the set of trajectories, $T = \{t, t'\}$. The shuffle of α with β on the set T of trajectories is

$$\alpha \, \sqcup\!\sqcup_T \, \beta = \alpha \, \sqcup\!\sqcup_t \, \beta \cup \alpha \, \sqcup\!\sqcup_{t'} \, \beta =$$

$$= \{a_1a_2a_3b_1b_2a_4a_5a_6a_7b_3a_8b_4b_5, a_1a_2a_3b_1b_2a_4a_5a_6a_7b_3b_4a_8b_5,$$

$$a_1a_2a_3b_1b_2a_4a_5a_6b_3a_7a_8b_4b_5, a_1a_2a_3b_1b_2a_4a_5a_6b_3a_7b_4a_8b_5,$$

$$a_1b_1a_2a_3a_4a_5b_2b_3b_4a_6b_5a_7a_8, a_1b_1a_2a_3a_4a_5b_2b_3b_4b_5a_6a_7a_8,$$

$$b_1a_1a_2a_3a_4a_5b_2b_3b_4a_6b_5a_7a_8, b_1a_1a_2a_3a_4a_5b_2b_3b_4b_5a_6a_7a_8\}.$$

It was pointed out already in [5] that customary operations for the parallel composition of words can be obtained as special cases of the operation of shuffle on trajectories. We now summarize these facts, adding an observation concerning the versor n.

1. Let T be the set $T = \{r, u\}^*$. Then $\sqcup\!\sqcup_T = \sqcup\!\sqcup$, the shuffle operation.
2. Assume that $T = (ru)^*(r^* \cup u^*)$. Now $\sqcup\!\sqcup_T = \sqcup\!\sqcup_l$, the literal shuffle.
3. For $T = n^*(r^* \cup u^*)$, we have $\sqcup\!\sqcup_T = \sqcup\!\sqcup_{cl}$, the co-literal shuffle.
4. If $T = r^*u^*r^*$, then $\sqcup\!\sqcup_T = \longleftarrow$, the insertion operation.
5. Assume that $T = r^*u^*$. It follows that $\sqcup\!\sqcup_T = \cdot$, the catenation operation.
6. For $T = u^*r^*$, we have $\sqcup\!\sqcup_T = \circ$, the anti-catenation operation.
7. Assume that $T = r^*u^* \cup u^*r^*$. It follows that $\sqcup\!\sqcup_T = \odot$, the bi-catenation operation.

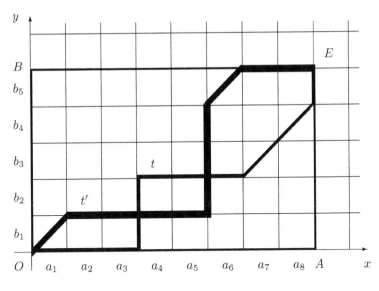

Fig. 1.

4   Determinism versus Nondeterminism. Algebraic Properties

We begin with some straightforward definitions.

Definition 4.1. *A nondeterministic trajectory t is* deterministic *if $|t|_n = 0$, that is, $t \in \{r, u\}^*$.*

Definition 4.2. *Two sets of trajectories, T_1 and T_2 are* equivalent *iff for all languages L_1 and L_2 it follows that $L_1 \sqcup\!\!\sqcup_{T_1} L_2 = L_1 \sqcup\!\!\sqcup_{T_2} L_2$.*

The following result is now immediate.

Proposition 4.1. *For each set T of nonderministic trajectories, there exists an equivalent set T' of deterministic trajectories.*

Proof. Consider the finite substitution $f : \{r, u, n\}^* \longrightarrow \{r, u\}^*$, defined as: $f(r) = r$, $f(u) = u$ and $f(n) = \{ru, ur\}$.
   It is easy to see that T is equivalent with $T' = f(T)$ and, moreover, T' is a set of deterministic trajectories.

$\square$

   The finite substitution f defined above is essential in characterizing the difference between deterministic and nondeterministic trajectories. We make the *convention* that in the sequel f will always denote this substitution.

The algebraic properties of the shuffle on a set T of nondeterministic trajectories, such as commutativity and associativity, are closely related to the corresponding properties of the shuffle on the equivalent set T' of deterministic trajectories. For instance, the operation $\sqcup\!\sqcup_T$ is associative iff the operation $\sqcup\!\sqcup_{T'}$ is associative, where T' is a set of deterministic trajectories equivalent with T.

For a set T of deterministic trajectories, the algebraic properties of the operation $\sqcup\!\sqcup_T$ are investigated in [5]. We recall here only one fact, concerning the property of associativity.

Definition 4.3. *Consider the sets* $V = \{r, u\}$ *and* $D = \{x, y, z\}$. *Define the substitutions* σ *and* τ *by*

$$\sigma \,,\, \tau : V^* \longrightarrow \mathcal{P}(D^*),$$

$$\sigma(r) = \{x, y\} \,,\, \sigma(u) = \{z\},$$

$$\tau(r) = \{x\} \,,\, \tau(u) = \{y, z\}.$$

Consider the morphisms φ *and* ψ:

$$\varphi \,,\, \psi : V^* \longrightarrow D^*,$$

$$\varphi(r) = x \,,\, \varphi(u) = y,$$

$$\psi(r) = y \,,\, \psi(u) = z.$$

Proposition 4.2. *([5]) Let* T *be a set of trajectories. The following conditions are equivalent:*

(i) T *is an associative set of trajectories.*
(ii) $\sigma(T) \cap (\varphi(T) \sqcup\!\sqcup z^*) = \tau(T) \cap (\psi(T) \sqcup\!\sqcup x^*).$

For each set of nondeterministic trajectories, T, the operation $\sqcup\!\sqcup_T$ is distributive over the union, both on the right and on the left. Hence, we obtain the following important result:

Proposition 4.3. *If* T *is an associative set of nondeterministic trajectories and if* T *has a unit element, then for any alphabet* Σ,

$$\mathcal{S} = (\mathcal{P}(\Sigma^*), \cup, \sqcup\!\sqcup_T, \emptyset, \lambda)$$

is a semiring.

We introduce next a new operation between nondeterministic trajectories and sets of nondeterministic trajectories.

Definition 4.4. *The sum of two versors from* $\{r, u, n\}$, *denoted* $\oplus$, *is defined as follows:* $x \oplus x = x$, *for all* $x \in \{r, u\}$, $x \oplus y = n$ *otherwise.*
The operation $\oplus$ *is extended to the set* $\{r, u, n, \lambda\}$: $\lambda \oplus x = x \oplus \lambda = x$, *for all* $x \in \{r, u, n, \lambda\}$.

Note that $(\{r, u, n, \lambda\}, \oplus, \lambda)$ is a commutative monoid.

Definition 4.5. *The sum of two nondeterministic trajectories, denoted also by* $\oplus$ *is defined as:*

$$a_1 \ldots a_n \oplus b_1 \ldots b_m = \begin{cases} (a_1 \oplus b_1) \ldots (a_n \oplus b_n) b_{n+1} \ldots b_m, & \text{if } n \leq m, \\ (a_1 \oplus b_1) \ldots (a_m \oplus b_m) a_{m+1} \ldots a_n, & \text{if } m < n, \end{cases}$$

where $a_i, b_j \in V$.

The sum of two sets of nondeterministic trajectories T_1 *and* T_2 *is defined as:*

$$T_1 \oplus T_2 = \bigcup_{t_1 \in T_1, t_2 \in T_2} t_1 \oplus t_2.$$

It is easy to prove the following result.

Proposition 4.4. $(\mathcal{P}(V^*), \oplus, \lambda)$ *is a commutative monoid. Moreover,*

$$\mathcal{S}_\oplus = (\mathcal{P}(V^*), \oplus, \cup, \lambda, \emptyset)$$

is a commutative semiring.

5   Shuffle on Nondeterministic Trajectories of Regular and Context-Free Languages

Let $\Sigma_1 = \{a_1 \mid a \in \Sigma\}$ and $\Sigma_2 = \{a_2 \mid a \in \Sigma\}$ be two "copies" of Σ. Define the morphisms $g : \Sigma^* \longrightarrow \Sigma_1^*$, $g(a) = a_1$, $a \in \Sigma$, and $h : \Sigma^* \longrightarrow \Sigma_2^*$, $h(a) = a_2$, $a \in \Sigma$. Then the following proposition is a representation result for languages of the form $L_1 \amalg_T L_2$.

Proposition 5.1. *For all languages* L_1 *and* L_2, $L_1, L_2 \subseteq \Sigma^*$, *and for all sets* T *of nondeterministic trajectories, there exist a morphism* φ *and a regular language* R, *such that*

$$L_1 \amalg_T L_2 = \varphi((g(L_1) \amalg h(L_2) \amalg f(T)) \cap R).$$

Proof. Let R be the regular language $R = (r\Sigma_1 \cup u\Sigma_2)^*$ and consider the morphism

$$\varphi : (\Sigma_1 \cup \Sigma_2 \cup \{r, u\})^* \longrightarrow \Sigma^*,$$

defined by $\varphi(a_1) = a$, $\varphi(a_2) = a$ and $\varphi(r) = \varphi(u) = \lambda$.
It is easy to see that Proposition 5.1 holds for this choice of φ and R.

$\square$

Consequently, we obtain also the following result.

Corollary 5.1. *For all languages* L_1 *and* L_2, $L_1, L_2 \subseteq \Sigma^*$, *and for all sets* T *of nondeterministic trajectories, there exists a gsm* M *such that*

$$L_1 \amalg_T L_2 = M(g(L_1) \amalg h(L_2) \amalg f(T)).$$

Proposition 5.2. *Let L_1, L_2 and T, $T \subseteq \{r, u, n\}^*$ be three languages.*

(i) if all three languages are regular languages, then $L_1 \sqcup_T L_2$ is a regular language.

(ii) if two languages are regular languages and the third one is a context-free language, then $L_1 \sqcup_T L_2$ is a context-free language.

Proof. The results follow from the above Proposition 5.1 and the closure properties of regular and context-free languages.

$\square$

For a different proof concerning deterministic sets of trajectories, the reader is referred to [5], Section 5.

6   Fairness

Fairness is a property of the parallel composition of processes to the effect that, roughly speaking, each action of a process is performed with not too much delay in regard to actions of other processes. That is, the parallel composition is "fair" with both processes that are performed.

Definition 6.1. *Let $T \subseteq \{r, u, n\}^*$ be a set of trajectories and let m be an integer, $m \geq 1$. T has the m-fairness property iff for all $t \in T$ and for all t' such that $t = t't''$ for some $t'' \in \{r, u, n\}^*$, it follows that:*

$$\mid \,|t'|_r - |t'|_u \,\mid\, \leq m.$$

This means that all trajectories from T are contained in the region of the plane bounded by the line $y = x - m$ and the line $y = x + m$, see Figure 2, for $m = 4$.

The set $T = n^*$ has the m-fairness property for all $m \geq 1$. The operations of shuffle ($\sqcup$), catenation ($\cdot$) and insertion ($\longleftarrow$) do not have the m-fairness property for any $m \geq 1$. The following result follows by the definition.

Proposition 6.1. *Assume that T is a set of deterministic trajectories having the m-fairness property and that T' is a set of nondeterministic trajectories satisfying the equation $g(T') = T$, where the projection $g : \{r, u, n\}^* \longrightarrow \{r, u\}^*$ is defined by*

$$g(r) = r, \ g(u) = u, \ g(n) = \lambda.$$

Then also T' has the m-fairness property.

Definition 6.2. *Let m be a fixed number, $m \geq 1$. Define the language F_m as:*

$$F_m = \{t \in V^* \mid \, |t'|_r - |t'|_u \,\mid\, \leq m, \ for \ all \ t' \ such \ that \ t = t't'', t'' \in V^* \}.$$

Clearly, a set T of trajectories has the m-fairness property if and only if $T \subseteq F_m$.

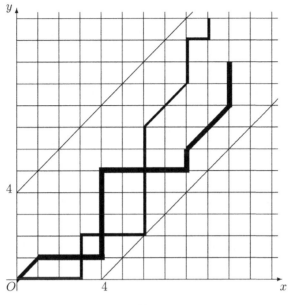

Fig. 2.

We omit the straightforward proof of the following result.

Proposition 6.2. *For every $m \geq 1$, the language F_m is a regular language.*

Corollary 6.1. *Given a context-free set T of trajectories and an integer $m \geq 1$, it is decidable whether or not T has the m-fairness property.*

For our final results, we refer to [3,?,?].

Proposition 6.3. *The fairness property is preserved in the transition to the commutative closure.*

Proposition 6.4. *The fairness property is not preserved in the transition to the associative closure.*

7   Conclusion

We have introduced the notion of a nondeterministic trajectory, and studied its basic properties in the control of the shuffle operation. Our approach has been theoretical. Indeed, ⊔ defines a partial order between words having pleasing properties, [6]. However, the situation is somewhat different in connection with ⊔$_T$, where T is a set of trajectories.

On the practical side, shuffle on nondeterministic trajectories provides a useful tool to the study of a variety of problems in the area of parallel computation and in the theory of concurrency. The method of shuffling words and languages offers a uniform global approach to the problem of finding parallel composition operations.

Another important problem seems to be the problem of parallelization of languages. Not much work has been done in this direction.

One can also investigate problems of parallelization in connection with the Turing complexity classes (time and space). Finding good parallelizations of problems can produce significant improvements with respect to the time and space complexity.

Other aspects from the theory of concurrency and parallel computation, such as priorities, the existence of critical sections, communication, the use of re-entrant routines, can be studied using *semantic constraints* on the shuffle operation. Indeed, these aspects are more related to the inner structure of the words to be shuffled and, therefore, cannot be investigated using only syntactic constraints. We like to emphasize that perhaps the most useful and realistic types of constraints are mixed, that is, apply both syntactic and semantic constraints.

Of special interest is to extend these operations to more complex objects, such as graphs, networks or different types of automata. In this way one could obtain a still more general framework to the study of parallelism and concurrency.

References

1. J.S. Golan, *The Theory of Semirings with Applications in Mathematics and Theoretical Computer Science*, Longman Scientific and Technical, Harlow, Essex, 1992.
2. W. Kuich and A. Salomaa, *Semirings, Automata, Languages*, EATCS Monographs on Theoretical Computer Science, Springer-Verlag, Berlin, 1986.
3. A. Mateescu, "On (Left) Partial Shuffle", *Results and Trends in Theoretical Computer Science*, LNCS 812, Springer-Verlag, (1994) 264 - 278.
4. A. Mateescu and G.D. Mateescu, "Associative Closure and Periodicity of ω-words", RAIRO, Informatique Theorique et Applications, 32, (1998) 153 - 174.
5. A. Mateescu, G. Rozenberg and A. Salomaa, "Shuffle on Trajectories: Syntactic Constraints", Theoretical Computer Science, 197, (1998) 1 - 56. (Fundamental Study)
6. G. Rozenberg and A. Salomaa (Eds.), *Handbook of Formal Languages,* Springer-Verlag, 1997, Vol. 1 - 3.
7. A. Salomaa, *Formal Languages*, Academic Press, New York, 1973.

Binary Patterns in Infinite Binary Words[*]

Antonio Restivo and Sergio Salemi

University of Palermo,Dipartimento di Matematica ed Applicazioni,
Via Archirafi 34, 90123 Palermo, Italy
{restivo,salemi}@dipmat.math.unipa.it

Abstract. In this paper we study the set $P(w)$ of binary patterns that can occur in one infinite binary word w, comparing it with the set $F(w)$ of factors of the word. Since the set $P(w)$ can be considered as an extension of the set $F(w)$, we first investigate how large is such extension, by introducing the parameter $\Delta(w)$ that corresponds to the cardinality of the difference set $P(w) \setminus F(w)$. Some non trivial results about such parameter are obtained in the case of the Thue-Morse and the Fibonacci words. Since, in most cases, the parameter $\Delta(w)$ is infinite, we introduce the pattern complexity of w, which corresponds to the complexity of the language $P(w)$. As a main result, we prove that there exist infinite words that have pattern complexity that grows more quickly than their complexity. We finally propose some problems and new research directions.

1 Introduction

The study of patterns goes back to the beginning of last century with the papers of Axel Thue (cf. [16], [17]) on repetitions on words, repetitions corresponding to *unary* patterns. Such study was extended in [2], and independently in [18], to arbitrary patterns, providing a very general framework for researches on avoidability, i.e. researches concerning words that do not follow, or avoid, certain patterns. An important reference on this topic, including very recent contributions, is [5].

Since the work of Thue, several papers have been devoted to study properties of repetitions occurring in words (cf. [9],[12],[11] for recent contributions on the subject). On the other hand, infinite words have been also studied by investigating properties of the set of their factors. In particular, infinite words can be classified in terms of their *complexity*, i.e. the function that counts, for any positive integer n, the number of factors of length n (cf.[1]).

In the present paper we are interested in the study of the set $P(w)$ of *binary* patterns that occur in a given infinite *binary* word w. Since the alphabet of patterns and that of ordinary words are the same binary alphabet $\{a, b\}$, we can consider the set $F(w)$ of factors of the infinite word w as a subset of the set $P(w)$. Moreover, if w contains a repetition, i.e. it contains as factor a word of

[*] Partially supported by MURST projects: *Bioinformatica e Ricerca Genomica*

W. Brauer et al. (Eds.): Formal and Natural Computing, LNCS 2300, pp. 107–116, 2002.
© Springer-Verlag Berlin Heidelberg 2002

the form v^k, for some $k \geq 2$, then a^k belongs to $P(w)$. In this way, the study of the language $P(w)$ generalizes, at the same time, the study of the factors and that of repetitions occurring in w.

The fact that the language $P(w)$ is an extension of the language $F(w)$ leads to investigate how large is such extension. We start the investigation by analysing what happens for two famous infinite words: the Thue-Morse word w_T and the Fibonacci word w_F. We first report a result of D. Guaiana (cf. Theorem 3) which states that all binary patterns $p \neq aabaa$ (and, by symmetry $p \neq bbabb$) of w_T are factors of w_T, i.e. $P(w_T) \setminus F(w_T) = \{aabaa, bbabb\}$. A similar property does not hold for the Fibonacci word: indeed we prove (cf. Theorem 4) that the language $P(w_F) \setminus F(w_F)$ is infinite. We then introduce, for a given infinite word w, the parameter $\Delta(w) = Card(P(w) \setminus F(w))$, and we pose, in particular, the problem to characterize those infinite words w such that $\Delta(w)$ is finite.

Since, in most cases, the parameter $\Delta(w)$ is infinite, we then introduce the *pattern complexity* of an infinite word w, which is the function that counts, for any positive integer n, the number of elements of $P(w)$ of length n. In comparing complexity and pattern complexity, we show that, for some words w (for instance, for periodic words) the complexity and the pattern complexity have the same rate of growth. However, as a main result, we prove (cf. Corollary 8) that there exist infinite words having pattern complexity that grows more quickly than their complexity. Such a result is obtained as a consequence of a theorem of independent interest (cf. Theorem 7) stating the surprising fact that there exists a *single* Sturmian word that contains as patterns all the factors of *all* Sturmian words.

The results of the present paper show the relevance of the notion of pattern complexity in the study of infinite words. Further problems and new research directions about such a notion are proposed at the end of the paper.

Some of the results of the present paper are reported, without proof, in [15].

2   Factors and Patterns

In order to define patterns, in general one makes use of two distinct alphabets. The first one, A, is the usual alphabet on which ordinary words are constructed. The second alphabet, E, is used in patterns. Its elements are usually called *variables*, and words in E^* are called *patterns*. This distinction is meant to help the understanding of the roles of the different words used. However, in the present paper, we treat a pattern as an ordinary word, and, moreover, we consider only binary alphabets, which amounts to take $A = E = \{a, b\}$.

Given an infinite word $w \in A^\omega$, a finite word $v \in A^*$ is a *factor* of w if there exists a finite word $u \in A^*$ and an infinite word $z \in A^\omega$ such that $w = uvz$. Denote by $F(w)$ the set of factors of the infinite word w.

Given an infinite word $w \in A^\omega$, a finite word $p \in A^*$ *occurs as pattern in w*, or simply *is a pattern of w*, if there exists an *injective* morphism h from A^* into

A^* such that $h(p) \in F(w)$. Denote by $P(w)$ the set of patterns of the infinite word w.

Remark 1. The usual definition of pattern in literature (cf.[6],[5]) only requires that the morphism h is non-erasing. However, in the binary case, if the morphism h is not injective, then the words $h(a)$ and $h(b)$ are both powers of the same word. This leads to some trivial consequences in the case of *repetitive* words. Recall that an infinite word w is repetitive if it contains as factors arbitrarily large powers, i.e. if, for any positive integer n, there exists a finite word u such that $u^n \in F(w)$. If we allow, in the definition of pattern, non-injective morphisms, every words of A^* trivially occurs as pattern in an infinite repetitive word. In order to avoid such trivial cases, we restrict ourselves to injective morphisms.

The language $P(w)$ is not, in general, recursive. In the special case of infinite words that are fixed points of morphisms (cf.[6],[5]), by using some arguments developed in Mignosi and Séébold [13] one can obtain the following result (cf.[4]).

Theorem 2. *Let w be an infinite word that is fixed point of a morphism. Given finite word p, it is decidable whether p is a pattern of w, i.e. whether $p \in P(w)$.*

In the study of the patterns that occur in a given infinite word w, it is of particular interest to investigate the relationships between the set of patterns of w and the set of factors of w. The hypothesis $E = A = \{a, b\}$, implies that $F(w) \subseteq P(w)$, i.e. the language $P(w)$ is an extension of the language $F(w)$. The problem is how large is this extension.

We start our investigation by analysing what happens for two famous infinite words: the Thue-Morse word and the Fibonacci word. These two words are among the most simple obtained as fixed points of morphisms, and still they have endless number of interesting combinatorial properties and are ubiquitous in combinatorics on words.

Recall that the Thue-Morse infinite word

$$w_T = abbabaabbaababbabaababbaabbaba...$$

is the fixed point of the morphism $\mu : a \mapsto ab, b \mapsto ba$. Daniela Guaiana proved in [8] the following surprising result.

Theorem 3. *(D. Guaiana). If p is a binary pattern occurring in the Thue-Morse word w_T such that $p \neq aabaa$ (and, by symmetry, $p \neq bbabb$), then p is a factor of w_T. In other terms:*

$$P(w_T) = F(w_T) \cup \{aabaa, bbabb\}.$$

One can ask the question whether a similar property holds true for the Fibonacci word w_F. Recall that the Fibonacci infinite word

$$w_F = abaababaabaababaababaabaababa...$$

is the fixed point of the morphism $\varphi : a \mapsto ab, b \mapsto a$.

Theorem 4. *There exist infinitely many binary patterns occurring in w_F that are not factors of w_F, i.e.*

$$Card(P(w_F) \setminus F(w_F)) = \infty.$$

Proof. Given a finite word $x = a_1...a_n$, denote by x^R the *reversal* of x, i.e. $x^R = a_n...a_1$. A word x is a *palindrome* if $x = x^R$. By well known properties of the Fibonacci word (cf.[11]) one has that, for all $n \geq 0$:

$$\varphi^{2n+1}(a) = uab \qquad\qquad \text{where } u = u^R \qquad\qquad (1)$$
$$\varphi^{2n+2}(a) = vba \qquad\qquad \text{where } v = v^R \qquad\qquad (2)$$
$$\varphi^{2n+3}(a) = vbauab = uabvab. \qquad\qquad\qquad\qquad\qquad (3)$$

Moreover, from Corollary 28 in [14], one has that

$$bub \ \in \ A^* \setminus F(w_F). \qquad\qquad (4)$$

By taking into account (1) and (2) one derives:

$$\varphi(uab) = \varphi(u)\varphi(ab) = \varphi(u)aba = \varphi(ub)ba.$$

It follows that $v = \varphi(ub)$ and then we can write:

$$av = \varphi(b)\varphi(ub) = \varphi(bub).$$

On the other hand, since v is a palindrome, one has:

$$(va)^R = a(v)^R = av = \varphi(bub).$$

It follows that:

$$va = (\varphi(bub))^R = \tilde{\varphi}((bub)^R) = \tilde{\varphi}(bub),$$

where $\tilde{\varphi} : a \mapsto ba, b \mapsto a$. Since, by equations (3), va is factor of $\varphi^{2n+3}(a)$, and then it is a factor of w_F, one derives that bub is a pattern occurring in w_F. By taking into account (4), one can conclude that $bub \in P(w_F) \setminus F(w_F)$. □

Given an infinite word w, define

$$\Delta(w) = Card(P(w) \setminus F(w)).$$

By previous results, $\Delta(w_T) = 2$ and $\Delta(w_F) = \infty$. Notice that there exist words w such that $\Delta(w) = 0$. It suffices to consider *complete* words, i.e. words such that $F(w) = A^*$.

In the study of the parameter $\Delta(w)$ of an infinite word w, it is of particular interest to consider special families of infinite words, as, for instance, words that are fixed points of morphisms, or words of "low" complexity (and, in particular, words with linear complexity).

Denote by $\mathcal{F}$ the family of binary infinite words that are fixed point of morphisms, and denote by $\mathcal{L}$ the family of binary infinite words that are of linear complexity (see below for a definition of complexity). Previous results lead in a natural way to ask the following questions.

- Does there exist a word w in $\mathcal{F}$ (or in $\mathcal{L}$) such that $\Delta(w) = 0$?
- Does the property $\Delta(w) = 2$ uniquely characterize (among the words in $\mathcal{F}$, or in $\mathcal{L}$) the Thue-Morse word?
- Characterize (among the words in $\mathcal{F}$, or in $\mathcal{L}$) the words w such that $\Delta(w)$ is finite.

Remark 5. Given a factorial language L, denote by $P(L)$ the set of patterns of words in L. With this notation, if w is an infinite word, then $P(w) = P(F(w))$. For any language L over the alphabet $\{a, b\}$, denote by $\overline{L}$ the closure of L by the automorphism interchanging a and b. By definition, $P(L)$ is invariant under such automorphism, i.e. $\overline{P(L)} = P(L)$. There is then a lack of symmetry in comparing, for a given infinite word w over $\{a, b\}$, the languages $F(w)$ and $P(w)$. Indeed $\overline{P(w)} = P(w)$, whereas the same property does not hold, in general, for $F(w)$. One can erroneously suppose that the difference in the behaviours of the Thue-Morse word and the Fibonacci word, stated in Theorem 3 and Theorem 4 respectively, is a consequence of this asymmetry. In fact the set of factors of the Thue-Morse word w_T is invariant under the interchanging of a and b $(\overline{F(w_T)} = F(w_T))$, whereas the same property does not hold for the Fibonacci word $(\overline{F(w_F)} \neq F(w_F))$. However, a minor variation on the arguments used in the proof of Theorem 4 shows that $Card(P(w_F) \setminus \overline{F(w_F)}) = \infty$.

Taking into account previous remark, it appears more appropriate to compare $P(w)$ and $\overline{F(w)}$, and to introduce, together with the parameter $\Delta(w)$, the parameter $\overline{\Delta}(w)$, defined as follows:

$$\overline{\Delta}(w) = Card(P(w) \setminus \overline{F(w)}).$$

One can then reformulate previous problems for the parameter $\overline{\Delta}(w)$.

3   Pattern Complexity

In most cases, the parameter $\Delta(w)$ (the parameter $\overline{\Delta}(w)$, resp.), introduced in the previous section, is infinite. For a more accurate analysis we take then into account the notion of "complexity". Given an infinite word w, its (factor) *complexity* (cf. [1],[6]) is the function

$$f_w(n) = Card(F(w) \cap A^n).$$

In a similar way, we introduce the *pattern complexity* of an infinite word w, that is defined as follows:

$$p_w(n) = Card(P(w) \cap A^n).$$

By the inclusion $F(w) \subseteq P(w)$, one has that $f_w(n) \leq p_w(n)$, for all $n \geq 0$.

In the comparison between factors and patterns, a complete word w, i.e. such that $F(w) = A^*$, corresponds to an extremal case: $\Delta(w) = 0$ and $f_w(n) = p_w(n)$. However complete words also correspond, in some sense, to the *trivial* case. If we leave out such trivial case, an interesting problem, posed in the previous section, is whether there exists an infinite word w such that $\Delta(w) = 0$. In the case of the Thue-Morse word (cf. Theorem 3), "almost all" patterns are factors. In particular, its (factor) complexity $f_{w_T}(n)$ coincides with its pattern complexity $p_{w_T}(n)$, for all $n \neq 5$.

The search for words having "small" difference between complexity and pattern complexity, leads to investigate the case of periodic words. Recall that an infinite word w is *periodic* if $w = v^\omega$, for some finite word v. Remark that, given a periodic word w, in general $\Delta(w) = \infty$. Consider, for instance, the word $w = (abb)^\omega$: one has that $a^2 a^* \cup (ab)^2 (ab)^* \subseteq P(w) \setminus F(w)$. As to concern the complexity, it is well known (cf. [1],[6]) that, if w is periodic, its complexity is upper bounded by a constant. The following proposition shows that the same property holds true for the pattern complexity.

Proposition 6. *If w is an infinite periodic word, then there exists a positive integer K such that $p_w(n) \leq K$, for all $n \geq 0$.*

Proof. By hypothesis, $w = v^\omega$, for some finite word v. We first prove that there exists a finite set H of morphisms from A^* into A^*, such that, if $p \in P(w)$, then $h(p) \in F(w)$, for some $h \in H$. The set H is defined as follows:

$$H = \{h \mid max\{\mid h(a) \mid, \mid h(b) \mid\} \leq \mid v \mid\}.$$

If $p \in P(w)$, then, by definition, there exists a morphism g from A^* into A^* such that $g(a) = (v_1)^n r_1$ and $g(b) = (v_2)^m r_2$, where n, m are non-negative integers, v_1, v_2 are conjugates of the word v, and r_1, r_2 are prefixes of v_1 and v_2 respectively. Consider the morphism $h \in H$, defined as follows: $h(a) = r_1$ and $h(b) = r_2$. It is easy to verify that $h(p) \in F(w)$. As a consequence, since, in our definition of pattern, we take into account only injective morphisms, the number of patterns corresponding to the same element of $F(w)$ is bounded by $Card(H)$. The thesis of the proposition follows then from the fact that the function $f_w(n)$ is upper bounded by a constant. $\square$

One can now ask the question whether there exist infinite words having pattern complexity that grows more quickly than their complexity. An answer is given by analysing non periodic words of minimal complexity, i.e. *Sturmian* words.

Recall (cf. [3]) that a Sturmian word w is, by definition, a word of complexity $f_w(n) = n + 1$. It is well known that there exist infinitely many Sturmian words (actually their set is *uncountable*). Let us denote by St the set of all factors of all Sturmian words, i.e. $v \in St$ iff there exists a Sturmian word w such that $v \in F(w)$. The following theorem states the surprising fact that there exists a *single* Sturmian word that contains as patterns all the factors of all Sturmian words.

Theorem 7. *There exists a Sturmian word z such that $St \subseteq P(z)$.*

In [10] has been explicitly computed the complexity of the language St, i.e. the function $f_{St}(n) = Card(St \cap A^n)$. Moreover it is shown that $f_{St}(n) = \Theta(n^3)$. One derives the following corollary.

Corollary 8. *There exists an infinite word w such that $f_w(n) = n + 1$ and $p_w(n) \geq \Theta(n^3)$.*

In order to prove Theorem 7, let us recall some known facts about Sturmian words (cf. [3]). A special subfamily of the family of Sturmian words is that of *characteristic* Sturmian words, having the property that, for any Sturmian word x, there exists a characteristic Sturmian word y such that $F(x) = F(y)$. So, for the proof of Theorem 7, we can limit ourselves to consider only characteristic Sturmian words.

The characteristic Sturmian words can be constructed by the *standard method*: one defines a family of finite words, called *standard words*, and every characteristic Sturmian word is the limit of a sequence of standard words.

Consider two functions ρ_1 and ρ_2 from $A^* \times A^*$ into $A^* \times A^*$:

$$\rho_1(u, v) = (u, uv)$$

$$\rho_2(u, v) = (vu, v).$$

ρ_1 and ρ_2 are also known as the *Rauzy rules*. Any word $d \in \{1, 2\}^*$ defines recursively a mapping (denoted again by d) as follows:

$$\epsilon(u, v) = (u, v)$$
$$di(u, v) = \rho_i d(u, v) \qquad \text{where } i \in \{1, 2\}.$$

Denote by (u_d, v_d) the pair of words $d(a, b)$. The words u_d, v_d are called *standard words*. The following lemma is an immediate consequence of previous definitions.

Lemma 9. *For $d \in \{1, 2\}^*$ consider a factorization $d = ps$. Let (u_d, v_d), (u_p, v_p), (u_s, v_s) be the pairs of standard words corresponding to d, p and s respectively. Then $u_d = h_p(u_s)$, $v_d = h_p(v_s)$, where h_p denotes the morphism from A^* into A^* defined as follows: $h_p : a \mapsto u_p, b \mapsto v_p$.*

It is well known (cf. [3]) that any characteristic Sturmian word can be obtained as follows. Let $t \in \{1,2\}^\omega$ be an infinite word over the alphabet $\{1,2\}$ and denote by $t(j)$ its prefix of length j. The sequences of standard words $(u_{t(j)})_{j \geq 0}$ and $(v_{t(j)})_{j \geq 0}$ both converge to the same characteristic Sturmian word x. t is called the *rule-sequence* of x and it is denoted by $\delta(x)$.

We are now ready to prove Theorem 7.

Proof of Theorem 7. Let z be a characteristic Sturmian word such that its rule-sequence $\delta(z)$ is a complete word, i.e. $F(\delta(z)) = \{1,2\}^*$. Let w be an arbitrary word in St. This means that there exists a characteristic Sturmian word x such that $w \in F(x)$. We shall prove that $w \in P(z)$. Let $\delta(x) \in \{1,2\}^\omega$ be the rule-sequence of x and denote by d_w the smallest prefix of $\delta(x)$ such that $w \in F(u_{d_w}) \cup F(v_{d_w})$. Suppose that $w \in F(u_{d_w})$ (in the alternative case, the proof is analogous). One can write: $u_{d_w} = u_1 w u_2$. Since $F(\delta(z)) = \{1,2\}^*$, then $d_w \in F(\delta(z))$. It follows that there exists a prefix t_w of $\delta(z)$ such that

$$t_w = p d_w$$

for some word $p \in \{1,2\}^*$. By the Lemma 9, one has

$$u_{t_w} = h_p(u_{d_w}),$$

where $h_p : a \mapsto u_p, b \mapsto v_p$. It follows that

$$u_{t_w} = h_p(u_1 w u_2) = h_p(u_1) h_p(w) h_p(u_2).$$

Since $u_{t_w} \in F(z)$, one has that $w \in P(z)$, i.e. w is a pattern of z. This concludes the proof.   □

4   Concluding Remarks

The results reported in the present paper suggest some new problems and research directions. Most of the problems can be referred to a possible classification of infinite words in terms of the "difference" between the set of its patterns and the set of its factors.

A first interesting problem, related to Corollary 8, is to search for other non trivial infinite words having pattern complexity that grows more quickly than their complexity. In particular, one can ask the question whether there exists an infinite binary word for which the gap between complexity and pattern complexity is exponential.

A more general problem is to develop a classification of infinite words in terms of their pattern complexity. One can, in particular, approach the problem by considering special family of infinite words, as, for instance, words that are fixed points of morphisms. In [7] Ehrenfeucht, Lee and Rozenberg have proved the remarkable results that, for an infinite word that is fixed point of a morphism, the complexity is at most quadratic. As a specific problem, one can ask whether an analogous result holds true by taking into account the pattern complexity.

The results of the present paper and the problems just posed are referred only to the binary case (binary words and binary patterns). Another interesting problem is to develop a generalization for arbitrary alphabets, by introducing the appropriate definitions.

In conclusion, we believe that the notion of pattern complexity can have a relevant role in the study of infinite words and that other results about this notion are still to be discovered.

References

1. Allouche, J.P.: Sur la complexité des suites infinies. Bull. Belg. Math. Soc. **1** (1994) 133–143
2. Bean, D.R., Ehrenfeucht, A., McNulty, G.F.: Avoidable Patterns in Strings of Symbols. Pacific J. Math. **85** (1984) 261–294
3. Berstel, J., Séébold, P.: Sturmian Words. In: Lothaire, M. (Ed.): Algebraic Combinatorics on Words. Chap. 2. Cambridge University Press (2001)
4. Cassaigne, J.: Motifs evitables et regularites dans les mots. These de Doctotat, Universite Paris VI, Report LITP TH 94.04 (1994)
5. Cassaigne, J.: Unavoidable Pattern. In: Lothaire, M. (Ed.): Algebraic Combinatorics on Words. Chap. 3. Cambridge University Press (2001)
6. Choffrut, C., Karhumaki, J.: Combinatorics on Words. In: Rozenberg, G., Salomaa, A. (Eds.) The Handbook of Formal Languages. Springer, Berlin (1997)
7. Ehrenfeucht, A., Lee, K.P., Rozenberg, G.: Subword Complexities of Various Classes of Deterministic Developmental Languages without Interactions. Theoret. Comput. Sci. **1** (1975) 59–75
8. Guaiana, D.: On the Binary Patterns of the Thue-Morse Infinite Word. Internal Report, University of Palermo (1996)
9. Kolpakov, R., Kucherov, G.: On Maximal Repetitions in Words. In: *Proc. 12-th International Symposium on Fundamentals of Computer Science* Lecture Notes in Comput. Sci., Vol. 1684. Springer-Verlag (1999) 374–385
10. Mignosi, F.: On the Number of Factors of Sturmian Words. Theor. Comp. Sci. **82** (1991) 71–84
11. Mignosi, F., Pirillo, G.: Repetitions in the Fibonacci Infinite Word. RAIRO Theoretical Informatics and Applications **26**(3) (1992) 199–204
12. Mignosi, F., Restivo, A.: Periodicity. In: Lothaire, M. (Ed.): Algebraic Combinatorics on Words. Chap. 8. Cambridge University Press (2001)
13. Mignosi, F., Séébold, P.: If a DOL Language Is k-power-free Then It Is Circular. In: *Proc. ICALP'93*, Lecture Notes in Comput. Sci., Vol. 700. Springer-Verlag (1993)
14. Mignosi, F., Restivo, A., Sciortino, M.: Words and Forbidden Factors. Theoret. Comput. Sci., to appear
15. Restivo, A., Salemi, S.: Patterns and Words. In: *Proc. 5th International Conference DLT 2001, Wien, Austria, July 16-21*, Lecture Notes in Comput. Sci., to appear
16. Thue, A.: Über unendliche Zeichenreihen. Kra. Vidensk. Selsk. Skrifter. I. Mat. Nat. Kl., Christiana **7** (1906)

17. Thue, A.: Über die gegenseitige Lage gleicher Teile gewisser Zeichenreihen. Kra. Vidensk. Selsk. Skrifter. I. Mat. Nat. Kl., Christiana **12** (1912)
18. Zimin, A.I.: Blocking Sets of Terms. Math. USSRSb **47** (1979) 353–364

Part II

Graph Transformations

A Sight-seeing Tour of the Computational Landscape of Graph Transformation*

Hans-Jörg Kreowski

University of Bremen, Department of Computer Science
P.O. Box 33 04 40, 28334 Bremen, Germany
kreo@informatik.uni-bremen.de

Abstract. In this paper, the basic features of graph transformation are introduced as a kind of sight-seeing tour of the computational landscape which is based on the application of rules to graphs.

1 Introduction

In this paper, the basic features of graph transformation are introduced as a kind of sight-seeing tour of the computational landscape which is based on the application of rules to graphs. Four selected sites are visited – two known, two unknown.

The first, frequently visited place. A binary relation on graphs is computed by starting from initial graphs and repeating rule applications as long as terminal graphs are derived.

The second, well-known place. The computed relation becomes a function if the derivation process is confluent and the reduced graphs are terminal or if the derivation process is properly regulated.

The third, rather unknown place. The computed relation becomes a function if the derived graphs are re-interpreted as values in a suitable domain. If, for example, a recursive graph language is interpreted as TRUE and its complement as FALSE, then each computed relation can be re-interpreted as a computable test of some graph property. The property holds for an initial graph if it is related to a graph in the given language. Otherwise the test fails.

The fourth, brand-new place. Inspired by genetic algorithms and DNA computing, one may transform sets or multisets of graphs rather than single graphs in a rule-based way. This leads to a novel type of parallel graph transformation by which, for example, NP-complete problems can be solved in a polynomial number of steps.

All the visited places are described in some detail and illustrated by typical examples. But the tour does not provide a complete survey.

---

* This research was partially supported by the EC TMR Network GETGRATS (General Theory of Graph Transformation Systems) and the ESPRIT Working Group APPLIGRAPH (Applications of Graph Transformation).

W. Brauer et al. (Eds.): Formal and Natural Computing, LNCS 2300, pp. 119–137, 2002.

2   Computing Binary Relations on Graphs

One encounters quite a number of graph transformation approaches in the literature that differ from each other with respect to the type of graphs, the kind of rules and the way of rule applications (see [Roz97] for some of the most frequently used approaches). But in all cases, a graph can be derived from a graph by the application of a rule, such that a rule defines a binary relation on graphs. Given a set of rules, one may close the union of these relations under sequential composition and get a description of the effect of a derivation process. As one can see from many examples and other rule-based frameworks like Chomsky grammars and term rewriting, one needs in addition means to identify initial and terminal objects to know where computations may start and stop. Moreover, it is very helpful to provide devices for the regulation of the derivation process. Altogether, this leads to the notion of a transformation unit that encapsulates a set of rules, two graph class expressions to specify initial and terminal graphs, and a control condition. Semantically, such a unit computes a binary relation between initial and terminal graphs. For technical simplicity, transformation units are introduced for a particular type of graphs and rules and a particular way of rule application.

2.1   Graphs, Subgraphs, and Graph Morphisms

Let Σ be a label alphabet.

A *graph* is a system $G = (V, E, F)$ where V is a set of *nodes*, $E \subseteq V \times \Sigma \times V$ is a set of *edges* and $F \subseteq V \times \Sigma$ is a set of *flags*.

If nothing else is said, this is subject to the condition that $(v, a, v') \in E$ implies $v \neq v'$ and $(v', a, v) \in E$. This means that loops are forbidden. A pair of edges (v, a, v') and (v', a, v) may be seen as a single undirected edge labeled with a and incident to v and v'. Accordingly, it will be graphically displayed in the form $\bullet\!\!\overset{a}{\text{---}}\!\!\bullet$. Instead of loops, nodes may have flags, which may be interpreted as node labels. A flag (v, a) is depicted as $\bullet\!\!-\!\!\boxed{a}$.

The components of a graph G may be denoted by V_G, E_G, and F_G, respectively.

The class of all graphs is denoted by $\mathcal{G}_\Sigma$.

G is a *subgraph* of G', denoted by $G \subseteq G'$, if $V \subseteq V'$, $E \subseteq E'$, and $F \subseteq F'$.

Let $G = (V, E, F)$ and $G' = (V', E', F')$ be graphs. Then a mapping $g: V \to V'$ with $(g(v), a, g(v')) \in E'$ for all $(v, a, v') \in E$ and $(g(v), a) \in F'$ for all $(v, a) \in F$ is called *graph morphism* from G to G', denoted by $g: G \to G'$.

Let $g: G \to G'$ be a graph morphism. Then $g(G) = (g(V), g(E), g(F))$ with $g(E) = \{(g(v), a, g(v')) \mid (v, a, v') \in E\}$ and $g(F) = \{(g(v), a) \mid (v, a) \in F\}$ is a subgraph of G'.

2.2   Rules, Direct Derivations, and Derivations

A *rule* r consists of a *left-hand side* graph L, a *right-hand side* graph R, and a set of *gluing nodes* V_K with $V_K \subseteq V_L$ and $V_K \subseteq V_R$. It may be denoted by $r: L \to_{V_K} R$, or $r: L \to R$ if the gluing nodes are clear from the context.

Let $G \in \mathcal{G}_\Sigma$ and $r\colon L \to_{V_K} R$ be a rule. Then r is *applied to* G in the following way:

(i) A matching of L in G is fixed by a graph morphism $g\colon L \to G$,

(ii) $g(L)$ is removed from G up to gluing nodes, leading to

$$Z = (V_G - (g(V_L) - g(V_K)), E_G - g(E_L), F_G - g(F_L)).$$

(iii) R is added to Z by merging the gluing nodes with their images under g, leading to $H = (V_Z + (V_R - V_K), E_Z \cup h(E_R), F_Z \cup h(F_R))$ where $h\colon V_R \to V_H$ is given by $h(v) = g(v)$ for $v \in V_K$ and $h(v) = v$ otherwise.

The constructions in (ii) and (iii) are required to yield graphs. This is denoted by $G \Rightarrow_r H$ and called a *direct derivation* from G to H through r.

Z is a graph (and then a subgraph of G) if and only if the *contact condition* holds, i.e. for each node that is removed, all incident edges and flags are removed too.

Let Z be a graph. Then H is a graph (with subgraph Z) if and only if the *loop condition* holds, i.e. $g(v) \neq g(v')$ for all $(v, a, v') \in E_R$ with $v, v' \in V_K$. Otherwise h would map this edge to a forbidden loop.

In (iii), the set of nodes of the derived graph is defined as the disjoint union of V_Z and $V_R - V_K$, which is only unique up to a renaming of elements. Hence the derived graph is only unique up to isomorphism.

A sequence $G_0 \Rightarrow_{r_1} G_1 \Rightarrow_{r_2} \cdots \Rightarrow_{r_n} G_n$ of direct derivations is a *derivation* from $G = G_0$ to $H = G_n$. The sequence of applied rules $r_1 \cdots r_n$ is called *application sequence*. The number n is the *length*.

Let P be a set of rules with $r_1, \ldots, r_n \in P$. Then the derivation above may be shortly denoted by $G \overset{n}{\underset{P}{\Rightarrow}} H$ or $G \overset{*}{\underset{P}{\Rightarrow}} H$.

2.3 Graph Class Expressions

A *graph class expression* may be any syntactic entity X that specifies a class of graphs $SEM(X) \subseteq \mathcal{G}_\Sigma$.

A typical example is a subset $\Delta \subseteq \Sigma$ with $SEM(\Delta) = \mathcal{G}_\Delta \subseteq \mathcal{G}_\Sigma$. In particular, a special label $* \in \Sigma$ is assumed that is invisible in displayed graphs, i.e. edges carry no label and flags are empty (cf., e.g., the initial graph in Figure 2). This allows one to identify the class $\mathcal{G}$ of unlabeled graphs as a subclass of $\mathcal{G}_\Sigma$. It will be denoted by the expression *unlabeled* with $\mathcal{G} = SEM(unlabeled) = \{G \in \mathcal{G}_{\{*\}} \mid F_G = V \times \{*\}\}$. Similarly, the expression *all nodes* x for $x \in \Sigma$ specifies the class of all graphs G with $F_G = V \times \{x\}$, i.e. all nodes are flagged by x only.

Another famous type of graph class expressions is given by sets of rules. Let P be a set of rules. Then $SEM(P)$ contains all *P-reduced graphs* to which none of the rules in P can be applied.

2.4 Control Conditions

A *control condition* may be any syntactic entity C that cuts the derivation process down.

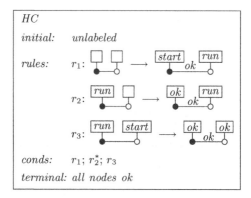

Fig. 1. The transformation unit HC

A typical example is a regular expression over a set of rules (or any other language-defining device). Let C be a regular expression specifying the language $L(C)$. Then a derivation with application sequence s is *permitted* by C if $s \in L(C)$.

In the following, all examples are of this kind except the control condition in Figure 4. There the Kleene star stating that "certain rules are applied as long as one likes" is replaced by an exclamation mark which requires that "the rules are applied as long as possible."

2.5   Transformation Units

A *transformation unit* is a system $tu = (I, P, C, T)$ where I and T are graph class expressions to specify the *initial* and the *terminal* graphs resp., P is a set of rules, and C is a control condition.

Such a transformation unit specifies a binary relation $SEM(tu) \subseteq SEM(I) \times SEM(T)$ that contains a pair of graphs (G, H) if and only if there is a derivation $G \overset{*}{\underset{P}{\Rightarrow}} H$ permitted by C.

Example 2.1.   1. As a first example, a transformation unit HC is specified in Figure 1. The initial graphs of HC are unlabeled, and there are three rules. The first rule takes two adjacent nodes with empty flags and replaces one of these by a *start*-flag, the other by a *run*-flag, and the unlabeled edge by an *ok*-edge. The gluing nodes of this rule and all further sample rules are all nodes that occur in the left-hand side and the right-hand side in the same color. According to the control condition, the first rule must be applied first and then never again. Afterwards the second rule can be applied as often as one likes. It takes the *run*-flagged node and a neighbor with empty flag connected by an unlabeled edge and changes *run* into *ok*, fills the empty flag by *run* and replaces the unlabeled edge by an *ok*-edge. In this way, a path of *ok*-edges is created that never visits a node twice. Eventually, the third

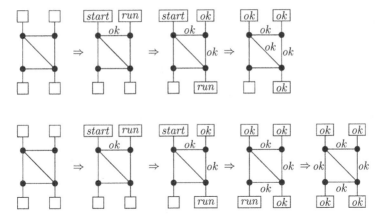

Fig. 2. Two computations of HC

rule must be applied to obtain a permitted derivation. This works only if the *run*-node and the *start*-node are connected by an unlabeled edge. This is labeled with *ok* and *run* and *start* are changed into *ok*, thereby closing a simple cycle of *ok*-edges and *ok*-nodes. The resulting graph is accepted as terminal if all nodes have got *ok*-flags, such that the generated cycle turns out to be a Hamiltonian one. The two derivations shown in Figure 2 illustrate this. While both start in the same initial graph, the first derivation produces a cycle of length 3 and the second one a cycle of length 4. Only the derived graph of the second derivation is terminal because all nodes have *ok*-flags.

Altogether, the semantic relation of HC is characterized in the following way: $(G, H) \in SEM(HC)$ if and only if G is unlabeled, H equals G if *ok* is changed into $*$ wherever it occurs, $H \in SEM(all\ nodes\ ok)$, and the *ok*-edges form a Hamiltonian cycle. In other words, HC computes all Hamiltonian cycles of all input graphs.

2. In a quite similar way, the transformation unit HP shown in Figure 3 computes all Hamiltonian paths of all unlabeled graphs.

3. The third example, see Figure 4, does something different. Again computations start in unlabeled graphs, and again the first rule must be applied first and never again. The left-hand side is empty, such that it matches trivially and the right-hand side is added disjointly. This is the "handle" consisting of a path of length two. The two outer nodes are flagged with A and B resp., the inner node is C-flagged. Now the control condition requires $(r_2|r_3)!$. This is a modified regular expression where the Kleene-$*$ is replaced by ! meaning that the rules r_2 and r_3 must be applied as long as possible rather than as long as one likes. The rule r_2 connects the A-node with nodes that have empty flags (this is all initial nodes) and fills the flags by 1. The rule r_2 does the same with the B-node and the nodes with 1-flags, changing the latter into 2. In this way the new A-node and B-node become connected by edges with all original initial nodes. At the end, all flags are emptied.

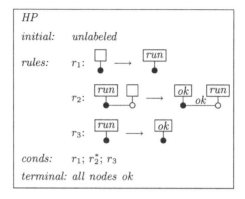

Fig. 3. The transformation unit *HP*

4. The significance of the construction is the following. If the initial graph has got a Hamiltonian path, it can be completed to a Hamiltonian cycle of the corresponding terminal graph by going from the ends of the path to the *A*-node and the *B*-node resp. and closing the cycle by passing the *C*-node. Conversely, if one removes the three added nodes from a Hamiltonian cycle of a graph derived by a permitted derivation, one gets a Hamiltonian path in the initial graph of this derivation.

   The kind of rule application introduced above is a variant of the double-pushout approach (see, e.g., [CMR+97]). But a direct derivation is not characterized explicitly as a double pushout because this fact is not used in this paper. The notion of a transformation unit has been introduced in [KKS97, KK99a, KK99b] as a structuring concept for graph transformation systems. Here the structuring

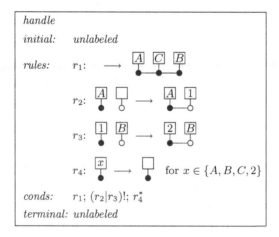

Fig. 4. The transformation unit *handle*

component is omitted and the computational aspect is emphasized. In addition to the cited papers, one can find more about graph class expressions and control conditions in [Kus00a, Kus00b].

It should be noted that a direct derivation can be constructed in polynomial time. To find a graph morphism $g: L \to G$, one may have to check all mappings from V_L to V_G in the worst case. But this is polynomially bounded if the set of rules is finite and fixed. All the rest of the construction can be done in linear time. If the form of the host graph and the rule are appropriate, a direct derivation can be performed in linear or even constant time as the examples above demonstrate.

Using the effective construction of direct derivations, where the disjoint union of sets of nodes is explicitly chosen in some appropriate way, the semantic relation $SEM(tu)$ of a transformation unit $tu = (I, P, C, T)$ is recursively enumerable if $SEM(I)$ is recursively enumerable and $SEM(T)$ and the control condition are decidable. $SEM(tu)$ can be computed as follows:

(i) Enumerate the graphs of $SEM(I)$.
(ii) For each $G \in SEM(I)$, enumerate all derivations starting in G together with their application sequences.
(iii) For each derived graph $\overline{G}$, check whether $\overline{G} \in SEM(T)$ or not.
(iv) If yes, check whether the respective application sequence belongs to $L(C)$.
(v) If yes, put $(G, \overline{G})$ into $SEM(tu)$.

Altogether, graph transformation as introduced provides a computational framework for binary relations on graphs.

Habel and Plump [HP01] have recently shown that a similar kind of graph transformation approach is computationally complete. Litovsky and Métivier (together with various coauthors) [LM93, LMS95, MS97, LMS98, BM98, LMS99] have advocated the usefulness of a special type of graph transformation (so-called graph relabeling) as a suitable framework to study various kinds of graph algorithms.

3   Computing Functions

As most rule-based frameworks, graph transformation is nondeterministic in general because various rules may match in various places such that the next derivation step is rarely uniquely determined. This is fine if one wants to compute a nondeterministic relation. Many games like chess, go, solitaire, etc. are of this kind; they would be awfully boring if one never had any choice. Language generation is of this kind where a single initial object should allow to derive usually infinitely many items. But if one wants to compute a function, nondeterminism can be a nuisance. Graph algorithms, for instance, are often required to be functional. How long is the shortest path from A to B? How much is the sum of distances of a minimum spanning tree? How many nodes have odd degree? In particular, decision problems ask for either "yes" or "no," and not for "yes and no" or "neither yes nor no."

There are at least three ways to deal with functional behavior within a nondeterministic framework.

Required Functionality. In the same way a nondeterministic Turing machine can compute a (partial) function, one may just require that the semantic relation of a transformation unit be a function.

Let $tu = (I, P, C, T)$ be a transformation unit and $f: SEM(I) \to SEM(T)$ be a (partial) function. Then tu *computes* f if $SEM(tu) = f$.

This is easily defined, but has some disadvantages. As graph transformation provides a general computational approach, it is undecidable whether a transformation unit computes a function or not. Moreover, even if a function is computed, there may be derivations that never end in a terminal graph but in a deadlock, or can be prolonged ad infinitum.

Regulated Functionality. One may use the control conditions to get a functional behavior of transformation units. A possibility is that the control condition restricts the derivation process such that a derivation starting in an initial graph and being the prefix of a permitted derivation can be prolonged in only one way. For example, the rules may be ordered, and if a rule has several matches in a graph, they may be ordered too in some way. Then the computation can be done according to these orders by applying always the smallest rule with its smallest match. In other words, evaluation strategies can be applied in the framework of graph transformation that correspond to the basic ideas how functional or logical programs or systems of recursive equations are interpreted in a deterministic way. It is beyond the scope of this paper to follow this line of consideration.

Termination and Confluence. It is well known and often used at least in the area of term rewriting that a binary relation $R \subseteq A \times A$ for some set A has unique reduced normal forms if it is terminating and confluent. Clearly, this can be applied to the derivation process of a transformation unit. But to make it more useful, one should take the control conditions into account as is done in the following.

Definition 3.1. Let $tu = (I, P, C, T)$ be a transformation unit.

1. Let $G \in SEM(I)$. Let $G \overset{*}{\underset{P}{\Rightarrow}} G'$ and $G' \overset{*}{\underset{P}{\Rightarrow}} G''$ be derivations with application sequences s and s' resp. Let $L(C)$ be the language specified by C and $Prefix(L(C))$ its prefix closure, i.e.

$$Prefix(L(C)) = \{u \mid uv \in L(C) \text{ for some } v\}.$$

   Then $G \overset{*}{\underset{P}{\Rightarrow}} G'$ is called a *permitted prefix* if $s \in Prefix(L(C))$, and $G' \overset{*}{\underset{P}{\Rightarrow}} G''$ a *permitted prolongation* of the prefix $G \overset{*}{\underset{P}{\Rightarrow}} G'$ if $ss' \in Prefix(L(C))$.
2. Graphs that are derived by permitted prefixes are also called *permitted*. The class of permitted graphs is denoted by $Permit(tu)$.
3. A graph G' is called tu-*reduced* if it is permitted and each permitted prolongation $G' \overset{*}{\underset{P}{\Rightarrow}} G''$ has length 0, i.e. there is no proper permitted prolongation starting in G'.

4. tu is *terminating* if, for each initial graph $G \in SEM(I)$, there is an upper bound $b(G) \in \mathbb{N}$ such that $n \leq b(G)$ for each permitted prefix $G \underset{P}{\overset{n}{\Rightarrow}} G'$. The function $b\colon SEM(I) \to \mathbb{N}$ given in this way is called *termination bound*.

5. tu is *confluent* if, for each initial graph $G \in SEM(I)$ and each two permitted prefixes $G \underset{P}{\overset{*}{\Rightarrow}} G_1$ and $G \underset{P}{\overset{*}{\Rightarrow}} G_2$, there are two permitted prolongations $G_1 \underset{P}{\overset{*}{\Rightarrow}} \overline{G}$ and $G_2 \underset{P}{\overset{*}{\Rightarrow}} \overline{G}$ for some graph $\overline{G}$.

It is not difficult to show the following result.

Observation 3.2. Let $tu = (I, P, C, T)$ be a transformation unit.

1. Let $val\colon Permit(tu) \to \mathbb{N}$ be a valuation function with $val(G') > val(G'')$ for each permitted prolongation $G' \underset{P}{\Rightarrow} G''$. Then tu is terminating.

2. Let $SEM(T)$ consist of tu-reduced graphs, and let tu be confluent. Then $SEM(tu)$ is a partial function from $SEM(I)$ to $SEM(T)$.

3. Let tu be terminating and confluent. Let $G \in SEM(I)$, and $SEM(T)$ consist of tu-reduced graphs. Then there is a unique tu-reduced graph $\overline{G}$ such that each permitted prefix $G \underset{P}{\overset{*}{\Rightarrow}} G'$ can be prolonged by a permitted prolongation $G' \underset{P}{\overset{*}{\Rightarrow}} \overline{G}$. Moreover, $(G, \overline{G}) \in SEM(tu)$ if $\overline{G} \in SEM(T)$, and $SEM(tu)$ is undefined for G otherwise.

Remark. This tu-reduced normal form of G can be constructed inductively in the following way:

- Start with $G_0 = G$.
- Assume that $G_0 \underset{P}{\Rightarrow} \cdots \underset{P}{\Rightarrow} G_i$ is already constructed accordingly.
- Then either G_i is tu-reduced, and one is done. Or there is a permitted prolongation $G_i \underset{P}{\Rightarrow} G_{i+1}$.

This procedure stops after a finite number of steps because tu is terminating.

Proof (of Observation 3.2).

1. Because $\lambda \in Prefix(L(C))$, $G \underset{P}{\overset{0}{\Rightarrow}} G$ for $G \in SEM(I)$ is a permitted prefix. Therefore, $SEM(I) \subseteq Permit(tu)$ such that one may choose $b(G) = val(G)$. Consider now a permitted prefix $G = G_0 \underset{P}{\Rightarrow} G_1 \underset{P}{\Rightarrow} \cdots \underset{P}{\Rightarrow} G_n$. Then $G_i \in Permit(tu)$ and $val(G_{i+1}) > val(G_i)$ for $i = 1, \ldots, n$. As $val(G) = val(G_0)$ and $val(G_n) \geq 0$, this implies $n \leq val(G) = b(G)$.

2. Let $G \in SEM(I)$ and $G_1, G_2 \in SEM(T)$ with $(G, G_1), (G, G_2) \in SEM(tu)$. Then there are permitted derivations $G \underset{P}{\overset{*}{\Rightarrow}} G_1$ and $G \underset{P}{\overset{*}{\Rightarrow}} G_2$, which are in particular permitted prefixes.
   Because tu is confluent, there are permitted prolongations $G_1 \underset{P}{\overset{*}{\Rightarrow}} \overline{G}$ and $G_2 \underset{P}{\overset{*}{\Rightarrow}} \overline{G}$ for some graph $\overline{G}$. By assumption, G_1 and G_2 are tu-reduced such that both these derivations have length 0. In other words, $G_1 = \overline{G} = G_2$.

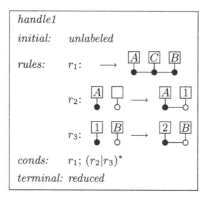

Fig. 5. The transformation unit *handle1*

3. Using the procedure in the remark above, there is always a permitted prefix $G \overset{*}{\underset{P}{\Rightarrow}} \overline{G}$ for some *tu*-reduced graph $\overline{G}$. Due to Point 2 of the observation, any other permitted prefix $G \overset{*}{\underset{P}{\Rightarrow}} G'$ can be prolonged to $G' \overset{*}{\underset{P}{\Rightarrow}} G''$ together with a prolongation $\overline{G} \overset{*}{\underset{P}{\Rightarrow}} G''$. Because $\overline{G}$ is *tu*-reduced, one gets $G'' = \overline{G}$. If $\overline{G} \in SEM(T)$, it follows $(G, \overline{G}) \in SEM(tu)$ by definition. Conversely, if $(G, \overline{\overline{G}}) \in SEM(tu)$, there is a permitted derivation $G \overset{*}{\underset{P}{\Rightarrow}} \overline{\overline{G}}$ with $\overline{\overline{G}} \in SEM(T)$. Then $\overline{G} = \overline{\overline{G}}$. And hence $SEM(tu)$ is undefined for G if $\overline{G} \notin SEM(T)$.   □

Example 3.1. Consider the transformation unit *handle1* in Figure 5. According to the control condition, derivations are permitted where r_1 is applied in the first step, and r_2 and r_3 are applied in all the following steps. The prefix closure of these permitted derivations contains the derivations of initial graphs of length 0 in addition. Consider now the valuation function that counts nodes with the empty flag twice, nodes with a 1-flag once, and adds 1 if there is no A-flag around. Hence the application of r_1 to an unlabeled graph reduces the valuation by 1. If r_2 is applied, one node changes an empty flag into a 1-flag. If r_3 is applied, then a 1-flag is replaced by a 2-flag. All other flags are unchanged such that again the valuation decreases in both cases. Altogether, *handle1* is terminating.

It is also easy to see that *handle1* is confluent. The rule r_1 can be applied at the beginning only, with a unique result. The rule r_2 is applicable as long as there are empty flags. Because all nodes have empty flags at the beginning, they get connected with the A-flagged node while the empty flags are replaced by 1-flags. The rule r_3 is applicable as long as there are 1-flags. If the 1-flags are replaced by 2-flags, all original nodes get connected to the B-flagged nodes. Therefore, there is always a unique reduced result, independent of the order in which the rules r_2 and r_3 are applied.

Similarly, one can show that the transformation unit *handle2* in Figure 6 computes a partial function that is defined in particular on graphs with A-, B-,

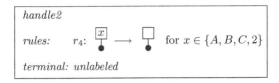

Fig. 6. The transformation unit *handle2*

C-, and 2-flags only, such as the results of *handle1*. Obviously, the composition of the functions computed by *handle1* and *handle2* is a total function on unlabeled graphs that coincides with the semantic relation of the transformation unit *handle*.

It should be noted that the control condition of *handle1* plays an important role. If rule r_1 could be applied in an unregulated way, the transformation unit would neither be terminating nor confluent and had no reduced graphs. This illustrates that it is very important to deal with permitted prefixes rather than arbitrary derivations.

Termination and confluence have been studied in the context of graph transformation and term graph rewriting by Plump [Plu93, Plu98, Plu99]. For regulated rewriting of term graphs, see also [SPvE93]. Moreover, various aspects of confluence have been investigated for various graph transformation approaches by many authors (see [CMR+97, EHK+97, EKMR99]).

4   Solving Decision Problems

In this section, a further way to compute functions within a nondeterministic framework is considered. If terminal graphs are interpreted as values of another suitable domain, this interpretation may turn the semantic relation of a transformation unit into a function. The idea applies in particular to the domain of truth values {TRUE, FALSE}. A terminating transformation unit solves a decision problem if terminal graphs are interpreted as TRUE (and an initial graph that does not derive into a terminal graph yields FALSE). Such a problem belongs to the class *NP* if the termination bound is polynomial in the size of the initial graphs.

Definition 4.1. Let $tu = (I, P, C, T)$ be a terminating transformation unit with the termination bound $b: SEM(I) \to \mathbb{N}$.

1. A function $d: SEM(I) \to \{\text{TRUE}, \text{FALSE}\}$ is called a *decision problem*.
2. *tu computes* (or *solves*) d if the following holds for all $G \in SEM(T)$:

$$d(G) = \text{TRUE} \text{ if and only if } (G, \overline{G}) \in SEM(tu) \text{ for some } \overline{G} \in SEM(T).$$

   This is denoted by $COMP(tu) = d$.

3. *tu* is called *polynomial* if there is a polynom p such that, for all $G \in SEM(I)$, $b(G) \le p(size(G))$ where $size(G)$ is the number of nodes of G, and if the membership problem of $SEM(T)$ can be solved in polynomial time.
4. The class of all decision problems that are solved by polynomial transformation units is denoted by NP_{GT}.

Remarks. 1. If *tu* is terminating, there is only a finite number of permitted prefixes $G \overset{*}{\underset{P}{\Rightarrow}} G'$ for each $G \in SEM(I)$. Hence, it can be checked effectively whether a terminal graph is derived or not.
2. All explicit examples of graph class expressions in Point 2.3 of Section 2 specify obviously graph languages with polynomial membership problems.
3. The computational framework given by terminating and polynomial transformation units in particular is still nondeterministic because there may be a permitted prefix $G \overset{*}{\underset{P}{\Rightarrow}} G'$ with a *tu*-reduced graph G', but $G' \notin SEM(T)$, and also a permitted derivation $G \overset{*}{\underset{P}{\Rightarrow}} \overline{G}$ with $\overline{G} \in SEM(T)$. In the polynomial case, it takes polynomial time to build up a single permitted prefix and to check whether its derived graph is terminal or not. Both points together justify the denotation NP_{GT}. The same reasoning shows that a decision problem $d: SEM(I) \to \{\text{TRUE}, \text{FALSE}\}$ which is solved by a polynomial transformation unit belongs to the class of *NP*-problems if one ignores that $SEM(I)$ is a set of graphs while *NP*-problems have sets of words as input domain. Nevertheless, the result may be stated explicitly.

Observation 4.2. $NP_{GT} \subseteq NP$.

It is beyond the scope of this paper to prove that also the converse inclusion holds because the proof requires quite a technical machinery. But the idea is simple. One simulates the computational steps of a Turing machine by the application of graph transformation rules.

That graph transformation provides a framework to study *NP*-problems is also illustrated by the following example.

Example 4.1. 1. In Example 3.1 it is shown that *handle1* is terminating with the termination bound $2 \cdot size(G) + 1$ such that *handle1* turns out to be polynomial. Because the rule r_4 can be applied to each node at most four times (emptying the flags A, B, C, and 2), *handle2* is also polynomial. This implies that also the transformation unit *handle* in Example 2.1 is polynomial because its longest permitted derivations are sequential compositions of permitted derivations of *handle1* and *handle2*. Together with the reasoning in Example 3.1, *handle* specifies a polynomial function on unlabeled graphs. Accordingly, *handle*(G) denotes the unique graph $\overline{G}$ with $(G, \overline{G}) \in SEM(handle)$ for each unlabeled graph G.
2. The transformation unit *HP* in Example 2.1 is polynomial because the rules r_1 and r_3 are applied only once and the rule r_2 $(size(G) - 2)$ times at most. The reasoning in 2.1.1 shows that *HC* decides whether a given unlabeled

graph is Hamiltonian, i.e. has a Hamiltonian cycle, or not. Let $hc\colon \mathcal{G} \to \{$TRUE, FALSE$\}$ be defined by $hc(G) =$ TRUE if there is a Hamiltonian cycle in G and $hc(G) =$ FALSE otherwise. Then we have $COMP(HC) = hc$.

Similarly, HP in 2.1.2 is also polynomial and solves the decision problem hp that tests an unlabeled graph for a Hamiltonian path, this is $COMP(HP) = hp$.

In other words, $hc, hp \in NP_{GT}$. Moreover, it is shown in 2.1.4 that $hp(G) =$ TRUE if and only if $hc(handle(G)) =$ TRUE for all unlabeled graphs G. This means that $handle$ provides a reduction of the Hamiltonian-path problem to the Hamiltonian-cycle problem. The fact is quite well known in the area of graph algorithms. But it may be interesting to know that graph transformation constitutes a framework that allows one such considerations in a systematic way.

5   Graph Multiset Transformation

In this section, a new type of graph transformation, called graph multiset transformation, is introduced that is inspired by the concepts of genetic algorithms and DNA computing (see, e.g., [Adl94, PRS98]). Adleman's seminal experiment demonstrates how combinatorial problems may be solved using DNA. Roughly speaking, a tube is filled with certain quantities of properly chosen DNA strands. Then their reactions according to the Watson–Crick complementarity produces DNA molecules, a selection of which represents solutions. Similarly, a genetic algorithm transforms a "population of individuals" step by step into one of "fitter" individuals by means of "mutation," "cross-over," and "selection." If, for example, the individuals are solutions of an optimization problem that differ from the optimum, then the genetic algorithm may yield solutions that are closer to or even meet the optimum. Replacing tubes of molecules and populations of individuals by multisets of graphs, and chemical reactions and evolution by operations by rule applications, one gets the concept of graph multiset transformation.

It is based on ordinary graph transformation. The underlying data structures are finite multisets of graphs. In each derivation step, some of the graphs of a given actual multiset are directly derived into graphs by applying ordinary rules, yielding a new actual multiset where the deriving graphs are replaced by the derived ones. This idea is formalized in the following way. The notions and notations of multisets are recalled in the Appendix.

Definition 5.1. Let P be a set of rules. Let $M\colon \mathcal{G}_\Sigma \to \mathbb{N}$ be a finite multiset of graphs and $M' \leq M$ a multi-subset of M. Let $G_1 \cdots G_n \in Perm(M')$ be one of the sequential representations of M' and $G'_1 \cdots G'_n \in \mathcal{G}^*_\Sigma$ be another sequence of graphs with $G_i \underset{P}{\Rightarrow} G'_i$ for all $i = 1, \ldots, n$. Let $M'' = MS(G'_1 \cdots G'_n)$ be the multiset of $G'_1 \cdots G'_n$.

Then M *directly derives* the graph multiset $\overline{M} = M - M' + M''$, denoted by $M \underset{P}{\Rightarrow} \overline{M}$.

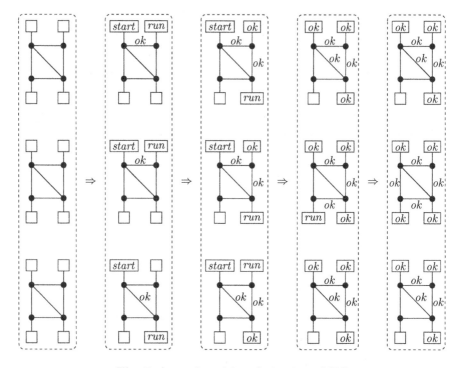

Fig. 7. A graph multiset derivation of HC

Remarks.   1. Note that the derived multiset does not depend on the choice of
the sequential representation of M' because each permutation of $G_1 \cdots G_n$
corresponds to the respective permutation of $G'_1 \cdots G'_n$ and the multisets of
sequences are invariant with respect to permutation.

2. A sequence $M_0 \underset{P}{\Rightarrow} M_1 \underset{P}{\Rightarrow} \cdots \underset{P}{\Rightarrow} M_n$ of direct derivations of multisets of graphs
defines a *(graph multiset) derivation* from $M = M_0$ to $\overline{M} = M_n$ of length n in
the usual way. Such derivations are shortly denoted by $M \underset{P}{\overset{n}{\Rightarrow}} \overline{M}$ or $M \underset{P}{\overset{*}{\Rightarrow}} \overline{M}$.

Example 5.1. Using the rules of the transformation unit HC in Example 2.1.1,
Figure 7 shows a graph multiset derivation starting from three copies of the same
graph and deriving a multiset of three graphs in four steps.

It is easy to see that graph multiset derivations correspond to derivations
of the graphs in the multisets and that therefore the lengths of graph multiset derivations are bounded if and only if the lengths of graph derivations are
bounded.

Observation 5.2.   1. Let $M \underset{P}{\overset{*}{\Rightarrow}} \overline{M}$ be   a   graph   multiset   derivation   and
$G_1 \cdots G_n \in Perm(M)$ a sequential representation of M. Then there is a
sequence $\overline{G_1} \cdots \overline{G_n} \in Perm(\overline{M})$ such that $G_i \underset{P}{\overset{*}{\Rightarrow}} \overline{G_i}$ for all $i = 1, \ldots, n$.

2. Let $G_1 \cdots G_n, \overline{G_1} \cdots \overline{G_n} \in \mathcal{G}_\Sigma^*$ be sequences of graphs with $G_i \underset{P}{\overset{*}{\Rightarrow}} \overline{G_i}$ for all $i = 1, \ldots, n$. Then $MS(G_1 \cdots G_n) \underset{P}{\overset{*}{\Rightarrow}} MS(\overline{G_1} \cdots \overline{G_n})$.

3. Let M be a multiset of graphs and $b \in \mathbb{N}$. Then the following hold. If $M \underset{P}{\overset{k}{\Rightarrow}} \overline{M}$ implies $k \leq b$, then, for all $G \in car(M)$, $G \underset{P}{\overset{l}{\Rightarrow}} \overline{G}$ implies $l \leq b$.

   And, conversely, if $G \underset{P}{\overset{l}{\Rightarrow}} \overline{G}$ implies $l \leq b$ for all $G \in car(M)$, then there is a constant c such that $M \underset{P}{\overset{k}{\Rightarrow}} \overline{M}$ implies $k \leq c \cdot b$.

This means that graph multiset transformation is a kind of parallel graph transformation that has the same termination properties as ordinary graph transformation discussed above. Therefore, graph multiset transformation can be used as a computational framework similarly to graph transformation. In particular, a terminating transformation unit can solve a decision problem on its initial graphs by means of graph multiset transformation. The computation starts with multiple copies of an initial graph and yields TRUE if some terminal graph occurs in one of the derived multisets. Decision problems that are solved by polynomial transformation units form the class P_{GMST}. The idea is that the lengths of graph multiset derivations are polynomially bounded and that TRUE is computed in a single derivation with high probability if the multiplicity of the initial graph is chosen large enough.

Definition 5.3. Let $tu = (I, P, C, T)$ be a terminating transformation unit. Let $d \colon SEM(I) \to \{\text{TRUE}, \text{FALSE}\}$ be a decision problem.

Then tu *computes* d *by graph multiset transformation* (GMST) if the following holds.

For each $G \in SEM(I)$, there are a multiset M_G with carrier set $car(M_G) = \{G\}$, a graph multiset derivation $M_G \underset{P}{\overset{*}{\Rightarrow}} \overline{M}$ the underlying derivations of which are permitted, and a graph $\overline{G} \in car(\overline{M}) \cap SEM(T)$ if and only if $d(G) = \text{TRUE}$.

Remarks. 1. If tu computes d by graph multiset transformation, this may be denoted by $d = COMP_{GMST}(tu)$.
2. P_{GMST} denotes the set of all decision problems that are computed by polynomial transformation units.
3. If tu is polynomial and G an initial graph, the number of permitted derivations starting in G is bounded by a number exponential in the size of G. If now the multiplicity of G in M_G is chosen larger and the derivation $M_G \underset{P}{\overset{*}{\Rightarrow}} \overline{M}$ is long, the probability is high that most permitted derivations starting in G occur in $M_G \underset{P}{\overset{*}{\Rightarrow}} \overline{M}$. Therefore the probability is high to find the proper value of $d(G)$ in a single graph multiset derivation with a polynomial number of steps. This justifies the denotation P_{GMST}.

As a first result on polynomial graph multiset transformation and as the main result of this section, one can show that the classes NP_{GT} and P_{GMST} coincide.

Theorem 5.4. $NP_{GT} = P_{GMST}$.

Proof. $d \in NP_{GT}$ means that there is a polynomial transformation unit $tu = (I, P, C, T)$ with $COMP(tu) = d$. By definition, the following holds for all $G \in SEM(I)$: $d(G) = \text{TRUE}$ if and only if there is a derivation $G \overset{*}{\underset{P}{\Rightarrow}} \overline{G}$ with $\overline{G} \in SEM(T)$. This derivation induces a graph multiset derivation $MS(G) \overset{*}{\underset{P}{\Rightarrow}} MS(\overline{G})$ according to the observation above. Because $car(MS(G)) = \{G\}$ and $\overline{G} \in car(MS(\overline{G})) = \{\overline{G}\}$ and hence $\overline{G} \in car(MS(\overline{G})) \cap SEM(T)$, one gets that $d(G) = \text{TRUE}$ if and only if there is a derivation $M_G \overset{*}{\underset{P}{\Rightarrow}} \overline{M}$ with $M_G = MS(G)$ and $\overline{M} = MS(\overline{G})$ and there is a graph $\overline{G}$ with $\overline{G} \in car(\overline{M}) \cap SEM(T)$. In other words, $d = COMP_{GMST}(tu)$ and, hence, $d \in P_{GMST}$.

Conversely, let $d \in P_{GMST}$, this is $d = COMP_{GMST}(tu)$ for some polynomial transformation unit $tu = (I, P, C, T)$. By definition, this means for all $G \in SEM(I)$ that $d(G) = \text{TRUE}$ if and only if there are a graph multiset derivation $M_G \overset{*}{\underset{P}{\Rightarrow}} \overline{M}$ with $car(M_G) = \{G\}$ and $\overline{G} \in car(\overline{M}) \cap SEM(T)$. Due to the observation above, this induces a derivation $G \overset{*}{\underset{P}{\Rightarrow}} \overline{G}$. Because $\overline{G} \in SEM(T)$, it follows that $d = COMP(tu)$ and, hence, $d \in NP_{GT}$.   □

The very first considerations on graph multiset transformation are somewhat straightforward. Further research is needed to see the significance and usefulness in a brighter light. For example, the rule application may be supplemented by a copying mechanism (like the polymerase chain reaction for DNA molecules). Then a next derivation step may continue from $M + M$ if the multiset M is formerly derived. This would allow to start the computation from a small number of copies of the initial graphs rather than from a large number.

6   Conclusion

In this paper, four selected sites of the computational landscape of graph transformation have been visited. Two of them are quite frequented: the computation of a binary relation of initial and terminal graphs by iterated rule application on one hand, and the restriction of this computation in a functional way by means of regulated rewriting like confluence and termination on the other hand. The other two sites are new. The computed binary relation on graphs solves a decision problem on graphs if all derivations terminate and the derivability of terminal graphs means that the property holds. This allows in particular to identify a graph-transformational counterpart of the class NP and provides a framework to study NP-completeness in a systematic way. Finally, graph multiset transformation has been introduced as a new type of parallel graph transformation. It has been easy to see that NP-problems with graph-transformational solutions can be solved by means of graph multiset transformation in a polynomial number of steps with arbitrarily high probability.

Future research will show whether this new framework given by graph transformation and graph multiset transformation allows one to shed more light on the mysteries of the class NP.

Acknowledgement

I would like to thank Frank Drewes, Renate Klempien-Hinrichs and the anonymous referee for their valuable hints and comments on the draft version of this paper.

References

[Adl94]   L.M. Adleman. Molecular Computation of Solutions to Combinatorial Problems. *Science*, 226:1021–1024, 1994.

[BM98]   Anne Bottreau and Yves Métivier. Minor Searching, Normal Forms of Graph Relabelling: Two Applications Based on Enumerations by Graph Relabelling. In M. Nivat, Editor, *Proc. Foundations of Software Science and Computation Structures (FoSSaCS'98)*, volume 1378 of *Lecture Notes in Computer Science*, pages 110–124. Springer, 1998.

[CMR⁺97]   Andrea Corradini, Ugo Montanari, Francesca Rossi, Hartmut Ehrig, Reiko Heckel, and Michael Löwe. Algebraic Approaches to Graph Transformation – Part I: Basic Concepts and Double Pushout Approach. In Rozenberg [Roz97], chapter 3, pages 163–245.

[EEKR99]   Hartmut Ehrig, Gregor Engels, Hans-Jörg Kreowski, and Grzegorz Rozenberg, Editors. *Handbook of Graph Grammars and Computing by Graph Transformation, Vol. 2: Applications, Languages and Tools*. World Scientific, Singapore, 1999.

[EHK⁺97]   Hartmut Ehrig, Reiko Heckel, Martin Korff, Michael Löwe, Leila Ribeiro, and Annika Wagner. Algebraic Approaches to Graph Transformation – Part II: Single Pushout Approach and Comparison with Double Pushout Approach. In Rozenberg [Roz97], chapter 4, pages 247–312.

[EKMR99]   Hartmut Ehrig, Hans-Jörg Kreowski, Ugo Montanari, and Grzegorz Rozenberg, Editors. *Handbook of Graph Grammars and Computing by Graph Transformation, Vol. 3: Concurrency, Parallelism, and Distribution*. World Scientific, Singapore, 1999.

[HP01]   Annegret Habel and Detlef Plump. Computational Completeness of Programming Languages Based on Graph Transformation. In F. Honsell and M. Miculan, Editors, *Proc. Foundations of Software Science and Computation Structures (FoSSaCS 2001)*, volume 2030 of *Lecture Notes in Computer Science*, pages 230–245. Springer, 2001.

[KK99a]   Hans-Jörg Kreowski and Sabine Kuske. Graph Transformation Units and Modules. In Ehrig et al. [EEKR99], pages 607–638.

[KK99b]   Hans-Jörg Kreowski and Sabine Kuske. Graph Transformation Units with Interleaving Semantics. *Formal Aspects of Computing*, 11(6):690–723, 1999.

[KKS97]   Hans-Jörg Kreowski, Sabine Kuske, and Andy Schürr. Nested Graph Transformation Units. *International Journal on Software Engineering and Knowledge Engineering*, 7(4):479–502, 1997.

[Kus00a]   Sabine Kuske. More about Control Conditions for Transformation Units. In H. Ehrig, G. Engels, H.-J. Kreowski, and G. Rozenberg, Editors, *Proc. Theory and Application of Graph Transformations (TAGT'98)*, volume 1764 of *Lecture Notes in Computer Science*, pages 323–337. Springer, 2000.

[Kus00b]   Sabine Kuske. *Transformation Units—A Structuring Principle for Graph Transformation Systems*. PhD thesis, University of Bremen, 2000.

[LM93]   Igor Litovsky and Yves Métivier. Computing with Graph Rewriting Systems with Priorities. *Theoretical Computer Science*, 115(2):191–224, 1993.

[LMS95]   Igor Litovsky, Yves Métivier, and Éric Sopena. Different Local Controls for Graph Relabeling Systems. *Mathematical Systems Theory*, 28(1):41–65, 1995.

[LMS98]   Igor Litovsky, Yves Métivier, and Éric Sopena. Checking Global Graph Properties by Means of Local Computations: The Majority Problem. *Theoretical Computer Science*, 194(1–2):245–246, 1998.

[LMS99]   Igor Litovsky, Yves Métivier, and Éric Sopena. Graph Relabelling Systems and Distributed Algorithms. In Ehrig et al. [EKMR99], chapter 1, pages 1–56.

[MS97]   Yves Métivier and Éric Sopena. Graph Relabelling Systems: A General Overview. *Computers and Artificial Intelligence*, 16(2):167–185, 1997.

[Plu93]   Detlef Plump. Hypergraph Rewriting: Critical Pairs and Undecidability of Confluence. In Sleep et al. [SPvE93], chapter 15, pages 201–213.

[Plu98]   Detlef Plump. Termination of Graph Rewriting Is Undecidable. *Fundamenta Informaticae*, 33(2):201–209, 1998.

[Plu99]   Detlef Plump. Term Graph Rewriting. In Ehrig et al. [EEKR99], chapter 1, pages 1–61.

[PRS98]   Gheorghe Păun, Grzegorz Rozenberg, and Arto Salomaa. *DNA Computing*. Springer, 1998.

[Roz97]   Grzegorz Rozenberg, Editor. *Handbook of Graph Grammars and Computing by Graph Transformation, Vol. 1: Foundations*. World Scientific, Singapore, 1997.

[SPvE93]   M.R. Sleep, M.J. Plasmeijer, and M.C.J.D. van Eekelen, Editors. *Term Graph Rewriting. Theory and Practice*. John Wiley, 1993.

Appendix

This appendix recalls the notions and notations of multisets used in the paper.

1. Let X be a set. Then a multiset (over X) is a mapping $M: X \to \mathbb{N}$, where $M(x)$ is the *multiplicity* of x in M.
2. The *carrier* of M contains all elements of X with positive multiplicity, i.e.

$$car(M) = \{x \in X \mid M(x) > 0\}.$$

3. A multiset is *finite* if its carrier is a finite set.
4. Let M and M' be multisets. Then M' is a *multi-subset* of M, denoted by $M' \leq M$, if $M'(x) \leq M(x)$ for all $x \in X$.
5. Let M and M' be multisets. Then the *sum* (*difference*) of M and M' is the multiset defined by

$$(M \pm M')(x) = M(x) \pm M'(x) \text{ for all } x \in X.$$

Here $+$ and $-$ are the usual sum and difference of non-negative integers with $m - n = 0$ if $m \leq n$ in particular.

6. Each sequence $w \in X^*$ induces a multiset by counting the number of occurrences of each x in w, i.e., for all $x, y \in X$ and $w \in X^*$,

$$MS(\lambda)(x) = 0$$
$$MS(yw)(x) = \ \textit{if } x = y \textit{ then } MS(w)(x) + 1 \textit{ else } MS(w)(x).$$

7. Let M be a multiset. Then the set of all sequences w with $MS(w) = M$ is denoted by $Perm(M)$. An element of $Perm(M)$ is called a *sequential representation* of M. Note that $Perm(M)$ contains all permutations of w if $MS(w) = M$.

Local Action Systems and DPO Graph Transformation*

Dirk Janssens

Department of Mathematics and Computer Science, U.I.A.
Universiteitsplein 1, 2610 Antwerp, Belgium
`dirk.janssens@ua.ac.be`

Abstract. A comparison between DPO graph rewriting and Local Action Systems is presented. It is shown that, as far as the sequential behaviour is concerned, each Local Action Systems can be simulated by a set of Double Pushout productions and vice versa. The encoding used is fairly straightforward, and it is easy to give conditions under which it preserves the finiteness of the sets of productions involved. As far as the sequential behaviour is concerned, it is shown that the situation is more complicated, and that the constructions presented are not satisfactory in the sense that atomic steps which are parallel independent in one system do not give rise to parallel independent steps in the simulating system.

1 Introduction

Graph rewriting based on the double pushout (DPO) construction has been introduced in [5] several decades ago. This type of graph rewriting systems is by far the most well-known, and a large amount of material about them has appeared in the literature. For a recent overview, see, e.g., [4]. Nevertheless, numerous other types of graph rewriting systems have been proposed, often motivated by concrete applications. Many of these graph rewriting systems are based on the idea that a rewrite consists of a combination of a replacement and an embedding operation. In order to obtain a uniform theory of graph rewriting, and to make the results about DPO graph rewriting available to a wider range of applications, it is important to consider the relationship between the main representatives of the embedding-based approach and DPO graph rewriting. The aim of this paper is to contribute to that, in particular for the case of Local Action Systems.

In graph rewriting based on replacement and embedding, a production consists of three components: a graph l, an occurrence of which is removed when the production is applied, a graph r, an occurrence of which replaces the removed occurence of l, and additional information needed to establish edges between the newly created occurrence of r and the part of the original graph that does not

---

* Partially supported by the EC TMR Network GETGRATS (General Theory of Graph Transformation Systems) and Esprit Working Group APPLIGRAPH through Universitaire Instelling Antwerpen.

W. Brauer et al. (Eds.): Formal and Natural Computing, LNCS 2300, pp. 138–157, 2002.

belong to the removed occurrence of l. The graph l is called the left-hand side of the production, r is called the right-hand side and the mechanism for establishing the edges is called the embedding mechanism. Local Action Systems (LAS) are an example of a graph rewriting system based on replacement and embedding. They are intended as a unifying framework for graph rewriting systems based on embedding, such as NLC [8], NCE [6], Actor Grammars [7] and others. The relationship between Local Action Systems and these types of graph rewriting is discussed in [9].

A distinguishing feature of LAS is that their theory is largely based on the notion of a process, in the sense of "true concurrency". Processes are an important notion in the theory of concurrency; e.g., since each process describes a (possibly large) set of sequential computations, processes are an important tool in dealing with the problem of state explosion in the verification of concurrent systems. A process theory of DPO graph rewriting has als been developed, [3,2], but there are significant methodological differences between the way the notion of a process is obtained in both approaches, and hence a comparison between them on the basis of their process theory seems difficult. For this reason the comparison between the two types of graph rewriting is based on the more traditional notion of a derivation sequence.

First a number of basic definitions is recalled, and then the sequential behaviour is considered: it is shown that each Local Action System can be simulated by a set of Double Pushout productions and vice versa. The first result, the construction of a set of DPO productions for a Local Action System, may be viewed as a simple case of the material presented in [1], but there only an encoding *into* the DPO formalism is considered. Then the concurrent behaviour is considered: the notion of a direct derivation in an LAS is generalized to the concurrent case, and it is shown that the relationship between the concurrent behaviour of both types of graph rewriting systems is more complicated than in the sequential case: it is shown that the straightforward encodings used in the sequential case do not preserve parallel independence. Evidently this raises the question whether other encodings exist that do preserve the concurrent behaviour, but there is reason to believe that such encodings would have to be at least rather sophisticated, if they exist at all.

2   Comparing the Sequential Behavour

The sequential behaviour of a graph rewriting system is completely determined by its direct derivations. In this section it is shown that each LAS can be encoded by a set of DPO productions such that the sequential behavior is preserved. On the other hand, it is shown that each set of DPO productions can be encoded by an LAS in such a way that the sequential behaviour is preserved, on the condition that the derivation steps of the LAS are restricted by imposing a counterpart of the dangling edge condition.

In the LAS from [7,9], the embedding mechanism acts on both node and edge labels. One of the aims of this choice was to show that node and edge labels can be treated in essentially the same way, and to suggest an extension from graph structures to hypergraph structures where one has to deal not only with unary and binary functions, representing labeled nodes and edges, but with n-ary functions representing hyperedges. In the version presented in this paper however, it is sufficient to consider the embedding mechanism for edge labels, and hence the component of the embedding mechanism acting on node labels is omitted. Also, one considers only LAS where induced subgraphs are rewritten. In [7] a more general way of matching a left-hand side was allowed, using a partial order on the labels. The LAS considered in his paper are the special case where this partial order is trivial: the equality of labels. For DPO graph rewriting, only the case where morphisms are injective is considered. This is a nontrivial restriction, but nevertheless the class of graph rewriting systems obtained in this way is still meaningful, and a lot of concrete examples and applications of it have been reported.

LAS and DPO productions operate on different types of graphs: the former manipulate graph structures, whereas the latter manipulate graphs where nodes and edges are considered as two sorts, related by explicit source and target function. Evidently, the results presented require the definition of constructions transforming graphs of one type into graphs of the other type.

2.1   Local Action Systems: Graph Structures and Labels

The objects manipulated by Local Acion Systems are graph structures; i.e. discrete structures consisting of a set of nodes equipped with two labelling functions: one for the node labels and one for the edge labels. Throughout the paper, Δ^v and Δ^e denote fixed sets of node and edge labels.

Definition 1. A graph structure *is a 3-tuple* $g = (V_g, g^v, g^e)$ *such that* V_g *is a finite set,* g^v *is a function from* V_g *into* Δ^v *and* g^e *is a function from* $V_g \times V_g$ *into* Δ^e.

For each subset X of V_g, $g|_X$ denotes the substructure of g induced by X; hence $g|_X = (X, g^v|_X, g^e|_{X \times X})$, where $g^v|_X$ and $g^e|_{X \times X}$ are the restrictions of g^v and g^e to X and $X \times X$, respectively.

The embedding mechanism of the LAS approach requires the possibility to combine edge labels with each other. For that reason it is assumed that the set of edge labels Δ^e is a commutative monoid instead of a set; the monoid operation is denoted by $+$ and the neutral element by $\mathbf{0}$. Informally, the set of pairs (x, y) such that $g^e(x, y) \neq \mathbf{0}$ may be viewed as the set of edges of g.

2.2   Local Action Systems: Direct Derivations

The theory of LAS is based on a process notion in the sense of true concurrency. The theory of DPO graph rewriting, however, is usually presented using the notion of a direct derivation. Thus, in order to investigate the relationship between the two types of graph rewriting, a more traditional definition of LAS, based on the notion of a direct derivation, is presented in this subsection. It describes how a new graph structure can be derived from a given graph structure by the application of a production; the possibility of a parallel application of several productions is not considered here. It will be treated in Section 3.

The essential part of the definition is the embedding mechanism. It is based on the transformation of edge labels by operations which are specified as part of the production that is applied. In fact, for each pair (x, y), where x is a node of the left-hand side of the production and y is a node of its right-hand side, a pair (d^s, d^t) of such operations is specified; informally speaking, d^s acts on the source side of an edge and d^t acts on the target side. The action of d^s and d^t is *local* to x and y in the sense that d^s and d^t are used only to determine labels of edges incident to y on the basis of labels of edges incident to x. Hence the name Local Action Systems. The operations d^s, d^t are assumed to be endomorphisms. They are also required to commute, in order to guarantee that the source and target sides of edges are treated in a symmetric way.

Formally, throughout the paper, let T^s, T^t denote sets of endomorphisms of Δ^e such that, for each $d^s \in T^s$, $d^t \in T^t$ and $a \in \Delta^e$, $d^s(d^t(a)) = d^t(d^s(a))$. **0** and **1** denote the constant zero function and the identity function on Δ^e, respectively. Obviously both are endomorphisms.

Definition 2. *An* LAS production *is a 3-tuple (l, r, D) such that l and r are graph structures, $V_l \cap V_r = \emptyset$, and $D = (D^s, D^t)$, where $D^s : V_l \times V_r \to T_s$ and $D^t : V_l \times V_r \to T_t$ are functions. A* Local Action System *is a set of LAS productions.*

The application of a (concrete) production to a (concrete) graph structure is defined as follows.

Definition 3. *Let g, h be graph structures and let $\pi = (l, r, D)$ be an LAS production. π is* applicable *to g if $V_r \cap (V_g \setminus V_l) = \emptyset$ and $g|_{V_l} = l$. If π is applicable to g, then $g \overset{\pi}{\underset{c}{\Longrightarrow}} h$ is a* concrete direct derivation *if h the graph structure such that*

1. $V_h = (V_g \setminus V_l) \cup V_r$,
2. $h^v(x) = \begin{cases} g^v(x), & \text{if } x \in (V_g \setminus V_l) \\ r^v(x), & \text{if } x \in V_r \end{cases}$
3. h^e *is defined by:*
   (a) *If $x, y \in V_g \setminus V_l$, then $h^e(x, y) = g^e(x, y)$.*
   (b) *If $x \in V_r$ and $y \in V_g \setminus V_l$, then*

$$h^e(x, y) = \sum_{z \in V_l} D^s(z, x)(g^e(z, y))$$

   (c) *If $x \in V_g \setminus V_l$ and $y \in V_r$, then*

$$h^e(x, y) = \sum_{z \in V_l} D^t(z, y)(g^e(x, z))$$

(d) If $x, y \in V_r$, then

$$h^e(x, y) = r^e(x, y) + \sum_{u, w \in V_l} (D^s(u, x) \circ D^t(w, y))(g^e(u, w))$$

Definition 4. *Let g, h be graph structures and let $\pi = (l, r, D)$ be an LAS production. Then $g \stackrel{\pi}{\Longrightarrow} h$ if there exist $\tilde{g}, \tilde{h}$, isomorphic to g and h, respectively, such that $\tilde{g} \stackrel{\pi}{\underset{c}{\Longrightarrow}} \tilde{h}$ is a concrete direct derivation.*

When drawing graph structures and productions, the following conventions are used. For a pair of nodes (x, y) of a graph structure g, $g^e(x, y)$ is only repesented if it is nonzero. For a production $\pi = (l, r, D)$, the upper part of the figure represents l, the lower part represents r, and only the nonzero components of D are explicitly given, in the form of pairs $(D^s(x, y), D^t(x, y))$.

Example 1. Let $\Delta^v = \{a, b, c\}$, let Δ^e be the set of subsets of $\{\alpha, \beta, \gamma, \delta\}$, let $\cup$ be the monoid operation on Δ^e and let θ, ϕ, ψ be the endomorphisms on Δ^e determined by

$$\theta(\{\gamma\}) = \{\gamma, \beta\}, \theta(X) = X \text{ if } \gamma \notin X$$
$$\phi(\{\alpha\}) = \{\beta\}, \phi(X) = X \text{ if } \alpha \notin X$$
$$\psi(\{\alpha\}) = \{\delta\}, \psi(X) = X \text{ if } \alpha \notin X$$

Figure 1 depicts a graph structure over Δ^v, Δ^e, Figure 2 depicts a LAS production π and Figure 3 depicts the result of the application of π to the graph structure of Figure 1.

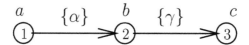

Fig. 1. A graph structure.

2.3   DPO Graph Rewriting: Graphs and Labels

In this subsection, basic notions of DPO graph rewriting are recalled. Only the case where all morphisms are injective is considered. This is a nontrivial restriction, but nevertheless the class of graph rewriting systems obtained in this way is meaningful, and a lot of concrete examples and applications of it have been reported in the literature. The formal results comparing Local Action Systems and Algebraic graph rewriting require an encoding of graphs into graph structures; in order to obtain such an encoding only finite graphs are considered, i.e. graphs that have finite sets of edges and of nodes.

Let Σ^v, Σ^e be sets. Σ^v and Σ^e are used as sets of node labels and of edge labels, respectively.

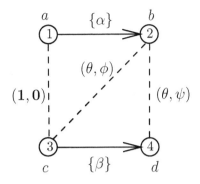

Fig. 2. A LAS production.

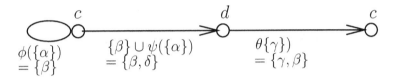

Fig. 3. Result of production application.

Definition 5. *A (finite) graph is a system $G = (V_G, E_G, s_G, t_G, l_G^v, l_G^e)$, where V_G and E_G are finite sets, and $s_G, t_G : E_G \to V_G$, $l_G^v : V_G \to \Sigma^v$ and $l_G^e : E_G \to \Sigma^e$ are functions.*

V_G is the set of nodes of G, E_G is its set of edges, s_G is its source function, t_G is its target function, l_G^v is its node label function, and l_G^e is its edge label function. Throughout the paper, capital letters G, H, K, ... are used to denote graphs, and small letters g, h, k, ... are used to denote graph structures. For $x, y \in V_G$ and $\sigma \in \Sigma^e$, $E_G^\sigma(x, y)$ denotes that set of σ-labeled edges from x into y in G:

$$E_G^\sigma(x, y) = \{e \in E_G \mid s_G(e) = x, t_G(e) = y \text{ and } l_G^e(e) = \sigma\}.$$

A graph G is *simple* if, for each $x, y \in V_G$, $\#\{e \in E_G \mid s_G(e) = x \text{ and } t_G(e) = y\} \leq 1$. In this paper, only injective graph morphisms are used. Hence a *graph morphism* $f : G \to G'$ is a pair $(f_V : V_G \to V_{G'}, f_E : E_G \to E_{G'})$ of injective functions which preserve sources, targets and labels; i.e. $f_V \circ t_G = t_{G'} \circ f_E$, $f_V \circ s_G = s_{G'} \circ f_E$, $l_{G'}^v \circ f_V = l_G^v$ and $l_{G'}^e \circ f_E = l_G^e$.

In DPO graph rewriting a production is defined as follows.

Definition 6. *a DPO production is a 5-tuple (L, λ, K, ρ, R) where L, K and R are graphs and $\lambda : K \to L$ and $\rho : K \to R$ are injectice morphisms.*

The objects under consideration in this paper are sets of productions, rather than grammars (where also a start graph is given). The way graphs are transformed by applying productions is formalized by the notion of a direct derivation.

Definition 7. *Let G and H be graphs, let $\nu = (L, \lambda, K, \rho, R)$ be a DPO production and let $m : L \to G$ be an injective graph morphism. A* direct derivation *from G to H using ν via m is a diagram of the form depicted in Figure 4, where both the left and the right square are pushouts in GRAPH, the category of graphs and graph morphisms.*

A direct derivation as depicted in Figure 4 is denoted by $G \stackrel{\nu,m}{\Longrightarrow} H$ or $G \stackrel{\nu}{\Longrightarrow} H$. In the case considered here, where all morphisms are injective, $G \stackrel{\nu,m}{\Longrightarrow} H$ if

1. no edge from $E_G - m(E_L)$ is incident with a node of $m(V_L - \lambda_V(V_K))$ - this is called the *dangling edge condition.*
2. H is isomorphic to the graph H' where $V_{H'} = V_G - m(V_L - \lambda_V(V_K)) \cup (V_R - \rho_V(V_K))$ and $E_{H'} = E_G - m(E_L - \lambda_E(E_K)) \cup (E_R - \rho_E(E_K))$, i.e. H' is constructed by deleting the items that are not preserved - those of $m(L - \lambda(K))$ - and adding the items that are created - those of $R - \rho(K)$. (It is assumed that G and R are disjoint.)

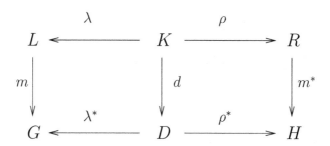

Fig. 4. A direct derivation.

2.4   Encoding of a Local Action System by a Set of DPO Productions

The sequential behaviour of a graph transformation system is determined by its direct derivations steps: applications of a production to a graph. It is shown in this subsection that, as far as the sequential behaviour is concerned, Local Action Systems and Double Pushout graph rewriting are equivalent in the following sense: let P be an LAS with alphabets Δ^v, Δ^e for node labels and edge labels, respectively. A construction is presented that yields a set of DPO productions P' such that each direct derivation in P corresponds to a direct derivation in P'. On the other hand, each direct derivation between simple graphs in P' corresponds to a direct derivation in P. Thus for each LAS there exists a set DPO productions that has essentially the same direct derivations, and vice versa. Formally, the result requires an encoding of graphs into graph structures; this encoding is defined next.

Firstly, one needs to define the sets of labels of P': its set of labels is Δ^v and its set of edges is $\Delta^e \setminus \{0\}$. The following operation is used to relate simple graphs to graph structures. For a finite set X, let $\#X$ denote the number of elements of X.

Definition 8. *Let G be a simple graph over Δ^v and $\Delta^e \setminus \{0\}$. Then $str(G)$ is the graph structure g over Δ^v, Δ^e where $V_g = V_G$, $g^v = l_G^v$ and g^e is defined by*

$$g^e(x, y) = \begin{cases} \delta, & \text{if } \#E_G^\delta(x, y) = 1 \\ 0, & \text{otherwise} \end{cases}$$

for each $x, y \in V_g$.

Next, consider the encoding of productions. The following notion is used.

Definition 9. *For a graph structure g, a neighbourhood extension of g is a graph structure h such that $h|_{V_g} = g$, $g^e(x, y) = 0$ for each $x, y \in V_h \setminus V_g$, and for each x in $V_h \setminus V_g$ there exists an $y \in V_g$ such that either $h^e(x, y) \neq 0$ or $h^e(y, x) \neq 0$.*

A graph g and a neighbourhood exrtension of g are depicted in Figure 5.

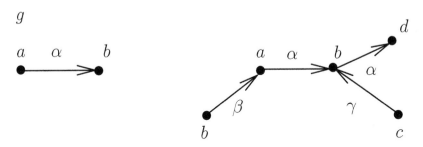

Fig. 5. A graph structure and a neighbourhood extension of it.

For each production $\pi = (l, r, D)$ of P, let $nex(\pi)$ be a fixed set of neighbourhood extensions of l such that each neighborhood extension of l is isomorphic to exactly one element of $nex(\pi)$ and, for each $\bar{l} \in nex(\pi)$, $V_{\bar{l}} \cap V_r = \emptyset$.

1. For a a neighbourhood extension $\bar{l}$ of l, $dpo(\pi, \bar{l})$ is the set of DPO productions (L, λ, K, ρ, R) such that $\bar{l} = str(L)$, $\bar{l}|_{V_{\bar{l}} \setminus V_l} = str(K)$, $str(R) = h$ where $\bar{l} \xRightarrow[c]{\pi} h$, and λ, ρ are inclusions.

2. The DPO encoding of π is the set

$$dpo(\pi) = \bigcup_{\bar{l} \in\ nex(\pi)} dpo(\pi, \bar{l}).$$

3. A DPO encoding of P is a set P' of DPO productions such that P' contains exactly one production from $dpo(\pi, \bar{l})$ for each π in P and each $\bar{l} \in nex(\pi)$.

Note that $dpo(\pi, \bar{l})$ is in general a set and not a singleton because $str(G)$ does not determine the choice of the set E_G.

Example 2. For the LAS productions π_1, π_2 depicted in Figure 6, $dpo(\pi_1)$ and $dpo(\pi_2)$ contain the DPO productions ν_1 and ν_2, depicted in Figure 7, respectively.

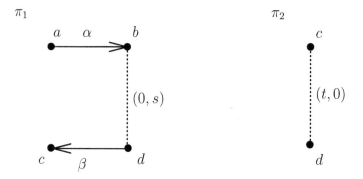

Fig. 6. LAS productions π_1 and π_2.

Next, the relationship between the direct derivations in P and in its DPO encodings is considered. So, let P' be a fixed DPO encoding of P.

Lemma 1. *Let $g \overset{\pi}{\underset{c}{\Longrightarrow}} h$ be a direct derivation in P, let $G \overset{\nu}{\Longrightarrow} H$ be a direct derivation in P', and assume that $g = str(G)$, $\pi = (l, r, D)$, $\nu = (L, \lambda, K, \rho, R) \in dpo(\pi)$, and all arrows in the diagram of Figure 4 are inclusions. Then $h = str(H)$.*

Proof. Since all arrows in the diagram of Figure 4 are inclusions, $V_H = (V_G \backslash V_L) \cup V_R$. Since V_K, V_l and V_r are pairwise disjoint, $V_L = V_K \cup V_l$ and $V_R = V_K \cup V_r$. Thus $V_H = (V_G \setminus V_L) \cup V_R = (V_G \setminus (V_l \cup V_K)) \cup (V_K \cup V_r) = (V_g \setminus V_l) \cup V_r = V_h$. It follows from the fact that m, m^*, λ^* and ρ^* are graph morphisms that $h^v = l_H^v$. Finally, consider the edges of H. One has to show that, for each $\delta \in \Delta^e \setminus \{\mathbf{0}\}$, $E_H^\delta(x, y) \neq \emptyset$ if and only if $h^e(x, y) = \delta$. This is sufficient because it implies that, if $E_H^\delta(x, y) = \emptyset$ for each $\delta \in \Delta^e \setminus \{\mathbf{0}\}$, then $h^e(x, y) \neq \delta$ for each $\delta \in \Delta^e \setminus \{\mathbf{0}\}$, and hence $h^e(x, y) = \mathbf{0}$. Consider four cases.

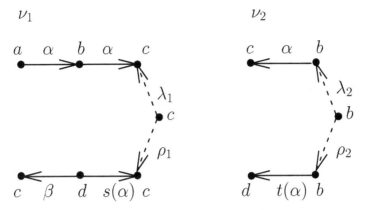

Fig. 7. DPO encodings of π_1 and π_2.

1. $x, y \in V_r$. Then it follows from the way a direct derivation is constructed in DPO graph rewriting that $E_H^\delta(x, y) \neq \emptyset$ if and only if $E_R^\delta(x, y) \neq \emptyset$. It follows from the construction of ν that the latter holds if and only if $h^e(x, y) = \delta$.
2. $x, y \in V_g \backslash V_l$. Then it follows from the way a direct derivation is constructed in DPO graph rewriting that $E_H^\delta(x, y) \neq \emptyset$ if and only if $E_D^\delta(x, y) \neq \emptyset$ and hence, if and only if $E_G^\delta(x, y) \neq \emptyset$. The latter holds if and only if $g^e(x, y) = \delta$, and it follows from (a) of Definition 3 that this holds if and only if $h^e(x, y) = \delta$.
3. $x \in V_r$, $y \in V_g \backslash V_l$. Then it follows from the way a direct derivation is constructed in DPO graph rewriting that $E_H^\delta(x, y) \neq \emptyset$ if and only if $E_R^\delta(x, y) \neq \emptyset$ and $y \in V_K$. It follows from the construction of ν that $E_R^\delta(x, y) \neq \emptyset$ if and only if $h^e(x, y) = \delta$.
4. $x \in V_g \backslash V_l$, $y \in V_r$. This case is analogous to case 3.

Theorem 1. *There exists a direct derivation $g \overset{\pi}{\Longrightarrow} h$ in P if and only if there exist simple graphs G, H and a direct derivation $G \overset{\nu}{\Longrightarrow} H$ in P' such that $str(G) = g$, $str(H) = h$ and $\nu \in dpo(\pi)$.*

Proof. (if) Let G, H be simple graphs and let $G \overset{\nu}{\Longrightarrow} H$, where $\nu = (L, \lambda, K, \rho, R)$, $\pi = (l, r, D)$ and $\nu \in dpo(\pi)$. Let $\tilde{G}$ and $\tilde{H}$ be graphs isomorphic to G and H, respectively, and such that $\tilde{G} \overset{\nu}{\Longrightarrow} \tilde{H}$, where all arrows in the corresponding diagram (i.e. the counterpart of the one from Figure 4) are inclusions. It follows from the fact that the dangling edge condition is satisfied that all edges in $\tilde{G}$ between nodes of V_l belong to E_L, and thus $str(\tilde{G})\big|_{V_l} = l$. Thus π is applicable to $str(\tilde{G})$, and it follows from Lemma 1 that $str(\tilde{G}) \overset{\pi}{\Longrightarrow} str(\tilde{H})$. It follows that $g \overset{\pi}{\Longrightarrow} h$, since g is isomorphic to $str(\tilde{G})$ and h is isomorphic to $str(\tilde{H})$.

(only if) For graph structures k, l such that $V_l \subseteq V_k$ and $k|_{V_l} = l$, let the neighbourhood extension of l in k be the graph structure $\bar{l}$ such that

$$V_{\bar{l}} = V_l \cup \{x \in V_k \setminus V_l \mid \text{ there exists a node } y \in V_l \text{ such that}$$
$$k^e(x, y) \neq \mathbf{0} \text{ or } k^e(y, x) \neq \mathbf{0}\},$$

$\bar{l}^v = k^v|_{V_{\bar{l}}}$, and $\bar{l}^e$ is defined by

$$\bar{l}^e(x, y) = \begin{cases} \mathbf{0}, & \text{if } x, y, \in V_{\bar{l}} \setminus V_l, \\ k^e(x, y), & \text{otherwise.} \end{cases}$$

Assume that $g \overset{\pi}{\Longrightarrow} h$. Let $\tilde{g}$ and $\tilde{h}$ be isomorphic to g and h, respectively, and such that $\tilde{g} \overset{\pi}{\underset{c}{\Longrightarrow}} \tilde{h}$ and the neighbourhood extension $\bar{l}$ of l in g belongs to $nex(\pi)$. Let $\nu = (L, \lambda, K, \rho, R)$ be the production of P' that belongs to $dpo(\pi, \bar{l})$. It follows from the construction of $\bar{l}$ that there exists a graph $\tilde{G}$ such that $str(\tilde{G}) = \tilde{g}$, L is a subgraph of $\tilde{G}$, and the inclusion of L in $\tilde{G}$ satisfies the dangling edge condition. Hence there exists a graph $\tilde{H}$ such that $\tilde{G} \overset{\nu}{\Longrightarrow} \tilde{H}$ and all arrows in the corresponding diagram are inclusions. It follows from Lemma 1 that $str(\tilde{G}) \overset{\pi}{\Longrightarrow} str(\tilde{H})$. Since $\tilde{g}$ is isomorphic to g and $\tilde{h}$ is isomorphic to h, there exist G and H, isomorphic to $\tilde{G}$ and $\tilde{H}$, respectively, such that $str(G) = g$, $str(H) = h$ and $\nu \in dpo(\pi)$. This completes the proof.

The set of DPO productions constructed for a LAS has in general an infinite number of productions, even if the LAS is finite. It makes sense to view an LAS production as a particular way to specify an infinite set of DPO productions, where each possible neighbourhood of the original production gives rise to a DPO production. Evidently, one can ensure that the set of DPO productions is finite by imposing additional restrictions on the LAS considered: e.g. one may require that the set of edge labels is finite and that the graph structures considered have bounded degree (for graph structures, edges with label $\mathbf{0}$ are not counted in defining the degree).

2.5 Encoding of a Set of DPO Productions by a Local Action System

Let P be a set of DPO productions with alphabets Σ^v, Σ^e of node labels and edge labels, respectively. A construction is presented that yields a LAS P' such that each direct derivation in P corresponds to a direct derivation in P'. On the other hand, direct derivations of P' correspond to direct derivations of P, but only to those that obey a restriction corresponding to the dangling edge condition of DPO graph rewriting.

Firstly, the alphabets Δ^v, Δ^e of P' are defined: $\Delta^v = \Sigma^v$, and Δ^e is the free monoid generated by Σ^e. Thus Δ^e may be viewed as the set of functions from Σ^e into the set of natural numbers, where the monoid operation is the elementwise sum; i.e. $(\delta_1 + \delta_2)(x) = \delta_1(x) + \delta_2(x)$, for each $\delta_1, \delta_2 \in \Delta^e$ and each $x \in \Sigma^e$. Each $a \in \Sigma^e$ may be identified with the function δ_a, where $\delta_a(a) = 1$

and $\delta_a(x) = 0$ for each $x \neq a$. In this way Σ^e may be viewed as a subset of Δ^e. Finally, let $T^s = T^e = \{\mathbf{0}, \mathbf{1}\}$.

The following operation is used to relate graphs over Σ^v, Σ^e and graph structures over Δ^v, Δ^e.

Definition 10. *Let G be a graph over Σ^v, Σ^e. Then $stru(G)$ is the graph structure g such that $V_g = V_G$, $g^v = l^v_G$, and, for each $\sigma \in \Sigma^e$, $g^e(x, y)(\sigma) = \#E^\sigma_G(x, y)$*

Thus the node labels remain unchanged and $g^e(x, y)$ is the function mapping $\sigma \in \Sigma^e$ into the number of σ-labeled edges from x into y in G. For each graph structure g over Δ^v, Δ^e there exists a graph G over Σ^v, Σ^e such that $stru(G) = g$. If two graphs G, G' are such that $stru(G) = stru(G')$, then G and G' are isomorphic: G and G' differ only in the choice of concrete elements in E_G and $E_{G'}$. Thus $stru(G)$ faithfully encodes G.

Next, consider the productions. Let $\nu = (L, \lambda, K, \rho, R)$ be a DPO production over Σ^v, Σ^e such that $V_L \cap V_R = \emptyset$, λ is an inclusion and ρ is injective. Then $las(\nu)$ is the set of LAS productions (l, r, D) such that $V_l = V_L$, $V_r = V_R$, $l^v = l^v_L$, $r^v = l^v_R$, $D : V_l \times V_r \to T^s \times T^t$ is defined by

$$D(x, y) = \begin{cases} (\mathbf{1}, \mathbf{1}), & \text{if } x \in V_K \text{ and } y = \rho(x) \\ (\mathbf{0}, \mathbf{0}), & \text{otherwise} \end{cases}$$

and $l^e : V_l \times V_l \to \Delta^e$, $r^e : V_r \times V_r \to \Delta^e$ are defined by

$$l^e(x, y)(\sigma) \begin{cases} \geq \#E^\sigma_L(x, y), & \text{if } x, y \in V_K \\ = \#E^\sigma_L(x, y), & \text{otherwise} \end{cases}$$

$$r^e(x, y)(\sigma) = \begin{cases} 0, & \text{if } x, y \in \rho(V_K) \\ \#E^\sigma_R(x, y), & \text{otherwise} \end{cases}$$

for each $\sigma \in \Sigma^e$.

Hence l differs from $stru(L)$ by the fact that the $l^e(x, y)(\sigma)$ may be larger than $\#E^\sigma_L(x, y)$ if $x, y \in V_K$. This is needed because in LAS graph rewriting it is required that the left-hand side of a production matches exactly the subgraph where it is applied, whereas in DPO graph rewriting there may be "dangling edges" incident to K. On the other hand, r differs from $stru(R)$ by the fact that edges between nodes of K are "left out" (encoded by 0). This is needed because these edges, or their encoding, are preserved by the embedding mechanism of the encoded production.

An LAS encoding of P is defined as follows. Let $\tilde{P}$ be a set of DPO productions obtained by replacing each production ν in P by a production $\tilde{\nu} = (L, \lambda, K, \rho, R)$ such that $V_L \cap V_R = \emptyset$, λ is an inclusion and ρ is injective. Then $P' = \cup_{\tilde{\nu} \in \tilde{P}} las(\tilde{\nu})$. Thus P' is not uniquely determined, because it is dependent on the choice of $\tilde{\nu}$. Throughout the remainder of this section, let P' be a fixed LAS encoding of P.

Example 3. For the DPO productions ν_3, ν_4 depicted in Figure 8, $las(\nu_3)$ and $las(\nu_4)$ contain the LAS productions π_3 and π_4, depicted in Figure 9, respectively.

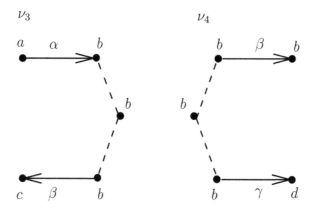

Fig. 8. DPO productions ν_3 and ν_4.

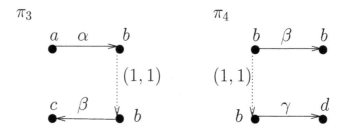

Fig. 9. LAS encodings of ν_3 and ν_4.

The direct derivations of P' that correspond to direct derivations of P are restricted in the sense that one has to take into account the dangling edge condition. This restiction is formally defined as follows.

Definition 11. *Let* $g \overset{\pi}{\underset{c}{\Rightarrow}} h$ *be a concrete direct derivation in* P'. *Let* $\pi \in las(L, \lambda,\ K, \rho, R)$. $g \overset{\pi}{\underset{c}{\Rightarrow}} h$ *is restricted if* $g^e(x, y) = g^e(y, x) = \mathbf{0}$ *for each pair of nodes* x, y *such that* $x \in V_g \backslash V_L$ *and* $y \in V_L \backslash V_K$. *A direct derivation* $g \overset{\pi}{\Rightarrow} h$ *is restricted if there exist graph structures* $\tilde{g}$, $\tilde{h}$, *isomorphic to* g *and* h, *respectively, such that there exists a concrete direct derivation* $\tilde{g} \overset{\pi}{\underset{c}{\Rightarrow}} \tilde{h}$ *that is restricted.*

Lemma 2. *Let* $G \overset{\nu}{\Rightarrow} H$ *be a direct derivation in* P, *let* $g \overset{\pi}{\underset{c}{\Rightarrow}} h$ *be a concrete direct derivation in* P', *and assume that* $\nu = (L, \lambda, K, \rho, R)$, $V_L \cap V_R = \emptyset$, $\pi \in las(\nu)$, *and* $stru(G) = g$. *Assume that* $\lambda, \lambda^*, m, m^*$ *and* d *in the diagram of Figure 4 are inclusions. Moreover, assume that the restriction of* ρ^* *to* $G|_{V_G \backslash V_L}$ *is also an inclusion. Then* $h = stru(H)$.

Proof. It follows from the assumptions that $V_H = (V_G \setminus V_L) \cup V_R = (V_g \setminus V_l) \cup V_r = V_h$. Since ρ^* and m^* are graph morphisms, $h^v = l_H^v$. Finally, consider the edges of H. One has to show that, for each $x, y \in V_H$ and each $\sigma \in \Sigma^e$, $h^e(x, y) = \#E_H^\sigma(x, y)$. Let $\pi = (l, r, D)$. Consider four cases:

1. $x, y \in V_R \setminus \rho(V_K)$. Then $\#E_H^\sigma(x, y) = \#E_R^\sigma(x, y)$ because of the way a direct derivation is constructed in DPO graph rewriting, $\#E_R^\sigma(x, y) = r^e(x, y)(\sigma)$ because of the way $dpo(\nu)$ is constructed, and $r^e(x, y)(\sigma) = h^e(x, y)(\sigma)$ because it follows from the construction of D that, in (d) of Definition 3, all terms but the first one are zero.

2. $x, y \notin V_R \setminus \rho(V_K)$. Then $\#E_H^\sigma(x, y) = \#E_D^\sigma(\rho^{*-1}(x), \rho^{*-1}(y)) = \#E_G^\sigma(\rho^{*-1}(x), \rho^{*-1}(y))$ because of the way a direct derivation is constructed in DPO graph rewriting, and $\#E_G^\sigma(\rho^{*-1}(x), \rho^{*-1}(y)) = h^e(x, y)(\sigma)$ because of the form of D (either $x = \rho^*(x)$ or $D(\rho^{*-1}(x), x) = (\mathbf{1}, \mathbf{1})$, and similarly for y).

3. $x \in V_R \setminus \rho(V_K)$ and $y \notin V_R \setminus \rho(V_K)$. Then $\#E_H^\sigma(x, y) \neq 0$ implies that $y \in \rho(V_K)$, because of the dangling edge condition, and $\#E_H^\sigma(x, y) = \#E_R^\sigma(x, y)$. It follows from the construction that $D(z, x) = (\mathbf{0}, \mathbf{0})$, for each $z \in V_l$, and thus, from (d) of Definition 3, $h^e(x, y)(\sigma) = r^e(x, y)(\sigma) = \#E_R^\sigma(x, y)$ if $y \in \rho(V_K)$. Thus $h^e(x, y)(\sigma) = \#E_H^\sigma(x, y)$ if $\#E_H^\sigma(x, y) \neq 0$ or $\#E_H^\sigma(x, y) = 0$ and $y \in \rho(V_K)$. On the other hand, if $y \notin \rho(V_K)$, then $\#E_H^\sigma(x, y) = 0$ and it follows from the construction of D and (b) of Definition 3 that $h^e(x, y)(\sigma) = 0$. Thus also in this case $h^e(x, y)(\sigma) = \#E_H^\sigma(x, y)$.

4. $x \notin V_R \setminus \rho(V_K)$ and $y \in V_R \setminus \rho(V_K)$. This case is analogous to case 3.

Theorem 2. *There exists a direct derivation $G \overset{\nu}{\Longrightarrow} H$ in P if and only if there exists a restricted direct derivation $stru(G) \overset{\pi}{\Longrightarrow} stru(H)$ in P' such that $\pi \in las(\nu)$.*

Proof. Let $\tilde{\nu} = (L, \lambda, K, \rho, L)$ be the DPO production used in the construction of $las(\nu)$.

(if) Let G, H be graphs such that there exists a restricted direct derivation $stru(G) \overset{\pi}{\Longrightarrow} stru(H)$ in P' with $\pi \in las(\nu)$. Let $\pi = (l, r, D)$. Then there exists a concrete restricted direct derivation $\tilde{g} \overset{\pi}{\underset{c}{\Longrightarrow}} \tilde{h}$ in P' such that $\tilde{g}, \tilde{h}$ are isomorphic to $stru(G)$ and $stru(H)$, respectively. It follows from $\tilde{g}|_{V_l} = l$ that there exists a graph $\tilde{G}$ such that $\tilde{G}$ is isomorphic to G and L is a subgraph of $\tilde{G}$. Moreover, since $\tilde{g} \overset{\pi}{\underset{c}{\Longrightarrow}} \tilde{h}$ is restricted the inclusion of L into $\tilde{G}$ satisfies the dangling edge condition. Thus one may construct a graph $\tilde{H}$ such that $\tilde{G} \overset{\tilde{\nu}}{\Longrightarrow} \tilde{H}$ in P and the conditions of Lemma 2 are satisfied for $\tilde{G} \overset{\tilde{\nu}}{\Longrightarrow} \tilde{H}$ and $\tilde{g} \overset{\pi}{\underset{c}{\Longrightarrow}} \tilde{h}$. It follows from Lemma 2 that $stru(\tilde{H}) = \tilde{h}$. Since $stru(H)$ and $\tilde{h}$ are isomorphic, H and $\tilde{H}$ are isomorphic. Since G and $\tilde{G}$ are isomorphic and ν and $\tilde{\nu}$ are isomorphic, it follows that $G \overset{\nu}{\Longrightarrow} H$.

(only if) Let $G \overset{\nu}{\Longrightarrow} H$ in P. It follows that $G \overset{\tilde{\nu}}{\Longrightarrow} H$. Since there is a match $m : L \to G$, the construction of $las(\nu)$ implies that there exists a production

$\pi = (l, r, D) \in las(\tilde{\nu})$ and a graph structure $\tilde{g}$ such that $\tilde{g}$ and $stru(G)$ are isomorphic, and $\tilde{g}|_{V_l} = l$. It follows that there exists a graph structure $\tilde{h}$ and graphs $\tilde{G}$, $\tilde{H}$ such that $\tilde{G}$ and G are isomorphic, $\tilde{H}$ and H are isomorphic, and the conditions of Lemma 2 are satisfied for $\tilde{G} \overset{\tilde{\nu}}{\Longrightarrow} \tilde{H}$ and $\tilde{g} \overset{\pi}{\underset{c}{\Longrightarrow}} \tilde{h}$. It follows from Lemma 2 that $stru(\tilde{H}) = \tilde{h}$. Thus $\tilde{h}$ and $stru(H)$ are isomorphic, because $\tilde{H}$ and H are isomorphic. Since $\tilde{g}$ and $stru(G)$ are isomorphic, it follows that there exists a restricted direct derivation $stru(G) \overset{\pi}{\Longrightarrow} stru(H)$ in P'.

The LAS obtained from a given finite set of DPO productions may be infinite; this is caused by the fact that, for a graph G, there exist infinitely many graphs G' on the same set of nodes such that G is a subgraph of G'. Again, the problem disappears if one requires that the set of edge labels is finite and that the graphs considered have bounded degree. If one generalizes the notion of a match for LAS in the way presented in [7], then the construction can be modified in such a way that each DPO production gives rise to just one LAS production.

3   Comparing the Concurrent Behaviour

One of the most interesting potential applications of graph rewriting systems is their use in the modeling of concurrency. For DPO graph rewriting, the relationship between parallel and sequential graph rewriting has been extensively investigated, see e.g. [10,11,4]. A central issue in this context is the need to determine when two direct derivations can be executed in parallel: either they are combined into a parallel derivation step, or, in the interleaving view, that they can be executed in any order without changing the resulting graph. It has been demonstrated that the presence of such potential parallellism is captured by the notion of *parallel independence* of direct derivations; it is defined as follows.

Definition 12. *Let* G, H_1, H_2 *be graphs, let* $\nu_1 = (L_1, \lambda_1, K_1, \rho_1, R_1)$, $\nu_2 = (L_2, \lambda_2, K_2, \rho_2, R_2)$ *be DPO productions and let* $G \overset{\nu_1, m_1}{\Longrightarrow} H_1$, $G \overset{\nu_2, m_2}{\Longrightarrow} H_2$ *be direct derivations. They are* parallel independent *if* $m_1(L_1) \cap m_2(L_2) \subseteq m_1(\lambda_1(K_1)) \cap m_2(\lambda_2(K_2))$.

In the case of LAS graph rewriting, the parallel application of productions is defined in [7] using LAS processes. However, for the purpose of this paper an equivalent definition is used, which is a straightforward generalization of Definition 3. It uses the notion of a production *occurrence*: an occurence of an LAS production (l, r, D) is an isomorphic copy of it; i.e. an LAS production (l', r', D') such that there exists bijective functions $h_l : V_l \to V_{l'}$ and $h_r : V_r \to V_{r'}$ that preserve the structure: for each $x, x' \in V_l$ and each $y, y' \in V_r$, $l^v(x) = l'^v(h_l(x))$, $l^e(x, x') = l'^e(h_l(x), h_l(x'))$, $r^v(y) = r'^v(h_r(y))$, $r^e(y, y') = r'^e(h_r(y), h_r(y'))$, and $D(x, y) = D'((h_l(x), h_r(y))$.

Definition 13. *Let* g, h *be graph structures and let* $\Pi = \{\pi_1, \dots, \pi_k\}$ *be a set of occurrences of productions, where* $\pi_i = (l_i, r_i, D_i)$ *for* $1 \le i \le k$. Π *is applicable* to g if the sets V_{l_i} and V_{r_i} are pairwise disjoint, $(\cup_{i=1}^k V_{r_i}) \cap (V_g \setminus \cup_{i=1}^k V_{l_i}) = \emptyset$ and $g|_{V_{l_i}} = l_i$ for each $1 \le i \le k$. If π is applicable to g, then $g \overset{\Pi}{\underset{c}{\Longrightarrow}} h$ is a concrete parallel derivation if h the graph structure such that

1. $V_h = (V_g \setminus \cup_{i=1}^k V_{l_i}) \cup (\cup_{i=1}^k V_{r_i})$,
2. $h^v(x) = \begin{cases} g^v(x), & \text{if } x \in (V_g \setminus \cup_{i=1}^k V_{l_i}) \\ r_i^v(x), & \text{if } x \in V_{r_i} \end{cases}$
3. h^e is defined by:
   (a) If $x, y \in V_g \setminus \cup_{i=1}^k V_{l_i}$, then $h^e(x,y) = g^e(x,y)$.
   (b) If $x \in V_{r_i}$ and $y \in V_g \setminus \cup_{i=1}^k V_{l_i}$, then

$$h^e(x,y) = \sum_{z \in V_{l_i}} D_i^s(z,x)(g^e(z,y))$$

   (c) If $x \in V_g \setminus \cup_{i=1}^k V_{l_i}$ and $y \in V_{r_i}$, then

$$h^e(x,y) = \sum_{z \in V_{l_i}} D_i^t(z,y)(g^e(x,z))$$

   (d) If $x, y \in V_{r_i}$, then

$$h^e(x,y) = r_i^e(x,y) + \sum_{u,w \in V_{l_i}} (D_i^s(u,x) \circ D_i^t(w,y))(g^e(u,w))$$

   (e) If $x \in V_{r_i}, y \in V_{r_j}, i \ne j$, then

$$h^e(x,y) = \sum_{\substack{u \in V_{l_i} \\ w \in V_{l_j}}} (D_i^s(u,x) \circ D_j^t(w,y))(g^e(u,w)).$$

Hence the only new clause is (e), which describes the way two right-hand sides are connected. In LAS graph rewriting, two direct derivations can be executed in parallel if they rewrite disjoint subgraphs. Hence, at first sight, LAS graph rewriting allows less parallelism, because disjointness of the rewritten subgraphs is obviously a stronger requirement than parallel independence: in Definition 12 $m_1(L_1) \cap m_2(L_2) = \emptyset$ implies $m_1(L_1) \cap m_2(L_2) \subseteq m_1(\lambda_1(K_1)) \cap m_2(\lambda_2(K_2))$. However, one has to keep in mind that the left-hand side of a DPO production contains the image of the interface graph K, which is, intuitively, a part that is preserved. In a LAS production, there is no need for such a preserved part, and hence, when modeling the same application, one may expect the left-hand sides of LAS productions to be smaller than those of the corresponding DPO productions.

In the remaining part of this section it is shown that the constructions from Section 2, transforming an LAS into a set of DPO productions and vice versa, do not faithfully preserve the concurrent behaviour of these systems. For both constructions, examples are given where the transformation, applied to concurrent productions (parallel independent productions, in the case of DPO graph rewriting), does not yield concurrent productions of the transformed system. Although this does not prove that it is impossible to find other encodings that do preserve the concurrent behaviour, there seems to be reason to believe that such encodings are not straightforward.

First consider the construction transforming an LAS into a set of DPO productions. Two LAS productions can be applied whenever their left-hand sides are disjoint; there may be edges connecting the left-hand sides and these edges may be changed in nontrivial way by the embedding mechanism. The fact that the DPO productions that encode an LAS production have in general a larger left-hand side than the original production leads to situations where the transformed versions of LAS productions cannot be applied in the way that is needed to obtain the desired concurrent behaviour. Consider, e.g., the productions π_1, π_2 from Example 2, and consider their concurrent application to the graph g of Figure 10, depicted in Figure 11.

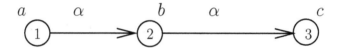

Fig. 10. The graph structure g.

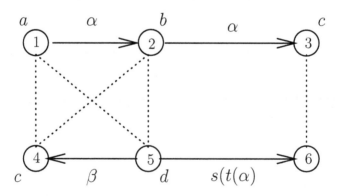

Fig. 11. Concurrent application of π_1 and π_2.

The corresponding application of the DPO productions ν_1, ν_2 from Figure 7 would require the matching morphisms to be chosen as depicted in Figure 12, but the corresponding direct derivations are obviously not parallel independent, since that would require $\{2,3\} \subseteq \{2\} \cap \{3\}$.

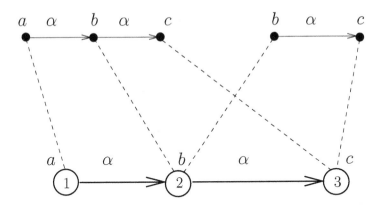

Fig. 12. Applications of ν_1, ν_2.

One may wonder whether this is only a property of the particular encoding of LAS productions chosen here, and whether other encodings exist where the DPO productions do have the same concurrent behaviour as the original LAS; thus in the situation considered here the encoding would yield parallel independent direct derivations. Such encoding, however, would not be straightforward: e.g., the α-labelled edge between nodes 2 and 3 of Figure 11 cannot be represented by a single item. Indeed, since the label α is transformed by both π_1 and π_2, one would expect its encoding to be changed by both the encodings of π_1 and π_2. But, since the left-hand sides in parallel independent direct derivations overlap only in items that are preserved, this would imply that the label remains unchanged.

The second construction, transforming a set of DPO productions into an LAS, has a similar problem. Consider the productions ν_3, ν_4 from Example 3 and their parallel independent application depicted in Figure 13. This time, the required application of π_3 and π_4 is not possible because the concurrent application of productions with overlapping left-hand sides is not allowed in an LAS.

Again, one may consider other encodings. Since LAS direct derivations are independent only if the rewritten subgraphs are disjoint, one may try to encode DPO productions by LAS productions in such a way that the left-hand sides of the LAS productions are smaller than in the encoding considered here. However, there seems to be no obvious way to do this.

A last remark pointing to the possibility that encodings between LAS and DPO graph rewriting that preserve the concurrent behaviour may be hard to find is the following. Let $g_{n,a}$ be the complete graph on n nodes, where all nodes are labeled by a (edge labels are not needed). It is easy to write an LAS with only one production that can change $g_{n,a}$ into $g_{n,b}$ in one parallel step, for each

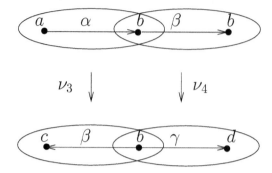

Fig. 13. Concurrent application of ν_3, ν_4.

n (each production occurrence simply replaces one labeled node, the embedding mechanism is the identity). On the other hand, a set of parallel independent DPO direct derivations rewriting a connected graph must be such that at least some of the interface graphs have a nonemty set of nodes, because of the dangling edge condition. But these nodes have images in both the original graph and the result graph of the parallel derivation, and hence their labels are preserved.

References

1. K. Barthelmann, *Describing Göttler's Operational Graph Grammars with Pushouts*, in "4th International Workshop on Graph Grammars and Their Application to Computer Science" Springer Lecture Notes in Computer Science **532** (1991), 98-112.
2. P. Baldan, A. Corradini, H. Ehrig, M. Löwe, U. Montanari and F. Rossi, *Concurrent Semantics of Algebraic Graph Transformations*, in "Handbook of Graph Grammars and Computing by Graph Transformation", **Vol. 3**, World Scientific (1999), 107-187.
3. A. Corradini, U. Montanari and F. Rossi, Graph Processes, *Fundamenta Informaticae*, **26** (1996), 241-265.
4. A. Corradini, H. Ehrig, R. Heckel, M. Löwe, U. Montanari and F. Rossi, *Algebraic Approaches to Graph Transformation*, in "Handbook of Graph Grammars and Computing by Graph Transformation", **Vol. 1**, World Scientific (1997), 163-245.
5. H. Ehrig, M. Pfender and H.J. Schneider, *Graph-Grammars: an Algebraic Approach*, In "Proceedings IEEE Conf. on Automata and Switching Theory", 167-180, 1973.
6. J. Engelfriet and G. Rozenberg, Node Replacement Graph Grammars, in "Handbook of Graph Grammars and Computing by Graph Transformation", **Vol. 1**, World Scientific, 1-94, 1997.
7. D. Janssens, Actor Grammars and Local Actions, in *Handbook of Graph Grammars and Computing by Graph Transformation*, **Vol. 3**, World Scientific (1999), 57-106.
8. D. Janssens and G. Rozenberg, On the Structure of Node Label Controlled Graph Languages, Information Sciences **20** (1980), 191-216.

9. D. Janssens and N. Verlinden, *A Framework for ESM and NLC: Local Action Systems*, in "6th International Workshop on Theory and Application of Graph Transformation", Springer Lecture Notes in Computer Science **1764** (2000), 194-214.

10. H.-J. Kreowski, *Manipulation von Graphmanipulationen*, PhD Thesis, Technische Universität Berlin (1977).

11. H.-J. Kreowski, *Is Parallelism Already Concurrency? Part 1: Derivations in Graph Grammars*, in "3rd International Workshop on Graph Grammars and Their Application to Computer Science", Springer Lecture Notes in Computer Science **291** (1987), 343-360.

Bisimulation Equivalences for Graph Grammars[*]

Paolo Baldan, Andrea Corradini, and Ugo Montanari

Dipartimento di Informatica, Università di Pisa
Corso Italia, 40 56125 Pisa, Italy
{baldan, andrea, ugo}@di.unipi.it

Abstract. Along the years the concurrent behaviour of graph grammars has been widely investigated, and, in particular, several classical approaches to the semantics of Petri nets have been extended to graph grammars. Most of the existing semantics for graph grammars provide a (possibly concurrent) operational model of computation, while little interest has been devoted to the definition of abstract observational semantics. The aim of this paper is to introduce and study a behavioural equivalence over graph grammars, inspired by the classical *history preserving bisimulation*. Several choices are conceivable according to the kind of concurrent observation one is interested in. We concentrate on the basic case where the concurrent nature of a graph grammar computation is described by means of a prime event structure. As it happens for Petri nets, history preserving bisimulation can be studied in the general framework of *causal automata* — a variation of ordinary automata introduced to deal with history dependent formalisms. In particular, we prove that history preserving bisimulation is decidable for finite-state graph grammars, by showing how the problem can be reduced to deciding the equivalence of finite causal automata.

1 Introduction

Graph grammars have been shown to be a powerful formalism for the specification of concurrent and distributed systems, which properly generalizes Petri nets. Along the years their truly concurrent behaviour has been deeply studied and a consolidated theory of concurrency is now available [Roz97, EKMR99]. In particular, several classical approaches to the semantics of Petri nets, like process and unfolding semantics, have been extended to graph grammars (see, e.g., [CMR96, Rib96, BCM98a, BCM99]).

Most of the existing semantics for graph grammars define a (possibly concurrent) operational model of computation, which gives a concrete description of the behaviour of the system in terms of non-effective (e.g., infinite, non-decidable) structures. Thus they cannot be used directly to reason about the modelled system. Indeed, these operational models are intended to represent the basis for the definition of more abstract semantics, which take into account only some aspects

---

[*] Research partially supported by the EC TMR Network GETGRATS, by the ESPRIT Working Group APPLIGRAPH and by the MURST project TOSCA.

W. Brauer et al. (Eds.): Formal and Natural Computing, LNCS 2300, pp. 158–187, 2002.

of interest for the system at hand, disregarding inessential details. At this level one can define effective techniques for checking the equivalence of systems with respect to the selected observations, for verifying if a system satisfies a given property or for synthesizing a system satisfying a given property. Roughly, we can distinguish two main approaches to system verification based on abstract semantics. First, one can verify a system by checking its equivalence with a special system which is known to be "correct". For instance, the fact that a system is secure with respect to external attacks can be checked by verifying that the system in isolation is semantically equivalent to the system under a generic attack. Alternatively one can develop a logic, adequate with respect to the abstract semantics, which is interpreted over the class of systems at hand. Then to verify that a system satisfies a certain property, expressed as a formula in the logic, one checks if it is a model (in logical sense) for the formula, hence the name *model checking* for this approach.

Some effort has been devoted to the development of logics suited to specify the dynamics of graph transformation systems, with special interest in the integration of graphical specifications and temporal logic constraints (see, e.g., [HEWC97, Hec98, Koc99, GHK00]), but the study of abstract behavioural semantics and of the corresponding logics has received little attention. Here we move some steps in this direction, introducing an abstract semantics for graph grammars based on the classical *history preserving bisimulation* (*HP-bisimulation*, for short) [RT88, DD90], a behavioural equivalence which, differently from ordinary bisimulation, takes into account the concurrency properties of a system. Informally, two systems are HP-bisimilar if every event in the first one can be simulated by an event in the second one with an equivalent causal history and vice versa. History preserving bisimulation on ordinary P/T nets [RT88, BDKP91] relies on the notions of process and deterministic *prime event structure* (PES) associated to a process. Roughly speaking, two nets N_0 and N_1 are HP-bisimilar if for any process π_0 of N_0 we can find a process π_1 of N_1 such that the associated deterministic PES's are isomorphic. Whenever π_0 can perform an action becoming a process π_0', also π_1 can perform the same action becoming π_1' and vice versa. Moreover the isomorphism between the PES's associated to π_0 and π_1 is required to be extensible to an isomorphism between the PES's associated to π_0' and π_1'. Intuitively, history preserving bisimulation is more appropriate than ordinary bisimulation whenever in a system we are interested not only in the events which might happen, but also in the dependency relations between such events. For instance, imagine to have a system where a subset of actions is considered critical and suppose that for security reasons critical actions must not be influenced by non-critical actions. This property, which can be seen as a form of non-interference [GM82], can be formalized by asking that critical actions do not causally depend on non-critical actions and it is invariant for transformations of the system which preserve HP-bisimilarity.

A basic source of inspiration for our work is the close relation existing between graph grammars and Petri nets. The simple but crucial observation is that Petri nets are essentially rewriting systems on multisets, i.e., the markings of the net, which can be seen, in turn, as discrete graphs labelled over the places of the net. Hence graph grammars can be viewed as a generalization of Petri nets: they allow to give a more structured description of the state in term of a proper graph and to specify "contextual" rewriting steps where part of the state is preserved. In this respect graph grammars are closer to some generalizations of nets in the literature, called nets with read (test) arcs or contextual nets (see, e.g., [JK95, MR95, Vog97]), where transitions can be enriched with a context, i.e., with the possibility of checking the presence of tokens in the places of the net, without consuming such tokens.

Indeed, our study of HP-bisimulation for graph grammars is guided by the work on ordinary Petri nets [MP97, Vog91], which has been generalized to contextual nets in [BCM00b]. Graph grammars come equipped with a notion of deterministic (graph) process [CMR96, BCM98a] and with an event structure model [BCM99, Bal00], and thus the notion of HP-bisimulation can be generalized to graph grammars. We show that HP-bisimulation is decidable for *finite-state* graph grammars, called here, by analogy with Petri nets, *n-safe* graph grammars. To this aim, as in [MP97, BCM00b], we resort to *causal automata* [MP97], a variation of ordinary automata where states are sets of names (or events) and transitions allow for the creation of new names and the deallocation of old ones. A generalization of causal automata, called *history-dependent automata* (*HD-automata*), has been proposed as a general framework to study history-dependent formalisms, like CCS with causal and location semantics or with value-passing, and the π-calculus with the ordinary, early or late, or noninterleaving semantics [MP98, Pis99].

The (possibly infinite) transition system of processes of a graph grammar, which is used to define HP-bisimulation, is translated to a causal automaton via a construction which respects (preserves and reflects) bisimilarity. The automaton is proved to be finite exactly for finite-state graph grammars. Thus HP-bisimilarity of any two finite-state graph grammars can be checked by verifying the bisimilarity of the corresponding automata. This can be done concretely by using the algorithm proposed in [MP97], which after removing from the states of the automaton the events which are useless, i.e., never referenced in the future, translates the causal automaton into an ordinary automaton. Then the standard techniques for ordinary transition systems can be used to check bisimilarity or to obtain a minimal realization. More recent works [Pis99, MP00] show that a minimal realization exists and can be constructed in the class of causal automata themselves (actually, in the mentioned papers, the general case of HD-automata is worked out and a suitable extension of HD-automata, the so-called *automata with symmetries*, must be introduced to get this result). As it happens for ordinary automata, also a causal automaton can be seen as a coalgebra for a suitable functor and the minimal realization arises as the image in the final coalgebra of the given automaton.

It is worth mentioning that when considering formalisms more expressive than ordinary nets, like nets with read or inhibitor arcs, or graph grammars themselves, the dependencies between events in a computation become more complex than causality and conflict. For instance, the possibility of specifying "read-only" operations over the state leads to an asymmetric form of conflict: if an event e reads a resource which is consumed by another event e', then the execution of e' disables e, while the converse does not hold, i.e., e can precede e' in a computation. Hence the causal structure of a process can be described at various degrees of abstraction. At a basic level it can be represented as a deterministic PES, a labelled partial order which describes only the precedences between events, disregarding their origin. But we can also consider finer descriptions in terms of event structures which "observe", for instance, new kind of dependencies arising from the possibility of preserving part of the state in a rewriting step or from the need of maintaining the integrity of its graphical structure. In this paper we will concentrate on the basic case only, just hinting at the other possibilities.

The rest of the paper is structured as follows. First in Section 2 we present the basics of graph grammars and the notion of (deterministic) graph process. In Section 3 we introduce HP-bisimulation for graph grammars. In Section 4 we review causal automata and the corresponding notion of causal bisimulation. Then in Section 5 we show how a (finite-state) graph grammar can be mapped to a (finite) causal automaton via a transformation which respects HP-bisimilarity, thus offering the possibility of deciding HP-bisimulation and of building a minimal automaton for a given grammar up to HP-bisimilarity. Finally, in Section 6 we draw some conclusions and directions for future work. In particular we hint at the possibility of defining different notions of HP-bisimulation which arise by considering finer observations of the causal history of events. Furthermore we give some ideas about the logical counterpart of history preserving bisimulation, presenting a logic in the style of Hennessy-Milner which can be shown to be adequate.

2   Typed Graph Grammars and Processes

This section briefly introduces typed graph grammars [CMR96], a variation of classical DPO graph grammars [Ehr87, CMR+97] where the rewriting takes place on so-called *typed graphs*, namely graphs labelled over a structure (the *graph of types*) that is itself a graph. After some basic definitions and a discussion about the relationship between graph grammars and (contextual) Petri nets, we will recall the notion of *process* for a typed graph grammar [CMR96, BCM98a], which plays a basic role in the definition of history preserving bisimulation.

2.1   Typed Graph Grammars

Let **Graph** be the category of (directed, unlabelled) graphs and total graph morphisms. For a graph G we will denote by N_G and E_G the (disjoint) sets of *nodes* and *edges* of G, and by $s_G, t_G : E_G \to N_G$ its *source* and *target* functions. Given a graph TG, a *typed graph* G over TG is a graph $\langle G \rangle$, together with a morphism $t_G : \langle G \rangle \to TG$. A morphism between TG-typed graphs $f : G_1 \to G_2$

is a graph morphisms $f : \langle G_1 \rangle \rightarrow \langle G_2 \rangle$ consistent with the typing, i.e., such that $t_{G_1} = t_{G_2} \circ f$. A typed graph G is called *injective* if the typing morphism t_G is injective. More generally, for a fixed $n \in \mathbb{N}$, the graph is called *n-injective* if for any item x in TG, $|t_G^{-1}(x)| \leq n$, namely if the number of instances of "resources" of any type x is bounded by n. The category of TG-typed graphs and typed graph morphisms is denoted by TG-**Graph** and can be synthetically defined as the comma category (**Graph** $\downarrow TG$).

Fixed a graph TG of types, a *(TG-typed graph) production* $(L \xleftarrow{l} K \xrightarrow{r} R)$ is a pair of *injective* typed graph morphisms $l : K \rightarrow L$ and $r : K \rightarrow R$, where $\langle L \rangle$, $\langle K \rangle$ and $\langle R \rangle$ are finite graphs. It is called *consuming* if morphism $l : K \rightarrow L$ is not surjective. The typed graphs L, K, and R are called the *left-hand side*, the *interface*, and the *right-hand side* of the production, respectively.

Definition 1 (typed graph grammar). *A (TG-typed) graph grammar $\mathcal{G}$ is a tuple $\langle TG, G_s, P, \pi \rangle$, where G_s is the start (typed, finite) graph, P is a finite set of production names, and π is a function which associates a graph production to each production name in P. A labelled graph grammar is a pair $\langle \mathcal{G}, \lambda_{\mathcal{G}} \rangle$, where $\mathcal{G}$ is a graph grammar and $\lambda_{\mathcal{G}} : P \rightarrow$ Act is a function from P to a fixed set of action names Act.*

We will denote by $Elem(\mathcal{G})$ the set $N_{TG} \cup E_{TG} \cup P$. Furthermore, we will assume that for each production name $q \in P$ the corresponding production $\pi(q)$ is $L_q \xleftarrow{l_q} K_q \xrightarrow{r_q} R_q$. The components of a graph grammar $\mathcal{G}$ will be denoted by TG, G_s, P and π, possibly with subscripts.

Since in this paper we work only with typed notions, we will usually omit the qualification "typed", and, sometimes, we will not indicate explicitly the typing morphisms. Moreover, we will consider only *consuming* grammars, namely grammars where all productions are consuming: this corresponds, in the theory of Petri nets, to the usual requirement that transitions must have non-empty pre-set.

Definition 2 (direct derivation). *Let $\mathcal{G}$ be a graph grammar. Given a typed graph G, a production $q \in P$, and a match (i.e., a graph morphism) $g : L_q \rightarrow G$, a direct derivation δ from G to H using q (based on g) exists, written $\delta : G \Rightarrow_q H$ (or $\delta : G \Rightarrow_{\mathcal{G}} H$), if and only if the diagram*

$$
\begin{array}{ccccc}
q : L_q & \xleftarrow{l_q} & K_q & \xrightarrow{r_q} & R_q \\
{\scriptstyle g}\downarrow & & {\scriptstyle k}\downarrow & & \downarrow{\scriptstyle h} \\
G & \xleftarrow{b} & D & \xrightarrow{d} & H
\end{array}
$$

*can be constructed, where both squares have to be pushouts in TG-**Graph**. For a labelled grammar, if $\lambda_{\mathcal{G}}(q) = a$, in this situation we write $\delta : G \Rightarrow_q^a H$ (or $\delta : G \Rightarrow_{\mathcal{G}}^a H$).*

A derivation in $\mathcal{G}$ is a sequence of direct derivations (in $\mathcal{G}$) beginning from the start graph G_s.

Roughly speaking, the rewriting step removes from the graph G the items of the left-hand side which are not in the image of the interface, namely $L_q - l_q(K_q)$, producing in this way the graph D. Then the items in the right-hand side which are not in the image of the interface, namely $R_q - r_q(K_q)$, are added to D, obtaining the final graph H. Notice that the interface graph K_q (common part of L_q and R_q) specifies both what is preserved and how the added subgraph has to be connected to the remaining part. Given a match $g : L_q \to G$ as in the above diagram, the pushout complement of l_q and g (i.e., a graph D with morphisms k and b such that the left square is a pushout) exists if and only if the *gluing condition* is satisfied. This consists of two parts:

- *identification condition*, requiring that if two distinct nodes or edges of L_q are mapped by g to the same image, then both must be in the image of l_q;
- *dangling condition*, stating that no edge in $G - g(L_q)$ should be incident to a node in $g(L_q - l_q(K_q))$ (because otherwise the application of the production would leave such an edge "dangling").

2.2   Relation with Petri Nets

Many definitions and constructions in this paper are better understood keeping in mind the relation between Petri nets and DPO graph grammars. The basic observation (which belongs to the folklore, see, e.g., [Cor96]) is that a P/T Petri net is essentially a rewriting system on multisets, and that, given a set A, a multiset of A can be represented as a discrete graph typed over A. In this view a P/T net can be seen as a graph grammar acting on discrete graphs typed over the set of places, the productions being (some encoding of) the net transitions: a marking is represented by a set of nodes (tokens) labelled by the place where they are, and, for example, the Petri net transition t in the top part of Fig. 1 is represented by the graph production depicted aside. Notice that the interface is empty since nothing is explicitly preserved by a net transition. It is not difficult to show that this encoding satisfies the properties one would expect, namely that there is a precise correspondence between transition firings in the original net and derivations in the corresponding grammar.

The considered encoding of nets into grammars enlightens the dimensions in which graph grammars properly extend nets. First of all grammars allow for a more structured description of state, that is a general graph rather than a multiset (discrete graph). Furthermore, graph grammars allow for productions where the interface graph may not be empty, thus specifying a "context" consisting of items that have to be present for the productions to be applied, but which are not affected by the application. The context can be interpreted as a part of the state which is accessed in a "read-only" way by the rewriting step, and, consistently with this view, several rewriting steps can be applied in parallel sharing (part of) the context. In this respect, graph grammars are closer to some generalizations of Petri nets in the literature, called nets with read (test) arcs or contextual nets (see, e.g., [JK95, MR95, Vog97]), which generalize classical nets by adding the possibility of checking for the presence of tokens which are not

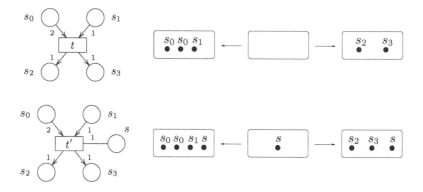

Fig. 1. Petri net transitions and corresponding DPO productions.

consumed. Concretely, a transition of a contextual net, besides the pre-set and post-set, has also a context specifying tokens which must be present to enable the transitions, but which are not affected by the firing. For instance, in the bottom left part of Fig. 1, place s is a context for transition t', and hence t', to be enabled, requires a token in s which is not consumed. It is clear that the context of a contextual net transition closely corresponds to the interface graph of a DPO production, so that contextual nets can be seen as special graph grammars acting on discrete graphs, but with productions which can have a non-empty interface (see the encoding of transition t' as a DPO graph production in the bottom right part of Fig. 1).

2.3   Processes of Typed Graph Grammars

Graph processes [CMR96, BCM98a] arise from the idea of equipping graph grammars with a semantics which on the one hand explicitly represents events and relationships among them, and on the other hand uses graph grammars themselves as semantic domain. Analogously to what happens for Petri nets, a *graph process* of a graph grammar $\mathcal{G}$ is defined as an "occurrence grammar" $\mathcal{O}$, i.e., a grammar satisfying suitable acyclicity and conflict freeness constraints, equipped with a mapping from $\mathcal{O}$ to $\mathcal{G}$. This mapping is used to associate to the derivations in $\mathcal{O}$ corresponding derivations in $\mathcal{G}$. The basic property of a graph process is that the derivations in $\mathcal{G}$ which are in the range of such mapping constitute a full class of *shift*-equivalent derivations, i.e., of derivations which differ only for the order of "independent" rewriting steps. Therefore the process can be regarded as an abstract representation of such a class and plays a role similar to a *canonical derivation* [Kre77].

It is worth remarking that in the definitions of occurrence grammar and of graph process, later in this section, we will slightly depart from the original proposal in [CMR96], as we will use explicitly the relation of asymmetric conflict (as we already did, e.g., in [BCM99]). A first step towards the definition of (deterministic) occurrence grammar is a suitable notion of safety for grammars [CMR96], generalizing that for P/T nets. More generally, we extend to graph grammars the notion of n-safety, which amounts to the property of being finite-state.

Definition 3 (safe grammar). *For a fixed $n \in \mathbb{N}$, we say that a graph grammar $\mathcal{G}$ is n-safe if, for all H such that $G_s \Rightarrow^* H$, H is n-injective. A 1-safe grammar will be simply called* safe.

The definition can be understood by thinking of nodes and edges of the type graph as a generalization of places in Petri nets. In this view the number of different items of a graph which are typed on a given item of the type graph corresponds to the number of tokens contained in a place, and thus the condition of (n-) safety for a Petri net marking, which requires each place to contain at most 1 (n) tokens, is generalized to typed graphs by the (n-) injectivity of the typing morphism. In the following, to mean that a graph grammar $\mathcal{G}$ is n-safe for some $n \in \mathbb{N}$ we will simply say that $\mathcal{G}$ is n-safe.

In particular, safe graph grammars can be given a visual net-like representation, where the items of the type graph and the productions play, respectively, the role of places and transitions. In fact, if $\mathcal{G}$ is a safe graph grammar, then each graph $\langle\langle G\rangle, t_G\rangle$ reachable in $\mathcal{G}$ can be identified with the subgraph $t_G(\langle G\rangle)$ of the type graph TG and thus it can be represented by suitably decorating the nodes and edges of the type graph. Concretely, a node is drawn as a filled circle, if it belongs to $t_G(\langle G\rangle)$ and as an empty circle, otherwise, while an edge is drawn as a plain (bold) line if it belongs to $t_G(\langle G\rangle)$ and as a dotted line otherwise. For instance, in the right part of Fig. 2, forgetting about the productions q_i and the corresponding connections, one can see a representation of the start graph G_s of the graph grammar presented in the left part: nodes B, C, D are filled since they belong to G_s, while node A is empty and edge L is dotted since they are not in G_s.

With this identification, in each derivation of a safe grammar beginning from the start graph a production q can be applied only to the subgraph of the type graph which is the image via the typing morphism of its left-hand side, i.e., to $t_{L_q}(\langle L_q\rangle)$. Therefore according to its typing, we can think that a production *produces*, *preserves* and *consumes* items of the type graph. Using a net-like language, we speak of *pre-set* $\bullet q$, *context* $\underline{q}$ and *post-set* $q\bullet$ of a production q. This is expressed by representing productions as arrow-shaped boxes, connected to the consumed and produced resources by incoming and outgoing arrows, respectively, and to the preserved resources by undirected lines. Fig. 2 presents a safe graph grammar and its net-like pictorial representation. To have a lighter presentation in the examples, we assume that the action label of each production q in grammar $\mathcal{G}$ is the name q of the production itself.

The notions of pre-set, post-set and context of a production have a clear interpretation only for safe grammars. However for technical reasons it is preferable to define them for general graph grammars.

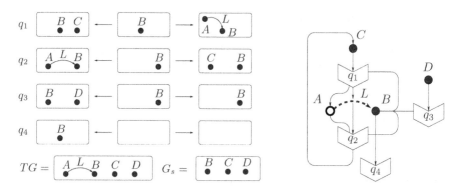

Fig. 2. A grammar $\mathcal{G}$ and its net-like representation.

Definition 4 (pre-set, post-set, context). *Let $\mathcal{G}$ be a graph grammar. For any $q \in P$ we define*

$$^\bullet q = t_{L_q}(\langle L_q \rangle - l_q(\langle K_q \rangle)) \qquad q^\bullet = t_{R_q}(\langle R_q \rangle - r_q(\langle K_q \rangle))$$

$$\underline{q} = t_{K_q}(\langle K_q \rangle)$$

seen as sets of nodes and edges, and we say that q consumes, produces and preserves items in $^\bullet q$, $q^\bullet$ and $\underline{q}$, respectively. Similarly for a node or an edge x in TG we write $^\bullet x$, $\underline{x}$ and $x^\bullet$ to denote the sets of productions which produce, preserve and consume x, respectively.

For instance, for grammar $\mathcal{G}$ in Fig. 2, the pre-set, context and post-set of production q_1 are $^\bullet q_1 = \{C\}$, $\underline{q_1} = \{B\}$ and $q_1^\bullet = \{A, L\}$, while for the node B, $^\bullet B = \emptyset$, $\underline{B} = \{q_1, q_2, q_3\}$ and $B^\bullet = \{q_4\}$.

We next introduce the relations of causality and asymmetric conflict, representing the dependencies between events in a graph grammar.

Definition 5 (causal relation). *The causal relation of a grammar $\mathcal{G}$ is the binary relation $<$ over $Elem(\mathcal{G})$ defined as the least transitive relation satisfying: for any node or edge x in the type graph TG and for productions $q, q' \in P$*

1. *if $x \in ^\bullet q$ then $x < q$;*
2. *if $x \in q^\bullet$ then $q < x$;*
3. *if $q^\bullet \cap \underline{q'} \neq \emptyset$ then $q < q'$.*

As usual $\leq$ denotes the reflexive closure of $<$. Moreover, for $x \in Elem(\mathcal{G})$ we write $\lfloor x \rfloor$ for the set of causes of x in P, namely $\{q \in P \mid q \leq x\}$. We will denote by $Min(\mathcal{G})$ and $Max(\mathcal{G})$ the sets of items of TG which are minimal and maximal, resp., with respect to $\leq$.

The first two clauses of the definition of relation $<$ are obvious. The third one formalizes the fact that if an item is generated by q and preserved by q', then q', to be applied, requires that q had already been applied.

Notice that the fact that an item is preserved by q and consumed by q', i.e., $\underline{q} \cap {}^\bullet q' \neq \emptyset$, does not imply $q < q'$. Actually, since q must precede q' in any computation where both appear, in such computations q acts as a cause of q'. However, differently from a true cause, q is not necessary for q' to be applied. Therefore we can think of the relation between the two productions as a *weak* form of *causal dependency*. Equivalently, we can observe that the application of q' prevents q to be applied, so that q can never follow q' in a derivation. But the converse is not true, since q *can* be applied before q'. Thus this situation can also be interpreted naturally as an *asymmetric conflict* between the two productions (see, e.g., [BCM99]). For instance, in the grammar $\mathcal{G}$ of Fig. 2 there is an asymmetric conflict between productions q_3 and q_4, since $B \in \underline{q_3} \cap {}^\bullet q_4$.

Definition 6 (asymmetric conflict). *The asymmetric conflict relation of a grammar $\mathcal{G}$ is the binary relation $\nearrow$ over the set P of productions, defined by:*

1. *if $\underline{q} \cap {}^\bullet q' \neq \emptyset$ then $q \nearrow q'$;*
2. *if ${}^\bullet q \cap {}^\bullet q' \neq \emptyset$ and $q \neq q'$ then $q \nearrow q'$;*
3. *if $q < q'$ then $q \nearrow q'$.*

Point (1) has been discussed above. By point (2), the symmetric conflict arising when two productions q and q' consume a common resource is represented as an asymmetric conflict in both directions $q \nearrow q'$ and $q' \nearrow q$. Finally, point (3) formalizes the intuition that asymmetric conflict can be seen as a weak form of causality and thus it is implied by causality.

A *(deterministic) occurrence grammar* is now defined as a special grammar satisfying suitable requirements of acyclicity and absence of conflicts, which will allow to view its productions as single event occurrences.

Definition 7 ((deterministic) occurrence grammar). *A* (deterministic) occurrence grammar *is a graph grammar $\mathcal{O} = \langle TG, G_s, P, \pi \rangle$ such that*

1. *each edge or node x in TG is created by at most one production in P, namely $|{}^\bullet x| \leq 1$;*
2. *$\nearrow_\mathcal{O}$ is acyclic and finitary; thus $(\nearrow_\mathcal{O})^*$ and $\leq_\mathcal{O}$ are finitary partial orders;[1]*
3. *$Min(\mathcal{O})$ and $Max(\mathcal{O})$, with the graphical structure inherited from TG, are well-defined subgraphs of TG; furthermore the start graph G_s coincides with $Min(\mathcal{O})$ (typed by the inclusion);*
4. *for each production $q : L_q \xleftarrow{l_q} K_q \xrightarrow{r_q} R_q$, the typing t_{L_q} is injective on the "consumed part" $\langle L_q \rangle - l_q(\langle K_q \rangle)$, and similarly t_{R_q} is injective on the "produced part" $\langle R_q \rangle - r_q(\langle K_q \rangle)$.*

Intuitively, conditions (1)–(4) recast in the framework of graph grammars the analogous conditions of occurrence contextual nets [BCM98b, VSY98]. In particular the acyclicity of $\nearrow$ corresponds to the requirement of absence of conflicts in

---

[1] A relation $r \subseteq X \times X$ is called *finitary* if for any $x \in X$ the set $\{y \in X : y\,r\,x\}$ is finite. Furthermore r^* denotes the reflexive and transitive closure of a relation r.

occurrence Petri nets. Condition (4) is closely related to safety and requires that each production consumes and produces items with "multiplicity" one. Observe that, together with acyclicity of $\nearrow$, it disallows the presence of some productions which surely could never be applied, because they fail to satisfy the identification condition with respect to the typing morphism.

Since the start graph of an occurrence grammar $\mathcal{O}$ is determined by $Min(\mathcal{O})$, we often do not mention it explicitly. Observe that, by the defining conditions, each occurrence grammar is safe.

A (deterministic) process for a graph grammar, analogously to what happens for ordinary and contextual nets, is an occurrence grammar endowed with a mapping to the original grammar and it can be seen as a representative of a set of shift equivalent derivations of $\mathcal{G}$.

Definition 8 (graph process). *Let $\mathcal{G} = \langle TG, G_s, P, \pi \rangle$ be a typed graph grammar. A (finite marked) process for $\mathcal{G}$ is a mapping $\varphi : \mathcal{O}_\varphi \to \mathcal{G}$, such that $\mathcal{O}_\varphi = \langle TG_\varphi, P_\varphi, \pi_\varphi \rangle$ is an occurrence grammar and $\varphi = \langle \varphi_T, \varphi_P, \iota_\varphi \rangle$, where*

1. *$\varphi_T : TG_\varphi \to TG$ is a graph morphism;*
2. *$\varphi_P : P_\varphi \to P$ is a function mapping each production $q' : (L' \leftarrow K' \to R')$ in P_φ to an isomorphic production $q = \varphi_P(q') : (L \leftarrow K \to R)$ in P and*
3. *the ι_φ component associates to each production $q' \in P_\varphi$ a triple of isomorphisms $\iota_\varphi(q') = \langle \iota_\varphi^L(q') : L \to L', \iota_\varphi^K(q') : K \to K', \iota_\varphi^R(q') : R \to R' \rangle$, making the diagram in the left part of Fig. 3 commute. Furthermore it includes an isomorphism $\iota_\varphi^s : \langle G_s \rangle \to \langle G_{s\varphi} \rangle$, which makes the diagram in the right part of Fig. 3 commute.*

We denote by $Min(\varphi)$ and $Max(\varphi)$ the graphs $Min(\mathcal{O})$ and $Max(\mathcal{O})$. The same graphs typed over TG by the restrictions of φ_T are denoted by $^\bullet\varphi$ and $\varphi^\bullet$ and called, respectively, the source *and* target *graphs of the process (observe that $^\bullet\varphi \simeq G_s$).*

We call initial process *of $\mathcal{G}$ any process φ with an empty set of productions (and thus with $TG_\varphi \simeq \langle G_s \rangle$).*

For instance, Fig. 4 presents several processes of grammar $\mathcal{G}$ in Fig. 2 (for the moment ignore the fact that processes are partly shaded). For each process we only give the net-like representation of the underlying occurrence grammar. The mapping over the original grammar is implicitly represented by the labelling.

It is worth observing, that because of the dangling condition, a production q which consumes a node n can be applied only if there are no edges with source or target in n which remain dangling after the application of q. In other words, the presence of an edge e with source or target in n such that $e \notin {}^\bullet q$ *inhibits* the application of q (in [Bal00] this observation represents the basis to establish a close correspondence between graph grammars and nets with inhibitor arcs). For example, in the grammar $\mathcal{G}$ of Fig. 2, edge L inhibits production q_4 since q_4 consumes node B which is the target of L. Observe that productions q_1 and q_2, respectively, produce and consume such an edge, and therefore, once q_1 has been applied, q_4 can occur only after the application of q_2. That is, in a process

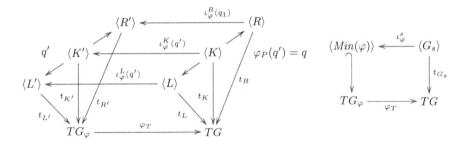

Fig. 3. Graph processes.

where all q_1, q_2 and q_4 are applied, they must occur exactly in this order. Indeed, q_1 and q_2, to act on edge L must produce or preserve its target node B (in this case they both preserve B) and thus, by definition of asymmetric conflict, we have $q_1 \nearrow q_4$ and $q_2 \nearrow q_4$. Hence in a deterministic computation where q_1, q_2 and q_4 occur, the relation $\nearrow$ already imposes the correct order of application for them. This holds in general: there is no need to consider explicitly the inhibiting effects due to the dangling condition in a graph process, as they are subsumed by the asymmetric conflict relation. Note that this does not hold in the case of inhibitor nets, for which the definition of process becomes more involved [Bal00].

3   History Preserving Bisimulation on Graph Grammars

As mentioned in the introduction, the theory of concurrency for graph grammars has been deeply studied and a number of concurrent operational models for graph grammars has been proposed in the literature. However, until now the problem of defining suitable abstract behavioural semantics for graph grammars has been given little attention.

Observe that the notions of (labelled) graph grammar and of direct derivation are enough to define ordinary bisimulation over graph grammars. Intuitively, two systems are bisimilar if every action of the first one can be simulated by an action of the second one, and vice versa. Formally, given two graph grammars $\mathcal{G}_1$ and $\mathcal{G}_2$, a *simulation* of $\mathcal{G}_1$ into $\mathcal{G}_2$ is a relation $\mathcal{R}$ between (abstract) graphs typed over TG_1 and TG_2, respectively, such that if $G_1 \mathcal{R} G_2$ and $G_1 \Rightarrow^a_{\mathcal{G}_1} H_1$ then there exists H_2 such that $G_2 \Rightarrow^a_{\mathcal{G}_2} H_2$ and $H_1 \mathcal{R} H_2$. The relation $\mathcal{R}$ is a *bisimulation* if both $\mathcal{R}$ and $\mathcal{R}^{-1}$ are simulations, and $\mathcal{G}_1$ and $\mathcal{G}_2$ are *bisimilar* if their initial graphs are related by a bisimulation.

Ordinary bisimulation is an "interleaving" equivalence, in the sense that it is not able to capture the concurrency properties of a system. For instance, it equates the parallel composition of two systems and the nondeterministic choice of their possible sequentializations. Here we are interested in the so-called *history preserving bisimulation*, a behavioural equivalence which, instead, takes into account the dependencies among events. Roughly speaking, it equates two systems if each action of the first one can be simulated by an action of the second one with an equivalent history, and vice versa. In this section, relying on the work already developed on contextual nets [BCM00a], the notion of graph process is taken as a basis to extend this idea to the case of graph grammars. As a description of the "concurrent structure" of a computation we consider the *(labelled) prime event structure* (PES) underlying a process, i.e., a partially ordered structure where the elements represent events (occurrences of productions) and the partial order represents the dependencies between events. This amounts to observing the precedences between events, without taking care of their origin. We mentioned that such precedences can arise both as ordinary causal dependencies, induced by the flow of information, and as dependencies induced by read-only operations and inhibiting effects related to the dangling condition. Other finer observations, taking into account the diverse nature of these precedences, are conceivable and will be discussed in the conclusions.

The basic ingredient for the definition of history preserving bisimulation is a transition system, associated to each graph grammar, where states are processes. The initial state is the empty process, corresponding to the start graph, and any process can be extended by the "application" of any production which is enabled in its final (maximal) graph.

Definition 9 (process moves). *Given two processes φ and φ' of a labeled graph grammar $\mathcal{G}$, we write $\varphi \xrightarrow{a}_{e} \varphi'$, saying that φ moves to φ' performing action a, if*

- $P_{\varphi'} = P_{\varphi} \cup \{e\}$, *with $e \notin P_{\varphi}$ and $\lambda_{\mathcal{G}}(\varphi'_P(e)) = a$;*
- TG_{φ} *is a subgraph of $TG_{\varphi'}$;*
- ${}^{\bullet}e$ *and $\underline{e}$ are included in $Max(\varphi)$;*
- φ_T, φ_P, π_{φ} *and ι_{φ} and are the restrictions to $\mathcal{O}_{\varphi}$ of the components of φ'.*

Fig. 4 presents a sequence of processes φ_i for the grammar $\mathcal{G}$ of Fig. 2, such that each φ_i moves to φ_{i+1} (the process φ_3 is not represented explicitly). For instance $\varphi_0 \xrightarrow{q_1}_{e_1} \varphi_1$.

To each process φ of a graph grammar $\mathcal{G}$ we can naturally associate a (deterministic labelled) PES where events are the productions of the underlying occurrence graph grammar, causality is the transitive closure of the asymmetric conflict relation and each event is labelled by the action label of the corresponding production in $\mathcal{G}$.

Definition 10 (prime event structure for processes). *Let φ be a process of a labelled graph grammar $\mathcal{G}$. The PES associated to φ is defined as:*

$$ev(\varphi) = \langle P_{\varphi}, (\nearrow_{\varphi})^*, \lambda_{\mathcal{G}} \circ \varphi_P \rangle.$$

Based on the notions of process and of event structure associated to a process, *history preserving (HP-) bisimulation* is readily defined.

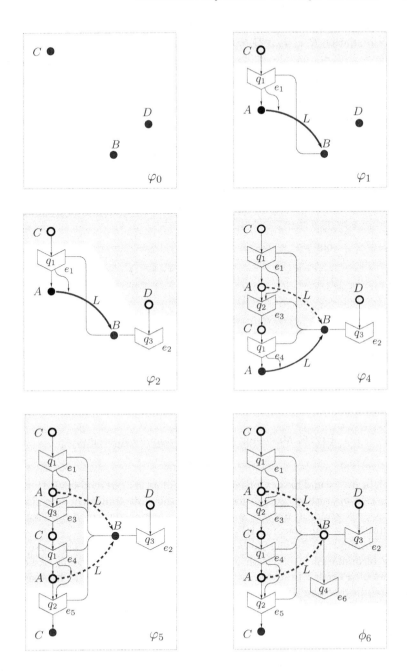

Fig. 4. A sequence of process moves for grammar $\mathcal{G}$ in Fig. 2, starting from an initial process. For any process the non-shaded part represents the corresponding partial process.

Definition 11 (HP-bisimulation). *Let $\mathcal{G}_1$ and $\mathcal{G}_2$ be labelled graph grammars. An HP-simulation $\mathcal{R}$ of $\mathcal{G}_1$ in $\mathcal{G}_2$ is a set of triples $\langle \varphi_1, f, \varphi_2 \rangle$ where φ_i is a process of $\mathcal{G}_i$ for $i \in \{1, 2\}$, and $f : ev(\varphi_1) \to ev(\varphi_2)$ is an isomorphism of PES's, such that*

1. $\langle \varphi_0(\mathcal{G}_1), \emptyset, \varphi_0(\mathcal{G}_2) \rangle \in \mathcal{R}$, with $\varphi_0(\mathcal{G}_i)$ initial process of $\mathcal{G}_i$ for $i \in \{1, 2\}$;
2. $\langle \varphi_1, f, \varphi_2 \rangle \in \mathcal{R} \wedge \varphi_1 \xrightarrow[e_1]{a} \varphi_1' \ \Rightarrow\ \varphi_2 \xrightarrow[e_2]{a} \varphi_2' \wedge \langle \varphi_1', f', \varphi_2' \rangle \in \mathcal{R} \wedge f'_{|ev(\varphi_1)} = f$.

An HP-bisimulation between $\mathcal{G}_1$ and $\mathcal{G}_2$ is a set of triples $\mathcal{R}$ such that $\mathcal{R}$ and $\mathcal{R}^{-1} = \{ \langle \varphi_2, f^{-1}, \varphi_1 \rangle : \langle \varphi_1, f, \varphi_2 \rangle \in \mathcal{R} \}$ are HP-simulations. The labelled graph grammars $\mathcal{G}_1$ and $\mathcal{G}_2$ are HP-bisimilar, written $\mathcal{G}_1 \sim_{hp} \mathcal{G}_2$, if there is an HP-bisimulation $\mathcal{R}$ between $\mathcal{G}_1$ and $\mathcal{G}_2$.

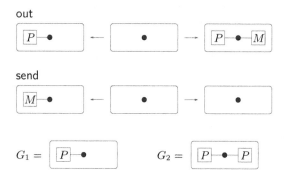

Fig. 5. Modelling the transmission of messages.

Both ordinary and history preserving bisimulation represent an abstraction of the concrete operational semantics based on the shift equivalence, in the sense that any two graph grammars with the same concurrent model of computation [Roz97] are bisimilar and HP-bisimilar.

Concerning the relationship between ordinary bisimulation and history preserving bisimulation over graph grammars, quite obviously, being based on a more detailed observation, the latter is finer than the former. To have a better understanding of the difference between the two semantics consider the productions in Fig. 5, which are intended to model the generation and delivery of messages in a single node of a network. Edges labelled by P and M represent processes and messages, respectively. Rule **out** represents the generation of a message by a process, while rule **send** represents the delivery of the message: since we consider a single node of the newtwork the message which is sent simply disappears. This minimal subsystem is only aimed at illustrating some concepts in a setting as simple as possible: to make the model more realistic one could make explicit the reception of messages, the entire network could be represented as a graph and new rules could be added to represent message delivery over the network. Let $\mathcal{G}_1$ and $\mathcal{G}_2$ be the graph grammars with rules out and send, and with initial graph G_1 and G_2, respectively. It is easy to see that $\mathcal{G}_1$ and $\mathcal{G}_2$ are bisimilar, but not HP-bisimilar. In fact, each out operation performed by a process causally depends on the previous one and each send operation causally depends on the out operation which generated the corresponding message. Therefore in $\mathcal{G}_1$ there is a single chain of causally dependent out operations, while in $\mathcal{G}_2$ there can be two concurrent out operations, as shown by the corresponding event structures in Fig. 6.

It is worth observing that extending the grammars with an explicit rule modelling the receive operation, the (deterministic components of the) event structures would closely correspond to Message Sequence Charts [RGG96], a graphical and textual language for the description and specification of the inter-actions between system components.

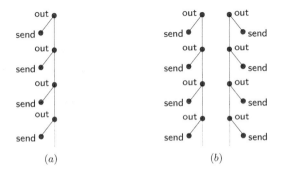

Fig. 6. The event structures corresponding to the graph grammars (a) $\mathcal{G}_1$ and (b) $\mathcal{G}_2$.

4   Causal Automata

In this section we review *causal automata*, a generalization of ordinary automata introduced in [MP97] as an appropriate model for history dependent formalisms (see also [MP98, Pis99], where more general models, called HD-automata, are presented). Here causal automata will be used as an abstract framework where HP-bisimulation over graph grammars can be studied. In particular the decidability of HP-bisimulation for finite-state graph grammars will be proved by showing that the problem can be reduced to the bisimilarity of finite causal automata.

Causal automata extend ordinary automata by allowing sets of names to appear explicitly in the states and labels of the automata. The names are local, namely they do not have a global identity, and the correspondence between the names of the source and those of the target states of each transition is specified explicitly. This allows for a compact representation of systems since states differing only for the concrete identity of the names can be identified. Moreover causal automata provide a mechanism for the generation of new names: the problem of choosing a fresh name disappears in this formalism where a new name is simply a name which does not correspond to any name in the source state. In the specific case of Petri nets and graph grammars, names are identities of transitions in a process (events) and the correspondence between names allows to represent causal dependencies.

Definition 12 (causal automaton). *Let $\mathcal{N}$ be a fixed infinite countable set of names (event names) and let* Act *be a fixed set of labels. A causal automaton is a tuple $\mathcal{A} = \langle Q, n, \longmapsto, q_0 \rangle$, where*

- Q *is the set of* states;
- $n : Q \to \mathcal{P}_{fin}(\mathcal{N})$ *is a function associating to each state a finite set of names;*
- $\longmapsto$ *is a set of transitions, each of the form $q \xmapsto[M]{a}_\sigma q'$, with*
  - *q, q' the source and target states;*
  - *$a \in$ Act the label;*
  - *$M \subseteq n(q)$ the set of dependencies of the transition;*
  - *$\sigma : n(q') \hookrightarrow n(q) \cup \{\star\}$ the injective inverse renaming function;*
- *$q_0 \in Q$ is the initial state; it is required that $n(q_0) = \emptyset$.*

For each state $q \in Q$ the set of names $n(q)$ is used to represent the past events which can (but not necessarily will) be referenced by future transitions. Conceptually, each transition $q \xmapsto[M]{a}_\sigma q'$ depends on the past events mentioned in M. Due to the local scope of names, the function $\sigma : n(q') \hookrightarrow n(q) \cup \{\star\}$ is needed to relate the names of the target state to those of the source. The event mapped to $\star$ (if any) represents the new event generated by the considered transition. In the following the components of a causal automaton will be often denoted by using the name of the automaton as subscript.

The notion of bisimulation on causal automata (CA-bisimulation) takes into account the fact that a state has attached a set of local names. Hence a bisimulation not only relates states, but also the corresponding sets of local names.

Definition 13 (CA-bisimulation). *Let $\mathcal{A}$ and $\mathcal{B}$ be two causal automata. A CA-simulation $\mathcal{R}$ of $\mathcal{A}$ in $\mathcal{B}$ is a set of triples $\langle q, \delta, p \rangle$, where $q \in Q_\mathcal{A}$, $p \in Q_\mathcal{B}$ and δ is a partial injective function from $n_\mathcal{A}(q)$ to $n_\mathcal{B}(p)$, such that*

1. *$\langle q_{0\mathcal{A}}, \emptyset, q_{0\mathcal{B}} \rangle \in \mathcal{R}$;*
2. *if $\langle q, \delta, p \rangle \in \mathcal{R}$ and $q \xmapsto[M]{a}_\sigma q'$ in $\mathcal{A}$ then*

   - *$p \xmapsto[\delta(M)]{a}_\rho p'$ in $\mathcal{B}$ for some p' and*
   - *$\langle q', \delta', p' \rangle \in \mathcal{R}$ for some δ' such that $\delta^\star \circ \sigma = \rho \circ \delta'$, where $\delta^\star$ is defined as $\delta \cup \{(\star, \star)\}$ (see the diagram below).*

$$
\begin{array}{ccc}
n_\mathcal{A}(q) \cup \{\star\} & \xrightarrow{\ \delta^\star\ } & n_\mathcal{B}(p) \cup \{\star\} \\
\sigma \uparrow & & \uparrow \rho \\
n_\mathcal{A}(q') & \xrightarrow[\ \delta'\ ]{} & n_\mathcal{B}(p')
\end{array}
$$

A CA-bisimulation *between $\mathcal{A}$ and $\mathcal{B}$ is a set of triples $\mathcal{R}$ such that $\mathcal{R}$ and $\mathcal{R}^{-1} = \{\langle p, \delta^{-1}, q \rangle : \langle q, \delta, p \rangle \in \mathcal{R}\}$ are CA-simulations. The automata $\mathcal{A}$ and $\mathcal{B}$ are CA-bisimilar, written $\mathcal{A} \sim_{ca} \mathcal{B}$, if there exists a bisimulation $\mathcal{R}$ between $\mathcal{A}$ and $\mathcal{B}$.*

In [MP97] an algorithm has been proposed for checking the CA-bisimilarity of (finite) causal automata. Given a causal automaton $\mathcal{A}$, first the "useless" names, i.e., names never referenced by future transitions, are removed from the states of the automaton. For instance, in the case of Petri nets, the useless names are the events that belong to a state because they have generated a token which still exists, but which is never used later by any other event. Then the basic step of the algorithm constructs an ordinary labelled transition system $Unf(\mathcal{A})$, called the unfolding of $\mathcal{A}$, such that $\mathcal{A} \sim_{ca} \mathcal{B}$ iff the associated transition systems $Unf(\mathcal{A})$ and $Unf(\mathcal{B})$ are bisimilar. Finally, standard algorithms (e.g., a partition/refinement algorithm) can be used to verify bisimilarity on the ordinary transition systems or to obtain a minimal equivalent transition system.

As mentioned in the introduction, some more recent works [Pis99, MP00] show that, considering a generalization of the model, the so-called automata with symmetries, a minimal realization exists and can be constructed in the class of causal (or, more generally, HD) automata themselves. A causal automaton can be seen as a coalgebra of a suitable functor and the minimal realization arises as the image in the final coalgebra of the given automaton.

Abstraction homomorphisms [CFM83, Cas87], which are also called zig-zag morphisms [vB84] or transition preserving homomorphisms [FM90], are defined in the setting of ordinary automata as morphisms which "preserve" and "reflect" transitions. The existence of an abstraction homomorphism ensures that the source and target automata are bisimilar. The next definition generalizes this idea to causal automata.

Definition 14 (abstraction homomorphism). *Let $\mathcal{A}$ and $\mathcal{B}$ be causal automata. An* abstraction homomorphism $\mathsf{h} : \mathcal{A} \to \mathcal{B}$ *is a pair* $\mathsf{h} = \langle h, \{h_q\}_{q \in Q_{\mathcal{A}}} \rangle$ *where* $h : Q_{\mathcal{A}} \to Q_{\mathcal{B}}$ *is a function and for all* $q \in Q_{\mathcal{A}}$, $h_q : n_{\mathcal{B}}(h(q)) \to n_{\mathcal{A}}(q)$ *is an injective function, such that* $h(q_{0\mathcal{A}}) = q_{0\mathcal{B}}$ *and*

- *if* $q \xmapsto[M]{a}_\sigma q'$ *in $\mathcal{A}$ then* $h(q) \xmapsto[h_q^{-1}(M)]{a}_\rho h(q')$ *in $\mathcal{B}$, with* $\sigma \circ h_{q'} = h_q^\star \circ \rho$ *(see Fig. 7.(a));*
- *if* $h(q) \xmapsto[M]{a}_\rho p'$ *in $\mathcal{B}$ then* $q \xmapsto[h_q(M)]{a}_\sigma q'$ *in $\mathcal{A}$ for some q', with* $h(q') = p'$ *and* $\sigma \circ h_{q'} = h_q^\star \circ \rho$ *(see Fig. 7.(b)).*

Intuitively, via an abstraction homomorphism $\mathsf{h} : \mathcal{A} \to \mathcal{B}$ several states of $\mathcal{A}$ can collapse into a single state of $\mathcal{B}$, in a way that respects the behaviour and the naming. In particular, observe that for any state $q \in Q_{\mathcal{A}}$, the function h_q maps the names of $h(q)$ (in $\mathcal{B}$) into the names of q (in $\mathcal{A}$). The idea is that the names of q which are not in the image of h_q can be safely removed, obtaining

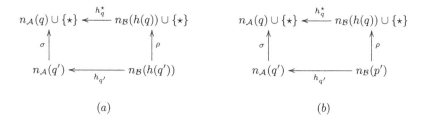

Fig. 7. Diagrams for abstraction homomorphisms.

an equivalent system, namely, in a sense, they are "useless". Indeed, also in this setting, the existence of an abstraction homomorphism $h : \mathcal{A} \to \mathcal{B}$ is sufficient to conclude the bisimilarity of $\mathcal{A}$ and $\mathcal{B}$.

Lemma 15. *Let $\mathcal{A}$ and $\mathcal{B}$ be causal automata. If there exists an abstraction homomorphism $h : \mathcal{A} \to \mathcal{B}$ then $\mathcal{A} \sim_{ca} \mathcal{B}$.*

It is worth observing that, as for ordinary automata, the above lemma does not provide a necessary condition. In [MP98], following the approach of [JNW96], abstraction homomorphisms have been described as open maps in a category of causal automata and it has been shown that two causal automata are CA-bisimilar if and only if they are related by a span of open maps.

5   Deciding HP-bisimulation on Graph Grammars

In this section we show that it is possible to associate to any graph grammar $\mathcal{G}$ a causal automaton $\mathcal{A}_{hp}(\mathcal{G})$, via a construction which respects HP-bisimulation, i.e., such that two graph grammars $\mathcal{G}_1$ and $\mathcal{G}_2$ are HP-bisimilar if and only if $\mathcal{A}_{hp}(\mathcal{G}_1)$ and $\mathcal{A}_{hp}(\mathcal{G}_2)$ are CA-bisimilar. Furthermore, for finite-state graph grammars, the corresponding automaton is proved to be finite and thus the general algorithms for causal automata mentioned in Section 4 can be used to check the bisimilarity of graph grammars and to construct a minimal realization.

First, note that, as in the case of Petri nets, the definition of HP-bisimulation on graph grammars relies on the transition system of processes and process moves, which is infinite for any non-trivial system exhibiting a cyclic behaviour. To reduce it to a finite causal automaton, or, in general, to a finite transition system, at least in the case of finite-state systems, the leading idea, already present in [DD90], is that not all the information carried by a process is relevant for deciding HP-bisimulation. Hence processes may be replaced by more compact structures where part of the past history is discarded.

For ordinary nets, as observed in [Vog91, MP97], one can restrict the attention only to the set of events which produced at least one token in the current state and to the causal ordering among them. In the case of contextual nets one must keep information not only about the events which produced a token in the current state ("producers"), but also about the events which read a token in the current state ("readers"). Fortunately, among the readers, which can be unbounded even for a safe net, only the maximal ones play a significant role, while the others can be safely discarded. This allows to obtain a finite description of the transition system of processes for finite-state contextual nets [BCM00b].

We will show that the construction proposed for contextual nets can be generalized to graph grammars. This can be better understood by recalling that, as already observed, for a deterministic computation of a graph grammar the asymmetric conflicts induced by the possibility of expressing "contextual" rewritings (read operations) play a significant role in the ordering of events, while the inhibiting effects between production occurrences related to the dangling condition can be disregarded since they are subsumed by such asymmetric conflicts.

The next definition formalizes the notions of producer and of (maximal) reader for a process of a graph grammar.

Definition 16 (producers and (maximal) readers). *Given a process φ of a graph grammar $\mathcal{G}$, we define*

- *the set of* producers
    $$p(\varphi) = \{q \in P_\varphi : q^\bullet \cap Max(\varphi) \neq \emptyset\};$$
- *the set of* readers
    $$r(\varphi) = \{q \in P_\varphi : \underline{q} \cap Max(\varphi) \neq \emptyset\};$$
- *the set of* maximal readers
    $$mr(\varphi) = \{q \in r(\varphi) : \exists x \in \underline{q} \cap Max(\varphi). \ q \text{ is } \nearrow_\varphi -\text{maximal in } \underline{x}\}.$$

For instance, for process φ_5 of Fig. 4, the set of producers is $p(\varphi_5) = \{e_5\}$, the set of readers is $r(\varphi_5) = \{e_1, e_2, e_3, e_4, e_5\}$, while the maximal readers are $mr(\varphi_5) = \{e_2, e_5\}$.

A crucial observation is that for any *n-safe* graph grammar $\mathcal{G}$ the sets $p(\varphi)$ and $mr(\varphi)$, with φ ranging over the processes of $\mathcal{G}$ are *bounded*. In the sequel, given a graph G we will denote by $|G|$ the cardinality of the (disjoint) union of the node and edge sets of G. More generally, with abuse of notation, a graph will be sometimes identified with the set consisting of the (disjoint) union of its node and edge sets, and we will use on graphs the ordinary set-theoretical relations and operations.

Lemma 17. *Let $\mathcal{G}$ be a n-safe graph grammar. Then, for any process φ of $\mathcal{G}$ we have $|p(\varphi)| \leq n \cdot |TG_\mathcal{G}|$ and $|mr(\varphi)| \leq (n \cdot |TG_\mathcal{G}|)^2$.*

Proof (sketch). By the basic properties of graph processes, for any process φ, the graph $\varphi^\bullet$, namely $Max(\varphi)$ typed over $TG_\mathcal{G}$ by the restriction of φ_T, is reachable in $\mathcal{G}$. Since any graph reachable in $\mathcal{G}$ is *n*-injective, we can establish the following bound for the number of items (nodes and edges) of $Max(\varphi)$,

$$|Max(\varphi)| \leq n \cdot |TG_\mathcal{G}|.$$

Hence it is immediate to conclude that $n \cdot |TG_{\mathcal{G}}|$ is a bound also for the cardinality of $p(\varphi)$ since for each $q, q' \in p(\varphi)$ we have $q^{\bullet} \cap Max(\varphi) \neq \emptyset$ and $q^{\bullet} \cap q'^{\bullet} = \emptyset$.

Furthermore, for any item x in $Max(\varphi)$ the set A_x of maximal events in x consists of concurrent events. Hence also the corresponding pre-set $^{\bullet}A_x$ is concurrent and therefore $|{}^{\bullet}A_x|$ is bounded by $n \cdot |TG_{\mathcal{G}}|$. Since productions are consuming, i.e., they have a non-empty pre-set, and for any $q, q' \in A_x$ it must be $^{\bullet}q \cap {}^{\bullet}q' = \emptyset$, we conclude that $n \cdot |TG_{\mathcal{G}}|$ is a bound also for the cardinality of A_x. Therefore the number of productions in $mr(\varphi)$ is bounded by $(n \cdot |TG_{\mathcal{G}}|)^2$. □

We next define partial processes, which represent abstractions of graph processes where only a relevant part for discriminating non HP-bisimilar states is kept, namely the target graph of the process (i.e., the subgraph consisting of the maximal items), the producers, the maximal readers and their dependencies. For technical reasons we first introduce pre-partial processes which are required to satisfy weaker requirements.

Definition 18 (pre-partial process). *A* pre-partial process *of a graph grammar $\mathcal{G}$ is a tuple $\gamma = \langle G_\gamma, E_\gamma, \ll_\gamma, \lambda_\gamma, post_\gamma, cont_\gamma \rangle$, where*

- *G_γ is a $TG_{\mathcal{G}}$-typed graph;*
- *E_γ is a set of events;*
- *$\ll_\gamma \subseteq E_\gamma \times E_\gamma$ is a partial order;*
- *$\lambda_\gamma : E_\gamma \to \mathsf{Act}$ is a labelling function over a fixed set of actions Act;*
- *$cont_\gamma, post_\gamma : E_\gamma \to \mathcal{P}(N_{\langle G_\gamma \rangle} \cup E_{\langle G_\gamma \rangle})$ are functions which map each $e \in E_\gamma$ to the sets of items in $\langle G_\gamma \rangle$ which are read and produced, respectively, by e.*

For any $x \in \langle G_\gamma \rangle$ we denote by $cont_\gamma(x)$ the set of readers of x, i.e., the set $\{e \in E_\gamma : x \in cont_\gamma(e)\}$.

An isomorphism of pre-partial processes $i : \gamma_1 \to \gamma_2$ is a pair of functions $i = \langle i_T, i_E \rangle$ where $i_T : G_{\gamma_1} \to G_{\gamma_2}$ is an isomorphism of $TG_{\mathcal{G}}$-typed graphs and $i_E : E_{\gamma_1} \to E_{\gamma_2}$ is a bijection such that i_E establishes an isomorphism of labelled partial orders between $\langle E_{\gamma_1}, \ll_{\gamma_1}, \lambda_{\gamma_1} \rangle$ and $\langle E_{\gamma_2}, \ll_{\gamma_2}, \lambda_{\gamma_2} \rangle$ and, for any $e \in E_{\gamma_1}$, $post(i_E(e)) = i_T(post(e))$ and $cont(i_E(e)) = i_T(cont(e))$.

As for ordinary graph process, for any pre-partial process γ we define the sets of producers and of maximal readers.

Definition 19. *Let γ be a pre-partial process. The* set *of* producers *of γ is defined as $p(\gamma) = \{e \in E_\gamma : post_\gamma(e) \neq \emptyset\}$. The set of* maximal readers *of γ is defined as $mr(\gamma) = \{e \in E_\gamma : \exists x \in cont_\gamma(e). \ e \text{ is } \ll_\gamma\text{-maximal in } cont_\gamma(x)\}$.*

Partial processes are defined as pre-partial processes where each event is a producer or a maximal reader.

Definition 20 (partial process). *A* partial process *of a graph grammar $\mathcal{G}$ is a pre-partial process γ such that $E_\gamma = p(\gamma) \cup mr(\gamma)$. The* initial partial process *for $\mathcal{G}$ is the partial process over the initial graph, with an empty set of events, i.e., $\gamma_0 = \langle G_{s\mathcal{G}}, \emptyset, \emptyset, \emptyset, \emptyset, \emptyset \rangle$.*

An obvious construction associates to each pre-partial process the corresponding partial process.

Definition 21. *Given any pre-partial process* γ*, the corresponding partial process, denoted by* $Cut(\gamma)$*, is defined as follows:*

- $G_{Cut(\gamma)} = G_\gamma$*;*
- $E_{Cut(\gamma)} = p(\gamma) \cup mr(\gamma)$*;*

and $\ll_{Cut(\gamma)}$*,* $\lambda_{Cut(\gamma)}$*,* $post_{Cut(\gamma)}$ *and* $cont_{Cut(\gamma)}$ *are the restrictions to* $E_{Cut(\gamma)}$ *of the corresponding relations and functions of* γ*.*

Given any process φ of a graph grammar, we can construct a corresponding partial process by keeping only the producers and the maximal readers of φ. Technically this is done by first constructing a pre-partial process and then using the operation $Cut(\cdot)$.

Definition 22 (partial process associated to a process). *Let* φ *be a process of a graph grammar* $\mathcal{G}$*. The corresponding partial process, denoted by* $\gamma(\varphi)$*, is defined as* $Cut(\gamma)$ *where* γ *is the pre-partial process satisfying*

- $G_\gamma = \varphi^\bullet = \langle Max(\varphi), \varphi_{T|Max(\varphi)} \rangle$*;*
- $E_\gamma = P_\varphi$*;*
- $\ll_\gamma = (\nearrow_\varphi)^*$*;*
- $\lambda_\gamma = \lambda_{\mathcal{G}} \circ \varphi_P$*;*
- *for any* $q \in E_\gamma$*,* $cont_\gamma(q) = \underline{q} \cap Max(\varphi)$ *and* $post_\gamma(q) = q^\bullet \cap Max(\varphi)$*.*

In Fig. 4, for every process φ_i, the corresponding partial process $\gamma(\varphi_i)$ is obtained by considering only the non-shaded part. The next lemma makes explicit the easy fact that the events in the partial process associated to a process φ are exactly the producers and the maximal readers of the original process φ.

Lemma 23. *Let* $\mathcal{G}$ *be a labelled graph grammar and let* φ *be a process of* $\mathcal{G}$*. Then* $p(\gamma(\varphi)) = p(\varphi)$ *and* $mr(\gamma(\varphi)) = mr(\varphi)$*.*

Next we introduce a *move relation* on partial processes: given a partial process γ, whenever a production of the original grammar is applicable to the graph G_γ, the partial process can evolve accordingly. This leads to a transition system of partial processes which represents the first step in the construction of the causal automaton associated to a graph grammar.

Definition 24 (partial processes move). *Given two partial processes* γ *and* γ' *of a labelled graph grammar* $\mathcal{G}$ *we write* $\gamma \xrightarrow[e_0]{a} \gamma'$*, and we say that* γ *moves to* γ' *performing the action* a *if* $\gamma' = Cut(\gamma'')$ *where* γ'' *is a pre-partial process satisfying the following conditions: there is a production* $q \in P_{\mathcal{G}}$

$$q : L_q \xleftarrow{l_q} K_q \xrightarrow{r_q} R_q$$

and a match $m : L_q \to G_\gamma$ *such that, if* $X = m(\langle L_q \rangle - l_q(\langle K_q \rangle))$ *and* $C = m(l_q(\langle K_q \rangle))$, *then*

- $G_\gamma \Rightarrow_q^a G_{\gamma''}$ *using match* m; *more specifically we assume that* $\langle G_\gamma \rangle - X \subseteq \langle G_{\gamma''} \rangle$, *i.e., the items which are preserved remains concretely the same;*
- $E_{\gamma''} = E_\gamma \cup \{e_0\}$ *and* $e_0 \notin E_\gamma$;
- $\ll_{\gamma''} = (\ll_\gamma \cup \{(e, e_0) : e \in E_\gamma \land (post(e) \cap (X \cup C)) \cup (cont(e) \cap X) \neq \emptyset\})^*$;
- $\lambda_{\gamma''}(e) = \lambda_\gamma(e)$ *for any* $e \in E_\gamma$ *and* $\lambda_{\gamma''}(e_0) = a = \lambda_{\mathcal{G}}(q)$;
- *for any* $e \in E_\gamma$, $post_{\gamma''}(e) = post_\gamma(e) - X$, $cont_{\gamma''}(e) = cont_\gamma(e) - X$, *and* $cont_{\gamma''}(e_0) = C$, $post_{\gamma''}(e_0) = \langle G_{\gamma''} \rangle - \langle G_\gamma \rangle$.

As mentioned above, a partial process γ of a grammar $\mathcal{G}$ can perform a move when there exists a production q in $\mathcal{G}$ which is applicable to its graphical component G_γ. The graph $G_{\gamma'}$ underlying the new partial process is obtained by rewriting G_γ using q. Observe that the new event e_0, representing the occurrence of q, depends on the events which have generated a graph item which is consumed or read by q (causality), and also on the events which have read an item consumed by q (asymmetric conflict). The functions *cont* and *post* are extended to the new event e_0, but they must be updated also to take into account the fact that some items of G_γ might have been deleted. Consequently an event might cease to be a producer or a maximal reader and thus, by effect of the application of $Cut(\cdot)$, some events can disappear. A sequence of partial process move is exemplified in Fig. 4, if we consider only the non-shaded parts.

To each process and partial process move we associate the set of maximal (weak or strong) causes of the executed production, which will play a basic role in the definition of the automaton. In fact, to observe the partial order associated to an evolving computation it is sufficient to look, step by step, only at the immediate maximal causes of each single production (the other dependencies being implicitly given by the transitivity of the partial order).

Definition 25 (immediate and maximal causes). *The set of* immediate (weak or strong) causes *of a process move* $\varphi \xrightarrow{a}_e \varphi'$ *is defined as* $\mathsf{IC}(\varphi \xrightarrow{a}_e \varphi') = \{q \in P_\varphi : q^\bullet \cap (\underline{e} \cup {}^\bullet e) \neq \emptyset \lor \underline{q} \cap {}^\bullet e \neq \emptyset\}$. *We denote by* $\mathsf{MC}(\varphi \xrightarrow{a}_e \varphi')$ *the set of* maximal causes, *namely the subset of* $\nearrow_\varphi$-maximal elements of $\mathsf{IC}(\varphi \xrightarrow{a}_e \varphi')$.

The set of immediate causes *of a partial process move* $\gamma \xrightarrow{a}_e \gamma'$, *adopting the notation of Definition 24, is defined by* $\mathsf{IC}(\gamma \xrightarrow{a}_{e_0} \gamma') = \{e \in E_\gamma : (post_\gamma(e) \cap (X \cup C)) \cup (cont_\gamma(e) \cap X) \neq \emptyset\}$. *The set of* maximal causes $\mathsf{MC}(\gamma \xrightarrow{a}_{e_0} \gamma')$ *is the subset of* $\ll_\gamma$-maximal immediate causes.

For example, considering transition $\varphi_5 \xrightarrow{q_4}_{e_6} \varphi_6$ in Fig. 4, the immediate causes are $\{e_1, e_2, e_3, e_4, e_5\}$, while the immediate maximal causes are $\{e_2, e_5\}$.

The next lemma relates the transition system of processes and the transition system of partial processes.

Lemma 26. *Let $\mathcal{G}$ be any labelled graph grammar.*

1. *If φ and φ' are processes of $\mathcal{G}$ and $\varphi \xrightarrow[e]{a} \varphi'$ then we have $\gamma(\varphi) \xrightarrow[e]{a} \gamma(\varphi')$, with $\mathsf{MC}(\varphi \xrightarrow[e]{a} \varphi') = \mathsf{MC}(\gamma(\varphi) \xrightarrow[e]{a} \gamma(\varphi'))$;*

2. *If φ is a process of $\mathcal{G}$ and $\gamma(\varphi) \xrightarrow[e]{a} \gamma'$ then there exists a process φ' of $\mathcal{G}$, such that $\varphi \xrightarrow[e']{a} \varphi'$, with γ' and $\gamma(\varphi')$ isomorphic and $\mathsf{MC}(\gamma(\varphi) \xrightarrow[e]{a} \gamma') = \mathsf{MC}(\varphi \xrightarrow[e']{a} \varphi')$.*

It is worth noting that we cannot replace point (2) above with the stronger "if $\gamma(\varphi) \xrightarrow[e]{a} \gamma'$ then there exists a process φ' of $\mathcal{G}$, such that $\varphi \xrightarrow[e]{a} \varphi'$, with $\gamma' = \gamma(\varphi')$", since in general the event e and the new graph items in $G_{\gamma'}$ can appear in φ.

By Lemma 26 we conclude that if a partial process γ of a graph grammar $\mathcal{G}$ is reachable from an initial partial process via a finite sequence of moves, then $\gamma = \gamma(\varphi)$ for some process φ of $\mathcal{G}$. Hence, when the graph grammar $\mathcal{G}$ is n-safe, the definition of $\gamma(\varphi)$ and Lemmata 17 and 23 allow us to conclude the validity of the following result.

Lemma 27. *For any n-safe labelled graph grammar the set of partial processes reachable from the initial process (and taken up to isomorphism) is finite.*

We are now ready to present the construction of the causal automaton associated to a graph grammar for checking HP-bisimilarity. To obtain a "compact" automaton (with a finite number of states for n-safe graph grammar) we must consider partial processes up to isomorphism. To this aim we fix a standard representative in each class of isomorphic partial processes. Furthermore we consider a normalization function **norm** such that for any partial process γ, $\mathbf{norm}(\gamma) = \langle \gamma', i \rangle$, where γ' is the standard representative in the isomorphism class of γ and $i : \gamma' \to \gamma$ is a chosen partial process isomorphism. We assume that the names of the productions in any (partial) process γ are taken from $\mathcal{N}$, namely that $E_\gamma \subseteq \mathcal{N}$.

Definition 28 (causal automaton for HP-bisimulation). *Let $\mathcal{G}$ be a labelled graph grammar. The HP-causal automaton associated to $\mathcal{G}$ is the automaton $\mathcal{A}_{hp}(\mathcal{G}) = \langle Q, n, \longmapsto, q_0 \rangle$, having (standard representatives of) partial processes as states. The initial state q_0 is the standard representative γ_0 of the initial partial processes of $\mathcal{G}$ and whenever $\gamma \in Q$ then*

- $n(\gamma) = E_\gamma$;
- *if $\gamma \xrightarrow[e]{a} \gamma'$ and $\mathbf{norm}(\gamma') = \langle \gamma'', i \rangle$ then $\gamma'' \in Q$ and $\gamma \xmapsto[M]{a}{}_\sigma \gamma''$ where*

  - $\sigma : E_{\gamma''} \hookrightarrow E_\gamma \cup \{\star\}$ *is defined as $\sigma = (id_{E_\gamma} \cup \{(e, \star)\}) \circ i_E$;*
  - $M = \mathsf{MC}(\gamma \xrightarrow[e]{a} \gamma')$.

Observe that the renaming function in a transition of the causal automaton is obtained from the isomorphism given by the normalization function **norm**, simply by redirecting the new name e to $\star$ (if e belongs to $E_{\gamma'}$). As anticipated, the maximal causes of a process move are used as dependencies in the automaton transition.

The states of the automaton are standard representatives of partial processes reachable from the initial partial process. Hence by Lemma 27 we deduce that for any n-safe graph grammar the above defined automaton has a finite number of states (and also a finite number of transitions leaving from each state, since the number of productions is finite). Vice versa, if the graph grammar is not n-safe for some n, then the automaton will have an infinite number of states.

Theorem 29. *Let $\mathcal{G}$ be a labelled graph grammar. Then $\mathcal{G}$ is n-safe for some n iff the automaton $\mathcal{A}_{hp}(\mathcal{G})$ is finite.*

To effectively build the automaton we can perform an inductive construction based on Definition 28. The only thing to observe is that, given a partial process γ, there might be infinitely many moves $\gamma \xrightarrow{a}_{e} \gamma'$ since the event e can be chosen arbitrarily among the unused events in $\mathcal{N}$ and a similar consideration holds for the new graph items in $G_{\gamma'}$. However, without loss of generality, we can limit our attention only to some partial process moves, called the *representative* moves, where the newly generated name and items are chosen in a canonical way. For instance we can suppose that the set of names $\mathcal{N}$ is well-ordered and assume that a transition $\gamma \xrightarrow{a}_{e} \gamma'$ to be representative must satisfy $e = \min(\mathcal{N} - P_{\gamma})$.

The main result now states that there is a precise correspondence between HP-bisimulation on graph grammars and CA-bisimulation on causal automata. Hence HP-bisimilarity of graph grammars can be checked on the corresponding automata.

Theorem 30. *Let $\mathcal{G}_1$ and $\mathcal{G}_2$ be two labelled graph grammars. Then $\mathcal{G}_1 \sim_{hp} \mathcal{G}_2$ if and only if $\mathcal{A}_{hp}(\mathcal{G}_1) \sim_{ca} \mathcal{A}_{hp}(\mathcal{G}_2)$.*

Proof (sketch). The proof is organized in two steps. First observe that the transition system of processes of a graph grammar $\mathcal{G}$ can be seen itself as a causal automaton $\mathcal{A}_{pr}(\mathcal{G}) = \langle Q, n, \longmapsto, q_0 \rangle$, where

- Q is the set of processes φ of $\mathcal{G}$ and $n(\varphi) = P_\varphi$ for any process φ;
- $\varphi \xrightarrow{a}_{M}{}_{\sigma} \varphi'$ if, according to Definition 9, $\varphi \xrightarrow{a}_{e} \varphi'$, $M = \mathsf{MC}(\varphi \xrightarrow{a}_{e} \varphi')$, and the naming $\sigma : P_{\varphi'} \to P_\varphi \cup \{\star\}$ is defined as the identity for $x \in P_{\varphi'} - \{e\}$, while $\sigma(e) = \star$;
- the initial state q_0 is any initial process of $\mathcal{G}$.

Then, it is possible to prove that HP-bisimulation on graph grammars coincides with CA-bisimulation on the causal automata of processes, namely $\mathcal{G}_1 \sim_{hp} \mathcal{G}_2$ iff $\mathcal{A}_{pr}(\mathcal{G}_1) \sim_{ca} \mathcal{A}_{pr}(\mathcal{G}_2)$.

The second step of the proof shows that, for any graph grammar $\mathcal{G}$ there exists an abstraction homomorphism $\mathsf{h} : \mathcal{A}_{pr}(\mathcal{G}) \to \mathcal{A}_{hp}(\mathcal{G})$, and thus, by Lemma 15,

$\mathcal{A}_{pr}(\mathcal{G}) \sim_{ca} \mathcal{A}_{hp}(\mathcal{G})$. The abstraction homomorphism $\mathsf{h} = \langle h, \{h_\varphi\}_\varphi \rangle$ can be defined as follows: for any process φ (state of $\mathcal{A}_{pr}(\mathcal{G})$), if $\mathtt{norm}(\gamma(\varphi)) = \langle \gamma', i \rangle$ then $h(\varphi) = \gamma'$ and $h_\varphi : E_{\gamma'} \to P_\varphi$ is simply i_E. To prove that h satisfies the conditions in Definition 14 one essentially resorts to Lemma 26.

Summing up, by the above considerations we have that $\mathcal{A}_{pr}(\mathcal{G}_i) \sim_{ca} \mathcal{A}_{hp}(\mathcal{G}_i)$ for $i \in \{1,2\}$, and moreover $\mathcal{A}_{pr}(\mathcal{G}_1) \sim_{ca} \mathcal{A}_{pr}(\mathcal{G}_2)$ iff $\mathcal{G}_1 \sim_{hp} \mathcal{G}_2$. Hence the thesis easily follows. □

By Theorems 29 and 30 we immediately conclude the desired decidability result.

Corollary 31. *HP-bisimulation on n-safe graph grammars is decidable.*

It is worth observing that, in this setting, due to the Turing completeness of graph grammars, differently from what happens for ordinary and contextual nets, the property of being n-safe for some n, i.e., the property of being finite-state, is not decidable.

6   Conclusions

In this paper we have introduced an abstract semantics for graph grammars inspired by the classical history preserving bisimulation. Extending the work already developed on ordinary and contextual P/T nets, we have shown how history preserving bisimulation on graph grammars can be studied in the general framework of causal automata. A translation of graph grammars into causal automata has been proposed, which respects (preserves and reflects) history preserving bisimulation. The translation produces finite automata for finite-state graph grammars, thus allowing to reuse the algorithms existing for this general formalism in order to decide bisimulation and to obtain a minimal realization.

We conclude by discussing two possible directions of further investigation which we find interesting: on the one hand the possibility of defining different notions of history preserving bisimulation by considering observations of the causal history of a computation finer than the associated PES; on the other hand the development of a logic in the style of Hennessy-Milner for HP-bisimulation.

6.1   Refining the Observation

The notion of HP-bisimulation considered in this paper is obtained by taking as observation of a concurrent computation of a graph grammar the PES underlying the corresponding graph process. We have already mentioned that this corresponds to observe only the precedences between events, confusing the weak causality deriving from the possibility of preserving part of the state in a rewriting step, the inhibiting effects related to the dangling condition and the "strong" causality deriving from the flow of information. It could be reasonable to consider, instead, equivalences which arise by assuming different, finer descriptions of concurrent computations.

For instance, a natural refinement consists of distinguishing the flow of information from the other dependencies. This is easily achieved by extracting from a process a different event structure, which is called *asymmetric event structure* [BCM98b, BCM00a] where causality and asymmetric conflict are kept separate. The asymmetric event structure associated to a graph process φ is defined as

$$aev(\varphi) = \langle P_\varphi, \leq_\varphi, \nearrow_\varphi, \lambda_{\mathcal{G}} \circ \varphi_P \rangle.$$

Then the corresponding bisimulation, which can be called *read history preserving (RHP-) bisimulation*, is defined as HP-bisimulation, by simply refining the observation, namely by changing $ev(\varphi_i)$ with $aev(\varphi_i)$ in Definition 11.

Any RHP-bisimulation relating two graph grammar $\mathcal{G}_1$ and $\mathcal{G}_2$ is also an HP-bisimulation. In fact if φ_1 and φ_2 are processes of $\mathcal{G}_1$ and $\mathcal{G}_2$, respectively, and $f : aev(\varphi_1) \rightarrow aev(\varphi_2)$ is an isomorphism of asymmetric event structures then it is easy to see that f is also an isomorphism of PES's between $ev(\varphi_1)$ and $ev(\varphi_2)$. Therefore $\mathcal{G}_1 \sim_{rhp} \mathcal{G}_2$ implies $\mathcal{G}_1 \sim_{hp} \mathcal{G}_2$. As for contextual nets, the converse implication, instead, does not hold. Regarding the decidability of RHP-bisimulation, the natural extension of the construction which has been introduced for HP-bisimulation consists of considering partial processes where all the readers (not only the maximal ones) are kept. Unfortunately in this way the construction produces a causal automaton which may be infinite also for safe graph grammars. Indeed, the decidability of RHP-bisimulation is an open question already for contextual nets [BCM00b].

6.2   Hennessy-Milner Logic for HP-bisimulation

The ordinary bisimulation over transition systems has a logical counterpart, the so-called Hennessy-Milner logic [HM85], a kind of modal logic with two basic modalities which can be interpreted as *possibility* and *necessity*. The syntax of formulae is the following

$$\phi ::= \text{true} \mid \phi \wedge \phi \mid \neg\phi \mid \langle a \rangle \phi.$$

The formula constructed with the "*diamond*" modality $\langle a \rangle \phi$, where a is an action and ϕ a formula, intuitively is satisfied by any state from which an a-action can be executed leading to a state which satisfies ϕ. The dual modality, i.e., the "*box*" modality $[a]\phi$, can be defined as $\neg\langle a \rangle \neg\phi$. It is satisfied by all the states where any a-action leads to a state that satisfies ϕ. Hennessy-Milner logic can be shown to be *adequate* for bisimulation in the sense that, two states of a transition system are bisimilar if and only if they satisfy the same set of formulae [HM85].

An interesting direction of further research is the study of an analogue of Hennessy-Milner logic for HP-bisimulation, which has been initiated in [Bar99]. The basic syntax of formulae is the following

$$\phi ::= \text{true} \mid \phi \wedge \phi \mid \neg\phi \mid \text{EX}\{n, a, M\}\phi.$$

The *existential* modality allows to construct a formula $\mathsf{EX}\{e, a, M\}\phi$ which, intuitively, is satisfied by a state where an action a can be executed, which generates a new name (or event) e directly caused by the set of events in M, leading to a state which satisfies ϕ. Also in this case there is a dual *universal* modality: the formula $\mathsf{AX}\{n, a, M\}\phi$, defined as $\neg\mathsf{EX}\{e, a, M\}\neg\phi$, is satisfied by a state where any action a which can be executed, generates a new name (or event) e directly caused by the set of events in M, leading to a state which satisfies ϕ.

Like ordinary Hennessy-Milner logic is naturally interpreted over transition systems (labelled graphs), this variation of the logic has a natural interpretation over causal automata, but also over the transition system of processes of a net or of a graph grammar. The possibility of declaring new names/events in a formula is reflected, at semantical level, by the the presence in the model of a kind of environment which links the events in the current state and the names "declared" in the formula. An *adequateness* result for such a logic over causal automata has been proved in [Bar99] showing that two automata $\mathcal{A}_1$ and $\mathcal{A}_2$ are CA-bisimilar iff they satisfy the same set of formulae. Resorting to our results, adequateness for the logic over graph grammars would be easily proved by showing that for any labelled graph grammar $\mathcal{G}$

$$\mathcal{G} \Vdash \phi \quad \Leftrightarrow \quad \mathcal{A}_{pr}(\mathcal{G}) \Vdash \phi.$$

where "$\Vdash$" means "is a model of".

As in the case of ordinary Hennessy-Milner logic, the expressiveness would greatly benefit form the introduction of some "recursion" operator, e.g., minimal/maximal fix-point operators in the style of the μ-calculus (ν-calculus). This should be done by retaining some interesting properties of the logic, like decidability, at least for a significant fragment.

Acknowledgements. We are grateful to the anonymous referees for their insightful comments and suggestions.

References

[Bal00]   P. Baldan. *Modelling Concurrent Computations: From Contextual Petri Nets to Graph Grammars*. PhD thesis, Department of Computer Science, University of Pisa, 2000. Available as technical report n. TD-1/00.

[Bar99]   R. Bartolini. Model checking di proprietà causali di reti di Petri. MSc thesis, University of Pisa, 1999. (In Italian).

[BCM98a]   P. Baldan, A. Corradini, and U. Montanari. Concatenable Graph Processes: Relating Processes and Derivation Traces. In *Proceedings of ICALP'98*, volume 1443 of *LNCS*, pages 283–295. Springer Verlag, 1998.

[BCM98b]   P. Baldan, A. Corradini, and U. Montanari. An Event Structure Semantics for P/T Contextual Nets: Asymmetric Event Structures. In M. Nivat, Editor, *Proceedings of FoSSaCS '98*, volume 1378 of *LNCS*, pages 63–80. Springer Verlag, 1998.

[BCM99]   P. Baldan, A. Corradini, and U. Montanari. Unfolding and Event Struc-
            ture Semantics for Graph Grammars. In W. Thomas, Editor, *Proceedings
            of FoSSaCS '99*, volume 1578 of *LNCS*, pages 73–89. Springer Verlag,
            1999.

[BCM00a]   P. Baldan, A. Corradini, and U. Montanari. Contextual Petri Nets, Asym-
            metric Event Structures and Processes. To appear in *Information and
            Computation.*, 2000.

[BCM00b]   P. Baldan, A. Corradini, and U. Montanari. History Preserving Bisimula-
            tions for Contextual Nets. In D. Bert and C. Choppy, Editors, *WADT'99
            Conference Proceedings*, number 1827 in LNCS, pages 291–310. Springer
            Verlag, 2000.

[BDKP91]   E. Best, R. Devillers, A. Kiehn, and L. Pomello. Concurrent Bisimulations
            in Petri Nets. *Acta Informatica*, 28(3):231–264, 1991.

[Cas87]   I. Castellani. Bisimulations and Abstraction Homomorphisms. *Journal of
            Computer and System Sciences*, 34(2/3):210–235, 1987.

[CFM83]   I. Castellani, P. Franceschi, and U. Montanari. Labeled Event Structures:
            A Model for Observable Concurrency. In D. Bjørner, Editor, *Proceedings
            of IFIP TC2 Working Conference on Formal Description of Programming
            Concepts – II*, pages 383–389. North-Holland, 1983.

[CMR96]   A. Corradini, U. Montanari, and F. Rossi. Graph Processes. *Fundamenta
            Informaticae*, 26:241–265, 1996.

[CMR+97]   A. Corradini, U. Montanari, F. Rossi, H. Ehrig, R. Heckel, and M. Löwe.
            Algebraic Approaches to Graph Transformation I: Basic Concepts and
            Double Pushout Approach. In G. Rozenberg, Editor, *Handbook of Graph
            Grammars and Computing by Graph Transformation. Volume 1: Founda-
            tions*. World Scientific, 1997.

[Cor96]   A. Corradini. Concurrent Graph and Term Graph Rewriting. In U. Mon-
            tanari and V. Sassone, Editors, *Proceedings of CONCUR'96*, volume 1119
            of *LNCS*, pages 438–464. Springer Verlag, 1996.

[DD90]   P. Darondeau and P Degano. Causal Trees: Interleaving + Causality. In
            Proc. 18th École de Printemps sur la Semantique de Parallelism, number
            469 in LNCS, pages 239–255. Springer Verlag, 1990.

[Ehr87]   H. Ehrig. Tutorial Introduction to the Algebraic Approach of Graph-
            Grammars. In H. Ehrig, M. Nagl, G. Rozenberg, and A. Rosenfeld, Edi-
            tors, *Proceedings of the 3rd International Workshop on Graph-Grammars
            and Their Application to Computer Science*, volume 291 of *LNCS*, pages
            3–14. Springer Verlag, 1987.

[EKMR99]   H. Ehrig, J. Kreowski, U. Montanari, and G. Rozenberg, Editors. *Hand-
            book of Graph Grammars and Computing by Graph Transformation, Vol.
            2: Concurrency, Parallelism and Distribution*. World Scientific, 1999.

[FM90]   G. Ferrari and U. Montanari. Towards the Unification of Models of Con-
            currency. In A. Arnold, Editor, *Proceedings of CAAP '90*, volume 431 of
            LNCS, pages 162–176. Springer-Verlag, 1990.

[GHK00]   F. Gadducci, R. Heckel, and M. Koch. A Fully Abstract Model for Graph-
            Interpreted Temporal Logic. In H. Ehrig, G. Engels, H.J. Kreowski, and
            G. Rozenberg, Editors, *Proceedings of TAGT'98*, volume 1764 of *LNCS*,
            pages 310–322. Springer Verlag, 2000.

[GM82]   J. A. Goguen and J. Meseguer. Security Policies and Security Models. In
            Proceedings 1982 IEEE Symposium on Security and Privacy, pages 11–20.
            IEEE Computer Society, 1982.

[Hec98]   R. Heckel. *Open Graph Transformation Systems: A New Approach to the Compositional Modelling of Concurrent and Reactive Systems*. PhD thesis, TU Berlin, 1998.

[HEWC97]   R. Heckel, H. Ehrig, U. Wolter, and A. Corradini. Integrating the Specification Techniques of Graph Transformation and Temporal Logic. In *Proceedings of MFCS'97*, number 1295 in LNCS. Springer Verlag, 1997.

[HM85]   M. Hennessy and R. Milner. Algebraic Laws for Indeterminism and Concurrency. *Journal of the ACM*, 32:137–162, 1985.

[JK95]   R. Janicki and M. Koutny. Semantics of Inhibitor Nets. *Information and Computation*, 123:1–16, 1995.

[JNW96]   A. Joyal, M. Nielsen, and G. Winskel. Bisimulation from Open Maps. *Information and Computation*, 127(2):164–185, 1996.

[Koc99]   M. Koch. *Integration of Graph Transformation and Temporal Logic for the Specification of Distributed Ssystems*. PhD thesis, TU Berlin, 1999.

[Kre77]   H.-J. Kreowski. *Manipulation von Graphmanipulationen*. PhD thesis, Technische Universität Berlin, 1977.

[MP97]   U. Montanari and M. Pistore. Minimal Transition Systems for History-Preserving Bisimulation. In *14th Annual Symposium on Theoretical Aspects of Computer Science*, volume 1200 of *LNCS*, pages 413–425. Springer Verlag, 1997.

[MP98]   U. Montanari and M. Pistore. History-Dependent Automata. Technical Report TR-98-11, Dipartimento di Informatica, 1998. Available as ftp://ftp.di.unipi.it/pub/techreports/TR-98-11.ps.Z.

[MP00]   U. Montanari and M. Pistore. Structured Coalgebras and Minimal HD-automata. In M. Nielsen and B. Roman, Editors, *Proc. of MFCS 2000*, volume 1983 of *LNCS*, pages 569–578. Springer Verlag, 2000.

[MR95]   U. Montanari and F. Rossi. Contextual Nets. *Acta Informatica*, 32(6), 1995.

[Pis99]   M. Pistore. *History Dependent Automata*. PhD thesis, Department of Computer Science, University of Pisa, 1999.

[RGG96]   E. Rudolph, J. Grabowski, and P. Graubmann. Tutorial on Message Sequence Charts. *Computer Networks and ISDN Systems*, 28(12):1629–1641, 1996.

[Rib96]   L. Ribeiro. *Parallel Composition and Unfolding Semantics of Graph Grammars*. PhD thesis, Technische Universität Berlin, 1996.

[Roz97]   G. Rozenberg, Editor. *Handbook of Graph Grammars and Computing by Graph Transformation, Vol. 1: Foundations*. World Scientific, 1997.

[RT88]   A. Rabinovich and B. A. Trakhtenbrot. Behavior Structures and Nets. *Fundamenta Informaticæ*, 11(4):357–404, 1988.

[vB84]   J. van Bentham. Correspondence Theory. In *Handbook of Philosophical Logic*, volume II. Reidel, 1984.

[Vog91]   W. Vogler. Deciding History Preserving Bisimilarity. In J. Leach Albert, B. Monien, and M. Rodríguez-Artalejo, Editors, *Proceedings of ICALP'91*, volume 510 of *LNCS*, pages 495–505. Springer-Verlag, 1991.

[Vog97]   W. Vogler. Efficiency of Asynchronous Systems and Read Arcs in Petri Nets. In *Proceedings of ICALP'97*, volume 1256 of *LNCS*, pages 538–548. Springer Verlag, 1997.

[VSY98]   W. Vogler, A. Semenov, and A. Yakovlev. Unfolding and Finite Prefix for Nets with Read Arcs. In *Proceedings of CONCUR'98*, volume 1466 of *LNCS*, pages 501–516. Springer-Verlag, 1998.

Part III

Petri Nets

High-Level Net Processes

Hartmut Ehrig[1], Kathrin Hoffmann[1], Julia Padberg[1], Paolo Baldan[2], and
Reiko Heckel[3]

[1] Technical University of Berlin, Germany
{ehrig,hoffmann,padberg}@cs.tu-berlin.de
[2] University of Pisa, Italy
baldan@di.unipi.it
[3] University of Paderborn, Germany
reiko@upb.de

Abstract. The notion of processes for low-level Petri nets based on occurrence nets is well known and it represents the basis for the study of the non-sequential behavior of Petri nets. Processes for high-level nets N are often defined as processes of the low level net $Flat(N)$ which is obtained from N via a construction called "flattening". In this paper we define high-level processes for high-level nets based on a suitable notion of high-level occurrence nets. The flattening of a high-level occurrence net is in general not a low-level occurrence net, due to so called "assignment conflicts" in the high-level net. The main technical result is a syntactical characterization of assignment conflicts. But the main focus of this paper is a conceptual discussion of future perspectives of high-level net processes including concurrency and data type aspects. Specifically, in the second part of the paper, we discuss possible extensions of high-level net processes, which are formally introduced for algebraic high-level nets in the first part of this paper. Of special interest are high-level processes with data type behavior, amalgamation, and other kinds of constructions, which are essential aspects for a proposed component concept for high-level nets.

1 Introduction

High-level nets are one of the most important examples of integrated data type and process modeling techniques for concurrent and distributed systems (see [EGH92, Jen92]). For low-level Petri nets the notion of nondeterministic and deterministic processes is an essential concept to capture their non-sequential truly concurrent behavior. Especially in the case of elementary net systems and safe place/transition nets this has been worked out in a fully satisfactory way by Rozenberg, Winskel, Nielsen, Goltz, Reisig, Degano, Meseguer, Montanari and other authors [NPW81, GR83, Roz87, Win87, Win88, DMM89, Eng91, MMS97] leading to different notions of deterministic and nondeterministic processes and to a truly concurrent semantics of Petri nets in terms of prime algebraic domains and event structures. The situation is already slightly more difficult in the case of non-safe place/transition nets. In order to capture a satisfactory notion of

W. Brauer et al. (Eds.): Formal and Natural Computing, LNCS 2300, pp. 191–219, 2002.

causality and conflict in the case of multiple tokens on one place, the dichotomy between the "individual token" and "collective token" views has been developed in the literature and coined as such by van Glabbeck and Plotkin in [vGP95]. On the basis of the individual token interpretation Meseguer, Montanari and Sassone [MMS97] have extended Winskel's adjunction between safe Petri nets and prime event structures to general place/transition nets. Since the flattening of high-level nets in general leads to non-safe place/transition nets, processes for general place/transition nets are a prerequisite to study the concurrent behavior of a high-level net N via the flattening $Flat(N)$ using the corresponding semantics and techniques of low-level nets. Especially, this allows to define processes of a high-level net N as low-level processes of the flattening $Flat(N)$ of N. This view of processes of high-level nets or an equivalent presentation has been mainly considered in the literature up to now.

In this paper we claim, however, that a more adequate view of processes for high-level nets should capture the distinction between the data processing and the concurrency aspect of processes in the sense of basic procedures for concurrent and distributed systems in software engineering and communication technology. For this purpose we propose a notion of high-level process for high-level nets which is defined independently of flattening.

The essential idea is to generalize the concept of occurrence net from the low-level to the high-level case. This means that the net structure of a high-level occurrence net has similar properties like a low-level occurrence net, like unitarity, conflict freeness, and acyclicity. But we drop the idea that an occurrence net captures essentially one concurrent computation. Instead, a high-level occurrence net and a high-level process are intended to capture a set of different concurrent computations corresponding to different input parameters of the process. This is in some sense analogous to procedures in programming languages, where a procedure works on a set of input parameters: Each instantiation or call of the procedure with suitable input parameters leads to a run of the procedure and hence to one specific computation. In fact, high-level processes can be considered to have a set of initial markings for the input places of the corresponding occurrence net, whereas there is only one implicit initial marking of the input places for low-level occurrence nets.

The paper is organized as follows. First in Section 2 we define high-level processes for algebraic high-level nets (AHL-nets) without initial marking. The case with initial markings is discussed in Section 4. In Section 3, we review the flattening of AHL-nets (see e.g. [EPR94]) and apply it to high-level processes. As expected, the flattening of a high-level process is in general not a low-level process, due to so called "assignment conflicts", which may occur in high-level occurrence nets. As main technical result we give a syntactical characterization of assignment conflicts. The main idea, however, is that a high-level process of a high-level net N corresponds to a set of low-level processes of the flattening $Flat(N)$ of N.

In Section 4, we discuss possible extensions of our basic notion of high-level processes. The first extension is that from algebraic-high level nets to that of other types of high-level nets in the framework of parameterized net classes ([EP97a, EP97b, PE01]) and abstract Petri nets [Pad96]. Another extension is that from AHL-processes in Section 2 to open AHL-processes in the sense of open nets and open processes studied for Place/Transition nets most recently in the paper [BCEH01]. As mentioned already, another important extension is the case of AHL-processes with a set of initial markings, which also allows to define a data type behavior of high-level processes. This extension allows to consider AHL-nets and AHL-processes as an instantiation of the general concept of integrated data type and process modeling techniques in [EO01a] and leads to a component concept for AHL-nets with AHL-processes in the sense of [EO01b]. Last but not least we discuss in Section 4 how well-known constructions of low-level processes, like unfolding and concatenation can be extended to high-level processes. Moreover, we propose also new constructions for low-level and high-level processes via process terms based on constructions like sequential and parallel composition as well as amalgamation of processes in the sense of [BCEH01]. This should allow to define process types based on nets and net processes in analogy to data types [EM85] as advocated in [EMP97] already.

Acknowledgements

We are grateful to the referees of the paper for several useful comments and to Claudia Ermel and Maria Oswald for careful figure drawing and typing.

2   Algebraic High-Level Processes

In this section we review the concept of algebraic high-level net and we give a formal definition of algebraic high-level processes based on a suitable high-level notion of occurrence net. The well known example of dining philosophers in the high-level case (see [EPR94, PER95]) serves as running example.

The version of AHL-nets defined below is similar to [EPR94, PER95] but for the fact that places are typed, that is, the data elements on these places and the terms occurring in the inscriptions of the attached arcs are required to be of a specified sort. This typing reduces the set of possible markings and helps to keep the unfolding of a high-level net manageable.

Definition 2.1 (Algebraic High-Level Net).
An *algebraic high-level net (AHL-net)*,

$$N = (SPEC, P, T, pre, post, cond, type, A)$$

consists of an algebraic specification $SPEC = (S, OP, E; X)$ with equations E and additional variables X over the signature (S, OP) (see [EM85]), sets P and T of places and transitions, respectively, pre- and post-domain functions

$$pre, post : T \rightarrow (T_{OP}(X) \otimes P)^{\oplus}$$

assigning to each transition $t \in T$ the pre- and post-domains $pre(t)$ and $post(t)$ (see Remark 1), respectively, a firing condition function

$$cond : T \to \mathcal{P}_{fin}(EQNS(S, OP, X))$$

assigning to each transition $t \in T$ a finite set $cond(t)$ of equations over the signature (S, OP) with variables X, a type function

$$type : P \to S$$

assigning to each place $p \in P$ a sort $type(p) \in S$, and an (S, OP, E)-algebra A (see [EM85]).

$\triangle$

Remarks

1. Denoting by $T_{OP}(X)$ the set of terms with variables X over the signature (S, OP) (see [EM85]), and by $M^{\oplus}$ the free commutative monoid over a set M, the set of all type-consistent arc inscriptions $T_{OP}(X) \otimes P$ is defined by

$$T_{OP}(X) \otimes P = \{(term, p) | term \in T_{OP}(X)_{type(p)}, p \in P\}.$$

   Thus, $pre(t)$ (and similar $post(t)$) is of the form $pre(t) = \sum_{i=1}^{n}(term_i, p_i)$ $(n \geq 0)$ with $p_i \in P, term_i \in T_{OP}(X)_{type(p_i)}$. This means, $\{p_1, \ldots, p_n\}$ is the pre-domain of t with arc-inscription $term_i$ for the arc from p_i to t if the $p_1, \ldots, p_n$ are pairwise distinct (unary case) and arc-inscription $term_{i1} \oplus \cdots \oplus term_{ik}$ for $p_{i1} = \cdots = p_{ik}$ (multi case).

2. The proposed version of AHL-nets is similar to [EPR94, PER95], but for the use of free commutative monoids $M^{\oplus}$ (cf. [MM90]) instead of free Abelian groups M^{ab}. In this paper the use of $M^{\oplus}$ is more suitable than M^{ab} in order to compare the high level with the classical low level case of place/transition nets. Moreover, as discussed above, places are typed. Therefore, the cartesian product $T_{OP}(X) \times P$ used in [PER95] has been replaced by its subset $T_{OP}(X) \otimes P$. Consequently a marking m is now an element $m \in (A \otimes P)^{\oplus}$ with

$$A \otimes P = \{(a, p) | a \in A_{type(p)}, p \in P\}.$$

3. The case of AHL-nets and corresponding AHL-processes with initial markings $init \in (A \otimes P)^{\oplus}$ will be discussed in Section 4.

Enabling and firing of transitions are defined as follows.

Definition 2.2 (Algebraic High-Level Net).
Given an AHL-net as above and a transition $t \in T$, $Var(t)$ denotes the set of variables occurring in $pre(t), post(t)$, and $cond(t)$. An assignment $asg_A : Var(t) \to A$ is called consistent if the equations $cond(t)$ are satisfied in A under asg_A.

The marking $pre_A(t, asg_A)$ – and similarly $post_A(t, asg_A)$ – is defined for $pre(t) = \sum_{i=1}^{n}(term_i, p_i)$ by

$$pre_A(t, asg_A) = \sum_{i=1}^{n}(\overline{asg_A}(term_i), p_i),$$

where $\overline{asg_A} : T_{OP}(Var(t)) \to A$ is the extension of the assignment asg_A to an evaluation of terms (see [EM85]).

A transition $t \in T$ is enabled under a consistent assignment $asg_A : Var(t) \to A$ and marking $m \in (A \otimes P)^{\oplus}$, if

$$pre_A(t, asg_A) \leq m,$$

In this case, the successor marking m' is defined by

$$m' = m \ominus pre_A(t, asg_A) \oplus post_A(t, asg_A)$$

where $pre_A(t, asg_A)$ and similar $post_A(t, asg_A)$ is defined for $pre(t) = \sum_{i=1}^{n}(term_i, p_i)$ by

$$pre_A(t, asg_A) = \sum_{i=1}^{n}(\overline{asg_A}(term_i), p_i).$$

$\triangle$

Example 2.3 (Dining Philosophers).
In analogy to [PER95] the AHL-net $DIPHI$ for dining philosophers (with n philosophers) is given in Figure 1 together with the algebraic specification

$\underline{diphi} = \underline{sorts} : philo, fork$

$\quad\quad \underline{opns} : p_1, \ldots, p_n :\to philo$
$\quad\quad\quad\quad f_1, \ldots, f_n :\to fork$
$\quad\quad\quad\quad ls : philo \to fork$
$\quad\quad\quad\quad rs : philo \to fork$
$\quad\quad \underline{eqns} : ls(p_1) = f_n$
$\quad\quad\quad\quad ls(p_i) = f_{(i-1)} \quad (i = 2 \ldots n)$
$\quad\quad\quad\quad rs(p_i) = f_i \quad (i = 1 \ldots n),$

additional variables $X = \{x : philo; y, z : fork\}$, $type(THINK) = type(EAT) = philo$, $type(FORK) = fork$ and initial $\underline{diphi}$-algebra A with $A_{philo} = \{P_1, \ldots, P_n\}$ and $A_{fork} = \{F_1, \ldots, F_n\}$. The usual initial marking for the dining philosophers is to have all philosophers $P_1 \ldots P_n$ on place THINK and all forks $F_1 \ldots F_n$ on place FORK, i.e.

$$init = \sum_{i=1}^{n}(P_i, THINK) \oplus \sum_{i=1}^{n}(F_i, FORK).$$

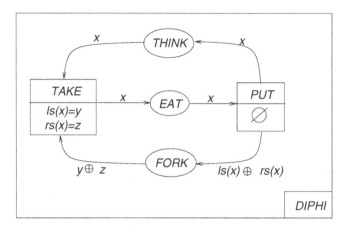

Fig. 1. AHL Net for Dining Philosophers

◊

Definition 2.4 (Category of AHL-Nets).

The category **AHL-net** has AHL-nets N as objects and AHL-net-morphisms $f : N_1 \to N_2$ as arrows where $f = (f_{SPEC}, f_P, f_T, f_A)$ with

- $f_{SPEC} : SPEC_1 \to SPEC_2$ is a specification morphism with sort part $f_s : S_1 \to S_2$, signature part $f_{OP} : (S_1, OP_1, X_1) \to (S_2, OP_2, X_2)$ and extension $f_{OP}^\#$ to terms and equations such that the restrictions $f_{OP}|_{Var(t_1)} : Var(t_1) \to Var(f_T(t_1))$ of f_{OP} to variables of transitions are bijective;
- $f_P : P_1 \to P_2$ *and* $f_T : T_1 \to T_2$ are functions;
- $f_A : A_1 \to A_2$ is induced by an isomorphism $f_a : A_1 \xrightarrow{\sim} V_{f_{SPEC}}(A_2)$ in the category of $SPEC_1$-algebras (see [EM85]) requiring that the following diagrams commute separately for pre- and post-functions.

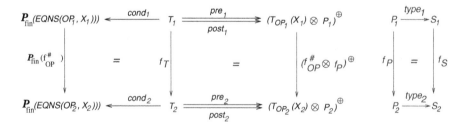

△

Remark Although this definition is slightly different from those in [PER95] and [EGP99] we still have the existence of pushouts and other HLR-properties as stated in the mentioned papers. These properties allow to define the union of nets via pushouts and net transformations via double pushouts in the sense of high-level replacement systems (see [EGP99]). The bijectivity of f_{OP} on variables of transitions is used in Fact 3.2.2.

Definition 2.5 (AHL-Occurrence Net).

A (deterministic) *AHL-occurrence net* K is an AHL-net

$$K = (SPEC, P, T, pre, post, cond, type, A)$$

such that for all $t \in T$ with $pre(t) = \sum_{i=1}^{n}(term_i, p_i)$ and notation $\bullet t = \{p_1, \ldots, p_n\}$ and similarly $t\bullet$ we have

1. (*Unarity*): $\bullet t, t\bullet$ are sets rather than multisets for all $t \in T$, i.e., for $\bullet t$ the places $p_1 \ldots p_n$ are pairwise distinct. Hence $|\bullet t| = n$ and the arc from p_i to t has a unary arc-inscription $term_i$ (rather than a proper sum of terms as in Remark 1 of Definition 2.1).
2. (*No Forward Conflicts*): $\bullet t \cap \bullet t' = \emptyset$ for all $t, t' \in T, t \neq t'$
3. (*No Backward Conflicts*): $t\bullet \cap t'\bullet = \emptyset$ for all $t, t' \in T, t \neq t'$
4. (*Partial Order*): the causal relation $< \subseteq (P \times T) \cup (T \times P)$ defined by the transitive closure of

$$\{(p, t) \in P \times T \mid p \in \bullet t\} \cup \{(t, p) \in T \times P \mid p \in t\bullet\}$$

is a finitary strict partial order, i.e. the partial order is irreflexive and for each element in the partial order the set of its predecessors is finite.

$\triangle$

Remarks

1. Conditions 1-4 are exactly those for occurrence nets in the case of – low-level place/transition nets with $pre(t) = \sum_{i=1}^{n} p_i$ (see [MM90]) and do not take into account possible assignment conflicts formally introduced in Definition 3.7. This means that the flattening $Flat(K)$ of an AHL-occurrence net K may not be a low-level occurrence net (see Example 3.5.2).
2. If we drop the unarity condition, K is called an *AHL- multi-occurrence net*.
3. We only define deterministic AHL-occurrence nets leading to deterministic AHL-processes. The nondeterministic case can be obtained by dropping the second condition "no forward conflicts" because conflicts are allowed in nondeterministic processes.

Definition 2.6 (AHL-process).

A *(deterministic) AHL-process* of an AHL-net N is an AHL-net morphism $p : K \to N$, where K is a (deterministic) AHL-occurrence net with the same data type part $(SPEC, A)$, which is preserved by p, i.e. $p_{SPEC} = id_{SPEC}$ and $p_A = id_A$.

$\triangle$

Remarks

1. This definition generalizes that of (deterministic) processes of Place/Transition nets which is obtained in the special case where $SPEC$ consists of one sort and A of one element (black token) only.
2. If K is an AHL-multi-occurrence net, then $p : K \rightarrow N$ is called *AHL-multi-process*. *AHL-multi-process* seem to be an interesting alternative to AHL-processes in the high-level case as shown in the following examples.
3. We only define deterministic AHL-processes, but nondeterministic processes are obtained if K is a nondeterministic AHL-occurrence net (see Remark 3 of Definition 2.5).

Example 2.7 (AHL-processes of Dining Philosophers).
The AHL-net $COURSE_1$ resp. $COURSE_2$ in Figure 2 with the same data type part as that of $DIPHI$ in Example 2.3 is a (deterministic) AHL-occurrence net resp. AHL-multi-occurrence net, because $COURSE_2$ violates the unitarity condition (see Definiton 2.5.1). Moreover, we obtain a (deterministic) AHL- process $p_1 : COURSE_1 \rightarrow DIPHI$ resp. (deterministic) AHL- multi-process $p_2 : COURSE_2 \rightarrow DIPHI$ by defining the morphisms p_1 and p_2 as suggested by the labelling in Figure 2:

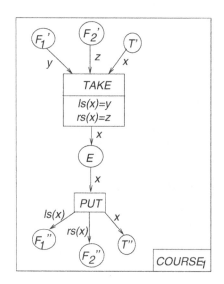
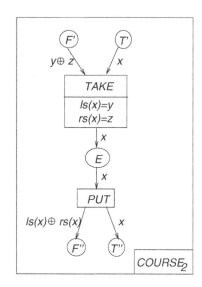

Fig. 2. AHL-process and AHL-multi process of AHL-net $DIPHI$ with AHL-occurrence net $COURSE_1$ and AHL-multi occurrence net $COURSE_2$

More precisely, $p_1 : COURSE_1 \rightarrow DIPHI$ maps F_1', F_2', F_1'', F_2'' to FORK, T' and T'' to THINK and E to EAT in $DIPHI$. Similarly $p_2 : COURSE_2 \rightarrow$

$DIPHI$ maps F', F'' to FORK, T', T'' to THINK, and E to EAT, while transitions are mapped identically in both cases.

The mappings $p_1 : COURSE_1 \rightarrow DIPHI$ and $p_2 : COURSE_2 \rightarrow DIPHI$ are both AHL-net morphisms preserving the data type parts. We only show compatibility of p_1 for TAKE with pre-domains:

$$
\begin{aligned}
(id \otimes p_{1_P})^{\oplus}(pre_1(TAKE)) &= (id \otimes p_{1_P})^{\oplus}((y, F_1') \oplus (z, F_2') \oplus (x, T')) \\
&= (y, FORK) \oplus (z, FORK) \oplus (x, THINK) \\
&= pre_{DIPHI}(TAKE) \\
&= pre_{DIPHI}(p_{1_T}(TAKE))
\end{aligned}
$$

It is interesting to note that the two processes of $DIPHI$ in Figure 2 have different behaviors as formally shown for their flattenings in Section 3.

Finally let us note that we have an AHL-net morphism $f : COURSE_1 \rightarrow COURSE_2$ which maps F_1' and F_2' to F' and F_1'' and F_2'' to F''. This leads to an AHL-multi-process morphism (f, id_{DIPHI}) from p_1 to p_2 (see below). $\Diamond$

Definition 2.8 (Category of AHL-processes).
Given AHL-processes $p_1 : K_1 \rightarrow N_1$ and $p_2 : K_2 \rightarrow N_2$ an AHL-process morphism is a pair (f_K, f_N) of AHL-net morphisms such that the following diagram commutes:

$$
\begin{array}{ccc}
K_1 & \xrightarrow{\ p_1\ } & N_1 \\
{\scriptstyle f_K}\downarrow & = & \downarrow{\scriptstyle f_N} \\
K_2 & \xrightarrow[\ p_2\ ]{} & N_2
\end{array}
$$

The category **AHL-Proc** has AHL-processes as objects and AHL-process morphisms as arrows. Similarly **AHL-Multi-Proc** is the category consisting of AHL-multi-processes as objects and AHL-process morphisms between AHL-multi-processes as morphisms. $\triangle$

AHL-Proc and **AHL-Multi-Proc** are well-defined because they form diagram categories over **AHL-Net** (see Definition 2.4).

Remark In the case of low-level nets there is also another view how to define a category of processes: Inspired by the "arrows as computations" philosophy, in [DMM89] a category of processes is defined where processes are viewed as arrows of a category in which objects are the possible states of the net (markings) and the source and target of a process are the starting and final state for the process itself.

3 Flattening of AHL-processes

In this section we review the well-known flattening construction from AHL-nets to Place/Transition nets and apply it to construct the flattening of AHL-processes introduced in the previous section. We will see that the flattening of an AHL-process is in general not a low- level process of place/transition nets, because the flattening may contain forward and/or backward conflicts. We call a place of an AHL-occurrence net K to be in forward resp. backward assignment conflict if there is a corresponding place in $Flat(K)$ which is in forward resp. backward conflict. The main result of this section is a characterization of assignment conflicts for AHL-processes. Moreover, we discuss the relationship between the AHL-process of an AHL-net N and the low-level processes of the flattening $Flat(N)$ of N.

Definition 3.1 (Place/Transition Nets and Processes).
A *Place/Transition net (P/T net)*,

$$N = (P, T, pre, post)$$

consists of sets P and T of places and transitions respectively, and pre- and post-domain functions

$$pre, post : T \rightarrow P^{\oplus}$$

where $P^{\oplus}$ is - as in Definition 2.1 - the free commutative monoid over P.
   A *P/T net morphism* $f : N_1 \rightarrow N_2$ is given by $f = (f_P, f_T)$ with functions $f_P : P_1 \rightarrow P_2$ and $f_T : T_1 \rightarrow T_2$ such that the following diagram commutes separately for pre- and post-functions:

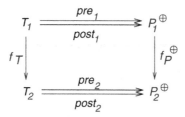

$\triangle$

   The category **Net** consists of P/T nets as objects and P/T-net morphisms as morphisms.
   A *(deterministic) P/T process* of a P/T net N is a P/T net morphism $p : K \rightarrow N$, where K is a (deterministic) occurrence net, i.e. a net satisfying conditions 1-4 of Definition 2.5.

Remark The case of nondeterministic P/T processes can be obtained by dropping condition 2 which requires the absence of no forward conflicts. A slightly more restrictive notion of nondeterministic processes is considered in [Eng91]. If condition 1 is dropped, K is called multi-occurrence net and $p : K \to N$ a P/T multi-process of N.

Definition 3.2 (Flattening).

1. Given an AHL-net $N = (SPEC, P, T, pre, post, cond, type, A)$, the flattening *Flat(N)* of N is a P/T net

$$Flat(N) = (CP, CT, pre_A, post_A)$$

   defined by
   - $CP = A \otimes P = \{(a, p) | a \in A_{type(p)}, p \in P\}$, called *colored places*;
   - $CT = \{(t, asg) | t \in T, asg : Var(t) \to A, \text{ s.t. all equations } e \in cond(t)$ are valid in A under $asg\}$, called *consistent transition assignments*;
   - $pre_A(t, asg) = \sum_{i=1}^{n} (\overline{asg}(term_i), p_i)$ for $pre(t) = \sum_{i=1}^{n} (term_i, p_i)$ where $term_i \in T_{OP}(X)_{type(p_i)}$ and $\overline{asg} : T_{OP}(Var(t)) \to A$ is the extension of the assignment $asg : Var(t) \to A$ to terms (see [EM85]);
   - $post_A(t, asg) = \sum_{i=1}^{m} (\overline{asg}(term_i'), p_i')$ for $post(t) = \sum_{i=1}^{m} (term_i', p_i')$.
2. Given an AHL-net morphism $f : N_1 \to N_2$ with $f = (f_{SPEC}, f_P, f_T, f_A,)$, the *flattening Flat(f)* of f is a P/T-net morphism given by

$$Flat(f) = (f_A \otimes f_P : CP_1 \to CP_2, f_C : CT_1 \to CT_2)$$

where f_C is defined by $f_C(t_1, asg_1) = (f_T(t_1), asg_2)$ with asg_2 given by

(bijectivity of f_{OP} on variables of transitions is required in Definition 2.3).

$\triangle$

Fact 3.3 (Flattening Functor).

The flattening conctruction defined in Definition 3.2 is well-defined and can be turn into a functor

$$Flat : \textbf{AHL-net} \to \textbf{Net}$$

$\triangle$

Proof

1. Flat (N) is a well-defined P/T net if we show $pre_A(t, asg), post_A(t, asg) \in CP^\oplus = (A \otimes P)^\oplus$. In fact we have $\overline{asg}(term_i) \in A_{type(p_i)}$ because $term_i \in T_{OP}(X)_{type(p_i)}$
   by definition of $pre(t) \in (T_{OP}(X) \otimes P)^\oplus$. This implies $pre_A(t, asg) = \sum_{i=1}^{n}(\overline{asg}(term_i), p_i) \in (A \otimes P)^\oplus$ and similarly for $post_A(t, asg)$.
2. For symmetry reasons it suffices to show commutativity of

$$
\begin{array}{ccc}
CT_1 & \xrightarrow{\ pre_{1A}\ } & CP_1^\oplus = (A_1 \otimes P_1)^\oplus \\
\Big\downarrow{\scriptstyle f_C} & & \Big\downarrow{\scriptstyle (f_A \otimes f_P)^\oplus} \\
CT_2 & \xrightarrow{\ pre_{2A}\ } & CP_2^\oplus = (A_2 \otimes P_2)^\oplus
\end{array}
$$

Given $(t_1, asg_1) \in CT_1$ we have for $pre_1(t_1) = \sum_{i=1}^{n}(term_i, p_i)$

$$
(f_A \otimes f_P)^\oplus(pre_{1A}(t_1, asg_1)) = (f_A \otimes f_P)^\oplus\Big(\sum_{i=1}^{n}(\overline{asg_1}(asg_1)(term_i), p_i\Big)
$$
$$
= \sum_{i=1}^{n}(f_A(\overline{asg_1}(term_i)), f_P(p_i)) \qquad (1)
$$

$$
(pre_{2A}(f_C(t_1, asg_1)) = (pre_{2A}(f_T(t_1), asg_2)
$$
$$
= \sum_{i=1}^{n}(\overline{asg_2}(f_{OP}^{\#}(term_i)), f_P(p_i)) \qquad (2)
$$

where the last equation holds, because f AHL-net morphism implies:

$$
pre_2(f_T(t_1)) = (f_{OP}^{\#} \otimes f_P)^\oplus\Big(\sum_{i=1}^{n}(term_i, (p_i))\Big)
$$
$$
= (f_{OP}^{\#} \otimes f_P)^\oplus\Big(\sum_{i=1}^{n}(term_i, p_i)\Big)
$$
$$
= \sum_{i=1}^{n}(f_{OP}^{\#}(term_i), f_P(p_i)).
$$

Comparing (1) and (2) is suffices to show

$$
\overline{asg_2}(f_{OP}^{\#}(term_i)) = f_A(\overline{asg_1}(term_i)) \quad (i = 1 \ldots n). \qquad (3)
$$

For (3) it is sufficient to show commutativity of (5) in the following diagram:

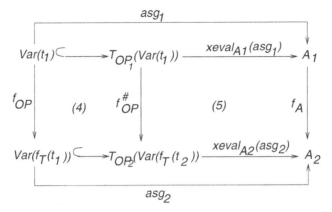

But due to commutativity of (4) and the outer diagram by definition of asg_2 diagram (5) commutes because $TOP_1(Var(t_1))$ is a free construction (see [EM85]).

3. Obviously we have $Flat(f) = id_{Flat(N)}$ for $f = id_N$. We can show $Flat(g \circ f) = Flat(g) \circ Flat(f)$ by composing the corresponding diagrams in part 2 of the proof and using the properties

$$(g \circ f)_C = g_C \circ f_C \text{ and } ((g \circ f)_A \otimes (g \circ f)_P)^\oplus = (g_A \otimes g_P)^\oplus \circ (f_A \otimes f_P)^\oplus.$$

Example 3.4 (Flattening of Dining Philosophers).
Given the AHL-net $DIPHI$ for dining philosophers in Example 2.3 we obtain the following flattening

$$Flat(DIPHI) = (CP, CT, pre_A, post_A)$$

with

- $CP = A \otimes P = \{(P_i, T), (P_i, E), (F_i, F) | i = 1 \ldots n\}$
- $CT = \{(TAKE, asg_i), (PUT, asg_i) | asg_i(x) = P_i, i = 1 \ldots n\}$
  where $T = THINK, E = EAT, F = FORK$ and $asg_i(y), asg_i(z)$ are uniquely determined by $asg_i(x) = P_i$ and the equations $ls_A(x) = y$ and $rs_A(x) = z$. The net $Flat(DIPHI)$ in the case $n = 3$ is shown in Figure 3:

◇

Remark 3.5 (Flattening of AHL-processes).
As we will show in the following examples, an AHL- process $p : K \to N$ can be flattened to

$$Flat(p) : Flat(K) \to Flat(N),$$

but $Flat(p)$ is not necessarily a P/T process of $Flat(N)$. In the first example $Flat(p)$ corresponds to a set of P/T-processes and in the second one $Flat(K)$ is

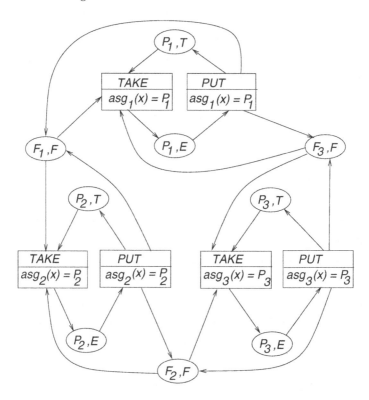

Fig. 3. Flattening of Dining Philosophers ($n = 3$)

not a low-level occurrence net, although K is a high-level occurrence net. This is due to the fact that K has assignment conflicts which become conflicts in $Flat(K)$. In Definition 3.7 we will formally define assignment conflicts and in Fact 3.8 we will give a characterization of them.

$\Diamond$

Example 3.6 (Flattening of AHL-processes).

1. The AHL-process $p_1 : COURSE_1 \rightarrow DIPHI$ (see 2.7) has the flattening

$$Flat(p_1) : Flat(COURSE_1) \rightarrow Flat(DIPHI)$$

where $Flat(DIPHI)$ is given in example 3.4, $Flat(COURSE_1)$ in Figure 4 and $Flat(p_1)$ maps places (P_i, T') and (P_i, T'') to (P_i, T), (P_i, E) to (P_i, E), and (F_i, F'_j), (F_i, F''_j) to (F_i, F) for $i \in \{1, 2, 3\}, j \in \{1, 2\}$.
Obviously $Flat(p_1)$ corresponds to three processes of $Flat(DIPHI)$ with usual initial marking $init = \sum_{i=1}^{3}(P_i, T) \oplus (F_i, F)$. Since we have not considered initial markings up to now, $Flat(p_1)$ is formally a (single) process

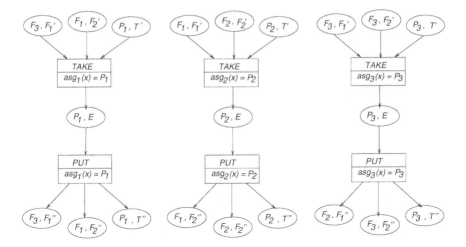

Fig. 4. Flattening of AHL-process $p_1 : COURSE_1 \rightarrow DIPHI$

of $Flat(DIPHI)$. The usual interpretation of $Flat(p_1)$ would have as initial marking one token on each input place, which would be mapped to the marking

$$init_2 = \sum_{i=1}^{3}(P_i, T) \oplus 2(F_i, F)$$

where two forks are on each fork place. This would avoid conflicts, but does not correspond to the problem of shared resources. Taking into account initial markings (see Subsection 4.4), $Flat(p_1)$ is not a process of $(Flat(DIPHI), init)$, but only a set of three single processes.

2. The flattening of the AHL-multi-process $p_2 : COURSE_2 \rightarrow DIPHI$ (see Example 2.7) leads to the following flattening:

$$Flat(p_2) : Flat(COURSE_2) \rightarrow Flat(DIPHI)$$

where $Flat(DIPHI)$ is given in Example 3.4, $Flat(COURSE_2)$ in Figure 5 and $Flat(p_2)$ maps places (P_i, T') and (P_i, T'') to (P_i, T'), (P_i, E) to (P_i, E), and (F_i, F'), (F_i, F'') to (F_i, F) for $i \in \{1, 2, 3\}$.

The P/T net $Flat(COURSE_2)$ is neither an occurrence net, nor a multi-occurrence net, although $COURSE_2$ is an AHL-multi-occurrence net. Especially $COURSE_2$ has no forward and backward conflicts, but $Flat(COURSE_2)$ has three forward conflicts for places (F_i, F') and 3 backward conflicts for places (F_i, F''), $i \in \{1, 2, 3\}$.

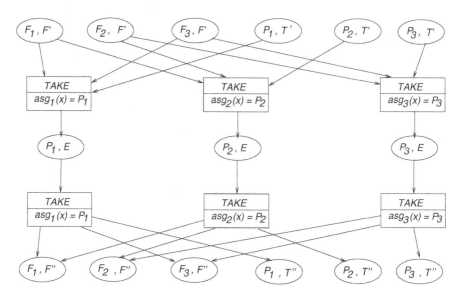

Fig. 5. Flattening of AHL-multi-process $p_2 : COURSE_2 \to DIPHI$

In fact we have in $COURSE_2$

$$pre(TAKE) = (x, T') \oplus (y, F') \oplus (z, F').$$

This implies for asg_1 with $asg_1(x) = P_1,\quad asg_1(y) = F_3,\quad asg_1(z) = F_1$:

$$pre_A(TAKE, asg_1) = (P_1, T') \oplus (F_3, F') \oplus (F_1, F').$$

But (F_1, F') is also in the pre-domain of $(TAKE, asg_2)$ leading to a forward conflict in $Flat(COURSE_2)$.

According to the following definition of assignment conflicts (see Definition 3.7) the place F' of $COURSE_2'$ is in forward assignment conflict, because (F_1, F') defines a forward conflict in the flattening $Flat(COURSE_2)$ of $COURSE_2$.

3. If we drop the equations of transition $TAKE$ of $COURSE_1$ and $DIPHI$, then $COURSE_1'$ is an AHL-process of $DIPHI'$ and we have two different consistent assignments asg_1, asg_1' with $asg_1(x) = P_1, asg_1(y) = F_3, asg_1(z) = F_1$ and $asg_1'(x) = P_1, asg_1'(y) = F_1, asg_1'(z) = F_3$ leading to a forward assignment conflict for place T', because (P_1, T') is in the pre-domain of the transitions $(TAKE, asg_1)$ and $(TAKE, asg_1')$. Note that asg_1 is not a consistent assignment for $COURSE_1$ and $DIPHI$, such that we have no transition $(TAKE, asg_1')$ in $Flat(COURSE_1)$ and $Flat(DIPHI)$.

This example shows that also AHL-processes may have assignment conflicts, while Example 2 has shown assignment conflicts for the AHL-multi-process $p_2 : COURSE_2 \to DIPHI$.

$\Diamond$

Definition 3.7 (Assignment Conflicts).
Given a (deterministic) AHL-occurrence net

$$K = (SPEC, P, T, pre, post, cond, type, A)$$

a place $p \in P$ is in *forward* (resp. *backward) assignment conflict* in K if there is a data $a \in A_{type(p)}$ such that the place $(a, p) \in A \otimes P$ defines a forward (resp. backward) conflict in the flattening $Flat(K)$ of K.

$\triangle$

Remark According to definition 2.5 $(a, p) \in A \otimes P$ defines a forward (resp. backward) conflict in $Flat(K)$ if there are distinct transitions $(t, asg), (t', asg') \in CT$ with

$$(a, p) \in [pre_A(t, asg)] \cap [pre_A(t', asg')]$$

(forward conflict) resp.

$$(a, p) \in [post_A(t, asg)] \cap [post_A(t', asg')]$$

(backward conflict).

In the following we give a characterization for forward and backward assignment conflicts:

Theorem 3.8 (Characterization of Assignment Conflicts).
Given a (deterministic) AHL-occurrence net K as in 3.7 a place $p \in P$ is in forward (resp. backward) assignment conflict in K if and only if the following *assignment conflict condition* is satisfied:

There is a transition $t \in T$ with $pre(t) = \sum_{i=1}^{n}(term_i, p_i)$ (resp. $post(t) = \sum_{i=1}^{n}(term_i, p_i)$) such that $p = p_i$ for some $i \in \{1, \dots, n\}$ and there are consistent assignments $asg \neq asg'$ with

$$\overline{asg}(term) = \overline{asg'}(term) = a$$

for some $a \in A_{type(p)}$ and $term = term_i$ as shown in Figure 6.

$\triangle$

Remark In the case of AHL-multi-occurrence nets K the assignment condition is slightly more general because we require the existence of $t \in T$ with $p = p_i = p_j$ for some

$i, j \in \{1, \dots, n\}$ and consistent assignments $asg \neq asg'$ with

$$\overline{asg}(term_i) = \overline{asg'}(term_j) = a \in A_{type(p)}$$

which includes the condition above for $i = j$.

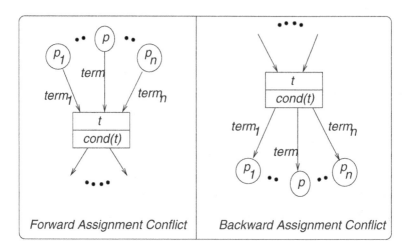

Fig. 6. Forward and Backward Assignment Conflicts with $(t, asg) \neq (t, asg') \in CT$ and $\overline{asg}(term) = \overline{asg'}(term)$

Proof For symmetry reasons it suffices to consider forward conflicts.

Necessity of Assignment Conflict Condition

Given a place $p \in P$ in forward assignment conflict we have $(a, p) \in A \otimes P, (t, asg) \neq (t', asg') \in CT$ with

$$(a, p) \in [pre_A(t, asg)] \cap [pre_A(t', asg')].$$

Let $pre(t) = \sum_{i=1}^{n}(term_i, p_i)$ and $pre(t') = \sum_{j=1}^{m}(term'_j, p'_j)$ then

$$pre_A(t, asg) = \sum_{i=1}^{n}(\overline{asg}(term_i), p_i), pre_A(t', asg') = \sum_{j=1}^{m}(\overline{asg'}(term'_j), p'_j)$$

which means that we have $i \in \{1, \ldots, n\}$, $j \in \{1, \ldots, m\}$ with

$$(a, p) = (\overline{asg}(term_i), p_i) = (\overline{asg'}(term'_j), p'_j).$$

This implies $p = p_i = p'_j$ and $a = \overline{asg}(term_i) = (\overline{asg'}(term'_j)$.

Case 1 ($t \neq t'$) In this case we have $p = p_i = p'_j \in \bullet t \cap \bullet t'$ for $t \neq t'$ and hence a forward conflict in K, which contradicts the fact that K is an AHL-occurrence net.

Case 2 ($t = t'$) In this case $p = p_i = p'_j$ and $pre(t) = pre(t')$ implies $term_i = term'_j$ such that we have for $term = term_i$ the assignment conflict condition

$$\overline{asg}(term) = \overline{asg'}(term) = a$$

with $asg \neq asg'$, because $(t, asg) \neq (t', asg')$ and $t = t'$.

Sufficiency of Assignment Conflict Condition:
Given the assignment conflict condition we have $asg \neq asg'$ with

$$(a, p) \in [pre_A(t, asg)] \cap [pre_A(t', asg')].$$

This implies $(t, asg) \neq (t, asg')$ and hence (a, p) defines a forward conflict in $Flat(K)$, i.e. a forward assignment conflict for p in K.

Remark In the case of an AHL-multi-occurrence net K case 2 above allows $term_i \neq term_j$ for $p_i = p'_j$ and hence the slightly more general assignment conflict condition.

Remark 3.9 (Relationship between High-Level and Low-Level Processes).

1. Given an AHL-process $p : K \to N$ we have seen already that
   $Flat(p) : Flat(K) \to Flat(N)$ is not necessarily a low-level process of $Flat(N)$ because K may have an assignment conflict which causes a conflict in $Flat(K)$. But if K has no assignment conflicts, then $Flat(K)$ has no conflicts and $Flat(p)$ is a low-level process. Moreover, even in the general case with assignment conflicts of K each low-level process $q : L \to Flat(K)$ defines a low-level process $q' = Flat(p) \circ q : L \to Flat(N)$ of $Flat(N)$. In this way we obtain the set of all *low-level* processes of $Flat(N)$ *associated* to $p : K \to N$.
2. Vice versa let us call a low-level process $q' : L \to Flat(N)$ *high-level-representable*, if there is an AHL-process $p : K \to N$ and a P/T-process $q : L \to Flat(K)$ such that $q' = Flat(p) \circ q : L \to Flat(N)$. For example let L_1, L_2, L_3 be the three connected low-level occurrence nets in Figure 4 leading to low-level processes $q'_i = Flat(DIPHI)$ $(i = 1 \ldots 3)$. Then each of these processes is high-level representable by the AHL-process $p_1 : COURSE_1 \to DIPHI$, where
   $q'_i : L_i \to Flat(COURSE_1)$ is the embedding of L_i into $Flat(COURSE_1)$ in Figure 4.
   In general, we claim that (under mild assumptions which we dont know yet) each low-level process $q' : L \to Flat(N)$ is high-level representable by some AHL-processes $p : K \to N$, where the net structures of K and L coincide, i.e. the skeleton of K is isomorphic to L. In other words, $q' : L \to Flat(N)$ can be lifted to a high-level process $p : K \to N$ with some $q : L \to Flat(K)$.

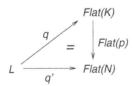

◇

4   Future Perspectives

In this section, we discuss several extensions of AHL-processes and flattening introduced in the previous sections. Each of these extensions can be considered in its own right, but most of them can be also combined with each other. A more detailed presentation of most of these extensions will be given in forthcoming papers.

4.1   High-Level Net Processes

We have defined processes for AHL-nets in Section 2, where AHL-nets, however, are only one specific type of high-level nets. Of course the question arises how far this can be generalized to other types of high-level nets, like colored nets or predicate transition nets. In [EP97a, EP97c, PE01] we have introduced the notion of parameterized net classes, which can be instantiated to a great variety of low-level and high-level net classes in the literature including colored nets [Jen92] and predicate transition nets [Gen91]. The categorical theory of parameterized net classes is based on the notion of abstract Petri nets introduced in [Pad96]. This notion relies on an institution for the data type part and on a net structure functor $Net : \textbf{Sets} \rightarrow \textbf{Sets}$ for the net structure part. In [Pad96] the instantiation for P/T nets is given by $Net(P) = P^{\oplus}$ and for AHL-nets by $Net(P) = (T_{OP}(X) \times P)^{\oplus}$. The basic concepts of a theory of abstract Petri nets are developed, including the category of abstract Petri nets and a flattening construction from high-level to low-level abstract Petri nets. But a concept of processes for abstract Petri nets generalizing processes for elementary nets and P/T nets is not yet considered in [Pad96] or elsewhere. As discussed in Section 2 the main problem is to find a suitable notion of occurrence net in the case of high-level nets. In fact, our notion of AHL-occurrence net and process in Definitions 2.5 and 2.6 can be generalized to abstract Petri nets, if we are able to define the pre-domain $\bullet t$ and the post-domain $t \bullet$ of a transition $t \in T$. The present version of abstract Petri nets in [Pad96] does not allow to define these domains as subsets of the set of places P. For this purpose an idea could be to extend the notion of abstract Petri nets by a natural transformation

$$[\ \ ] : Net \rightarrow \mathcal{P}$$

from the net-structure functor $Net : \textbf{Sets} \rightarrow \textbf{Sets}$ to the power set functor $\mathcal{P} : \textbf{Sets} \rightarrow \textbf{Sets}$, where the family of functions

$$[\ \ ]_P : Net(P) \rightarrow \mathcal{P}(P)$$

is intended to define for each marking $m \in Net(P)$ over a set P of places the subset $[m]_P \subseteq P$ of places occurring in the marking m. In the case of P/T nets we have $Net(P) = P^{\oplus}$ and $[]_P : P^{\oplus} \rightarrow \mathcal{P}(P)$ can be defined for $m = \sum_{i=1}^{n}(\lambda_i, p_i)$ with $p_i \in P$ and $\lambda_i \in \textbf{N} - \{0\}$ by

$$[m]_P = \{p_1, \ldots p_n\} \subseteq P.$$

Similarly in the case of AHL-nets with $Net(P) = (T_{OP}(x) \times P)^{\oplus}$ and $m = \sum_{i=1}^{n}(term_i, p_i)$ with $p_i \in P$ and $term_i \in T_{OP}(X)$ by

$$[m]_P = \{p_1, \ldots p_n\} \subseteq P.$$

In both cases we obtain a natural transformation, which means in the case of P/T nets commutativity of the following diagram for each function $f : P_1 \rightarrow P_2$.

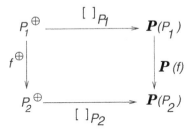

In fact, we have for $m = \sum_{i=1}^{n}(\lambda_i, p_i)$

$$\mathcal{P}(f)([m]_{P_1}) = \mathcal{P}(f)\{p_1, \ldots p_m\} = \{f(p_1), \ldots f(p_m)\}$$
$$= [\sum_{i=1}^{n}(\lambda_i, f(p_i))]_{P_2} = [f^{\oplus}(m)]_{P_2}.$$

Using this natural transformation we are able to define pre-domain $\bullet t$ and post-domain $t\bullet$ of a transition $t \in T$ by

$$\bullet t = [pre(t)]_P \subseteq P \quad and \quad t\bullet = [post(t)]_P \subseteq P$$

With these notions we can generalize at least the conflict- and partial order conditions in Definition 2.5 to abstract Petri nets. In order to define unarity we must be able to distinguish between set and multisets which would require an additional extension of abstract Petri nets.

Finally let us note that AHL-nets as defined in Definition 2.1 of this paper are slightly different from those in [PER95] and [Pad96]. In our case we have

$$Net(P) = (T_{OP}(X) \times P)^{\oplus},$$

where $T_{OP}(X) \otimes P \subseteq T_{OP}(X) \times P$ depends on the type function $type : P \rightarrow S$, which is not present in the definition of AHL-nets in [PER95] and [Pad96]. In fact, our definition is much more adequate in the case of flattening: Otherwise in our running example (and similar for most other examples) the places of the flattened net would include also pairs $(P_i, FORK)$ and $(F_i, THINK)$, where philosophers P_i are on the place $FORK$ or forks F_i on the place $THINK$. On the other hand Net in our case is no longer a functor $Net : \mathbf{Sets} \rightarrow \mathbf{Sets}$, but a slightly different functor $Net : (\mathbf{Sets} \downarrow S) \rightarrow \mathbf{Sets}$, because $type : P \rightarrow S$ is an element of the comma category $\mathbf{Sets} \downarrow S$.

This, however, would require an extension of the notion of abstract Petri nets in [Pad96].

4.2   Higher Order Net Processes

In [Hof00, Hof01] we have introduced the concept and formal definition of Algebraic Higher Order Nets to model flexible business processes. Algebraic Higher Order Nets are AHL-nets where the data type part is extended by higher order types, sorts and functions. This allows to have functions as data items on places which are typed by higher order sorts, such that different functions may be activated and applied during run time. This feature is especially useful to model flexible business processes, where the choice of different functions would require different nets, in the case of ordinary AHL-nets, but can be modeled with a single Algebraic Higher Order Net using different functions as tokens. For a restricted class of Algebraic Higher Order Nets it is possible to define an unfolding operation leading to an AHL-net. This is similar in some sense to the flattening construction of AHL-nets leading to Place/Transition nets discussed in Section 3. But in general Algebraic Higher Order Nets are more expressive than AHL-nets.

AHL-nets in contrast to Algebraic Higher Order Nets are adequate in application domains, where the context is known from the very beginning. The system can be modeled by a Petri net with a fixed net structure, that is, changes of the environment can only be modeled by changing the structure of Petri nets. But in other application domains like business processes it is also desirable to support the fact that an organisation of a system is not fixed once and for all. Rather, a large variety of changes e.g. replacing one task by another refined task can occur. In such application domains it is useful to use Algebraic Higher Order Nets. In [Hof01] we have used Algebraic Higher Order Nets in an example of logistic processes and discussed different kinds of changes which are supported by this formalism. In a forthcoming paper this example will be extended to a whole case study where specific scenarios will be modeled as processes for AHL-nets and Algebraic Higher Order Nets.

In fact, the main difference between Algebraic Higher Order Nets and AHL-nets consist in the use of higher order functions in the data type part. This means that the extension of high-level occurrence nets and processes to higher order occurrence nets and higher order processes seems to be quite natural and will be studied as part of ongoing work.

4.3   Open AHL-processes

In [BCEH01] we have formally defined the notion of open P/T net and process of such P/T nets leading to a compositional modeling of reactive systems. The main result in [BCEH01] is an amalgamation theorem which allows the amalgamation and decomposition of open P/T nets. This kind of result is not possible for ordinary P/T nets, because ordinary P/T nets cannot take into account the behavior of the environment. On the other hand this is the essential new feature of open nets, where in addition to producing and consuming tokens from places by firing of transitions we have open places, where so called "invisible actions" can produce or consume tokens on these open places. The intuitive idea is that the open places are the interface towards the environment. The "invisible actions" of one open net component can be interpreted as the consequence of the firing of transitions of other open net components which belong to the environment of the first component sharing the open places as interface places.

This idea of open net has been applied to the modeling of interorganizational workflows in the sense of [vdA98] and on a conceptual level to interoperability in train control systems [PJE+01]. In the second application open high-level processes have been introduced on a conceptual level already, and called scenario nets in [PJE+01]. In this paper we have defined AHL-processes, which can be extended to open nets in the sense of [BCEH01]. In fact, the idea of open places in [BCEH01] allows to define open AHL-nets, open AHL-net morphisms and open AHL-processes of open AHL-nets. As far as we can see it is possible to extend on one hand the theory of open nets and processes of P/T nets in [BCEH01] to open AHL-nets and processes, and on the other hand the flattening of AHL-processes in this paper to open AHL-processes.

4.4   AHL-processes with Initial Marking

For low-level processes $p : K \to N$ it is implicitly assumed that we have an initial marking $init_K$, where each input place of the occurrence net K contains exactly one token. Moreover, if N has an initial marking $init_N$ then it is assumed that $p(init_K) = init_N$. Sometimes it is useful to require $p(init_K) \leq init_N$ or $p(init_K) \geq init_N$.

For high-level processes $p : K \to N$ of an AHL-net with initial marking $init_N$ we propose to have a set of markings $INIT_K$, where each $init_K \in INIT_K$ is a marking of all input places of K, i.e.

$$[init_K] = \{p \in P_K | \neg \exists \quad t \in T_K : \quad p \in [post_K(t)]\},$$

and $p(init_K) = init_N$. Here $[m]$ denotes the set of all places occurring in m i.e. for $m = \sum_{i=1}^{n}(term_i, p_i)$ we have $[m] = \{p_1, \ldots p_n\}$, where unitarity of K implies that $p_1, \ldots p_n$ are pairwise disjoint. The idea to have a set $INIT_K$ of initial markings for the high-level process corresponds to the idea that the process should be defined for different input parameters $init_K \in INIT_K$.

In our running example of dining philosophers we should have n initial markings for the process $p_1 : COURSE_1 \to DIPHI$ (resp. multi-process $p_2 : COURSE_2 \to DIPHI$) if $DIPHI$ has the standard initial marking

$$init_{DIPHI} = \sum_{i=1}^{n}(P_i, THINK) + \sum_{i=1}^{n}(F_i, FORK)$$

In fact, the n initial markings of $COURSE_1$

$$init^{(i)}_{COURSE_1} = (P_i, T'_1) \oplus (ls_A(P_i), F'_1) \oplus (rs_A(P_i), F'_2) \qquad (i = 1 \ldots n)$$

correspond to the n cases, where each philosopher $P_i (i = 1 \ldots n)$ has his associated forks. For the multi-process we would have

$$init^{(i)}_{COURSE_2} = (P_i, T') \oplus (ls_A(P_i), F') \oplus (rs_A(P_i), F') \quad (i = 1 \ldots n),$$

where we have two tokens on F', i.e. the two forks of P_i.

Of course, it would make no sense to have the initial marking

$$init_{COURSE_1} = (P_1, T') \oplus (F_1, F'_1) \oplus (F_2, F'_2)$$

In this case the transition $TAKE$ could not fire, because the left-side fork of P_1 is F_3 and the right-side fork is F_1. However, it is probably not useful to force by definition that K can fire for each initial marking $init_K \in INIT_K$. But it is interesting to analyze under which condition there is - up to independence of firing - only one firing sequence in K leading from the initial marking $intit_K$ to some final marking fin_K of K, i.e. fin_K contains only tokens on output places of K. For this purpose it makes sense to extend the flattening construction of Section 3 to the case with initial markings:

A marking m in the high-level case of AHL-net N is given by

$$m = \sum_{i=1}^{n} (a_i, p_i) \in (A \otimes P)^{\oplus}.$$

In fact, m can also be interpreted as a marking of the low-level net $Flat(N)$, because $A \otimes P$ is the set of places of $Flat(N)$. Hence for $(N, init)$ we obtain $Flat(N, init)$, where $init$ is initial marking of N and $Flat(N)$.

For a high-level process $p : K \to N$ with set of initial markings $INIT_K$ of K and initial marking $INIT_N$ of N we obtain the following flattenings

$$Flat(p) : Flat(K, init_K) \to Flat(N, init_N) \, for \, all \, init_K \in INIT_K.$$

As pointed out already $Flat(K)$ is not necessarily a low-level occurrence net. Moreover, $init_K$ is not necessarily a marking of all the input places of $Flat(K)$. For example, $init^{(1)}_{COURSE_1}$ is only a marking for three of the nine input places of $Flat(COURSE_1)$ in Figure 4, where we have $n = 3$ philosophers. But for each initial marking of $COURSE_1$ we obtain one subnet of $Flat(COURSE_1)$ leading to a well-defined low-level process of $Flat(DIPHI, init_{DIPHI})$.

In general, each high-level process $p : K \to N$ with initial markings $INIT_K$ and $init_N$ defines a set of low-level processes of $Flat(N)$ given by

$$LL(p, INIT_K) = \{q' : L \rightarrow Flat(N, init_N) | q' = Flat(p) \circ q \text{ for some low-level}$$
$$\text{process}$$
$$q : L \rightarrow Flat(K, init_K) \text{ with } init_K \in INIT_K\}.$$

Vice versa, given a low-level process $q' : L \rightarrow Flat(N, init_N)$ we call q' *high-level representable*, if there is an AHL-process $p : K \rightarrow N$ with initial markings $INIT_K$ and $init_N$ and a low-level process $q : L \rightarrow Flat(K, init_K)$ for some $init_K \in INIT_K$ with $q' = Flat(p) \circ q$. Again the problem arises under which assumptions low-level processes are high- level representable and which sets of low-level processes are realizable by one high-level process.

4.5   AHL-processes with Data Type Behavior

In order to define the data type behavior of AHL-processes it makes sense to consider processes $p : K \rightarrow N$ not only with initial markings $INIT_K$ and $init_N$ as discussed above, but also with finite sequences of input and output places (i.e. an arbitrary but fixed order of finite sets instead of arbitrary sets) IN and OUT given by

$$IN = (p_1 \ldots p_n) \text{ and } OUT = (p'_1 \ldots p'_m).$$

Let $s_i = type(p_i)$ $(i = 1 \ldots n)$ and $s_j = type(p'_j)$ $(i = 1 \ldots m)$ then we can define input and output parameter sets

$$A = A_{s_1} \times \cdots \times A_{s_n} \text{ and } B = A_{s'_1} \times \cdots \times A_{s'_m},$$

where A is the data type algebra of the AHL-nets K and N.

The set of all possible final markings of the out-put places of K is given for $OUT = (p'_1 \ldots p'_m)$ by

$$FIN_K = \{fin_K \in (A \otimes P)^{\oplus} | \quad \exists b = (a'_1 \ldots a'_m) \in B, fin_K = \sum_{j=1}^{m}(a'_j, p'_j)\}$$

In this case let data $(fin_K) = (a'_1 \ldots a'_n) = b \in B$. Similarly let $data(init_K) = (a_1 \ldots a_n) = a \in A$ for $init_K = \sum_{i=1}^{n}(a_i, p_i)$.

With these preliminaries we can define the *data type behavior* of $(p_i, INIT_K)$ by
$data - type - beh(p, INIT_K)$
$= \{(a, b) \in A \otimes B | \quad \exists init_K \in INIT_K, \exists fin_K \in FIN_K, \text{ and } \exists \text{ firing sequence}$
from $init_K$ to fin_K in K with $data(init_K) = a$ and $data(fin_K) = b\}$.

In the case of our process $p_1 : COURSE_1 \rightarrow DIPHI$ we have

$$A = A_{fork} \times A_{fork} \times A_{philo} = B$$

and the data type behavior of $(p_1, INIT_{COURSE_1})$ is a partial identity

$data - type - beh(p_1, INIT_{COURSE_1}) : A \rightarrow B$ defined on the following input parameter values

$$(F_n, F_1, P_1), (F_1, F_2, P_2), \ldots, (F_{n-1}, F_n, P_n).$$

In each case there is exactly one firing sequence from the corresponding initial to the corresponding final marking.

In general it seems to be useful to analyze high-level processes $p : K \rightarrow N$ with $(INIT_K, init_N)$ concerning consistency and completeness. Consistency would require that for each $init_K \in INIT_K$ there is at least one (or exactly one up to independence of firing) firing sequence from $init_K$ to some final marking $fin_K \in FIN_K$. Completeness means that $INIT_K$ contains all those markings of the input places $init$, such that there exists a firing sequence to some $fin_K \in FIN_K$.

AHL-nets and processes with data type behavior as discussed above are an important example for the instantiation of the integration paradigm in [EO01a] of integrated data type and process modeling techniques.

4.6   Construction of Low- and High-Level Net Processes

There are several different kinds of process constructions which should be considered for high-level nets:

1. A well-known construction of nondeterministic processes in the low-level case is the *unfolding* of a given net. It is certainly interesting to extend the unfolding constructions and results to open low-level nets in the sense of [BCEH01] on one hand and to high-level nets on the other hand. Especially this is interesting in view of an event structure semantics for these types of Petri nets generalizing the well-known Winskel adjunction of [Win88].
2. The idea of *concatenable processes* [DMM89, MMS97] is another important issue which should be extended to open and high-level nets respectively and also in combination. This allows sequential composition of processes, while parallel composition should be defined via coproducts or tensor products. In the case of open nets both constructions should be a special case of amalgamation in the sense of [BCEH01].
3. Using the constructions above it should be possible to define *process terms* built up from basic processes in analogy to data type terms built up from data type operations (see [EM85]). The closure of a given set of processes w.r.t. process terms would correspond to the construction of all terms and the term algebra respectively. This allows to define *process types* as nets together with a given set of processes for these nets as advocated in [EMP97] already and to study process types in analogy to data types in [EM85].
4. Given a net morphism $f : N_1 \rightarrow N_2$, the *translation* of a process $p_1 : L \rightarrow N_1$ is given by $p_2 = f \circ p : L \rightarrow N_2$ and the *restriction* $p_1 : L_1 \rightarrow N_1$ of a process $p_2 : L_2 \rightarrow N_2$ can be defined via the following pullback

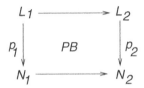

provided that the corresponding pullback construction exists for the corresponding net class and L_1 becomes an occurrence net. See [BCEH01] for the restriction of open processes for open P/T-nets.

4.7 Component Concept for Low- and High-Level Nets

In [EO01a, EO01b] we have introduced a components concept for integrated data type and process modeling techniques. The basic idea - in analogy to the algebraic module specification concept in [EM90] - is to have for each component an import specification IMP, export specification EXP, body specification BOD and two types of morphisms

$$i : IMP \to BOD \quad and \quad e : EXP \to BOD$$

connecting import and export with the body specification.

An integrated data type and process specification according to [EO01a] is defined on 4 layers: the data type layer 1, the data state and transformation layer 2, the process layer 3, and the system architecture layer 4.

In the case of AHL-nets N layer 1 consists of the algebraic specification $SPEC$ of N, in layer 2 the data states correspond to markings of N and transformations between data states are defined by firing of the transitions of N, and processes in layer 3 should be high-level processes of N as defined in this paper, or open AHL-processes as discussed in 4.1. Up to now, however, there is no component concept for AHL-nets corresponding to layer 4, or to the general component concept in [EO01b]. An instantiation of the general component concept leads to the following ideas of a component concept for AHL-nets.

Roughly spoken import, export and body consist of (open) AHL-nets N_I, N_E, and N_B respectively together with a set of (open) AHL-processes in each case. The morphism $e : EXP \to BOD$ is based on an (open) AHL-net morphism $f_e : N_E \to N_B$ such that the export processes are restrictions (see Subsection 4.7) of corresponding body processes. The morphism $i : IMP \to BOD$ is constructive in the sense of [EO01b]. This means that on one hand the import processes are translated along $i : IMP \to BOD$ to become body processes. On the other hand the body net N_B and the body processes are constructed from corresponding parts of the import and new parts introduced in the body. Especially the body net N_B might be constructed as union (pushout) of N_I and some auxiliary net N_{aux}. In the case of open AHL-nets and processes (see Subsection 4.3) the new body processes might be constructed by amalgamation of import processes of N_I and auxiliary processes of N_{aux}. But also other constructions in the sense of Subsection 4.6 could be used to construct new body processes.

Another alternative - also proposed in Subsection 4.6 and [EO01b] - would be to define the morphism $e : EXP \rightarrow BOD$ by a suitable net transformation in the sense of [PER95] and $i : IMP \rightarrow BOD$ as net inclusion. This corresponds to the idea that the relationship between export and body is a refinement.

In fact, both alternatives discussed above are not only useful for a component concept of high-level nets, but also for low-level nets, which are also discussed as instantiation of the general integration paradigm in [EO01a, EO01b].

References

[BCEH01] P. Baldan, A. Corradini, H. Ehrig, and R. Heckel. Compositional Modeling of Reactive Systems Using Open Nets. In *Proc. of CONCUR'01*, 2001. To appear.

[DMM89] P. Degano, J. Meseguer, and U. Montanari. Axiomatizing Net Computations and Processes. In *Proc. of LICS'89*, pages 175–185, 1989.

[EGH92] H. Ehrig, M. Große-Rhode, and A. Heise. Specification Techniques for Concurrent and Distributed Systems. Technical Report 92/5, Technical University of Berlin, jan. 1992. Invited paper for 2nd Maghr. Conference on Software Engineering and Artificial Intelligence, Tunis,1992.

[EGP99] H. Ehrig, M. Gajewsky, and F. Parisi-Presicce. *High-Level Replacement Systems with Applications to Algebraic Specifications and Petri Nets*, chapter 6, pages 341–400. Number 3: Concurrency, Parallelism, and Distribution in Handbook of Graph Grammars and Computing by Graph Transformations. World Scientific, 1999.

[EM85] H. Ehrig and B. Mahr. *Fundamentals of Algebraic Specification 1: Equations and Initial Semantics*, volume 6 of *EATCS Monographs on Theoretical Computer Science*. Springer Verlag, Berlin, 1985.

[EM90] H. Ehrig and B. Mahr. *Fundamentals of Algebraic Specification 2: Module Specifications and Constraints*, volume 21 of *EATCS Monographs on Theoretical Computer Science*. Springer Verlag, Berlin, 1990.

[EMP97] H. Ehrig, A. Merten, and J. Padberg. How to Transfer Concepts of Abstract Data Types to Petri Nets. *EACTS Bulletin*, 62:106–104, 1997.

[Eng91] J. Engelfriet. Branching Processes of Petri Nets. *Acta Informatica*, 28:575–591, 1991.

[EO01a] H. Ehrig and F. Orejas. A Conceptual and Formal Framework for the Integration of Data Type and Process Modeling Techniques. In *Proc. GT-VMT 2001, ICALP 2001 Satellite Workshops*, pages 201–228, Heraclion, Greece, 2001.

[EO01b] H. Ehrig and F. Orejas. A Generic Component Concept for Integrated Data Type and Process Specification Techniques. Technical report, Technische Universität Berlin, FB Informatik, 2001.

[EP97a] H. Ehrig and J. Padberg. A Uniform Approach to Petri Nets. In Ch. Freksa, M. Jantzen, and R. Valk, Editors, *Foundations of Computer Science: Potential - Theory - Cognition*, pages 219–231. Springer, LNCS 1337, 1997.

[EP97b] H. Ehrig and J. Padberg. Introduction to Universal Parametrized Net Classes. In H. Weber, H. Ehrig, and W. Reisig, Editors, *MoveOn-Proc. der DFG-Forschergruppe "Petrinetz-Technologie"*, pages 39–51, Technische Universität Berlin, 1997. Forschungsberichte des Fachbereichs Informatik.

[EP97c]   C. Ermel and J. Padberg. Formalization of Variables in Algebraic High-Level Nets. Technical Report 97-19, Technical University Berlin, 1997.

[EPR94]   H. Ehrig, J. Padberg, and L. Ribeiro. Algebraic High-Level Nets: Petri Nets Revisited. In *Recent Trends in Data Type Specification*, pages 188–206. Springer Verlag, 1994. Lecture Notes in Computer Science 785.

[Gen91]   H.J. Genrich. Predicate/Transition Nets. In *High-Level Petri Nets: Theory and Application*, pages 3–43. Springer Verlag, 1991.

[GR83]   U. Goltz and W. Reisig. The Non-Sequential Behaviour of Petri Nets. In *Information and Computation*, volume 57, pages 125–147. Academic Press, 1983.

[Hof00]   K. Hoffmann. Run Time Modification of Algebraic High Level Nets and Algebraic Higher Order Nets Using Folding and Unfolding Construction. In *Proceeding of the 3rd Internation Workshop Communication Based Systems*, pages 55–72. Kluwer Academic Publishers, 2000.

[Hof01]   K. Hoffmann. Flexible Modellierung mit Algebraischen Higher Order Netzen. In *Proceeding of the Workshop Modellierung 2001*, pages 101–110.

[Jen92]   K. Jensen. *Coloured Petri Nets. Basic Concepts, Analysis Methods and Practical Use*, volume 1: Basic Concepts. Springer Verlag, EATCS Monographs in Theoretical Computer Science Edition, 1992.

[MM90]   J. Meseguer and U. Montanari. Petri Nets Are Monoids. *Information and Computation*, 88(2):105–155, 1990.

[MMS97]   J. Meseguer, U. Montanari, and V. Sassone. On the Semantics of Place/Transition Petri Nets. *Mathematical Structures in Computer Science*, 7:359–397, 1997.

[NPW81]   M. Nielsen, G. Plotkin, and G. Winskel. Petri Nets, Event Structures and Domains, Part 1. *Theoretical Computer Science*, 13:85–108, 1981.

[Pad96]   J. Padberg. *Abstract Petri Nets: A Uniform Approach and Rule-Based Refinement*. PhD thesis, Technical University Berlin, 1996. Shaker Verlag.

[PE01]   J. Padberg and H. Ehrig. Introduction to Parametrized Net Classes. In H. Ehrig, G. Juhás, J. Padberg, and G. Rozenberg, Editors, *Advances in Petri Nets: Unifying Petri Nets*, LNCS. Springer, 2001.

[PER95]   J. Padberg, H. Ehrig, and L. Ribeiro. Algebraic High-Level Net Transformation Systems. *Mathematical Structures in Computer Science*, 5:217–256, 1995.

[PJE⁺01]   J. Padberg, L. Jansen, H. Ehrig, E. Schnieder, and R. Heckel. Cooperability in Train Control Systems Specification of Scenarios Using Open Nets. *Journal of Integrated Design and Process Technology*, 5:3–21, 2001.

[Roz87]   G. Rozenberg. Behaviour of Elementary Net Systems. In W. Brauer, W. Reisig, and G. Rozenberg, Editors, *Advances in Petri Nets 1986*, pages 60–94. Springer Verlag Berlin, LNCS 254, 1987.

[vdA98]   W.M.P. van der Aalst. The Application of Petri Nets to Workflow Management. *The Journal of Circuits, Systems and Computers*, 8:21–66, 1998.

[vGP95]   R. v. Glabbeck and G. Plotkin. Configuration Structures. In *Proc. 10th LICS Symposium*. IEEE, 1995.

[Win87]   G. Winskel. Petri Nets, Algebras, Morphisms, and Compositionality. *Information and Computation*, 72:197–238, 1987.

[Win88]   G. Winskel. Event Structures. In W. Brauer, W. Reisig, and G. Rozenberg, Editors, *Petri Nets: Applications and Relationships to Other Models of Concurrency*, pages 324 – 392. Springer, LNCS 255, 1988.

Petri Net Control for Grammar Systems

Maurice ter Beek and Jetty Kleijn*

LIACS, Leiden University, P.O.Box 9512, 2300 RA Leiden, The Netherlands
kleijn@liacs.nl

Abstract. It is demonstrated how Petri nets may be used to control the derivations in systems of cooperating grammars. This allows to define grammar systems with a concurrent rewriting protocol. Some basic properties are established.

1 Introduction

A grammar system consists of grammars and a protocol prescribing their co-operation. The first grammar systems appearing as such in the literature are the cooperating grammar systems defined in 1978 in [MR78] and [MRV78] by G. Rozenberg and his two Ph.D. students R. Meersman and D. Vermeir. These systems derived from a study of two-level substitution mechanisms by focussing on the collaboration and communication between multiple rewriting systems. Some ten years later, the link between grammar systems and the blackboard model for problem solving ([Nii89]) was established and a grammatical theory of cooperation protocols was developed (see [CDKP94] and [DPR97]). Two basic classes of grammar systems are distinguished: cooperating distributed (CD) grammar systems (introduced in [CK89] and [CD90]) and parallel communicating (PC) grammar systems ([PS89]). Like the cooperating grammar systems of [MR78], CD grammar systems are sequential in nature. The grammars work on a common sentential form and at each moment during the rewriting process only one of them is active. On the other hand in a PC grammar system the grammars work simultaneously, each on its own sentential form. The operations are synchronized (by means of a global clock): in each time unit the grammars either all rewrite their current string or they communicate through queries which leads to the sending of sentential forms from one component to another. Since their introduction many variations of CD and PC grammar systems have been formulated not just by varying the type of the participating grammars, but rather by defining and investigating various protocols modelling aspects of distributed computations (derivations) in grammar systems. For the sequential CD grammar systems, e.g., one distinguishes so-called modes of derivations to control the de-activation of the active grammar in a derivation of the system, whereas for the simultaneously operating grammars in a PC grammar system, protocols for the transfer of sentential forms have been a main focus of research.

---

* corresponding author

W. Brauer et al. (Eds.): Formal and Natural Computing, LNCS 2300, pp. 220–243, 2002.

This paper demonstrates how Petri nets may be used to control the derivations in grammar systems, thus creating an explicit possibility for the study of concurrent rewriting protocols. We propose to use a control mechanism based on Petri nets that has been developed within the framework of Vector Controlled Concurrent Systems. These systems were introduced in a two part paper ([KKR90] and [KKR91]) by G. Rozenberg together with H.C.M. Kleijn and N.W. Keesmaat as the beginning of the latter's Ph.D. research ([Kee96]). A Vector Controlled Concurrent System (VCCS) consists of concurrently operating sequential components together with a mechanism which synchronizes and controls their behaviour. The specific control mechanism we have in mind is the Generalized Individual Token Net Controller (GITNC), investigated in detail in [KK97] and apparently well suited for implementation in grammar systems. A GITNC is a (finite) labelled Petri net with individual tokens — one for each component — which monitor the progress of the components. It controls the operation of the system as a whole by allowing or disallowing certain synchronizations depending on the current marking (the distribution of the individual tokens over the places). Therefore the transitions of the GITNC are labelled by vectors which describe a synchronous execution of components' actions. Such a vector label has one entry for each component: a non-empty entry represents an action to be executed by the corresponding component, while an empty entry indicates that that component is not involved (remains idle) in the synchronization. Moreover, this vector labelling is consistent in the sense that a transition uses the token associated to a certain component if and only if that component is involved in the synchronization described by its vector label. The occurrence of a transition of a GITNC implies a combined action of those components whose tokens are used by the transition. These components then execute synchronously the actions in the vector which labels the transition. A GITNC is a finite state device and may be seen as a finite automaton with vectors as its action labels. However in contrast with a finite automaton, a GITNC has a distributed state space and allows concurrent execution of transitions which do not use a common token. This implies that synchronizations which involve different components can occur independently of each other (and hence also in any order). Using simply regular control languages (over an alphabet of vectors) rather than GITNC languages would destroy the potential concurrency in the computations of the controlled system (see [KK97]).

Thus we introduce Petri net (PN) grammar systems as consisting of a number of grammars and a GITNC which describes a concurrent protocol for rewriting in the participating grammars. (Actually, some initial ideas concerning this subject were presented at the MFCS Workshop on Grammar Systems in Brno in 1998 and the Seminar Recent Trends in Language Theoretic Models of Multi-Agent Systems in Budapest in 1999.) Within a PN grammar system, the grammars are viewed as separate entities. Hence, each has its own sentential form to work on just like in a PC grammar system. The grammars collaborate by synchronizing their actions (rewriting steps) subject to the control exercised by the GITNC. A system derivation in a PN grammar system starts from the axioms of the grammars with the controller in an initial marking. At each moment during the derivation rewritings are applied synchronously according to the labels of the transitions that occur. When all components have derived a terminal string and the GITNC is in one of its final markings, the derivation has been successful.

As follows from the above, the grammars in a PN grammar system cooperate subject to a regular control language. However because of its implementation as a GITNC, this protocol is explicitly concurrent and PN grammar systems are essentially concurrent grammar systems. Moreover like CD and PC grammar systems, also PN grammar systems are related to the blackboard approach of problem solving. The grammars correspond to knowledge sources, which each possesses some knowledge to solve the problem, and their sentential forms represent the blackboard with the current state of the problem's solution. Rewriting corresponds to changing the state of the blackboard. The problem solving strategy is reflected in the cooperation protocol and the solutions are represented by the thus generated terminal strings. In a PN grammar system, the grammars work on separate regions of a common blackboard and a separately defined control mechanism allows to concurrently pursue multiple lines of reasoning. So the model proposed here relates to the blackboard paradigm as discussed in [Cor91] and [CL92].

After having defined Generalized Individual Token Net Controllers, we introduce PN grammar systems consisting of context-free grammars and a GITNC enforcing synchronized applications of productions. Some initial observations are made relating to concurrency in the derivations of a PN grammar system and the vector languages defined by PN grammar systems are discussed. In particular the vector languages of PN grammar systems with regular component grammars are characterized. In a concluding section we point out some topics which may warrant further investigations.

2   Preliminaries

We assume some familiarity with basic notions from the theory of formal languages ([RS97]), regulated rewriting ([DPS97]), and Petri nets ([RR98]). The paper is however to a large extent self-contained and knowledge of grammar systems or GITNCs is not a prerequisite.

We use $\subset$ to denote strict set inclusion. For a set V, its powerset is denoted by $\mathcal{P}(V)$. All functions considered are total. As ususal, if $f : V \to W$ is a function and U is a subset of V, then $f(U) = \{f(u) \mid u \in U\}$. Let $n \in \mathbb{N}$, the set of non-negative integers. Then $[n] = \{1, \ldots, n\}$ with $[0] = \emptyset$. Let $V_1, \ldots, V_n$ be sets. We refer to the elements of the cartesian product $V_1 \times \cdots \times V_n$ as (n-dimensional) vectors. Given an n-dimensional vector $v = (v_1, \ldots, v_n)$ and $i \in [n]$, the i-th entry of v is obtained by applying the projection function $proj_i(v) = v_i$.

An alphabet is a finite, possibly empty, set of symbols. Let Σ be an alphabet. A word (over Σ) is a finite sequence (concatenation) of symbols (from Σ). The empty word is denoted by λ. A language (over Σ) is a set of words (over Σ). Σ^* is the set of all words over Σ. Recall that Σ^* is a free monoid generated by Σ with λ as its unit element.

Let $n \in \mathbb{N}$ and let $\Sigma_1, \ldots, \Sigma_n$ be alphabets. An (n-dimensional) vector letter (over $\Sigma_1, \ldots, \Sigma_n$) is a tuple $(\sigma_1, \ldots, \sigma_n)$ with $\sigma_i \in \Sigma_i \cup \{\lambda\}$ for all $i \in [n]$ and $(\sigma_1, \ldots, \sigma_n) \neq (\lambda, \ldots, \lambda)$. By $tot(\Sigma_1, \ldots, \Sigma_n)$ we denote the set of all vector letters over $\Sigma_1, \ldots, \Sigma_n$. An n-dimensional vector alphabet (over $\Sigma_1, \ldots, \Sigma_n$) is a finite, possibly empty, subset of $tot(\Sigma_1, \ldots, \Sigma_n)$. Since vector alphabets are alphabets, all terminology and notation for alphabets, words and languages can be carried over. Next to normal concatenation, also component-wise concatenation can be considered in the context of vectors. An (n-dimensional) word vector (over $\Sigma_1, \ldots, \Sigma_n$) is a tuple $(v_1, \ldots, v_n)$ with $v_i \in \Sigma_i^*$ for all $i \in [n]$. The component-wise concatenation of two word vectors $v = (v_1, \ldots, v_n)$ and $w = (w_1, \ldots, w_n)$ is defined by $v \circ w = (v_1 w_1, \ldots, v_n w_n)$. Thus $v \circ w$ is again a word vector. The support of an n-dimensional word vector v tells which entries of v are not λ: $support(v) = \{i \in [n] : v(i) \neq \lambda\}$.

Let $\Theta \subseteq tot(\Sigma_1, \ldots, \Sigma_n)$ be a vector alphabet. A word vector over Θ is a finite component-wise concatenation of vector letters from Θ. An (n-dimensional) vector language (over Θ) is a set of (n-dimensional) word vectors (over Θ). $\Theta^\otimes$ is the set of all word vectors over Θ. Thus $(tot(\Sigma_1, \ldots, \Sigma_n))^\otimes = \Sigma_1^* \times \cdots \times \Sigma_n^*$ and $\Theta^\otimes$ with component-wise concatenation is a monoid generated by Θ with the n-dimensional word vector $(\lambda, \ldots, \lambda)$ as its unit element. In general $\Theta^\otimes$ is not a free monoid. We have, e.g., $(\lambda, b, d) \circ (a, c, \lambda) = (a, b, d) \circ (\lambda, c, \lambda) = (a, bc, d)$. To *collapse* a sequence of vector letters into a word vector, we define the (monoid) homomorphism $coll_\Theta$ from Θ^* to $\Theta^\otimes$ by $coll_\Theta(\sigma) = \sigma$ for all $\sigma \in \Theta$. Hence $coll_\Theta(\sigma\tau) = \sigma \circ \tau$ for all vector letters σ and τ in Θ. The subscript Θ is usually omitted. Thus, e.g., $coll((\lambda, b, d)(a, c, \lambda)) = (\lambda, b, d) \circ (a, c, \lambda) = (a, bc, d)$.

A (context-free) grammar is a construct $G = (\Sigma, \Delta, S, \Pi)$, where Σ and Δ are two disjoint alphabets, $S \in \Sigma$, and Π is a finite set of pairs $(A, x) \in \Sigma \times (\Sigma \cup \Delta)^*$. We call Σ the non-terminal alphabet, Δ the terminal alphabet, S the axiom, and the elements of Π the productions of G. Usually, a production (A, x) is written as $A \to x$. Productions of the form $A \to \lambda$ are called λ-productions. If G does not have λ-productions, then it is called λ-free. If all productions in Π are of the form $A \to aB$, $A \to a$, or $A \to \lambda$ with $A, B \in \Sigma$ and $a \in \Delta$, then G is called a regular grammar.

A string x directly derives a string y in G by applying $\pi = A \to x \in \Pi$, notation $x \Longrightarrow_G^\pi y$, if $x = w_1 A w_2$ and $y = w_1 x w_2$ for some $w_1, w_2 \in (\Sigma \cup \Delta)^*$. The subscript G may be omitted if G is clear from the context. We write $x \Longrightarrow_G y$ or $x \Longrightarrow y$ if $x \Longrightarrow_G^\pi y$ for some production π of G. The transitive and reflexive closure of $\Longrightarrow$ and $\Longrightarrow_G$ are denoted by $\Longrightarrow^*$ and $\Longrightarrow_G^*$, respectively. $L(G)$, the language generated by G, is defined by $L(G) = \{w \in \Delta^* \mid S \Longrightarrow^* w\}$. A language is called context-free (regular) if it is generated by a context-free (regular) grammar.

3   Generalized Individual Token Net Controllers

In this section we introduce the Generalized Individual Token Net Controllers from [KK97]. A GITNC has an underlying structure which is a special type of

Petri net suitable to control and record the progress of individual sequential components. Such Petri nets are called Individual Token Nets and like ordinary Petri nets, they consist of places (drawn as circles), transitions (rectangles) and arcs (arrows) between them. The difference lies in the specification of a set of individual tokens and the special arc inscriptions. The individual tokens are to be related on a one-to-one basis to the sequential components, while the arc inscriptions describe the flow of these tokens through the net.

Definition 1. *An* Individual Token Net *(ITN) is a construct* $N = (P, T, F, I)$ *where* P, T, *and* I *are finite mutually disjoint sets, and* F *is a function from* $(P \times T) \cup (T \times P)$ *to* $\mathcal{P}(I)$.
P is the set of places *of* N; T *is the set of* transitions *of* N; I *is the set of* individual tokens *of* N; *and* F *is the* flow function *of* N, *assigning to each pair* $(x, y) \in (P \times T) \cup (T \times P)$ *a subset of* I *such that, for all* $t \in T$,
(i) for all distinct $p, p' \in P$: $F(p, t) \cap F(p', t) = \emptyset$ *and* $F(t, p) \cap F(t, p') = \emptyset$;
(ii) $\bigcup_{p \in P} F(p, t) = \bigcup_{p \in P} F(t, p)$.   □

Let N be an ITN as specified in the above definition. The flow function F describes for each transition t, its input places (those p such that $F(p, t) \neq \emptyset$) and its input tokens ($\bigcup_{p \in P} F(p, t)$); its output places (those p such that $F(t, p) \neq \emptyset$) and its output tokens ($\bigcup_{p \in P} F(t, p)$). The conditions on F guarantee that, for any given transition, no individual token appears more than once as an input token or more than once as an output token. Moreover, for each transition, its set of input tokens is the same as its set of output tokens. Consequently, a transition either does not use a token at all or it uses it exactly once as input and once as output, a property which in [KKR90] is called 1-throughput.

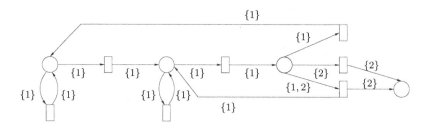

Fig. 1. An ITN with individual tokens $\{1, 2\}$.

This is the basis of the firing rule for ITNs. A transition t can fire (occur) if each of its input places p contains the individual tokens specified in $F(p, t)$. When t occurs, its input tokens are consumed and in each ouput place q of t new tokens as described by $F(t, q)$ are produced. This defines the dynamics of an ITN once we have determined its state space. The states of an ITN, or in Petri net terminology its markings, consist of a distribution of the individual tokens over the places. According to the intuition that the individual tokens are used to follow individual sequential components, we require that in every marking each token appears exactly once. Firing a transition preserves this property, because the transitions are 1-throughput.

Definition 2. *Let* $N = (P, T, F, I)$ *be an ITN.*

(1) A marking with individual tokens of N (it-marking of N), is a function $M : P \to \mathcal{P}(I)$ such that for all distinct $p, p' \in P$: $M(p) \cap M(p') = \emptyset$ and $\bigcup_{p \in P} M(p) = I$. $\mathcal{M}_N$ is the set of all it-markings of N.

(2) Let $t \in T$ and let $M \in \mathcal{M}_N$ be an it-marking of N. Then t has concession in M, notation $M[t\rangle_N$, if $F(p, t) \subseteq M(p)$ for all $p \in P$.

(3) Let $t \in T$ and let $M, M' \in \mathcal{M}_N$ be two it-markings of N. Then t fires from M to M', notation $M[t\rangle_N M'$, if $M[t\rangle_N$ and $M'(p) = (M(p) - F(p, t)) \cup F(t, p)$ for all $p \in P$.

(4) Let $m \geq 0$, let $t_1, \ldots, t_m \in T$, and let $M, M' \in \mathcal{M}_N$. Then $t_1 \cdots t_m$ is a firing sequence of N leading from M_0 to M_m, notation $M_0[t_1 \cdots t_m\rangle_N M_m$, if there exist it-markings $M_0, \ldots, M_m$ of N such that $M_{j-1}[t_j\rangle_N M_j$ for all $1 \leq j \leq m$. □

We have $M[\lambda\rangle_N M$ for all $M \in \mathcal{M}_N$. This follows from (4) above when $m = 0$. Sometimes it is convenient to consider it-markings from a dual viewpoint and to know for each individual token, the place where it resides rather than specifying per place the individual tokens it contains. If $M : P \to \mathcal{P}(I)$ is an it-marking of the ITN $N = (P, T, F, I)$, then we associate with M the function $\overline{M} : I \to P$ defined by $\overline{M}(i) = p$ if $i \in M(p)$. Note that M can be recovered from $\overline{M}$, because $M(p) = \{i \mid \overline{M}(i) = p\}$ for all places p.

When used to control the behaviour of the components of a system, the transitions of a GITNC model synchronous occurrences of components' actions. They are labelled with vectors indicating which actions from which components participate in the synchronization. To facilitate the reasoning about tokens corresponding to components which in turn correspond to the entries in the vectors, we assume that the individual tokens of an ITN form the set $[n]$, where $n \geq 1$ is the number of components of the system. From now on n is fixed. The vector labelling a transition has to be consistent with the components synchronizing through that transition: the i-th entry of the label is empty if and only if the synchronization does not involve the i-th component, that is, the i-th token is neither input nor output to that transition. Thus we arrive at the intermediate notion of an ITN $N = (P, T, F, [n])$ with vector labels. By $use(t) = \bigcup_{p \in P} F(p, t) = \bigcup_{p \in P} F(t, p)$ we denote the set of tokens used by transition t in N.

Definition 3. *A (n-dimensional) Vector Labelled Individual Token Net, (n-) VLITN, is a construct $N = (P, T, F, [n], \Theta, l)$, where $(P, T, F, [n])$ is an ITN, Θ is an n-dimensional vector alphabet, and $l : T \to \Theta$ is a labelling of the transitions such that $support(l(t)) = use(t)$ for all $t \in T$.* □

The terminology and notation introduced for ITNs is carried over to VLITNs in the standard way through their underlying ITNs.

N_1:

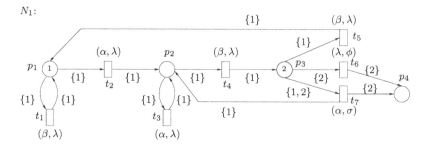

Fig. 2. A 2-VLITN with an it-marking.

Distinguishing initial and final it-markings leads to the notion of a Generalized Individual Token Net Controller.

Definition 4. *A (n-dimensional) Generalized Individual Token Net Controller, (n-)GITNC, is a construct $C = (N; \mathcal{M}_{in}, \mathcal{M}_{fin})$ where N is an n-VLITN, $\mathcal{M}_{in} \subseteq \mathcal{M}_N$ is the set of initial it-markings of C and $\mathcal{M}_{fin} \subseteq \mathcal{M}_N$ is the set of final it-markings of C.* □

In a GITNC individual tokens follow the progress of individual sequential components. Since the transitions are 1-throughput, each token uniquely determines a sequential subnet (a state machine). Thus a GITNC can be viewed as being composed of finite state machines each monitoring the behaviour of a component. The transitions of the GITNC represent synchronized combinations of state-action transitions from the state machines. The vector label of a transition combines the action labels of the state machine transitions involved and has an empty component for a state machine if and only if that state machine is not involved in the synchronization.

   A GITNC exercises its control through its firing rule. The vector labels of the transitions in a firing sequence leading from an initial it-marking to a final one describe a history of synchronizations taking place between the components. Thus the labelled firing sequences form a control language which describes in which order the synchronizations may take place. Component-wise concatenating (collapsing) the vector labels of a firing sequence yields a word vector. These word vectors, collected in the vector language of the system, describe which combinations of individual behaviours of the components are allowed by the GITNC without referring to the underlying decomposition in vector labels.

Definition 5. *Let $C = (N; \mathcal{M}_{in}, \mathcal{M}_{fin})$ be a GITNC with $N = (P, T, F, [n], \Theta, l)$.*

(1) $FS(C) = \{u \in T^* \mid M[u\rangle_N M', M \in \mathcal{M}_{in} \text{ and } M' \in \mathcal{M}_{fin}\}$ is the set of firing sequences of C.
(2) $L(C) = l(FS(C))$ is the language of C.
(3) $V(C) = coll(l(FS(C)))$ is the vector language of C. □

The label function l is extended in the standard way to a homomorphism for sequences of transitions by $l(\lambda) = \lambda$ and $l(t_1 \cdots t_k) = l(t_1) \cdots l(t_k)$.

Example 1. Consider the 2-GITNC C_1 defined by the 2-VLITN N_1 of Fig. 2, with the it-marking M defined by $\overline{M}(1) = p_1$ and $\overline{M}(2) = p_3$ depicted in that figure as its single initial it-marking, and all it-markings of N_1 as its final it-markings. Then, e.g., $t_1t_2t_4t_5t_6 \in FS(C)$ and hence $(\beta, \lambda)(\alpha, \lambda)(\beta, \lambda)(\beta, \lambda)(\lambda, \phi) \in L(C_1)$. Also, $t_1t_2t_4t_6t_5$ and $t_6t_1t_2t_4t_5$ are firing sequences of C_1 and thus $(\beta, \lambda)(\alpha, \lambda)$ $(\beta, \lambda)(\lambda, \phi)(\beta, \lambda)$ and $(\lambda, \phi)(\beta, \lambda)(\alpha, \lambda)(\beta, \lambda)(\beta, \lambda) \in L(C_1)$. Each when collapsed yields the word vector $(\beta\alpha\beta\beta, \phi) \in V(C_1)$. Yet another firing sequence of C_1 is $t_2t_4t_7t_4$ and thus $(\alpha, \lambda)(\beta, \lambda)(\alpha, \sigma)(\beta, \lambda) \in L(C_1)$ and $(\alpha\beta\alpha\beta, \sigma) \in V(C_1)$. It is easily seen that $V(C) = \{(w, \sigma) \mid w \in \{\alpha, \beta\}^*, \alpha\beta\alpha$ occurs exactly once in $w\}$ $\cup \{(w, x) \mid w \in \{\alpha, \beta\}^*, x = \lambda$ or $x = \phi$, and $\alpha\beta\alpha$ does not occur in $w\}$.   □

By $\mathcal{L}_n(GITNC)$ we denote the family of n-GITNC languages and the family of n-GITNC vector languages is denoted by by $\mathcal{V}_n(GITNC)$.

GITNCs are finite state devices and consequently define regular languages. In general, regular languages over vector letters can be defined as the languages accepted by vector labelled finite automata. These automata are however sequential in nature, whereas a GITNC has a distributed state space implying that the occurrences of transitions are not necessarily ordered. In particular, whenever two transitions which do not use a common token occur consecutively in a firing sequence, they can occur in either order. Due to the consistency of the vector labelling this implies that whenever two vector labels which have disjoint supports occur consecutively in a labelled firing sequence of the GITNC, also the labelled firing sequence with these two occurrences interchanged will belong to the language of the GITNC (see also Example 1). Consequently, the regular languages (over vector letters) defined by GITNCs have a particular structure and not every regular language over vector letters (of the same dimension) can be implemented as the language of a GITNC. In fact, as discussed in [KK97], GITNC languages are related to regular trace languages.

However, when vector languages are considered, the situation changes. The vector language of a vector labelled finite automaton is defined, just as for a GITNC, by applying component-wise concatenation to (collapsing) the words in its language. The vector languages thus obtained are exactly the rational relations (see, e.g., [Ber79]). It was shown in [KK97] how changing the underlying vector alphabet makes it possible to transform a vector labelled finite automaton into a GITNC with the same vector language, but not necessarily the same language. Let now $\mathcal{L}_n(REG)$ denote the family of regular languages over n-dimensional vector alphabets and let $n\mathcal{RAT}$ be the family of n-dimensional rational relations or equivalently, the collapses of the languages in $\mathcal{L}_n(REG)$. Then we have

Theorem 1. *([KK97])*

(1) $\mathcal{L}_1(GITNC) = \mathcal{L}_1(REG)$.
(2) $\mathcal{L}_n(GITNC) \subset \mathcal{L}_n(REG)$ *if* $n \geq 2$.
(3) $\mathcal{V}_n(GITNC) = n\mathcal{RAT}$.   □

4   PN Grammar Systems

We are now ready to define PN grammar systems in which context-free grammars cooperate by synchronizing the application of their productions under the control of a GITNC. The productions of the grammars are given names and the vectors labelling the transitions of the GITNC are vector letters over these alphabets of names.

Definition 6. *An (n-dimensional) PN grammar system, (n-)PNGS, is a construct $\Gamma = ((G_1, \Theta_1, \varphi_1), \ldots, (G_n, \Theta_n, \varphi_n); C)$ where, for each $i \in [n]$, $G_i = (\Sigma_i, \Delta_i, S_i, \Pi_i)$ is a grammar, the i-th component grammar of Γ, Θ_i is an alphabet (of labels), $\varphi_i : \Pi_i \to \Theta_i$ is a function assigning labels to the productions of G_i, and $C = (N; \mathcal{M}_{in}, \mathcal{M}_{fin})$ with VLITN $N = (P, T, F, [n], \Theta, l)$ is an n-GITNC, the controller of Γ, with $\Theta \subseteq tot(\Theta_1, \ldots, \Theta_n)$.*
Γ is called regular *if all of its components are regular grammars.* □

For the rest of this section Γ is an arbitrary n-dimensional PN grammar system as specified in the above definition.

The component grammars of a PN grammar system each have their own sentential form and so the states of the system are described by the current sentential forms of the grammars and the current it-marking of the controller.

Definition 7. *A* configuration *of Γ is a tuple $(v_1, \ldots, v_n; M)$ with $v_i \in (\Sigma_i \cup \Delta_i)^*$ for all $i \in [n]$, and $M \in \mathcal{M}_N$ an it-marking of C.*
Let $\gamma = (v_1, \ldots, v_n; M)$ be a configuration of Γ. Then
(1) γ is an initial *configuration of Γ if $v_i = S_i$ for all $i \in [n]$ and $M \in \mathcal{M}_{in}$.*
(2) γ is a final *configuration of Γ if $v_i \in \Delta_i^*$ for all $i \in [n]$ and $M \in \mathcal{M}_{fin}$.* □

A configuration changes when a transition fires and this entails a synchronized application of productions to which its vector label refers. Thus a production can only be applied by a component grammar to its current sentential form if this can happen synchronously with the application of productions by other grammars in accordance with the vector label of a transition with concession. Dually, a transition with concession can only occur if the productions to which it refers can actually be applied in the sentential forms.

Definition 8. *(1) Let $t \in T$ and let $\gamma = (v_1, \ldots, v_n; M)$ be a configuration of Γ. Then t can* occur *(in Γ) at γ, notation $\gamma \vdash_\Gamma^t$, if $M[t\rangle_N$ and if, for all $i \in [n]$, $proj_i(l(t)) \neq \lambda$ implies that there is a production $\pi = A \to w \in \Pi_i$ such that $\varphi_i(\pi) = proj_i(l(t))$ and A appears in v_i.*
(2) Let $t \in T$ and let $\gamma = (v_1, \ldots, v_n; M)$ and $\gamma' = (w_1, \ldots, w_n; M')$ be two configurations of Γ. Then γ is transformed into γ' by the occurrence of t (in Γ), notation $\gamma \vdash_\Gamma^t \gamma'$, if $M[t\rangle M'$ and for all $i \in [n]$, $v_i = w_i$ whenever $proj_i(l(t)) = \lambda$, otherwise $v_i \Longrightarrow_{G_i}^\pi w_i$ where $\pi \in \Pi_i$ is such that $\varphi_i(\pi) = proj_i(l(t))$. □

We write $\gamma \vdash_\Gamma \delta$ if there exists a $t \in T$ such that $\gamma \vdash_\Gamma^t \delta$. The subscript Γ may be omitted if there is no danger of confusion with which system we are dealing.

A successful run of a PN grammar system starts in an initial configuration and leads by to a final one a sequence of successive transformations. Thus the system operates by synchronizing the derivation steps of its component grammars according to the control exercised by its controller through firing sequences. The resulting combinations of terminal strings form the vector language of the system.

Definition 9. *The* vector language generated by Γ, *denoted by* $V(\Gamma)$, *is defined by* $V(\Gamma) = \{(v_1, \ldots, v_n) \in \Delta_1^* \times \cdots \times \Delta_n^* \mid (S_1, \ldots, S_n; M) \vdash^* (v_1, \ldots, v_n; M') \text{ for some } M \in \mathcal{M}_{in}, M' \in \mathcal{M}_{fin}\}.$ □

By $\mathcal{V}_n(PNGS)$ we denote the family of vector languages generated by n-PNGSs and the family of vector languages generated by n-dimensional regular PN grammar systems is denoted by $\mathcal{V}_n(regPNGS)$.

Example 2. Let $\Gamma = ((G_1, \Theta_1, \varphi_1), (G_2, \Theta_2, \varphi_2); C_1)$ be the regular 2-PNGS with C_1 as in Example 1, $G_1 = (\{S\}, \{a, b\}, S, \Pi_1)$ and $G_2 = (\{S\}, \{s, f\}, S, \Pi_2)$ where $\Pi_1 = \{S \rightarrow aS, S \rightarrow a, S \rightarrow bS, S \rightarrow b\}$ and $\Pi_2 = \{S \rightarrow s, S \rightarrow f\}$. The productions are labelled by $\varphi_1(S \rightarrow aS) = \varphi_1(S \rightarrow a) = \alpha$, $\varphi_1(S \rightarrow bS) = \varphi_1(S \rightarrow b) = \beta$, and $\varphi_2(S \rightarrow s) = \sigma$ and $\varphi_2(S \rightarrow f) = \phi$.
The initial configuration of the system is $(S, S; M)$. At $(S, S; M)$ the three transitions t_1, t_2, and t_6 can occur. If t_1 occurs, then the configuration is changed in either $(bS, S; M)$ or $(b, S; M)$, depending on which production labelled by β is chosen to be applied. If t_6 occurs, then the configuration is changed in $(S, f; M_1)$ with $\overline{M_1}(1) = p_1$ and $\overline{M_1}(2) = p_4$.
Consider the firing sequence $t_1 t_2 t_4 t_5 t_6$ labelled by $(\beta, \lambda)(\alpha, \lambda)(\beta, \lambda)(\beta, \lambda)(\lambda, \phi)$. On basis of this sequence we obtain the transformation sequence $(S, S; M) \vdash (bS, S; M) \vdash (baS, S; M_2) \vdash (babS, S; M_3) \vdash (babb, S; M) \vdash (babb, f; M_1)$ with $\overline{M_2}(1) = p_2$ and $\overline{M_2}(2) = p_3$, $\overline{M_3}(1) = \overline{M_3}(2) = p_3$. Since every it-marking is final and both grammars have derived a terminal word we have $(babb, f) \in V(\Gamma)$. If for the last occurrence of β we would have chosen to apply $S \rightarrow bS$ rather than $S \rightarrow b$, then the non-final configuration $(babbS, f; M_1)$ would have resulted. If at the occurrence of t_2, we would have chosen to apply $S \rightarrow a$ instead of $S \rightarrow aS$, then we would have $(S, S; M) \vdash (bS, S; M) \vdash (ba, S; M_2)$ and t_4 can no longer occur, since the first grammar has produced a terminal word. The only transition that can still occur is t_6 entailing a rewriting by the second grammar.
Observe that the firing sequences $t_1 t_2 t_4 t_6 t_5$ and $t_6 t_1 t_2 t_4 t_5$ also give rise to the generation of $(babb, f)$, since both define the same vector word $(\beta\alpha\beta\beta, \phi)$ which enforces the successive application of productions labelled by β, α, β, and β respectively by the first grammar and the application of $S \rightarrow f$ in the second grammar.
A successful run of Γ controlled by the firing sequence $t_2 t_4 t_7 t_4$ labelled by $(\alpha, \lambda)(\beta, \lambda)(\alpha, \sigma)(\beta, \lambda)$, leads to $(abab, s; M_4)$ or $(ababS, s; M_4)$ with $\overline{M_4}(1) = p_3$ and $\overline{M_4}(2) = p_4$. The application of $S \rightarrow s$ by G_2 is synchronized with the application of a production labelled by α in order to signal the introduction by G_1 of a subword aba. As long as this has not happened, transition t_6 can occur which implies the application of the production $S \rightarrow f$ by G_2 and prohibits the introduc-

tion of aba by G_1. Thus we have $V(\Gamma) = \{(w,s) \mid w \in \{a,b\}^*, aba$ occurs exactly once in $w\} \cup \{(w,f) \mid w \in \{a,b\}^*, w \neq \lambda$, and aba does not occur in $w\}$. A special property of this PN grammar system is the one-to-one correspondence between the labels of the productions (α, β, σ, and ϕ) and the terminal symbols (a, b, s, and f) they introduce. As will become clear in Section 5.2, this induces a strong similarity between the vector language of a regular PNGS and the vector languages of its GITNC.

Finally, note that without the control of C_1, the grammar G_1 can generate all non-empty words over $\{a,b\}$. □

As an immediate consequence of the definitions we have that the vector language of a PN grammar system consists of those combinations of terminal words for which there exists an approved (by the controller) combination of sequences of productions applied in the component grammars.

Corollary 1. $V(\Gamma) = \{(v_1, \ldots, v_n) \in \Delta_1^* \times \cdots \times \Delta_n^* \mid$ there exists an $x \in V(C)$ such that, for all $i \in [n]$, $S_i \Longrightarrow_{G_i}^* v_i$ by applying the sequence of productions $proj_i(x)\}$. □

In the PN grammar system Γ, the control exercised by the GITNC C concerns the *application* of productions. *Listing* the productions as abstract entities rather than applying them describes the effect of the cooperation protocol enforced by the GITNC on the rewriting steps within the grammars. The result is a vector language of the form $(Sz_1 \times \cdots \times Sz_n) \cap V(C)$ where Sz_i is the Szilárd language (consisting of labelled sequences of productions that can be successfully applied) of the i-th component grammar. This vector language describes which sequences of productions in the component grammars can be successfully combined in a system derivation. It represents the concurrency in the derivations of a PN grammar system resulting from its rewriting protocol. This corresponds to the set-up of the model of Vector Controlled Concurrent Systems where the concurrent behaviours of a VCCS are given in the form of word vectors representing successful synchronized combinations of sequential behaviours of the components.

The potential concurrency in the derivations in a PN grammar systems is due to the fact that without the control exercised by the GITNC the grammars work independently, that is, concurrently, each on their own sentential form. The protocol represented by the GITNC enforces certain synchronized applications of productions. Since however, as observed before, the GITNC is itself a concurrent device with a distributed state space, synchronizations involving disjoint groups of grammars can still be executed concurrently. As we explain next, this allows to "speed up" the allowed derivation sequences represented in the language of the controller without affecting the protocol itself as represented in its vector language.

The grammars of Γ are sequential rewriting systems. Productions are applied one after the other. In C we have one individual token for each grammar and the occurrences of transitions which use a common individual token are always ordered by their use of this token. Let us say that two transitions t and t' are independent if they do not use a common individual token, i.e. $use(t) \cap use(t') = \emptyset$.

A non-empty subset U of T is called independent if every pair of distinct transitions in U is independent. Independent transitions can be fired concurrently which we formalize in a step semantics as is usually done for Petri nets. Thus, for an it-marking $M \in \mathcal{M}_N$ and an independent set $U \subseteq T$, we say that U is a step at M, notation $M[U\rangle_N$, if $M[t\rangle_N$ for all $t \in U$. The effect of a step U occurring at an it-marking M is the accumulated effect of the transitions forming the step. Thus firing U leads from M to M', notation $M[U\rangle_N M'$, with M' defined by $M'(p) = (M(p) - \bigcup_{t \in U} F(p,t)) \cup \bigcup_{t \in U} F(t,p)$ for all $p \in P$. Note that M' is again an it-marking. Since the transitions forming a step at a given it-marking all use their own subset of the individual tokens, they can fire in any order from that it-marking. More precisely, $M[U\rangle_N M'$ if and only if U is an independent set and $M[t_1 \cdots t_k\rangle_N M'$ for every permutation $t_1 \cdots t_k$ of the elements of U.
Steps may be fired consecutively. We write $M[U_1 \cdots U_k\rangle_N M'$ if for all $1 \leq j \leq k$, U_j is an independent set and there exist it-markings $M_0 = M, M_1, \ldots, M_k = M'$ such that $M_{j-1}[U_j\rangle_N M_j$ for all $1 \leq j \leq k$.
Because of the consistency of the vector labelling, independency of transitions is equivalent with their vector labels having disjoint supports. Thus the componentwise concatenation of the vector labels of independent transitions forms a vector letter. Formally, if $U \subseteq T$ is an independent set, then $proj_i(l(t_1) \cdots l(t_k)) \in proj_i(\Theta) \cup \{\lambda\}$ for every $i \in [n]$ and for every permutation $t_1 \cdots t_k$ of the elements of U. Now we can unambiguously associate to U a vector label $l_{step}(U)$ defined by $l_{step}(U) = coll(l(t_1) \cdots l(t_k))$ where $t_1 \cdots t_k$ is any permutation of the elements of U. It is immediate that allowing steps with vector label function l_{step} does not add to the vector language of a GITNC $C = (N; \mathcal{M}_{in}, \mathcal{M}_{fin})$. Moreover, $l_{step}(\{t\}) = l(t)$ for all $t \in T$ and every firing sequence of C can be considered as a step sequence.

Lemma 1. $V(C) = \{coll(l_{step}(u)) \mid u = U_1 \cdots U_k \text{ with } U_j \subseteq T \text{ for all } 1 \leq j \leq k \text{ and } M[u\rangle_N M' \text{ for some } M \in \mathcal{M}_{in} \text{ and } M' \in \mathcal{M}_{fin}\}$. $\qquad\square$

We extend the definition of transformations to transformations by occurrences of steps as follows. Let $U \subseteq T$ be an independent set and let $\gamma = (v_1, \ldots, v_n; M)$ be a configuration of Γ. Then U can occur at γ, if $M[U\rangle_N$ and if, for all $i \in [n]$, $proj_i(l_{step}(U)) \neq \lambda$ implies that there is a production $\pi = A \to w \in \Pi_i$ such that $\varphi_i(\pi) = proj_i(l_{step}(U))$ and A has an occurrence in v_i. If $U \subseteq T$ occurs at $\gamma = (v_1, \ldots, v_n; M)$, then γ is transformed into $\gamma' = (w_1, \ldots, w_n; M')$ by the occurrence of U, notation $\gamma \vdash^U_{step} \gamma'$, if $M[U\rangle_N M'$ and for all $i \in [n]$, $v_i = w_i$ whenever $proj_i(l_{step}(U)) = \lambda$, otherwise $v_i \Longrightarrow^\pi_{G_i} w_i$ where $\pi \in \Pi_i$ is such that $\varphi_i(\pi) = proj_i(l_{step}(U))$. We write $\gamma \vdash_{step} \gamma'$ if $\gamma \vdash^U_{step} \gamma'$ for some step U.
Thus, by Corollary 1 and Lemma 1, the derivations in Γ can be based on the step semantics of C.

Theorem 2. $V(\Gamma) = \{(v_1, \ldots, v_n) \in \Delta_1^* \times \cdots \times \Delta_n^* \mid (S_1, \ldots, S_n; M) \vdash^*_{step} (v_1, \ldots, v_n; M') \text{ for some } M \in \mathcal{M}_{in}, M' \in \mathcal{M}_{fin}\}$. $\qquad\square$

The step semantics offers the possibility to "speed up" the (sequential) derivation processes in a PN grammar system since independent rewritings by the component grammars of a PN grammar system may be executed simultaneously. The vector labels assigned to steps show that the step semantics translates concurrency into synchronization. These two phenomema are however not the same. Concurrency is based on independence and implies that independent derivation steps in the component grammars may be executed in any order and also synchronously. Synchronization of productions on the other hand is a tool that can be used to guarantee that different components will simultaneously reach a given state from a given state and hence, unlike concurrency, implies a dependence between the components.

5   Vector Languages of PN Grammar Systems

Definition 9 describes the result of the work of a PN grammar system Γ in terms of vectors consisting of those combinations of terminal words for which the component grammars have a cooperation strategy approved by the controller. There are of course more options to define the result of a successful run of a PN grammar system. As for PC grammar systems, one might, e.g., decide to focus on the result of one (central) grammar and thus define a language rather than a vector language. Or one could consider the *concatenated language of Γ*, obtained by concatenating the strings of the generated word vectors into one terminal string: $L_\bullet(\Gamma) = \{v_1 \cdots v_n \mid (v_1, \ldots, v_n) \in V(\Gamma)\}$. Yet another option is to define the *agreement language of Γ* by considering only those terminal strings on which the components agree: $L_\cap(\Gamma) = \{w \mid$ there exists a $(v_1, \ldots, v_n) \in V(\Gamma)$ such that for all $i \in [n]$, $v_i = w$ or $v_i = \lambda\}$. In terms of the blackboard model, both the vector language and the concatenated language present a view of the blackboard as a whole once all knowledge sources (the grammars) have come to a conclusion. In case of agreement however, a solution is only accepted if all knowledge sources offering an answer have come to the same conclusion.

In this introduction of PN grammar systems we opt for the vector language as the description of the result of the collaboration of the grammars, since it appears as the more general definition which forms a basis for other definitions.

5.1   A Normal Form

In order to control the derivations of the grammars in a PN grammar system, productions are assigned labels and these are combined into vectors expressing the allowed synchronizations. Different productions from the same grammar may have the same label. This makes it possible to efficiently represent the intended synchronizations in a succinct GITNC (see Example 2). A disadvantage may be the ambiguity of the vector labels which in this set-up can represent different combinations of productions. As we show next, this ambiguity can be avoided. In fact, every PNGS can effectively be transformed into a PNGS which defines the same vector language and in which the vector labels have only entries referring to unique productions. Let Γ be a PNGS specified as in Definition 6.

Definition 10. Γ *is in normal form if, for all distinct $i, j \in [n]$, $\Sigma_i \cap \Sigma_j = \emptyset$, φ_i is a bijection, and $\Theta \subseteq tot(\varphi_1(\Pi_1), \ldots, \varphi_n(\Pi_n))$.*   □

Thus a PNGS is in normal form if the productions of the grammars and the entries of the vector labels of the controller are in one-to-one correspondence, and moreover all participating grammars have their own sets of non-terminals. It is not difficult to show, that this is indeed a normal form. Only when productions share a label, one has to be a bit careful.

Theorem 3. *For every PN grammar system, a PN grammar system in normal form and generating the same vector language can be constructed.*

Proof. Consider Γ. It is clear that the requirement of disjoint sets of non-terminals can easily be satisfied without affecting the vector language of Γ by renaming the non-terminal symbols with the obvious modifications in the set of productions and the definition of the label functions. Hence $\Sigma_i \cap \Sigma_j = \emptyset$, for all distinct $i, j \in [n]$ is considered to already hold for Γ.

Assume that for some $i \in [n]$, there are two distinct productions $\pi, \pi' \in \Pi_i$ such that $\varphi_i(\pi) = \varphi_i(\pi')$. Let us fix such i, π, and π'. For π' we add a new label θ to Θ_i and define a new label function φ_i' by $\varphi_i'(\pi') = \theta$ and $\varphi_i'(\rho) = \varphi_i(\rho)$ for all $\rho \in \Pi_i - \{\pi'\}$. For each transition t of C such that $proj_i(l(t)) = \varphi_i(\pi)$, we add a new transition t' with the same neighbourhood relations as t has. Each new transition t' is labelled by the same vector label as t except that the i-th entry is replaced by θ. The construction is illustrated in Fig. 3.

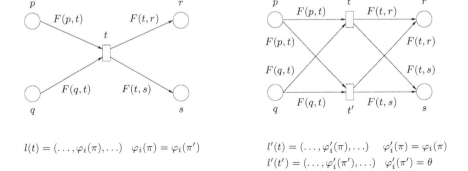

Fig. 3. A transition t with an ambiguous i-th entry in its vector label is split. The implicit choice between the productions π or π' is modelled explicitly using a (Petri net) conflict between t and a new transition t'.

Each new transition is 1-throughput and consistently labelled and so we obtain a new PN grammar system Γ'. That Γ' generates the same vector language as Γ is easy to prove. We repeat this procedure until no component grammar is left with different productions which have the same label associated to them. As the last step we remove for each component grammar all labels that are not assigned to productions and we obtain the desired bijection between labels and productions.

Finally, transitions which have a vector label with a non-empty entry that does not occur as the label of a production in the corresponding grammar can never be used to transform a configuration of the PN grammar system. Hence we can delete all such transitions without affecting the generated vector language. The remaining transitions are all labelled by vector letters over the labelling alphabets of the productions, as required.   □

5.2   Expressive Power

In a 1-dimensional PN grammar system there is only one grammar which works under the control of its GITNC. For a derivation to be successful, the order in which the productions are applied has to form a sequence belonging to the language of the controller. Thus, by Theorem 1, these grammar systems can be considered to be context-free grammars with a regular control language (see, e.g., [DPS97]) and so $\mathcal{V}_1(PNGS)$ can be identified with $\mathcal{L}(RC)$, the family of regularly controlled context-free languages (without appearance checking). However, since we deal with vectors (in this case 1-dimensional), the formal relationship is as follows.

Theorem 4. $proj_1(\mathcal{V}_1(PNGS)) = \mathcal{L}(RC)$.   □

This family is incomparable with the family of context-sensitive languages, and strictly included in the family of recursively enumerable languages. When λ-productions are not allowed, the resulting family is strictly inbetween the families of context-free and context-sensitive languages.

To describe the vector languages of more dimensional PN grammar systems appears to be more complicated and we give only a first impression. Again one could use grammars with some form of regulated rewriting (see [DPS97]) and describe, e.g., using matrix grammars the concatenated versions of the vector languages. In matrix grammars, rewriting is based on finite sequences of productions which have to be applied consecutively. In a PN grammar system in normal form, each component has its own set of non-terminals and without the risk of confusing grammars we can apply the productions in a vector one after the other. Thus by concatenating the components' sentential forms and applying the synchronized rules in a vector sequentially as if it were a matrix, the concatenated version of the vector language is derived. That the sequence of productions to be used is determined by the (regular) control of the GITNC poses no problems, since regular control can be included in matrix grammars. Hence the concatenated vector languages of PN grammar systems can be generated by context-free matrix grammars (without appearance checking). Since the context-free matrix grammars and the regularly controlled context-free grammars define the same family of languages, this shows that as far as the concatenated vector languages of PN grammar systems are concerned, one grammar is as good as many.

Example 3. Let $\Gamma = ((G_1, \Theta_1, \varphi_1), (G_2, \Theta_2, \varphi_2), (G_3, \Theta_3, \varphi_3); C)$ be the 3-PNGS with $G_1 = (\{S\}, \{a, b\}, S, \Pi_1)$, $G_2 = (\{A\}, \{a\}, A, \Pi_2)$, $G_3 = (\{B\}, \{b\}, B, \Pi_3)$, with the productions and labelling of G_1 given by:

$\varphi_1(S \rightarrow \lambda) = \phi$, $\varphi_1(S \rightarrow LR) = \omega$, $\varphi_1(L \rightarrow aL) = \varphi_1(L \rightarrow a) = \alpha_L$ and
$\varphi_1(R \rightarrow aR) = \varphi_1(R \rightarrow a) = \alpha_R$, $\varphi_1(L \rightarrow bL) = \varphi_1(L \rightarrow b) = \beta_L$ and
$\varphi_1(R \rightarrow bR) = \varphi_1(R \rightarrow b) = \beta_R$;
the productions and labelling of G_2 are given by:
$\varphi_2(A \rightarrow \lambda) = \phi$, $\varphi_2(A \rightarrow A) = \varphi_2(A \rightarrow \lambda) = \omega$, $\varphi_2(A \rightarrow aA) = \varphi_2(A \rightarrow a) = \alpha$;
and those of G_3 by:
$\varphi_3(B \rightarrow \lambda) = \phi$, $\varphi_3(B \rightarrow B) = \varphi_3(B \rightarrow \lambda) = \omega$, $\varphi_3(B \rightarrow bB) = \varphi_3(B \rightarrow b) = \beta$.
The GITNC C consists of the VLITN N depicted in Fig. 4 with one and the
same initial and final it-marking M which assigns each of the three tokens 1,2,
and 3 to the place in the middle.

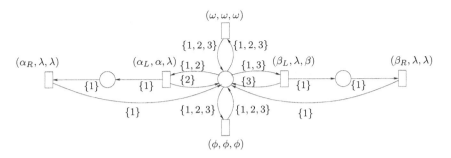

Fig. 4. The VLITN N underlying C of Example 3.

Since every transition of N uses token 1, grammar G_1 is involved in every transformation of a configuration of Γ and the control exercised by C is sequential. Initially only two transitions can occur. The transition labelled by (ϕ, ϕ, ϕ)
transforms the initial configuration $(S, A, B; M)$ into $(\lambda, \lambda, \lambda; M)$ and the rewriting stops. If the transition labelled by (ω, ω, ω) starts the rewriting process,
then the initial configuration is transformed into one of the four configurations
$(LR, X, Y; M)$ with $X \in \{A, \lambda\}$ and $Y \in \{B, \lambda\}$. To rewrite LR the control
either switches to the left part of N or to its right part. The consecutive occur-
rences of the two left-most transitions labelled by $(\alpha_L, \alpha, \lambda)$ and $(\alpha_R, \lambda, \lambda)$ force
G_1 to generate an a using either $L \rightarrow aL$ or $L \rightarrow a$ followed by $R \rightarrow aR$ or
$R \rightarrow a$. In that case, the second grammar G_2 has to synchronize by rewriting
A and producing an a (hence A still has to be present in the second sentential
form). When the right-most transitions occur, G_1 is forced to generate a b using
either $L \rightarrow bL$ or $L \rightarrow b$ followed by $R \rightarrow bR$ or $R \rightarrow b$. Then the third grammar
G_3 has to synchronize by rewriting B and adding a b to its sentential form. This
process is repeated. Thus, on the one hand, the GITNC forces the first grammar (by a regular control mechanism) to generate the non-context-free language
$\{ww \mid w \in \{a, b\}^*\}$. On the other hand G_2 and G_3 are forced to keep track,
respectively, of $\#_a w$ the number of occurrences of a in the word w generated
from L, and of $\#_b w$ the number of occurrences of b in the word w generated
from L. They may only terminate when no more a's or b's, respectively, will be

introduced by G_1, or conversely, as soon as they terminate, grammar G_1 can no longer introduce a's or b's by rewriting L. Hence Γ generates the vector language $\{(ww, a^n, b^m) \mid w \in \{a, b\}^*, n = \#_a w, \text{ and } m = \#_b w\}$.   □

The components of the vector language generated by a PN grammar system cannot simply be viewed as generated by a component grammar under the control of the corresponding subnet of the GITNC, since the control not only depends on the subnet but also on the behaviour of the other components. Both the synchronization constraints within the GITNC and the requirement that it must be possible to execute the productions associated to transitions synchronously have to be taken into account. The vector language of the system is in general strictly contained in the cartesian product of the (controlled) languages of its component grammars (see Example 3). Hence, simply using the projection function will not lead to a proper characterization of the structure of more-dimensional vector languages of PN grammar systems. For regular PN grammar systems we do have such a description. We will next demonstrate that the vector languages of these systems are precisely the rational relations, which form a class strictly larger than the cartesian products of regular languages.

Regular PN Grammar Systems From Theorem 1 we know that every rational relation can be defined as the vector language of a GITNC. Thus it is fairly easy to prove — by adding "dummy" grammars — that every rational relation can be generated by a regular PN grammar system.

Lemma 2. $n\mathcal{R}\mathcal{A}\mathcal{T} \subseteq \mathcal{V}_n(regPNGS)$.

Proof. Let $R \in n\mathcal{R}\mathcal{A}\mathcal{T}$ and let C be an n-GITNC such that $V(C) = R$. By Theorem 1 such C exists. Let $C = (N; \mathcal{M}_{in}, \mathcal{M}_{fin})$ with $N = (P, T, F, [n], \Theta, l)$. We add regular grammars $G_1, \ldots, G_n$ to C and change the vector labels of the transitions of N by replacing each non-empty entry with (a label referring to) a regular production that generates the original entry as a terminal symbol. For each $i \in [n]$, we let $G_i = (\{S_i\}, proj_i(\Theta), S_i, \Pi_i)$, with $\Pi_i = \{S_i \to \theta S_i \mid \theta \in proj_i(\Theta)\} \cup \{S_i \to \lambda\}$. The VLITN N' is N extended with new transitions t_M where $M \in \mathcal{M}_{fin}$ (note that $\mathcal{M}_{fin}$ is a finite set). Thus $N' = (P, T \cup \{t_M \mid M \in \mathcal{M}_{fin}\}, F', [n], \bigcup_{i \in [n]} \Pi_i, l')$ where for all $t \in T$ and $p \in P$, $F'(p, t) = F(p, t)$ and $F'(t, p) = F(t, p)$; furthermore, for all $M \in \mathcal{M}_{fin}$ and $p \in P$, $i \in F'(p, t_M) = F'(t_M, p)$ if and only if $\overline{M}(i) = p$. We label the productions of the G_i by identity. The vector labelling l' of the transitions of N' is defined by $proj_i(l'(t)) = S_i \to \theta S_i$ if $t \in T$ and $proj_i(l(t)) = \theta$, and $proj_i(l'(t_M)) = S_i \to \lambda$ for all $M \in \mathcal{M}_{fin}$ and $i \in [n]$. Clearly, $C' = (N'; \mathcal{M}_{in}, \mathcal{M}_{fin})$ is a GITNC. Let $\Gamma = ((G_1, \Pi_1, \varphi_1), \ldots, (G_n, \Pi_n, \varphi_n); C')$ where φ_i is the identity on Π_i for each $i \in [n]$. Thus Γ is a regular PNGS. The firing of a transition t in N corresponds to the transformation of a configuration by the occurrence of t in Γ: $M[t\rangle_N M'$ if and only if $(x_1 S_1, \ldots, x_n S_n; M) \vdash_\Gamma^t (y_1 S_1, \ldots, y_n S_n; M')$ with for all $i \in [n]$, whenever $proj_i(l(t)) = \lambda$, then $y_i = x_i$; otherwise $y_i = x_i \theta S_i$ where $\theta = proj_i(l(t))$. The transitions t_M are used to check that the final it-marking

M has been reached and when such a transition occurs, the non-terminals S_i are erased: $\gamma \vdash_{\Gamma}^{t_M} \gamma'$ for some $M \in \mathcal{M}_{fin}$ if and only if γ' is a final configuration $(x_1, \ldots, x_n; M)$ of Γ and $\gamma = (x_1 S_1, \ldots, x_n S_n; M)$. From these observations it follows that $V(C) = V(\Gamma)$ and so $R = V(C) \in \mathcal{V}_n(regPNGS)$. $\qquad \square$

To prove that the regular PN grammar systems generate exactly the rational relations, we provide a construction which incorporates the grammars of a regular PNGS into its GITNC in such a way that the resulting GITNC defines the same vector language as the original system. Then, again by Theorem 1, we may conclude that $\mathcal{V}_n(regPNGS)$ is included in $n\mathcal{RAT}$.

Let Γ be a fixed regular n-PNGS in normal form. Hence the productions of its component grammars are in one-to-one correspondence with their label. Thus the vector labels of the transitions can have productions as entries and there is no need to define label functions for the productions. Thus we specify Γ by $\Gamma = (G_1, \ldots, G_n; C)$ where, for all $i \in [n]$, $G_i = (\Sigma_i, \Delta_i, S_i, \Pi_i)$ is a regular grammar and $C = (N; \mathcal{M}_{in}, \mathcal{M}_{fin})$ is an n-GITNC with VLITN $N = (P, T, F, [n], \Theta)$ and $\Theta \subseteq tot(\Pi_1, \ldots, \Pi_n)$. In the construction we assume that each G_i is λ-free. The idea behind the incorporation construction (see also Fig. 5) is to replace in the vectors labelling the transitions, every production by the terminal symbol it introduces. Thus a vector label $(\ldots, A \to aB, \ldots)$ is replaced by the vector label $(\ldots, a, \ldots)$. In order to faithfully implement the synchronizations of the productions, we have to keep track of the non-terminals. Therefore for each place p we will have copies (p, A), where A is a non-terminal symbol. Token i in place (p, A) in the new net represents the situation that token i resides in place p in the original net while A is the current non-terminal in the sentential form of the i-th component. (Note that we can speak of *the* non-terminal since G_i is regular.) The original places will still be present in the new net and token i in place p in the new net corresponds with token i in place p in the original net while the sentential form of the i-th component is a terminal string. A transition t labelled with a vector with $A \to aB$ as its i-th component, which in the original net consumes token i from place p and produces token i in place q, in the new net will take token i from place (p, A) and put it in place (q, B). If the i-th component of the label of t is $A \to a$, then in the new net t will still take token i from place (p, A) but now put it in place q rather than in (q, B). The original places p will not be input places of transitions. The initial it-markings of the new net are copies of the original initial it-markings in the sense that if the original marking had token i in place p, then the copy has token i in place (p, S_i). The final it-markings are not changed.

In the construction we use the following notation and terminology.

Let $\pi \in \bigcup_{i \in [n]} \Pi_i$ be a production of Γ and let G_j be the component grammar it belongs to. Note that since Γ is in normal form, there is only one index j such that $\pi \in \Pi_j$. Since G_j is a λ-free regular grammar, either $\pi = A \to aB$ or $\pi = A \to a$ for some $A, B \in \Sigma_j$ and $a \in \Delta_j$. In both cases, we refer to A as the left-hand side of π and write $lhs(\pi) = A$.

If $\pi = A \to aB$, then B is called the right-hand side of π, denoted by $rhs(\pi) = B$. If $\pi = A \to a$ with $A \in \Sigma_j$ and $a \in \Delta_j$, then π is said to be terminating.

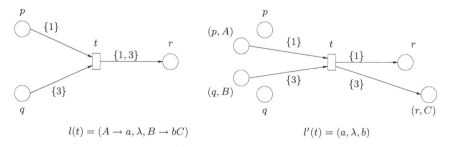

Fig. 5. The incorporation construction illustrated.

a is the symbol introduced by π, denoted by $sym_j(\pi)$. This leads, for each $i \in [n]$, to the definition of a homomorphism $sym_i : \Pi_i^* \to \Delta_i^*$ defined by $sym_i(\rho) = b$ if $\rho = X \to bY$ with $b \in \Delta_i$. The homomorphism $lsym : \Theta^* \to \Delta^{\otimes}$ is defined by combining these homomorphisms and applying them to vectors. Thus $lsym(\rho_1, \ldots, \rho_n) = (sym_1(\rho_1), \ldots, sym_n(\rho_n))$. Observe that $sym_i(\rho_i) = \lambda$ if and only if $\rho_i = \lambda$.

Definition 11. The controller incorporating $G_1, \ldots, G_n$ into C is the construct $inc(\Gamma) = (N'; \mathcal{M}'_{in}, \mathcal{M}_{fin})$ with $N' = (P', T, F', [n], \Delta, l')$ where,
$P' = P \cup (P \times \bigcup_{i \in [n]} \Sigma_i)$,
F' is defined as follows:
$\quad$ for all $t \in T$, for all $p \in P$
$F'(p, t) = \emptyset$,
$F'(t, p) = \{i \mid i \in F(t, p)$ and $proj_i(l(t))$ is terminating$\}$,
$\quad$ for all $t \in T$, for all $(p, A) \in P \times \bigcup_{i \in [n]} \Sigma_i$
$F'((p, A), t) = \{i \mid i \in F(p, t)$ and $lhs(proj_i(l(t))) = A\}$,
$F'(t, (p, A)) = \{i \mid i \in F(t, p)$ and $rhs(proj_i(l(t))) = A\}$,
$\Delta = tot(\Delta_1, \ldots, \Delta_n)$,
$l' : T \to \Delta$ is defined by $l'(t) = lsym(l(t))$ and
$\mathcal{M}'_{in} = \{M' \mid \exists M \in \mathcal{M}_{in}$ such that for all $i \in [n] : \overline{M'}(i) = (\overline{M}(i), S_i)\}$. $\qquad \square$

This construction resembles the one used in [KKR91] to prove that regular languages can be incorporated into GITNCs. Now however, the situation is more complicated because here we incorporate grammars.

$\quad$ Before comparing the vector languages of $inc(\Gamma)$ and Γ, we observe that the incorporation construction indeed yields a GITNC.

Lemma 3. $inc(\Gamma)$ is a GITNC.

Proof. To prove the statement we have to show that the transitions of N' are 1-throughput (conditions 1 and 2 in Definition 1), that the vector labelling of the transitions is consistent (Definition 3), and that $\mathcal{M}'_{in}$ and $\mathcal{M}_{fin}$ consist of it-markings of N' (Definition 4).
The last requirement is clearly fulfilled, since $\mathcal{M}_{fin}$ is not changed and each element of $\mathcal{M}'_{in}$ is defined by specifying per token the place where it resides

and hence is an it-marking. The vector labelling is consistent, because in N the transitions are consistently labelled and all productions introduce a terminal symbol (there are no λ-productions). Finally, N' has the same transitions as N has and the flow function F' is derived from F. They only differ where the flow of a token i from (to) a place p to (from) a transition t according to F is redirected by F' from (to) a place (p, A) to (from) t where A is uniquely determined by the production in the i-th entry of $l(t)$. Hence, like N, also N' is 1-throughput. $\square$

Now we are ready to prove that $inc(\Gamma)$ defines the same vector language as Γ.

Lemma 4. $V(inc(\Gamma)) = V(\Gamma)$.

Proof. To prove that $V(\Gamma) \subseteq V(inc(\Gamma))$ we relate the configurations of Γ and their transformations to it-markings and the firing of transitions in N'. With each configuration $\gamma = (v_1, \ldots, v_n; M')$ of Γ we associate an it-marking M_γ of N' defined as follows. $\overline{M_\gamma}(i) = \overline{M'}(i)$ for all $i \in [n]$ such that v_i is a terminal string, that is, in this case M_γ has token i in the same place as M'. For all $i \in [n]$, such that $v_i = xA$ for some $x \in \Delta_i^*$ and $A \in \Sigma_i$, token i is assigned to the A-copy of the place where M' puts it, thus $\overline{M_\gamma}(i) = (\overline{M'}(i), A)$. As a consequence, M_γ is an initial it-marking of $inc(\Gamma)$ whenever γ is an initial configuration of Γ. Furthermore, M_γ is a final it-marking of $inc(\Gamma)$ if and only if γ is a final configuration of Γ.

We first prove that a transformation $\gamma \vdash^t \delta$ implies that $M_\gamma[t\rangle M_\delta$ in N'. Let $\gamma = (v_1, \ldots, v_n; M_1)$ and $\delta = (w_1, \ldots, w_n; M_2)$ and let $t \in T$ be such that $\gamma \vdash^t \delta$. Let i be an input token of t. Thus $i \in F'(p', t)$ for some $p' \in P'$. Since in N' places from P are never input to any transition, this implies that $p' = (p, A)$ for some $p \in P$ and $A \in \Sigma_i$. From the definition of F' it then follows that $i \in F(p, t)$ and $lhs(proj_i(l(t))) = A$. Since t can occur at γ in Γ, we deduce that $\overline{M_1}(i) = p$ and that the last symbol of v_i is an A. Hence $\overline{M_\gamma}(i) = (p, A) = p'$. We conclude that $F'(p', t) \subseteq M_\gamma(p')$ for all $p' \in P'$ and so t has concession in N' in the it-marking M_γ. Now, let M be the it-marking such that $M_\gamma[t\rangle_{N'} M$. We prove that $M = M_\delta$. Let i be a token used by t in N'. Thus $i \in F'(p', t)$ for some $p' \in P'$. Hence, as above, there is $p \in P$ such that $i \in F(p, t)$, and there is $A \in \Sigma_i$ such that $p' = (p, A)$, $lhs(proj_i(l(t))) = A$, and $v_i = xA$ for some $x \in \Delta_i^*$. Let $q \in P$ be the output place of t in N for token i, that is $\overline{M_2}(i) = q$. The occurrence of t at γ implies that v_i is rewritten using the production $proj_i(l(t))$. This production is either $A \to aB$ or $A \to a$ for some $a \in \Delta_i$ and $B \in \Sigma_i$. If $proj_i(l(t)) = A \to aB$, then $w_i = xaB$ and the definition of F'' implies that $\overline{M}(i) = (q, B) = \overline{M_\delta}(i)$. If $proj_i(l(t)) = A \to a$, then $w_i = xa$ and the definition of F'' implies that $\overline{M}(i) = q = \overline{M_\delta}(i)$. A token i which is not used by t in N' is also not used by t in N and so v_i is not rewritten if t occurs. Consequently, $\overline{M}(i) = \overline{M_\gamma}(i) = \overline{M_\delta}(i)$. We conclude that $M = M_\delta$.

Consider a word vector $(w_1, \ldots, w_n) \in V(\Gamma)$. Hence there is a successful run $\gamma_0 \vdash^{t_1} \cdots \vdash^{t_k} \gamma_k$ of Γ such that γ_0 is an initial configuration of Γ and γ_k is a final configuration of Γ. From the above we know that $M_{\gamma_0}[t_1\rangle \cdots [t_k\rangle M_{\gamma_k}$ in N', M_{γ_0} is an initial it-marking of $inc(\Gamma)$, and M_{γ_k} is a final it-marking of $inc(\Gamma)$. Thus

$t_1 \cdots t_k \in FS(inc(\Gamma))$. Let $i \in [n]$. In each transformation step $\gamma_{j-1} \vdash^{t_j} \gamma_j$, either the i-th string is not rewritten, in which case $proj_i(l(t_j)) = proj_i(l'(t_j)) = \lambda$, or it is rewritten according to the production $proj_i(l(t_j))$ which adds the terminal symbol $sym(proj_i(l(t_j))) = proj_i(l'(t))$ to the right of the terminals in the i-th string. So, after the successful sequence of transformations $\gamma_0 = (S_1, \ldots, S_n; M'_0)$ $\vdash^{t_1} \cdots \vdash^{t_k} (w_1, \ldots, w_n; M'_k) = \gamma_k$, we have $w_i = proj_i(l'(t_1)) \cdots proj_i(l'(t_k))$ and hence $(w_1, \ldots, w_n) = coll(l'(t_1) \cdots l'(t_k)) \in V(inc(\Gamma))$.

To prove that $V(inc(\Gamma)) \subseteq V(\Gamma)$ we consider once more the relation between the configurations of Γ and the it-markings of N'. When associating to a configuration $\gamma = (v_1, \ldots, v_n; M')$ of Γ the it-marking M_γ of N', the terminal parts of the v_i are not considered. Hence each it-marking M of N' is related to infinitely many configurations of Γ. However, as we show next, every firing sequence of $inc(\Gamma)$, determines a unique sequence of transformations in Γ in such a way that the it-markings encountered in the firing sequence are associated to the respective configurations in the transformation sequence. Let $k \geq 0$, let $M_0 \in \mathcal{M}'_{in}$, and let $M_0[t_1) \cdots [t_k) M_k$ in N' for some transitions $t_1, \ldots, t_k$ and it-markings $M_1, \ldots, M_k$. Set $\gamma_0 = (S_1, \ldots, S_n; M'_0)$, with for all $i \in [n]$, $\overline{M'_0}(i) = p$ whenever $\overline{M_0}(i) = (p, S_i)$. Since M_0 is an initial it-marking of $inc(\Gamma)$, this is well defined and γ_0 is an initial configuration with M_0 as its associated it-marking. Let $1 \leq j \leq k$ and assume that $\gamma_{j-1} = (v_1, \ldots, v_n; M'_{j-1})$ has already been defined and is such that M_{j-1} is the it-marking of N' associated to γ_{j-1}. We first show that t_j can occur at γ_{j-1} in Γ. Let i be an input token for t_j in N. Hence $i \in F(p, t_j)$ for some $p \in P$. The definition of F' implies that i is also an input token for t_j in N'. In particular, there is a non-terminal $A \in \Sigma_i$ such that $i \in F'((p, A), t_j)$. Since t_j has concession in M_{j-1}, it follows that $\overline{M_{j-1}}(i) = (p, A)$. Combining this with the fact that M_{j-1} is the it-marking associated to γ_{j-1}, we obtain that $\overline{M'_{j-1}}(i) = p$ and $v_i = xA$ for some $x \in \Delta_i^*$. Since t_j uses i, the i-th entry of its vector label in N is not empty and we have $proj_i(l(t_j)) \in \Pi_i$. From the definition of F' it follows that $lhs(proj_i(l(t_j))) = A$ and hence v_i can be rewritten using this production. Consequently, t_j has concession in M_{j-1} and the productions in its vector label can be applied to the corresponding v_i and so t_j can occur at γ_{j-1}. We define γ_j to be the configuration obtained by the transformation of γ_{j-1} by the occurrence of t_j. Thus $\gamma_{j-1} \vdash^{t_j} \gamma_j$. We show that M_j is the it-marking of N' associated to γ_j. Let i be an input token of t_j in N. Then $v_i = xA$ for some $x \in \Delta_i^*$ and $A \in \Sigma_i$ is the left-hand side of the production $\pi = proj_i(l(t_j)) \in \Pi_i$. If π is a terminating production $A \to a$ with $a \in \Delta_i$, then v_i is rewritten into the terminal string xa. By the construction, $i \in F'(t_j, q)$, where q is the output place of t_j in N such that $i \in F(t_j, q)$. Thus, $\overline{M_j}(i) = \overline{M'_j}(i)$ as required. If $\pi = A \to aB$ with $a \in \Delta_i$ and $B \in \Sigma_i$, then v_i is rewritten into xaB. By the construction, $i \in F'(t_j, (q, B))$. Thus, $\overline{M_j}(i) = (\overline{M'_j}(i), B)$ as required. If i is not an input token of t_j in C, then the occurrence of t_j does not affect i and it entails no rewriting of v_i. Hence nothing is changed with respect to the i-th component: $\overline{M'_j}(i) = \overline{M'_{j-1}}(i)$ and v_i is not changed. In N' token i is also not used by t_j and $\overline{M_j}(i) = \overline{M_{j-1}}(i)$. Consequently, also in this case $\overline{M'_j}(i)$ satisfies the requirements.

Now consider a word vector $(w_1, \ldots, w_n) \in V(inc(\Gamma))$. Hence there is a firing sequence $t_1 \cdots t_k$ with $t_j \in T$ for all $1 \leq j \leq k$, and there are it-markings $M_0, \ldots, M_k$ of N' where M_0 is initial and M_k is final, such that $M_0[t_1\rangle \cdots [t_k\rangle M_k$ and $(w_1, \ldots, w_n) = coll(l'(t_1) \cdots l'(t_k))$. From the above we deduce that in Γ, there are configurations $\gamma_0, \ldots, \gamma_k$ such that $\gamma_0 \vdash^{t_1} \cdots \vdash^{t_k} \gamma_k$ and M_j is the associated it-marking of γ_j for each $0 \leq j \leq k$. Thus γ_0 is an initial configuration of Γ and $\gamma_k = (v_1, \ldots, v_n; M'_k)$ is a final configuration of Γ. Hence $(v_1, \ldots, v_n) \in V(\Gamma)$. Since $(v_1, \ldots, v_n) = coll(l'(t_1) \cdots l'(t_k)) = (w_1, \ldots, w_n)$ it follows that $(w_1, \ldots, w_n) \in V(\Gamma)$. $\qquad\square$

Using this result we can prove

Lemma 5. $\mathcal{V}_n(regPNGS) \subseteq \mathcal{V}_n(GITNC)$.

Proof. For the λ-free regular PN grammar systems, the result follows from the incorporation construction and Lemma 4. In case Γ is a regular n-PNGS with λ-productions, each production $A \to \lambda$ is replaced by a production $A \to \$$ where $\$$ is a new symbol. Then the incorporation construction is applied. The resulting GITNC defines a regular language L over a vector alphabet in which some vectors have entries $\$$ instead of λ. By Lemma 4, the vector language $coll(L)$ coincides with $V(\Gamma)$ once all occurrences of $\$$ have been replaced by λ. Regular languages are closed under (arbitrary) homomorphisms and so we can define a homomorphism h which maps every vector letter to the corresponding vector letter which has λ instead of $\$$ and the resulting language $h(L)$ will also be regular. Thus $V(\Gamma) = coll(h(L)) \in n\mathcal{R}\mathcal{A}\mathcal{T} = \mathcal{V}_n(GITNC)$ by Theorem 1. $\quad\square$

Combining Lemmas 2 and 5 with Theorem 1 shows that the vector languages of regular n-PNGSs coincide with the n-dimensional rational relations.

Theorem 5. $\mathcal{V}_n(regPNGS) = \mathcal{V}_n(GITNC) = n\mathcal{R}\mathcal{A}\mathcal{T}$. $\qquad\square$

From this result we can deduce that $proj_1(\mathcal{V}_1(regPNGS)) = \mathcal{L}_1(REG)$ (cf. Theorem 4). This is consistent with the well-known fact that adding regular control to regular grammars does not lead to an increase of the generative power, and contrasts with the effect of adding regular control to context-free grammars.

6   Conclusion

The theory of grammar systems is concerned with the study and development of grammatical models for distributed computations and cooperation. By viewing the grammars in a grammar system as concurrently operating partners subject to certain synchronization constraints, a link has been established with the theory of Vector Controlled Concurrent Systems. This has made it possible to use the Petri net based vector control mechanism of GITNCs to model concurrent rewriting protocols. This paper is clearly no more than an introduction proposing a definition and establishing some basic facts. A lot of work is still to be done before concurrent rewriting protocols for grammar systems and in particular the possibilities of PN grammar systems are fully understood.

A topic worth investigating is the optimalization of derivations on basis of both the structure of the controller and the form of the productions. Different criteria can be used here, like minimizing the number of steps in a derivation sequence, avoiding delays for component grammars, minimizing the number of synchronization partners in the vector labels, and reducing the size of the controller.

Also the connections between PN grammar systems and other models for regulated rewriting deserve more study. In a GITNC a transition can occur if the non-terminals forming the left-hand sides of the productions in its vector label occur in the sentential forms to be rewritten. This makes it difficult if not impossible to implement in the current PN grammar systems the appearance checking often used in regulated rewriting. For Petri nets, inhibitor arcs are an extension well suited to model situations in which a certain condition has to be tested (see, e.g., [Pet81]). Perhaps PN grammar systems with GITNCs extended with inhibitor arcs have sufficient modelling power to simulate appearance checking. PN grammar systems are appealingly close to PC grammar systems. A feature of PC grammar systems which the PN grammar systems lack, is the possibility to communicate through queries, but also bounded communication and non-communicating variants have been studied ([CDKP94], [IP94]). The rewriting in a PC grammar system is synchronized in the sense that at each step of the derivation process, all grammars with a not yet terminal sentential form have to apply a production. There are variants of the model in which the synchronizations are subject to additional constraints like rules synchronization which only allows fixed combinations of productions in rewriting steps (see, e.g., [CV01]). In [Mit00], PC finite automata systems are considered with synchronizations between state-action transitions resembling the synchronizations in regular PN grammar systems. Furthermore PC grammar systems with components not necessarily regular or context-free have been investigated. Hence insight in properties of PN grammar systems may come from results obtained for variants of the PC grammar systems model. On the other hand dynamic (state-dependent) and concurrent control on derivations as exercised by a GITNC is not part of PC grammar systems. In this sense, the introduction of PN grammar systems may be perceived as broadening the spectrum of the study of grammatical models for cooperation.

References

[Ber79] J. Berstel, *Transductions and Context-Free Languages*, Teubner, Stuttgart, 1979.

[Cor91] D.D. Corkill, Blackboard Systems. *AI Expert* 6, 9 (1991), 40-47.

[CD90] E. Csuhaj-Varjú and J. Dassow, On Cooperating Distributed Grammar Systems. *J. Inf. Process. Cybern. EIK* 26 (1990), 49-63.

[CDKP94] E. Csuhaj-Varjú, J. Dassow, J. Kelemen and Gh. Păun, *Grammar Systems. A Grammatical Approach to Distribution and Cooperation*, Gordon and Breach, London, 1994.

[CK89] E. Csuhaj-Varjú and J. Kelemen, Cooperating Grammar Systems: A Syntactical Framework for the Blackboard Model of Problem Solving. In *Proc. AI and Information-Control Systems of Robots '89* (I. Plander, Ed.), North-Holland Publ. Co., 1989, 121-127.

[CV01] E. Csuhaj-Varjú and Gy. Vaszil, On Context-Free Parallel Communicating Grammar Systems: Synchronization, Communication, and Normal Forms. *Theoretical Computer Science* 255 (2001), 511-538.

[CL92] N. Carver and V. Lesser, The Evolution of Blackboard Control Architectures. In *Expert Systems with Applications, Special Issue on The Blackboard Paradigm and Its Applications* 7, 1 (1994), 1-30.

[DPR97] J. Dassow, Gh. Păun and G. Rozenberg, Grammar Systems. In [RS97] vol. 2 (1997), 155-213.

[DPS97] J. Dassow, Gh. Păun and A. Salomaa, Grammars with Controlled Derivations. In [RS97] vol. 2 (1997), 101-154.

[IP94] C.-M. Ionescu and O. Procopiuc, Bounded Communication in Parallel Communicating Grammar Systems. *J. Inf. Process. Cybern. EIK* 30 (1994), 97-110.

[Kee96] N.W. Keesmaat, *Vector Controlled Concurrent Systems.* Ph.D. thesis, Leiden University, 1996.

[KK97] N.W. Keesmaat and H.C.M. Kleijn, Net-Based Control versus Rational Control: The Relation between ITNC Vector Languages and Rational Relations. *Acta Informatica* 34 (1997), 23-57.

[KKR90] N.W. Keesmaat, H.C.M. Kleijn and G. Rozenberg, Vector Controlled Concurrent Systems, Part I: Basic Classes. *Fundamenta Informaticae* 13 (1990), 275-316.

[KKR91] N.W. Keesmaat, H.C.M. Kleijn and G. Rozenberg, Vector Controlled Concurrent Systems, Part II: Comparisons. *Fundamenta Informaticae* 14 (1991), 1-38.

[MR78] R. Meersman and G. Rozenberg, Cooperating Grammar Systems. *Lect. Notes in Comp. Sci.* 64 (1978), Springer-Verlag, 364-374.

[MRV78] R. Meersman, G. Rozenberg and D. Vermeir, Cooperating Grammar Systems. *Techn. Report 78-12,* Univ. Antwerp, Dept. Math., 1978.

[Mit00] V. Mitrana, On the Degree of Communication in Parallel Communicating Finite Automata Systems. *J. Automata, Languages and Combinatorics* 5 (2000), 301-314.

[Nii89] P.H. Nii, Blackboard Systems. In *The Handbook of Artificial Intelligence* vol. 4 (A. Barr, P.R. Cohen and E.A. Feigenbaum, Eds.), Addison-Wesley, 1989.

[Pet81] J.L. Peterson, *Petri Net Theory and the Modeling of Systems*, Prentice Hall, 1981.

[PS89] Gh. Păun and L. Santean, Parallel Communicating Grammar Systems: The Regular Case. *A. Univ. buc., Ser. Matem.-Inform.* 38 (1989), 55-63.

[RR98] *Lectures on Petri Nets I: Basic Models* (W. Reisig and G. Rozenberg, Eds.) Lect. Notes in Comp. Sci. 1491, Springer-Verlag, 1998.

[RS97] *Handbook of Formal Languages* (G. Rozenberg and A. Salomaa, Eds.), Springer-Verlag, 1997.

Regular Event Structures and Finite Petri Nets: A Conjecture

P.S. Thiagarajan* **

School of Computing
National University of Singapore
3 Science Drive 2
Singapore 117543
thiagu@comp.nus.edu.sg

Abstract. We formulate the notion of a regular event structures and conjecture that they correspond exactly to finite 1-safe Petri nets. We offer a partial result in support of the conjecture. This result is in terms of a natural subclass of regular event structures that admit a sensible labeling with Mazurkiewicz trace alphabets.

1 Introduction

A classic result in concurrency theory is that the non-interleaved branching time behavior of 1-safe Petri nets can be represented as prime event structures [NPW]. Since then, this relationship between Petri nets and event structures has been strengthened in various ways [NRT, WN]; so much so, these two classes of objects can now be viewed as being strongly equivalent.

Here we venture a conjecture that relates Petri nets and event structures in the presence of a *finiteness* assumption. To be precise, we ask : What is the property of event structures that corresponds to a 1-safe Petri net being finite ?

Finite 1-safe Petri nets are important because they constitute a basic model of finite state distributed systems. Indeed, a good deal of research has been done on succinctly representing the event structure unfolding of a 1-safe Petri net (for a sample of the literature, see [Mc, E, ERV]). Here, the simple but basic observation due to Ken McMillan [Mc] is that if the 1-safe Petri net is finite, then its potentially infinite event structure unfolding can be represented as a *finite* object. The conjecture we formulate places this observation in a general setting.

More precisely, we define the notion of *regular* event structures and conjecture that finite 1-safe Petri nets and regular event structures correspond to each other. It turns out that this is a smooth generalization of the classical case where finite transition systems and regular trees correspond to each other. It is worth noting

---

* A major part of this work was done at BRICS, Computer Science Department, University of Aarhus, Aarhus, Denmark.
** On leave from Chennai Mathematical Institute, 92 G.N. Chetty Road, Chennai, India

W. Brauer et al. (Eds.): Formal and Natural Computing, LNCS 2300, pp. 244–253, 2002.

that the notion of a regular tree is fundamental in the setting of branching time temporal and modal logics [Tho]. We expect regular event structures to play a similar role in non-interleaved branching time settings. Admittedly, we still lack at present an effective temporal/modal logic over labeled event structures but we believe such a logic will appear eventually when suitable semantic restrictions have been identified.

In the next section we define regular event structures and formulate the conjecture. In section 3, we present a partial result in support of the conjecture. We show that the subclass of regular event structures that admit a sensible labeling in terms of a Mazurkiewicz trace alphabet correspond to 1-safe Petri nets. This is nice because even in the classical setting the glue that holds together Petri nets and event structures is the theory of Mazurkiewicz traces. In the concluding section we point to some possible strategies for settling the conjecture.

There exist a variety of models strongly related to 1-safe Petri nets, particularly in the setting of transition systems, as detailed in [WN]. A meta-conjecture is that a suitable version of our conjecture holds uniformly across all these models. Here we have concentrated on 1-safe Petri nets for a number of reasons. Firstly, this is one of the earliest and simplest concurrency models and it is widely known. Secondly, both the notions of a state and a transition are explicitly local and hence the conjecture is in a more demanding form. Finally, the occasion that has inspired this paper deserves a net treatment.

2   The Conjecture

To define regular event structures, we start with a notation concerning posets. Let $(X, \leq)$ be a poset and $Y \subseteq X$. Then $\downarrow Y = \{x \mid \exists y \in Y, x \leq y\}$. Whenever Y is a singleton with $Y = \{y\}$ we will write $\downarrow y$ instead of $\downarrow \{y\}$.

A prime event structure is a triple $ES = (E, \leq, \#)$ where $(E, \leq)$ is a poset and $\# \subseteq E \times E$ is an irreflexive and symmetric relation such that the following conditions are met:

 - $\downarrow e$ is a finite set for every $e \in E$.
 - For every $e_1, e_2, e_3 \in E$, if $e_1 \# e_2$ and $e_2 \leq e_3$ then $e_1 \# e_3$.

E is the set of events and $\leq$ is the causality relation. $\#$ is the conflict relation.

Throughout what follows, we shall refer to prime event structures as just event structures.

As usual, the states of a prime event structure will be called configurations. Let $ES = (E, \leq, \#)$ be an event structure. We say that $c \subseteq E$ is a configuration iff $c = \downarrow c$ and $(c \times c) \cap \# = \emptyset$. It is easy to see that $\emptyset$ is always a configuration and more interestingly, $\downarrow e$ is a configuration for every event e. We let C_{ES} denote the set of finite configurations of ES.

Let $c \in C_{ES}$. We define $\#(c) = \{e' \mid \exists e \in c. \ e \# e'\}$. The substructure rooted at c is denoted by $ES \backslash c$ and is defined to be the triple $ES \backslash c = (E', \leq', \#')$ where

- $E' = E - (c \cup \#(c))$.
- $\leq'$ is $\leq$ restricted to $E' \times E'$.
- $\#'$ is $\#$ restricted to $E' \times E'$.

It is easy to observe that $ES \backslash c$ is also an event structure.

Let $ES_i = (E_i, \leq_i, \#_i)$, $i = 1, 2$ be a pair of event structures. We say that ES_1 and ES_2 are isomorphic – and denote this by $ES_1 \equiv ES_2$ – iff there exists a bijection $f : E_1 \to E_2$ such that $e_1 \leq_1 e'_1$ iff $f(e_1) \leq_2 f(e'_1)$ and $e_1 \#_1 e'_1$ iff $f(e_1) \#_2 f(e'_1)$ for every $e_1, e'_1 \in E_1$.

Finally, for the event structure $ES = (E, \leq, \#)$ we define the equivalence relation $R_{ES} \subseteq C_{ES} \times C_{ES}$ via:

$$c \, R_{ES} \, c' \text{ iff } ES \backslash c \equiv ES \backslash c'.$$

The set of events enabled at a configuration will also play a role in the definition of a regular event structure. To this end, let $ES = (E, \leq, \#)$ be an event structure. Then we say that $e \in E$ is enabled at $c \in C_{ES}$ iff $e \notin c$ and $c \cup \{e\} \in C_{ES}$. Let $en(c)$ be the set of events enabled at the configuration c.

Definition 1. *The event structure ES is regular iff R_{ES} is of finite index and there exists an integer k such that $|en(c)| \leq k$ for every $c \in C_{ES}$.*

Intuitively, the transition system associated with ES is required to be a boundedly-branching dag with finite number of isomorphism classes ; thus generalizing the standard notion of a regular tree [Tho]. The condition requiring the bounded-branching property is independent of R_{ES} being required to be of finite index.

To see this, let $ES = (E, \leq, \#)$ be an event structure with $E = \mathbf{N}^*$ where $\mathbf{N}$ is the set of non-negative integers and $\leq$ is given by : $e \leq e'$ iff e is a prefix of e'. Further, $e \# e'$ iff neither e is a prefix of e' nor e' is a prefix of e. Clearly ES is an event structure and R_{ES} is of finite index. Indeed, there is just one isomorphism class. Yet, at every configuration, an infinite number of events are enabled thus violating the second condition of the above definition.

We next define a 1-safe Petri net to be a quadruple $\mathcal{N} = (S, T, F, M_{in})$ where (S, T, F) is a net and $M_{in} \subseteq B$ is the initial marking. (S, T, F) is a net in the sense that S is a set of S-elements (local states), T is the set of T-elements (local transitions) with $S \cap T = \emptyset$. Furthermore $F \subseteq (S \times T) \cup (T \times S)$ is the flow relation. We say that $\mathcal{N}$ is finite if both S and T are finite sets.

The basic result shown in [NPW] says that every 1-safe Petri net unfolds into an event structure. Later results appearing in a uniform setting (see [WN] for exact references) show in fact 1-safe Petri nets and event structures represent each other in a strong sense. We shall begin by recalling how one associates an event structure with a 1-safe petri net.

Fix $\mathcal{N} = (S, T, F, M_{in})$, a 1-safe Petri net. As usual, for $x \in S \cup T$, we set $^\bullet x = \{y \mid (y, x) \in F\}$ and $x^\bullet = \{y \mid (x, y) \in F\}$. The dynamics of $\mathcal{N}$ are captured by the associated transition system $TS_{\mathcal{N}} = (RM_{\mathcal{N}}, \to_{\mathcal{N}}, M_{in})$ where $RM_{\mathcal{N}} \subseteq 2^S$ and $\to_{\mathcal{N}} \subseteq RM_{\mathcal{N}} \times T \times RM_{\mathcal{N}}$ are the least sets satisfying:

- $M_{in} \in RM_{\mathcal{N}}$.
- Suppose $M \in RM_{\mathcal{N}}$ and $t \in T$ such that ${}^{\bullet}t \subseteq M$ and $(t^{\bullet} - {}^{\bullet}t) \cap M = \emptyset$. Then $M' \in RM_{\mathcal{N}}$ and $M \xrightarrow{t}_{\mathcal{N}} M'$ where $M' = (M - {}^{\bullet}t) \cup t^{\bullet}$.

We next extend the relation $\to_{\mathcal{N}}$ to sequences of transitions. Denoting this extension by $\Longrightarrow_{\mathcal{N}}$, we define $\Longrightarrow_{\mathcal{N}} \subseteq RM_{\mathcal{N}} \times T^{\star} \times RM_{\mathcal{N}}$ via :

- $M \xrightarrow{\epsilon}_{\mathcal{N}} M$ for every M in $RM_{\mathcal{N}}$.
- Suppose $M \xrightarrow{\sigma}_{\mathcal{N}} M'$ with $\sigma \in T^{\star}$ and $M' \xrightarrow{t}_{\mathcal{N}} M''$ then $M \xrightarrow{\sigma t}_{\mathcal{N}} M''$.

This leads to the notion of the set of firing sequences of $\mathcal{N}$ denoted $FS_{\mathcal{N}}$ which is given by:

$\sigma \in FS_{\mathcal{N}}$ iff there exists $M \in RM_{\mathcal{N}}$ such that $M_{in} \xrightarrow{\sigma}_{\mathcal{N}} M$.

We will extract the event structure unfolding of $\mathcal{N}$ from $FS_{\mathcal{N}}$ using the theory of Mazurkiewicz traces. For basic material concerning this rich theory, which we shall assume, the reader is referred to [DR]. Here we wish to merely recall that a (Mazurkiewicz) trace alphabet is a pair $M = (\Sigma, I)$ where Σ is a finite non-empty alphabet set and $I \subseteq \Sigma \times \Sigma$ is an irreflexive and symmetric relation called the independence relation. D is the dependence relation given by $D = (\Sigma \times \Sigma) - I$. Further, $\sim_I$ is the least equivalence relation induced by I over $\Sigma^{\star}$ satisfying : $\sigma_1 ab \sigma_2 \sim_I \sigma_1 ba \sigma_2$ whenever $\sigma_1, \sigma_2 \in \Sigma^{\star}$ and $(a, b) \in I$.

Returning to $\mathcal{N}$, we first note that $(T, I_{\mathcal{N}})$ is a trace alphabet where $I_{\mathcal{N}}$ is given by : $t_1 \, I_{\mathcal{N}} \, t_2$ iff $({}^{\bullet}t_1 \cup t_1^{\bullet}) \cap ({}^{\bullet}t_2 \cup t_2^{\bullet}) = \emptyset$.

We let $\sim_{\mathcal{N}}$ denote the equivalence (congruence) induced by $I_{\mathcal{N}}$ over $T^{\star}$. For σ in $T^{\star}$, we let $< \sigma >$ be the $\sim_{\mathcal{N}}$-equivalence class (trace) containing σ.

A simple but crucial fact is that in case $\mathcal{N}$ is finite, $FS_{\mathcal{N}}$ is a prefix-closed regular subset of $T^{\star}$. A second important fact is that $FS_{\mathcal{N}}$ is trace-closed. In other words, if $\sigma \in FS_{\mathcal{N}}$ then $< \sigma > \subseteq FS_{\mathcal{N}}$.

We next define the relation $\sqsubseteq$ over $T^{\star}/ \sim_{\mathcal{N}}$ as follows:

$< \sigma > \sqsubseteq < \sigma' >$ iff there exists σ_1 in $< \sigma >$ and σ_1' in $< \sigma' >$ such that σ_1 is a prefix of σ_1'.

Finally, for σ in $T^{\star} - \{\epsilon\}$, we let $last(\sigma)$ be the last letter appearing in σ. We define $< \sigma >$ to be a *prime* trace iff σ is a non-null sequence and for every σ' in $< \sigma >$, it is the case that $last(\sigma) = last(\sigma')$. Thus for a prime trace $< \sigma >$, it makes sense to define $last(< \sigma >)$ via: $last(< \sigma >) = last(\sigma)$

At last, we can define $ES_{\mathcal{N}} = (E, \leq, \#)$ where:

- $E = \{< \sigma > \mid \sigma \in FS_{\mathcal{N}} \text{ and } < \sigma > \text{ is prime}\}$.
- $\leq$ is $\sqsubseteq$ restricted to $E \times E$.
- Let $e, e' \in E$. Then $e \# e'$ iff there does *not* exist $\sigma \in FS_{\mathcal{N}}$ such that $e \sqsubseteq < \sigma >$ and $e' \sqsubseteq < \sigma >$.

It is easy to check $ES_{\mathcal{N}}$ is a prime event structure. We have now arrived at the main point of the paper :

CONJECTURE:

The event structure ES is regular iff there exists a *finite* 1-safe Petri net $\mathcal{N}$ such that ES and $ES_{\mathcal{N}}$ are isomorphic.

Thus our conjecture says that for 1-safe Petri nets, finiteness at the net level corresponds to regularity at the event structure level. One half of the conjecture is easy :

Proposition 1. *Suppose $\mathcal{N}$ is a finite 1-safe Petri net and the event structure ES is isomorphic to $ES_{\mathcal{N}}$. Then ES is a regular event structure.*

This result follows from a series of standard definitions and observations which we shall now sketch.

It turns out that there is a very close relationship between the dynamics of $\mathcal{N}$ and $ES_{\mathcal{N}}$. This can be brought out through the map $Config$ which assigns a configuration of $ES_{\mathcal{N}}$ to each firing sequence of $\mathcal{N}$ and the map Tr which assigns a trace (contained in $FS_{\mathcal{N}}$) to each configuration of $ES_{\mathcal{N}}$. Both these maps can be defined inductively as follows:

- $Config(\epsilon) = \emptyset$ and $Tr(\emptyset) = \{\epsilon\}$.
- Suppose σt is in $FS_{\mathcal{N}}$ with $Config(\sigma) = c$. Then $Config(\sigma t) = c \cup \{e\}$ where e is the unique event enabled at c satisfying $last(e) = t$. Next suppose $c' = c \cup \{e\}$ is configuration such that e is enabled at c and $Tr(c) = < \sigma >$. Then $Tr(c') = < \sigma t >$ where $last(e) = t$.

It is not difficult to verify that that the maps $Config$ and Tr are well-defined. One can in fact show that the map $Config$ can be consistently extended to $FS_{\mathcal{N}}/\sim_{\mathcal{N}}$ via : $Config(< \sigma >) = Config(\sigma)$. Further, one can now associate a reachable marking of $\mathcal{N}$ with each configuration of $ES_{\mathcal{N}}$ with the help of the map $Mark$ given by :

$Mark(c) = M$ iff $M_{in} \overset{\sigma}{\Longrightarrow}_{\mathcal{N}} M$ where $Tr(c) = < \sigma >$.

The point is, it is straightforward to show that the event structure rooted at c ($ES_{\mathcal{N}} \backslash c$) is isomorphic to the event structure unfolding of the 1-safe Petri net whose underlying net is that of $\mathcal{N}$ but whose initial marking is $Mark(c)$. Thus the equivalence relation $R_{\mathcal{N}}$ which sets two configurations c and c' to be equivalent just in case $Mark(c) = Mark(c')$ will be of finite index *and* it will be a refinement of the equivalence relation $R_{ES_{\mathcal{N}}}$. Consequently, $R_{ES_{\mathcal{N}}}$ is of finite index as well. Further, at most $|T|$ events are enabled at any configuration of $ES_{\mathcal{N}}$. Thus $ES_{\mathcal{N}}$ is regular and therefore ES is too.

The second half of the conjecture turns out to be surprisingly difficult to show. More precisely, we do not know how to do it. One source of difficulty is that there could be more than one isomorphism relating two configurations and there seems to be no good way of fixing these isomorphisms globally and uniformly.

In the next section we identify regular *trace* event structures which are regular event structures that admit a sensible labeling (of the events) by the letters of a Mazurkiewicz trace alphabet. It turns that our conjecture goes through for this subclass. In fact, our conjecture is equivalent to the statement that every regular event structure is also a regular trace event structure.

Even the proof of the fact that regular trace event structures correspond to finite 1-safe Petri nets is not straightforward . It uses in an essential way

Zielonka's theorem [Zie] ; a deep result with a notoriously difficult proof. Hence on second thought, it is perhaps *not* surprising that the main conjecture is difficult to prove.

3   Regular Trace Event Structures

Our goal here is to formulate the notion of regular trace event structures and argue that our conjecture holds for this subclass of event structures. The proof is quite technical and requires the introduction a variety of notions related to Zielonka's theorem. The details can be found in [Thi]. For the sake of brevity, we shall just summarize the main arguments here.

We will formulate regular trace event structures as the underlying event structures of certain kinds of labeled event structures. To be specific we will consider event structures whose events are labeled with the letters of a Mazurkiewicz trace alphabet.

Until further notice, we fix a trace alphabet M with $M = (\Sigma, I)$ and recall that D is the dependence relation given by $D = (\Sigma \times \Sigma) - I$.

Next we need two derived relations associated with event structures. Let $ES = (E, \leq, \#)$ be an event structure. Then $\lessdot \subseteq E \times E$ is defined as: $e \lessdot e'$ iff $e < e'$ (i.e. $e \leq e'$ and $e \neq e'$) and for every e'', if $e \leq e'' \leq e'$ then $e = e''$ or $e'' = e'$.

The minimal conflict relation $\#_\mu \subseteq E \times E$ is defined via:

$$e \#_\mu e' \text{ iff } (\downarrow e \times \downarrow e') \cap \# = \{(e, e')\}.$$

Definition 2. *An M-labeled event structure is a structure* $LES = (ES, \lambda)$ *where* $ES = (E, \leq, \#)$ *is an event structure and and* $\lambda : E \to \Sigma$ *is a labeling function which satisfies :*

(LES1) $e \#_\mu e'$ *implies* $\lambda(e) \neq \lambda(e')$

(LES2)   *If* $e \lessdot e'$ *or* $e \#_\mu e'$ *then* $(\lambda(e), \lambda(e')) \in D$

(LES3)   *If* $(\lambda(e), \lambda(e')) \in D$ *then* $e \leq e'$ *or* $e' \leq e$ *or* $e \# e'$.

□

The restrictions (LES2) and (LES3) on the labeling function ensure that the concurrency relation associated with an event structure (unordered events that are not in conflict) respects the the indepence relation of M. The restriction (LES1) demands that the natural Σ-labeled transition system associated with LES is deterministic. As pointed out in [Thi], an M-labeled event structure is just an event structure representation of the objects studied in [PK].

In what follows we will often represent the M-labeled $LES = (ES, \lambda)$ with $ES = (E, \leq, \#)$ as $LES = (E, \leq, \#, \lambda)$. We will also say that ES is the *underlying event structure* of LES.

Let $LES = (E, \leq, \#, \lambda)$ be an M-labeled event structure and $c \in C_{ES}$. As before, $\#(c) = \{e' \mid \exists e \in c.\ e \# e'\}$. We denote the substructure rooted at c as $LES \backslash c$ and define it to be the quadruple $LES \backslash c = (E', \leq', \#', \lambda')$ where

- $E' = E - (c \cup \#(c))$.
- $\leq'$ is $\leq$ restricted to $E' \times E'$.
- $\#'$ is $\#$ restricted to $E' \times E'$.
- λ' is λ restricted to E'.

Again, it is an easy observation that $LES \backslash c$ is also an M-labeled event structure.

Let $LES_i = (E_i, \leq_i, \#_i, \lambda_i)$, $i = 1, 2$ be a pair of M-labeled event structures. We say that ES_1 and ES_2 are isomorphic – and again denote this by $LES_1 \equiv LES_2$ – iff there exists a bijection $f : E_1 \to E_2$ such that $e_1 \leq_1 e_1'$ iff $f(e_1) \leq_2 f(e_1')$ and $e_1 \#_1 e_1'$ iff $f(e_1) \#_2 f(e_1')$ for every $e_1, e_1' \in E_1$. Furthermore we require $\lambda_2(f(e_1)) = \lambda_1(e_1)$ for every $e_1 \in E_1$.

Finally, for the M-labeled event structure $LES = (ES, \lambda)$, the equivalence relation $R_{LES} \subseteq C_{ES} \times C_{ES}$ is given by:

$$c\ R_{LES}\ c' \text{ iff } LES \backslash c \equiv LES \backslash c'.$$

We can now define regular trace event structures in two steps.

Definition 3. *The M-labeled event structure LES is regular iff R_{LES} is of finite index.*

Unlike the case of (unlabeled) event structures we do not have to demand here that at every configuration only a bounded number of events are enabled. Due to the condition (LES1) in the definition of an M-labeled event structure we are guaranteed that at each configuration at most $|\Sigma|$ events are enabled.

Definition 4. *The event structure ES is a regular trace event structure iff there exists a trace alphabet M and a regular M-labeled event structure LES such that ES is isomorphic to the underlying event structure of LES.*

It is clear from the definition that every regular trace event structure is also a regular event structure. It turns out that the converse is equivalent to our conjecture. This will follow from the main result of this section :

Theorem 1. *ES is a regular trace event structure iff there there exists a finite 1-safe Petri net $\mathcal{N}$ such that ES and $ES_{\mathcal{N}}$ are isomorphic.*

Before considering the proof of Theorem 1, we shall establish one of its interesting consequences mentioned above.

Corollary 1. *The conjecture of the previous section holds iff every regular event structure is also a regular trace event structure.*

To see this, suppose every regular event structure is also a regular trace event structure. Then by Theorem 1, every regular trace event structure is isomorphic to the event structure unfolding of some finite 1-safe Petri net. Thus every regular event structure is also isomorphic to the event structure unfolding of some finite 1-safe Petri net. This establishes the conjecture.

Next assume that the conjecture holds and let ES be a regular event structure. Then ES is isomorphic to $ES_{\mathcal{N}}$ for some finite 1-safe Petri net $\mathcal{N}$. Let $\mathcal{N} = (S, T, F, M_{in})$. Define now $LES_{\mathcal{N}} = (ES_{\mathcal{N}}, \lambda)$ where $ES_{\mathcal{N}}$ is the event structure unfolding of $\mathcal{N}$ defined in the previous section with $ES_{\mathcal{N}} = (E, \leq, \#)$ and $\lambda : E \to T$ is the labeling function given by :

$\lambda(e) = last(e)$ for every e in E.

It is easy to verify that $LES_{\mathcal{N}}$ is a $(T, I_{\mathcal{N}})$-labeled regular event structure. Thus $ES_{\mathcal{N}}$ is a regular trace event structure and consequently, every regular event structure is also a regular trace event structure.

Through the rest of the section, we will sketch a proof of Theorem 1. Again, the details can be found in [Thi].

Suppose ES is an event structure and there exists a finite 1-safe Petri net $\mathcal{N}$ such that ES and $ES_{\mathcal{N}}$ are isomorphic. Then by the the construction of $LES_{\mathcal{N}}$ above, we can conclude that $ES_{\mathcal{N}}$ is a regular trace event structure and hence ES is also a regular trace event structure.

So assume that ES is isomorphic to the underlying event structure of a regular M-labeled event structure LES. For convenience and without loss of generality let us assume that, in fact, ES *is* the underlying event structure of LES with $ES = (E, \leq, \#)$ and $M = (\Sigma, I)$. We now extract $L \subseteq \Sigma^{\star}$ from LES via :

- $\epsilon \in L$ and $config(\epsilon) = \emptyset$.
- Assume inductively that $\sigma \in L$ and that $config(\sigma) = c$ is a configuration. Suppose e is enabled at c and $c' = c \cup \{e\}$ and $\lambda(e) = a$. Then $\sigma a \in L$ and $config(\sigma a) = c'$. (From the definition of an event structure it will follow that c' is indeed a configuration).

Using the fact that LES is regular, it is not difficult to establish that L is a recognizable trace language over M. We now define $\sigma \in L$ to be *prime* iff there exists a letter $a \in \Sigma$ such every σ' which is *trace equivalent* to σ ends with the letter a. Let $pr(L)$ be then set of prime elements of L. Then we can show that $pr(L)$ is a recognizable trace language. Hence by Zielonka's theorem [Zie], there exists a deterministic asynchronous automaton $\mathcal{A}$ the language recognized by which is $pr(L)$. Now using $\mathcal{A}$ and the so-called gossip automaton [MS] we can construct a deterministic asynchronous automaton $\mathcal{B}$ which has the following pleasant properties :

- For every $\sigma \in \Sigma^{\star}$, the string σ is accepted iff $\mathcal{B}$ has a run over σ.
- The language accepted by $\mathcal{B}$ is L.

A crucial fact to note here is that L is prefix-closed.

We can then extract a Σ-labeled 1-safe Petri net $\mathcal{N}$ from $\mathcal{B}$ and show that it has the required property.

4   Concluding Remarks

At present, we have no good ideas for settling the conjecture. Perhaps one could gain some insight by considering *behavioral* subclasses of event structures. For instance, one could look at conflict-free event structures and then confusion-free event structures. But even the argument for conflict-free event structures appears to be non-trivial [N].

Given a regular event structure ES, one could try to manufacture a trace alphabet M_{ES} and a labeling function to obtain a regular M_{ES}-labeled event structure LES whose underlying event structure is ES. To get at M_{ES}, one might attempt to cover ES by a finite number of *sequential* components. The details however appear to be daunting.

Perhaps the conjecture is false. In this case, we conjecture that any counter-example and the argument that it is a counter-example will be quite horrendous.

5   Acknowledgments

I thank Mogens Nielsen for a number of very fruitful discussions.

References

[DR]   V. Diekert and G. Rozenberg: The Book of Traces, World Scientific, Singapore (1995)

[E]   J. Esparza: Model Checking Using Net Unfoldings, *Science of Computer Programming 23* (1996) 151-195

[ERV]   J. Esparza, S. Roemer and W. Vogler: An Improvement of McMillan's Unfolding Algorithm, *Proc. of TACAS'96, LNCS 1055* (1996) 87-106.

[Mc]   K.L. McMillan: A Technique of a State Space Search Based on Unfolding, *Formal Methods in System Design 6(1)* (1995) 45-65.

[MS]   M. Mukund and M.S. Sohoni: Keeping Track of the Latest Gossip: Bounded Time-Stamps Suffice, *Proc. FST & TSC'93, LNCS 761* (1993) 388-399.

[N]   M. Nielsen: Private communication (2001).

[NPW]   M. Nielsen, G. Plotkin and G. Winskel: Petri Nets, Event Structures and Domains I, *Theor. Comput. Sci.*, 13 (1980) 86-108.

[NRT]   M. Nielsen, G. Rozenberg and P.S. Thiagarajan: Transition Systems, Event Structures and Unfoldings, *Information and Computation, 118(2)*, (1995) 191-207.

[PK]   W. Penczek and R. Kuiper: Traces and Logic, In: V. Diekert and G. Rozenberg (Eds.), *The Book of Traces*, World Scientific, Singapore (1995) 307-379.

[RT]   B. Rozoy and P.S. Thiagarajan: Event Structures and Trace Monoids, *Theoretical Computer Science*, 91 (1991) 285-313.

[Thi]   P.S. Thiagarajan: Regular Trace Event Structures, *Technical Report, BRICS RS-96-32*, Computer Science Department, Aarhus University, Aarhus, Denmark (1996).

[Tho]   W. Thomas: Automata on Infinite Objects, In: J. van Leeuwen (Ed.) *Handbook of Theoretical Computer Science, Volume B*, North-Holland, Amsterdam (1990) 130-191.

[Wal]   I. Walukiewicz. Private communication.

[WN]   G. Winskel and M. Nielsen: Models for Concurrency, *In: Handbook of Logic in Computer Science, Vol.IV*, Eds.: S. Abramsky, D. Gabaay and T.S.E. Maibaum, Oxford University Press, (1995).

[Zie]   W. Zielonka: Notes on Finite Asynchronous Automata, *R.A.I.R.O. – Inf. Théor. et Appl.*, 21 (1987) 99-135.

Part IV

Concurrent Computing

Towards Team-Automata-Driven Object-Oriented Collaborative Work

Gregor Engels[1] and Luuk Groenewegen[2]

[1] University of Paderborn, Dept. of Mathematics and Computer Science
33095 Paderborn, Germany
engels@uni-paderborn.de
[2] Leiden University, Dept. of Computer Science
P.O. Box 9512, 2300 RA Leiden, The Netherlands
luuk@liacs.nl

Abstract. The paper studies and compares two different approaches to model communication and cooperation. The approaches are team automata, a well-defined variant of communicating automata, and statecharts, heavily used in object-oriented modelling methods. The comparison yields interesting insights for modelling communication and cooperation. In particular, the differences between action-based, synchronous and state-based, asynchronous communication are elucidated.

1 Introduction and Problem Situation

Automata theory, computer supported collaborative work (CSCW) and object-orientation (OO) are rather different fields of computer science. Although communication, cooperation, coordination and collaboration (CCCC) are being studied within each of these fields, notions or approaches from the different fields are usually not combined and integrated.

The question then rises, whether such a combination and integration of notions and approaches could be more clarifying and more precise with respect to CCCC than notions and approaches from one field alone. A reasonable expectation is, a combination of complementary notions or approaches in its turn complements the understanding already reached by each notion or approach in separation. This is the more interesting, as communication alone is not yet fully understood, and cooperation, coordination and collaboration are even less clear. So it is worthwhile to try some or other combination of notions and approaches from these fields, and to find out whether their complementarity leads to more understanding.

As already mentioned, such combinations and integrations are usually not studied. A positive exception is the research of Rozenberg and colleagues addressing team automata (TAs), see [3, 12, 13], where automata theory is geared towards collaborative phenomena from CSCW. Right at the beginning of the abstract in [13] it is being phrased as follows: "Team automata provide a framework for capturing notions like coordination, collaboration and cooperation in

W. Brauer et al. (Eds.): Formal and Natural Computing, LNCS 2300, pp. 257–276, 2002.

distributed systems. They consists of an abstract specification of components of a system and allow one to describe different interconnection mechanisms based upon the concept of 'shared actions'."

The following terminology from the citation in particular, is most inviting for researchers in the field of OO to join in the effort of combining and integrating ideas from the three fields: framework for coordination, collaboration and cooperation in distributed systems (3 C's out of CCCC, and the other C implicitly); components of a system; abstract specification thereof; interconnection mechanisms; shared actions. The notions this terminology is referring to, all belong to the kernel notions OO is focussing on.

So, given the problem situation put forward by the above question, and given the expectation concerning the complementary value of combining and integrating notions and approaches, we structure the paper as follows. After this introductory Section 1, we give a short impression of object-orientation (OO) in Section 2, and of team automata (TA) in Section 3. Taking the final TA from [13] as our leading example, we discuss similarities between OO and TAs in Section 4. Section 5 then discusses some different structuring of the same example, as it is not uncommon in OO, by explicitly separating the sending part of the automaton in a component from the receiving part. Continuing this line of thought we extend the example in Section 6, by also separating the internal part of the component's automaton. In so doing we are able, among other things, to model rather different collaborative strategies. Discussion and conclusions are presented in Section 7, together with some ideas for future work.

2   Object-Orientation (OO)

During the last decade, OO has become a most dominant paradigm in software engineering, from its early requirements engineering phase to its later integration and deliver phases as well as its maintenance phase. See the abundance of conferences and books addressing general OO, patterns, the Unified Modeling Language (UML) and its variants, and also UML's precursing languages. Two properties in particular lie at the root of the success story of OO. The first property is fundamental: OO advertizes and strongly supports the software engineering (SE) principles separation of concerns and hiding, making them key notions of OO. This is rather in line with the relevance of the seven SE principles mentioned in [9]. The second property is above all things practical: OO covers many different, already existing, successful modelling and programming approaches, by incorporating and integrating them; moreover, in this respect it is not limitative, but extensible. As the UML has become the vehicle for OO, we shall restrict ourselves to the UML. So we shall present our visualizations according to the UML diagrams. From these diagrams we shall only need two for this paper: the class/object diagram and the statechart diagram, see e.g. [1].

Although these two properties are very valuable and profitable, many improvements of OO are still needed. Among these needed improvements are various kinds of consistency between diagrams parts, between different diagrams of the same kind and also between different kinds of diagrams, see e.g. [5]. This is particularly true for those diagrams or diagram parts representing dynamic aspects. The scenarios for example as modelled by sequence charts should correspond to the behaviour descriptions of the objects involved as given by their statechart diagrams.

The topic of CCCC mentioned in the introduction, is another example of one that needs improvement. In [6] it has been proposed to discriminate not only between synchronous communication and various gradations of asynchronous communication, but also between the start of the communication and the end of it. It is by means of the notions of subprocess and trap as used in SOCCA, see [4, 2], that the different details can be expressed in a sufficiently fine-grained manner.

In [7, 8] a certain form of behavioural consistency between UML-RT components, so-called capsules, is defined. Based on this notion of consistency it can be investigated whether (combined) capsule behaviour is compliant with a (required) protocol and specified protocol roles. The problem situation is a particular combination of (behavioural) consistency and CCCC. As only a first step towards understanding of the problem situation has been set, a sufficiently satisfactory solution seems to be rather far off yet. So here we have a combination of the previously mentioned two examples of what needs improvement in OO.

The above discussion clearly stresses the necessity of a much better understanding and also of a formal underpinning of OO's consistency and of CCCC (in the OO context). It is in particular in the combination of behavioural consistency and CCCC, that we see a useful complementarity between OO and TAs. About a direct result of this complementarity, to be discussed in this paper, we want to say the following. Based on a careful combination of ideas from TA and OO, any communication going from one sender component to one receiver component will be structured according to two parts, one external and one internal.

The external part is between the two components. The external part can be considered as synchronous - it is in fact based on action-sharing, as we will see. Moreover, it guarantees a certain behavioural consistency, to be referred to as matching, of the two components through the behavioural similarity of two threads, one in each component. The matching of the two threads follows so straightforwardly from their structural specification through the TA-like language description, that we tend to categorize this external part of the communication as syntactical.

The internal part of the communication is inside each component. The internal part can be considered as asynchronous. It is such that it guarantees internal behavioural consistency between the various threads of one component through behaviour influencing, based on (internal) state-sharing. Within one component, the current state of one internal thread then determines which part of the behaviour in another internal thread is allowed. So this part of the communication is about behavioural consequences of internal communication, where the threads involved do not have a similarity in their structure (their languages can be arbitrarily different). Therefore we tend to categorize the internal part of the communication as semantical.

It is perhaps clarifying to make one more observation. With respect to the communication from one sender component to one receiver component, there is exactly one external part, but there are two internal parts: one is inside the receiver, which is probably self evident as the consequences of receiving usually consist of 'starting to behave accordingly'; the other internal part is inside the sender. The latter is maybe less obvious. An intuitive clarification is, sending is more or less irrevocable, so it also expresses a certain commitment. This commitment is reflected in - again - 'starting to behave accordingly', in this case by the sending component.

Enough announcements and intuition. We continue by introducing TAs and by comparing OO and TAs, the topics of the next two sections.

3   Team Automata (TAs)

In this section, we present a rather brief introduction to the notion of TA. For more information see e.g. [3, 12, 13] as mentioned above. A TA is a composition of component automata (CAs). The composition is more or less a Cartesian product of the CAs, but for the possibility to choose extra coordination between CAs' actions. The coordination takes the form of so-called shared actions. Each CA is a normal automaton with states, actions and (labeled) transitions, but their actions come into two categories: internal and external actions; in addition, the external actions also come into two categories, output and input actions. The coordination is as follows. Each internal action is not coordinated at all with whatever other action, so the transition corresponding to such an action is completely independent of the actions (and corresponding transitions) in the other CAs. They are only locally (i.e. within the same automaton) visible, and cannot be observed by the other CAs. But the external actions are observable by the other CAs and the coordination between them is: if two or more CAs participate in the same external action, they perform the corresponding transitions simultaneously. Such a combined transition of the CAs is reflected in a transition of the TA, where exactly those coordinates of the Cartesian product are involved corresponding to the participating CAs. Such a TA's transition then corresponds to the 'shared action' mentioned above.

Whether a CA is involved in such a shared action, depends on whether it participates in the particular external action which is at the basis of the shared action. The choice for these participations is called an interconnection strategy. The choice actually depends on what one wants to model. In this context the categories output and input actions are important: the concrete set of CAs participating in one particular external action consists of two disjoint subsets, those automata for which the external action is an output action - the sending subset - and the other automata (of that same set) for which the external action is an input action - the receiving subset. The automata in the sending subset are supposed to send information to the ones in the receiving subset, which are supposed to receive that information right then. Note that each shared action has its own sending set as well as receiving set. The freedom in choosing an interconnection strategy is essential for the following property: TA's can model a wide range of architectures for interacting hardware components and / or (groups of) people.

An interesting example of a TA is presented in [13]. It models so-called meta access right (MAR) control. 'Access' refers to file access rights: no right at all; the ("single") right to read; the ("double") right to read and to write. 'Meta' refers to the following level structure for controlling these rights. Level 0 models a person having such a file access right (or not) as well as acting according to that right. Level l ($l = 1,2,...,n$) models a person having (or not) the right to change (both grant and revoke) the right for a person on level l-1: no right to grant anything; the ("single") right to grant the "single" right to a person having none; the ("double") right to grant the "double" right to a person having single right. Revoking is always allowed, from double to single and from single to none. By means of two figures we visualize these ideas.

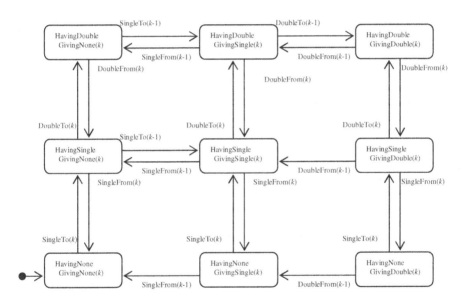

Fig. 1. Component automaton for level k ($k= 0,1,...,n$) of the meta access right (MAR) team automaton.

Figure 1 presents the CA for level k ($k=0,1,...,n$). In view of the readability we prefer long identifiers as state names and transition labels. (The occurrence of 'Giving' in the various state names does not refer to an action taking place, but to an action's result, consisting of the continuation of a right after it has been changed.) The starting state is indicated by means of an incoming unlabeled arc, starting from a black dot. The labels of the horizontal transitions are the output actions. The labels of the vertical transitions are the input actions. There are no internal actions. The interconnection strategy connects output actions of the level k automaton $(1 \leq k \leq n)$ with input actions of the level k-1 automaton. Output actions of level 0 are not connected (they are the actual - single right - read decisions and the - double right - read and write decisions). Neither are the input actions of level n connected (there is no higher level). One could even argue that the input actions on level n as well as the output actions on level 0 are internal.

As Figure 1 presents exactly one CA, it models exactly one coordinate of the Cartesian product that corresponds to the complete TA. This Cartesian product is, partially only, presented in the next figure. Note that we did not incorporate any phrasing like 'Grant' or 'Revoke' in the labeling of the horizontal transitions, e.g. GrantSingleTo(k-1) instead of SingleTo(k-1) and, similarly, RevokeDoubleFrom(k-1) instead of DoubleFrom(k-1). This would have been indeed more clarifying for the horizontal labels, but not for the vertical labels. There one would prefer 'Granted' or 'Revoked', e.g. SingleTo(k)Granted instead of SingleTo(k) and DoubleFrom(k)Revoked instead of DoubleFrom(k). But this is against the required equality of the labels referring to the actions to be shared.

The TA of these CAs, being their Cartesian product, is too large to visualize. We give an impression of it by showing in Figure 2 some states from the Cartesian product space together with each transition between them. The central state of the figure is the one where on each level the person has the single right and is giving the single right to the person on the lower level. The transition labels with an extra * as prefix to the action in the label, are the input actions on level n and the output actions on level 0, which might be considered as internal.

In line with the example in [13], we will restrict ourselves to the following interconnection strategy: each shared action has a sending set of at most one CA and also has a receiving set of at most one CA. Such sets do not change within the context of one model; in particular, it is always the same CA, if any ever, that sends a certain output (correponding to a certain shared action) to always the same CA, if any ever, receiving it as input (corresponding to the same shared action).

Here ends our short introduction to TAs, as the example gives a good impression of their modelling expressivity with respect to CCCC. The next topic we want to touch upon, is a comparison of OO and TAs.

4 Object-Orientation and Team Automata

TAs are built from automata, CAs. The diagram in OO (UML) coming closest to an automaton, is the statechart diagram, very similar to the original statechart proposed in [10]. Setting aside the different forms - sequential or concurrent - of hierarchical refinement of a state into one or more (different) statecharts as well as everything coming with that, such as shallow and deep history, synch state and the Petri net-like synchronization bar, a statechart consists of a set of states

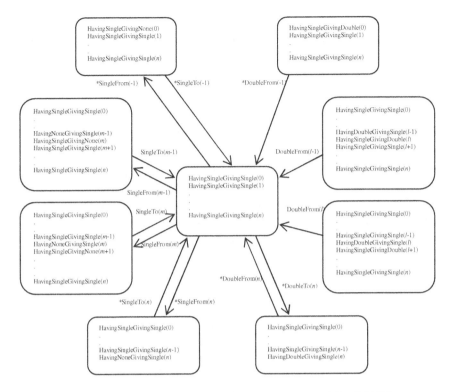

Fig. 2. Team automaton modelling meta access right (MAR).

and of labeled transitions from one state to another. So a statechart is a state transition diagram, like an automaton. The main difference with the CAs in a TA is in the transition labels.

In general, a transition label in a statechart consists of three parts: event part, condition part and action part, in this order. Each of these parts may be missing. Figure 3 presents the UML notation for a labeled statechart transition between two states, from state FromState to state ToState. The name of a state is written inside its graphical symbol, the rounded oblong. If there is an additional horizontal line below the name, the space below that line can be used for further refinement of the state into one or more statecharts, its substatecharts, consisting of so-called substates of the original so-called superstate. If there are two or more substatecharts of the same superstate, they are separated by means of a dashed line. In that case the superstate is a so-called AND-superstate, being a parallel composition of its substatecharts.

In a statechart, transition labels exhibit some structure in accordance to the three parts. The square brackets together with what they enclose, are the condition part; the slash is the beginning of the action part. The event part is either

Fig. 3. UML's labeling of statechart transitions.

missing or it contains one event, in this case anOccurrence. Such an event is the analogue of an input action in a CA: when it arrives from outside this statechart, it triggers the transition for which this event constitutes the event part - without event part no triggering is needed; see [1] for more details - provided that the statechart is in the state from where this transition is outgoing and moreover provided, the condition in the condition part evaluates to true (right then). Such conditions have no analogue in CAs. As we shall see below, they play a particular role in statecharts. If there is an action part in the transition thus triggered, all actions listed in the part are performed in one go. This is another difference with CAs and TAs, where only one action can occur in a transition label, so only one action is performed when the transition takes place. The actions themselves however, constitute another analogue with CAs and TAs. Unless special key words are used in the action, it is something without side effects to other statecharts, similar to internal actions. If the action consists of the key word *send* followed by an event prefixed by some reference to the statechart that is to receive the event, it is the analogue of an output action. The statechart rules then say, the transition labeled with such a send action, takes place simultaneously with the transition of the receiving statechart where this event constitutes the event part, if such a transition exists outgoing from the current state of the receiving statechart and if the condition part evaluates to true. If such a transition does not exist, the transition labeled with the send action takes place on its own; the event then is said to be lost.

So the action sharing as in TAs is also present in statecharts. In addition, via the condition part a statechart can check the current state of another statechart. This is state sharing (data sharing in a different context), not present in CAs and TAs. It is not uncommon to restrict the state sharing to statecharts being substatecharts of the same superstate. The underlying idea is, within the same superstate, i.e. within the same (super)statechart, substatecharts can share all information at will. For the moment, this is all very loose and informal. It is in clarifying the border between where to use action sharing and where to use state sharing, that TAs might be of substantial help, to be discussed from the next section on.

In order to clarify the above, we present an example statechart corresponding to the CA from Figure 1, thus modelling a person on meta access right level k. Figure 4 is a most straightforward translation of that CA, adapting the transition labels only. Furthermore, in order to facilitate future use of the statechart in other diagrams, we present it as a substatechart of state MARLevel(k). But usually we shall refer to the substatechart as if its name is MARLevel(k). Note that Figure 4 represents the levels 1,...,n-1 only, as for level 0 sending is meaningless and for level n the arriving events are meaningless. So MARLevel(n) is the same automaton as in Figure 4, with the actual parameter value n instead of k, but the labels of the vertical transitions are just not there. Similarly, MARLevel(0) is the same automaton, with the actual parameter value 0 instead of k, but here the labels of the horizontal transitions are missing. (In both cases an unlabeled transition reflects an internal (,anonymous, autonomous) action resulting in a state change.)

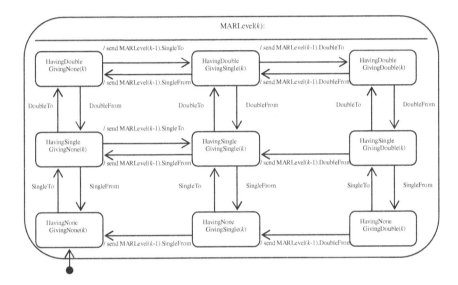

Fig. 4. Meta access right statechart MARLevel(k) for level k (k= 1,2,...,n-1); straightforward translation of Fig. 1.

An example of a rather different statechart is present in Figure 5, to be studied in the next section. As we observe here already, it consists of one state being an AND-superstate, itself consisting of two substatecharts. The internal communication between these two substatecharts is on the basis of state-sharing, as the conditions in substatechart MAR(k)Giving depend on the state in the other substatechart MAR(k)Having; the value of the condition depends on the current state of the other substatechart, i.e. the state MAR(k)Having is in, exactly at the moment of the evaluation of the condition. For instance, the condition part [HavingDouble(k)] evaluates to true if and only if MAR(k)Having is right then in state HavingDouble(k).

So far we have concentrated on similarities between the formalisms of TAs and OO. Now we are to discuss similarities between OO's key notions and TAs, against the background of the OO key notions mentioned. One such an interesting similarity between TAs and OO is: also a TA, by consisting of clearly separated components - the CAs - separates concerns. But - and this is a very promising difference - the TA by itself additionally composes its constituting CAs into a well defined whole - the TA - thereby establishing consistency in the formal manner of TAs.

Through its CAs, a TA offers a nice structure for separating concerns: those tasks, responsibilities in reality belonging to a member of a certain team, can be modelled with one CA of the TA modelling the whole team. This comes very close to OO's modularization, which is separation of concerns, of any model into classes/objects. Hiding is reflected in the internal actions as well as through the states - only external actions can be shared. As TAs are far more formal than the UML and than statecharts in particular (at this moment - not everything has reached its definitive form), the consistency of these CAs within the TA, being a kind of counterpart of the separation into CAs, is clearly well understood and expressed. In addition, any TA can figure as a CA of an even larger TA. Furthermore, through the choice of an interconnection strategy the structure of the actual CCCC is influenced, what comes down to controlling the actual visibility within the composition, as if smaller, consistent (with respect to CCCC in particular) groupings of CAs exist within the framework of the TA.

Apart from the mentioned similarities between TAs and OO we see an even larger lot of interesting differences. Based on the similarities, the differences and their complementarity are to be addressed in the remainder of the paper.

5   Revisiting the Meta Access Right Team Automaton, with Object-Oriented Manners

While studying the meta access right TA and in particular its statechart translation as indicated in Figure 4, we got the strong feeling that, at least in this case, the CA for one person on level k is itself a kind of Cartesian product of two smaller automata, one for the vertical transitions, registrating the current right of the person, the other for the horizontal transitions, exercising the supervision of the person on the next lower level by granting and revoking her access rights. Depending on her current right, the person on level k to a greater or less extent has restrictions on her horizontal i.e. supervising behaviour. This feeling was actually based on experience with multi-threading within classes / objects and (instantiated) package instances, a typical example of separation of concerns: complicated behaviour is separated into a consistent parallel composition of much simpler sequential behaviours, see e.g. [4, 2, 11].

Figure 5 visualizes this idea. It is the more interesting, as it adds a specific structuring to the original model. The additional structuring is typical for OO, being an example of separation of concerns: the whole input part of the CA is separated from the whole output part. The input part, called MAR(k)Having, reflects the person registering her rights. The output part, called MAR(k)Giving, reflects her activities of supervising the level below. Again, we have to treat the levels 0 and n separately. In substatechart MAR(n)Having there are no transition labels at all. In substatechart MAR(0)Giving the action parts are empty; so the send actions are not performed, but the conditions are still in place.

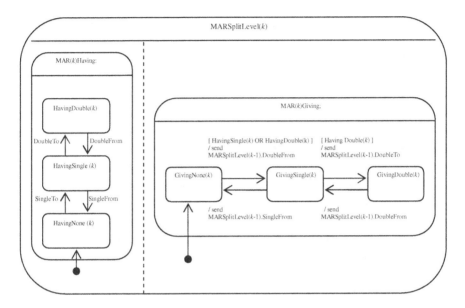

Fig. 5. Meta access right statechart MARSplitLevel(k) for level k (k= 1,2,...., n-1).

Another interesting thing to observe, concerns the difference in the type of the communication taking place. The communication between two different levels is synchronous as it takes place through the sending and simultaneous receiving of events. It is based on action sharing and there is no delay involved. Moreover, a one-to-one mapping exist between the two sets of states of the sending and receiving statechart respectively and also between their two sets of transitions, such that the current state of one statechart is (always) matching the current state of the other and such that a transition taking place in one statechart is matching the transition simultaneously taking place in the other, where 'is matching' means 'is related to according to the one-to-one mapping'.

On the other hand, the communication between the two statecharts on the same level is much more asynchronous of nature, although it is in disguise. Here the communication is based on state sharing. The inspecting statechart MAR(k)Giving, through its condition parts, communicates *at leisure* with the statechart MAR(k)Having whose current state is being inspected. One can argue that the latter informs the former asynchronously by entering a new state, and the former only takes note of this information when it needs it, possibly much later, asynchronously indeed. An extra and somewhat unusual feature of this communication is, the information is not consumed (deleted) by receiving or using it. On the contrary, the information continues to exist as the current state of MAR(k)Having, so it can be inspected (used) without destroying it. It is overridden (replaced) by new information only when MAR(k)Having again enters a new state, i.e. when MAR(k)Having receives new information.

The synchronous communication, the one between two different levels, is exactly the same as the communication in a TA between two CAs. The asynchronous communication, the internal communication within one level, is rather different, however, certainly not exactly the same as the communication in a TA between two CAs.

Figures 6 and 7 illustrate the above observations concerning the meta access right example in the following structured way. Figure 6 visualizes the original, unsplit situation: the (type of) person on level k is represented by the class Person(k). The person's responsibility to grant and revoke the rights of the person on the next lower level is expressed through the relationship supervises, with Person(k) in the role of sender and Person(k-1) in the role of receiver. The behaviour of the class is specified through statechart MARLevel(k) - more precise: through the one substatechart of state MARLevel(k). This substatechart thus realizes class Person(k) in a behavioural manner. To express this we use a dependency (relationship) stereotyped with ¡¡realize¿¿. As both class and statechart together specify level(k) we have expressed this by means of the package Level(k) as a container for the class and the statechart. By means of a note we remind the reader about the character of the communication.

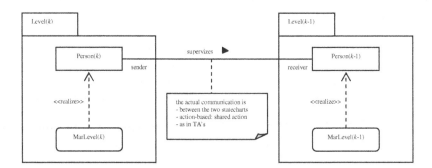

Fig. 6. Packages for two adjacent levels in the Meta Access Right example; the unsplit situation.

Figure 7 visualizes the split level situation, where each MARSplitLevel(k) statechart consists of two substatecharts. To be able to discriminate between this and other splitted situations, we refer to this one as the split-into-two situation. For the supervises relationship we have the same characteristics as in the unsplit situation. In addition there is the communication within one statechart MARSplitLevel(k), which has rather different characteristics. We shall refer to the latter as internal communication (within one level); the former will be referred to as external communication (between two different levels).

Summarizing this particular combination of TAs and OO, we observe the following. Internal communication is not TA-like, as it is based on state sharing; it is asynchronous in character, and it does neither destroy nor change the communicative information by using it. External communication however is TA-like, as it is based on action sharing: one send and one receive are connected; it is synchronous in character and it does destroy the communicative information by using it. The latter feature is compensated by the modelled effect of the output action (receive action): the new state entered stores that information (until new interobject communication is being received).

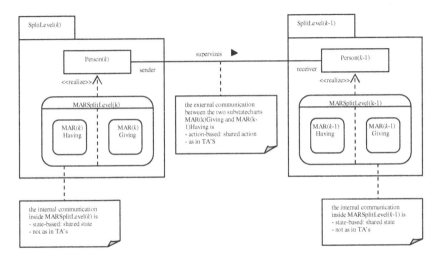

Fig. 7. Packages for two adjacent levels in the meta access right (MAR) example; the split-into-two situation.

6 Remodelling General Team Automata, with More Object-Oriented Manners

In the previous section we did the following. Starting from a given TA, we have given an OO model of the same situation such that the TA is still recognizable in it: each CA was formulated as a statechart for one class / object. This statechart has the same behaviours as the original CA (see Figure 6). As these statecharts communicate in exactly the same way as the CAs, the statecharts together have the same behaviour as the original TA.

Then we splitted the various statecharts into two parts according to the two different concerns of input part and output part. The thus splitted statechart has the same behaviours as the unsplitted statechart, so it still has the same behaviours as the original CA (see Figure 7). Hence, all properties valid for the CA and TA behaviours, are also valid for the statechart behaviours, although the splitted statecharts from Figure 7 together do not at all form a TA. Questions then arising are:

- can such a translation from CAs to statecharts as well as splitting of the statecharts be performed for a larger class of TAs.
- are there perhaps more concerns to separate, i.e. not always splitting a statechart into two substatecharts but into more if wanted.

With respect to the first question we can say the following. Sending and receiving are the apparent analogues of an output action and of an input action respectively. As in statecharts sending and receiving only takes place between two statecharts, this means that only TAs are being considered with an interconnection strategy, such that with respect to action sharing always (at most) one output action is being shared with (at most) one input action. This means that in any shared action either two CAs are participating or one. It also means, external communication is exclusively based on action sharing.

Pursuing the OO way of separating different concerns slightly further, we apply the same idea to the internal actions, thereby affirmatively answering the second question. This means, any statechart is modelled as a superstate comprising three substatecharts: one for the input actions, one for the output actions and one for the other actions and activities. The communication between these three substatecharts takes place exclusively via the conditions in the transition labels of such a substatechart, concerning the current state of the other two substatecharts. So internal communication is exclusively based on (internal) state sharing.

Figure 8 presents the structural consequences of this idea applied to the MARlevels. As the superstatechart for one level now consists of three substatecharts, we have adapted the names accordingly. As name of the (new) internal part we have chosen MAR-3(k)Maintaining, suggesting that the internal part, both based on the right the person has received from the next higher level and on the right she gives to the next lower level, determines (i.e. computes) the right she deems reasonable to act according to. So the person on level k then maintains her right in accordance with some personal view, insight, responsibility, which is possibly different from the right she is actually having as it has been given to her from one level higher. Note that Figure 8 illustrates an example only, although it still is fairly general. To make the example more concrete, we consider the situation where the right she has, the right she maintains and the right she gives are computed as follows. The right she has is completely in accordance with the right given to her by the person on the next higher level. The right she is giving is always less than or equal to the right she is maintaining. Upgrading the right she is maintaining, immediately follows upgrading the right she is having, provided the two rights were equal immediately before the latter upgrading (the

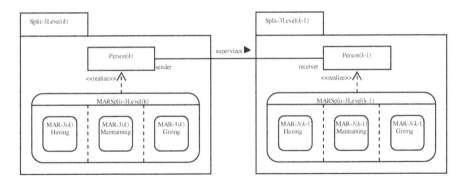

Fig. 8. Packages for two adjacent levels in the Meta Access Right example; the split-into-three situation.

first of the two in time) happened. Downgrading the right she is maintaining, only happens as soon as she is giving none; the new right she will start maintaining then, is equal to the right she is having right then. Whereas the transitions of MAR-3(k)Giving generally happen at leisure, those of MAR-3(k)Maintaining take place the moment the condition for it holds. This more concrete version of the example in Figure 8 is supported by Figure 9, where we have visualized the consequences for one statechart MARSplit-3Level(k). Pursuing the OO way of separating different concerns slightly further, we apply the same idea to the internal actions, thereby affirmatively answering the second question. This means, any statechart is modelled as a superstate comprising three substatecharts: one for the input actions, one for the output actions and one for the other actions and activities. The communication between these three substatecharts takes place exclusively via the conditions in the transition labels of such a substatechart, concerning the current state of the other two substatecharts. So internal communication is exclusively based on (internal) state sharing.

An interesting question now coming up is, can we, inversely so to say, construct a suitable CA from the three statecharts constituting one level? As a matter of fact, this turns out to be rather straightforward. First we construct a Cartesian product of the three state spaces, e.g. with coordinate order (MAR-3(k)Having, MAR-3(k)Maintaining, MAR-3(k)Giving). Then we add the transitions within a separate coordinate only, exactly mirroring the transitions from the corresponding original state space in such a way that the conditions are superfluous, as the state the transition is leaving from, actually meets the condition. Furthermore, the input actions are exactly the incoming events appearing as labels in the MAR-3(k)Having statechart and, omitting the "/send MARSplit-3Level(k-1)."-part, the output actions are exactly the sent events appearing in the labels of the MAR-3(k)Giving statechart. Figure 10 summarizes this, where we have abbreviated state names and actions as: HN_k for HavingNone(k), MS_k for MaintainingSingle(k), etc. and SF_k for SingleFrom(k), DT_{k-1} for DoubleTo(k-

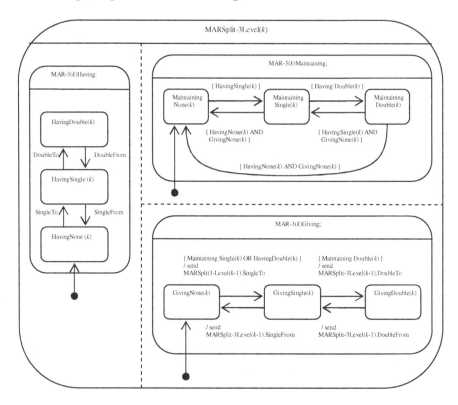

Fig. 9. Meta access right statechart MARSplit-3Level(k) for level k (k= 1,2,...,
n-1).

1), etc. Transitions in the first coordinate MAR-3(k)Having are horizontal (right-
left), transitions in the second coordinate MAR-3(k)Maintaining are vertical
(up-down) and transitions in the third coordinate MAR-3(k)Giving are askew
(back-front). Observe how we indeed specify the immediate occurrence of the
transitions in the MAR-3(k)Maintaining coordinate. This means, if in a state a
vertical transition can be made, no other transitions leave that state.

The construction of such a CA (of a much larger TA) is relatively easy, once
the separated concern specification via UML's substatecharts has been formulated. And these substatecharts are themselves relatively easy to build because
of the *divide et impera* approach: one type of action at a time, together with what
is triggering them. A direct building of such a CA is much more complicated,
as might follow from the question how to organize the state space when even
the dimensions are not clear. On the other hand, from the CA description many
consequences are pleasantly clearly visualized. To mention a few: some states of
the Cartesian product space are not reachable (and hence they are not drawn):

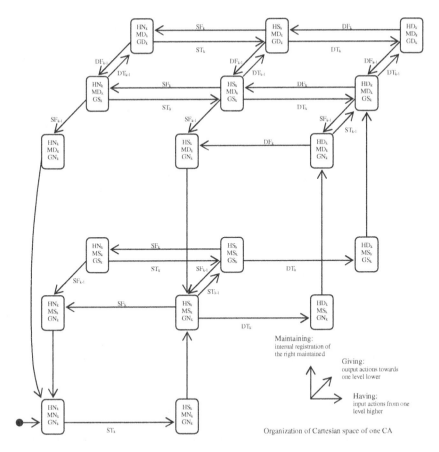

Fig. 10. CA corresponding to statechart MARSplit-3Level(k) for level k ($k=$ 1,2,...,n-1).

e.g. states with a higher right in the Giving coordinate than in the Maintaining coordinate (simply forbidden); if the Maintaining right is lower than the Having right (at most one grade), this is immediately corrected by upgrading the Maintaining right, a vertical step to the next higher right (without other steps being allowed); if the Maintaining right is higher than the Having right (one or two grades), this is corrected only, and in that case even immediately, if the current Giving right is no right at all (none), so the vertically downward transitions occur in the front plane only and where they occur, no other transition is allowed.

In our opinion the example of the thus constructed TA nicely illustrates the complementarity of TAs and OO. As this complementarity is the main topic of this paper, we postpone its discussion to the next (last) section.

7   Discussion and Conclusions

After our last example in the previous section we mentioned complementarity between TAs and OO. This complementarity was the main thing we were hoping to clarify by writing this paper. The complementarity consists of an impact of OO on TAs as well as an impact of TAs on OO. In the example we found the impact of OO on TAs in the step-wise, process-like way, starting from a UML description of a certain structure with well-separated substatecharts, first to construct the various Cartesian product CAs from it and then to build the TA from these CAs. The separation of concerns allows for modelling the behaviour in one thread (concern), depending on the behaviour of the other threads only through their current states. In the Cartesian product CA these dependencies reduce to the dependency on the current (Cartesian product) state, which is the normal dependency for state-transition systems.

By varying how a thread's transitions actually depend on the current state in the other threads (of the same object), we vary the computation as performed by such a thread. As the receiving thread exactly matches the corresponding sending thread in a different object, the actual dependency of a thread's computation on the receiving thread comes down to one possible variant for a collaboration: one concrete collaborative strategy for the receiving object. As the dependencies can be varied rather easily, different collaborative strategies can be modelled as easily. In combination with the straightforward construction of a Cartesian product CA on the basis of the threads of one object, collaborative strategies for such CAs can be as easily varied as for our type of multi-threaded objects.

In the example we moreover found the impact of TAs on OO in the two parts of any communication: the external communication between the components or objects and the internal communication between the various threads of one object. As the external communication is the TA-way of communicating, based on action sharing, this is modelled through sending and receiving of a particular event. In a synchronous way the receiving object (component) is informed about the sending object; the receiving actually enables new behaviour, which becomes possible only because of the receiving; the enabling of new behaviour is registrated in the current state of the thread that actually receives the sending. In addition, the sending object similarly registrates which new behaviour of itself is enabled by its own sending, in the current state of the thread that actually sends the sending. Both enablings are identically registrated, as the behaviours of both the sending and the receiving thread are matching. Matching of the two sets of behaviours is a direct consequence of the structuring of the two threads. This is a matter of form, so, apart from being synchronous, external communication is categorized as being syntactical of nature.

The internal communication does not exist within the TA approach, since within one CA there is no communication between the coordinates of the same Cartesian product. It is the separation of concerns resulting in different threads within one object, that necessitates this communication. Because of our particular structuring, the internal communication is completely based on state sharing. The internal communication determines which part of the behaviours of the various threads are enabled on the basis of the registrating performed by the receiving thread. In addition, the internal communication indeed establishes for each thread one of the enabled behaviours. So the internal communication not only is asynchronous of nature as it is based on state sharing, but it is also semantical of nature as it describes the (internal) behavioural consequences of the receiving.

We consider this insight as a very clarifying extension of the results in [6], where communication was categorized according to start or end as well as according to synchronous and three different gradations of asynchronous.

In doing this research we have, inspired by the approach taken in [13], restricted ourselves to a rather simple interconnection strategy for TAs: for each action to be shared both the sending set and the receiving set consist of exactly one CA; moreover, both sets do not vary depending on the behaviour of the system. In future research it might be interesting to consider more complex interconnection strategies too.

Acknowledgement We would like to thank Jetty Kleijn for pointing out some improvements to Section 3.

References

[1] G. Booch, J. Rumbaugh, and I. Jacobson. The Unified Modeling Language User Guide. *Addison-Wesley, Reading, Mass.*, 1999.

[2] T. de Bunje, G. Engels, L.P.J. Groenewegen, A. Matsinger, and M. Rijnbeek. Industrial Maintenance Modelled in SOCCA: An Experience Report. *In W. Schäfer (Ed.): Proc. of the 4th Int. Conf. on the Software Process, IEEE Press*, pages 13 – 26, 1996.

[3] C.A. Ellis. Team Automata for Groupware Systems. *In J. Clifford, B. Lindsay, D. Mayer (Eds.): Proc. of the GROUP'97 Int. ACM SIGGROUP Conf. on Supporting Group Work: The Integration Challenge, Phoenix, Arizona, ACM Press*, pages 415–424, 1997.

[4] G. Engels and L.P.J. Groenewegen. SOCCA: Specifications of Coordinated and Cooperative Activities. *In A. Finkelstein, J. Kramer, B.A. Nuseibeh (Eds.): Software Process Modelling and Technology, Research Studies Press, Taunton*, pages 71 – 102, 1994.

[5] G. Engels and L.P.J. Groenewegen. Object-Oriented Modeling: A Roadmap. *In A. Finkelstein (Ed.): The Future of Software Engineering. 22nd Int. Conf. on Software Engineering, Limerick, Eire, ACM Press*, pages 103 – 116, 2000.

[6] G. Engels, L.P.J. Groenewegen, and G. Kappel. Coordinated Cooperation of Objects. *In M. Papazoglou, S. Spaccapietra, Z. Tari (Eds.): Advances in Object-Oriented Data Modeling, MIT Press, Cambridge, Mass.*, pages 307 – 331, 2000.

[7] G. Engels, L.P.J. Groenewegen, and J. Küster. Modelling Concurrent Behaviour through Consistent Statechart Views. *In G. Reggio, A. Knapp, B. Rumpe, B. Selic, R. Wieringa (Eds.): Dynamic Behaviour in UML Models: Semantic Questions, ¡¡UML¿¿2000 Workshop Proceedings, York, UK*, pages 44 – 49, 2000.

[8] G. Engels, J. Küster, L.P.J. Groenewegen, and R. Heckel. A Methodology for Specifying and Analyzing Consistency of Object-Oriented Behavioral Models. In

Volker Gruhn, Editor, *Proceedings of the 8th European Software Engineering Conference (ESEC), Vienna, Austria*, pages 186–195, Sep. 2001.

[9] C. Ghezzi, M. Jazayeri, and D. Mandrioli. Fundamentals of Software Engineering. Prentice-Hall, 1991.

[10] D. Harel. Statecharts: A Visual Formalism for Complex Systems. *Sc. of Computer Programming*, pages 231 – 274, July 1987.

[11] P.J. 't Hoen. *Towards Distributed Development of Large Object-Oriented Models. Views of Packages as Classes.* PhD thesis, Leiden University, 2001.

[12] M.H. ter Beek, C.A. Ellis, J. Kleijn, and G. Rozenberg. Synchronizations in Team Automata for Groupware Systems. Technical report, Leiden Institute of Advanced Computer Science, Leiden University, 1999. Techn. Rep. TR-99-12.

[13] M.H. ter Beek, C.A. Ellis, J. Kleijn, and G. Rozenberg. Team Automata for Spatial Access Control. In W. Prinz, M. Jarke, Y. Rogers, K. Schmidt, and V. Wulf, Editors, *Proceedings of the 7th European Conference on Computer-Supported Cooperative Work (ECSCW), Bonn, Germany*, pages 59–77. Kluwer Academic Publishers, Dordrecht, 2001.

Grammars as Processes

Javier Esparza

Laboratory for Foundations of Computer Science
Division of Informatics, University of Edinburgh,
James Clerk Maxwell Building, Mayfield Road,
Edinburgh, EH9 3JZ, United Kingdom.

1 Preface

In 1999 I met Grzegorz Rozenberg in Amsterdam, while I was attending the
ETAPS conference and he was taking part in a meeting. The next day I was
giving a talk with the title "Grammars as Processes", and Grzegorz, who had
seen it announced in the program, asked me about it. We had little time, and
so I could barely sketch the contents. I think Grzegorz would have liked the
talk, because it pointed out an interesting connection between two of his oldest
loves, formal languages and concurrency theory, and showed how a model of
computation derived from this connection has a natural application in the area
of program analysis. He would have also liked to see how an abstract result
obtained by Büchi in 1964 on regular canonical systems was the basis to new
algorithms for the analysis of software.

This paper is a written version of the talk, and it also surveys the new results
obtained since 1999. Sections 3 and 4 are taken from the Ph. D. Thesis of Richard
Mayr [21], and have also been published in [22].

2 An Intuitive Introduction

Grammars count among the oldest tools in computer science. They are one of
the few formal concepts that a speaker can safely use in front of an audience
of computer scientists without having to introduce them. The "grammars as
processes" research program proposes to look at grammars from a different point
of view; not as language generators, but as generators of *behaviours* (formally
captured as labelled transition systems). The purpose of this paper is to convince
you, the reader, that this is an interesting thing to do, both from a theoretical
and from a practical point of view.

In order to look at grammars in this way, we will wear three different pairs
of glasses. The first pair is already waiting for us in Figure 1. It is called the
Sequential Model, for reasons that will be clear soon. Let us look at a production
of a left-linear grammar like

$$X \to aY$$

If we now put our glasses on, what we see is

$$X \xrightarrow{a} Y$$

W. Brauer et al. (Eds.): Formal and Natural Computing, LNCS 2300, pp. 277–297, 2002.
© Springer-Verlag Berlin Heidelberg 2002

Fig. 1. The Sequential Model

We interpret X and Y as *processes*, and interpret the production as:

Process X can perform the action a and become process Y

Readers familiar with process algebras are now raising their eyebrows, since this idea is at least 20 years old. But let us see how far can we take the analogy. The other possible productions in a left-linear grammar have the form

$$X \to a$$

If we put our glasses on, we see

$$X \xrightarrow{a} \epsilon$$

where ϵ denotes the empty word. We interpret this production as:

Process X can perform the action a and *terminate*

So through the glasses the empty word is seen as the terminated process which cannot execute any further actions.

If we now look at a context-free production like

$$X \to aYZ$$

through our glasses, what we see is

$$X \xrightarrow{a} Y \cdot Z$$

with the following interpretation:

Process X can perform the action a and become the *sequential composition* of the processes Y and Z

This is why the glasses are called the Sequential Model. The intuition for $Y \cdot Z$ is that the process Y must execute and terminate before Z can start its execution. You may object that the usual rewriting rule for grammars does not reflect this. If $Z \to a$ is a production, then YZ can be rewritten into Ya, whereas the production $Z \xrightarrow{a} \epsilon$ should not be applicable to $Y \cdot Z$, because Y has not terminated yet. This objection is correct. In order to match the intuition, we need to change the inference rule for the application of productions. Without glasses we see the usual rule

$$\frac{X \to w}{uXv \to uwv}$$

but if we put our glasses on we see the *prefix rewriting* rule

$$\frac{X \xrightarrow{a} w}{X \cdot v \xrightarrow{a} w \cdot v}$$

Notice that in the context-free case the two rewriting rules are equivalent with respect to the generated languages: Every word generated by a context-free grammar can be generated through a leftmost derivation, and this derivation corresponds to prefix rewriting. However, they are not equivalent with respect to the generated behaviours.

Grammars with prefix rewriting have been less studied than ordinary ones, but they have a distinguished origin. They were introduced by Büchi in [4] under the name of *regular canonical systems*, as a variant of Post's canonical systems. An updated presentation can be found in Chapter 5 of Büchi's unfinished book [5].

Let us now consider a non-context-free production like

$$XY \to aZ$$

If we put our glasses on, what we see is

$$X \cdot Y \xrightarrow{a} Z$$

This has a natural interpretation in terms of *value passing* between processes. Imagine we wish to model the sequential composition of two processes, X and Y, where X somehow computes a boolean and Y passes this boolean to the environment by executing the actions t or f. If, for the sake of simplicity, we assume that X computes the boolean nondeterministically, then the system can be modelled by the productions

$$X \xrightarrow{a} T \quad T \cdot Y \xrightarrow{t} \epsilon$$
$$X \xrightarrow{a} F \quad F \cdot Y \xrightarrow{f} \epsilon$$

The two productions on the right model passing the boolean from X to Y. The two possible executions of $X \cdot Y$ are

$$X \cdot Y \xrightarrow{a} T \cdot Y \xrightarrow{t} \epsilon$$
$$X \cdot Y \xrightarrow{a} F \cdot Y \xrightarrow{f} \epsilon$$

as expected.

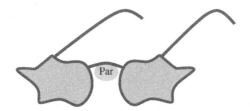

Fig. 2. The Concurrent Model

It is now time to try the second pair of glasses, waiting for us to collect in Figure 2. It is the *Concurrent Model.* The Concurrent and Sequential models have the same effect when we look through them at linear productions. However, if we look at a context-free production like

$$X \to aYZ$$

through the new glasses, what we see is

$$X \xrightarrow{a} Y \parallel Z$$

which we interpret as:

> Process X can perform the action a and become the *parallel composition* of the processes Y and Z

We interpret $\parallel$ as a commutative operator, i.e., we consider $Y \parallel Z$ and $Z \parallel Y$ as the same term. We model concurrency as interleaving: "a and b can occur concurrently" is considered equivalent to "a and b can occur in any order, and both orders lead to the same final result." Under this proviso, we can take the following rule for applying productions in the presence of parallel composition:

$$\frac{t \xrightarrow{a} t'}{t \parallel u \xrightarrow{a} t' \parallel u}$$

If only context-free productions are allowed, processes can be created but they cannot interact, only coexist. Interaction is elegantly introduced by non-context-free productions. For instance, if we look at

$$XY \to aZV$$

through our new glasses, we see

$$X \parallel Y \xrightarrow{a} Z \parallel V$$

which we can interpret as:

> Processes X and Y can have a rendez-vous by jointly executing the action a and become the processes Z and V

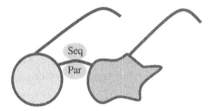

Fig. 3. The final model

The third and final model of glasses is shown in Figure 3, and combines the former two. If we put these glasses on we see productions like

$$X \xrightarrow{a} (Z \parallel V) \cdot U$$

which can be interpreted as a **parbegin–parend**: Z and V are started in parallel, and after both of them terminate— i.e., after both of them become the empty word—execution is continued with U.

Summarizing, the "grammars as processes" approach allows to model a variety of control mechanisms of programming languages in a simple way. The next section presents a formal syntax and semantics of the model.

3   Process Rewrite Systems

Let $Act = \{a, b, \ldots\}$ and $Cons = \{\epsilon, X, Y, \ldots\}$ be sets of *actions* and *process constants*, respectively. *Process terms* over Act and $Cons$ are given by

$$t ::= \epsilon \mid X \mid t_1 \cdot t_2 \mid t_1 \| t_2$$

where ϵ denotes the empty term. We introduce a syntactic equivalence relation $\equiv$ defined by the axioms

$$t_1 \cdot (t_2 \cdot t_3) \equiv (t_1 \cdot t_2) \cdot t_3$$
$$t_1 \parallel (t_2 \parallel t_3) \equiv (t_1 \parallel t_2) \parallel t_3$$
$$t_1 \parallel t_2 \equiv t_2 \parallel t_1$$
$$\epsilon \cdot t \equiv t \cdot \epsilon \equiv t \equiv \epsilon \parallel t \equiv t \parallel \epsilon$$

and by the two inference rules below, stating that $\equiv$ is a congruence.

$$\frac{t \equiv t'}{t \cdot u \equiv t' \cdot u} \qquad \frac{t \equiv t'}{t \parallel u \equiv t' \parallel u}$$

A *process rewrite system* (PRS) over $Cons$ and Act is a finite set Δ of *productions* of the form $t_1 \xrightarrow{a} t_2$, where t_1, t_2 are process terms such that $t_1 \not\equiv \epsilon$ and a is an action. The semantics of a PRS is a labelled transition system. A *labelled transition system* is a triple (S, L, R), where S is a set of *states*, L is a set of *labels*, and $R \subset S \times L \times S$ is a *transition relation*. We denote $(s, l, s') \in R$ by $s \xrightarrow{l} s'$. The labelled transition system associated to a PRS has the set of all process terms as states, and the set *Act* as labels. For each action a, $t \xrightarrow{a} t'$ belongs to R if it can be derived from the productions in Δ using the following inference rules:

$$\frac{(t \xrightarrow{a} t') \in \Delta}{t \xrightarrow{a} t'} \qquad \frac{u \equiv t \quad u' \equiv t' \quad u \xrightarrow{a} u'}{u \xrightarrow{a} u'}$$

$$\frac{t \xrightarrow{a} t'}{t \cdot u \xrightarrow{a} t' \cdot u} \qquad \frac{t \xrightarrow{a} t'}{t \parallel u \xrightarrow{a} t' \parallel u}$$

Figures 4 and 5 show two PRSs together with the transition systems they generate.

$$R \xrightarrow{a} A \qquad A \xrightarrow{a} A \parallel A \qquad B \xrightarrow{b} B \parallel B$$
$$R \xrightarrow{b} B \qquad A \xrightarrow{b} A \parallel B \qquad B \xrightarrow{a} A \parallel B$$

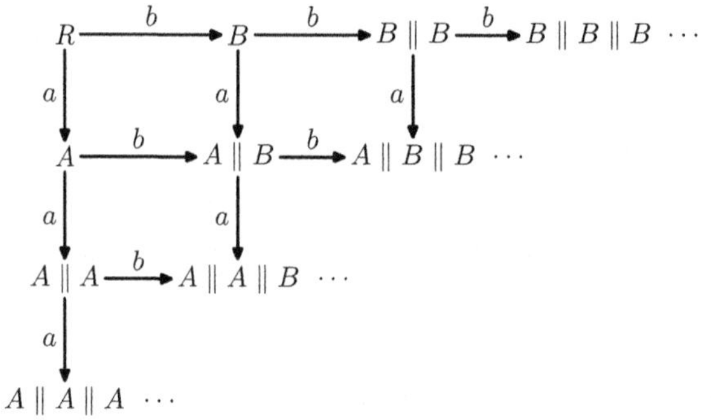

Fig. 4. An example with parallel composition

4   A Process Hierarchy

Grammars are customarily classified according to the Chomsky hierarchy. We introduce a similar hierarchy for PRSs, taken from [22]. We distinguish four classes of process terms:

- **1.** Terms consisting of a single process constant like X.
- **S.** Terms consisting of a single constant or a sequential composition of constants like $X \cdot Y \cdot Z$.

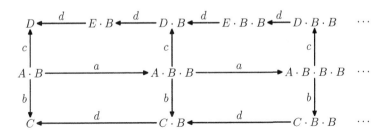

$$A \cdot B \xrightarrow{a} A \cdot B \cdot B \qquad C \cdot B \xrightarrow{d} C$$
$$A \cdot B \xrightarrow{b} C \qquad D \cdot B \xrightarrow{d} E \cdot B$$
$$A \cdot B \xrightarrow{c} D \qquad E \cdot B \xrightarrow{d} D$$

Fig. 5. An example with sequential composition

- **P.** Terms consisting of a single constant or a parallel composition of constants like $X \parallel Y \parallel Z$.
- **G.** General process terms with arbitrary sequential and parallel composition.

We obtain classes of PRSs by restricting the class of terms that can appear in the left-hand-side and in the right-hand side of a production. Given two classes of terms α and β, we denote by (α, β) the class of PRSs whose productions have α terms on the left and β terms on the right of the arrow. As in the Chomsky hierarchy, it only makes sense to consider classes in which β is at least as general as α (the remaining classes are uninteresting). Also, we do not allow the empty term in the left-hand-side of a production, but we always allow it in the right-hand-side. In this way we obtain the process hierarchy shown in Figure 6.

Basing on previous work [23], Mayr has shown that the hierarchy is strict with respect to bisimulation equivalence, i.e., no two classes generate the same transition systems up to bisimulation [22]. For instance, the transition system of Figure 5 cannot be generated (up to bisimulation) by any $(1, S)$-PRS. Incidentally, strictness does not hold for language equivalence, because the classes $(1, S)$ and (S, S) generate the same languages. So, in particular, some $(1, S)$-PRS generates the same language as the (S, S)-PRS in Figure 5, but no $(1, S)$-PRS is bisimilar to it.

4.1 Is the Process Hierarchy Interesting?

Since the process hierarchy mimics the Chomsky hierarchy, we can ask ourselves why is the Chomsky hierarchy interesting and try to find similar arguments for the process hierarchy. The main two reasons for the relevance of the Chomsky hierarchy are probably the following:

- Its classes have interesting machine characterisations (finite and pushdown automata, Turing machines ...), which allow to manipulate the languages generated by grammars and decide their properties.

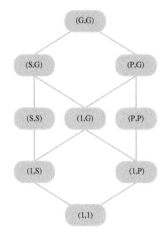

Fig. 6. The process hierarchy

- It is the undisputed formal basis for the lexicographic and syntactic analysis of programming languages, which provides an extremely important application making the hierarchy relevant outside pure theory.

We claim that two similar reasons can be used to support the relevance of the process hierarchy. In the rest of this section we show that the classes of the hierarchy have natural machine characterisations. In the next section we claim that the process hierarchy is a natural formal basis for control-flow analysis of programs. Or more daringly: In the same way that *grammars as language acceptors/generators* are an adequate basis for the syntactic analysis of programs, we claim that *grammars as processes* are an adequate basis for the analysis of their control-flow.

4.2   Machine Characterisations

We start with the following proposition.

Proposition 1. *The labelled transition systems generated by (S,S)-PRSs are exactly those generated by pushdown automata (up to relabelling of states).*

For this to make sense we must first define the transition system generated by a pushdown automaton. The states of the transition system are all pairs (q, w), where q is a control state of the automaton and w is a word of stack symbols. The labels are the letters of the input alphabet. The transition relation contains $(q, w) \xrightarrow{a} (q', w')$ whenever this is a transition allowed by the transition function of the automaton.

One direction of the proof of Proposition 1 is simple. It is easy to see that a pushdown automaton can be encoded as a subclass of (S,S)-PRS in which the left-hand-sides of productions have length at most 2: If $(q, s_1 s_2 \ldots s_n) \in \delta(q, a, s)$, where δ is the transition function of the automaton, add a production $q \cdot s \xrightarrow{a} q \cdot s_1 \cdot s_2 \cdot \ldots \cdot s_n$ to the PRS. This shows that the transition systems generated by pushdown automata can also be generated by $S, S)$-PRS. The other direction is a bit more complex. Caucal shows in [7] that any (S, S)-PRS is equivalent—generates the same transition system up to relabelling of states— to an (S, S)-PRS in which the left-hand-sides of productions have length at most 2.

The following proposition has an even simpler proof.

Proposition 2. *The labelled transition systems generated by (P, P)-PRSs are exactly those generated by labelled (place/transition) Petri nets.*

Given a labelled place/transition Petri net, construct a PRS as follows. Take a constant for each place, and for each a-labelled transition having places $p_1, \ldots, p_n$ in its preset and places $p'_1, \ldots, p'_m$ in its postset add a production

$$p_1 \parallel \ldots \parallel p_n \xrightarrow{a} p'_1 \parallel \ldots \parallel p'_n$$

to the PRS.

The class $(1, S)$ corresponds to pushdown automata with one single control state. It is also equivalent to the class of context-free processes [6] and to Basic Process Algebra [2], the core of the ACP process algebra. $(1, P)$ is equivalent to the class of labelled Petri nets in which every transition has exactly one input place, and to a fragment of CCS called Basic Parallel Processes [15]. $(1, G)$ has been studied under the name Process Algebra [6]. Finally, the class $(1, 1)$ generates finite transition systems, and so it is equivalent to finite automata when seen as transition systems.

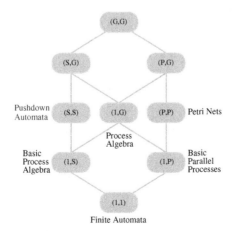

Fig. 7. Machine characterisations of the classes

These correspondences allow to describe PRSs as a process algebra combining the sequential composition operator of ACP and the synchronisation mechanism of Petri nets, with the goal of keeping a strong link to computational machines.

5   The Process Hierarchy and Control-Flow Analysis

The thesis of this section is that PRSs constitute a very adequate tool for control-flow analysis of programs. On the one hand, they provide a simple semantics to sophisticated control mechanisms, like procedures, spawning of processes, multiple threads, and synchronisation. On the other hand, as shown in the last section, they are closely related to computational models for which a large collection of analysis and verification techniques have been developed. So PRSs are a natural interface between theoretical results and software analysis.

In the area of program analysis it is customary to represent the flow of control of programs in terms of flow-graphs. We use flow-graphs with program instructions attached to the edges. Figure 8 shows the flow-graph of a program consisting of two procedures, Π_0 and Π_1. Π_0 is the main procedure. The flow-

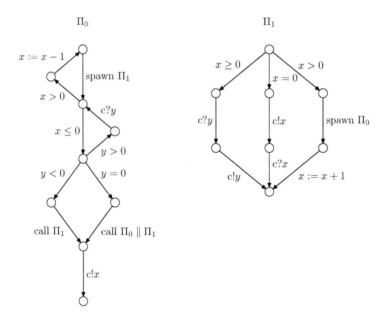

Fig. 8. A flow-graph

graph contains procedure calls (call Π_1), parallel procedure calls (call $\Pi_1 \parallel \Pi_1$), a process creation primitive, (spawn Π_0, spawn Π_1) and the well-known primitives $c?x$ and $c!expr$ for rendez-vous communication. As usual, $c!expr$ denotes sending the value of *expr* through the channel c, while $c?x$ denotes receiving a value through channel c which is assigned to the variable x. Sending and receiving must occur together in a single atomic action. In general, we assume that the graph corresponding to a procedure has a unique distinguished initial node. In figures, this is always the topmost node.

Control-flow analysis abstracts from data. This means that we are allowed to take a conditional branch in a flow-graph even if the condition attached to it does not hold. In this way we add to the *real* executions of the program *spurious* executions. The semantics of the flow-graph is the set of all executions, real or spurious. Any property holding of all executions of the program will also hold, in particular, of its real executions.

Flow-graphs of plain while programs have one single component (the main procedure) whose edges are labelled with assignments or boolean conditions. In this case, the executions of a flow-graph are just the maximal paths of the graph, where a path is maximal if it is infinite or it is finite and its last node has no successors. In the presence of procedures, the flow-graph has several components, and a denotational definition of the set of executions becomes more complicated, since "jumps" to procedures and correct nesting of calls and returns have to be accounted for. Papers on program analysis usually define the executions of these flow-graphs (if at all) with the help of an inlining operator, which replaces an edge corresponding to a procedure call by the graph of the called procedure. If procedures are recursive or mutually recursive, inlining does not terminate, but a "limit" infinite flow-graph can still be defined as a suitable fixpoint, and executions are then defined as the maximal paths of this limit. This is already somewhat involved. If parallelism and synchronisation are added, a denotational definition becomes more complicated; in fact, papers dealing with these issues usually provide no formal definition at all. For instance, recent papers like [25, 24] give the semantics in English.

In contrast, it is remarkably simple to give an operational definition of the set of all executions. Just convert the flow-graph into a PRS with a distinguished *initial process constant*, and declare the executions to be the maximal paths of the associated transition system which start at this constant. The conversion proceeds as follows. The set of process constants is the set of nodes of the flow-graph (although we use lowercase for the nodes and uppercase for the constants for clarity). The initial constant is the one corresponding to the initial node of the main procedure. The productions of the PRS are described in Figure 9. For each edge labelled by an assignment or a boolean condition, we generate the production shown in the upper left part of the figure (the figure shows the case of an assignment). For each edge labelled by a procedure call, we generate the production shown in the upper right, where I denotes the constant corresponding to the initial node of procedure Π. The productions corresponding to a parallel procedure call and a spawn operation are shown in the middle row of the figure, where $I_1, \dots I_n$ denote the initial nodes of the procedures $\Pi_1, \dots, \Pi_n$. Notice that the production for the parallel call correctly models that all the parallel processes must terminate before execution can be resumed; this is due to the

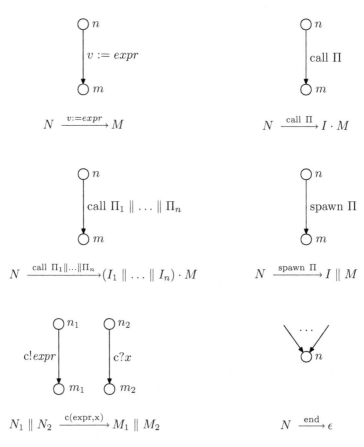

Fig. 9. PRS semantics of flow-graphs

fact that a parallel composition of processes is equivalent to ϵ only if all its components are equivalent to ϵ. For each (unordered) *pair* of edges labelled by an input and an output on the same channel, we generate the production shown in the lower left of the figure. Finally, for each node n without successors (end node of a procedure), we generate the production $N \xrightarrow{\text{end}} \epsilon$, as shown in the lower right.

If we consider a hierarchy of programs corresponding to more and more sophisticated control structures, we observe that the translations into PRSs match corresponding classes of the process hierarchy. Flat while-programs translate into the class $(1, 1)$. If we add procedures, we move to the class $(1, S)$. Through the addition of parallel threads through primitives for parallelism and process creation we jump to $(1, G)$. Finally, synchronisation between threads requires to use (P, G). If procedures are allowed to return a value from a finite domain, (sometimes called *multiple exit* procedures in other models, since the exit taken by the procedure is used to encode the value), we obtain the classes (S, S), (S, G), and (G, G), respectively.

5.1 The PRS Communication Policy: Pros and Cons

The presence of procedures leads to the distinction between global and local variables. Local variables are incarnated anew whenever the procedure is called; their values must be stored before the call and restored after the call is completed.

If we add procedures to a language with communication through channels, we find a similar distinction between global and local *channels*. Consider the flow-graph of Figure 10.

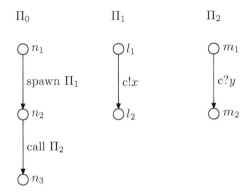

Fig. 10. The difference between global and local channels

Π_0 first spawns the process Π_1 and then calls the process Π_2. Should Π_1 and Π_2 be able to communicate or not? This depends on our assumptions on the nature of channel c. If the channel is globally defined, then communication can take place. On the contrary, if the channel is locally defined in, say, Π_1, then its existence is only known to Π_1 itself, to the processes Π_1 was called in parallel with (none in our example), and to the processes spawned by these processes (again, none). Communication is then forbidden.

The assumption underlying the PRS-semantics of flow-graphs is that *all channels are local*. Let us see why. The PRS-semantics of the flow-graph of Figure 10 is given by

$$N_1 \xrightarrow{\text{spawn } \Pi_1} (N_2 \parallel L_1) \qquad L_1 \parallel M_1 \xrightarrow{c(x,y)} L_2 \parallel M_2$$
$$N_2 \xrightarrow{\text{call } \Pi_2} M_1 \cdot N_3 \qquad L_2 \xrightarrow{\text{end}} \epsilon$$
$$N_3 \xrightarrow{\text{end}} \epsilon \qquad M_2 \xrightarrow{\text{end}} \epsilon$$

The only possible execution is

$$N_1 \xrightarrow{\text{spawn } \Pi_1} (N_2 \parallel L_1) \xrightarrow{\text{call } \Pi_2} (M_1 \cdot N_3) \parallel L_1$$

The production $L_1 \parallel M_1 \xrightarrow{c(x,y)} L_2 \parallel M_2$ is not applicable because this requires $L_1 \parallel M_1$ or $M_1 \parallel L_1$ to be a subterm of $(M_1 \cdot N_3) \parallel L_1$, which is not the case. In general, a production with a left-hand-side of the form $(X \parallel Y)$ cannot be applied to a term of the form $(X \cdot t \parallel Y \cdot t')$ if $t \neq \epsilon$ or $t' \neq \epsilon$. Intuitively, if we say that Y is a child of X in $Y \cdot X$ and a sibling of X in $X \parallel Y$, then a constant is only allowed to communicate with its siblings, but not with its aunts or nieces. Communication with, say, aunts, can be allowed by adding productions of the form $(M_1 \cdot N_3) \parallel L_1 \xrightarrow{c(x,y)} (M_2 \cdot N_3) \parallel L_2$. In a similar way we could allow communication with grand-aunts etc.. However, communication with arbitrary ancestors is not possible, since it requires an infinite number of productions.

Global channels have the same advantages and disadvantages as global variables. Global variables can be useful and reduce the size of code, but they can also be dangerous, since badly programmed procedures may have undesired side-effects which modify the values of global variables, when they should not. Similarly, global channels can be useful, but they allow any process to communicate with any other, whether that is intended or not.

However, global channels have another specific disadvantage: They make flow-graphs Turing-powerful, which implies that all interesting verification problems are undecidable. Even though we have not formally defined the concept of global channel, let us formulate this as a theorem and sketch a proof.

Proposition 3. *Flow-graphs with global communication channels are Turing-powerful.*

Proof. The proof shows that counter machines, a Turing-powerful model (see for instance Section 8.5.3 of [16]), can be simulated by flow-graphs with global channels. Counter machines consist of counters and a finite control. The control can increase or decrease the counters by one unit, and it can test if they are zero (i.e., it can decide which action to perform next according to whether a counter is zero or not). We simulate a counter by means of the flow-graph shown in Figure 11. The channels are *inc*, *dec*, *zero*, and *nonzero* with the obvious meanings: increase the counter, decrease, and test for zero. Since the values sent or received during communication are irrelevant, we write *inc*? instead of *inc*?x, and similarly for the other channels. The number stored in the counter is simulated by the number of calls of the procedure C which have not terminated yet. Observe that a communication on channel *zero* is only possible if this number is 0. The control of a particular counter machine can be easily simulated by a flow-graph which communicates with the counters through their channels (the names of the channels need renaming so that the sets of channels of any two counters are disjoint). The final flow-graph consists of the procedures C_{0i}, C_i for all the counters, the procedure for the finite control, say *Control*, and a main procedure which just calls $C_{01}, \ldots, C_{0n}$, and *Control* in parallel.

Globality of channels is essential for this proof: If channels are local, the *Control* procedure can communicate with C_0 but not with C, and so in particular the counter cannot exceed the value 1.

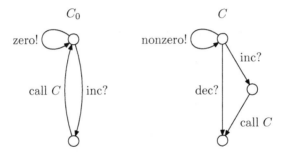

Fig. 11. A flow-graph simulating a counter

In contrast to this result, there are interesting verification problems which are decidable for flow-graphs with local channels. We prove this by translating the flow-graphs into PRSs and applying known results. In particular, we have the following theorem:

Proposition 4. *Given a flow-graph with local channels and one of its nodes, the existence of a computation that visits this node is a decidable problem.*

Proof. We first translate the flow-graph into a PRS. The node, say n, which we wish to visit becomes a process constant N. The initial node of the main procedure becomes another constant, say I. We add to the PRS a production $N \xrightarrow{yes} \epsilon$, where *yes* is a new action not appearing anywhere else in the PRS. Computations that visit n correspond to paths in the transition system of the PRS that start at I and contain an edge labelled by *yes*. Mayr has shown that the existence of these paths can be reduced to solving a number of instances of the word problem for Petri nets and for pushdown automata, both of which are known to be decidable [22].

6   Flow-Graph Analysis Using PRSs

We have shown that PRSs provide a simple semantics to sophisticated control mechanisms, like procedures, spawning of processes, multiple threads, and synchronisation. We still have to show that the theoretical results behind the process hierarchy can be applied to control flow analysis. This has been the subject of a number of papers, whose results we now survey.

(S, S)-PRSs: The class of PRSs most studied so far is (S, S), corresponding to pushdown automata, and including the PRSs modelling flow-graphs with procedure calls. Given a PRS Δ over sets *Cons* and *ACt*, we say that a process term t' is *reachable* from another term t if the transition system of the PRS contains a path leading from t to t'. The following theorem is the heart of all the work done on this class:

Theorem 1. *Let Δ be a (S, S)-PRS over a set Cons of constants, and let $L \subseteq$ Cons* be a regular set. The set of terms reachable from L (the* successors *of L) is regular, and an automaton recognising this set can be effectively constructed from an automaton recognising L.*[1] *The same result holds for the set of terms from which L can be reached (the* predecessors *of L).*

This result has an interesting history. It was first proved by Büchi in 1964, where he expressed it in terms of regular canonical systems [4]; it can also be found in Chapter 5 of his unfinished book [5]. The result has been rediscovered at least twice: Book and Otto prove it for monadic rewriting systems in [3], while Caucal proves it for prefix rewriting [7].

In [12] it was shown that this theorem leads to new solutions for a variety of classical control-flow analysis problems, like comptuting the sets of live variables or very busy expressions. In order to convey the main idea behind the solutions, let us sketch the procedure for a somewhat simpler problem, namely that of determining if a program variable v needs to be initialised. This is the case if some execution of the flow-graph uses the value of v (i.e., executes an assignment with v on the right-hand-side or checks a boolean condition involving v) before v is assigned a value.

Since we have given flow-graphs a PRS semantics, this problem can now be reformulated in PRS terms. We assume that the set Act contains two subsets of actions, a set Use containing the actions that use the variable v, and a set Def containing the actions that assign values to it. Let C_{Use} be the set of process constants to which productions with actions in Use can be applied. Then, v needs to be initialised if the transition system of the PRS contains a path of the form

$$I \xrightarrow{a_1} t_1 \xrightarrow{a_2} t_2 \dots t_{n-1} \xrightarrow{a_n} N \cdot t'$$

where I is the constant corresponding to the initial node of the main procedure, $a_1, \dots, a_n \in (Act - Def)$, and $N \in C_{Use}$.

Now, we proceed as follows. We first compute the set of process terms reachable from I by means of productions whose actions belong to $Act - Def$. This set can be infinite, but by Theorem 1 we can compute a finite automaton that recognises it. It is then easy to check if the automaton accepts some term of the form $N \cdot t'$.

In order to make Theorem 1 the basis of competitive systems for flow-graph analysis it is necessary to develop efficient algorithms for the computation of the automata. This was done in [11] for (S, S)-PRSs in which the left-hand-side of a production has length at most 2. The time and space complexity of the procedures must be analysed in detail. Let n_C and n_Δ be the number of constants and productions of the PRS, and let n_Q, n_δ be the number of states and transitions of the automaton accepting L. Then, an automaton recognising all successors of L can be computed in $O(n_C n_\Delta(n_Q + n_\Delta) + n_C n_\delta)$ time and space. An automaton recognising all predecessors of L can be computed in $O(n_Q^2 n_\Delta)$ time and $O(n_Q n_\Delta + n_\delta)$ space. For (S, S)-PRSs which model flow-graphs, we

---

[1] Here we are identifying the term $X_1 \cdot \ldots \cdot X_n$ and the word $X_1 \ldots X_n$.

can measure the complexity in terms of the numbers n_P and n_E of procedures and edges, respectively. An automaton recognising all successors of L can be computed in $O(n_E(n_Q+n_P)+n_\delta)$ time and space, and an automaton recognising all predecessors in $O(n_Q^2 n_E)$ time and $O(n_Q n_E + n_\delta)$ space.[2]

Paper [11] contains experimental results on an implementation, not only of the algorithms for the computation of predecessors and successors, but also of a model-checker for (S, S)-PRSs based on them. The checker allows to uniformly solve analysis problems by formulating them in the temporal logic LTL.

$(1, G)$-*PRSs:* The class $(1, G)$, which includes the PRS models of flow-graphs with procedure calls, parallelism and process creation, but without synchronisation, has also been studied. Lugiez and Schnoebelen observed in [20] that Büchi's result, which holds for the class $(1, S)$ as a subclass of (S, S), could be generalised to $(1, G)$ in a very elegant way. In the case of $(1, S)$, terms are made out of constants and sequential composition, and so a set of terms can be identified with a set of words over the alphabet of process constants. This is no longer possible for $(1, G)$, because terms now contain both sequential and parallel composition. But a set of terms can still be identified with a set of trees, namely the syntax trees of the terms.[3] So it makes sense to speak of a regular set of terms as a set of terms recognised by a tree automaton. Lugiez and Schnoebelen show that Büchi's result still holds: Given a $(1, G)$-PRS and a regular set of terms L, the sets of predecessors and successors of L are regular, and tree automata recognising them can be effectively computed from a tree automaton recognising L. However, just as for the (S, S) class, it is necessary to provide efficient algorithms for the computation of the tree automata. This was done in [14], and the paper also shows how to apply the algorithms to common program analysis problems. However, in this case the algorithms have not been efficiently implemented yet.

It is interesting to note that more involved analysis problems are undecidable for flow-graphs with procedure calls and parallelism, but without synchronisation. Müller-Olm and Seidl have recently shown that this is the case for optimal slicing [24].

(P, G)-*PRSs:* The class (P, G), which includes the PRS models of flow-graphs which procedure calls, parallelism, and synchronisation through local channels has been less studied. Mayr shows in [21] that the reachability problem and a generalisation of it, the reachable property problem, are decidable. These results can be used to prove decidability of some control-flow problems. Proposition 4

---

[2] These are results for procedures which do not return a value. See [1] for a more detailed analysis in a similar model.

[3] There is a technical subtlety here. In the definition of PRS we work with a structural congruence stating that parallel composition is associative and commutative. This is important in the presence of synchronisation: Otherwise the production $X \parallel Y \xrightarrow{a} Z$ would be applicable to $(X \parallel Y) \parallel V$ but not to $X \parallel (Y \parallel V)$. However, in the class $(1, G)$ the left-hand-side of a production is always a single constant, and this problem does not appear. It is then possible to work directly with terms instead of with equivalence classes of terms.

shows that the reachability of program points is decidable, and the same holds for other simple problems like Possible Rendezvous (determining if two given statements $c?x$ and $c!y$ may synchronise with each other), or May Happen in Parallel (determining if two given statements may ever execute in parallel).

These results are in sharp contrast with undecidability results recently presented in the literature. Ramalingam shows in [25] that even the simplest analysis problems, like reachability of a point in a program, are undecidable for a set of Ada communicating procedures each of which may call itself recursively. In Ada, a concurrent program is a statically specified set of tasks. Each task is essentially a collection of sequential and possibly recursive procedures, with a distinguished main procedure. The only concurrency primitive he uses for the undecidability proof is rendezvous communication: a task T may *invoke* an *entry* $S.E$ belonging to a task S; S may *accept* this entry. So, in our language of flow-graphs, if T wants to communicate with S, then it does so by means of a channel named S, which is globally and statically defined before the computation starts. So, apart from technicalities, Ramalingam's result is the one we sketched in Proposition 3. Notice that neither process creation nor mutual recursion are required for the proof: It suffices to have three processes, two of which call themselves recursively. However, global channels are essential. Notice that Proposition 4 shows decidability for a model with local channels only, but allowing for process creation and mutual recursion with unrestricted interplay between the two.

The complexity of analysis problems for the (P, G) class is necessarily high. The reason is that it properly includes the class (P, P), which corresponds to place/transition Petri nets. Since all interesting analysis problems for Petri nets are know to be EXPSPACE-hard, there is no hope of finding algorithms with a good worst-case complexity. However, a bad worst-case complexity does not necessarily mean that analysis algorithms for this class will not be useful in practice. For instance, there has been recent success in the analysis of a model called broadcast protocols [13], which also contains Petri nets as special case. Delzanno has implemented an algorithm and used it to automatically verify safety properties of many different cache-coherence protocols in a few seconds [9]. Further work on the (P, G) class is needed.

7   History and Related Work

The history of process rewrite systems and its applications to program analysis is not easy to reconstruct, because the researchers involved in it have communicated intensely and have had a variety of motivations.

The idea of using grammars to describe transition systems can be traced back to Caucal [7], who uses pushdown automata to define and study a class of graphs. Caucal presents pushdown automata as (S, S)-PRSs.

A grammar-based view of Petri nets is presented by Huynh in [17, 18]. He calls his model "commutative grammars", and studies both the context-free and the general case, which correspond to the classes (P, P) and $(1, P)$, respectively. However, he still looks at this grammars mostly as language generators. Other authors have studied these classes as generators of transition systems, with the classes presented through their machine characterizations. For instance, in [8] $(1, P)$ is presented as a subset of the CCS process algebra, while in [15, 10] it is presented as a subclass of Petri nets.

The idea of integrating different classes of transition systems into a unified model by means of a Chomsky-like hierarchy can also be traced back to [7]. However, only the sequential case is considered in his paper. Moller introduces two different hierarchies in [23], one for the sequential and one for the parallel case. The process hierarchy as presented here, allowing for mixed terms with both sequential and parallel combinators, was introduced by Mayr in his Ph.D. Thesis [21] and later published in [22].

The decidability and complexity of verification problems for the classes of the hierarchy has been the subject of many papers. Surveys (a bit outdated) can be found in [23] and [6].

The idea of applying PRSs to model the semantics of flow-graphs was first presented in [12]. However, it builds upon ideas by Steffen [29]—later refined by Steffen and Schmidt [27, 26]—on the relationship between program analysis and model-checking.

The program analysis algorithms of Section 6 can be seen as a development of Büchi's result on canonical systems, but also as an automata-theoretic approach to program analysis problems. A different approach based on fixpoint techniques has been introduced and developed by Knoop, Müller-Olm, Seidl, Steffen, and others (see for instance [19, 28]). This approach predates the automata-theoretic. Today the two approaches influence each other.

8   Conclusions

We have introduced Process Rewrite Systems, a process algebra having strong connections with well known computational models like pushdown automata and Petri nets. PRSs have not been defined by an individual or a few individuals; instead, they are the result of a synthesis process in which results were obtained by a large number of people, and then a model able to encompass them was defined. We have argued that PRSs are an excellent interface between strong theoretical results and applications, with program analysis playing a distinguished rôle.

Grzegorz, I hope you enjoyed the talk!

References

[1] R. Alur, K. Etessami, and M. Yannanakis. Analysis of Recursive State Machines. In *Proceedings of CAV '01*, LNCS 2102:207–220, 2001.

[2] J. C. M. Baeten and W. P. Weijland. *Process Algebra. Cambridge Tracts in Theoretical Computer Science*, vol. 18, Cambridge University Press, 1990.

[3] R. Book and F. Otto. *String-Rewriting Systems*. Springer-Verlag, 1993.

[4] J. R. Büchi. Regular Canonical Systems and Finite Automata. *Arch. Math. Logik Grundlagenforschung*, 6:91–111, 1964.

[5] J. R. Büchi and D. Siefkes. *Finite Automata, Their Algebras and Grammars.* Springer-Verlag, 1988.

[6] O. Burkart and J. Esparza. More Infinite Results. *EATCS Bulletin*, 62:138–159, 1997.

[7] D. Caucal. On the Regular Structure of Prefix Rewriting. *Theoretical Computer Science*, 106(1):61–86, November 1992.

[8] S. Christensen, Y. Hirshfeld, and F. Moller. Bisimulation Equivalence Is Decidable for All Basic Parallel Processes. In *Proceedings of CONCUR '93*, LNCS 715:143–157, 1993.

[9] G. Delzanno. Automatic Verification of Parameterized Cache Coherence Protocols. In *Proceedings of CAV '00*, LNCS 1885:53–68, 2000.

[10] J. Esparza. Petri Nets, Commutative Context-Free Grammars, and Basic Parallel Processes. *Fundamenta Informatica*, 31:13–26, 1997.

[11] J. Esparza, D. Hansel, P. Rossmanith, and S. Schwoon. Efficient Algorithms for Model Checking Pushdown Systems. In *Proceedings of CAV '00*, LNCS 1885:232–247, 2000.

[12] J. Esparza and J. Knoop. An Automata-Theoretic Approach to Interprocedural Data-Flow Analysis. *Proceedings of FOSSACS '99*, LNCS 1578:14–30, 1999.

[13] J. Esparza, A. Finkel, and R. Mayr. On the Verification of Broadcast Protocols. In *Proceedings of LICS '99*, 352–359. IEEE Computer Society, 1999.

[14] J. Esparza and A. Podelski. Efficient Algorithms for Pre and Post on Interprocedural Parallel Flow Graphs. In *Proceedings of POPL '00*, 1–11, ACM Press, 2000.

[15] Y. Hirshfeld. Petri Nets and the Equivalence Problem. In *Proceedings of CSL '93*, LNCS 832:165–180, 1994.

[16] J.E. Hopcroft, R. Motwani, and J.D. Ullman. *Introduction to Automata Theory, Languages, and Computation.* Addison-Wesley, 2001.

[17] D.T. Huynh. Commutative Grammars: The Complexity of Uniform Word Problems. *Information and Control*, 57(1):21–39, 1983.

[18] D.T. Huynh. The Complexity of Equivalence Problems for Commutative Grammars. *Information and Control*, 66(1/2):103–121, 1985.

[19] J. Knoop. *Optimal Interprocedural Program Optimization.* LNCS 1428, 1998.

[20] D. Lugiez and Ph. Schnoebelen. The Regular Viewpoint on PA-processes. In *Proceedings of CONCUR '98*, LNCS 1466:50–66, 1998.

[21] R. Mayr. *Decidability and Complexity of Model Checking Problems for Infinite-State Systems.* Ph.D. thesis, Technische Universität München, 1998.

[22] R. Mayr. Process Rewrite Systems. *Information and Computation*, 156(1/2):264–286, 2000.

[23] F. Moller. Infinite Results. In *Proceedings of CONCUR '96*, LNCS 1119:195–216, 1996.

[24] M. Müller-Olm and H. Seidl. On Optimal Slicing of Parallel Programs. In *Proceedings of STOC '01*, 647–656, ACM Press, 2001.

[25] G. Ramalingam. Context-Sensitive Synchronization-Sensitive Analysis Is Undecidable. *ACM Transactions on Programming Languages and Systems*, 22(2):416–430, 2000.

[26] D.A. Schmidt and B. Steffen. Program Analysis as Model Checking of Abstract Interpretations. In *Proceedings of SAS '98*, LNCS 1503:351–380, 1998.

[27] D.A. Schmidt. Data Flow Analysis Is Model Checking of Abstract Interpretation. In *Proceedings of POPL '98*, 38–48, ACM Press, 1998.

[28] H. Seidl and B. Steffen. Constraint-Based Inter-procedural Analysis of Parallel Programs. In *Proceedings of ESOP '00*, LNCS 1782:351–365, 2000.

[29] B. Steffen. Data Flow Analysis as Model Checking. In *Proceedings of TACS '91*, LNCS 526:346–364, 1991.

Temporal Concurrent Constraint Programming: Applications and Behavior

Mogens Nielsen and Frank D. Valencia

BRICS[*], Department of Computer Science, University of Aarhus,
Ny Munkegade, building 540, 8000 Århus C, Denmark
`fvalenci@brics.dk`

Abstract The *ntcc* calculus is a model of non-deterministic temporal concurrent constraint programming. In this paper we study behavioral notions for this calculus. In the underlying computational model, concurrent constraint processes are executed in discrete time intervals. The behavioral notions studied reflect the reactive interactions between concurrent constraint processes and their environment, as well as internal interactions between individual processes. Relationships between the suggested notions are studied, and they are all proved to be decidable for a substantial fragment of the calculus. Furthermore, the expressive power of this fragment is illustrated by examples.

1 Introduction

Concurrent constraint programming [19] has been studied extensively as a paradigm for specifying and programming reactive systems. One of the main features of ccp is that it is based on a declarative as well as operational computational model.

The fundamental primitive of a *constraint* is a partial information on values of variables (e.g. $x + y > 5$). The state of a computation (also called a *store*) is simply a set of constraints, and during a computation, a process may modify the state by telling information. Also, a process may condition its activity by asking for certain information to be entailed by the present store - operationally blocking its activity until other processes provide the requested information (if ever). In this way *concurrent* processes may communicate via the common store of constraints. Processes in ccp are built using the basic primitives of telling and asking constraints, and the operators of parallel composition, hiding and recursion.

The *temporal* ccp computational model introduced in [20] is an extension aimed at specifying timed systems following the paradigms of Synchronous Languages ([2]). Time is conceptually divided into discrete intervals (or time units). In a particular time interval, a ccp process receives a stimulus (i.e. a constraint) from the environment, it executes with this stimulus as the initial store, and

---

[*] Basic Research in Computer Science, Centre of the Danish National Research Foundation.

W. Brauer et al. (Eds.): Formal and Natural Computing, LNCS 2300, pp. 298–321, 2002.

when it reaches its resting point, it responds to the environment with the resulting store. Also the resting point determines a residual process, which is then executed in the next time interval.

This temporal ccp model is inherently deterministic. In [17] a nondeterministic version of the calculus was introduced, adding e.g. (non-deterministic) guarded choice and unbounded-finite delay as new operators in the language of processes. The extension was argued to be consistent with the declarative flavor of ccp, i.e. to free the programmer from over-specifying a deterministic solution, when a non-deterministic simple solution is more appropriate (following the arguments behind Dijkstra's language of guarded commands). Furthermore, it was argued that a very important benefit of allowing the specification of non-deterministic behavior arises when modeling the interaction among several components running in parallel, in which one component is part of the environment of the others. These systems often need non-determinism to be modeled faithfully.

In this paper we introduce and study various notions of behavior for the *ntcc* calculus: the input-output and the language equivalence and their congruences, all motivated operationally and/or logically. The notions are related, and they are all proved to be decidable for a substantial fragment of the calculus. The decidability for the complete calculus is left open.

Furthermore, we illustrate the expressive power of our fragment of *ntcc* by modeling constructs such as cells and some applications involving the programming of RCX[TM] controllers, and a version of a Predator/Prey (Pursuit) game.

2   The Calculus

In this section we present the syntax and an operational semantics of the ntcc calculus. First we recall the notion of constraint system.

2.1   Constraint Systems

Concurrent constraint languages are parameterized by a *constraint system*. Basically, a constraint system defines the underlying universe of the particular language. It provides a signature from which syntactically denotable objects in language called *constraints* can be constructed, and an entailment relation specifying interdependencies between such constraints. For our purposes it will suffice to consider the notion of constraint system based on First-Order Predicate Logic, as it was done in [24][1]

Definition 1. *A constraint system is a pair* (Σ, Δ) *where* Σ *is a signature specifying functions and predicate symbols, and* Δ *is a consistent first-order theory.*

Given a constraint system (Σ, Δ), let $\mathcal{L}$ be the underlying first-order language $(\Sigma, \mathcal{V}, \mathcal{S})$, where $\mathcal{V}$ is a countable set of variables and $\mathcal{S}$ is the set of logical

---

[1] See [22] for a more general notion of constraints based on Scott's information systems.

symbols $\wedge$, $\vee$, $\Rightarrow$, $\neg$, $\exists$, **true** and **false** which denote logical conjunction, disjunction, implication, negation, existential quantification and the always true and false predicates, respectively. *Constraints,* denoted by $c, d, \ldots$ are first-order formulae over $\mathcal{L}$. We say that c *entails* d in Δ, written $c \vdash d$, if the formula $c \Rightarrow d$ holds in all models of Δ. We shall require $\vdash$ to be decidable. We say that c is equivalent to d, written $c \approx d$, iff $c \vdash d$ and $d \vdash c$. We define the (relevant) *free-variables* of c as $fv(c) = \{x \in \mathcal{V} \mid \exists_x c \not\approx c\}$ (e.g., $fv(x = x \wedge y > 1) = \{y\}$).

Henceforth, $\mathcal{C}$ is a set of constraints modulo $\approx$ in (Σ, Δ). The set $\mathcal{C}$ is closed wrt conjunction and existential quantification and it represents the constraints under consideration in the underlying constraint system.

2.2   Process Syntax

Processes P, Q, $\ldots \in Proc$ are built from constraints $c \in \mathcal{C}$ and variables $x \in \mathcal{V}$ in the underlying constraint system by the following syntax:

$$P, Q, \ldots ::= \; \textbf{tell}(c) \;\; \mid \sum_{i \in I} \textbf{when } c_i \textbf{ do } P_i \mid P \parallel Q \; \mid \textbf{local } x \textbf{ in } P$$
$$\mid \;\; \textbf{next } P \mid \textbf{unless } c \textbf{ next } P \mid \; ! P.$$

The only move or action of process **tell**(c) is to add the constraint c to the current store, thus making c available to other processes in the current time interval. The guarded-choice $\sum_{i \in I} \textbf{when } c_i \textbf{ do } P_i$, where I is a finite set of indexes, represents a process that, in the current time interval, must non-deterministically choose one of the P_j $(j \in I)$ whose corresponding constraint c_j is entailed by the store. The chosen alternative, if any, precludes the others. If no choice is possible then the summation is precluded. We use $\sum_{i \in I} P_i$ as an abbreviation for the "blind-choice" process $\sum_{i \in I} \textbf{when } (\textbf{true}) \textbf{ do } P_i$. We use **skip** as an abbreviation of the empty summation and "$+$" for binary summations.

Process $P \parallel Q$ represents the parallel composition of P and Q. In one time unit (or interval) P and Q operate concurrently, "communicating" via the common store. We use $\prod_{i \in I} P_i$, where I is finite, to denote the parallel composition of all P_i. Process **local** x **in** P behaves like P, except that all the information on x produced by P can only be seen by P.

The process **next** P represents the activation of P in the next time interval. Hence, a move of **next** P is a unit-delay of P. The process **unless** c **next** P is similar, but P will be activated only if c cannot be inferred from the current store. The "unless" processes add (weak) time-outs to the calculus, i.e., they wait one time unit for a piece of information c to be present and if it is not, they trigger activity in the next time interval. We use $\textbf{next}^n(P)$ as an abbreviation for $\textbf{next}(\textbf{next}(\ldots(\textbf{next } P)\ldots))$, where **next** is repeated n times.

The operator "!" is a delayed version of the replication operator for the π−calculus ([15]): $!P$ represents $P \parallel \textbf{next } P \parallel \textbf{next}^2 P \parallel \ldots$, i.e. unboundely many copies of P but one at a time. The replication operator is the only way of defining infinite behavior through the time intervals.

Our process language is essentially the language of the calculus ntcc from [17], but in order to unify and to simplify the presentation of our technical results, we have omitted the unbounded finite delay operator. As we shall clarify, it is not clear to what extent all our results generalize to the full language of ntcc.

2.3   An Operational Semantics

Operationally, the current information is represented as a constraint $c \in \mathcal{C}$, so-called *store*. Our operational semantics is given by considering transitions between *configurations* γ of the form $\langle P, c \rangle$. We define Γ as the set of all configurations. Following standard lines, we extend the syntax with a construct **local** (x, d) **in** P, which represents the evolution of a process of the form **local** x **in** Q, where d is the local information (or store) produced during this evolution. Initially d is "empty", so we regard **local** x **in** P as **local** $(x, \mathbf{true})$ **in** P.

We need to introduce a notion of free variables that is invariant wrt the equivalence on constraints. We can do so by defining the "relevant" free variables of c as $fv(c) = \{x \in \mathcal{V} \mid \exists_x c \not\approx c\}$. For the bound variables, define $bv(c) = \{x \in \mathcal{V} \mid x$ occurs in $c\} - fv(c)$. Regarding processes, define $fv(\mathbf{tell}(c)) = fv(c)$, $fv(\sum_i \mathbf{when}\ c_i\ \mathbf{do}\ P_i) = \bigcup_i fv(c_i) \cup fv(P_i)$, $fv(\mathbf{local}\ x\ \mathbf{in}\ P) = fv(P) - \{x\}$. The bound variables and the other cases are defined analogously.

Definition 2 (Structural Congruence). *Let $\equiv$ be the smallest congruence over processes satisfying the following laws:*

1. $(Proc/_{\equiv}, \|, \mathbf{skip})$ *is a symmetric monoid.*
2. $P \equiv Q$ *if they only differ by a renaming of bound variables.*
3. $\mathbf{next\ skip} \equiv \mathbf{skip}$ $\qquad \mathbf{next}(P \parallel Q) \equiv \mathbf{next}\ P \parallel \mathbf{next}\ Q$.
4. $\mathbf{local}\ x\ \mathbf{in\ skip} \equiv \mathbf{skip}$ $\quad \mathbf{local}\ x\ y\ \mathbf{in}\ P \equiv \mathbf{local}\ y\ x\ \mathbf{in}\ P$.
5. $\mathbf{local}\ x\ \mathbf{in\ next}\ P \equiv \mathbf{next}(\mathbf{local}\ x\ \mathbf{in}\ P)$.
6. $\mathbf{local}\ x\ \mathbf{in}\ (P \parallel Q) \equiv P \parallel \mathbf{local}\ x\ \mathbf{in}\ Q \quad if \quad x \notin fv(P)$.

We extend $\equiv$ to configurations by defining $\langle P, c \rangle \equiv \langle Q, c \rangle$ if $P \equiv Q$.

The reduction relations $\longrightarrow\ \subseteq \Gamma \times \Gamma$ and $\Longrightarrow\ \subseteq Proc \times \mathcal{C} \times \mathcal{C} \times Proc$ are the least relations satisfying the rules appearing in Table 1. The *internal transition* $\langle P, c \rangle \longrightarrow \langle Q, d \rangle$ should be read as "P with store c reduces, in one internal step, to Q with store d". The *observable transition* $P \xRightarrow{(c,d)} Q$ should be read as "P on input c reduces, in one time unit, to Q with store d". As in tcc, the store does not transfer automatically from one interval to another.

We now give a description of the operational rules. Rules TELL, CHOICE, PAR and LOC are standard [22]. Rule UNLESS says that if c is entailed by the current store, then the execution of the process P (in the next time interval) is precluded. Rule REPL specifies that the process $!\,P$ produces a copy P at the current time unit, and then persists in the next time unit. Rule STRUCT simply says that structurally congruent processes have the same reductions.

Rule OBS says that an observable transition from P labeled by (c, d) is obtained by performing a terminating sequence of internal transitions from $\langle P, c \rangle$ to $\langle Q, d \rangle$, for some Q. The process to be executed in the next time interval, $F(Q)$ ("future" of Q), is obtained by removing from Q what was meant to be executed only in the current time interval and any local information which has been stored in Q, and by "unfolding" the sub-terms within **next** R expressions. More precisely:

Definition 3 (Future Function). *The partial function* $F : Proc \rightharpoonup Proc$ *is defined as follows:*

$$F(P) = \begin{cases} Q & \text{if } P = \mathbf{next}\ Q \text{ or } P = \mathbf{unless}\ c\ \mathbf{next}\ Q \\ F(P_1) \parallel F(P_2) & \text{if } P = P_1 \parallel P_2 \\ \mathbf{local}\ x\ \mathbf{in}\ F(Q) & \text{if } P = \mathbf{local}\,(x,c)\ \mathbf{in}\ Q \\ \mathbf{skip} & \text{if } P = \sum_{i \in I} \mathbf{when}\ c_i\ \mathbf{do}\ P_i \end{cases}$$

Remark: Function F does not need to be total since whenever we apply F to a process P (Rule OBS in Table 1), all replications operators in P occur within a next construction.

TELL	$\langle \mathbf{tell}(c), d \rangle \longrightarrow \langle \mathbf{skip}, d \wedge c \rangle$
CHOICE	$\langle \sum_{i \in I} \mathbf{when}\ c_i\ \mathbf{do}\ P_i, d \rangle \longrightarrow \langle P_j, d \rangle \quad$ if $d \vdash c_j$, for $j \in I$
PAR	$\dfrac{\langle P, c \rangle \longrightarrow \langle P', d \rangle}{\langle P \parallel Q, c \rangle \longrightarrow \langle P' \parallel Q, d \rangle}$
LOC	$\dfrac{\left\langle P, c \wedge \dot{\exists}_x d \right\rangle \longrightarrow \langle Q, c' \rangle}{\langle \mathbf{local}\,(x,c)\ \mathbf{in}\ P, d \rangle \longrightarrow \left\langle \mathbf{local}\,(x,c')\ \mathbf{in}\ Q, d \wedge \dot{\exists}_x c' \right\rangle}$
UNLESS	$\langle \mathbf{unless}\ c\ \mathbf{next}\ P, d \rangle \longrightarrow \langle \mathbf{skip}, d \rangle \quad$ if $d \vdash c$
REPL	$\langle\, !\, P, c \rangle \longrightarrow \langle P \parallel \mathbf{next}\, !\, P, c \rangle$
STRUCT	$\dfrac{\gamma_1 \equiv \gamma_1' \quad \gamma_1' \longrightarrow \gamma_2' \quad \gamma_2' \equiv \gamma_2}{\gamma_1 \longrightarrow \gamma_2}$
OBS	$\dfrac{\langle P, c \rangle \longrightarrow^* \langle Q, d \rangle \nrightarrow}{P \xrightarrow{(c,d)} F(Q)}$

Table 1. An operational semantics for ntcc. The upper part defines the internal transitions while the lower part defines the observable transitions. The function F, used in OBS, is given in Definition 3

Interpreting Processes Runs. Henceforward we use α, α' to represent elements of C^{ω}. Let us consider the sequence of observable transitions

$$P = P_1 \xrightarrow{(c_1, c_1')} P_2 \xrightarrow{(c_2, c_2')} P_3 \xrightarrow{(c_3, c_3')} \ldots$$

This sequence can be interpreted as a *interaction* between the system P and an environment. At the time unit i, the environment provides a *stimulus* c_i and P_i produces c_i' as *response*. We then regard (α, α') as a *reactive* observation of P. If $\alpha = c_1.c_2.c_3.\ldots$ and $\alpha' = c_1'.c_2'.c_3'\ldots$, we represent the above interaction as $P \xrightarrow{(\alpha, \alpha')} {}^{\omega}$. Given P we shall refer to the set of all its reactive observations as the *input-output behavior* of P.

Alternatively, if $\alpha = \texttt{true}^{\omega}$, we can interpret the run as an interaction among the parallel components in P without the influence of an external environment (i.e., each component is part of the environment of the others). In this case α is called the *empty* input sequence and α' is regarded as a *timed* observation of such an interaction in P. We shall refer to the set of all timed observations of a process P as the *language* of P.

In section 4 we study in detail input-output behavior and language of processes.

Notation 1 *Throughout the paper we use the following notation on transitions:*
1) $P \longrightarrow Q$ *iff*   *for some* c, $\langle P, c \rangle \longrightarrow \langle Q, c' \rangle$.
2) $P \Longrightarrow Q$ *iff* $P \longrightarrow^* P' \not\longrightarrow$ *and* $Q = F(P')$.
3) $P \xLongrightarrow{c} Q$ *iff* $P \xrightarrow{(\texttt{true}, c)} Q$.
4) $P \xLongrightarrow{\alpha} {}^{\omega}$ *iff* $P \xrightarrow{(\texttt{true}^{\omega}, \alpha)} {}^{\omega}$.

2.4 A Logic of ntcc Processes

A relatively complete formal system for proving whether or not an ntcc process satisfies a linear-temporal property was introduced in [17]. In this section we summarize these results.

We extend the ccp notion of strongest postcondition of a process P ([6]), $sp(P)$, to our setting. In ntcc, $sp(P)$ denotes the set of all infinite sequences that P can possibly output. More precisely,

Definition 4. *Given P its* strongest postcondition *is defined as*

$$sp(P) = \{\alpha' \mid for\ some\ \alpha : P \xrightarrow{(\alpha, \alpha')} {}^{\omega}\}.$$

Temporal Logic. We define a linear temporal logic for expressing properties of ntcc processes. The formulae $A, B, \ldots \in \mathcal{A}$ are defined by the grammar

$$A := c \mid A \dot{\Rightarrow} A \mid \dot{\neg} A \mid \dot{\exists}_x A \mid \bigcirc A \mid \Box A \mid \Diamond A,$$

where c denotes an arbitrary constraint. The intended meaning of the other symbols is the following: $\dot{\Rightarrow}$, $\dot{\neg}$ and $\dot{\exists}$ represent linear-temporal logic implication, negation and existential quantification. These symbols are not to be confused with the symbols $\Rightarrow, \neg$ and $\exists$ in the underlying constraint system. The symbols $\circ$, $\Box$, and $\Diamond$ denote the temporal operators *next*, *always* and *sometime*. We use $A \dot{\vee} B$ as an abbreviation of $\dot{\neg} A \dot{\Rightarrow} B$ and $A \dot{\wedge} B$ as an abbreviation of $\dot{\neg}(\dot{\neg} A \dot{\vee} \dot{\neg} B)$.

The semantics of the logic is given in Definition 5. The standard interpretation structures of linear temporal logic are infinite sequences of states [14]. In the case of ntcc, states are represented by constraints, thus we consider as interpretations the elements of $\mathcal{C}^\omega$.

Definition 5. *We say that* $\alpha \in \mathcal{C}^\omega$ *is a model of* A, *notation* $\alpha \models A$, *if* $\langle \alpha, 1 \rangle \models A$, *where:*

$\langle \alpha, i \rangle \models c$	*iff*	$\alpha(i) \vdash c$
$\langle \alpha, i \rangle \models \dot{\neg} A$	*iff*	$\langle \alpha, i \rangle \not\models A$
$\langle \alpha, i \rangle \models A_1 \dot{\Rightarrow} A_2$	*iff*	$\langle \alpha, i \rangle \models A_1$ *implies* $\langle \alpha, i \rangle \models A_2$
$\langle \alpha, i \rangle \models \circ A$	*iff*	$\langle \alpha, i+1 \rangle \models A$
$\langle \alpha, i \rangle \models \Box A$	*iff*	*for all* $j \geq i$ $\langle \alpha, j \rangle \models A$
$\langle \alpha, i \rangle \models \Diamond A$	*iff*	*there exists* $j \geq i$ *s.t.* $\langle \alpha, j \rangle \models A$
$\langle \alpha, i \rangle \models \dot{\exists}_x A$	*iff*	*there exists* $\alpha' \in \mathcal{C}^\omega$ *s.t.* $\exists_x \alpha = \exists_x \alpha'$ *and* $\langle \alpha', i \rangle \models A$,

where $\exists_x \alpha$ *represents the sequence obtained by applying* $\exists_x$ *to each constraint in* α. *Notation* $\alpha(i)$ *denotes the i-th element in* α. *We define* $\llbracket A \rrbracket$ *to be the collection of all models of* A, *i.e.* $\llbracket A \rrbracket = \{ \alpha \mid \alpha \models A \}$.

We shall say that P *satisfies* A iff every infinite sequence that P can possibly output satisfies the property expressed by A, i.e. $sp(P) \subseteq \llbracket A \rrbracket$. A relatively complete proof system for assertions $P \vdash A$, whose intended meaning is that P satisfies A, can be found in [17]. We shall write $P \vdash A$ if there is a derivation of $P \vdash A$ in this system.

3   Applications

Let us assume that the underlying constraint system is $FD[max]$ which has $\{\texttt{succ}, \texttt{prd}, +, \times, =, <, >, 0, 1, \ldots\}$ as signature and the set of sentences valid in arithmetic modulo max as theory. Henceforth, we designate Dom as the set $\{0, 1, \ldots, max - 1\}$ and use v and w to range over its elements.

It will be convenient to specify our applications using defining equations of the form $q(x_1, \ldots, x_m) \stackrel{\text{def}}{=} P_q$. In ntcc we encode definitions of this sort provided that P_q contains at most one occurrence of q which must be within the scope of a "**next**" and out of the scope of any "!". The reason for such a restriction is that we want to keep the response time of the system bounded: we do not want P_q to make unboundely many recursive calls within a time interval. The intended behavior of a call of q with arguments $t_1, \ldots, t_m$, written $\ulcorner q(t_1, \ldots, t_m) \urcorner$, when

$t_i = v_i$ in the current store, is that of $P_q[v_1/x_1, \dots, v_m/x_m]$ [2]. The encoding of a process definition requires the use of replication and, if the definition is recursive or it has at least one parameter, also hiding (see [18] for the exact details of the encoding).

3.1 Cell Example

Cells provide a basis for the specification and analysis of mutable and persistent data structures as shown for the π calculus. We assume that the signature is extended with an unary predicate symbol **change**. A *mutable cell* $x\colon (v)$ can be viewed as a structure x which has a current value v and can, in the future, be assigned a new value.

$$x\colon (z) \quad \overset{\text{def}}{=} \textbf{tell}(x = z) \; \| \; \textbf{unless change}(x) \; \textbf{next} \; x\colon (z)$$

$$g_{\text{exch}}(x, y) \overset{\text{def}}{=} \textstyle\sum_v \textbf{when} \; (x = v) \; \textbf{do} \; (\; \textbf{tell}(\text{change}(x)) \quad \| \; \textbf{tell}(\text{change}(y)) \; \| $$
$$\textbf{next}(\; \ulcorner x\colon (g(v)) \urcorner \;) \; \| \; \textbf{next}(\; \ulcorner y\colon (v) \urcorner) \;).$$

Definition $x\colon (z)$ represents a cell x whose value is z and it will be the same in the next time interval unless it is to be changed next (i.e., $\text{change}(x)$). Definition $g_{\text{exch}}(x, y)$ represents an exchange operation between the contents of x and y. If v is x's current value then $g(v)$ and v will be the next values of x and y respectively. In the case of functions that always return the same value (i.e. constants), we take the liberty of using that value as its symbol. For example, $\ulcorner x\colon (3) \urcorner \; \| \; \ulcorner y\colon (5) \urcorner \; \| \; \ulcorner 7_{exch}(x, y) \urcorner$ gives us the cells $x\colon (7)$ and $y\colon (3)$ in the next time interval. The assignment of v to a cell x, written $x \; := \; v$, can then be encoded as **local** y **in** $\ulcorner v_{\text{exch}}(x, y) \urcorner$ where the local variable y is used as dummy variable (cell).

The following temporal property states the invariant behavior of a cell, i.e., if it satisfies A now, it will satisfy A next unless it is changed.

Proposition 1. $\ulcorner x\colon (v) \urcorner \vdash (A \wedge \dot{\neg} \, \text{change}(x)) \Rightarrow \circ A$.

3.2 The Zigzagging Example

An RCX is a programmable, controller-based LEGO® brick used to create autonomous robotic devices ([13]). Zigzagging [7] is a task in which an (RCX-based) robot can go either forward, left, or right but (1) it cannot go forward if its preceding action was to go forward, (2) it cannot turn right if its second-to-last action was to go right, and (3) it cannot turn left if its second-to-last action was to go left. In order to model this problem, *without over-specifying it* , we use guarded choice. We use cells a_1 and a_2 to "look back" one and two time units,

---

[2] $[v_1/x_1, \dots, v_m/x_m]$ is the operation of (syntactical) replacement of every occurrence of the x_i by v_i

respectively. We use three distinct constants $\mathtt{f},\mathtt{r},\mathtt{l} \in Dom - \{0\}$ and extend the signature with the predicate symbols $\mathtt{forward},\mathtt{right},\mathtt{left}$.

$$GoF \quad \stackrel{\mathrm{def}}{=} \quad \ulcorner \mathtt{f}_{\mathrm{exch}}(a_1, a_2) \urcorner \parallel \mathbf{tell}(\mathtt{forward})$$

$$GoR \quad \stackrel{\mathrm{def}}{=} \quad \ulcorner \mathtt{r}_{\mathrm{exch}}(a_1, a_2) \urcorner \parallel \mathbf{tell}(\mathtt{right})$$

$$GoL \quad \stackrel{\mathrm{def}}{=} \quad \ulcorner \mathtt{l}_{\mathrm{exch}}(a_1, a_2) \urcorner \parallel \mathbf{tell}(\mathtt{left})$$

$$Zigzag \quad \stackrel{\mathrm{def}}{=} \quad !\, (\quad \mathbf{when}\ (a_1 \neq \mathtt{f})\ \mathbf{do}\ \ulcorner GoF \urcorner$$
$$+\, \mathbf{when}\ (a_2 \neq \mathtt{r})\ \mathbf{do}\ \ulcorner GoR \urcorner$$
$$+\, \mathbf{when}\ (a_2 \neq \mathtt{l})\ \mathbf{do}\ \ulcorner GoL \urcorner\ )$$

$$GoZigzag \quad \stackrel{\mathrm{def}}{=} \quad \ulcorner a_1\!:\!(0) \urcorner \parallel \ulcorner a_2\!:\!(0) \urcorner \parallel \ulcorner Zigzag \urcorner.$$

Initially cells a_1 and a_2 contain neither $\mathtt{f}, r$ nor $\mathtt{l}$. After a choice is made according to (1), (2) and (3), it is recorded in a_1 and the previous one moved to a_2. The property below states that the robot indeed goes right and left infinitely often.

Proposition 2. $\ulcorner GoZigzag \urcorner \vdash \Box(\Diamond \mathtt{right} \wedge \Diamond \mathtt{left})$.

3.3   Multi-agent Systems: The Pursuit Game Example

The Predator/Prey (or Pursuit) game [1] has been studied using a wide variety of approaches [11] and it has many different instantiations that can be used to illustrate different multi-agent scenarios [25]. As the Zigzagging example, instances of the Predator/Prey game have been modeled using autonomous robots [16]. Here we model a simple instance of this game.

The predators and prey move around in a discrete, grid-like toroidal world with square spaces; they can move off one end of the board and come back on the other end. Predators and prey move simultaneously. They can move vertically and horizontally in any direction. In order to simulate fast but not very precise predators and a slower but more maneuverable prey we assume that predators move two squares in straight line while the prey moves just one.

The goal of the predators is to "capture" the prey. A capture position occurs when the prey moves into a position which is within the three-squares line of a predator current move; i.e. if for some of the predators, the prey current position is either the predator current position, the predator previous position, or the square between these two positions. This simulates the prey deadly moving through the line of attack of a predator.

For simplicity, we assume that initially the predators are in the same row immediately next to each other, while the prey is in front of a predator (i.e, in the same column, above this predator) one square from it. The prey's maneuver to try to escape is to move in an unpredictable zigzagging around the world. The strategy of the predators is to cooperate to catch the prey. Whenever one of the predators is in front of the prey it declares itself as the leader of the attack and the other becomes its support. Therefore depending on the moves of the prey the role of leader can be alternated between the predators. The leader moves towards the prey, i.e. if it sees the prey above it then it moves up, if it sees the prey below it then it moves down, and so on. The support predator moves in the direction the leader moves, thus making sure it is always next to leader.

In order to model this example we extend the signature with the predicates symbols $\mathtt{right}_i, \mathtt{left}_i, \mathtt{up}_i, \mathtt{down}_i$ for $i \in \{0,1\}$. For simplicity we assume there are only two predators $Pred_0$ and $Pred_1$. We use the cells x_i, y_i and cells x, y for representing the current positions of predator i and the prey, respectively, in a $max \times max$ matrix (with $max = 2^k$ for some $k > 1$) representing the world. We also use the primed version of these cells to keep track of corresponding previous positions and cell l to remember which predator is the current leader. We can now formulate the capture condition. Predator i captures the prey with a horizontal move iff

$$x_i' = x = x_i \wedge (\ (y_i = y_i' - 2 \wedge (y = y_i' \vee y = y_i' - 1 \vee y = y_i' - 2)) \vee$$
$$(y_i = y_i' + 2 \wedge (y = y_i' \vee y = y_i' + 1 \vee y = y_i' + 2))\ )$$

and with a vertical move iff

$$y_i' = y = y_i \wedge (\ (x_i = x_i' - 2 \wedge (x = x_i' \vee x = x_i' - 1 \vee x = x_i' - 2)) \vee$$
$$(x_i = x_i' + 2 \wedge (x = x_i' \vee x = x_i' + 1 \vee x = x_i' + 2))\ ).$$

We define $\mathtt{capture}_i$ as the conjunction of the two previous constraints.

The process below models the behavior of the prey. The preys moves as in the Zigzagging example. Furthermore, the values of cells x, y and x', y' are updated according to the zigzag move (e.g., if it goes right the value of x is increased and x' takes x's previous value).

$$Prey \stackrel{\text{def}}{=} \ulcorner GoZigzag \urcorner \ \| \ !(\ \textbf{when forward do} \ \ulcorner \mathtt{succ}_{\mathrm{exch}}(y, y') \urcorner$$
$$+\ \textbf{when right} \quad \textbf{do} \ \ulcorner \mathtt{succ}_{\mathrm{exch}}(x, x') \urcorner$$
$$+\ \textbf{when left} \quad \textbf{do} \ \ulcorner \mathtt{prd}_{\mathrm{exch}}(x, x') \urcorner).$$

The process $Pred_i$ with $i \in \{0,1\}$ models the behavior of predator i. The operator $\oplus$ denotes binary summation.

$$Pred_i \stackrel{\text{def}}{=} \ !(\ \textbf{when } x_i = x \qquad\qquad \textbf{do}\ (\ulcorner l := i \urcorner \ \| \ \ulcorner Pursuit_i \urcorner)$$
$$+\ \textbf{when } l = i \wedge x_{i \oplus 1} \neq x \quad \textbf{do}\ \ulcorner Pursuit_i \urcorner$$
$$+\ \textbf{when } l = i \oplus 1 \wedge x_i \neq x \ \textbf{do}\ \ulcorner Support_i \urcorner \ ).$$

Thus whenever $Pred_i$ is in front of the prey (i.e. $x_i = x$) it declares itself as the leader by assigning i to the cell l. Then it runs process $Pursuit_i$ defined below and keep doing it until the other predator $Pred_{i \oplus 1}$ declares itself the leader. If the other process is the leader then $Pred_i$ runs process $Support_i$ defined below.

Process $Pursuit_i$, whenever the prey is above of corresponding predator ($y_i < y \wedge x_i = x$), tells the other predator that the move is to go up and increases by two the contents of y_i while keeping in cell y_i' the previous value. The other cases which correspond to going left, right and down can be described similarly.

$$Pursuit_i \overset{\text{def}}{=} \quad \textbf{when } (y_i < y \wedge x_i = x) \textbf{ do } (\ulcorner \texttt{succ}^2_{\text{exch}}(y_i, y_i') \urcorner \parallel \textbf{tell}(\texttt{up}_i))$$
$$+ \textbf{when } (y_i > y \wedge x_i = x) \textbf{ do } (\ulcorner \texttt{prd}^2_{\text{exch}}(y_i, y_i') \urcorner \parallel \textbf{tell}(\texttt{down}_i))$$
$$+ \textbf{when } (x_i < x \wedge y_i = y) \textbf{ do } (\ulcorner \texttt{succ}^2_{\text{exch}}(x_i, x_i') \urcorner \parallel \textbf{tell}(\texttt{right}_i))$$
$$+ \textbf{when } (x_i > x \wedge y_i = y) \textbf{ do } (\ulcorner \texttt{prd}^2_{\text{exch}}(x_i, x_i') \urcorner \parallel \textbf{tell}(\texttt{left}_i)).$$

The process $Support_i$ is defined according to the move decision of the leader. Hence, if the leader moves up (e.g. $\texttt{up}_{i\oplus 1}$) then the support predator moves up as well. The other cases are similar.

$$Support_i \overset{\text{def}}{=} \quad \textbf{when } \texttt{up}_{i\oplus 1} \quad \textbf{do } (\ulcorner \texttt{succ}^2_{\text{exch}}(y_i, y_i') \urcorner \parallel \textbf{tell}(\texttt{up}_i))$$
$$+ \textbf{when } \texttt{down}_{i\oplus 1} \quad \textbf{do } (\ulcorner \texttt{prd}^2_{\text{exch}}(y_i, y_i') \urcorner \quad \parallel \textbf{tell}(\texttt{down}_i))$$
$$+ \textbf{when } \texttt{right}_{i\oplus 1} \textbf{ do } (\ulcorner \texttt{succ}^2_{\text{exch}}(x_i, x_i') \urcorner \parallel \textbf{tell}(\texttt{right}_i))$$
$$+ \textbf{when } \texttt{left}_{i\oplus 1} \quad \textbf{do } (\ulcorner \texttt{prd}^2_{\text{exch}}(x_i, x_i') \urcorner \quad \parallel \textbf{tell}(\texttt{left}_i)).$$

We assume that initially $Pred_0$ is the leader and that it is in the first row in the middle column . The other predator is next to it in the same row. The prey is just above $Pred_0$. The process $Init$ below specifies these conditions. Let $p = max/2$.

$$Init \overset{\text{def}}{=} \prod_{i\in 0,1} (\ulcorner x_i : (p+i) \urcorner \parallel \ulcorner y_i : (0) \urcorner \parallel \ulcorner x_i' : (p+i) \urcorner \parallel \ulcorner y_i' : (0) \urcorner$$
$$\parallel \ulcorner x : (p) \urcorner \parallel \ulcorner y : (1) \urcorner \parallel \ulcorner x' : (p) \urcorner \parallel \ulcorner y_i' : (1) \urcorner \parallel \ulcorner l : 0 \urcorner.$$

The proposition states that the predators eventually capture the prey under our initial conditions.

Proposition 3. $Init \parallel Pred_0 \parallel Pred_1 \parallel Prey \vdash \Diamond(\texttt{capture}_0 \,\dot\vee\, \texttt{capture}_1).$

It is worth noticing that in the case of one single predator, say $Pred_0$, the prey may sometimes escape under the same initial conditions, i.e. $Init \parallel Pred_0 \parallel Prey \not\vdash \Diamond\texttt{capture}_0$. A similar situation occurs if the predators were not allowed to alternate the leader role.

4   Behavioral Equivalence

In this section we introduce notions of equality for our calculus. We wish to distinguish between the observable behavior of two processes if the distinction can somehow be detected by a process interacting with them. A natural observation we can make of a process is its input-output behavior, i.e. its infinite sequences of input-output constraints.

Furthermore, in Section 2.3 we mentioned that we can model the behavior of processes in which each component is part of the environment of the others. Thus the only "external" input is the empty one, i.e., $\textbf{true}^\omega$. Therefore, another interesting observation to make is the set of outputs on the empty sequence, which we shall call the language of a process.

We now introduce the observables and the corresponding equivalences we are interested in.

Definition 6. *Given P, the* input-output behavior *of P and the* language *of P are defined as*

$$io(P) = \{(\alpha, \alpha') \mid P \xrightarrow{(\alpha,\alpha')} {}^{\omega}\} \quad and \quad \mathcal{L}(P) = \{\alpha \mid P \xrightarrow{(\text{true}^{\omega},\alpha)} {}^{\omega}\},$$

respectively. For all P and Q, we define $P \sim_{io} Q$ iff $io(P) = io(Q)$ and $P \sim_{\mathcal{L}} Q$ iff $\mathcal{L}(P) = \mathcal{L}(Q)$.

Unfortunately, the equivalences $\sim_{io}$ and $\sim_{\mathcal{L}}$ are not preserved by process constructions, i.e. they are not *congruences*.

Example 1. Assume that a, b, c are non-equivalent constraints such that $c \vdash b \vdash a$. Let

$$P = \textbf{when true do tell}(a) \; + \; \textbf{when } (b) \textbf{ do tell}(c)$$
$$Q = \textbf{when true do tell}(a) \; + \; \textbf{when } (b) \textbf{ do tell}(c)$$
$$+$$
$$\textbf{when true do } (\textbf{tell}(a) \parallel \textbf{when } (b) \textbf{ do tell}(c))$$

and let $R = \textbf{when } a \textbf{ do tell}(b)$. We leave it to the reader to verify that we can distinguish P from Q if we make R to interact with them, i.e. although $P \sim_{io} Q$ (and thus $P \sim_{\mathcal{L}} Q$) we have $R \parallel P \not\sim_{\mathcal{L}} R \parallel Q$ (and thus $R \parallel P \not\sim_{io} R \parallel Q$).

Therefore, we ought to consider the largest congruences included in $\sim_{io}$ and $\sim_{\mathcal{L}}$, respectively. More precisely,

Definition 7. *For all P and Q, $P \approx_{io} Q$ iff for every process context $C[.]$, $C[P] \sim_{io} C[Q]$, and $P \approx_{\mathcal{L}} Q$ iff for every process context $C[.]$, $C[P] \sim_{\mathcal{L}} C[Q]$.*

As usual a process context $C[.]$ is a process term with a single hole such that placing a process in the hole yields a well-formed process. The relations $\approx_{io}$ and $\approx_{\mathcal{L}}$ are then our first proper notion of equality for the calculus.

It is important to point out that the mismatch between $\approx_{io}$ and $\sim_{io}$ arises from allowing nondeterminism. In fact, the following result follows from ([18], Theorem 3).

Definition 8. *A process P is said to be* deterministic *iff for every construct of the form $\sum_{i \in I} \textbf{when } c_i \textbf{ do } P_i$ in P, the c_i's are mutually exclusive.*

Proposition 4. *For all deterministic processes P and Q, $P \approx_{io} Q$ iff $P \sim_{io} Q$.*

The reason for using the name "deterministic process" is because given an input, the output of a process of this kind is always the same independently of the execution order of its parallel component [22].

Let us now see the relation between the different equivalences for arbitrary processes. The relation $\equiv$ denotes structural congruence (Definition 2). For technical purposes we consider the finite prefixes of the language of a process. Let $\mathcal{L}^i(P) = \{\alpha^i \mid \alpha \in \mathcal{L}(P)\}$ where α^i is the $i-th$ prefix of α and define $P \sim_{\mathcal{L}}^i Q$ iff $\mathcal{L}^i(P) = \mathcal{L}^i(Q)$. Obviously, relation $\sim_{\mathcal{L}}$ is weaker than $\sim_{io}$, however, the corresponding congruences coincide.

Theorem 1. $\equiv \subset \approx_{io} = \approx_{\mathcal{L}} \subset \sim_{io} \subset \sim_{\mathcal{L}} = \bigcap_{n \in \omega} \sim_{\mathcal{L}}^n$.

Proof. The proper inclusions are left for the reader to verify. The final equality follows from the fact that our calculus is finitely branching. Here we prove $\approx_{io} = \approx_{\mathcal{L}}$. The case $\approx_{io} \subseteq \approx_{\mathcal{L}}$ is trivial. We want to prove that $P \approx_{\mathcal{L}} Q$ implies $P \approx_{io} Q$. Suppose that $P \approx_{\mathcal{L}} Q$ but $P \not\approx_{io} Q$. Then there must exist a context $C[.]$ s.t $C[P] \not\approx_{io} C[Q]$. Consider the case $io(C[P]) \not\supseteq io(C[Q])$. Take an $\alpha = c_1.c_2 \ldots$ such that $(\alpha, \alpha') \in io(C[Q])$ but $(\alpha, \alpha') \notin io(C[P])$. There must then be a prefix of α' which differs from all other prefixes of sequences α'' s.t. $(\alpha, \alpha'') \in io(C[P])$. Suppose that this is the $n-$th prefix. One can verify that for the context

$$C'[.] = C[.] \parallel \prod_{i \leq n} \mathbf{next}^i \, \mathbf{tell}(c_i),$$

$\mathcal{L}(C'[P]) \neq \mathcal{L}(C'[Q])$. This contradicts our assumption $P \approx_{\mathcal{L}} Q$. The case $io(C[Q]) \not\supseteq io([P])$ is symmetric. Therefore $P \not\approx_{\mathcal{L}} Q$ as required. $\square$

We next investigate the type of contexts $C[.]$ in ntcc needed to verify $P \approx_{io} Q$ and focus on relation $\approx_{\mathcal{L}}$ as it is equivalent to $\approx_{io}$. The proposition below allows us to approximate the behavior of $!P$.

Proposition 5. *For all* $P, Q, n \geq 0$: $Q \parallel !P \sim_{\mathcal{L}}^n Q \parallel \prod_{i \leq n} \mathbf{next}^i P$.

The next proposition states that it is sufficient to consider parallel contexts.

Lemma 1. $P \approx_{\mathcal{L}} Q$ *iff for all* R, $R \parallel P \sim_{\mathcal{L}} R \parallel Q$.

Proof. Suppose that for all R, $P \parallel R \sim_{\mathcal{L}} Q \parallel R$. We can prove that for all contexts $C[.]$, $C[P] \parallel R \sim_{\mathcal{L}} C[Q] \parallel R$ for an arbitrary R. Here we outline the proof of the next and replication context cases. The other cases are trivial. For the next case we have $\mathbf{next} \, P \parallel R \xRightarrow{(c,c')} P \parallel R'$ iff $R \xRightarrow{(c,c')} R'$. Similarly, $\mathbf{next} \, Q \parallel R \xRightarrow{(c,c')} Q \parallel R'$ iff $R \xRightarrow{(c,c')} R'$. Thus, the result follows immediately from the initial assumption. As for the replication case, from the Prop. 5 for all n, $R \parallel !P \sim_{\mathcal{L}}^n R \parallel \prod_{i \leq n} \mathbf{next}^i P$ and $R \parallel !Q \sim_{\mathcal{L}}^n R \parallel \prod_{i \leq n} \mathbf{next}^i Q$. With the help of Theorem 1 ($\sim_{\mathcal{L}} = \bigcap_{n \in \omega} \sim_{\mathcal{L}}^n$) we get that $R \parallel !P \sim_{\mathcal{L}} R \parallel !Q$ if for all $n \geq 0$, $R \parallel !P \sim_{\mathcal{L}}^n R \parallel !Q$. The result now follows from the next and parallel cases. $\square$

Moreover, if $\mathcal{C}$ (i.e., the underlying set of constraints) is finite we have the notion of a *universal context*, i.e., a context that can distinguish any two processes iff they are not language (or input-output) congruent. Intuitively, the idea is to provide a single process that can simulate all possible interactions that a process can have with others.

Consider $R \parallel P$ with P and R as in Example 1. By telling information, process P provides information which influences the evolution of R, i.e., the constraint a. Similarly, R influences the evolution of P by providing the constraint b. Thus asking a and then telling b is one possible interaction a process can have with P while telling a and then asking b is a possible interaction a process can have with R. In general, interactions can be represented as strictly increasing and alternating sequences of ask and tell operations (see [22]).

In the following we write $c' \prec c$ iff $c \vdash c'$ and $c \not\vdash c'$. The assertion $S \subseteq_{fin} S'$ holds iff S is a finite subset of S'. Given $S \subseteq_{fin} \mathcal{C}$, $ic(S)$ denotes the set of strictly increasing sequences in S^*, i.e., $ic(S) = \{c_1 \ldots c_n \in S^* \mid c_1 \prec c_2 \prec \ldots \prec c_n\}$. Furthermore, we extend the underlying constraint system signature Σ to a signature Σ' with unary predicates tr_β for each $\beta \in C^*$. These predicates are "private" in the sense that they are only allowed to occur in the process contexts $\mathcal{U}^S[.]$ defined below.

Definition 9. *The* distinguishing context *wrt* $S \subseteq_{fin} \mathcal{C}$, *written* $\mathcal{U}^S[.]$, *is defined as*

$$! \left(\sum_{\beta \in ic(S)} \textbf{tell}(tr_\beta) \parallel \mathcal{T}_\beta \right) \parallel [.]$$

where for each $\beta \in S^*$, $\mathcal{T}_{c.\beta} = \textbf{tell}(c) \parallel \mathcal{W}_\beta$ *and* $\mathcal{W}_{c.\beta} = \textbf{when } c \textbf{ do } \mathcal{T}_\beta$ *with* $\mathcal{T}_\epsilon = \mathcal{W}_\epsilon = \textbf{skip}$.

Theorem 2. *Suppose that* $\mathcal{C}$ *is finite. Then* $P \approx_\mathcal{L} Q$ *iff* $\mathcal{U}^\mathcal{C}[P] \sim_\mathcal{L} \mathcal{U}^\mathcal{C}[Q]$.

Proof. The "only if" direction is trivial. Here we outline the proof of the "if" direction. From Lemma 1 it is sufficient to prove that $\mathcal{U}^\mathcal{C}[P] \sim_\mathcal{L} \mathcal{U}^\mathcal{C}[Q]$ implies $R \parallel P \sim_\mathcal{L} R \parallel Q$ for all R. Suppose that R is such that $R \parallel P \not\sim_\mathcal{L} R \parallel Q$. We want to prove that $\mathcal{U}^\mathcal{C}[P] \not\sim_\mathcal{L} \mathcal{U}^\mathcal{C}[Q]$.

Consider the case $\mathcal{L}(R \parallel P) \not\subseteq \mathcal{L}(R \parallel Q)$. Take an $\alpha = d_0.d_1 \ldots$ such that $\alpha \in \mathcal{L}(R \parallel P)$ and $\alpha \notin \mathcal{L}(R \parallel Q)$. Furthermore, suppose that $R_0 \parallel P_0 \xRightarrow{d_0} R_1 \parallel P_1 \xRightarrow{d_1} \ldots$ with $P = P_0$ and $R = R_0$.

We can represent the internal reduction of each $R_i \parallel P_i$ which gives us d_i and $R_{i+1} \parallel P_{i+1}$, as a sequence of internal transitions (or *interactions*) $\langle R_i^0 \parallel P_i^0, c_i^0 \rangle \longrightarrow^* \langle R_i^n \parallel P_i^n, c_i^n \rangle \not\longrightarrow$, with $R_i = R_i^0, P_i = P_i^0, c_i^0 = \textbf{true}, P_{i+1} = F(P_i^n), R_{i+1} = F(R_i^n)$ and $d_i = c_i^n$, satisfying

$$\langle P_i^0, a_i^0 \rangle \longrightarrow^* \langle P_i^1, a_i^1 \rangle$$
$$\langle P_i^1, a_i^1 \wedge b_i^1 \rangle \longrightarrow^* \langle P_i^2, a_i^2 \rangle$$
$$\vdots$$
$$\langle P_i^j, a_i^j \wedge b_i^j \rangle \longrightarrow^* \langle P_i^{j+1}, a_i^{j+1} \rangle$$

$$\langle R_i^0, b_i^0 \rangle \longrightarrow^* \langle R_i^1, b_i^1 \rangle$$
$$\langle R_i^1, a_i^1 \wedge b_i^1 \rangle \longrightarrow^* \langle R_i^2, b_i^2 \rangle$$
$$\vdots$$
$$\langle R_i^j, a_i^j \wedge b_i^j \rangle \longrightarrow^* \langle R_i^{j+1}, b_i^{j+1} \rangle$$

where for each $j \leq n$, $c_i^j = a_i^j \wedge b_i^j$. Let $\sigma_i = b_i^1.c_i^1 \ldots .b_i^n.c_i^n$. It is easy to see that $\langle \mathcal{T}_{\sigma_i} \parallel P_i^0, c_i^0 \rangle \longrightarrow^* \langle \mathcal{T}_\epsilon \parallel P_i^n, c_i^n \rangle \longmapsto\!\!\!\!\!/\;$ (see Definition 9). Note that sequence σ_i is increasing, thus by removing all constraint repetitions we get a strictly increasing sequence. Let β_i be such a sequence. One can verify that T_{β_i} can "mimic" R_i^0 interacting with P_i^0. More precisely, $\langle \mathcal{T}_{\beta_i} \parallel P_i^0, c_i^0 \rangle \longrightarrow^* \langle \mathcal{T}_\epsilon \parallel P_i^n, c_i^n \rangle \longmapsto\!\!\!\!\!/\;$. This implies:

$$\left\langle !(\sum_{\beta \in ic(\mathcal{C})} \textbf{tell}(tr_\beta) \parallel T_\beta) \parallel P_i^0, \textbf{true} \right\rangle \longrightarrow^* \langle \mathcal{T}_\epsilon \parallel P_i^n, d_i \wedge tr_{\beta_i} \rangle \longmapsto\!\!\!\!\!/ \qquad (1)$$

By observing that $last(\beta_i) = d_i$ (where $last(\beta_i)$ denotes the last element of β_i), one can show that R_i can mimic T_{β_i} interacting with any P' provided that the result is d_i. More precisely,:

$$\text{For all } P', \text{ if } \langle \mathcal{T}_{\beta_i} \parallel P', \textbf{true} \rangle \longrightarrow^* \langle \mathcal{T}_\epsilon \parallel P'', d_i \rangle \longmapsto\!\!\!\!\!/, \text{ where } P' \longrightarrow^* P'',$$
$$\text{then } \langle R_i^0 \parallel P', \textbf{true} \rangle \longrightarrow^* \langle R_i^n \parallel P'', d_i \rangle \longmapsto\!\!\!\!\!/ \qquad (2)$$

From (1), $\alpha' = (d_0 \wedge tr_{\beta_0}).(d_1 \wedge tr_{\beta_1}) \ldots \in \mathcal{L}(!(\sum_{\beta \in ic(\mathcal{C})} \textbf{tell}(tr_\beta) \parallel T_\beta) \parallel P)$ where β_i corresponds to the internal T_{β_i} selected to "mimic" R_i. We want to show α' is not in $\mathcal{L}(!(\sum_{\beta \in ic(\mathcal{C})} \textbf{tell}(tr_\beta) \parallel T_\beta) \parallel Q)$. Suppose it is. Then at time i, T_{β_i} must be selected in the execution of $!(\sum_{\beta \in ic(\mathcal{C})} \textbf{tell}(tr_\beta) \parallel T_\beta) \parallel Q$ that outputs α'. By using Property (2) (and observing our restriction on the use of tr_{β_i} predicates), one can inductively construct a sequence $R_0 \parallel Q_0 \overset{d_0}{\Longrightarrow} R_1 \parallel Q_1 \overset{d_1}{\Longrightarrow} \ldots$ with $Q = Q_0$, $R = R_0$. We conclude that $\alpha \in \mathcal{L}(R \parallel Q)$ thus contradicting the assumption about α.

The case of $\mathcal{L}(R \parallel Q) \not\subseteq \mathcal{L}(R \parallel P)$ is symmetric. $\square$

Therefore context $\mathcal{U}^{\mathcal{C}}[.]$ is the *universal* distinguishing context, provided that $\mathcal{C}$ is finite, as it can distinguish any two processes P and Q which are not language congruent.

It is interesting that even if $\mathcal{C}$ is not finite, we can construct specialized distinguishing contexts for arbitrary processes as stated in the following result. The idea is to choose a suitable finite set of constraints.

Definition 10. *Let $\Lambda \subset_{fin}$ Proc. Define $\mathcal{C}(\Lambda) \subseteq_{fin} \mathcal{C}$ as the set whose elements are* **true**, **false** *and all constraints resulting from the closure under conjunction and existential quantification of the constraints occurring in Λ's processes.*

Theorem 3. *For all $P, Q \in \Lambda \subset_{fin}$ Proc, $P \approx_{\mathcal{L}} Q$ iff $\mathcal{U}^{\mathcal{C}(\Lambda)}[P] \sim_{\mathcal{L}} \mathcal{U}^{\mathcal{C}(\Lambda)}[Q]$.*

Proof. The proof is the same as that of Theorem 2 except for the role of β_i which is now played by a sequence $\overline{\beta_i}$, defined below, that depends only on constraints in Λ's processes. More precisely, let $consq(c, S) = \{d \in S \mid c \vdash d\}$. Define $\overline{e}$ as the conjunction of all constraints in $consq(e, \mathcal{C}(\Lambda))$ and let $\overline{s}$ be the sequence that results from replacing each constraint e in a sequence s with $\overline{e}$. By definition every constraint in $\mathcal{C}(\Lambda)$ which can be inferred from e, can also be inferred from $\overline{e} \in \mathcal{C}(\Lambda)$. We proceed exactly as in the proof of Theorem 2 until properties (1) and (2), which we re-state as:

$$\left\langle !\left(\sum_{\beta \in ic(\mathcal{C}(\Lambda))} \mathbf{tell}(tr_\beta) \parallel \mathcal{T}_\beta \right) \parallel P_i^0, \mathbf{true} \right\rangle \longrightarrow^* \left\langle \mathcal{T}_\epsilon \parallel P_i^n, \overline{d_i} \wedge tr_{\overline{\beta_i}} \right\rangle \not\longrightarrow \quad (3)$$

and

$$\text{For all } P' \in \Lambda, \text{ if } \left\langle \mathcal{T}_{\overline{\beta_i}} \parallel P', \mathbf{true} \right\rangle \longrightarrow^* \left\langle \mathcal{T}_\epsilon \parallel P'', \overline{d_i} \right\rangle \not\longrightarrow, \text{ where } P' \longrightarrow^* P'',$$
$$\text{then } \left\langle R_i^0 \parallel P', \mathbf{true} \right\rangle \longrightarrow^* \left\langle R_i^n \parallel P'', d_i \right\rangle \not\longrightarrow \quad (4)$$

We then proceed as in the proof of Theorem 2; getting a contradiction out of (3) and (4). □

Therefore $\mathcal{U}^{\mathcal{C}(\Lambda)}$ is an universal context for Λ's processes. The ability of constructing distinguishing contexts for arbitrary processes is important as it can be used for proving decidability results for $\approx_{io}$ (note that $P \approx_\mathcal{L} Q$ iff $\mathcal{U}^{\mathcal{C}(\{P,Q\})}[P] \sim_\mathcal{L} \mathcal{U}^{\mathcal{C}(\{P,Q\})}[Q]$). It turns out that $\sim_\mathcal{L}$ is decidable for a significant fragment of the calculus. The languages of these processes can be recognized by automata over infinite sequences, more precisely Büchi Automata ([3]). We will elaborate on this in the next section.

4.1   Decidability and Characterization of Processes Languages

In this section we will characterize processes languages in terms of ω-regular languages (i.e., the languages accepted by Büchi automata). Recall that Büchi automata are ordinary nondeterministic finite-state automata equipped with an acceptance condition that is appropriate for ω-sequences: an ω-sequence is accepted if the automaton can read it from left to right while visiting a sequence of states in which some final state occurs infinitely often. This condition is called *Büchi acceptance* ([3]).

We aim at proving decidability of the relation $\sim_\mathcal{L}$ for a fragment of ntcc which we call *restricted-nondeterministic*.

Definition 11. *A process P is said to be* restricted-nondeterministic *iff for all* **local** x **in** Q **in** P, *for every construct of the form* $\sum_{i \in I}$ **when** c_i **do** Q_i **in** Q, *the c_i's are mutually exclusive. We use $Proc^r$ to denote the set of all restricted-nondeterministic processes.*

This fragment allows non-deterministic process (summations) out of the scope of local variables. In fact, all application examples in this paper (Section 3) belong to this fragment. Notice that each **local** x **in** $P \in Proc^r$ is deterministic in the sense of Definition 8.

We shall show that the languages of restricted-nondeterministic processes are ω-regular. We will also show that given a $P \in Proc^r$ we can construct a Büchi automaton recognizing the language of P. Then using the fact that language equivalence for Büchi automata is decidable [23], we conclude that $\sim_{\mathcal{L}}$ is decidable for restricted-nondeterministic processes and thus so are $\approx_{\mathcal{L}}$ and $\approx_{io}$ (see Theorem 3).

To illustrate the problem in trying to use finite-state machines for representing processes let us consider the following example.

Example 2. Let $Q = !!P$ with $P = \sum_{j \in J} \textbf{tell}(c_j)$. We have the following transition sequence (on input $\texttt{true}^\omega$):

$$Q \xRightarrow{d_1} Q \,\|!P \xRightarrow{d_2} Q \,\|!P \,\|!P \xRightarrow{d_3} \ldots \xRightarrow{d_n} Q \,\| \prod_n !P \xRightarrow{d_{n+1}} \ldots$$

This example illustrates that in a transition system where states are the elements of *Proc* it is possible to have infinite paths where all states are different up to structural congruence (i.e., there can be an infinite set of derivatives). Moreover, notice that in this particular example, the process at time i can output everything the process at time $i-1$ can, but not necessarily the other way round. This situation arises from the nondeterminism specified by P.

Nevertheless, we will show that after some time units the states can be identified up to $\approx_{\mathcal{L}}$. More precisely, the property we would like to have is that there exists t such that for all $k \geq t$, $\prod_k !P \approx_{\mathcal{L}} \prod_{k+1} !P$. In the above example for any $k \geq |J|$ we have $\prod_k !P \approx_{\mathcal{L}} \prod_{k+1} !P$ thus validating the property. Unfortunately, the property does not hold for processes out of $Proc^r$. Let us define an arbitrary-delay operation δP which delays P arbitrarily:

$$\delta P \stackrel{\text{def}}{=} P + \delta P.$$

The encoding in our calculus of the recursive definition of δP requires hiding over non-mutually exclusive summations (see [18]) thus it is out of $Proc^r$. Assume that $P = \textbf{tell}(c)$. Then two copies of δP can output c at two (arbitrary) points of time while a single copy cannot. In general one can prove that for any $k > 1$, $\mathcal{L}(\prod_k \delta P) \subset \mathcal{L}(\prod_{k+1} \delta P)$, thus invalidating the property.

The following property is needed in the proof of Lemma 2 which implies the property described above. It relates the language of processes with the language of processes arising at intermediate steps of the internal computations.

Proposition 6. $\alpha \in \mathcal{L}(P)$ *iff there are Q and c such that $\langle P, \texttt{true} \rangle \longrightarrow^* \langle Q, c \rangle$ and $Q \,\| \textbf{tell}(c) \xRightarrow{\alpha} {}^\omega$.*

We now introduce the notion of multiplicity of a process.

Definition 12. *Let $m : Proc^r \to Nat$. The multiplicity of P, $m(P)$ is defined as*

$m(\textbf{skip}) = 0$
$m(\textbf{tell}(c)) = 1$

$$m(\textstyle\sum_{i \in I} \textbf{when}\, c_i \,\textbf{do}\, P_i) = \textstyle\sum_{i \in I} m(P_i)$$
$$m(P \parallel Q) = max\{m(P), m(Q)\}$$
$$m(\textbf{local}\, x \,\textbf{in}\, P) = m(\textbf{next}\, P) = m(\textbf{unless}\, c \,\textbf{next}\, P) = m(!P) = m(P).$$

The value $m(P)$ is aimed to be the number of copies of P, after which, further copies are redundant. This is stated in the following lemma which is the key for decidability of $\sim_{\mathcal{L}}$.

Lemma 2. *Let $P \in Proc^r$. For all $k > m(P)$, $\prod_{k-1} P \approx_{\mathcal{L}} \prod_k P$.*

Proof. The proof proceeds by induction on the structure of $P \in Proc^r$. Here we show some cases. Suppose $k > m(P)$.

• Case $P = P_1 \parallel P_2$. From Theorem 1 we get $\prod_k(P_1 \parallel P_2) \approx_{\mathcal{L}} \prod_k P_1 \parallel \prod_k P_2$. Note that $k > m(P) \geq m(P_1)$ and $k > m(P) \geq m(P_2)$. Therefore, from the hypothesis $\prod_k P_1 \parallel \prod_k P_2 \approx_{\mathcal{L}} \prod_{k-1} P_1 \parallel \prod_{k-1} P_2 \approx_{\mathcal{L}} \prod_{k-1}(P_1 \parallel P_2)$ as required.

• Case $P = \textbf{next}\, Q$. We have $\prod_k \textbf{next}\, Q \approx_{\mathcal{L}} \textbf{next}\, \prod_k Q$ from Theorem 1. From $m(P) = m(Q)$, the hypothesis and Theorem 1, we get $\textbf{next}\, \prod_k Q \approx_{\mathcal{L}} \textbf{next}\, \prod_{k-1} Q \approx_{\mathcal{L}} \prod_{k-1} \textbf{next}\, Q$.

• Case $P = \,!Q$. We verify that $\prod_k !Q \approx_{\mathcal{L}} ! \prod_k Q$. From $m(P) = m(Q)$ and hypothesis we verify that $! \prod_k Q \approx_{\mathcal{L}} ! \prod_{k-1} Q \approx_{\mathcal{L}} \prod_{k-1} !Q$.

• Case $P = \sum_{u \in I} \textbf{when}\, c_u \,\textbf{do}\, P_u$. From Lemma 1 we know that it is enough to consider parallel contexts. Let E an arbitrary process and suppose that $\alpha = c.\alpha' \in \mathcal{L}(E \parallel \prod_k P)$ (1). We want to show that $\alpha \in \mathcal{L}(E \parallel \prod_{k-1} P)$. From (1) we know that there exists sequence of internal transitions $t = \langle E \parallel \prod_k P, \textbf{true} \rangle \longrightarrow^* \gamma_1 \longrightarrow^*, ..., \longrightarrow^* \gamma_n \longrightarrow^* \langle R, c \rangle \not\longrightarrow$ with $\alpha' \in \mathcal{L}(F(R))$ which contains only the initial and final configuration, and those configurations $\gamma_1, ..., \gamma_n$ in which a reduction from a P takes place, if any. By monotonicity of the store if t contains a configuration with store c s.t. $\langle P, c \rangle \longrightarrow$ then since a reduction of each P must eventually take place $n = k$ *(I)* otherwise $n = 0$ *(II)*.

(I). Suppose $n = k$. Define $E_0 = E$, $P_0 = \textbf{skip}$. For $0 < j \leq n$, each γ_j can be defined as $\left\langle E_j \parallel P_j \parallel \prod_{n-j} P, c_j \right\rangle$, where $\langle E_{j-1} \parallel P_{j-1}, c_{j-1} \rangle \longrightarrow^* \langle E_j, c'_j \rangle$ for some c'_j s.t. $\langle P, c'_j \rangle \longrightarrow \langle P_j, c_j \rangle$ (a reduction from one of the k $P's$). Notice $k > m(P) = \Sigma_{Q:P \longrightarrow Q} m(Q)$, so from the pigeon-hole principle there must be a process P', $P \longrightarrow P'$ with $r > m(P')$ configurations $\gamma_{j_1}, ... \gamma_{j_r}$ such that each corresponding $P_{j_1}, ..., P_{j_r}$ is P'. Let γ_i be the first among these configurations and let P_i be the process in such a configuration, i.e., $E_i \parallel P' \parallel \prod_{k-i} P$. From Proposition 6, we have $\alpha \in \mathcal{L}(P_i \parallel \textbf{tell}(c_i))$. As r copies of P' are eventually triggered, one can verify that $\alpha \in \mathcal{L}(E_i \parallel \prod_r P' \parallel \prod_{k-(i+r-1)} P \parallel \textbf{tell}(c_i))$. Since P' is a subprocess of P, from the hypothesis $\alpha \in \mathcal{L}(Q_i \parallel \textbf{tell}(c_i))$ with $Q_i = E_i \parallel \prod_{r-1} P' \parallel \prod_{k-(i+r-1)} P$. One can then construct the sequence

$$\left\langle E \parallel \textstyle\prod_{(k-1)} P, \text{true} \right\rangle \longrightarrow^* \left\langle E_i \parallel P' \parallel \textstyle\prod_{(k-1)-i} P, c_i \right\rangle$$
$$\longrightarrow \left\langle E_i \parallel \textstyle\prod_2 P' \parallel \textstyle\prod_{(k-1)-(i+1)} P, c_i \right\rangle$$
$$\vdots$$
$$\longrightarrow \left\langle E_i \parallel \textstyle\prod_{r-1} P' \parallel \textstyle\prod_{(k-1)-(i+r-2)} P, c_i \right\rangle = \langle Q_i, c_i \rangle .$$

From Proposition 6, $\alpha \in \mathcal{L}(E \parallel \prod_{(k-1)} P)$ as required.

(II). Suppose $n = 0$. Then $R = E' \parallel \prod_k P$ for some E' s.t. $\langle E, \text{true} \rangle \longrightarrow^*$ $\langle E', c \rangle \not\longrightarrow$. Trivially $\left\langle E \parallel \prod_{k-1} P, \text{true} \right\rangle \longrightarrow \langle R', c \rangle \not\longrightarrow$ with $R' = E' \parallel \prod_{k-1} P$. From the definition of $F(.)$, $F(P) \equiv \textbf{skip}$, thus $F(R) = F(E') \parallel \prod_k F(P) \equiv F(E') \equiv F(R') = F(E') \parallel \prod_{k-1} F(P)$. Hence $F(R) \approx_{\mathcal{L}} F(R')$ by Theorem 1, thus $\alpha' \in F(R')$. We then conclude $\alpha \in \mathcal{L}(E \parallel \prod_{k-1} P)$.

• Case $P = \textbf{local } x \textbf{ in } Q$. In this case P is a deterministic process. It is easy to verify that if P is a deterministic process then $P \approx_{\mathcal{L}} \prod_k P$ for any k, thus validating the property. □

The lemma below states that every language transition sequence over $Proc^r$ ultimately contains two language congruent processes.

Lemma 3. Let $P_0 \overset{c_1}{\Longrightarrow} P_1 \overset{c_2}{\Longrightarrow} \dots$ be an arbitrary language transition sequence where $P_0 \in Proc^r$. Then there are two processes P_m, P_n with $m < n$ such that $P_n \approx_{\mathcal{L}} P_m$.

Proof. Let $P_0 \overset{c_1}{\Longrightarrow} P_1 \overset{c_2}{\Longrightarrow} \dots$ be an arbitrary language transition sequence where $P_0 \in Proc^r$. It is sufficient to construct a sequence $P_0' \overset{c_1}{\Longrightarrow} \approx_{\mathcal{L}} P_1' \overset{c_2}{\Longrightarrow} \approx_{\mathcal{L}} \dots$ with $P_i \approx_{\mathcal{L}} P_i'$ for every $i \geq 0$ and two processes P_m', P_n' with $m < n$ satisfying $P_n' \equiv P_m'$ (Definition 2). We sketch such a construction next.

Every process P can be rewritten via $\equiv$ as $\prod_{i \in I} !R_i \parallel E$ where E is a replication-free processes. Hence $P_0 \overset{c_0}{\Longrightarrow} P_1 \overset{c_1}{\Longrightarrow} \dots$ can be rewritten as:

$$\prod_{i \in I_0} !R_i \parallel E_0 \overset{c_0}{\Longrightarrow} \prod_{i \in I_1} !R_i \parallel E_1 \overset{c_1}{\Longrightarrow} \dots \qquad (5)$$

where each E_u is a non-replicated processes. It is easy to verify that $I_0 \subseteq I_1 \subseteq \dots$ since new replicated processes can move up to the top level. Assume that k is such that satisfies $\prod_{i \in I_k} !R_i \approx_{\mathcal{L}} \prod_{i \in I_j} !R_i$ for any $j > k$. Such a k is guaranteed to exist from Lemma 2. Thus the sequence in (5) is point-wise $\approx_{\mathcal{L}}$-equivalent to the sequence

$$\prod_{i \in I_0} !R_i \parallel E_0 \overset{c_1}{\Longrightarrow} \dots \prod_{i \in I_k} !R_i \parallel E_k \overset{c_k}{\Longrightarrow} \approx_{\mathcal{L}} \prod_{i \in I_k} !R_i \parallel E_{k+1} \overset{c_{k+1}}{\Longrightarrow} \approx_{\mathcal{L}} \dots \qquad (6)$$

Now notice that both the E_j's $(j > k)$ and $\prod_{i \in I_k} R_i$ can have replicated processes $!R$ which can move up to the top level. However, $\prod_{i \in I_k} !R_i \parallel !R \approx_{\mathcal{L}} \prod_{i \in I_k} !R_i$ from our assumption about k. Therefore we can replace such replications with

skip. Given Q let us use $\widehat{Q}$ to denote the processes resulting from replacing each replicated process in Q with **skip**. We can then verify that the sequence

$$\prod_{i\in I_0} !R_i \parallel E_0 \stackrel{c_1}{\Longrightarrow} \ldots \prod_{i\in I_k} !\widehat{R}_i \parallel \widehat{E}_k \stackrel{c_k}{\Longrightarrow}\approx_{\mathcal{L}} \prod_{i\in I_k} !\widehat{R}_i \parallel \widehat{E}_{k+1} \stackrel{c_{k+1}}{\Longrightarrow}\approx_{\mathcal{L}} \ldots \quad (7)$$

is point-wise $\approx_{\mathcal{L}}$-equivalent to the one in (6). We claim the following:

Claim. For some $n > k$ there exists a m, with $k \leq m < n$ such that $\widehat{E}_m \equiv \widehat{E}_n$

Thus, for m and n in the above claim, it follows $\prod_{i\in I_k} !\widehat{R}_i \parallel \widehat{E}_m \equiv \prod_{i\in I_k} !\widehat{R}_i \parallel \widehat{E}_n$ thus proving the Lemma. Below we prove this claim.

Define the *next-depth* of a process Q, written $nd(Q)$, as the maximum number of nesting of next operations in Q. Let $D(Q,i) = \{Q' \mid Q \Longrightarrow^i Q'\}$, i.e. the set of all processes which Q can possibly evolve to in i times units. Trivially, if Q is replication-free then for all $u > nd(Q)$, $D(Q,u) = \{\text{skip}\}$ (2).

Let $R = \prod_{i\in I_k} \widehat{R}_i$, $Rr = \prod_{i\in I_k} !\widehat{R}_i$ and $E = \widehat{E}_k$. Without loss of generality assume that $nd(R) > nd(E)$ (by adding next-guarded skips we can always augment the next-depth of a process). Let $h = nd(R)$. At time k the processes E and R are the ones to be executed in parallel with Rr. At time $k+1$, a process in $D(E,1)$, a process in $D(R,1)$, and R which is a process in $D(R,0)$ are the ones to be executed with Rr. In general, at time $k+n$ there are $n+2$ processes $E' \in D(E,n)$, $Q_n \in D(R,n)$, $Q_{n-1} \in D(R,n-1), \ldots, Q_0 \in D(R,0)$ to be executed with Rr. If $n \geq h$, however, we know from (2) that at each following time unit it is enough to consider the process in the (finite) sets $D(R,0), \ldots, D(R,h)$ since $D(R,u) = \{\text{skip}\}$ for $u > h$. The are $w = |D(R,0)| \times \ldots \times |D(R,h)|$ many choices of the h process in these sets. Thus after $h + w$ time units at least one choice must be repeated. $\square$

By using the Lemma 3 we can prove that the set of derivatives of P, which we define as $S(P) = \{Q \mid P \stackrel{c_1}{\Longrightarrow} \ldots \stackrel{c_n}{\Longrightarrow} Q\}$, modulo $\sim_{\mathcal{L}}$ is finite.

Lemma 4. *For every $P \in Proc^r$, $S(P)/ \sim_{\mathcal{L}}$ is finite.*

Proof. Here we outline the proof. Consider the finitely-branching transition system graph of P with labeled transitions $\stackrel{c}{\Longrightarrow}$ modulo $\sim_{\mathcal{L}}$. One can verify that if the transition graph were infinite then it would have to have an infinite path $P \sim_{\mathcal{L}} Q_0 \stackrel{c_0}{\Longrightarrow}\sim_{\mathcal{L}} Q_1 \stackrel{c_1}{\Longrightarrow}\sim_{\mathcal{L}} Q_2 \ldots$, where all the Q_i's are different (modulo $\sim_{\mathcal{L}}$). But this would imply that there is a sequence $P = P_0 \stackrel{c_0}{\Longrightarrow} P_1 \stackrel{c_1}{\Longrightarrow} P_2 \ldots$ (with $P_i \sim_{\mathcal{L}} Q_i$ for all $i \geq 0$) where all the P_i's are different modulo $\approx_{\mathcal{L}}$ which is impossible according to Lemma 3 (Recall that from Theorem 1, $\approx_{\mathcal{L}} \subset \sim_{\mathcal{L}}$).$\square$

Given a restricted-nondeterministic process P, Lemma 4 above allows us to define a Büchi automaton $A_{P/\sim_{\mathcal{L}}}$ which accepts $\mathcal{L}(P)$. The set of states is $S(P)/ \sim_{\mathcal{L}}$ in Lemma 4. All states are accepting. The start state is P. There is transition from Q to Q' labeled by c iff $Q \stackrel{c}{\Longrightarrow} Q'$. It is easy to verify such an automaton accepts $\mathcal{L}(P)$.

Theorem 4. *For every* $P \in Proc^r$, $\mathcal{L}(P)$ *is an* ω-*regular language.*

The definition of $A_{P/\sim_{\mathcal{L}}}$ above does not give us an effective way of constructing the automaton. In Algorithm 1 we describe a method which given $P \in Proc^r$ constructs a Büchi automaton A_P accepting $\mathcal{L}(P)$.

First we need the following definitions: given Q and R let $r(R, Q)$ be the number of occurrences of R in Q at the top level. Let $Q \downarrow_R$ the process that results from replacing with **skip** each non-top-level occurrence of $!R$ in Q if $r(!R, Q) > m(!R)$ (See Definition 12). Let $Q \uparrow_R$ be the process that results from replacing with **skip**, $r(!R, Q) - m(!R)$ top-level occurrence of $!R$ in Q in some fixed order. Suppose that we enumerate all the replicated process in Q in some fixed order $R_1, \ldots, R_n$. Let us define $Q \downarrow$ as the process $Q \downarrow_{R_1} \cdots \downarrow_{R_n}$ and $Q \uparrow$ as $Q \uparrow_{R_1} \cdots \uparrow_{R_n}$. Recall that $\equiv$ denotes the structural congruence (Definition 2).

Remark 1. For each permutation π on $\{1, \ldots, m\}$,

$$Q \uparrow_{R_1} \cdots \uparrow_{R_m} \equiv Q \uparrow_{R_{\pi(1)}} \cdots \uparrow_{R_{\pi(m)}} \quad \text{and} \quad Q \downarrow_{R_1} \cdots \downarrow_{R_m} \equiv Q \downarrow_{R_{\pi(1)}} \cdots \downarrow_{R_{\pi(m)}}$$

The proposition below follows from Lemma 2.

Proposition 7. *For all* Q, $Q \downarrow \approx_{\mathcal{L}} Q \uparrow \approx_{\mathcal{L}} Q$.

Algorithm 1 Constructing the automaton A_P

Start by creating the initial state and label it with $(P \downarrow\uparrow)$. (1) Choose a state p' labeled by P' from the current transition graph and a reduction $P' \overset{c}{\Longrightarrow} Q$. The choice should satisfy that there is not already an edge labeled with c from p' to a state q with a label structurally congruent to $(Q \downarrow\uparrow)$. If such a choice is not possible we stop. If there is already a state q labeled with a process (structurally equivalent to) $(Q \downarrow\uparrow)$ then create an edge from p' to it with label c. Otherwise create a new state q with label $(Q \downarrow\uparrow)$ and an edge from p' to it with label c. Go to (1).

This algorithm assumes decidability of $\equiv$ which basically follows from the decidability of the π-calculus structural congruence *without* the replication axiom [15]. The termination of Algorithm 1 is based on the proof of Lemma 3. Basically, each path in the transition graph constructed by this method is constructed as in the proof of the lemma; if the method did not terminate then the construction would violate the claim in the proof. The partial correctness is easy to verify.

Theorem 5. *For all* $P \in Proc^r$, *one can effectively construct a Büchi automaton* A_P *accepting the set* $\mathcal{L}(P)$.

Therefore $\sim_{\mathcal{L}}$ is decidable for restricted-nondeterministic processes (Definition 6). Moreover, $\approx_{\mathcal{L}} = \approx_{io}$ is also decidable for these processes as we need to consider only one context to check whether two processes are language congruent (Theorem 3).

Corollary 1. *Relations* $\sim_{\mathcal{L}}$, $\approx_{\mathcal{L}}$ *and* $\approx_{io}$ *are decidable for restricted nondeterministic processes.*

5   Related Work and Concluding Remarks

Related Work. The work most closely related to our paper is that of tcc ([20]). Our proposal is a strict extension of tcc, in the sense that tcc can be encoded in (the deterministic fragment of) ntcc, while the vice-versa is not possible because tcc does not have constructs to express non-determinism. The input-output behavior of tcc has been studied in [20]. In tcc the input-output equivalence and congruence coincide as only deterministic processes are allowed. Therefore, there is no need for the study of universal or distinguishing contexts as in the ntcc case. In [20] it was shown that tcc processes can be compiled into (deterministic) finite-state automata. Moreover such a compilation is compositional. This result relies on determinacy of tcc processes. As shown in this paper, in ntcc the non-deterministic constructs are the ones which present technical difficulties to deal with when trying to represent them as finite-state machines. Other interesting extensions of tcc have been proposed in [9, 10, 21]. None of these, however, consider non-determinism.

The tccp calculus ([5]) is the only other proposal for a non-deterministic timed extension of ccp that we know of. As such, tccp provides a declarative language for the specification of (large) timed systems. One major difference with our approach is that the information about the store is carried through the time units, so the semantic setting is rather different. The notion of time is also different; in tccp each time unit is identified with the time needed to ask and tell information to the store. As for the constructs, unlike ntcc, tccp provides for arbitrary recursion. Like ntcc, the deterministic fragment of tccp can be used to program reactive systems. A store that grows monotonically, however, may be inadequate for the kind of application we have in mind, like RCX micro-controllers.

A proof system for reasoning about the correctness of tccp processes was recently introduced in [4]. The underlying temporal logic in [4] can be used for describing input-output behavior while the one in [17] for ntcc can only be used for the strongest-postcondition. As such the temporal logic of ntcc processes is less expressive than that one underlying the proof system of tccp, but it is also semantically simpler and defined as the standard linear-temporal logic of [14]. This may come in handy when using the Consequence Rule present in the proof systems of both [4] and [17].

Concluding Remarks. In this paper we introduced and studied different notions of equality for ntcc. We showed that the languages of restricted-nondeterministic processes can be characterized in terms of ω-languages. Furthermore, we described how to construct Büchi automata accepting the language of restricted-nondeterministic processes. This allowed us to prove decidability of language-equivalence for these processes. By proving the existence of distinguishing contexts, and that the input-output and language congruences coincide, we also proved decidability for these relations. On the practical side we show applications examples illustrating the expressiveness of (the restricted-nondeterministic fragment of) ntcc.

As an extension of this work, we have used the automata constructions in this paper for characterizing the strongest postcondition and input-output behavior of processes. This gives us some decidability results for these notions and also a simple execution model for restricted-nondeterministic processes.

Our current research includes the study of the decidability of $\approx_{\mathcal{L}}$ for arbitrary ntcc processes as it remains an open question. The plan for future research includes the extension of ntcc to a probabilistic model following ideas in [12] and [8]. This is justified by the existence of RCX program examples involving stochastic behavior which cannot be faithfully modeled with non-deterministic behavior. In a more practical setting we plan to define a programming language for RCX controllers based on ntcc.

Acknowledgments. We owe much to Catuscia Palamidessi, with whom we have worked on ntcc, for her insight into ccp issues. We would also like to thank Maurizio Gabbrielli, Paulo Oliva, Daniele Varacca, Pawel Sobocinski, Jesus Almansa for helpful comments on different aspects of ntcc. Finally, we thank the anonymous referees for their suggestions and remarks.

References

[1] M. Benda, V. Jagannathan, and R. Dodhiawala. On Optimal Cooperation of Knowledge Sources - An Empirical Investigation. Technical Report BCS-G2010-28, Boeing Advanced Technology Center, 1986.

[2] G. Berry and G. Gonthier. The ESTEREL Synchronous Programming Language: Design, Semantics, Implementation. *Science of Computer Programming*, 19(2):87–152, November 1992.

[3] J. R. Buchi. On a Decision Method in Restricted Second Order Arithmetic. In *Proc. Int. Cong. on Logic, Methodology, and Philosophy of Science*, pages 1–11. Stanford University Press, 1962.

[4] F. de Boer, M. Gabbrielli, and M. Chiara. A Temporal Logic for Reasoning about Timed Concurrent Constraint Programs. In *TIME 01*. IEEE Press, 2001.

[5] F. de Boer, M. Gabbrielli, and M. C. Meo. A Timed Concurrent Constraint Language. *Information and Computation*, 1999. To appear.

[6] F. S. de Boer, M. Gabbrielli, E. Marchiori, and C. Palamidessi. Proving Concurrent Constraint Programs Correct. *ACM Transactions on Programming Languages and Systems*, 19(5):685–725, 1997.

[7] J. Fredslund. The Assumption Architecture. Progress Report, Department of Computer Science, University of Aarhus, November 1999.

[8] V. Gupta, R. Jagadeesan, and P. Panangaden. Stochastic Processes as Concurrent Constraint Programs. In *Symposium on Principles of Programming Languages*, pages 189–202, 1999.

[9] V. Gupta, R. Jagadeesan, and V. Saraswat. Models for Concurrent Constraint Programming. In Ugo Montanari and Vladimiro Sassone, Editors, *CONCUR '96: Concurrency Theory, 7th International Conference*, volume 1119 of *Lecture Notes in Computer Science*, pages 66–83, 26–29 August 1996.

[10] V. Gupta, R. Jagadeesan, and V. Saraswat. Probabilistic Concurrent Constraint Programming. In *CONCUR '97: Concurrency Theory, 8th International Conference*, volume 1243 of *LNCS*, pages 243–257, 1–4 July 1997.

[11] T. Haynes and S. Sen. The Evolution of Multiagent Coordination Strategies. *Adaptive Behavior*, 1997.

[12] O. Herescu and C. Palamidessi. Probabilistic Asynchronous Pi-calculus. *FoSSaCS*, pages 146–160, 2000.

[13] H. H. Lund and L. Pagliarini. Robot Soccer with LEGO Mindstorms. *Lecture Notes in Computer Science*, 1604, 1999.

[14] Z. Manna and A. Pnueli. *The Temporal Logic of Reactive and Concurrent Systems, Specification*. Springer, 1991.

[15] R. Milner. *Communicating and Mobile Systems: The π-calculus*. Cambridge University Press, 1999.

[16] S. Nolfi and D. Floreano. Coevolving Predator and Prey Robots: Do "Arms Races" Arise in Artificial Evolution? *Artificial Life*, 4(4):311–335, 1998.

[17] C. Palamidessi and F. Valencia. A Temporal Concurrent Constraint Programming Calculus. In *Proc. of the Seventh International Conference on Principles and Practice of Constraint Programming*, 26 November 2001.

[18] C. Palamidessi and F. Valencia. A Temporal Constraint Programming Calculus. Technical Report RS-01-20, BRICS, University of Aarhus, June 2001. availabe via http://www.brics.dk/~fvalenci/publications.html.

[19] V. Saraswat. *Concurrent Constraint Programming*. The MIT Press, Cambridge, MA, 1993.

[20] V. Saraswat, R. Jagadeesan, and V. Gupta. Foundations of Timed Concurrent Constraint Programming. In *Proc. of the Ninth Annual IEEE Symposium on Logic in Computer Science*, pages 71–80, 4–7 July 1994.

[21] V. Saraswat, R. Jagadeesan, and V. Gupta. Timed Default Concurrent Constraint Programming. *Journal of Symbolic Computation*, 22(5–6):475–520, November–December 1996.

[22] V. Saraswat, M. Rinard, and P. Panangaden. The Semantic Foundations of Concurrent Constraint Programming. In *POPL '91. Proceedings of the Eighteenth Annual ACM Symposium on Principles of Programming Languages*, pages 333–352, 21–23 January 1991.

[23] A. Sistla, M. Vardi, and P. Wolper. The Complementation Problem for Buchi Automata with Applications to Temporal Logic. *Theoretical Computer Science*, 49:217–237, 1987.

[24] G. Smolka. A Foundation for Concurrent Constraint Programming. In *Constraints in Computational Logics*, volume 845 of *Lecture Notes in Computer Science*, Munich, Germany, September 1994. Invited Talk.

[25] P. Stone and M. Veloso. Multiagent Systems: A Survey from a Machine Learning Perspective. *Autonomous Robots*, 8:345–383, 2000.

Part V

Molecular Computing

Rewriting P Systems
with Conditional Communication

Paolo Bottoni[1], Anna Labella[1], Carlos Martín-Vide[2], and Gheorghe Păun[3]*

[1] Department of Computer Science, University of Rome "La Sapienza"
Via Salaria 113, 00198 Roma, Italy
`bottoni/labella@dsi.uniroma1.it`
[2] Research Group in Mathematical Linguistics
Rovira i Virgili University
Pl. Imperial Tàrraco 1, 43005 Tarragona, Spain
`cmv@astor.urv.es`
[3] Institute of Mathematics of the Romanian Academy
PO Box 1-764, 70700 Bucureşti, Romania
`gpaun@imar.ro, g_paun@hotmail.com`

Abstract. A membrane system (P system) is a model of computation inspired by some basic features of the structure and behaviour of living cells. In this paper we consider systems with string-objects processed by rewriting, with the communication controlled by conditions on the contents of the strings. Symbols, substrings (in an arbitrary place, or as a prefix/suffix), or the shape of the whole string are used as permitting and as forbidding conditions when moving strings from a membrane to a neighboring membrane. Many of the obtained variants lead to new characterizations of recursively enumerable languages (as expected, these characterizations indicate a trade-off between the number of membranes and the strength of the communication conditions used). Several open problems are also formulated.

1 Introduction

Membrane computing is a branch of molecular computing which abstracts from the way the alive cells process chemical compounds (as well as energy and information) in the complex compartmental structure defined by the various membranes present inside a cell. In short, we have a *membrane structure*, in the form of a hierarchical arrangement of membranes (in principle, understood as three dimensional vesicles, but a two dimensional representation is equivalent), embedded in a *skin* membrane. Each membrane delimits in a one-to-one manner a *region*. For an elementary membrane (that is, a membrane without any membrane inside) this is the space enclosed by it, while the region of a non-elementary membrane is the space in-between the membrane and the membranes directly

---

* Work supported by a grant of NATO Science Committee, Spain, 2000–2001, and by the Visiting professor programme of the University "La Sapienza" of Rome, Italy

W. Brauer et al. (Eds.): Formal and Natural Computing, LNCS 2300, pp. 325–353, 2002.

included in it. Each membrane is labeled; the one-to-one correspondence between membranes and regions associated with them makes it possible to refer the regions by the labels of membranes. Figure 1 illustrates these notions.

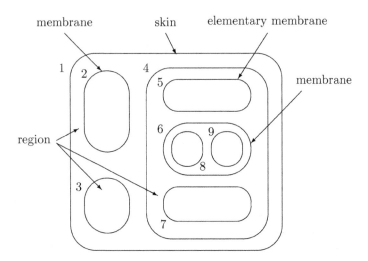

Fig. 1. A membrane structure

Each region contains *objects* and (*evolution*) *rules*. In this paper we consider the case when the objects are described by strings and the evolution rules are context-free rewriting rules. After rewriting a string, it is assumed that it is no longer present, and the result of the rewriting replaces it. (However, this is not essential for the variants of P systems we consider in this paper, but it is important for certain variants where the strings can influence each other.) In the basic variant of such a membrane system, a target indication is associated with each rule, specifying where the string obtained by a rewriting operation performed by that rule will be placed. Such indications are of the form *here* (the string remains in the same region), *out* (the string exits the region), in_j (the string is sent to the membrane with label j, providing that it is immediately inside the region where the rule is used), or, a weaker variant of the last command, *in* (the string is sent to one of the immediately inner membranes, nondeterministically choosing it).

In each step, each string which can be rewritten by a rule in its region is rewritten. (All the strings are processed in parallel, but the rewriting of each string is done sequentially: at each step only one rule per string is applied.) In this way, one gets *transitions* between the configurations of the system. A sequence of transitions is called a *computation*. The *result* of a halting computation (one which reaches a configuration where no rule can be applied) is the set of strings sent out of the system during the computation. Thus, a rewriting P system generates a language.

Priorities among rules or possibilities to control the membrane permeability were also considered in the literature. In most cases, characterizations of recursively enumerable languages were obtained. Results of this type can be found, e.g., in [4], [17], [8], [11], [12], [13], [14], [20].

In this paper we consider a variant of rewriting P systems where the communication of strings is not controlled by the evolution rules, but it depends on the contents of the strings themselves. This is achieved by considering certain types of *permitting* and *forbidding* conditions, based on the symbols or the substrings (arbitrary, or prefixes/suffixes) which appear in a given string, or on the shape of the string. By combining these variants we get a large number of classes of P systems, hence of families of languages generated by these systems. As expected, many of these families equal the family of recursively enumerable languages. In many cases, such results are obtained for systems with a small number of membranes. Several cases remain to be further investigated, for instance, when checking prefixes or suffixes: we do not know whether or not we can characterize the recursively enumerable languages by systems where only prefixes or only suffixes are checked (we *conjecture* that the answer is regative); when both prefixes and suffixes are used, we have obtained a characterization of recursively enumerable languages by systems without a bound on the number of membranes (but we *conjecture* that such a characterization holds also for a reduced number of membranes, as happens for almost all classes of P systems).

We emphasize the fact that this way of communicating strings through membranes is "more realistic" than that based on target indications associated with the rewriting rules, it corresponds to the biochemical situation where the objects (some of them strings, such as DNA molecules) can pass through membranes depending on their shape (size, polarization, other properties) and not depending on the last transformation applied to them (the last rewriting, in the basic model of P systems).

2 Language Theory Prerequisites

In this section we introduce some formal language theory notions and notations which will be used in this paper; for further details we refer to [19].

For an alphabet V, by V^* we denote the set of all strings over V, including the empty one, denoted by λ; V^+ denotes the set of all non-empty strings over V, that is, $V^+ = V^* - \{\lambda\}$. The set of symbols appearing in a string $x \in V^*$ is denoted by $alph(x)$ and the set of substrings of x is denoted by $Sub(x)$. A regular expression is said to be *elementary* if it has the star height at most one and uses the union at most for symbols in the alphabet. (For instance, $\{a, b\}^* cca^*$ is an elementary expression, while $a^* \cup ab$ is not.) We denote by $L(e)$ the language represented by a regular expression e. One can see that the language of an elementary regular expression can also be represented by a *pattern*, in the sense of [1], with each variable appearing only once (such a pattern is called *regular*) and with a *domain* associated with each variable, in the form of a star language U^*, where U is a set of symbols. For instance, $L(e)$ for the previous expression also corresponds to the pattern $XccY$, with X interpreted by any string from $\{a, b\}^*$ and Y interpreted by any string from a^*.

By *FIN, REG, LIN, CF, CS, RE* we denote the families of finite, regular, linear, context-free, context-sensitive, and recursively enumerable languages, respectively.

In the proofs from the subsequent sections we need the notions of a *matrix grammar with appearance checking*, of *Kuroda normal form*, and of a *pure context-free grammar*.

A matrix grammar with appearance checking is a construct $G = (N, T, S, M, F)$, where N, T are disjoint alphabets, $S \in N$, M is a finite set of sequences of the form $(A_1 \rightarrow x_1, \ldots, A_n \rightarrow x_n)$, $n \geq 1$, of context-free rules over $N \cup T$ (with $A_i \in N, x_i \in (N \cup T)^*$, in all cases), and F is a set of occurrences of rules in M (N is the nonterminal alphabet, T is the terminal alphabet, S is the axiom, while the elements of M are called matrices).

For $w, z \in (N \cup T)^*$ we write $w \Longrightarrow z$ if there is a matrix $(A_1 \rightarrow x_1, \ldots, A_n \rightarrow x_n)$ in M and the strings $w_i \in (N \cup T)^*, 1 \leq i \leq n+1$, such that $w = w_1, z = w_{n+1}$, and, for all $1 \leq i \leq n$, either (1) $w_i = w_i' A_i w_i'', w_{i+1} = w_i' x_i w_i''$, for some $w_i', w_i'' \in (N \cup T)^*$, or (2) $w_i = w_{i+1}$, A_i does not appear in w_i, and the rule $A_i \rightarrow x_i$ appears in F. (The rules of a matrix are applied in order, possibly skipping the rules in F if they cannot be applied – therefore we say that these rules are applied in the *appearance checking* mode.)

The language generated by G is defined by $L(G) = \{w \in T^* \mid S \Longrightarrow^* w\}$. The family of languages of this form is denoted by MAT_{ac}. When $F = \emptyset$ (hence we do not use the appearance checking feature), the generated family is denoted by MAT.

It is known that $CF \subset MAT \subset MAT_{ac} = RE$, the inclusions being proper. All one-letter languages in the family MAT are regular, see [10].

A matrix grammar $G = (N, T, S, M, F)$ is said to be in the *binary normal form* if $N = N_1 \cup N_2 \cup \{S, \#\}$, with these three sets mutually disjoint, and the matrices in M are in one of the following forms:

1. $(S \rightarrow XA)$, with $X \in N_1, A \in N_2$,
2. $(X \rightarrow Y, A \rightarrow x)$, with $X, Y \in N_1, A \in N_2, x \in (N_2 \cup T)^*$,
3. $(X \rightarrow Y, A \rightarrow \#)$, with $X, Y \in N_1, A \in N_2$,
4. $(X \rightarrow \lambda, A \rightarrow x)$, with $X \in N_1, A \in N_2$, and $x \in T^*$.

Moreover, there is only one matrix of type 1 and F consists exactly of all rules $A \rightarrow \#$ appearing in matrices of type 3; $\#$ is called a trap-symbol, because once introduced, it is never removed. A matrix of type 4 is used only once, in the last step of a derivation.

According to [6], for each matrix grammar there is an equivalent matrix grammar in the binary normal form.

For an arbitrary matrix grammar $G = (N, T, S, M, F)$, let us denote by $ac(G)$ the cardinality of the set $\{A \in N \mid A \rightarrow \alpha \in F\}$. From the construction in the proof of Lemma 1.3.7 in [6] one can see that if we start from a matrix grammar G and we get the grammar G' in the binary normal form, then $ac(G') = ac(G)$.

Improving the result from [16] (six nonterminals, all of them used in the appearance checking mode, suffice in order to characterize RE with matrix grammars), in [9] it was proved that four nonterminals are sufficient in order to characterize RE by matrix grammars and out of them only three are used in appearance checking rules. Of interest here is another result from [9]: if the total number of nonterminals is not restricted, then each recursively enumerable language can be generated by a matrix grammar G such that $ac(G) \leq 2$.

Consequently, to the properties of a grammar G in the binary normal form we can add the fact that $ac(G) \leq 2$. We will say that this is *the strong binary normal form* for matrix grammars.

A type-0 grammar $G = (N, T, S, P)$ is said to be in the *Kuroda normal form* if the rules from P are of one of the following two forms: $A \rightarrow x, AB \rightarrow CD$, for $A, B, C, D \in N$ and $x \in (N \cup T)^*$ (that is, besides context-free rules we have only rules which replace two nonterminals by two nonterminals).

A *pure* context-free grammar is a construct $G = (V, S, P)$, where V is an alphabet, $S \in V$ and P is a finite set of context-free rules over V. The generated languages is defined by $L(G) = \{w \in V^* \mid S \Longrightarrow^* w$ with respect to $P\}$ (all generated strings are accepted).

Convention. When comparing two languages, the empty string is ignored, that is, L_1 is considered identical with L_2 as soon as $L_1 - \{\lambda\} = L_2 - \{\lambda\}$.

3   Rewriting P Systems

We introduce here only the class of P systems with string-objects processed by rewriting, in the variant we will investigate in this paper. For other classes the reader is referred to the bibliography (an up-to-date bibliography of the area can be found at the web address `http://bioinformatics.bio.disco.unimib.it/psystems`).

A membrane structure is pictorially represented by a Euler-Venn diagram (like the one in Figure 1); mathematically, it can be represented in a natural way by a tree or by a string of matching parentheses. For instance, the structure from Figure 1 is represented by the expression

$$[_1 \ [_2 \ ]_2 \ [_3 \ ]_3 \ [_4 \ [_5 \ ]_5 \ [_6 \ [_8 \ ]_8 \ [_9 \ ]_9 \ ]_6 \ [_7 \ ]_7 \ ]_4 \ ]_1.$$

Of course, the same membrane structure may be represented by different parenthesis expressions (neighboring membranes in the same level can be permuted).

An extended *rewriting P system* (of degree $m \geq 1$) *with conditional communication* is a construct

$$\Pi = (V, T, \mu, M_1, \ldots, M_m, R_1, P_1, F_1, \ldots, R_m, P_m, F_m),$$

where:

1. V is the alphabet of the system;
2. $T \subseteq V$ is the *terminal alphabet*;
3. μ is a membrane structure with m membranes (injectively labeled by $1, 2, \ldots, m$);
4. $M_1, \ldots, M_m$ are finite languages over V, representing the strings initially present in the regions $1, 2, \ldots, m$ of the system;
5. $R_1, \ldots, R_m$ are finite sets of context-free *rules* over V present in region i of the system, P_i are *permitting conditions* and F_i are *forbidding conditions* associated with region $i, 1 \le i \le m$.

The conditions can be of the following forms:

1. *empty*: no restriction is imposed on strings, they either exit the current membrane or enter any of the directly inner membrane freely (but they cannot remain in the current membrane); we denote an empty permitting condition by $(true, X), X \in \{in, out\}$, and an empty forbidding condition by $(false, notX), X \in \{in, out\}$.
2. *symbols checking*: each P_i is a set of pairs $(a, X), X \in \{in, out\}$, for $a \in V$, and each F_i is a set of pairs $(b, notX), X \in \{in, out\}$, for $b \in V$; a string w can go to a lower membrane only if there is a pair $(a, in) \in P_i$ with $a \in alph(w)$, and for each $(b, notin) \in F_i$ we have $b \notin alph(w)$; similarly, for sending the string w out of membrane i it is necessary to have $a \in alph(w)$ for at least one pair $(a, out) \in P_i$ and $b \notin alph(w)$ for all $(b, notout) \in F_i$.
3. *substrings checking*: each P_i is a set of pairs $(u, X), X \in \{in, out\}$, for $u \in V^+$, and each F_i is a set of pairs $(v, notX), X \in \{in, out\}$, for $v \in V^+$; a string w can go to a lower membrane only if there is a pair $(u, in) \in P_i$ with $u \in Sub(w)$, and for each $(v, notin) \in F_i$ we have $v \notin Sub(w)$; similarly, for sending the string w out of membrane i it is necessary to have $u \in Sub(w)$ for at least one pair $(u, out) \in P_i$ and $v \notin Sub(w)$ for all $(v, notout) \in F_i$.
4. *prefix/suffix checking*: exactly as in the case of substrings checking, with the checked string being a prefix or a suffix of the string to be communicated.
5. *shape checking*: each P_i is a set of pairs $(e, X), X \in \{in, out\}$, where e is an elementary regular expression over V, and each F_i is a set of pairs $(f, notX), X \in \{in, out\}$, where f is an elementary regular expression over V; a string w can go to a lower membrane only if there is a pair $(e, in) \in P_i$ with $w \in L(e)$, and for each pair $(f, notin) \in F_i$ we have $w \notin L(f)$; similarly, for sending the string w out of membrane i it is necessary to have $w \in L(e)$ for at least one pair $(e, out) \in P_i$ and $w \notin L(f)$ for all $(f, notout) \in F_i$.

We say that we have conditions of the types *empty*, *symb*, *sub_k*, *pref_k*, *suff_k*, *patt*, respectively, where k is the length of the longest string in all P_i, F_i; when no upper bound on this length is imposed we replace the subscript by $*$.

A system is said to be *non-extended* if $V = T$.

The transitions in a system as above are defined in the following way. In each region, each string which can be rewritten is rewritten by a rule from that region. The rule to be applied and the nonterminal it rewrites are non-deterministically chosen. Each string obtained in this way is checked against the conditions P_i, F_i from that region. If it fulfills the requested conditions, then it will be immediately sent out of the membrane or to an inner membrane, if any exists; if it fulfills both *in* and *out* conditions, then it is sent either out of the membrane or to a lower membrane, nondeterministically choosing the direction – and nondeterministically choosing the inner membrane in the case when several directly inner membranes exist. If a string does not fulfill any condition, or it fulfills only *in* conditions and there is no inner membrane, then the string remains in the same region. A string which is rewritten and a string which is sent to another membrane is "consumed", we do not have a copy of it at the next step in the same membrane. If a string cannot be rewritten, then it is directly checked against the communication conditions, and, as above, it leaves the membrane (or remains inside forever) depending on the result of this checking.

That is, the rewriting has priority over communication: we first try to rewrite a string and only after that do we try to communicate the result of the rewriting or the string itself if no rewriting is possible on it.

As usual, a sequence of transitions forms a computation and the result of a halting computation is the set of strings over T sent out of the system during the computation. In the case of non-extended systems, all strings sent out are accepted. A computation which never halts yields no result. A string which remains inside the system or, in the case of extended systems, which exits but contains symbols not in T does not contribute to the generated language. The language generated in this way by a system Π is denoted by $L(\Pi)$.

The family of all languages $L(\Pi)$, computed as above by extended systems Π of degree at most $m \geq 1$ and with permitting conditions of type α and forbidding conditions of type β, is denoted by $ERP_m(\alpha, \beta)$, $\alpha, \beta \in \{empty, symb, sub_*, pref_*, suff_*, patt\} \cup \{sub_k, pref_k, suff_k \mid k \geq 1\}$; when using non-extended systems we get the family $RP_m(\alpha, \beta)$. When we use both prefix and suffix checking (each condition string may be checked both as a prefix or as a suffix, that is, we do not separately give sets of prefixes and sets of suffixes), then we will indicate this by *prefsuff_k*. If the degree of the systems is not bounded, then the subscript m is replaced by $*$.

4   Proof Mechanisms

The proofs of universality which follow in the next Section are based on the simulation of well known models of universal computating devices in normal forms.

In particular, we exploit the Kuroda normal form for type 0 grammars and the binary normal form for matrix grammars with appearance checking.

Rewriting steps in these normal forms are simulated by coordinating the sequential use of context-free rules. Such a coordination is achieved by introducing new non terminals derived from those of a grammar in normal form and tagged so that they can be rewritten only in coordination with others analogously tagged, and constraining their coordinate usage to occur only within some well-defined membranes. We anticipate here the general mechanisms that will be exploited in the next Section in which detailed proofs are presented.

In general, as will be shown in the next Section, the distinction between terminal and non terminal alphabets can be simulated by the use of an additional membrane letting only terminal symbols out. The proofs need therefore to consider only pure systems or extended systems with an empty forbidding condition. It is indeed easy to realise that forbidding has global scope, while permitting conditions can obtain a global effect only by constraining the complete form of a word, i.e. by expressing the constraint through patterns.

In particular, we will observe that patterns can constrain the simulation of Kuroda rewriting by allowing only the communication of words in which symbols derived from a rule of the form $AB \to CD$ are present in the correct sequence, i.e. $(A, r)[B, r]$, where r is a label indicating the originating rule. In this case communication is allowed towards a membrane where the original rule can be simulated in two steps.

Conversely, a forbidding condition needs only to check that symbols derived from the same rule appear in the correct order, by listing all possible incorrect occurrences of these symbols in the context of symbols related to other rules. Hence checking a substring of length two suffices.

This is not sufficient if the substring is checked in a permitting condition. A check on individual symbols is indeed needed in a forbidding condition to force strings containing derived non terminals to reach a membrane where they can be both used. In this case, the depth of the membrane system must increase for the rewriting to occur only in the innermost membrane. In general, the level of nesting is related to the decomposition of the Kuroda rules, which can occur through at most 4 levels. One can also observe that checking on single symbols is already powerful in that it forces directionality in the traversing of the membranes by preventing movements in the opposite direction. Finally, checking based on suffix/prefix strings can be used to constrain the location in which rules have to be applied.

For proofs based on the simulation of matrix grammars, special membranes are needed in order to simulate the use of rules on which appearance checking is based. Rewriting in these matrices means that the original rewriting in the matrix grammar would produce the trap symbol #. For the other rules at least two levels of nesting are needed to simulate the coupling of the rules in the binary normal form. In this case the check can be based on just one symbol, as needed for directing words with symbols deriving from a matrix to reach the correct membrane into which to simulate the matrix.

Hence a trade-off occurs between the complexity of the check and the depth of the membrane system, which remains in any case limited. The degree of branching of the membrane system is in general independent of the grammar. Hence, the results obtained hold for P systems with a fixed number of membranes. The only exception is the case of check based on prefixes and suffixes, where branching depends on the number of rules of the form $AB \rightarrow CD$ present in the original grammar (each simulated with 4 levels of nesting in independent subsystems) and on the number of symbols in the grammar (to consider that a prefix can start with any of the grammar symbols).

5 Generative Power

We start by mentioning some relations which directly follow from the definitions or can be easily proved; in all these relations α, β assume all possible values in the set $\{empty, symb, sub_*, pref_*, suff_*, prefsuff_*, patt\} \cup \{sub_k, pref_k, suff_k, prefsuff_k \mid k \geq 1\}$.

Lemma 1. (i) $ERP_*(\alpha, \beta) \subseteq RE$.
(ii) $RP_m(\alpha, \beta) \subseteq ERP_m(\alpha, \beta), m \geq 1$.
(iii) $RP_m(\alpha, \beta) \subseteq RP_{m+1}(\alpha, \beta), m \geq 1$.
(iv) $RP_m(empty, \beta) \subseteq RP_m(symb, \beta) = RP_m(sub_1, \beta) \subseteq RP_m(sub_*, \beta)$
$\subseteq RP_m(patt, \beta), m \geq 1$.
(v) $RP_m(\alpha_k, \beta) = RP_m(\alpha_{k+1}, \beta), m, k \geq 1, \alpha \in \{sub, pref, suff, prefsuff\}$.
The relations from (iii) – (v) are valid also in the case of families of language generated by extended systems; in all relations (ii), (iv), (v) the subscript m can also be $*$.

Lemma 2. $ERP_m(\alpha, \beta) \subseteq RP_{m+1}(\alpha, \beta)$, for all α, β such that $\beta \neq empty$ and $m \geq 1$.

Proof. Starting from a given system Π with the total alphabet V and the terminal alphabet T, with a selection of a type (α, β) such that β allows at least the checking of symbols, we add one further membrane around the skin membrane of Π, as the skin membrane of the new system, we introduce no rewriting rule into it, but only the permitting condition $(true, out)$ and the forbidding conditions $(a, notout)$, for all $a \in V - T$. If we denote by Π' the obtained system, then we clearly have $L(\Pi) = L(\Pi')$ (no rewriting is possible in the skin membrane of Π', hence the halting computations in Π are halting also in Π', but only strings over T can leave the system).   □

Corollary 1. $RP_*(\alpha, \beta) = ERP_*(\alpha, \beta)$ for all α, β such that $\beta \neq empty$.

We now pass to proving the universality results we have announced. They suggest a trade-off between the number of membranes and the permitting/forbidding conditions we use. We start by using strong conditions, and this makes possible characterizations of RE by systems with a reduced number of membranes.

Theorem 1. $RP_2(patt, empty) = RE$.

Proof. Let $G = (N, T, S, P)$ be a type-0 Chomsky grammar in the Kuroda normal form; assume that all non-context-free rules in P are labeled in a one-to-one manner. We construct the P system

$$\Pi = (V, V, [_1[_2 \ ]_2]_1, \{S\}, \emptyset, R_1, P_1, F_1, R_2, P_2, F_2),$$

with the following components:

$$V = T \cup N \cup \{(A,r), [B,r] \mid r : AB \to CD \in P\},$$
$$R_1 = \{A \to x \mid A \to x \in P\}$$
$$\cup \{A \to (A,r), B \to [B,r] \mid r : AB \to CD \in P\},$$
$$P_1 = \{(T^*, out)\}$$
$$\cup \{(N \cup T)^*(A,r)[B,r](N \cup T)^*, in) \mid r : AB \to CD \in P\},$$
$$F_1 = \{(false, notin), (false, notout)\},$$
$$R_2 = \{(A,r) \to C, \; [B,r] \to D \mid r : AB \to CD \in P\},$$
$$P_2 = \{((N \cup T)^*, out)\},$$
$$F_2 = \{(false, notout)\}.$$

At any moment, only one string is present in the system; initially, this is the axiom of G.

Only terminal strings can be sent out. A string which contains at least a nonterminal of G is either rewritten in the skin membrane, or it remains forever there, hence we get no output. A string from the skin membrane can be sent to the inner membrane only if it is of the form $x(A,r)[B,r]y$, for some rule $r : AB \to CD$ and $x, y \in (N \cup T)^*$, which ensures the correct simulation in membrane 2 of this rule; the string exits membrane 2 only after replacing (A,r) with C and $[B,r]$ with D. The context-free rules of P are simulated in the skin membrane. Consequently, $L(G) = L(\Pi)$. □

When checking only substrings we need non-empty forbidding conditions, or a bigger number of membranes (Theorem 3); in turn, checking substrings of length at most two suffices.

Theorem 2. $RP_2(empty, sub_2) = RE$.

Proof. For a type-0 Chomsky grammar in the Kuroda normal form $G = (N, T, S, P)$, with the non-context-free rules in P labeled in a one-to-one manner, we construct the P system

$$\Pi = (V, T, [_1[_2 \;]_2]_1, \{XSX\}, \emptyset, R_1, P_1, F_1, R_2, P_2, F_2),$$

with the following components:

$$V = T \cup N \cup \{A' \mid A \in N\} \cup \{X\}$$
$$\cup \{(A,r), [B,r] \mid r : AB \to CD \in P\},$$
$$R_1 = \{A \to x \mid A \to x \in P\}$$
$$\cup \{A \to (A,r), B \to [B,r] \mid r : AB \to CD \in P\}$$
$$\cup \{A \to A, \; A' \to A \mid A \in N\}$$
$$\cup \{X \to \lambda\},$$
$$P_1 = \{(true, out), (true, in)\},$$

$$F_1 = \{(X, notout)\} \cup \{(A, notout), (A', notout) \mid A \in N\}$$
$$\cup \{((A, r), notout), ([B, r], notout) \mid \text{ for all } A, B \in N \text{ and}$$
$$r \text{ a non-context-free rule in } P\}$$
$$\cup \{(A, r)\alpha, notin), ((A, r)(E, r'), notin), (\alpha[B, r], notin),$$
$$([B, r][E, r'], notin), ([B, r](E, r'), notin) \mid$$
$$\text{for all possible } A, B, E \in N, \alpha \in N \cup T \cup \{X\},$$
$$\text{and } r \text{ a non-context-free rule in } P\}, r \neq r'$$
$$R_2 = \{(A, r) \rightarrow C', \ [B, r] \rightarrow D' \mid r : AB \rightarrow CD \in P\},$$
$$P_2 = \{(true, out)\},$$
$$F_2 = \{((A, r)E', notout), (E'[B, r], notout) \mid A, B, E \in N\}.$$

The equality $L(G) = L(\Pi)$ is easy to be proved: as in the proof of Theorem 1, we can pass a string from membrane 1 to membrane 2 only if it is of the form $x(A, r)[B, r]y$, for $r : AB \rightarrow CD \in P$ and $x, y \in (N \cup T)^*$, maybe with x starting and y ending with X (the forbidding conditions prevent having further occurrences of symbols of the form $(E, p), [E, p]$ in the strings x, y; a string with only one occurrence of a symbol of the form $(E, p), [E, p]$ cannot be sent to the inner membrane); a string in $(N \cup T)^*$, maybe starting or ending with X, can be sent to membrane 2 after applying a rule $A \rightarrow A, A' \rightarrow A$, or $X \rightarrow \lambda$ in membrane 1, but it will exit immediately, unchanged; note also that only terminal strings with respect to G can be sent out of the system. □

At the price of using a larger number of membranes, we can obtain a characterization of RE by systems which check permitting substrings of length 2 and forbidding symbols.

Theorem 3. $RP_4(sub_2, symb) = RE$.

Proof. We start again from a type-0 Chomsky grammar in the Kuroda normal form $G = (N, T, S, P)$, with the non-context-free rules in P labeled in a one-to-one manner, and we construct the P system

$$\Pi = (V, T, [_1[_2[_3[_4 \ ]_4]_3]_2]_1, \{S\}, \emptyset, \emptyset, \emptyset, R_1, P_1, F_1, \ldots, R_4, P_4, F_4),$$

with the following components:

$$V = T \cup N \cup \{A', A'' \mid A \in N\} \cup \{\$, Z\}$$
$$\cup \{(A, r), [B, r] \mid r : AB \rightarrow CD \in P\},$$
$$R_1 = \{A \rightarrow x \mid A \rightarrow x \in P\}$$
$$\cup \{A \rightarrow (A, r) \mid r : AB \rightarrow CD \in P\}$$
$$\cup \{E \rightarrow E, \ E'' \rightarrow E \mid E \in N\},$$
$$P_1 = \{(\lambda, out)\} \cup \{((A, r), in) \mid r : AB \rightarrow CD \in P\},$$
$$F_1 = \{(E, notout), (E', notout) \mid E \in N\}$$
$$\cup \{((A, r), notout) \mid r : AB \rightarrow CD \in P\},$$

$$R_2 = \{B \to [B, r] \mid r : AB \to CD \in P\}$$
$$\cup \{E' \to E'', \; E'' \to Z \mid E \in N\},$$
$$P_2 = \{(E'', out) \mid E \in N\}$$
$$\cup \{([B, r], in) \mid r : AB \to CD \in P\},$$
$$F_2 = \{([B, r], notout) \mid r : AB \to CD \in P\}$$
$$\cup \{(E', notin), (E'', notin) \mid E \in N\},$$
$$R_3 = \{E' \to E \mid E \in N\},$$
$$P_3 = \{((A, r)[B, r], in) \mid r : AB \to CD \in P\}$$
$$\cup \{(E', out) \mid E \in N\},$$
$$F_3 = \{(\$, notin), (\$, notout)\},$$
$$R_4 = \{(A, r) \to C', \; [B, r] \to D' \mid r : AB \to CD \in P\},$$
$$P_4 = \{(C'D', out) \mid r : AB \to CD \in P\},$$
$$F_4 = \{(\$, notout)\}.$$

The symbol \$ never appears in a string, it is only used in some forbidding conditions which should always be false, while Z is a trap-symbol, once introduced it is never removed. A string can be sent from membrane 1 to membrane 2 only after using a rule of the form $A \to (A, r)$ associated with a rule $r : AB \to CD$ from P, and, conversely after using such a rule, the string *must* go to membrane 2 (this ensures the fact that exactly one such a rule is used). Similarly, a string can be sent from membrane 2 to membrane 3 after using one rule of the form $E \to [E, p]$ (if no rule of this form can be used, then the string remains forever in membrane 2 and we get no output). Membrane 3 just checks whether or not the two rules used in membranes 1 and 2 correspond to the same non-context-free rule of P and the symbols which were rewritten are adjacent. If this is the case, then the string enters membrane 4, where the rule $r : AB \to CD$ is simulated; only when both C' and D' are introduced can the string leave membrane 4. One primed symbol is replaced in membrane 3 with its non-primed variant and the string immediately exits. In membrane 2 we cannot use a rule of the form $E \to [E, p]$, because the string will remain forever here (it cannot exit because of $[E, p]$ and cannot go to membrane 3 because of the primed symbol; even after using a rule $E' \to E''$, we cannot send the string to membranes 1 or 3). Thus, we have to use the rule $E' \to E''$ and exit. Assume that in the skin membrane we introduce again a symbol (A, r) before using the rule $E'' \to E$. The string goes to membrane 2. If we use the rule $E'' \to Z$, then the trap-symbol is introduced. If we use a rule of the form $B \to [B, r]$, then the string will remain here forever (hence, eventually, the rule $E'' \to Z$ should be used). Therefore, in the skin membrane we have to remove the primes, and only after that can we start simulating another non-context-free rule of G. The context-free rules are simulated in the skin membrane at any time before using a rule $A \to (A, r)$. Thus, any derivation of G can be simulated in Π. Clearly, only terminal strings with respect to G can be sent out, so we have the equality $L(G) = L(\Pi)$.   □

By using one further membrane, as well as final selection by a terminal alphabet, we can completely avoid the checking of forbidding conditions:

Theorem 4. $RE = ERP_5(sub_2, empty)$.

Proof. We start again from a type-0 Chomsky grammar in the Kuroda normal form $G = (N, T, S, P)$, with the non-context-free rules in P labeled in a one-to-one manner, and we construct the P system

$$\Pi = (V, T, [_1[_2[_4\ ]_4]_2[_3[_5\ ]_5]_3]_1, \emptyset, \emptyset, \emptyset, \{S\}, \emptyset, R_1, P_1, F_1, \ldots, R_5, P_5, F_5),$$

with the following components:

$$
\begin{aligned}
V =\ & T \cup N \cup \{A', A'', A''' \mid A \in N\} \cup \{f, Z\} \\
& \cup \{(A, r), [B, r] \mid r : AB \to CD \in P\}, \\
R_1 =\ & \{f \to \lambda\} \\
& \cup \{A' \to Z,\ A''' \to Z, A'' \to A \mid A \in N\}, \\
P_1 =\ & \{\lambda, out)\} \\
& \cup \{((A, r)[B, r], in) \mid r : AB \to CD \in P\} \\
& \cup \{(A', in) \mid A \in N\}, \\
R_2 =\ & \{B \to [B, r] \mid r : AB \to CD \in P\} \\
& \cup \{E' \to E'', E''' \to Z \mid E \in N\}, \\
P_2 =\ & \{(f, out)\} \\
& \cup \{([B, r], out) \mid r : AB \to CD \in P\}, \\
R_3 =\ & \{(A, r) \to C',\ [B, r] \to Z \mid r : AB \to CD \in P\}, \\
P_3 =\ & \{(E', in), (E'', out) \mid E \in N\}, \\
R_4 =\ & \{A \to (A, r) \mid r : AB \to CD \in P\} \\
& \cup \{A \to x,\ A \to xf \mid A \to x \in P\} \\
& \cup \{A''' \to A \mid A \in N\}, \\
P_4 =\ & \{(f, out)\} \cup \{((A, r), out) \mid r : AB \to CD \in P\}, \\
R_5 =\ & \{[B, r] \to D'' \mid r : AB \to CD \in P\} \\
& \cup \{C' \to Z \mid C \in N\}, \\
P_5 =\ & \{(C'D'', out) \mid r : AB \to CD \in P\}.
\end{aligned}
$$

All sets of forbidding conditions consist of the pairs $(false, notin)$, $(false, notout)$.

This system works as follows. We start in membrane 4 with the axiom of G. The context-free rules of G can be simulated here. If a terminal rule $A \to xf$ is used in membrane 4, then the string exits; if it not terminal and a rule $B \to [B, r]$ is used in membrane 2, then the string goes to membrane 1 and from here out of the system; but since it is not terminal, it is not accepted in the generated language. If the string is terminal, then it exits (f is erased in the skin membrane) and is introduced in $L(\Pi)$.

Assume that a string w is rewritten in membrane 4 by a rule $A \to (A, r)$ associated with a rule $r : AB \to CD \in P$. It exits; if no rule can be applied in membrane 2, then no output is produced. Assume that a rule $E \to [E, p]$ is used in membrane 2. The string is immediately sent to membrane 1. If the two tuple symbols are not associated with the same rule from P, so that no rule can be used in the skin membrane, then the string is sent out of the system, but it is not a terminal one. Assume that the string is of the form $w_1(A, r)[B, r]w_2$, for some $r : AB \to CD \in P$. No rule can be applied in the skin membrane, but the string can be sent to a lower membrane. If it arrives back in membrane 2, then it will exit either unchanged – if no rule of the form $E \to [E, p]$ can be used – or after introducing one further symbol of the form $[E, p]$. The process is repeated; eventually, the string will arrive in membrane 3 (otherwise we either continue between membranes 1 and 2 or we send the string out and it is not terminal). In membrane 3, the unique copy of the symbol (A, r) is replaced by C' and the string is sent to membrane 5. Here we also replace a symbol $[E, p]$ with H''. The string exits only if the primed symbols, $C'H''$, correspond to a rule $r : AB \to CD \in P$, otherwise the rule $C' \to Z$ introduces the trap-symbol Z. Assume that we have a substring $C'D''$ associated with a rule $r : AB \to CD \in P$. The string is sent to membrane 3. If we had at least two symbols of the form $[E, p]$, then the trap-symbol is introduced, otherwise the string is sent to the skin membrane. Consequently, we have to replace exactly two symbols A, B with $(A, r), [B, r]$, in adjacent positions, hence this corresponds to simulating the rule $r : AB \to CD \in P$.

Now, in the skin membrane (if not using the rule $C' \to Z$) we use the rule $D'' \to D$ and the string is sent to one of membranes 2 and 3. From membrane 3 the string should enter unchanged membrane 4, and here the rule $C' \to Z$ is used. Thus, we have to send the string to membrane 2. We have here two cases. If we use a rule $E \to [E, p]$, then the string is sent back to the skin membrane, where the only applicable rule is $C' \to Z$ and no terminal string will be ever obtained. If in membrane 2 we use the rule $C' \to C'''$, then the string is sent to membrane 4, where again we have two cases. If we use the rule $C''' \to C$, then we have again a string over $(N \cup T)^*$, and the process can be iterated. If, before using the rule $C''' \to C$, we use a rule $A \to (A, r)$, then the string should go to membrane 2. If we use here the rule $C''' \to Z$, then the computation will produce nothing. If we use a rule $E \to [E, p]$, then the string is sent to membrane 1, where the only applicable rule is $C''' \to Z$.

Consequently, we have to completely simulate the rule $r : AB \to CD \in P$, ending by using the rule $C'' \to C$ in membrane 4. Thus, $L(G) = L(\Pi)$.   □

We do not know whether or not the number of membranes in the previous system can be decreased without decreasing the generative power. Anyway, somewhat surprisingly, one additional membrane with respect to those used in the system from the proof of Theorem 4 suffices in order to characterize RE even when checking only symbols as permitting conditions.

Theorem 5. $ERP_6(symb, empty) = RP_6(symb, symb) = RE$.

Proof. Let us consider a matrix grammar with appearance checking, $G = (N, T, S, M, F)$, in the strong binary normal form, that is with $N = N_1 \cup N_2 \cup \{S, \#\}$, with rules of the four forms mentioned in Section 2, and with $ac(G) \leq 2$. Assume that we are in the worst case, with $ac(G) = 2$, and let $B^{(1)}, B^{(2)}$ be the two symbols in N_2 for which we have rules $B^{(j)} \rightarrow \#$ in matrices of M. Let us assume that we have k matrices of the form $m_i : (X \rightarrow \alpha, A \rightarrow x), X \in N_1, \alpha \in N_1 \cup \{\lambda\}, A \in N_2$, and $x \in (N_2 \cup T)^*$, $1 \leq i \leq k$ (that is, without rules to be used in the appearance checking manner). Each matrix of the form $(X \rightarrow \lambda, A \rightarrow x), X \in N_1, A \in N_2, x \in T^*$, is replaced by $(X \rightarrow f, A \rightarrow x)$, where f is a new symbol. We continue to label the obtained matrix in the same way as the original one. The matrices of the form $(X \rightarrow Y, B^{(j)} \rightarrow \#), X, Y \in N_1$ (that is, with rules used in the appearance checking manner), are labeled by m_i, with $i \in lab_j$, for $j = 1, 2$, such that lab_1, lab_2 and $lab_0 = \{1, 2, \ldots, k\}$ are mutually disjoint sets.

We construct the extended P system (of degree 6)

$$\Pi = (V, T, \mu, M_1, \ldots, M_6, R_1, P_1, F_1, \ldots, R_6, P_6, F_6),$$

with the following components:

$$V = T \cup N_1 \cup N_2 \cup \{(X_i, j) \mid X \in N_1, 1 \leq i \leq k, 0 \leq j \leq k\}$$
$$\cup \{X_i \mid X \in N_1, i \in lab_1 \cup lab_2\}$$
$$\cup \{A_i, (A_i, j) \mid A \in N_2, 1 \leq i \leq k, 0 \leq j \leq k\}$$
$$\cup \{X', X'', X''' \mid X \in N_1\}$$
$$\cup \{f'', Z\},$$
$$\mu = [_1[_2[_3[_4 \ ]_4]_3]_2[_5 \ ]_5[_6 \ ]_6]_1,$$
$$M_1 = \{XA\}, \text{ for } (S \rightarrow XA) \text{ being the initial matrix of } G,$$
$$M_i = \emptyset, \text{ for all } i = 2, \ldots, 6,$$

and with the following triples $(R_i, P_i, F_i), 1 \leq i \leq 6$ (the membranes with labels 2, 3, 4 will be used for simulating matrices $m_i, 1 \leq i \leq k$, while membranes with labels 5, 6 will simulate the matrices with labels in lab_1, lab_2, respectively):

R_1: $X \rightarrow X_i$, for all matrices $m_i : (X \rightarrow Y, B^{(j)} \rightarrow \#)$, $i \in lab_j, j = 1, 2$,
$\quad A \rightarrow (A_i, 0)$, for $m_i : (X \rightarrow Y, A \rightarrow x), 1 \leq i \leq k$,
$\quad X_i \rightarrow Y'$, for all matrices $m_i : (X \rightarrow Y, D \rightarrow \alpha)$, $i \in lab_0 \cup lab_1 \cup lab_2$,
$\quad X'' \rightarrow X'''$, for all $X \in N_1$,
$\quad f'' \rightarrow \lambda$;
$P_1 = \{((A_i, 0), in) \mid A \in N_2, i \in lab_0\}$
$\quad \cup \{(X_i, in), (X', in), (X''', in) \mid X \in N_1, i \in lab_1 \cup lab_2\}$
$\quad \cup \{(a, out) \mid a \in T\}$;
$F_1 = \{(false, notin), (false, notout)\}$;

R_2: $X_i \rightarrow Z$, for all $X \in N_1, i \in lab_1 \cup lab_2$,
$\quad X \rightarrow (X_i, 0)$, for all $X \in N_1, 1 \leq i \leq k$,

$A_i \to x$, for all $m_i : (X \to Y, A \to x), 1 \leq i \leq k$,
$(A_i, j) \to Z$, for all $A \in N_2, 1 \leq j < i \leq k$,
$X'' \to Z$, for all $X \in N_1 \cup \{f\}$,
$X''' \to X$, for all $X \in N_1$;

$P_2 = \{((X_i, 0), in) \mid X \in N_1, 1 \leq i \leq k\}$
$\cup \{(X, out), (X'', out) \mid X \in N_1 \cup \{f\}\}$;

$F_2 = \{(false, notin), (false, notout)\}$;

R_3: $(X_i, j) \to (X_i, j+1)$, for all $X \in N_1, 0 \leq j < i \leq k$,
$(X_i, i) \to \alpha''$, for all $m_i : (X \to \alpha, A \to x), 1 \leq i \leq k, \alpha \in N_1 \cup \{f\}$;

$P_3 = \{((X_i, j), in) \mid X \in N_1, 1 \leq j \leq i \leq k\}$
$\cup \{(X'', out) \mid X \in N_1 \cup \{f\}\}$;

$F_3 = \{(false, notin), (false, notout)\}$;

R_4: $(A_i, j) \to (A_i, j+1)$, for all $A \in N_2, 0 \leq j < i \leq k$,
$(A_i, i) \to A_i$, for all $m_i : (X \to \alpha, A \to x), 1 \leq i \leq k, \alpha \in N_1 \cup \{f\}$,
$A_i \to Z$, for all $A \in N_2, 1 \leq i \leq k$;

$P_4 = \{((A_i, j), out) \mid A \in N_2, 1 \leq j < i \leq k\}$
$\cup \{(A_i, out) \mid A \in N_2, 1 \leq i \leq k\}$;

$F_4 = \{(false, notout)\}$;

and, for $j = 1, 2$,

$R_{4+j,1}$: $X_i \to Z$, for all $X \in N_1, i \notin lab_j$,
$(A_i, 0) \to Z$, for all $A \in N_2, i \in lab_0$,
$B^{(j)} \to Z$,
$X' \to X$, for all $X \in N_1$,
$X''' \to Z$, for all $Z \in N_1$;

$P_{4+j} = \{(a, out) \mid a \in T\}$;

$F_{4+j} = \{(false, notout)\}$;

Let us examine the work of this system.

Only strings over T are accepted in the generated language; Z is a trap-symbol, once introduced it will never be removed, hence the string will never turn to be terminal. From the skin membrane in any moment we can send out a string which contains at least one terminal symbol, but if any symbol not in T is present, then the string is not accepted in the generated language.

At any moment we have exactly one string in the system; initially, this is XA, for $(S \to XA)$ the start matrix of G. Assume that we have here a string of the general form, Xw, with $X \in N_1$ and $w \in (N_2 \cup T)^*$. We have to use a rule of the form $X \to X_i$, for $i \in lab_j, 1 \leq j \leq 3$, or of the form $A \to (A_i, 0)$, for some $A \in N_2, 1 \leq i \leq k$. In the first case we start the simulation of a matrix with appearance checking, in the second case we start the simulation of a matrix $m_i, 1 \leq i \leq k$ (without appearance checking). If no rule can be used, then the string exits, but it is not terminal.

Assume that we are in the former case. The string must be communicated to a lower level membrane, that is, one of membranes 2, 5, 6. In membranes

2 and those of 5, 6 which are different from $4 + j$ the only applicable rule is $X_i \rightarrow Z$, hence the computation will not produce a terminal string. If the string $X_i w$ arrives in the right membrane $4 + j$, that is, the membrane with $i \in lab_j$, and $B^{(j)}$ is not present in it, then no rule can be applied to it, at the next step the string exits unchanged; in this way we know that w does not contain the symbol $B^{(j)}$; if $B^{(j)}$ is present, then the symbol Z is introduced. In the skin membrane we use the rule $X_i \rightarrow Y'$ which corresponds to the matrix $m_i : (X \rightarrow Y, B^{(j)} \rightarrow \#)$ from M. The string is sent again to a lower membrane; if it arrives in membrane 2, then it will remain here forever, unchanged; from any membrane 5, 6 it exits with Y' replaced with Y. This completes the simulation of the matrix m_i. The obtained string is of the initial form, hence the process can be iterated. If in the skin membrane we do not use the rule $X_i \rightarrow Y'$, but a rule of the form $A \rightarrow (A_i, 0)$, then the string can be sent to a lower membrane; both in membrane 2 and in membranes 5, 6 there is only one applicable rule, $(A_i, 0) \rightarrow Z$, hence no terminal string will be obtained.

Assume now that we have introduced a symbol $(A_i, 0)$, corresponding to a matrix $m_i : (X \rightarrow \alpha, A \rightarrow x), 1 \leq i \leq k$, with $\alpha \in N_1 \cup \{f\}$. The string should be communicated to a lower membrane. In membranes 5, 6 the symbol Z will be introduced, hence we have to send it to membrane 2. The only applicable rule is $X \rightarrow (X_j, 0)$, for some $j \in lab_0$. The string is sent to membrane 3, where $(X_j, 0)$ is replaced with $(X_j, 1)$. The obtained string is sent to membrane 4, where $(A_i, 0)$ is replaced with $(A_i, 1)$. The string returns to membrane 3. From now on, the string will go back and forth between membranes 3 and 4, and the second component of the symbols $(A_i, s), (X_j, t)$ is alternatively increased.

Now, we distinguish three cases:

Case 1: $i < j$. This means that at some step in membrane 4 we receive from membrane 3 a string of the form $(X_j, i)w_1(A_i, i - 1)w_2$. We replace $(A_i, i - 1)$ with (A_i, i) and no communication is possible (note that $((A_i, i), out)$ is not in P_4), hence one more rewriting is necessary. We replace (A_i, i) with A_i and the string is sent out. In membrane 3 we replace (X_j, i) with $(X_j, i + 1)$ (this is possible, because $i+1 \leq j$), the string is sent back to membrane 4, where the trap-symbol is introduced (the rewriting has priority over checking the communication conditions).

Case 2: $i > j$. At some moment we produce in membrane 3 a string of the form $(X_j, j)w_1(A_i, j - 1)w_2$, which is sent to membrane 4. Here we replace $(A_i, j - 1)$ with (A_i, j), the string exits, in membrane 3 we replace (X_j, j) with α'', $\alpha \in N_1 \cup \{f\}$, and the string is sent out. In membrane 2 we can apply $(A_i, j) \rightarrow Z$ or $\alpha'' \rightarrow Z$, hence again the string will never lead to a terminal one.

Case 3: $i = j$. At some moment we pass from membrane 3 to membrane 4 a string $(X_i, i)w_1(A_i, i - 1)w_2$. In membrane 4 we replace $(A_i, i - 1)$ with (A_i, i) and, because we cannot exit, we replace this latter symbol with A_i. Returned in membrane 3, we replace (X_i, i) with α'' and we send the string $\alpha'' w_1 A_i w_2$ to membrane 2. We have to continue by using the rule $A_i \rightarrow x$ and the string $\alpha'' w_1 x w_2$ is sent to the skin membrane.

We have here two subcases. If we use the rule $\alpha'' \to \alpha'''$, then the string is sent to membrane 2 again (in membranes 5, 6 the trap-symbol Z will be introduced). The only applicable rule here is $\alpha''' \to \alpha$, which completes the simulation of the matrix m_i. Moreover, we have a string of the form we have started with, hence – if $\alpha \in N_1$ – the process can be iterated. If in the skin membrane we use a rule of the form $C \to (C_l, 0)$, then a string of the form $\alpha'' z_1 (C_l, 0) z_2$ is sent to one of membranes 2, 5, 6; in all of them the trap-symbol is immediately produced.

Therefore, the only correct way (that is, leading to a terminal string) to proceed is to correctly simulate matrices from M.

At the moment when a matrix $(X \to f, A \to x)$ is simulated, the computation must stop: if a string $f'' z_1 (C_l, 0) z_2$ is sent to any membrane 2, 5, 6, then the trap-symbol is produced, hence the rule $f'' \to \lambda$ must be used in membrane 1. The string should exit (no condition allows movement to a lower membrane). If it is terminal, then it belongs to the language $L(\Pi)$, if not, then it is "lost".

If at any moment we get a string of the form $Xw, w \in T^*$, then we will never get a terminal string: we can at most simulate matrices $m_i, i \in lab_1 \cup lab_2$, but we cannot remove the symbol from N_1 present in the string. In turn, if we obtain a string without any symbol from N_1, but containing symbols from N_2, then this means that it is of the form $f'' w$, hence as we have seen above, the computation cannot lead to a terminal string.

Consequently, $L(\Pi) = L(G)$, and we have the equality $EPR_6(symb, empty) = RE$.

For the non-extended case we replace all sets $F_i, 2 \leq i \leq 6$, with $\{(\$, notin), (\$, notout)\}$, where $\$$ is a new symbol, to be added to V, and we consider

$$F_1 = \{(\$, notin)\} \cup \{(\alpha, notout) \mid \alpha \in V - T\}.$$

No string containing symbols not in T can exit the system, but all the strings are processed as described above, hence the language is not changed. This completes the proof.   □

It is an *open problem* whether or not the previous result is optimal, or the number of used membranes can be decreased.

For the case of checking separately only prefixes or only suffixes of strings we have not found a universality result, while when using both prefix and suffix checking we can characterize RE by systems with a number of membranes which is not bounded. Improving this result (we believe that the hierarchy on the number of membranes collapses also in this case) and investigating the families $RP_m(\alpha, \beta)$ with at least one of α, β in $\{pref_k, suff_k \mid k \geq 1\}$ remain as tasks for the reader.

Theorem 6. $ERP_*(prefsuff_2, empty) = RE$.

Proof. Let us consider a type-0 grammar $G = (N, T, S, P)$ in Kuroda normal form, with k non-context-free rules labeled in an injective manner, $r_i : AB \to CD, 1 \leq i \leq k$. Consider a new symbol, $\$$, and assume that $N \cup T \cup \{\$\} =$

$\{E_1, \ldots, E_n\}$. We construct the P system Π, of degree $4k + 2n + 7$, with the following components:

$$V = T \cup N \cup \{A' \mid A \in N\}$$
$$\cup \{(A', r), (B, r) \mid r : AB \to CD \in P\}$$
$$\cup \{X, X', X'', Y, Y', Y'', Z, \$\},$$
$$\mu = [_1[_2[_3[_4[_5 \ ]_5]_4[_6[_{E_1}[_{E_1'} \ ]_{E_1'}]_{E_1} \cdots [_{E_n}[_{E_n'} \ ]_{E_n'}]_{E_n}]_6$$
$$[_7[_{r_1}[_{r_1'}[_{r_1''}[_{r_1'''} \ ]_{r_1'''}]_{r_1''}]_{r_1'}]_{r_1} \cdots [_{r_k}[_{r_k'}[_{r_k''}[_{r_k'''} \ ]_{r_k'''}]_{r_k''}]_{r_k'}]_{r_k}]_7]_3]_2]_1,$$

all sets M_i of axioms are empty, excepting M_5, which contains the unique string $X''\$SY$, and with the following sets of rules and associated strings to be checked as permitting conditions (all forbidding condition sets are of the form $\{(false, notin), (false, notout)\}$):

R_1: $Y'' \to \lambda$;
$P_1 = \{(a, out) \mid a \in T\}$;

R_2: $Y' \to Y''$,
    $X \to \lambda$,
    $\$ \to \lambda$,
    $Y \to Z$;
$P_2 = \{(Y'', out)\}$;

R_3: $\alpha \to \alpha'$, for all $\alpha \in N \cup T \cup \{\$\}$,
    $X' \to X''$,
    $Y \to Y'$,
    $B \to (B, r)$, for all $r : AB \to CD \in P$;
$P_3 = \{(\alpha'Y, in), (\alpha Y, out) \mid \alpha \in N \cup T \cup \{\$\}\}$
    $\cup \{(X'', in), (\$Y', out)\} \cup \{((B, r)Y, in) \mid r : AB \to CD \in P\}$;

R_4: $= \{\alpha' \to Z \mid \alpha \in N \cup T \cup \{\$\}\}$
    $\cup \{(B, r) \to Z \mid r : AB \to CD \in P\}$;
P_4: $= \{(X, out), (X'', out)\}$;

R_5: $A \to x$, if such a rule is in P,
    $X'' \to X$,
    $\alpha' \to Z$, for all $\alpha \in N \cup T \cup \{\$\}$,
    $(B, r) \to Z$, for all $r : AB \to CD \in P$;
$P_5 = \{(X, out)\}$;

R_6 contains no rule;
$P_6 = \{(X, in), (X', out)\}$;

R_7 contains no rule;

$$P_7 = \{(X, in), (X', out)\},$$

for each $i = 1, 2, \ldots, n$, we have:

R_{E_i}: $X' \to X'$,
$E_i' \to \lambda$,
$\alpha' \to Z$, for all $\alpha \in N \cup T \cup \{\$\}$ such that $\alpha \neq E_i$,
$(B, r) \to Z$, for all $r : AB \to CD \in P$;

$$P_{E_i} = \{(Y, in), (X', out)\};$$

$R_{E_i'}$: $X \to X'E_i$;

$$P_{E_i'} = \{(X', out)\};$$

and for each $i = 1, 2, \ldots, k$ we have:

R_{r_i}: $\alpha' \to Z$, for all $\alpha \in N \cup T \cup \{\$\}$,
$(B, r_i) \to \lambda$,
$(F, r_j) \to Z$, for all $1 \leq j \leq k, j \neq i, F \in N$,
$X' \to X'$,
$(A', r_i) \to Z$;

$$P_{r_i} = \{(Y, in), (X', out)\};$$

$R_{r_i'}$: $A \to (A', r_i)$,
$X' \to X'$;

$$P_{r_i'} = \{((A', r_i)Y, in), (X', out)\} \cup \{(\alpha Y, out) \mid \alpha \in N \cup T \cup \{\$\}\};$$

$R_{r_i''}$: $(A', r_i) \to \lambda$,
$X' \to X'$;

$$P_{r_i''} = \{(Y, in), (X', out)\};$$

$R_{r_i'''}$: $X \to X'CD$;

$$P_{r_i'''} = \{(X', out)\}.$$

For the reader's convenience, Figure 2 presents the shape of the membrane structure of the system Π.

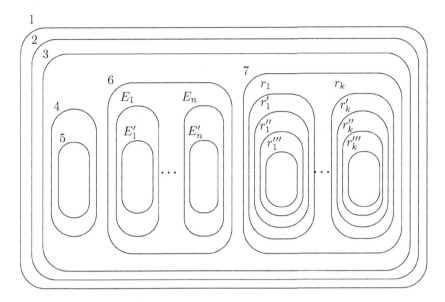

Fig. 2. The membrane structure of the system Π from the proof of Theorem 6

The idea of this construction is to simulate the non-context-free rules from P in the right end of the strings of Π, and, to this aim, the sentential forms of G are circularly permuted in Π; the symbol $ indicates the actual beginning of strings from G: if $Xw_1\$w_2Y$ is a sentential form of Π, then w_2w_1 is a sentential form of G. Z is a trap-symbol, once introduced, it cannot be removed, hence the string will never turn to be terminal.

We start from the string $X''\$SY$, initially present in membrane 5.

In membrane 5 we can simulate any context-free rule from P and the string, if not starting with X, will remain in the same region. After using the rule $X'' \rightarrow X$, it has to exit. From membrane 4, it immediately goes to membrane 3.

If in membrane 3 we use the rule $Y \rightarrow Y'$, then the string will go to membrane 2 only if it ends with $\$Y'$, which means that it is in the same permutation as in G. This is the way to produce a terminal string: the auxiliary symbol $X, \$$ are erased, Y' is replaced by Y'', the string is sent to the skin membrane, where Y'' is erased. If the string which is sent out of the system is terminal, then it is added to the language $L(\Pi)$, if not, then it is "lost".

Assume that in membrane 3 we have a string XwY and we use a rule $\alpha \rightarrow \alpha'$, for some $\alpha \in N \cup T \cup \{\$\}$. This will start the procedure of circularly permuting the string with one symbol: α is removed from the right end of the string and added in the left end of the string. Note that the nonterminals, the terminals, and the symbol $ are treated in the same manner. If the primed symbol is the rightmost one, then the condition to send the string to a lower membrane is fulfilled, otherwise the string is sent to membrane 2, because a condition $(\beta Y, out)$

is fulfilled, for some $\beta \in N \cup T \cup \{\$\}$. In membrane 2 we have to eventually use the rule $Y \to Z$ and no terminal string will be obtained. Thus, we have to prime the rightmost symbol of the string w, and the obtained string is sent to a lower level membrane. If it arrives in membrane 4, then the symbol Z is introduced by the rule $\alpha' \to Z$, if the string arrives in one of membranes 6 and 7, then it will be sent to a lower level membrane. In all membranes different from $[_\alpha \;]_\alpha$ the trap-symbol is introduced. In membrane $[_\alpha \;]_\alpha$ the symbol α' is removed and the string is sent to the inner membrane $[_{\alpha'} \;]_{\alpha'}$, where the same symbol α is introduced by the symbol X in the leftmost position; at the same time, X is replaced by X', which makes possible sending the string up to membrane 3. We have here several possibilities.

If we use the rule $Y \to Y'$ and the string is sent out (the special symbol $\$$ was adjacent to Y'), then we cannot remove X', hence the string will not lead to a terminal string. If we use a rule $\beta \to \beta'$, then either the string goes to membrane 2 and Z is introduced, or it goes to a lower membrane; in membrane 4 one introduces the trap-symbol by the rule $\beta' \to Z$, from membranes 6 and 7 we have to exit immediately, hence the process is repeated. Similar results are obtained if we use a rule $B \to (B, r)$, for some $r : AB \to CD \in P$. Thus, we have to use the rule $X' \to X''$, which implies that the string is sent to a lower level membrane. This should be membrane 4, otherwise the string remains forever in one of membranes 6 and 7. From membrane 4 the string is sent to membrane 5, where we can simulate context-free rules from P and eventually we have to use again the rule $X'' \to X$ and send to membrane 3 a string XzY (with z obtained by circularly permutingg the string w with a symbol, maybe also by using some context-free rules from P). The process can be iterated.

A similar procedure ensures the simulation of rules $r : AB \to CD$, in the membranes "protected" by membrane 7: a symbol B is replaced by (B, r) in membrane 3; if this is not done in the rightmost position, then the string has to exit and in membrane 2 one introduces the trap-symbol; if the string is of the form $Xw(B, r)Y$, then it goes to one of membranes 4, 6, or 7; in membrane 4 one introducees the trap-symbol, from membrane 6 the string is sent to a lower membrane and will introduce the trap-symbol. From membrane 7, the string is sent to a lower level membrane. If this is not the one associated with the rule r, then again the trap-symbol is introduced, otherwise in membrane $[_r \;]_r$ one removes (B, r) and one goes to the lower membrane. In membrane $[_{r'} \;]_{r'}$ one also replaces A by (A', r). If this is not done in the rightmost position, then the string has to exit, and in membrane $[_r \;]_r$ one introduces the trap-symbol. If A was the rightmost symbol, then the string goes one membrane below, where also (A', r) is erased. The string enters the lowest membrane associated with the rule r, where the rule $X \to X'CD$ completes the simulation of the rule. Because of X', the string can now exit all membranes associated with the rule r, and returns to membrane 3. Again the process can be iterated.

Consequently, we can correctly simulate all rules from P, and all strings which can be sent out of the system and are terminal precisely correspond to strings generated by terminal derivation of G. That is, $L(G) = L(\Pi)$, which concludes the proof.   □

6   The Remaining Families

"Below" the families considered in Theorems 1 – 5 there remain several families whose size is not precisely known. We will present here some results in this respect, especially about the families of languages generated by systems with only one membrane, but a systematic study of these families remains as a topic for further research.

Theorem 7. $RP_1(empty, symb) = CF$.

Proof. For a context-free grammar $G = (N, T, S, P)$ we consider the system $\Pi = (N \cup T, N \cup T, [_1 \ ]_1, \{S\}, P, \{(true, out)\}, \{(A, notout) \mid A \in N\})$, and we obviously have $L(G) = L(\Pi)$, that is, $CF \subseteq RP_1(empty, symb)$.

Conversely, consider a system $\Pi = (V, T, [_1 \ ]_1, M_1, R_1, P_1, F_1)$ with $P_1 = \{(true, out)\}$ and with $F_1 = \{(b_i, notout) \mid 1 \le i \le k\}$, for some $k \ge 1$, $b_i \in V, 1 \le i \le k$. Denote by $dom(R_1)$ the set $\{a \in V \mid a \to z \in R_1\}$. We construct the pure context-free grammar $G = (U, S, P)$ with

$$U = V \cup \{a' \mid a \in V\} \cup \{S, c\},$$

where S, c are new symbols, and with the following rules ($g(w)$ denotes the string obtained by priming all symbols from $w \in V^*$):

$$\begin{aligned}
P = \{&S \to g(w)c \mid w \in M_1, alph(w) \cap dom(R_1) = \emptyset, \\
&\text{and } alph(w) \cap \{b_1, \ldots, b_k\} = \emptyset, \\
&\text{or } z \Longrightarrow w \text{ by a rule from } R_1, (alph(z) \cup alph(w)) \cap \{b_1, \ldots, b_k\} = \emptyset\} \\
\cup\ \{&S \to w \mid w \in M_1, alph(w) \cap dom(R_1) \ne \emptyset\} \\
\cup\ \{&a \to z \mid a \to z \in R_1\} \\
\cup\ \{&b_i \to g(z)c \mid b_i \to z \in R_1, 1 \le i \le k\}.
\end{aligned}$$

Consider also the morphism h defined by $h(a) = h(a') = a, a \in V$, and $h(c) = \lambda$. We have the equality

$$L(\Pi) = h(L(G) \cap (V \cup V')^* c (V \cup V')^*) \cap \{w \in V^* \mid alph(w) \cap \{b_1, \ldots, b_k\} = \emptyset\} \cap T^*,$$

where $V' = \{a' \mid a \in V\}$. Indeed, the intersection with the regular language $(V \cup V')^* c (V \cup V')^*$ selects from the language $L(G)$ only those strings which contain exactly one occurrence of c, that is, they are either strings from M_1 which cannot be rewritten (but can be sent out), or they are obtained by a derivation step when a rule from R_1 is used. In the latter case, we either have rewritten an axiom w_1, obtaining a string w_2 such that both w_1 and w_2 contain no symbol $b_i, 1 \le i \le k$ (hence the derivation can have only one step), or a symbol $b_i, 1 \le i \le k$, appears either in w_1 or in w_2, and then a rule $b_i \to g(z)c$ is used during the derivation. Moreover, the intersection with $\{w \in V^* \mid alph(w) \cap \{b_1, \ldots, b_k\} = \emptyset\}$ ensures the fact that if a string of the form $x_1 g(z) c x_2$ is obtained by using such a rule, then we have $alph(x_1 z x_2) \cap \{b_1, \ldots, b_k\} = \emptyset$, hence it can be sent out. If further rules of the form $a \to y$ (without introducing the symbol c) are used for rewriting a string $x_1 g(z) c x_2$, then the string remains of the same form, and such rules were also possible to be used before using the rule $b_i \to g(z)c$ (the primed symbols prevent to use rules for rewriting the symbols from z), hence this does not lead to strings not in $L(\Pi)$. If a rule of the form $b_i \to g(y)c$ is used, then the obtained string is not in the intersection, because it contains two occurrences of c. The fact that the symbol c is introduced by a rule which removes a symbol $b_i, 1 \leq i \leq k$, ensures the fact that we finish the derivation in the moment when removing the last symbol from the forbidding set, hence the string is introduced in the language of $L(G)$ in the same moment when the corresponding string is sent out of the system Π.

The morphism h erases the primes and the symbol c, hence we return to a string from V^*. The intersection with T^* ensures the selection of terminal strings only.

All these operations preserve context-freeness, hence $L(\Pi) \in CF$.   □

Theorem 8. $ERP_1(empty, empty) = RP_1(empty, empty) = FIN$.

Proof. Let $\Pi = (V, T, [_1]_1, M_1, R_1, \{(true, out)\}, \{(false, notout)\})$ be a system with empty communication conditions. After each rewriting the string must exit the system, hence all computations have at most one step, which means that $L(\Pi)$ is finite. Conversely, we can take any finite language as M_1 and no rule in R_1. In this way, we just send out the strings from M_1, hence all finite languages are in $RP_1(empty, empty)$.   □

Lemma 1. $RP_1(symb, empty) - LIN \neq \emptyset$.

Proof. The system

$$\Pi = (\{a, b, c, d\}, \{a, b, c, d\}, [_1]_1, \{dd\},$$
$$\{d \to adb, d \to acb\}, \{(c, out)\}, \{(false, notout)\}),$$

generates the non-linear language

$$L(\Pi) = \{a^n cb^n a^m db^m, \ a^m db^m a^n cb^n \mid n \geq 1, m \geq 0\}.$$

(We can send out a string only if it contains the symbol c, hence immediately after using the rule $d \to acb$; the rule $d \to adb$ can be used any number $m \geq 0$ of times.)   □

Lemma 2. $ERP_1(symb, empty) \subseteq CF$.

Proof. The proof is similar (but simpler) to that of the inclusion $RP_1(empty, symb) \subseteq CF$ from the proof of Theorem 7, so we only present the construction needed (the notations for $dom(R_1), g, h, V'$ are the same as in the proof of Theorem 7). Let $\Pi = (V, T, [_1 \ ]_1, M_1, R_1, P_1, F_1)$ be a system with $P_1 = \{(b_i, out) \mid 1 \le i \le k\}$, for some $k \ge 1$, $b_i \in V, 1 \le i \le k$, and with $F_1 = \{(false, notout)\}$. We construct the pure context-free grammar $G = (U, S, P)$ with

$$U = V \cup \{a' \mid a \in V\} \cup \{S, c\},$$

where S, c are new symbols, and with the following rules:

$$P = \{S \to g(w)c \mid w \in M_1, alph(w) \cap dom(R_1) = \emptyset,$$
$$\text{and } alph(w) \cap \{b_1, \ldots, b_k\} \ne \emptyset\}$$
$$\cup \{S \to w \mid w \in M_1, alph(w) \cap dom(R_1) = \emptyset\}$$
$$\cup \{a \to z \mid a \to z \in R_1, alph(z) \cap \{b_1, \ldots, b_k\} = \emptyset\}$$
$$\cup \{a \to g(z)c \mid a \to z \in R_1, alph(z) \cap \{b_1, \ldots, b_k\} \ne \emptyset\}.$$

We have the equality

$$L(\Pi) = h(L(G) \cap (V \cup V')^* c(V \cup V')^*) \cap T^*,$$

consequently $L(\Pi) \in CF$.   □

This inclusion is proper. Actually, the following stronger result holds (which somehow completes the study of the families $ERP_1(symb, empty), RP_1(symb, empty)$:

Lemma 3. *All one-letter languages in $ERP_1(sub, empty)$ are finite.*

Proof. Consider a regular language $L \subseteq a^*$ and let $\Pi = (V, \{a\}, [_1 \ ]_1, M_1, R_1, P_1, \{(false, notout)\})$ be a system such that $L(\Pi) = L$. At least one condition from P_1 should be of the form (a^k, out) for some $k \ge 0$. Let k_0 be the smallest k with this property. All strings obtained by using a rule from R_1 and containing a substring a^j with $j \ge k_0$ is sent out of the system. Let $k_1 = \max\{|x| \mid \alpha \to x \in R_1\}$, $k_2 = \max\{|w| \mid w \in M_1\}$, and denote $t = \max\{k_0, k_1, k_2\}$.

No string of the form a^m with $m > 3t$ can be generated by the system Π. Indeed, in order to produce such a string we need a rewriting $w \Longrightarrow a^m$. Because $m > 3t$, we must have $|w| > 2t$, hence $w \notin M_1$. This means that in its turn, also w was obtained by a rewriting. However, because $t \ge k_0$, it follows that $a^{k_0} \in Sub(w)$. This means that w should be sent out immediately after obtaining it, hence the step $w \Longrightarrow a^m$ cannot be performed. This contradiction closes the proof.   □

Theorem 9. *The families $ERP_1(symb, empty), RP_1(symb, empty)$ are incomparable with REG, LIN, and strictly included in CF.*

However, REG is "almost included" into $RP_1(symb, empty)$:

Theorem 10. *For each regular language $L \subseteq T^*$ and $c \notin T$, the language $L\{c\}$ is in $RP_1(symb, empty)$.*

Proof. For a regular grammar $G = (N, T, S, P)$ and $c \notin T$ we consider the system $\Pi = (\{N \cup T \cup \{c\}, N \cup T \cup \{c\}, [_1 \ ]_1, \{S\}, \{A \rightarrow aB \mid A \rightarrow aB \in P\} \cup \{A \rightarrow ac \mid A \rightarrow a \in P\}, \{(c, out)\}, \{(false, notout)\})$. A string can be sent out only when c is present, which means that a derivation in G was completed, hence $L(\Pi) = L(G)\{c\}$. □

If we pass to systems with (at least) two membranes, then much more complex languages can be produced, even when using communication conditions of a weak type.

Theorem 11. $RP_2(empty, empty) - CF \neq \emptyset$.

Proof. The system

$$\Pi = (\{a, b, c, d_1, d_2\}, \{a, b, c, d_1, d_2\}, [_1[_2 \ ]_2]_1, \{d_1 d_2\}, \emptyset, R_1, P_1, F_1, R_2, P_2, F_2),$$
$$R_1 = \{d_1 \rightarrow ad_1 b\}, P_1 = \{(true, in), (true, out)\},$$
$$F_1 = \{(false, notin), (false, notout)\}, R_2 = \{d_2 \rightarrow cd_2\},$$
$$P_2 = \{(true, out)\}, F_2 = \{(false, notout)\},$$

generates the non-context-free language

$$L(\Pi) = \{a^{n+1} d_1 b^{n+1} c^n d_2 \mid n \geq 0\}.$$

Indeed, after a number of steps when the current string is moved between the skin membrane and the inner membrane (in such a step all symbols a, b, c increase by one the number of occurrences), the string can be sent out, which means that one further copy of a and b are produced. □

Theorem 12. $RP_2(empty, symb) - MAT \neq \emptyset$.

Proof. The system

$$\Pi = (\{a, b\}, \{a, b\}, [_1[_2 \ ]_2]_1, \{a\}, \emptyset, R_1, P_1, F_1, R_2, P_2, F_2),$$
$$R_1 = \{a \rightarrow bb\}, P_1 = \{(true, in), (true, out)\}, F_1 = \{(a, notin), (a, notout)\},$$
$$R_2 = \{b \rightarrow a\}, P_2 = \{(true, out)\}, F_2 = \{(b, notout)\},$$

generates the language

$$L(\Pi) = \{b^{2^n} \mid n \geq 0\}.$$

Assume that we have a string a^m in the skin membrane; initially, $m = 1$. We have to use the rule $a \rightarrow bb$ for all copies of a before communicating the obtained string. Thus, we have to obtain the string b^{2m}, which is either sent out of the system or to the inner membrane. In membrane 2 we have to use the rule $b \rightarrow a$ for all copies of b, otherwise the string cannot be communicated. Thus, we return to the skin membrane the string a^{2m} and the process is iterated. □

7   Final Remarks; Topics for Further Research

We have considered here a variant of rewriting P systems where communication is controlled by the contents of the strings, not by the rules used for obtaining these strings. Specifically, permitting and forbidding conditions were defined, depending on the symbols or the substrings of a given string, or depending on the shape of the string (whether or not it is of a given pattern). Several new characterizations of recursively enumerable languages were obtained, but the power of many classes of systems (especially with a small number of membranes) has remained to be clarified.

This approach can be seen as a counterpart of the approach in [3], where the use of rules (processing multisets, not strings as here) is controlled in a similar way, by the contents of a given membrane.

On the other hand, this work proceeds in the line of research on constraining application of context-free rules by the shape of the string to which a production is applied or into which an application results.

In [2] this was achieved in a setting where only one string was present and only a level was considered. The basic model proposd there was equivalent to what we could define as $ERP_1(patt, empty)$. This work shows how communication allows the complexity of the check on the produced words to be reduced, by distributing it over several membranes.

We have considered here only the rewriting case, but the same idea can be explored for all types of string-processing operations, in particular, for *splicing*. Actually, many other *research topics* remain to be investigated. We have already mentioned the need to further examine the families considered in Section 5, to improve the bounds in Theorems 3, 4, 5, and to find a characterization of RE as in Theorem 6 with a bounded number of membranes.

Here are three further research topics.

Remember that we have said that when a string fulfills both *in* and *out* conditions, it will go to one direction, nondeterministically chosen. An attractive case would be to *replicate* the string and send copies of it both out of the current membrane and to a lower level membrane. In this way we can produce additional strings, which is in general useful for solving NP-complete problems in polynomial (often, linear) time, by creating an exponential space and trading space for time (see [18] and references therein; in particular, this is the case of [12]).

In rewriting P systems we process in a parallel way different strings, present in the same membrane or in different membranes, but each string is rewritten in a sequential manner. The case of parallel rewriting, like in L systems, was considered in [11], with the following way of defining the communication: one counts how many rules from those applied to a string indicate to send the obtained string *out*, how many *in*, and how many *here*, and we send the string to the place which was indicated a largest number of times. This looks rather artificial; in the conditional case, the conditions are checked on the string obtained by rewriting, hence this difficulty does not appear, we can rewrite the string in any manner we like.

Finally, we can use patterns not only for defining the communication targets, but also for modifying the strings, thus replacing rewriting by another type of operation. This way of "growing" strings was already explored in the so-called *pattern grammars*, [7], or in other types of language generating mechanisms based on patterns, see [15]. The idea is simple: start with finite sets of terminal strings and of patterns in each membrane, interpret the variables from patterns by means of the available strings, and then evaluate the communication conditions; the terminals from a region can be variables in another region and conversely. In this way, all the work of the system would be based on using patterns.

References

1. D. Angluin, Finding Patterns Common to a Set of Strings, *J. Comput. System Sci.*, 21 (1980), 46–62.
2. P. Bottoni, A. Labella, P. Mussio, Gh. Păun, Pattern Control on Derivation in Context-Free Rewriting, *J. Automata, Languages, Combinatorics*, 3, 1, (1998), 3–28.
3. P. Bottoni, C. Martin-Vide, Gh. Păun, G. Rozenberg, Membrane Systems with Promoters/Inhibitors, submitted, 2000.
4. C. Calude, Gh. Păun, *Computing with Cells and Atoms*, Taylor and Francis, London, 2000.
5. J. Castellanos, A. Rodriguez-Paton, Gh. Păun, Computing with Membranes: P Systems with Worm-Objects, *IEEE 7th. Intern. Conf. on String Processing and Information Retrieval, SPIRE 2000*, La Coruna, Spain, 64–74.
6. J. Dassow, Gh. Păun, *Regulated Rewriting in Formal Language Theory*, Springer-Verlag, Berlin, 1989.
7. J. Dassow, Gh. Păun, A. Salomaa, Grammars Based on Patterns, *Intern. J. Found. Comput. Sci.*, 4, 1 (1993), 1–14.
8. R. Freund, C. Martin-Vide, Gh. Păun, Computing with Membranes: Three More Collapsing Hierarchies, submitted, 2000.
9. R. Freund, Gh. Păun, On the Number of Non-terminals in Graph-Controlled, Programmed, and Matrix Grammars, submitted, 2000.
10. D. Hauschild, M. Jantzen, Petri Nets Algorithms in the Theory of Matrix Grammars, *Acta Informatica*, 31 (1994), 719–728.
11. S.N. Krishna, R. Rama, On the Power of P Systems with Sequential and Parallel Rewriting, *Intern. J. Computer Math.*, 77, 1-2 (2000), 1–14.
12. S.N. Krishna, R. Rama, P Systems with Replicated Rewriting, *J. Automata, Languages, Conbinatorics*, to appear.
13. C. Martin-Vide, Gh. Păun, String Objects in P Systems, *Proc. of Algebraic Systems, Formal Languages and Computations Workshop*, Kyoto, 2000, RIMS Kokyuroku, Kyoto Univ., 2000.
14. C. Martin-Vide, Gh. Păun, Computing with Membranes. One More Collapsing Hierarchy, *Bulletin of the EATCS*, 72 (2000).
15. V. Mitrana, Patterns and Languages. An Overview, *Grammars*, 2, 2 (1999), 149–173.
16. Gh. Păun, Six Nonterminals Are Enough for Generating Each r.e. Language by a Matrix Grammar, *Intern. J. Computer Math.*, 15 (1984), 23–37.

17. Gh. Păun, Computing with Membranes, *Journal of Computer and System Sciences*, 61, 1 (2000), 108–143 (see also *Turku Center for Computer Science-TUCS Report* No 208, 1998, www.tucs.fi).
18. Gh. Păun, Computing with Membranes; Attacking NP-complete Problems, *Proc. Second Conf. Unconventional Models of Computing* (I. Antoniou, C.S. Calude, M.J. Dinneen, Eds.), Springer-Verlag, 2000.
19. G. Rozenberg, A. Salomaa, Eds., *Handbook of Formal Languages*, Springer-Verlag, Heidelberg, 1997.
20. Cl. Zandron, G. Mauri, Cl. Ferretti, Universality and Normal Forms on Membrane Systems, *Proc. Intern. Workshop Grammar Systems 2000* (R. Freund, A. Kelemenova, Eds.), Bad Ischl, Austria, July 2000, 61–74.

An Aqueous Algorithm for Finding the Bijections Contained in a Binary Relation

Tom Head

Mathematical Sciences, Binghamton University
Binghamton, New York 13902-6000, USA
tom@math.binghamton.edu

Abstract. Given a subset R of a set $A \times B$, one may ask whether R contains a subset F which is a bijective function from A onto B. A wet lab algorithm for answering this question is presented. Moreover, when such a bijection is contained in R, the algorithm produces a test tube containing a set of DNA plasmids, each of which encodes such a bijection. The number of steps required by the given procedure grows linearly with the number of ordered pairs in the relation R. All known algorithms for solving this bijection problem on conventional computers require a number of steps that grows exponentially in the number of pairs. Various forms of the Hamiltonian path problem are subsumed by the problem of finding such bijections. The algorithm presented is illustrated by outlining its application to the binary relation determined by the directed graph that occurs in the instance of the directed Hamiltonian path problem with which L. Adleman initiated DNA computing.

Key Words: Molecular computing, DNA computing, aqueous computing, Hamiltonian paths

1 Introduction

Since the appearance of the now classic paper [Ad'94] by L. Adleman, intense effort has been devoted to finding additional methods for encoding instances of algorithmic problems into sets of molecules in such a way that the problem solutions can be obtained through chemistry. This is now a world wide activity that is being recorded in an extensive journal literature that is being captured in a sequence of books that include [P'98] [PRS'98] [CCD'98] [ACD'01] & [CP'01]. Two valuable electronic bibliographies are also being maintained: [Fweb] & [Zweb]. The present article lies in this broad context, but also in the sub-context of *aqueous computing*. The abstract concept of aqueous computing has been explicated in several publications [H'00] & [H'01a,b,c] and exemplified with the reports of wet lab computations each of which has been carried out either at Leiden University [HRBBLS'00] or at Binghamton University [HYG'99] [YHG'00] & [HCNG'01]. Further aqueous computations are in progress at Tokyo Institute of Technology. Please consult these previous publications for the present scope

W. Brauer et al. (Eds.): Formal and Natural Computing, LNCS 2300, pp. 354–360, 2002.

and the projected future of aqueous computing. An attractive first background reading pertinent to the biomolecular procedures discussed here is [N'94]. For a more extensive reference consult [M'95].

The present article presents a new aqueous algorithm. Several technologies can be designed for implementing this algorithm in the aqueous manner. However, only one basic implementation is described here. Circular DNA molecules that contain a sequence of distinct restriction enzyme sites are suggested for encoding problem instances. Computational steps are suggested that alter the DNA sequences at selected enzyme sites in such a way that cutting with the restriction enzymes associated with the sites is no longer possible. Such disabled sites are said to have been *locked*. Solutions of problem instances are to be read by determining which sites have been locked and which sites have not been locked. This technology has been implemented successfully in previous computations [HCNG'01].

The problem treated here is that of finding all bijections that are contained in a given binary relation R in the product $A \times B$ of two equipotent finite sets A and B. This problem subsumes (and is virtually identical with) the algorithmic problem 'GT13' stated in [GJ'79, p.193]. The algorithm for solving this problem is given in Section 3 following the presentation in Section 2 of a careful sketch of specific biomolecular procedures for *locking* restriction enzyme sites. The solution of the bijections problem also provides solutions for various forms of Hamiltonian path problems. In Section 4 the directed graph that provided the instance of the directed Hamiltonian path problem treated in [Ad'94] is discussed as a specific instance of the algorithm presented here. This illustrates an alternate aqueous approach to the directed Hamiltonian path problem in which the latter problem is viewed as a sub-problem of the problem of finding bijections.

2 Technologies for Locking and Reading Restriction Enzyme Sites

Let P be a circular double stranded DNA molecule. Let E be a restriction enzyme that cuts at precisely one site S in P. Assume further that, when E cuts, it produces single stranded 5'-overhangs of length $s > 0$. To *lock* such a site S, we suggest the following three step procedure which we abbreviate as CEL: (1) **C**ut P with E to give a linear molecule L having 5'- overhangs of length s at each end. (2) **E**longate the double stranded portion of L by applying a DNA polymerase to fill-in under the 5'-overhangs to form a completely double stranded linear molecule L'. (3) **L**igate the resulting blunt ends of L' to re-create a circular plasmid. The three step CEL procedure introduces a duplication into the center of the original site S which (for almost all restriction enzymes E) results in a modification of the sequence at which E can no longer cut. (The site for the enzyme *Aci I* is not destroyed by CEL. This is an extremely rare phenomenon that should simply be avoided by appropriate choice of the enzymes that are placed in one to one correspondence with the ordered pairs in R.)

The CEL procedure for locking enzyme sites has been used successfully in Binghamton [HCNG'01]. It applies only to the case of enzymes that create 5'-overhangs, because DNA polymerase fills in only under 5'-overhangs, and not under 3'-overhangs. At Binghamton we have used for P a standard cloning plasmid that has allowed us to use sites for eight restriction enzymes each producing 4-base pair 5'-overhangs. Perhaps two or three more sites producing 5'-overhangs could be used. To go further with this same plasmid, it would be necessary to use sites for enzymes that produce 3'-overhangs. Consequently the following suggestion is included for modifying the CEL procedure to produce an alternate procedure, CTL, that may be successful for dealing with 3'-overhangs (as well as 5'-overhangs): CTL is identical with CEL except for the second of the three steps. The elongation step of CEL is replaced by: (2') **T**rim each of the overhangs from the ends of the linear molecule L using an exonuclease that attacks only single stranded DNA, but not double stranded DNA.

At the conclusion of the algorithm of Section 3 the condition (i.e., locked or not locked) of each of the sites can read in parallel. Let n is the number of site of the plasmid P that are in use. Suppose that a test tube T has been produced for which all plasmids contained in T have exactly the same locked/unlocked pattern of sites. This pattern can then be read as follows: Divide the content of T equally among n test tubes. Provide each of the resulting n tubes with one of the n restriction enzymes. Determine which sites have been cut, thereby determining the locked/unlocked pattern of the plasmids in the original tube T.

An attractive alternate method for locking restriction enzyme sites would be to *follow nature* by methylating the sites. Pros and cons of using methylation for locking sites in aqueous computing are discussed in [H'01b].

3   Finding the Bijections Contained in a Subset of $A \times B$

Let A and B be finite sets having the same cardinal number. Let R be a subset of the Cartesian product $A \times B$. We wish to determine whether R contains a subset F which constitutes a bijective function from A onto B. When such a bijection exists we wish to find representations for each such bijection. In this Section an aqueous procedure is described for deciding whether R contains such a bijection and, when one exists, producing a test tube that contains molecules that encode each such bijection.

Choose a circular double stranded DNA plasmid P that has sufficiently many restriction enzyme sites to allow the following one to one correspondence to be established: With each ordered pair (a, b) in R, associate a restriction enzyme site in P that meets the following two requirements: (1) the restriction enzyme having this site *does not produce blunt ends* when it cuts; and (2) this enzyme cuts P only at this one *unique site* in P. Distinct pairs in R must, of course, be associated with distinct restriction enzymes and the sites in P for the enzymes chosen must not overlap. It is convenient to mentally identify the set R with the set of enzyme sites with which R has been placed in one to one correspondence in this way.

Algorithm. This wet lab procedure is presented as a sequence of four macro steps: (1) Initialize Test Tube; (2) Lock Sites; (3) Cut Plasmids; and (4) Read.

{Initialize:}
Let T be a test tube in which a vast number of the plasmids P are dissolved in water;
{Comment: Each plasmid in T is interpreted as an encoding the binary relation R. In most cases a picomole would provide a sufficiently vast number of the plasmids.}

{Lock:}
For each a in A, let $(a, b_1), (a, b_2), ..., (a, b_{n(a)})$ be the set of all pairs in R having a as first coordinate:
    Divide the content of T equally into test tubes $T_1, T_2, ..., T_{n(a)}$.
    Parallel-For $i = 1$ to $n(a)$ do
      In T_i lock the site that corresponds to (a, b_i).
      Retain only the *plasmids* in T_i (i.e., purify).
    End Parallel-For.
    Pour each of the $n(a)$ tubes into a new tube T.
End For;
{Comment: T should now contain only plasmids that have exactly cardinal of A locked sites, one for each element of A. For each such plasmid, the ordered pairs that correspond to the locked sites should constitute a *function* from A *into* B.

{Cut:}
For each b in B, let $(a_1, b), (a_2, b), ..., (a_{n(b)}, b)$ be the set of all pairs in R having b as second coordinate.
    Divide the contents of T equally into test tubes $T_1, T_2, ..., T_{n(b)}$.
    Parallel-For $i = 1$ to $n(b)$ do
      To T_i add the restriction enzyme having the site that corresponds to (a_i, b).
      Retain only the plasmids in T_i (i.e., purify).
    End Parallel-For.
    Pour each of the $n(b)$ tubes into a new tube T.
End For;
{Comment: For each plasmid remaining in T, the set of edges that correspond to the locked sites should constitute a function from A *onto* B, i.e., a *bijection*.

{Read:} If T contains no plasmids, conclude that R contains *no* bijections of A onto B.
Otherwise, clone the plasmids using bacteria.
From each of sufficiently many of the resulting bacterial colonies, harvest the plasmids and determine which sites have been locked. This determination can be made by attempting to cut at each enzyme site with its associated restriction enzyme. (Sequencing can be used as an alternative to attempting the cuts.)
For each plasmid, the pairs (a, b) for which the associated sites of that plasmid have been locked constitute a bijection of A onto B.
End Algorithm.

When $A = B$, R is a binary relation in the set A and any bijections found in R are permutations of A.

Remark. In the algorithm above we applied the locking procedure to specify each of the functions from A into B. We then applied the cutting procedure to delete those functions from A into B that failed to be bijections. We could equally well have interchanged the roles of A and B and applied the locking procedure to specify each of the functions from B into A. We would then have applied the cutting procedure to delete those functions from B into A that fail to be bijections. For each specific instance of the general problem treated here, one of these two wet lab procedures may be more easily carried out then the other. This is illustrated in the next Section.

4   Example: Adleman's Graph in *Science*, 1994

Leonard Adleman initiated the field of DNA computing with [Ad'94]. In that paper he reported a wet lab solution of an instance of the directed Hamiltonian path problem. The graph he treated had seven vertices $\{0, 1, 2, 3, 4, 5, 6\}$ and fourteen edges. No edge entered vertex 0 and vertex 6 had no exit. In the present notation Adleman's graph is represented by the choices: $A = \{0, 1, 2, 3, 4, 5\}$; $B = \{1, 2, 3, 4, 5, 6\}$; and $R = \{(0, 1), (0, 3), (0, 6), (1, 2), (1, 3), (2, 1), (2, 3), (3, 2), (3, 4), (4, 1), (4, 5), (5, 1), (5, 2), (5, 6)\} = \{(0, 1), (2, 1), (4, 1), (5, 1), (1, 2), (3, 2), (5, 2), (0, 3), (1, 3), (2, 3), (3, 4), (4, 5), (0, 6), (5, 6)\}$.

We consider now the steps required to determine the bijections between A and B that R contains. If we apply locking to specify functions from A into B we note that this will result in $3 \times 2 \times 2 \times 2 \times 2 \times 3 = 144$ functions. If we apply locking to specify functions from B into A, we see that this will result in only $4 \times 3 \times 3 \times 1 \times 1 \times 2 = 72$ functions. *We prefer to keep the number of distinct molecular varieties in our test tubes as low as is convenient during molecular computations.* In the present case we prefer the second option which will provide the upper bound of 72 (rather than 144) on the number of distinct plasmid varieties occurring in any test tube during the computation. *We also prefer to keep the number of sequential steps in a molecular computation as small as is practical.* The B into A choice is better than the A into B choice in this respect also: If we wish to, we can take advantage of the two ones in the sequence 4, 3, 3, 1, 1, 2 above. The ones underscore the fact that the pairs (3,4) and (4,5) must occur in any bijection. This means that although there are 14 pairs in R, only 12 require a presence/non-presence decision to be made in determining the bijections. Note that this means that we need use only 12 restriction enzyme sites on the plasmid P, rather than 14. Locking will require only four sequential steps: a first step consisting of four parallel CELs, a second step consisting of three parallel CELs, a third step of three parallel CELs, and a fourth step of two parallel CELs. It is true that six sequential steps will be required in the cutting procedure, but 'cut & purify' is a much simpler and less error prone procedure than 'apply a CEL & purify'.

A careful consideration of what we should expect in the final tube T after locking followed by cutting gives three bijections: $\{(0,1),(1,2),(2,3),(3,4),(4,5),(5,6)\}$; $\{(0,3),(3,4),(4,5),(5,6),(1,2),(2,1)\}$; and $\{(0,6),(1,2),(2,3),(3,4),(4,5),(5,1)\}$. The first is the unique Hamiltonian path 0123456; the second consists of the shorter path, 03456, together with the cycle $1 \to 2 \to 1$; and the third consists of the shortest path, 06, together with the cycle $1 \to 2 \to 3 \to 4 \to 5 \to 1$. The reading portion of the procedure above should therefore be expected to find these *three* bijections represented by only three remaining distinct varieties of plasmids in the final tube T.

Any solutions that may exits for directed Hamiltonian paths in a directed graph, such as the one treated in [Ad'94], should always be found among the solutions of the problem of finding the bijections contained in the binary relation that is defined by the directed graph.

Acknowledgments

Partial support through DARPA/NSF CCR-9725021 and the Leiden Center for Natural Computing is gratefully recognized.

References

[Ad'94]   L. Adleman, Molecular Computation of Solutions to Combinatorial Problems, Science 266(1994)1021-1024.

[ACD'01]   I. Antoniou, C.S. Calude and M.J. Dineen, Eds., *Unconventional Models of Computation UMC'2K*, Springer, London (2001).

[CCD'98]   C.S. Calude, J. Casti & M.J. Dineen, Eds., *Unconventional Models of Computation*, Springer, Singapore (1998).

[CP'01]   C.S. Calude & Gh. Paun, *Computing with Cells and Atoms - An Introduction to Quantum, DNA and Membrane Computing*, Taylor & Francis, London, (2001).

[Fweb]   http://www.liacs.nl/home/pier/webPagesDNA

[GJ'79]   M.R. Garey & D.S. Johnson, *Computers and Intractibility - A Guide to the Theory of NP-completeness*, Freeman, New York (1979).

[H'00]   T. Head, Circular Suggestions for DNA Computing, in: *Pattern Formation in Biology, Vision and Dynamics*, Ed. by A. Carbone, M. Gromov & P. Prusinkiewicz (2000)325-335.

[H'01a]   T. Head, Splicing Systems, Aqueous Computing, and Beyond, in: *Unconventional Models of Computation UMC'2K*, Ed. by I. Antoniou, C.S. Calude and M.J. Dineen, Springer, London, (2001).

[H'01b]   T. Head, Writing by Methylation Proposed for Aqueous Computing, Chapter 31 of: *Where Mathematics, Computer Science, Linguistics and Biology Meet*, Ed. by C. Martin-Vide & V. Mitrana, (2001)353-360.

[H'01c]   T. Head, Biomolecular Realizations of a Parallel Architecture for Solving Combinatorial Problems, *New Generation Computing*, 19 (2001) 301-312..

[HCNG'01]   T. Head, X. Chen, M.J. Nichols, M. Yamamura & S. Gal, Aqueous Solutions of Algorithmic Problems: Emphasizing Knights on a 3 × 3, in: N. Jonoska & N.C. Seeman, Eds., *Pre-proceedings Workshop on DNA Computers #7*, U. South Florida, (2001) 219-230.

[HRBBLS'00]   T. Head, G. Rozenberg, R. Bladergroen, C.K.D. Breek, P.H.M. Lomerese & H. Spaink, Computing with DNA by Operating on Plasmids, *Bio Systems* 57(2000)87-93.

[HYG'99]   T. Head, M. Yamamura & S. Gal, Aqueous Computing: Writing on Molecules, in: *Proc. Congress on Evolutionary Computation 1999*, IEEE Service Center, Piscataway, NJ (1999)1006-1010.

[M'95]   R.A. Meyers, Ed., *Molecular Biology and Biotechnology - A Comprehensive Desk Reference*, VCH Publishers Inc., New York (1995).

[N'94]   D.S.T. Nicholl, *An Introduction to Genetic Engineering*, Cambridge Univ. Press, Cambridge, U.K. (1994).

[P'98]   Gh. Paun, Ed., *Computing with Biomolecules - Theory and Experiments*, Springer-Verlag, Berlin (1998).

[PRS'98]   Gh. Paun, G. Rozenberg & A. Salomaa, *DNA Computing - New Computing Paradigms*, Springer-Verlag, Berlin (1998).

[YHG'00]   M. Yamamura, T. Head & S. Gal, Aqueous Computing Mathematical Principles of Molecular Memory and Its Biomolecular Implementation, Chapter 2 in: *Genetic Algorithms 4*, Ed. by H. Kitano, (2000)49-73 (in Japanese).

[Zweb]   http://bioinformatics.bio.disco.unimib.it/psystems

Upper Bounds for Restricted Splicing

Hendrik Jan Hoogeboom and Nikè van Vugt

Universiteit Leiden, Institute of Advanced Computer Science
P.O. Box 9512, 2300 RA Leiden, The Netherlands

Abstract. We determine or improve upper bounds for non-iterated splicing in length-increasing, length-decreasing, same-length and self splicing mode.

1 Introduction

The cutting and recombination of DNA with the help of restriction enzymes has been abstracted as the splicing operation for formal languages, see for instance the introduction by Head, Păun, and Pixton [HPP97], or the relevant chapters in the book of Păun, Rozenberg, and Salomaa on computational models inspired by DNA computing [PRS98].

The splicing operation takes two strings, and cuts them in a position specified by a splicing rule. Then these strings are recombined after exchanging their postfixes (the parts of the strings following the cut). This operation can then be studied within the framework of formal language theory, in order to estimate its computational power. One may study its effect as a closure operation on language families, or one may study its power when applied iteratively as if it were a single step of a computing device. Most famous in this latter area is the result that the family of regular languages is closed under splicing (using a finite set of rules) [CH91]. In fact, for the Chomsky hierarchy the power of splicing has been extensively investigated, and optimal upper bounds within the hierarchy have been established (cf. [HPP97], or [PRS98]).

Here we concentrate on the non-iterative, single, application of the splicing operation applied to families of the Chomsky hierachy. What is open here is the power of some modes of restricted splicing, i.e., splicing where there are additional constraints on the two strings involved, as inspired by [PRS96, KPS96]. For instance, in same-length splicing both strings are required to be of the same length, and in self splicing both strings are assumed to be identical.

In particular, it is left open whether non-iterated splicing in one of the modes length-decreasing, same-length, and self splicing, stays within the context-sensitive languages when applied to regular languages, using context-free sets of rules. We will show that this is indeed the case for same-length and length-decreasing mode (Corollaries 8(1) and 12(1)), whereas self splicing generates every recursively enumarable language (up to a single marker, Corollary 16).

Moreover, we show that applying either of these splicing modes to context-free languages with finite or regular sets of rules, results in a context-sensitive

W. Brauer et al. (Eds.): Formal and Natural Computing, LNCS 2300, pp. 361–375, 2002.

language. This was open for same-length splicing (Corollary 8(2)) and self splicing (Corollary 14).

After defining the operation of splicing in Section 2, we explain our basic tools in Section 3. In the next three sections we discuss same-length splicing, length-increasing (and length-decreasing) splicing, and self splicing, respectively.

2   Splicing

A *splicing rule* over an alphabet V is an element of $(V^*)^4$. For such a rule $r = (u_1, v_1, u_2, v_2)$ and strings $x, y, z \in V^*$ we write

$$(x, y) \vdash_r z \text{ iff } x = x_1 u_1 v_1 y_1, \ y = x_2 u_2 v_2 y_2 \text{ and}$$
$$z = x_1 u_1 v_2 y_2, \text{ for some } x_1, y_1, x_2, y_2 \in V^*.$$

We say that the string z is obtained by *splicing* the strings x and y *using* the rule r.

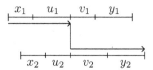

A *splicing system* (or *H system*) is a triple $h = (V, L, R)$ where V is an alphabet, $L \subseteq V^*$ is the *initial language* and $R \subseteq (V^*)^4$ is a set of splicing rules, the *splicing relation*.

To estimate the complexity of sets of rules using the familiar Chomsky hierarchy as a yard stick, splicing rules are commonly represented as strings rather than 4-tuples: a splicing rule $r = (u_1, v_1, u_2, v_2)$ is given as the string $Z(r) = u_1 \# v_1 \$ u_2 \# v_2$ (# and \$ are special symbols not in V), i.e., Z is a mapping from $(V^*)^4$ to $V^* \# V^* \$ V^* \# V^*$, that gives a *string representation* of each splicing rule. We extend Z in the natural way to a mapping from sets of splicing rules to languages. In agreement with this policy, we usually write, for instance, "regular set of splicing rules" when we mean a set of splicing rules of which the Z-representation is a regular language. It was argued in [HvV98] that this representation is quite robust: most of the other, related, representations do not change the position in the Chomsky hierarchy of the families resulting from (uniterated) splicing $\mathcal{F}_1$-languages using $\mathcal{F}_2$-rules.

In this paper we consider the setting where the general splicing operation $(x, y) \vdash_r z$ may only be applied in a certain context. We recall the definitions of certain types of restricted splicing from [PRS96, KPS96]. We splice in *(length-) increasing* mode (*in* for short) if the length of the resulting string is strictly greater than the lengths of the two input strings, in *(length-) decreasing* mode (*de*) if the length of the resulting string is strictly smaller than the lengths of the two input strings, in *same-length* mode (*sl*) if the two input strings have the same length, and in *self splicing* mode (*sf*) if the two input strings are equal.

We add *free* splicing (f) as a synonym for unrestricted splicing. Formally, for a splicing rule r we use the following relations.

$$
\begin{array}{lll}
\textit{free} & (x,y) \vdash_r^f z & \text{iff } (x,y) \vdash_r z \quad \text{unrestricted} \\
\textit{increasing} & (x,y) \vdash_r^{in} z & \text{iff } (x,y) \vdash_r z \text{ and } |z| > \max\{|x|,|y|\} \\
\textit{decreasing} & (x,y) \vdash_r^{de} z & \text{iff } (x,y) \vdash_r z \text{ and } |z| < \min\{|x|,|y|\} \\
\textit{same-length} & (x,y) \vdash_r^{sl} z & \text{iff } (x,y) \vdash_r z \text{ and } |x| = |y| \\
\textit{self} & (x,y) \vdash_r^{sf} z & \text{iff } (x,y) \vdash_r z \text{ and } x = y.
\end{array}
$$

Note that the requirement for length-increasing splicing can be reformulated in terms of the two input strings x and y, without explicitly mentioning the result z of the splicing. If we splice $x = x_1 u_1 v_1 y_1$ and $y = x_2 u_2 v_2 y_2$ using the rule $r = (u_1, v_1, u_2, v_2)$, it is in increasing mode iff $|x_1 u_1| > |x_2 u_2|$ and $|v_1 y_1| < |v_2 y_2|$. There is a similar formulation for length-decreasing splicing.

Let $h = (V, L, R)$ be a splicing system. With the splicing modes given above we define the (non-iterated splicing) languages

$$
\sigma_\mu(h) = \{\, z \in V^* \mid (x,y) \vdash_r^\mu z \text{ for some } x, y \in L \text{ and } r \in R \,\}
$$

for $\mu \in \{f, in, de, sl, sf\}$. Similarly we define the families

$$
S_\mu(\mathcal{F}_1, \mathcal{F}_2) = \{\, \sigma_\mu(h) \mid h = (V, L, R) \text{ with } L \in \mathcal{F}_1 \text{ and } \mathsf{Z}(R) \in \mathcal{F}_2 \,\}.
$$

A splicing system with $L \in \mathcal{F}_1$ and $\mathsf{Z}(R) \in \mathcal{F}_2$ is said to be of $(\mathcal{F}_1, \mathcal{F}_2)$ type.

Example 1. Let $h = (\{a, b, c\}, L, R)$ be the splicing system defined by

$$
L = c\, b^* a^* b^* c
$$
$$
R = \{\, (cb^m a^n, b^n c, c, b^m c) \mid m, n \geq 0 \}
$$

It is of (REG,LIN) type as the initial language L is regular, and the set of rules is linear: $\mathsf{Z}(R) = \{cb^m a^n \# b^n c \$ c \# b^m c \mid m, n \geq 0\}$.

The only splicings possible are of the form $(cb^m a^n \mid b^n c, c \mid b^m c) \vdash cb^m a^n b^m c$. If the splicing has to be done in length-increasing mode, then we must have $m + n + 1 > 1$ and $m + 1 > n + 1$, hence

$$
\sigma_{in}(h) = \{cb^m a^n b^m c \mid m, n \geq 0 \text{ and } m > n\}
$$

which is not a context-free language.   □

We only consider $\mathcal{F}_1 = $ REG, LIN, CF and $\mathcal{F}_2 = $ FIN, REG, LIN, CF, and in particular we are interested in upper bounds for the families $S_\mu(\mathcal{F}_1, \mathcal{F}_2)$ for the modes μ that we consider. Known results are from the papers [PRS98], which deals with finite sets of rules ($\mathcal{F}_2 = $ FIN) only, and [KPS96], which deals with sets of rules of arbitrary Chomsky complexity (contradicting its title). We repeat in Table 1 the parts of Tables 1, 2 and 3 from [KPS96] that summarize the lowest upper bounds within the Chomsky hierarchy for the families $S_\mu(\mathcal{F}_1, \mathcal{F}_2)$. The families of initial languages $\mathcal{F}_1$ are listed in the bottom row, the families of

	FIN	REG	LIN	CF	FIN	REG	LIN	CF	FIN	REG	LIN	CF
f	REG	REG	LIN	CF	CF	CF	RE	RE	CF	CF	RE	RE
in	REG	REG		CF+	CS	CS	CS	CS	CS	CS	CS	CS
de	REG	REG		CF+	CS	CS	RE	RE	CS	CS	RE	RE
sl	LIN	LIN	CF+			CF+	RE	RE	CF+		RE	RE
sf	CS	CS				CF+	RE	RE	CF+		RE	RE
	$\mathcal{F}_1 = $ REG				$\mathcal{F}_1 = $ LIN				$\mathcal{F}_1 = $ CF			

Table 1. Upper bounds of $S_\mu(\mathcal{F}_1, \mathcal{F}_2)$ within the Chomsky hierarchy [KPS96].

splicing rules $\mathcal{F}_2$ are in the top row, repeated for each of the three possible initial families $\mathcal{F}_1$.

For the entries marked with CF+ it is only known that the family contains a non-context-free language; it is not yet determined whether the smallest upper bound within the Chomsky hierarchy is CS or RE.

Note that although, for instance, the table contains the same bounds for the families $S_{sl}(\mathsf{REG}, \mathsf{FIN})$ and $S_{sl}(\mathsf{REG}, \mathsf{REG})$, this does not necessarily mean that they are equal: they only have the same upper bound in the Chomsky hierarchy. The same remark holds for the equality of the tables for $\mathcal{F}_1 = \mathsf{LIN}$ and $\mathcal{F}_1 = \mathsf{CF}$.

3   Basic Tools

We present our basic tools. First we define a language that captures both the initial language and the rules of a splicing system. Second, we recall the notion of valence grammar, a grammatical device modestly extending the context-free grammars.

3.1   Representing the System by a Language

The open problems indicated in Table 1 involve either a context-free (or even linear) initial language, and regular (or even finite) splicing rules, or vice versa. For unrestricted (free) non-iterated splicing the upper bounds for these two cases are determined in Lemma 3.3 and Lemma 3.6 of [HPP97]. We use the ideas from the proofs of these two lemma's to define, for each splicing system $h = (V, L, R)$, the language $C(L, R)$ which combines the initial language with the rules.

$$C(L, R) = \{\ x_1 u_1 \# v_1 y_1 \$ x_2 u_2 \# v_2 y_2 \ \mid\ x_1 u_1 v_1 y_1\,,\ x_2 u_2 v_2 y_2 \in L$$
$$\text{and } (u_1, v_1, u_2, v_2) \in R\}$$

This language turns out to be very helpful in determining upper bounds for (restricted) splicing families. Note that $\sigma_f(h) = \mathrm{join}(C(L, R))$, where join is the finite state transduction that erases the two $\#$'s, and everything in between, from a string in $C(L, R)$.

To construct $C(L, R)$ from L and R, we proceed as follows. It is straightforward to design a (non-deterministic) finite state transduction such that the language $Z(R)$, representing the rules, is transformed into the language $R' = \{x_1 u_1 \# v_1 y_1 \$ x_2 u_2 \# v_2 y_2 \mid u_1 \# v_1 \$ u_2 \# v_2 \in Z(R) \text{ and } x_1, y_1, x_2, y_2 \in V^*\}$. Also using a finite state transduction, the language $L' = \{x \# y \$ w \# z \mid xy, wz \in L\}$ can be constructed from $L \cdot \$ \cdot L$, the (marked) concatenation of the initial language L with itself. Clearly, $C(L, R) = L' \cap R'$.

Since both REG and CF are closed under finite state transductions and under concatenation, we either have $L' \in$ REG and $R' \in$ CF for splicing of (REG,CF) type, or $L' \in$ CF and $R' \in$ REG, for splicing of (CF,REG) type. Clearly in both cases $C(L, R) = L' \cap R'$ is a context-free language, and so is $\sigma_f(h) = \text{join}(C(L, R))$, proving the (known) upper bounds for (REG,CF) type and (CF,REG) type splicing.

Lemma 2. *Let $h = (V, L, R)$ be a splicing system of* (REG, CF) *type or* (CF, REG) *type. Then the language $C(L, R)$ is context-free.*

In the sequel we adapt this strategy to restricted splicing. In that case we have to put further restrictions on the pair of strings that is spliced. This leads us to consider particular subsets of the language $C(L, R)$.

In the case of same-length splicing for instance, we have to restrict ourselves to strings in $C(L, R)$ for which additionally $|x_1 u_1 v_1 y_1| = |x_2 u_2 v_2 y_2|$. The resulting language which we call $C_{sl}(L, R)$ again represents the system in the sense that $\sigma_{sl}(h) = \text{join}(C_{sl}(L, R))$. In the case of (REG, CF) type splicing, $C_{sl}(L, R)$ is in general no longer context-free, but context-sensitive. This means that the upper bound we obtain in this way for $S_{sl}(\text{REG}, \text{CF})$, i.e., by applying a finite state transduction to $C_{sl}(L, R)$, is RE rather than CS, as CS is not closed under finite state transductions (in particular it is not closed under erasing mappings).

However, it turns out that $S_{sl}(\text{REG}, \text{CF}) \subseteq$ RE is not the optimal upper bound that is valid within the Chomsky hierarchy. Hence the applicability of our method fails because of the poor closure properties of CS, and we have been looking for a natural family strictly in between CF and CS, closed under finite state transductions, and which contains the languages $C_\mu(L, R)$ for the splicing types μ we will consider. Such a family exists, and we discuss its characteristics in the next subsection.

3.2 Valence Grammars

Let $k \geq 1$. We use $\mathbb{Z}^k$ to denote the set of k-dimensional vectors over the integers, and the vector with all components zero is written as $\mathbf{0}$.

A *context-free valence grammar* over $\mathbb{Z}^k$ is a context-free grammar in which every production is assigned a vector from $\mathbb{Z}^k$, the valence of the production. A string belongs to the language of the grammar if it is derived in the usual, context-free, fashion, while additionally the valences of the productions used add up to zero.

Formally, such a grammar is a construct $G = (\Sigma, \Delta, R, S)$, where Σ is the alphabet, $\Delta \subseteq \Sigma$ is the terminal alphabet, $S \in \Sigma$ is the axiom, and R is a finite set of *rules*, each of which is of the form $[\pi, \boldsymbol{r}]$, where $\pi \in (\Sigma - \Delta) \times \Sigma^*$ is a context-free production, and $\boldsymbol{r} \in \mathbb{Z}^k$ is its associated valence.

For $x, y \in \Sigma^*$ and $\boldsymbol{v} \in \mathbb{Z}^k$ we write $(x, \boldsymbol{v}) \Rightarrow_G (y, \boldsymbol{v} + \boldsymbol{r})$ if there exist a rule $[A \rightarrow z, \boldsymbol{r}]$ and $x_1, x_2 \in \Sigma^*$, such that $x = x_1 A x_2$ and $y = x_1 z x_2$. The *language generated by* G equals $L(G) = \{\, w \in \Delta^* \mid (S, \boldsymbol{0}) \Rightarrow^* (w, \boldsymbol{0}) \,\}$.

The resulting family of valence languages over $\mathbb{Z}^k$ is denoted by $\mathsf{CF}(\mathbb{Z}^k)$. Valence grammars were introduced in [Păŭ80]. A good starting point for learning of their properties and for pointers to recent literature is the paper [FS00], presented as extended abstract in [FS97].

Example 3. (1) Consider the valence grammar G_1 over $\mathbb{Z}^2$, which has rules $[S \rightarrow aS, (+1, +1)]$, $[S \rightarrow bS, (-1, 0)]$, $[S \rightarrow cS, (0, -1)]$, and $[S \rightarrow \lambda, (0, 0)]$, where S is the axiom, and a, b, c are terminal symbols. Then $L(G_1) = \{\, w \in \{a, b, c\}^* \mid \#_a(w) = \#_b(w) = \#_c(w) \,\}$, as the first component of the valence forces $\#_a(w) = \#_b(w)$, while $\#_a(w) = \#_c(w)$ because of the second component. This is in fact a right-linear valence grammar.

(2) The same language can be obtained by a valence grammar over $\mathbb{Z}^1$ choosing rules $[S \rightarrow SS, (0)]$, $[S \rightarrow aSb, (+1)]$, $[S \rightarrow bSa, (+1)]$, $[S \rightarrow cS, (-1)]$, and $[S \rightarrow \lambda, (0)]$.

Note that this is essentially a context-free grammar for the language $\{\, w \in \{a, b, c\}^* \mid \#_a(w) = \#_b(w) \,\}$, augmented with an additional counter to compare the number of c's to the numbers of a's and b's. □

The right-linear valence grammars are a formalism equivalent to the blind counter automata of Greibach [Gre78]; these are finite state automata equipped with additional counters, each of which can be incremented and decremented independently. This storage is "blind" as the counters cannot be tested for zero during the computation, except implicitly at the end, as one only considers computations that lead from the initial state with empty counters to an accepting state with empty counters.

The context-free valence languages form a hierarchy within CS. Each $\mathsf{CF}(\mathbb{Z}^k)$ has very convenient closure properties; it is in fact a full semi-AFL.

Proposition 4. Let $k \geq 1$. $\mathsf{CF}(\mathbb{Z}^k)$ is closed under union, homomorphisms, inverse homomorphisms, and intersection with regular languages. Consequently $\mathsf{CF}(\mathbb{Z}^k)$ is closed under finite state transductions.

The closure under intersection with regular languages can be generalized as follows: the intersection of a context-free valence language over $\mathbb{Z}^k$ with a right-linear valence language over $\mathbb{Z}^\ell$ is a context-free valence language over $\mathbb{Z}^{k+\ell}$. We will use this fact in the sequel, in particular for $k = 0$, i.e., the intersection of a context-free language and a right-linear valence language over $\mathbb{Z}^\ell$ belongs to $\mathsf{CF}(\mathbb{Z}^\ell)$.

We end by giving two more examples of right-linear valence languages which are essential for our considerations.

Example 5. Let Σ be an alphabet, and let $\#, \$$ be two symbols not in Σ.
(1) Consider $D_{sl} = \{\, x_1 \# y_1 \$ x_2 \# y_2 \mid x_1, y_1, x_2, y_2 \in \Sigma^*, |x_1 y_1| = |x_2 y_2| \,\}$. It is generated by a right-linear valence grammar over $\mathbb{Z}^1$, with axiom S_0, and the following rules. Here a ranges over Σ.

$$[S_0 \rightarrow aS_0, (+1)], \quad [S_0 \rightarrow \#S_1, (0)],$$
$$[S_1 \rightarrow aS_1, (+1)], \quad [S_1 \rightarrow \$S_2, (0)],$$
$$[S_2 \rightarrow aS_2, (-1)], \quad [S_2 \rightarrow \#S_3, (0)], \quad \text{and}$$
$$[S_3 \rightarrow aS_3, (-1)], \quad [S_3 \rightarrow \lambda, (0)]$$

(2) $D_{in} = \{ x_1 \# y_1 \$ x_2 \# y_2 \mid x_1, y_1, x_2, y_2 \in \Sigma^*, |x_1| > |x_2| \text{ and } |y_2| > |y_1| \}$ is generated by the right-linear valence grammar over $\mathbb{Z}^2$, with axiom S_0, and the following rules; again, a ranges over Σ.

$$[S_0 \rightarrow aS_0, (+1, 0)], \quad [S_0 \rightarrow aS_0, (0, 0)], \quad [S_0 \rightarrow \#S_1, (0, 0)],$$
$$[S_1 \rightarrow aS_1, (0, -1)], \quad [S_1 \rightarrow \$S_2, (0, 0)],$$
$$[S_2 \rightarrow aS_2, (-1, 0)], \quad [S_2 \rightarrow \#S_3, (0, 0)], \quad \text{and}$$
$$[S_3 \rightarrow aS_3, (0, +1)], \quad [S_3 \rightarrow aS_3, (0, 0)], \quad [S_3 \rightarrow \lambda, (-1, -1)].$$

Observe that we have inequality $|x_1| \geq |x_2|$ rather than equality because symbols in the first segment do not have to be counted on the (first) counter as there is an alternative rule. The strictness of the inequality is forced by decreasing both counters in the final rule. $\qquad \Box$

4 Same-Length Splicing

We restrict splicing to cases where both inputs have the same length, i.e., mode $\mu = sl$. Precise upper bounds within the Chomsky hierarchy are missing for $S_{sl}(\mathcal{F}_1, \mathcal{F}_2)$ when (1) $\mathcal{F}_1 = \mathsf{REG}$ and $\mathcal{F}_2 = \mathsf{LIN}, \mathsf{CF}$ (two cases), and when (2) $\mathcal{F}_1 = \mathsf{LIN}, \mathsf{CF}$ and $\mathcal{F}_2 = \mathsf{FIN}, \mathsf{REG}$ (four cases).

All these families contain a non-context-free language. For $S_{sl}(\mathsf{REG}, \mathsf{LIN})$ this was shown in [KPS96, Lemma 8]; for $S_{sl}(\mathsf{LIN}, \mathsf{FIN})$ this follows from the fact that one may closely simulate the operation of doubling using splicing with finite rules, cf. Lemma 3 in [PRS98], obtaining from L the language $double(L) = \{xx \mid x \in L\}$.

We give an explicit example for the latter family $S_{sl}(\mathsf{LIN}, \mathsf{FIN})$.

Example 6. Let $h = (\{a, b, d\}, L, R)$ be the splicing system of (LIN,FIN) type defined by

$$L = \{a^n b^n d \mid n \geq 1\} \cup \{d\, a^n b^n \mid n \geq 1\}$$
$$R = \{ (b, d, d, a) \}$$

The form of the rule causes the first argument of each splicing to be of the form $a^k b^k d$, and the second argument of the form $d\, a^j b^j$, for some $k, j \geq 1$. Moreover, if we consider same-length splicing, we should have $k = j$. Then $(a^k b^k \mid d, d \mid a^k b^k) \vdash^{sl} a^k b^k a^k b^k$, using the only splicing rule in R. Consequently

$$\sigma_{sl}(h) = \{a^n b^n a^n b^n \mid n \geq 1\}$$

which is not context-free. $\qquad \Box$

We prove that in all six open cases the same-length splicing languages are context-free valence languages over $\mathbb{Z}^1$ and thus context-sensitive.

Theorem 7. $S_{sl}(\mathsf{REG}, \mathsf{CF}) \subseteq \mathsf{CF}(\mathbb{Z}^1)$ *and* $S_{sl}(\mathsf{CF}, \mathsf{REG}) \subseteq \mathsf{CF}(\mathbb{Z}^1)$.

Proof. Let $h = (V, L, R)$ be a splicing system. As described before, the language $C(L, R)$ codes the splicing ingredients in the free case, and can be used to obtain upper bounds. For the (REG,CF) and (CF,REG) types of splicing we have argued that $C(L, R)$ is a context-free language, see Lemma 2.

To extend the equality $\sigma_f(h) = \mathrm{join}(C(L, R))$ to same-length splicing we restrict $C(L, R)$ to pairs of initial strings having the same length: $\sigma_{sl}(h) = \mathrm{join}(C(L, R) \cap D_{sl})$, where $D_{sl} = \{\, x_1 \# y_1 \$ x_2 \# y_2 \mid x_1, y_1, x_2, y_2 \in \Sigma^*, |x_1 y_1| = |x_2 y_2| \,\}$.

Note that D_{sl} can be generated by a right-linear valence grammar over $\mathbb{Z}^1$, cf. Example 5(1), and consequently $C(L, R) \cap D_{sl}$ is an element of $\mathsf{CF}(\mathbb{Z}^1)$. This implies $\sigma_{sl}(h) \in \mathsf{CF}(\mathbb{Z}^1)$, as $\mathsf{CF}(\mathbb{Z}^1)$ is closed under finite state transductions, Proposition 4. □

We immediately have a minimal upper bound within the Chomsky hierarchy for the six open cases.

Corollary 8. (1) $S_{sl}(\mathcal{F}_1, \mathcal{F}_2) \subseteq \mathsf{CS}$ *for* $\mathcal{F}_1 = \mathsf{REG}$ *and* $\mathcal{F}_2 = \mathsf{LIN}, \mathsf{CF}$.
(2) $S_{sl}(\mathcal{F}_1, \mathcal{F}_2) \subseteq \mathsf{CS}$ *for* $\mathcal{F}_1 = \mathsf{LIN}, \mathsf{CF}$ *and* $\mathcal{F}_2 = \mathsf{FIN}, \mathsf{REG}$.

5   Length-Increasing (Decreasing) Splicing

We consider length-increasing splicing (mode $\mu = in$) and length-decreasing splicing ($\mu = de$). Although the specifications of these modes are rather similar, it must be observed that their power is not always equal, for instance, $S_{in}(\mathsf{CF}, \mathsf{CF}) \subseteq \mathsf{CS}$, while $S_{de}(\mathsf{CF}, \mathsf{CF}) - \mathsf{CS} \neq \varnothing$.

In [KPS96, p.238] the question is raised whether $S_\mu(\mathsf{REG}, \mathsf{LIN})$, $\mu = in, de$, contains a non-context-free language. Our Example 1 shows there is indeed such a language for increasing mode, for decreasing mode there is a simple variant (adapting an example given in the proof of Lemma 10 in [KPS96]).

Example 9. Replace the initial language of Example 1 by

$$L' = cb^* a^* b^* c \cup c^* b^* c$$

and let $h' = (\{a, b, c\}, L', R)$ with R as in Example 1. Now the only possible length-decreasing splicings are $(cb^m a^n \mid b^n c \, , \, c^\ell c \mid b^m c) \vdash^{de} cb^m a^n b^m c$, where $1 + m + n < \ell + 1$ and $m + 1 < n + 1$, thus

$$\sigma_{de}(h') = \{cb^m a^n b^m c \mid m, n \geq 0 \text{ and } m < n\}$$

which is not in CF. □

Consequently we have the following result.

Lemma 10. $S_\mu(\mathsf{REG}, \mathsf{LIN}) - \mathsf{CF} \neq \varnothing$ *for* $\mu = in, de$.

In fact, this already solves the minimal upper bounds for $S_{in}(\mathsf{REG}, \mathsf{LIN})$ and $S_{in}(\mathsf{REG}, \mathsf{CF})$ within the Chomsky hierarchy, as the inclusion $S_{in}(\mathsf{CS}, \mathsf{CS}) \subseteq \mathsf{CS}$ is known (Lemma 3 of [KPS96]).

For length-decreasing splicing we do not have such a convenient result. To remedy this, we prove that both $S_{de}(\mathsf{REG}, \mathsf{CF})$ and $S_{de}(\mathsf{CF}, \mathsf{REG})$ are subfamilies of $\mathsf{CF}(\mathbb{Z}^2)$, similar to the case of same-length splicing. For $S_{de}(\mathsf{REG}, \mathsf{CF})$ this answers the question whether the smallest upper bound in the Chomsky hierarchy is CS or RE, whereas for $S_{de}(\mathsf{CF}, \mathsf{REG})$ this improves the known upper bound CS. The argumentation works for increasing mode as well, so also in that case we obtain improved upper bounds within CS.

Theorem 11. $S_{\mu}(\mathsf{REG}, \mathsf{CF}) \subseteq \mathsf{CF}(\mathbb{Z}^2)$ and $S_{\mu}(\mathsf{CF}, \mathsf{REG}) \subseteq \mathsf{CF}(\mathbb{Z}^2)$, for $\mu = in, de$.

Proof. Let $h = (V, L, R)$ be a splicing system. Consider the language $C(L, R)$ constructed from L and R as before. It is context-free for splicing of $(\mathsf{REG}, \mathsf{CF})$ type or of $(\mathsf{CF}, \mathsf{REG})$ type, see Lemma 2. We now consider in splicing, argumentation for de splicing is completely symmetric.

It is easily seen that $\sigma_{in}(h) = \mathrm{join}(C(L, R) \cap D_{in})$, where D_{in} is the language $\{ x_1 \# y_1 \$ x_2 \# y_2 \mid x_1, y_1, x_2, y_2 \in \Sigma^*, |x_1| > |x_2| \text{ and } |y_2| > |y_1| \}$ from Example 5(2).

As $C(L, R)$ is context-free, and D_{in} is a right-linear valence language over $\mathbb{Z}^2$, we conclude that $\sigma_{in}(h)$ is in $\mathsf{CF}(\mathbb{Z}^2)$ using closure properties of these families. $\square$

Summarizing, we have found minimal upper bounds for both length-increasing and length-decreasing splicing within the Chomsky hierarchy.

Corollary 12. *For $\mu = in, de$ one has*

(1) $S_{\mu}(\mathsf{REG}, \mathcal{F}_2) \subseteq \mathsf{CS}$ *for $\mathcal{F}_2 = \mathsf{LIN}, \mathsf{CF}$.*
(2) $S_{\mu}(\mathcal{F}_1, \mathcal{F}_2) \subseteq \mathsf{CS}$ *for $\mathcal{F}_1 = \mathsf{LIN}, \mathsf{CF}$ and $\mathcal{F}_2 = \mathsf{FIN}, \mathsf{REG}$.*

6 Self Splicing

As self splicing takes a single string as both arguments for the splicing operation, the two splicing sites as described by the rules have to be located on that same string. As there are two possible orderings for the splicing sites for the first and second argument of the operation, the splicing may be in one of the following fashions.

First, we may splice according to the fashion $(x \mid yz, xy \mid z) \vdash xz$, i.e., the first site occurs before the second site. This means that a substring is removed from the input. In particular, when the second site occurs at the end of the string it is possible to model the quotient operation on languages, cf. Lemma 6 in [KPS96], as follows. Consider languages L_1, L_2, and let $L = L_1 d$, where d is a new symbol. Furthermore, let $R = \{ (\lambda, yd, d, \lambda) \mid y \in L_2 \}$. Then $\sigma_{sf}(V, L, R) = \{ x \mid xy \in L_1 \text{ for some } y \in L_2 \} = L_1 / L_2$. As a consequence $S_{sf}(\mathsf{LIN}, \mathsf{LIN}) - \mathsf{CS} \neq \varnothing$. In fact, this construction also works for the modes free splicing, length-decreasing splicing, and same-length splicing.

Second, we may splice according to the fashion $(xy \mid z, x \mid yz) \vdash xyyz$, i.e., the first site occurs *after* the second site. This means that a substring in the input is doubled. In particular, it is possible to model the doubling operation on languages, cf. Lemma 3 in [PRS98], as follows. Consider a language L_1, and let $L = cL_1d$, where c, d are new symbols. Furthermore, let $R = \{\ (\lambda, d, c, \lambda)\ \}$. Then $\sigma_{sf}(V, L, R) = c \cdot double(L_1) \cdot d = c \cdot \{\ xx \mid x \in L_1\ \} \cdot d$. As a consequence $S_{sf}(\mathsf{REG}, \mathsf{FIN}) - \mathsf{CF} \neq \varnothing$. In fact, this construction is a variant of Example 6, where doubling was obtained for same-length splicing.

We meet these operations of quotient and doubling later in this section, in Lemma 15 and Theorem 13.

The present state of knowledge concerning self splicing seems to be summarized by the two earlier conclusions $S_{sf}(\mathsf{LIN}, \mathsf{LIN}) \not\subseteq \mathsf{CS}$ and $S_{sf}(\mathsf{REG}, \mathsf{FIN}) \not\subseteq \mathsf{CF}$, and the inclusion $S_{sf}(\mathsf{REG}, \mathsf{REG}) \subseteq \mathsf{CS}$ ([KPS96], remark following Lemma 7). We extend this latter inclusion to a larger family of initial languages. To this end we will need deterministic two-way finite state transductions, i.e., relations realized by deterministic finite state automata with a two-way input tape and a one-way output tape. These machines are capable of writing a doubled copy of their input, which makes them suitable to simulate self splicing. We use 2DGSM to denote the family of deterministic two-way finite state transductions, and, in particular, 2DGSM(CF) denotes the family of languages obtained from CF by applying these transductions[1].

Theorem 13. $S_{sf}(\mathsf{CF}, \mathsf{REG}) \subseteq 2\mathsf{DGSM}(\mathsf{CF})$

Proof. Let $h = (V, L, R)$ be a splicing system with $L \in \mathsf{CF}$ and $Z(R) \in \mathsf{REG}$. As explained in the introduction to this section, $\sigma_{sf}(h)$ can be described as $L_{xz} \cup L_{xyyz}$, where

$$L_{xz} = \{\ xz \mid xyz \in L \text{ with } u_1 \in \mathrm{Suf}(x), v_1 \in \mathrm{Pref}(yz),$$
$$u_2 \in \mathrm{Suf}(xy), v_2 \in \mathrm{Pref}(z) \text{ for a } (u_1, v_1, u_2, v_2) \in R\ \} \text{ and}$$
$$L_{xyyx} = \{\ xyyz \mid xyz \in L \text{ with } u_1 \in \mathrm{Suf}(xy), v_1 \in \mathrm{Pref}(z),$$
$$u_2 \in \mathrm{Suf}(x), v_2 \in \mathrm{Pref}(yz) \text{ for a } (u_1, v_1, u_2, v_2) \in R\ \}$$

Let 1 and 2 be symbols not in V; we will use these symbols to mark the two splicing sites in a string, similarly to the symbol $\#$ in the strings of $C(L, R)$. So, let

$$L_{12} = \{\ x1y2z \mid xyz \in L \text{ with } u_1 \in \mathrm{Suf}(x), v_1 \in \mathrm{Pref}(yz),$$
$$u_2 \in \mathrm{Suf}(xy), v_2 \in \mathrm{Pref}(z) \text{ for a } (u_1, v_1, u_2, v_2) \in R\ \} \text{ and}$$
$$L_{21} = \{\ x2y1z \mid xyz \in L \text{ with } u_1 \in \mathrm{Suf}(xy), v_1 \in \mathrm{Pref}(z),$$
$$u_2 \in \mathrm{Suf}(x), v_2 \in \mathrm{Pref}(yz) \text{ for a } (u_1, v_1, u_2, v_2) \in R\ \}$$

---

[1] A generalized sequential machine, GSM, differs from a finite state transducer in that it is not allowed to read λ. For two-way machines the two notions are equivalent.

Note that $L_{12} \cup L_{21}$ can be obtained from L (and R) by a (nondeterministic, one-way) finite state transduction based on $Z(R)$. The transducer has to search for the two cutting points simultaneously, because the splicing sites u_1v_1 and u_2v_2 can overlap and the transducer is not allowed to go back on its input.

As CF is closed under finite state transductions, $L_{12} \cup L_{21}$ belongs to CF.

It is now straightforward to design a (deterministic) two-way finite state transduction that maps $L_{12} \cup L_{21}$ onto $L_{xz} \cup L_{xyyz}$, as follows. It copies its input from left to right until it arrives at the symbol 1. At that moment the machine moves to the symbol 2 without copying (forward or backward depending on whether the 2 was encountered before finding the 1). At the symbol 2 it resumes a left to right scan copying the input, stopping at the right end of the tape. □

As stated in [EY71, Theorem 3.4], 2DGSM(CF) is strictly contained in the family of context-sensitive languages. Hence we obtain an upper bound as required.

Corollary 14. $S_{sf}(\mathcal{F}_1, \mathcal{F}_2) \subseteq$ CS *for* $\mathcal{F}_1 =$ LIN, CF *and* $\mathcal{F}_2 =$ FIN, REG.

The construction for doubling discussed in the introduction of this section implies that also self splicings of (REG, LIN) type can yield languages outside CF. We show that they can even define non-context-sensitive languages, i.e., we prove that the smallest upper bound in the Chomsky hierarchy of $S_{sf}(\text{REG}, \text{CF})$ and $S_{sf}(\text{REG}, \text{LIN})$ is RE.

For context-free rules this is relatively easy, as we can directly simulate the quotient operation on linear languages using context-free splicing of regular languages. The result then follows, as every RE language can be written as the quotient of two linear languages ([LLR85]).

Lemma 15. *Let* L_1, L_2 *be linear languages over* Σ *and let* 1 *be a symbol not in* Σ. *Then* $1L_1/L_2 \in S_{sf}(\text{REG}, \text{CF})$.

Proof. Assume that L_1 and L_2 are linear languages with $L_1, L_2 \subseteq \Sigma^*$ for some alphabet Σ. Let $1, 2, 3 \notin \Sigma$ be new symbols, and define $h = (\Sigma \cup \{1, 2, 3\}, L, R)$ by

$$L = 1\Sigma^*2\Sigma^*3$$
$$R = \{ (1\,u, 2\,v\,3, 2\,w\,3, \lambda) \mid uv \in L_1, w \in L_2 \}$$

Since LIN is closed under concatenation with symbols and under shuffle with strings (but not under concatenation) we have $Z(R) = \{1u\#2v3\$ \mid uv \in L_1\} \cdot \{2w3\# \mid w \in L_2\} \in$ LIN $\cdot$ LIN $\subseteq$ CF.

We start by proving that $\sigma_{sf}(h) \subseteq 1L_1/L_2$. Let $x \in L$ and $(x, x) \vdash_r z$ for a rule $r = (1u, 2v3, 2w3, \lambda)$. Then, because of the form of the axioms and the first splicing site we must have $x = 1u2v3$. Moreover we have $2v3 = 2w3$, i.e., $v = w$, because we are considering self splicing. Clearly $(1u \mid 2v3 , 1u2v3 \mid \lambda) \vdash_r^{sf} z = 1u \in 1L_1/L_2$, since $uv \in L_1$ and $v = w \in L_2$ by construction.

Now take $z \in L_1/L_2$, i.e., there is a $y \in L_2$ such that $zy \in L_1$. According to the definition of h there is a splicing rule $r = (1z, 2y3, 2y3, \lambda) \in R$ and an axiom $1z2y3$, and so $(1z \mid 2y3 , 1z2y3 \mid \lambda) \vdash_r 1z \in \sigma_{sf}(h)$. □

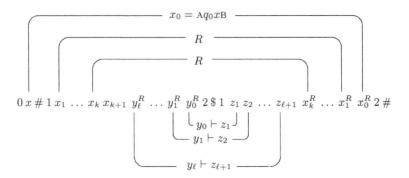

Fig. 1. The structure of strings in $K_\mathcal{M}$.

Corollary 16. *Let K be a language over Σ and let 1 be a symbol not in Σ. If $K \in \mathsf{RE}$, then $1K \in S_{sf}(\mathsf{REG}, \mathsf{CF})$.*

Since CS is closed under quotient with symbols, $1K \in \mathsf{CS}$ would imply $K \in \mathsf{CS}$. Consequently $K \in \mathsf{RE} - \mathsf{CS}$ implies $1K \in \mathsf{RE} - \mathsf{CS}$, thus the smallest upper bound in the Chomsky hierarchy of $S_{sf}(\mathsf{REG}, \mathsf{CF})$ is RE, as formulated in the following theorem.

Theorem 17. $S_{sf}(\mathsf{REG}, \mathsf{CF}) - \mathsf{CS} \neq \varnothing$.

The same result holds for $S_{sf}(\mathsf{REG}, \mathsf{LIN})$, i.e., we may replace the set of rules R for which $Z(R) \in \mathsf{LIN} \cdot \mathsf{LIN}$ by a set R with $Z(R) \in \mathsf{LIN}$, cf. the proof of Lemma 15. We cannot do this directly, as in that proof. Instead, we obtain this by reconsidering the proof in [LLR85] that every recursively enumerable language is the quotient of two linear languages. The main idea is that single steps of a Turing machine can be captured by a linear grammar, provided that we represent one of the two configurations involved by its mirror image. It is also possible to represent a series of steps of the Turing machine, steps which are unrelated however, as we cannot join them into a computation without further tricks (like intersection, quotient, or ... self splicing).

We describe now our approach to code series of Turing machine computational steps. Several markers are included in the language in order to use it in the splicing process.

Let $\mathcal{M}$ be a Turing machine with state set Q, initial state q_0, final state f and tape alphabet Γ. We denote the configurations of $\mathcal{M}$ by strings in $conf(\mathcal{M}) = \mathrm{A}\,\Gamma^*\,Q\,\Gamma^*\,\mathrm{B}$, where A, B are special symbols used to delimit the strings. The step relation of $\mathcal{M}$ is defined over $conf(\mathcal{M})$, and is denoted by $\vdash_\mathcal{M}$. We assume $\mathcal{M}$ recognizes strings x over Σ by starting in the initial configuration $\mathrm{A}\,q_0\,x\,\mathrm{B}$ and reaching a final configuration in $\mathrm{A}\,\Gamma^*\,f\,\Gamma^*\,\mathrm{B}$.

Let $0, 1, 2, \#, \$$ be symbols not in Σ. Using w^R to denote the mirror image of string w, define the language $K_\mathcal{M}$ to consist of the words

$$0\,x\,\#\,1\,x_1 \ldots x_k\,x_{k+1}\,y_\ell^R \ldots y_1^R\,y_0^R\,2\,\$\,1\,z_1\,z_2 \ldots z_{\ell+1}\,x_k^R \ldots x_1^R x_0^R\,2\,\#$$

where

$x \in \Sigma^*$, $x_0 = \text{A} \, q_0 \, x \, \text{B}$, $x_{k+1} \in \text{A} \, \Gamma^* f \, \Gamma^* \text{B}$,

$x_0, \ldots, x_{k+1}, y_0, \ldots, y_\ell, z_1, \ldots, z_{\ell+1} \in conf(\mathcal{M})$, for $k, \ell \geq 0$, and

$y_i \vdash_{\mathcal{M}} z_{i+1}$ for $0 \leq i \leq \ell$.

The structure of the strings in $K_{\mathcal{M}}$ is illustrated in Figure 1. A single step of a Turing machine induces just a local change in a configuration. It is an easy exercise to show that $K_{\mathcal{M}}$ is linear language, a variant of the language used in [LLR85].

Lemma 18. *For each Turing machine $\mathcal{M}$, $K_{\mathcal{M}} \in \mathsf{LIN}$.*

Theorem 19. *Let K be a language over Σ and let 0 be a symbol not in Σ. If $K \in \mathsf{RE}$, then $0K \in S_{sf}(\mathsf{REG}, \mathsf{LIN})$.*

Proof. Let $K = L(\mathcal{M})$ for a deterministic Turing machine $\mathcal{M}$, and let $K_{\mathcal{M}}$ be as defined above. Now $\sigma_{sf}(h) = 0K$ for the splicing system $h = (V, L, R)$ defined by

$$V = \Gamma \cup \{0, 1, 2\}$$
$$L = 0 \, \Sigma^* \, 1 \, (\Gamma \cup \{\text{A}, \text{B}\})^* \, 2$$
$$Z(R) = K_{\mathcal{M}}$$

Using Lemma 18, we observe that the system h is of $(\mathsf{REG}, \mathsf{LIN})$ type. The splicing rules of h are of the form

$$(\, 0 \, x \; , \; 1 \, x_1 \ldots x_{k+1} \, y_\ell^R \ldots y_1^R y_0^R \, 2 \; , \; 1 \, z_1 \ldots z_{\ell+1} \, x_k^R \ldots x_1^R x_0^R \, 2 \; , \; \lambda \,)$$

with $x_1, \ldots, x_{k+1}, y_0, \ldots, y_\ell, z_1, \ldots, z_{\ell+1} \in conf(\mathcal{M})$, $x_0 = \text{A} \, q_0 \, x \, \text{B}$ and $y_i \vdash_{\mathcal{M}} z_{i+1}$ for $0 \leq i \leq \ell$; x_{k+1} is a final configuration of $\mathcal{M}$.

Because of the form of the initial strings and of the rules, the first argument of the splicing must be of the form $0 \, x \, 1 \, x_1 \ldots x_{k+1} \, y_\ell^R \ldots y_1^R y_0^R \, 2$. Since we consider self splicing, this is also the second argument. The second splicing site now enforces the equality

$$x_1 \ldots x_{k+1} \, y_\ell^R \ldots y_1^R y_0^R = z_1 \ldots z_{\ell+1} \, x_k^R \ldots x_1^R x_0^R,$$

and the marking with A and B ensures that $k = \ell$, $x_i = z_i$ for $1 \leq i \leq k + 1$ and $y_j = x_j$ for $0 \leq j \leq k$. Hence $x_0 = \text{A} \, q_0 \, x \, \text{B}$ is the initial configuration of $\mathcal{M}$ for the input word x, $x_i = y_i \vdash_{\mathcal{M}} z_{i+1} = x_{i+1}$ for $0 \leq i \leq k$, and x_{k+1} is the final configuration of $\mathcal{M}$ for x. Thus $x_0 \vdash_{\mathcal{M}} x_1 \vdash_{\mathcal{M}} \ldots \vdash_{\mathcal{M}} x_{k+1}$ is an accepting configuration sequence for x. Consequently, if $0 \, x \, 1 \, x_1 \ldots x_{k+1} y_\ell^R \ldots y_1^R y_0^R 2$ splices with itself to give $0 \, x$, then $x \in L(\mathcal{M})$.

The reverse inclusion follows along the same lines (read backwards).   □

Again we obtain a negative result concerning the upper bound CS.

Theorem 20. $S_{sf}(\mathsf{REG}, \mathsf{LIN}) - \mathsf{CS} \neq \varnothing$.

	FIN	REG	LIN	CF	FIN	REG	LIN	CF	FIN	REG	LIN	CF
f	REG	REG	LIN	CF	CF	CF	RE	RE	CF	CF	RE	RE
in	REG	REG	$CF(\mathbb{Z}^2)$	$CF(\mathbb{Z}^2)$	$CF(\mathbb{Z}^2)$	$CF(\mathbb{Z}^2)$	CS	CS	$CF(\mathbb{Z}^2)$	$CF(\mathbb{Z}^2)$	CS	CS
de	REG	REG	$CF(\mathbb{Z}^2)$	$CF(\mathbb{Z}^2)$	$CF(\mathbb{Z}^2)$	$CF(\mathbb{Z}^2)$	RE	RE	$CF(\mathbb{Z}^2)$	$CF(\mathbb{Z}^2)$	RE	RE
sl	LIN	LIN	$CF(\mathbb{Z}^1)$	$CF(\mathbb{Z}^1)$	$CF(\mathbb{Z}^1)$	$CF(\mathbb{Z}^1)$	RE	RE	$CF(\mathbb{Z}^1)$	$CF(\mathbb{Z}^1)$	RE	RE
sf	2(CF)	2(CF)	RE	RE	2(CF)	2(CF)	RE	RE	2(CF)	2(CF)	RE	RE
	$\mathcal{F}_1 = $ REG				$\mathcal{F}_1 = $ LIN				$\mathcal{F}_1 = $ CF			

Table 2. Updated upper bounds for $S_\mu(\mathcal{F}_1, \mathcal{F}_2)$. We use 2(CF) as shorthand for 2DGSM(CF).

7   Conclusion

We have filled the open spots in Table 1, and improved some of the known CS upper bounds given there. In Table 2 we summarize the results on the upper bounds of the four modes that we considered. Note that not all bounds given in this summary meet the original goal set in [PRS98, KPS96], to give minimal upper bounds within the Chomsky hierarchy. To get these, replace the items $CF(\mathbb{Z}^1)$, $CF(\mathbb{Z}^2)$, and 2DGSM(CF) by CS.

We now have a full insight in the complexity of the restricted splicing modes we have considered. This picture is somewhat surprising. If we order the splicing modes according to their upper bounds, we obtain different outcomes depending on the complexity of the input languages and the rules. We list a few representative examples by comparing the upper bounds in the Chomsky hierarchy.

(REG, REG)	$f, in, de \prec sl \prec sf$
(REG, CF)	$f \prec sl, in, de \prec sf$
(CF, REG)	$f \prec sl, in, de, sf$
(CF, CF)	$in \prec f, de, sl, sf$

The picture is more complex in the case we consider the families $CF(\mathbb{Z}^k)$ and 2DGSM(CF) instead of CS. We postulate here that $CF(\mathbb{Z}^k)$ and 2DGSM(CF) are incomparable.

Apart from the fact that self splicing seems to be the most complex operation for all types of input language and rules, it seems hard to make general observations on the relative power of restricted splicing modes. One does note that the tables for linear and context-free initial languages coincide. However, we conjecture that, although these upper bounds are identical, the family $S_\mu(\text{LIN}, \mathcal{F})$ is strictly included in $S_\mu(\text{CF}, \mathcal{F})$. Similarly, we observe that for a fixed family of initial languages, the upper bounds obtained for FIN and REG rules are the same, and also the upper bounds obtained for LIN and CF rules are the same (with the exception of free splicing). For FIN and REG rules we have obtained some evidence that the families $S_\mu(\mathcal{F}, \text{FIN})$ and $S_\mu(\mathcal{F}, \text{REG})$ are equal for several modes of splicing, see [DHvV00] and the forthcoming thesis of the second author.

References

[CH91] K. Culik II, T. Harju. Splicing Semigroups of Dominoes and DNA, *Discrete Applied Mathematics*, 31:162–177, 1991.

[DHvV00] R. Dassen, H.J. Hoogeboom, N. van Vugt. A Characterization of Non-iterated Splicing with Regular Rules. In: *Where Mathematics, Computer Science and Biology Meet* (C. Martin-Vide, V. Mitrana, Eds.), Kluwer Academic Publishers, 2000, pages 319-327.

[EY71] R.W. Ehrich, S.S. Yau. Two-Way Sequential Transductions and Stack Automata. *Information and Control* 18:404–446, 1971.

[FS97] H. Fernau and R. Stiebe. Regulation by Valences. In: B. Rovan (Ed.) Proceedings of MFCS'97, Lecture Notes in Computer Science, vol. 1295, pages 239-248. Springer-Verlag, 1997.

[FS00] H. Fernau, R. Stiebe. Sequential Grammars and Automata with Valences. Technical Report WSI-2000-25, Wilhelm- Schickard-Institut für Informatik, Universität Tübingen, 2000. Submitted. Available via
http://www.informatik.uni-tuebingen.de/bibliothek/wsi-reports.html

[Gre78] S.A. Greibach. Remarks on Blind and Partially Blind One-Way Multicounter Machines. *Theoretical Computer Science* 7 (1978) 311- 324.

[HPP97] T. Head, Gh. Păun, D. Pixton. Language Theory and Molecular Genetics: Generative Mechanisms Suggested by DNA Recombination. In: *Handbook of Formal Languages* (G. Rozenberg, A. Salomaa, Eds.), volume 2, Springer-Verlag, 1997.

[HU79] J.E. Hopcroft, J.D. Ullman. *Introduction to Automata Theory, Languages, and Computation*, Addison-Wesley, 1979.

[HvV98] H.J. Hoogeboom, N. van Vugt. The Power of H Systems: Does Representation Matter? *Computing with Bio-molecules: Theory and Experiments* (G. Păun, Ed.), Springer-Verlag, Singapore, 255–268, 1998.

[KPS96] L. Kari, G. Păun, A. Salomaa. The Power of Restricted Splicing with Rules from a Regular Language, *Journal of Universal Computer Science*, 2(4):224-240, 1996.

[LLR85] M. Latteux, B. Leguy, B. Ratoandromanana. The Family of One-Counter Languages Is Closed under Quotient, *Acta Informatica* 22:579–588, 1985.

[Pău80] G. Păun. A New Generative Device: Valence Grammars. *Revue Roumaine de Mathématiques Pures et Appliquées* 6 (1980) 911-924.

[PRS95] Gh. Păun, G. Rozenberg, A. Salomaa. Computing by Splicing, *Theoretical Computer Science* 168:321–336, 1996.

[PRS96] Gh. Păun, G. Rozenberg, A. Salomaa. Restricted Use of the Splicing Operation, *International Journal of Computer Mathematics* 60:17–32, 1996.

[PRS98] Gh. Păun, G. Rozenberg, A. Salomaa. *DNA Computing. New Computing Paradigms*, Springer-Verlag, 1998.

Codes, Involutions, and DNA Encodings*

Lila Kari, Rob Kitto, and Gabriel Thierrin

Department of Computer Science, Univ. of Western Ontario
London, Ontario, N6A 5B7 Canada
{lila, kitto, gab}@csd.uwo.ca

> *If we knew what it was we were doing,*
> *it would not be called research, would it?*
> *(Albert Einstein)*

1 Introduction

DNA computing as a field started in 1994 when Leonard Adleman solved a hard computational problem entirely by manipulations of DNA molecules in a test tube [1]. The premise behind DNA computing is that DNA is capable of storing information, while various laboratory techniques that operate on and modify DNA strands (called bio-operations in the sequel) can be used to perform computational steps. Most DNA computations consists of three basic stages. The first is encoding the problem using single-stranded or double-stranded DNA. Then the actual computation is performed by employing a succession of bio-operations [14]. Finally, the DNA strands representing the solution to the problem are detected and decoded. Because of the nature of the substrate in which the data is encoded, namely DNA strands, problems can occur at the encoding stage which would not occur in an electronic medium. In order to describe these problems and our attempts at solutions, we now briefly present some basic molecular biology notions and notations.

DNA (deoxyribonucleic acid) is found in every cellular organism as the storage medium for genetic information. It is composed of units called nucleotides, distinguished by the chemical group, or base, attached to them. The four bases, are *adenine, guanine, cytosine* and *thymine*, abbreviated as A, G, C, and T. The names of the bases are also commonly used to refer to the nucleotides that contain them. Single nucleotides are linked together end–to–end to form DNA strands. A short single-stranded polynucleotide chain, usually less than 30 nucleotides long, is called an *oligonucleotide*. The DNA sequence has a *polarity*: a sequence of DNA is distinct from its reverse. The two distinct ends of a DNA sequence are known under the name of the $5'$ end and the $3'$ end, respectively. Taken as pairs, the nucleotides A and T and the nucleotides C and G are said to be complementary. Two complementary single–stranded DNA sequences with

---

* Research partially supported by Grants R0504A01 and R2824A01 of the Natural Sciences and Engineering Research Council of Canada.

W. Brauer et al. (Eds.): Formal and Natural Computing, LNCS 2300, pp. 376–393, 2002.

opposite polarity are called *Watson/Crick (W/C) complements* and will join together to form a double helix in a process called *base-pairing*, or *hybridization* [14].

In most proposed DNA-based algorithms, the initial DNA solution encoding the input to the problem will contain some DNA strands which represent single *codewords*, and some which represent strings of catenated codewords. Several attempts have been made to address the issue of "good encodings" by trying to find sets of codewords which are unlikely to form undesired bonds with each other by hybridization [3], [9], [8]. For example genetic and evolutionary algorithms have been developed which select for sets of DNA sequences that are less likely to form undesirable bonds [4], [5]. [6] has developed a program to create DNA sequences to meet logical and physical parameters such as uniqueness, melting temperatures and G/C ratio as required by the user. [7] has addressed the issue of finding an optimal word design for DNA computing on surfaces. [12] has designed a software for constraint-based nucleotide selection. [10] has investigated encodings for DNA computing in virtual test tubes. [15] used combinatorial methods to calculate bounds on the size of a set of uniform code words (as a function of codeword length) which are less likely to mishybridize.

In this paper, we only address some of the various possible issues that might arise in DNA encodings, namely undesirable intramolecular and intermolecular hybridizations of the following types. Firstly, it is undesirable for any single DNA strand (representing a codeword or a string of codewords) to form a hairpin structure, which can happen if either end of the strand binds to another section of that same strand. Secondly, it is undesirable for any strand representing a codeword to bind to another one representing a string of one or more codewords. If such undesirable hybridizations occur, they will in practice render the involved DNA strands useless for the subsequent computational steps.

We present an initial investigation into the algebraic structure of *DNA-compliant* languages: languages consisting of codewords (DNA strands) that avoid some or all of the above mentioned undesirable bindings. It is hoped that this will lead to a deeper understanding of what is necessary for encoding information in DNA, and will ultimately assist in solving the difficult problem of "good DNA encodings". The paper is organized as follows. Section 2 introduces some basic definitions and notations. Section 3 formalizes the problems we address and defines the notion of a DNA compliant language: a language of codewords that avoid the above undesirable bindings. Section 4 studies the simpler notions of complement-compliance and mirror-image compliance needed to solve the general case of DNA compliance. Section 5 connects these particular cases to DNA compliance, generalizes the notion of DNA compliance, and investigates languages with this generalized property. Section 6 investigates generalizations of some classical coding theory notions (infix, prefix, suffix codes, density, residues, ideals) inspired by this extension of the notion of DNA compliance.

2 Basic Definitions and Notations

In this section we define the basic algebraic, formal language theory and coding theory notions needed in this paper. For further formal language theory notions the reader is referred to [11] and for further coding theory and algebraic notions to [18], [13], [11].

A mapping $\alpha : S \to S$ of a set S into S is *bijective* if it is both injective and surjective. Every bijective mapping has an inverse α^{-1} that is also bijective and $\alpha\alpha^{-1} = \alpha^{-1}\alpha = \epsilon$ where ϵ is the identity mapping.

Definition 2.1. *An involution $\theta : S \to S$ of S is a mapping such that $\theta^2 = \epsilon$.*

It follows then that an involution θ is bijective and $\theta = \theta^{-1}$.

The identity mapping is a trivial example of involution.

Given an involution, the relation ρ_θ defined by $u\rho_\theta v$ if and only if $u = v$ or $v = \theta(u)$ is an equivalence of S and every class has one or two elements.

The product of involutions is not necessarily an involution. For example take $S = \{a, b, c\}$ and the involutions α and β defined by:

$$\alpha(a) = b, \alpha(b) = a, \alpha(c) = c \; ; \; \beta(a) = c, \beta(b) = b, \beta(c) = a$$

Then:

$$\alpha\beta(a) = c, \alpha\beta(b) = a, \alpha\beta(c) = b.$$

It is clear that the product $\alpha\beta$ is no more an involution as, for example, $(\alpha\beta)^2(a) = b \neq a$.

However if the involutions α, β commute, i.e. if $\alpha\beta = \beta\alpha$, then their product $\alpha\beta$ is an involution because;

$$(\alpha\beta)(\alpha\beta) = (\alpha\beta)(\beta\alpha) = \alpha(\beta^2)\alpha = \alpha^2 = \epsilon.$$

Let X^* be the free monoid generated by the finite alphabet X, let 1 denote the neutral element, i.e. the empty word, and let $X^+ = X^* \setminus \{1\}$. The catenation of two words $u, v \in X^*$ is denoted by uv or by $u.v$ and consists of the juxtaposition of the words. A mapping $\alpha : X^* \to X^*$ is called a *morphism* (*anti-morphism*) of X^* if $\alpha(uv) = \alpha(u)\alpha(v)$ (respectively $\alpha(uv) = \alpha(v)\alpha(u)$) for all $u, v \in X^*$. A bijective morphism (anti-morphism) is called an *isomorphism* (*anti-isomorphism*) of X^*.

Remark that a morphism or an anti-morphism α of X^* is completely determined by the image $\alpha(X)$ of the alphabet X. If α is a morphism (anti-morphism) of X^* that is also an involution, then $\alpha(X) = X$ since α is an involution and therefore a bijective function, and $\alpha(a) \neq 1$ for all $a \in X$.

Examples.

(1) Let $\mu : X^* \to X^*$ be the mapping $\mu(u) = v$ defined by:

$$u = a_1 a_2 \cdots a_k, \quad v = a_k \cdots a_2 a_1, \quad a_i \in X, 1 \leq i \leq k.$$

The word v is called the *mirror image* of u. Since $\mu^2 = \epsilon$, μ is an *involution* of X^*, and will be called the *mirror-involution* or simply the *m-involution* of X^*.

The m-involution of X^* is not a morphism but an *anti-morphism* of X^* because $\mu(uv) = \mu(v)\mu(u)$ for $u, v \in X^*$.

(2) A mapping $\gamma : X \to X$ of X into X can be extended to a morphism of X^* by $\gamma(a_1 a_2 \cdots a_k) = \gamma(a_1)\gamma(a_2) \cdots \gamma(a_k)$. If furthermore $\gamma^2 = \epsilon$, then this morphism of X^* is also an involution of X^*.

In the general case, an involution is just a mapping whose square is the identity and as such is not closely related to the algebraic structure of X^*. We give an example of an involution π of X^* that is neither a morphism nor an anti-morphism.

A *primitive word*, [18], w over X^+ is a word with the property that $w = u^p$ for some $p \geq 1$ and $u \in X^+$ implies $p = 1$ and $u = w$.

Let $u \in X^*$. If $u = 1$, then $\pi(u) = 1$. If $u \neq 1$, then $u = p^k$ where p is a primitive word and k a positive integer. If k is odd, then we define $\pi(u) = p^{k+1}$, and if k is even we define $\pi(u) = p^{k-1}$. Then clearly π is an involution which is not a morphism or an anti-morphism. For example take $u = a \in X$ and $v = a^2$. Then $\pi(uv) = \pi(a^3) = a^4$, $\pi(u) = a^2$ and $\pi(v) = a$. Hence $\pi(uv) \neq \pi(u)\pi(v)$ and $\pi(uv) \neq \pi(v)\pi(u)$.

Note. *The involutions considered in this paper being always either* morphisms *or an* anti-morphisms *of X^*, from now on an involution will always be implicitly assumed to be morphic or antimorphic.*

3   DNA-related Types of Compliance

The W/C complement of a single strand of DNA is the strand that would anneal to it in the process of base-pairing. For example, the Watson-Crick complement of $5' - AAACC - 3'$ is $3' - TTTGG - 5'$ which is the same as $5' - GGTTT - 3'$. If we consider the DNA alphabet $\Delta = \{A, C, G, T\}$, by convention, a word $a_1 a_2 \ldots a_n \in \Delta^*$, $n \geq 0$, represents the single DNA strand $5' - a_1 a_2 \ldots a_n - 3'$ in the 5' to 3' orientation.

Three involutions can be defined on Δ^*. The *m-involution* μ *(mirror-involution)*, which is an anti-morphism, has been formally defined in Section 2. The mapping $\gamma : \Delta \to \Delta$ defined by:

$$\gamma(A) = T, \gamma(T) = A, \gamma(C) = G, \gamma(G) = C,$$

associates to each nucleotide its complement and can be extended in the usual way to a morphism of Δ^* that is also an involution of Δ^*. This involution γ will be called the *complementary-involution* or simply the *c-involution of Δ^*.*

It is easy to see that γ and μ commute, i.e. $\gamma\mu = \mu\gamma$. Hence $\gamma\mu$, denoted by τ is also an involution of Δ^*, called the *W/C involution*. Furthermore τ is an anti-morphism. Note that, for $w \in \Delta^*$, $\tau(w)$ represents the W/C complement of w. Using our notations and convention, for example, $\tau(AAACC) = GGTTT$.

The following notations will also be used:

$$\gamma(u) = \bar{u}, \ \mu(u) = \tilde{u}, \ \gamma\mu(u) = \tau(u) = \overleftarrow{u}.$$

Let us assume that for encoding the input information to a computation, we use a set of single DNA strands, i.e., a finite set $K \subseteq \Delta^*$ of words, called also *codewords*. Due to the W/C complementarity, if the codewords are not carefully designed, they will stick to each other forming undesired double-stranded structures.

Some of the situations that should be avoided when designing the codewords are the following.

Situation 1. A codeword that sticks to itself by intramolecular hybridization: $uv \in K^*$, $u, v \in \Delta^*$ with

(i) $\overleftarrow{v}$ being a subword of u (Figure 1);
(ii) $\overleftarrow{u}$ being a subword of v (Figure 2).

Situation 2. Two codewords that stick to each other by intermolecular hybridization: $u, v \in K$ with $\overleftarrow{v}$ being a subword of u (Figure 3).

Situation 3. A codeword that sticks to the catenation of two other codewords, by intermolecular hybridization: $u_1, u_2, v \in K$ with $\overleftarrow{v}$ being a subword of $u_1 u_2$ (Figure 4).

Remark that *Situation 2* and *Situation 3* are closely related. Note also that if we consider the simplified version of *Situation 1* where $u, v \in K$ instead of $u, v \in \Delta^*$ then *Situation 1* becomes *Situation 2*. In view of these remarks, in this paper we will be dealing mainly with languages avoiding *Situation 2*.

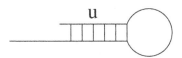

Fig. 1. Intramolecular hybridization leading to unwanted hairpin formations: $uv \in K^*$, $\overleftarrow{v}$ being a subword of u.

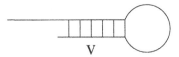

Fig. 2. Intramolecular hybridization leading to unwanted hairpin formations: $uv \in K^*$, $\overleftarrow{u}$ being a subword of v.

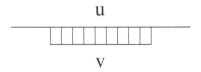

Fig. 3. Intermolecular hybridization between two codewords: $u, v \in K$, $\overleftarrow{v}$ being a subword of u.

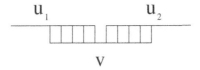

Fig. 4. Intermolecular hybridization between a composite codeword $u_1 u_2$ and a third codeword v: $u_1, u_2, v \in K$, $\overleftarrow{v}$ being a subword of $u_1 u_2$.

A simple (but not necessarily practical) solution to the above problems is the following. Take a language K over Δ such that $K^+ \subseteq \{A, C\}^+$. Then for every $u \in K^+$, $\overleftarrow{u} \notin K^+$. This means that there is no possibility for the occurences of the above *Situations 1, 2* or *3*.

The following definition formalizes a property of a language K which, if satisfied, ensures that the codewords of K avoid Situation 2 (Fig.3).

Definition 3.1. *A language $K \subseteq \Delta^*$ is called DNA compliant (DNA prefix-compliant, DNA suffix-compliant) iff:*

$$x \overleftarrow{v} y = u, u, v \in K \ \Rightarrow\ x = y = 1 \ (\overleftarrow{v} y = u \Rightarrow y = 1, \ y \overleftarrow{v} = u \Rightarrow y = 1).$$

In the following we shall sometimes refer to DNA compliant, DNA prefix-compliant, DNA suffix-compliant languages shortly as compliant, *p*-compliant, *s*-compliant languages.

Note that the preceding definition does not exclude the obviously undesirable case where two codewords in the language are exact W/C complements of each other. To eliminate this situation as well, we introduce the stronger notion of a strictly DNA compliant language.

Definition 3.2. *A language $K \subseteq \Delta^*$ is called strictly DNA compliant if it is DNA compliant and furthermore, for all $u, v \in K$ we have $u \neq \overleftarrow{v}$.*

4   The Complementarity and Mirror Involutions

Before addressing the general problem of DNA compliance that involves the W/C involution $\tau = \gamma\mu$, in this section we address separately the simpler cases involving the complementary involution γ and the mirror involution μ.

Definition 4.1. *A language $K \subseteq \Delta^*$ is called complementarity-compliant or c-compliant (respectively complementarity prefix compliant or cp-compliant) if $u \in K, x\bar{u}y = v \in K$ (resp. $\bar{u}y = v \in K$) implies $x = y = 1$.*

Definition 4.2. *A language $K \subseteq \Delta^*$ is called strictly c-compliant (cp-compliant) if it is c-compliant (cp-compliant) and for all $u, v \in K$ we have that $u \neq \bar{v}$.*

Let $\bar{K}^* = \{\bar{u} | u \in K^*\}$. Clearly $\bar{K}^*$ is a submonoid of Δ^* that is isomorphic to K^*.

Proposition 4.1. *A c-compliant (cp-compliant) language $K \subseteq \Delta^*$ is strictly c-compliant (cp-compliant) if and only if $K^* \cap \bar{K}^* = \{1\}$.*

Proof. Indeed, suppose K is a strictly c-compliant language and $K^* \cap \bar{K}^* \neq \{1\}$. Since $1 \in K^*$ and $1 \in \bar{K}^*$, there must be some $x \in \Delta^+$ such that $x \in K^*$ and $x \in \bar{K}^*$. Furthermore, $x \in \bar{K}^*$ implies $\bar{x} \in K^*$, from the definition of $\bar{K}^*$ and because γ is an involution.

Let $x = uv$, $u \in K$, $v \in K^*$. Let $\bar{x} = wz$, $w \in K$, $z \in K^*$. Suppose $|u| < |w|$. Then $\exists r \in \Delta^+$ such that $ur = \bar{w}$ (in fact, r will be a prefix of v). Since $r \neq 1$, K is not cp-compliant, and thus not c-compliant.

If $|w| < |u|$, the argument is the same. If $|w| = |u|$, then $w = \bar{u}$, and although K could be c-compliant, it is not *strictly* c-compliant. Thus $K^* \cap \bar{K}^* = \{1\}$.

Suppose K is a c-compliant language with $K^* \cap \bar{K}^* = \{1\}$ and that K is not strictly c-compliant. Then there is a $v \in \Delta^+$ such that $v, \bar{v} \in K$. But then v, $\bar{v} \in \bar{K}$, and thus $\{v, \bar{v}\} \subseteq K^* \cap \bar{K}^*$ - a contradiction.

The proof is similar for cp-compliant languages. ♣

Note that $K^* \cap \bar{K}^* = \{1\}$ does *not* imply that K is c-compliant, as shown by the example $K = \{ACC, TGGC\}$.

Proposition 4.2. *Let $K \subseteq \Delta^*$ be c-compliant language. Then $ux = \bar{v}y$, $u, v \in K$ implies $x = y$ and hence $u = \bar{v}$.*

Proof. If u is a prefix of $\bar{v}$, then $\bar{v} = ur$, $v = \bar{u}\bar{r}$. Since K is a cp-compliant language, then $\bar{r} = 1$, i.e. $r = 1$ and $u = \bar{v}$. If $\bar{v}$ is a prefix of u, then $u = \bar{v}s$ and similarly $s = 1$ and $u = \bar{v}$. ♣

Proposition 4.3. *If not empty, the intersection of c-compliant (cp-compliant) languages is a c-compliant (cp-compliant) language.*

Proof. Immediate. ♣

Similar results hold for the case of strictly c-compliant (cp-compliant) languages.

During computations, encodings for two different problems might be combined by, for example, catenating codewords from the two languages used for encoding the inputs of the two problems. The following proposition shows that this process preserves the property of c-compliance.

Proposition 4.4. *The catenation $K = K_1 K_2$ of (strictly) cp-compliant languages $K_1 \subseteq \Delta^*$ and $K_2 \subseteq \Delta^*$ is a (strictly) cp-compliant language.*

Proof. Let $u \in K$ and $\bar{u}x \in K$. Then $u = u_1 u_2$ with $u_1 \in K_1$, $u_2 \in K_2$, $\bar{u} = \bar{u}_1 \bar{u}_2$ and $\bar{u}_1 \bar{u}_2 x = c_1 c_2$, $c_1 \in K_1$, $c_2 \in K_2$.

If $|\bar{u}_1| \leq |c_1|$, then $\bar{u}_1 y = c_1$ for some $y \in \Delta^*$. Since K_1 is cp-compliant, $y = 1$ and $\bar{u}_1 = c_1$. Therefore $\bar{u}_2 x = c_2$ and $x = 1$ since K_2 is also cp-compliant.

If $|\bar{u}_1| > |c_1|$, then $\bar{u}_1 = c_1 z$ for some $z \in \Delta^*$. This implies $u_1 = \bar{\bar{u}}_1 = \bar{c}_1 \bar{z}$. Since $u_1, c_1 \in K_1$ and K_1 is cp-compliant, we have $\bar{z} = 1$, $z = 1$ and hence $\bar{u}_1 = c_1$, a contradiction.

Therefore $\bar{u}_1 \bar{u}_2 x = c_1 c_2$ implies $x = 1$ and hence $K_1 K_2$ is a cp-compliant language.

For the case of strict compliance, we have to show that $\bar{u}_1 \bar{u}_2 \neq c_1 c_2$. Suppose that $\bar{u}_1 \bar{u}_2 = c_1 c_2$. Then, as above, either $\bar{u}_1 y = c_1$ or $\bar{u}_1 = c_1 z$. Since both K_1 and K_2 are strictly compliant, this is impossible. ♣

Proposition 4.5. *Every (strictly) cp-compliant language can be embedded in a maximal (stricly) cp-compliant language.*

Proof. Suppose that $\Gamma = \{K_i \subseteq \Delta^* | i \in I\}$ is a chain of cp-compliant languages:

$$\cdots \subseteq K_j \subseteq \cdots \subseteq K_k \subseteq \cdots$$

Let $K = \bigcup_{i \in I} K_i$. It is easy to see that K is also a cp-compliant language. The proposition follows then from Zorn's Lemma. The proof is similar for the case of stricly cp-compliant languages. ♣

A language $L \subseteq X^*$ is called *dense* (right dense), [18], if for every $u \in X^*$, there exist $x, y \in X^*$ such that $xuy \in L (uy \in L)$. In the following we define an analogous notion, that of complementarity density. Proposition 4.6 then proves that a sufficient condition for a strictly cp-compliant language $K \subseteq \Delta^*$ to be maximal is that K^* be right c-dense.

Definition 4.3. *A language $K \subseteq \Delta^*$ is said to be right c-dense if for every $u \in \Delta^*$ there is $x \in \Delta^*$ such that $\bar{u}x \in K$.*

Proposition 4.6. *Let $K \subseteq \Delta^*$ be a stricly cp-compliant language. If K^* is right c-dense, then K is a maximal stricly cp-compliant language.*

Proof. Suppose K is not maximal. Then there is $v \notin K$ such that $T = K \cup \{v\}$ is a strictly cp-compliant language. The right c-density implies the existence of $x \in \Delta^*$ such that $\bar{v}x \in K^*$, i.e. $\bar{v}x = u_1 u_2 \cdots u_k$, $u_i \in K$. This implies either $\bar{v} = u_1 y$ or $u_1 = \bar{v}z$, i.e. $\bar{u}_1 \bar{y} = v \in T$ or $\bar{v}z = u_1 \in T$. Since T is a cp-compliant language, then either $\bar{y} = 1, \bar{u}_1 = v$ or $z = 1, \bar{v} = u_1$, a contradiction because of the strict compliance of T. ♣

The converse of Proposition 4.6 is not true as shown by the following example. Let $K = A\Delta^* \cup C\Delta^*$. This language over Δ is strictly cp-compliant and it is easy to see that it is maximal. Clearly the language K^* is not right c-dense.

Recall that, [18], a language $L \subseteq X^*$ is called *right-unitary* if $u \in L^*$, $ux \in L^*$ imply $x \in L^*$. The following definition is analogous to that of a right-unitary language and Proposition 4.7 relates the notions of right c-unitary and cp-compliance. It turns out that, given a right c-unitary language K^*, where $K \subseteq \Delta^*$, one can construct a cp-compliant language $K' \subseteq \Delta^*$.

Definition 4.4. *A language $K \subseteq \Delta^*$ is called right c-unitary if $u \in K^*$ and $\bar{u}x \in K^*$ imply $x \in K^*$.*

Example. Let $K = A\Delta^* \cup C\Delta^*$. Then K^+ is right c-unitary. Indeed suppose that $u, \bar{u}x \in K^+$. Every word in K^+ starts either with A or C and hence $\bar{u}x = Ty$ or Gy for some $y \in \Delta^*$, which is impossible. Hence $K = K^+$ is right c-unitary by default.

Proposition 4.7. *Consider $K \subseteq \Delta^*$ and let*

$$K' = K^+ \setminus [\bar{K}^+ K^+]$$

If K^* is right c-unitary then K' is cp-compliant.

Proof. Let $u \in K'$, $\bar{u}x \in K' \subseteq K^*$. As K^* is right c-unitary we have that $x \in K^*$, therefore

$$x = x_1 x_2 \ldots x_m, x_i \in K, 1 \le i \le m.$$

The word $u \in K' \subseteq K^*$ and therefore $\bar{u} \in \bar{K}^*$. If any of x_i, $1 \le i \le m$ would not be the empty word, $\bar{u}x$ would belong to $\bar{K}^+ K^+$ which would contradict the assumption about $\bar{u}x$. We can therefore conclude that $x_i = 1$ for all $1 \le i \le m$ which implies that K' is cp-compliant. ♣

In a similar manner to the c-involution, one can use the mirror involution to define m-compliant languages. A language $K \subseteq \Delta^*$ is called *m-compliant* (*mp-compliant, ms-compliant*) if $u \in K, x\tilde{u}y = v \in K (\tilde{u}y = v \in K, x\tilde{u} = v \in K)$ imply $x = y = 1$. If we add the condition that for any $u, v \in K$, $\tilde{u} \ne v$, then K will be *strictly m-compliant*. Informally, in an m-compliant language, the mirror image of a codeword cannot be a proper subword of another codeword. In a *strictly m*-compliant language, the mirror image of a codeword cannot be a subword of another codeword.

Example: $K = \{GGGA, CCG, TTAAA\}$ is strictly m-compliant, whereas $K' = \{GGGA, AGG\}$ is not m-compliant, and $K'' = \{GGGA, AGGG\}$ is m-compliant but not *strictly m*-compliant.

Using this definition of m-compliance, properties of m-compliant languages can be explored.

In contrast to the c-compliant case, the catenation $K = K_1 K_2$ of m-compliant languages over Δ is not necessarily an m-compliant language. Indeed, let $K_1 = \{CTG, TA\}$ and $K_2 = \{AT, GT\}$. Both K_1 and K_2 are m-compliant (in fact they are strictly m-compliant), but $\{CTGAT, TAGT\} \subset K$, so K is not m-compliant. Note that this example also demonstrates that the catenation of two ms-compliant languages is not necesarily ms-compliant.

A language consisting of a single codeword can fail to be strictly m-compliant. An example is $K = \{TAAT\}$. In contrast, any single-codeword language (except the empty word) will be strictly c-compliant.

A language which is both c-compliant and m-compliant will not necessarily be DNA compliant. Take for example $K = \{CGT, ACGA\}$. Then K is both m- and c- compliant, but is not DNA compliant. However, m- and c- compliance are still *related* to DNA compliance. Indeed in Section 5 we prove results that connect the three different types of compliance determined by two different involutions and their product, respectively. In particular, Corollary 5.1 gives a sufficient condition (involving the notions of c-compliance and m-compliance) for a language to be DNA compliant.

5 From DNA Compliance to Involution-Compliance

This section addresses the connections between the notions of c-compliance, m-compliance and the DNA compliance which was the original motivator of this study. Recall that the notions of c-compliance, m-compliance and DNA compliance were related respectively to the complementarity involution γ, the mirror involution μ and the Watson/Crick involution τ which is the product between the two, i.e., $\tau = \gamma\mu$. Instead of proving results related to the particular DNA-related involutions, we generalize from the DNA alphabet Δ to an arbitrary finite alphabet X and extend the notions of compliance to refer to arbitrary (morphic or anti-morphic) involutions of X^*. All the results obtained will have as corollaries results pertaining to the DNA-related involutions. In particular, Corollary 5.1 gives sufficient conditions for a c-compliant language to be DNA compliant, and for an m-compliant language to be DNA compliant.

Definition 5.1. *Let θ be an involution of X^*. A language $L \subseteq X^*$ is said to be θ-compliant (θ-p-compliant, θ-s-compliant) if:*

$$u, x\theta(u)y \in L \ (\theta(u)y \in L, x\theta(u) \in L) \ \Rightarrow \ x = y = 1.$$

The above condition prevents the image under θ of a word $u \in L$ to be a proper subword (prefix, suffix) of a word in L.

In order to eliminate also the case of two words $u, v \in L$ with $u = \theta(v)$, we strengthen the definition as follows.

Definition 5.2. *Let θ be an involution of X^* and $L \subseteq X^*$. A language L is said to be strictly θ-compliant (θ-p-compliant, θ-s-compliant) if it is θ-compliant (θ-p-compliant, θ-s-compliant) and, in addition, for each $u, v \in L$ we have that $u \neq \theta(v)$.*

Remark that if $\theta = \epsilon$, the identity involution, then the θ-compliant languages are respectively the infix, prefix and suffix codes. A *prefix code (suffix code)*, [18], [13], is a nonempty language $A \subseteq X^+$ with the property that $A \cap AX^+ = \emptyset$ ($A \cap X^+A = \emptyset$). An *infix code* is a language A with the property that for all $x, y, u \in X^*$ we have that $xuy \in L$ and $u \in L$ together imply $x = y = 1$.

In general θ-compliant languages are not infix codes. Let $L = \{A, C, AC\} \subseteq \Delta^*$. L is not an infix code, but a τ-compliant language relatively to the W/C involution τ.

An infix code is in general not θ-compliant. For example, the language $\{GG, ACCA\} \subseteq \Delta^*$ is an infix code, but $\tau(GG) = CC$ and $ACCA = A\tau(GG)A$, and hence the language is not τ-compliant.

Proposition 5.1. *If L is a θ-compliant language of X^* such that $\theta(L) \subseteq L$, then L is an infix code.*

Proof. Let $xuy \in L$ with $u \in L$. Since the involution θ is bijective, there is $v \in X^*$ such that $\theta(v) = u$ and hence $x\theta(v)y \in L$. Since $\theta(u) = v$ and $\theta(L) \subseteq L$, then $v \in L$. Because L is θ-compliant, $x = y = 1$ and therefore L is an infix code. ♣

The following results make the connection between c-compliance, m-compliance and DNA compliance.

Proposition 5.2. *Let θ_1 and θ_2 be two commuting involutions of X^*. If $L \subseteq X^*$ is a language such that $L \cup \theta_1(L)$ is θ_2-compliant, then L is $\theta_1\theta_2$-compliant.*

Proof. Let $\theta = \theta_1\theta_2$ and suppose that $L \cup \theta_1(L)$ is θ_2-compliant but is not θ-compliant. Then there exist $u, v \in L$ such that $u = x\theta(v)y$ with $xy \neq 1$. Let $T = \{u, v, \theta_1(u), \theta_1(v)\}$. Since $T \subseteq L \cup \theta_1(L)$, then T must be θ_2-compliant. From $u = x\theta(v)y$ follows $\theta_1(u) = \theta_1(x\theta(v)y)$.

If θ_1 is a morphism, then:

$$\theta_1(u) = \theta_1(x)\theta_1(\theta_1\theta_2(v))\theta_1(y) = \theta_1(x)\theta_2(v)\theta_1(y)$$

with $\theta_1(u), v \in T$. Since T is θ_2-compliant, this implies $\theta_1(x) = \theta_1(y) = 1$ and therefore $x = y = 1$, a contradiction with $xy \neq 1$. Hence L is θ-compliant.

If θ_1 is an antimorphism, then, since $\theta_1\theta_2 = \theta_2\theta_1$:

$$\theta_1(u) = \theta_1(y)\theta_1(\theta_1\theta_2(v))\theta_1(x) = \theta_1(y)\theta_2(v)\theta_1(x)$$

with $\theta_1(u), v \in T$. As above, we get a contradiction, hence L is θ-compliant. ♣

Corollary 5.1. *Let $L \subseteq \Delta^*$. If $L \cup \gamma(L)$ is μ-compliant or if $L \cup \mu(L)$ is γ-compliant, then L is DNA compliant, i.e. $\gamma\mu$-compliant.*

Furthermore, $K = \{AGT, CCCG\}$ is a DNA-compliant language for which $K \cup \tilde{K}$ is c-compliant and $K \cup \bar{K}$ is m-compliant, which means the sets of languages $\{K | K \cup \tilde{K}$ is c-compliant $\}$ and $\{K | K \cup \bar{K}$ is m-compliant $\}$ are non-empty subsets of the set of DNA-compliant languages.

Proposition 5.3. *Let θ be an involution of X^*. Then $L \subseteq X^*$ is θ-compliant iff $\theta(L)$ is θ-compliant.*

Proof. If $u, x\theta(u)y \in \theta(L)$, then $\theta(u), \theta(x)u\theta(y) \in L$ if θ is a morphism or $\theta(u), \theta(y)u\theta(x) \in L$ if θ is an antimorphism. In both cases, since L is θ-compliant, we have $\theta(x) = \theta(y) = 1$ and hence $x = y = 1$. Therefore $\theta(L)$ is θ-compliant.

Conversely, if $\theta(L)$ is θ-compliant, then, from the first part of the proof, it follows that $L = \theta(\theta(L))$ is also θ-compliant. ♣

The union of θ-compliant languages is not in general a θ-compliant language. For example let Δ be the DNA alphabet and τ be the W/C involution. Then $L_1 = \{A, AC\}$ and $L_2 = \{T, TG\}$ are both τ-compliant. However their union $L = \{A, T, AC, TG\}$ is not τ-compliant, because $A \in L$, $TG = \theta(A)G \in L$ with $G \neq 1$.

If L is θ-compliant, then any subset T of L is also θ-compliant. Indeed $u, x\theta(u)y \in T$ implies $u, x\theta(u)y \in L$ and hence $x = y = 1$.

The following generalizes Proposition 4.4.

Proposition 5.4. *If the involution θ of X^* is a morphism, then the catenation $L = L_1 L_2$ of θ-compliant (strictly θ-compliant) languages $L_1 \subseteq X^*$ and $L_2 \subseteq X^*$ is a θ-compliant (strictly θ-compliant) language.*

Proof. Let $u \in L$ and $x\theta(u)y \in L$. Then $u = u_1 u_2$ with $u_1 \in L_1$, $u_2 \in L_2$.

Since θ is a morphism, $\theta(u) = \theta(u_1)\theta(u_2)$ and $x\theta(u_1)\theta(u_2)y = c_1 c_2$, $c_1 \in L_1$, $c_2 \in L_2$.

If $|x\theta(u_1)| \leq |c_1|$, then $x\theta(u_1)z = c_1$ for some $z \in X^*$. Since L_1 is θ-compliant, then $x = z = 1$ and $\theta(u_1) = c_1$. Therefore $\theta(u_2)y = c_2$ and $y = 1$ since L_2 is θ-compliant.

If $|x\theta(u_1)| > |c_1|$, then $|\theta(u_2)y| < |c_2|$ and $z\theta(u_2)y = c_2$. Using a similar argument as above, we get $z = y = 1$.

Hence $u \in L$ and $x\theta(u)y \in L$ implies $x = y = 1$, i.e. L is θ-compliant.

For the case of strict compliance, we have to show that $\theta(u_1 u_2) = \theta(u_1)\theta(u_2) \neq c_1 c_2$. Suppose that $\theta(u_1)\theta(u_2) = c_1 c_2$. Then, as above either $\theta(u_1)z = c_1$ or $z\theta(u_2) = c_2$ which is impossible because of the strict compliance of both L_1 and L_2. ♣

If the involution θ is an anti-morphism of X^*, then the catenation of θ-compliant languages is not in general a θ-compliant language. Indeed, let τ be the W/C involution of Δ^*. The languages $\{CTG, AT\}$ and $\{AT, CA\}$ are both τ-compliant. However $L = \{CTGAT, ATCA\}$ which is included in their catenation, is not τ-compliant.

If θ is an involution of X^*, then a submonoid $S \subseteq X^*$ is said to be *right θ-unitary* if $u, \theta(u)x \in S$ implies $x \in S$.

The following proposition generalizes Proposition 4.7.

Proposition 5.5. *Let $L \subseteq X^+$ and let θ be an involution of X^*. Let*

$$T = L^+ \backslash (\theta(L)^+ L^+)$$

If L^* is right θ-unitary, then T is a θ-p-compliant language.

Proof. Let $u, \theta(u)x \in T \subseteq L^+$. Since L^* is right θ-unitary, $x \in L^*$. Suppose $x \neq 1$. Then:

$$x = x_1 x_2 \cdots x_m, \ x_i \in L, 1 \leq i \leq m.$$

The word $u \in L^+$ and therefore $\theta(u) \in \theta(L^+)$. If any of x_i, $1 \leq i \leq m$, would not be the empty word, $\theta(u)x$ would belong to $\theta(L)^+ L^+$ which would contradict the assumption about $\theta(u)x$. We can therefore conclude that $x_i = 1$ for all i, $1 \leq i \leq m$, which implies that T is θ-p-compliant. ♣

Proposition 5.6. *Let θ be an involution and a morphism of X^* and let $L \subseteq X^*$ be a nonempty language. If L is a θ-p-compliant language, then L^* is a right θ-unitary submonoid of X^*.*

Proof. Suppose that $u, \theta(u)x \in L^*$. If θ is a morphism of X^*, then:

$$u = u_1 u_2 \cdots u_k, \ u_i \in L, \theta(u)x = \theta(u_1)\theta(u_2) \cdots \theta(u_k)x = v_1 v_2 \cdots v_r, v_j \in L$$

Either $|\theta(u_1)| \le |v_1|$ or $|\theta(u_1)| > |v_1|$.

In the first case, we have $v_1 = \theta(u_1)z$ for some $z \in X^*$. Since L is θ-p-compliant and $u_1, v_1 \in L$, then $z = 1$ and $\theta(u_1) = v_1$.

In the second case, we have $\theta(u_1) = v_1 z$ with $z \ne 1$. But, as above, $u_1, v_1 \in L$ and the compliance condition implies $z = 1$, and $\theta(u_1) = v_1$.

Therefore $\theta(u_1) = v_1$ and by cancellation:

$$\theta(u_2) \cdots \theta(u_k)x = v_2 \cdots v_r$$

This reduction can be extended until we get $x = 1$ or $x = v_{k+1} \cdots v_r$ and hence $x \in L^*$, i.e. L^* is right θ-unitary. ♣

The following generalizes Proposition 4.1.

Proposition 5.7. *Let θ be a morphic involution. A θ-compliant (θ-p-compliant) language $L \subseteq X^*$ is strictly θ-compliant (strictly θ-p-compliant) if and only if $L^* \cap \theta(L)^* = \{1\}$.*

Proof. The proof given for the complementarity involution can be extended to this general case in the following way.

Suppose L is strictly θ-compliant and let $u \in L^* \cap \theta(L)^*$, $u \ne 1$. Then $u = u_1 x_1 = \theta(u_2 x_2) = \theta(u_2)\theta(x_2)$ with $u_1, u_2 \in L$, $u_1, u_2 \ne 1$, $x_1, x_2 \in L^*$.

If $|u_1| < |\theta(u_2)|$, then $\theta(u_2) = u_1 x$, $u_2 = \theta(u_1)\theta(x)$ with $x \ne 1$ and hence $\theta(x) \ne 1$, a contradiction since L is θ-compliant.

If $|u_1| \ge |\theta(u_2)|$, then $u_1 = \theta(u_2)x$. This implies $x = 1$ and $u_1 = \theta(u_2)$. Hence $u_2, \theta(u_2) \in L$, a contradiction with the strictness of L.

Therefore $L^* \cap \theta(L)^* = \{1\}$.

Suppose now L to be a θ-compliant language with $L^* \cap \theta(L)^* = \{1\}$. If L is not strictly θ-compliant, then there is a word $u \in X^+$ such that $u, \theta(u) \in L$. This implies $u, \theta(u) \in \theta(L)$. Thus, $\{u, \theta(u)\} \subseteq L^* \cap \theta(L)^*$, a contradiction. ♣

6   Maximality, Density, Residue, and Ideals

We have seen that in the particular case when θ is the indentity involution, θ-compliant (θ-p-compliant, θ-s-compliant) languages coincide with the classical infix codes (prefix codes, suffix codes). This suggests that other well-known notions from coding theory, like density, residue and ideals can be generalized from the particular case of the identity involution to the case of an arbitrary involution. This section investigates such generalizations and their properties.

The following proposition generalizes Proposition 4.5.

Proposition 6.1. *Let θ be an involution of X^*. Every θ-compliant (θ-p-compliant) language L can be embedded in a maximal θ-compliant (θ-p-compliant) language.*

Proof. The proof follows by showing first that the union of languages of any chain of θ-compliant (θ-p-compliant) languages containing L has the same property. Then, by Zorn's Lemma, it follows that the family of θ-compliant (θ-p-compliant) languages in X^* containing L has a maximal element. ♣

Proposition 6.2. *Let θ be an involution of X^*. Every strictly θ-compliant (θ-p-compliant) language L can be embedded in a strictly maximal θ-compliant (θ-p-compliant) language.*

Proof. Similar to the proof of the previous proposition. ♣

If $L \subseteq X^*$, let $Lg(L) = max\{|u| \mid u \in L\}$. It is known (see [18]) that, for every finite prefix code P with $Lg(P) = n$, there exists a maximal prefix code P' such that $P \subseteq P'$ and $Lg(P') = n$.

This result which is true for ϵ-p-compliant languages, cannot in general be extended to every θ-involution as shown by the following example.

Example. Let $X = \{a, b\}$ and the morphic involution θ of X^* defined by $\theta(a) = b$, $\theta(b) = a$. The language $L = \{a, a^2, ab\}$ is a stricly θ-p-compliant language. Let T be a maximal strictly θ-p-compliant language containing L. Remark first that $bX^* \cap T = \emptyset$. If not, let $by \in T$. Since $b = \theta(a)$ and $a \in T$, we have $\theta(a)y \in T$. Hence $y = 1$ and $a, \theta(a) \in T$, in contradiction with the strictness of T. If $u \in T$, then $u = ax$ and $\theta(u) = b\theta(x)$. Hence $\theta(T) \subseteq bX^*$.

We will show that T is infinite by showing that $a^+ \subseteq T$. We have $a, a^2 \in T$. Suppose that $a^k \in T$ and that $a^{k+1} \notin T$. Let $T' = T \cup a^{k+1}$. Then T' is not a strictly θ-p-compliant language. That means that one or both of the following situations hold:

(1) There is a word u such that $u, \theta(u) \in T'$ with $u = \theta(u)$. Since T is strictly θ-p-compliant, $u = a^{k+1}$ or $\theta(u) = a^{k+1}$. In the first case, $\theta(u) = b^{k+1} \notin T'$, a contradiction. In the second case, $u \in T$ and hence $\theta(u) \in bX^*$, a contradiction.

(2) T' is not θ-p-compliant, i.e. there are words $u, v \in T'$ such that $\theta(u)x = v$ with $x \neq 1$ and either $u \notin T$ or $v \notin T$.

If $v \notin T$, then $v = a^{k+1}$. From $\theta(T) \subseteq bX^*$ follows that $\theta(T') \subseteq bX^*$ and hence $\theta(u)x = bz = a^{k+1}$, a contradiction.

If $v \in T$, then $u \in T' \setminus T$, i.e. $u = a^{k+1}$ and

$$\theta(a^{k+1})x = b^{k+1}x = v \in bX^*$$

a contradiction since $bX^* \cap T = \emptyset$.

Therefore $a^{k+1} \in T$.

It follows then that every maximal θ-p-compliant language containing the finite language L is infinite, showing that the result for finite prefix codes cannot be extended to finite θ-p-compliant languages for every involution θ.

We now connect the notion of maximality to the notions of density, residue, and ideals generalized to arbitrary involutions.

The following definition is a further generalization of the notion of a dense language, from the particular case of the identity involution to that of an arbitrary involution.

Definition 6.1. *Let θ be an involution of X^*. A language $L \subseteq \Delta^*$ is said to be (right,left) θ-dense if for every $u \in \Delta^*$, there are $x, y \in \Delta^*$ such that $x\theta(u)y \in L$ ($\theta(u)y \in L$, $x\theta(u) \in L$).*

Based on the preceding definition, the following result now generalizes Proposition 4.6 in Section 4 dealing with the particular case of the complementary involution.

Proposition 6.3. *Let θ be an involution of X^* that is a morphism and let $L \subseteq X^*$ be a stricly θ-p-compliant language. If L^* is right θ-dense, then L is a maximal stricly θ-p-compliant language.*

Proof. Suppose L is not maximal. Then there is $v \notin L$ such that $T = L \cup \{v\}$ is a strictly θ-p-compliant language. The right θ-density of L^* implies the existence of $x \in \Delta^*$ such that $\theta(v)x \in L^*$, i.e. $\theta(v)x = u_1 u_2 \cdots u_k$, $u_i \in L$. This implies either $\theta(v) = u_1 y$ or $u_1 = \theta(v)z$, i.e. $\theta(u_1)\theta(y) = v \in T$ or $\theta(v)z = u_1 \in T$. Since T is a θ-p-compliant language, either $\theta(y) = 1$ and $\theta(u_1) = v$, or $z = 1$ and $\theta(v) = u_1$, a contradiction because of the strict compliance of T. ♣

Recall that, [18], the residue $R(L)$ of a language $L \subseteq X^*$ is defined as

$$R(L) = \{u|\ u \in X^*, X^*uX^* \cap L = \emptyset\}.$$

We can now generalize this notion from the identity involution to an arbitrary involution as follows.

Definition 6.2. *Let $L \subseteq X^*$ and let θ be an involution of X^*. The θ-residue $R_\theta(L)$ of L is defined by:*

$$R_\theta(L) = \{u|u \in X^*, \ X^*\theta(u)X^* \cap L = \emptyset\}$$

The right and the left θ-residue of L are defined similarly.

It is immediate that a language L is θ-dense if and only if its θ-residue is empty. Recall that, [18], a language $L \subseteq X^*$ is called a (right, left) ideal of X^* if $u \in L$, $x, y \in X^*$ imply $xuy \in L$ ($uy \in L$, $xu \in L$). The following definition generalizes the notion of ideal.

Definition 6.3. *Let θ be an involution of X^*. A language $L \subseteq X^*$ is called a (right, left) θ-ideal of X^* if $u \in L$, $x, y \in X^*$, implies $x\theta(u)y \in L$ ($\theta(u)y \in L$, $x\theta(u) \in L$).*

If θ is the identity involution, then the above notions correspond to the usual notions of residue and ideal.

Proposition 6.4. *Let θ be an involution of X^* and let L be a (right, left) θ-ideal of X^*. Then $\theta(L) = L$ and L is a (right, left) ideal of X^*.*

Proof. Let $u \in L$. Then $\theta(u) = 1.\theta(u).1 \in L$ and therefore $\theta(L) \subseteq L$. This implies $L \subseteq \theta(\theta(L)) \subseteq \theta(L)$ and hence $\theta(L) = L$. Since $u \in L$, there exists then $v \in L$ such that $\theta(v) = u$. Therefore $xuy = x\theta(v)y \in L$ and therefore L is an ideal. ♣

The previous proposition shows that every θ-ideal is an ideal, but the converse is not true in general. For example, the language $L = \Delta^* C \Delta^*$ is an ideal of Δ^*. However $C \in L$, but $\tau(C) = \overline{C} = G \notin L$. This implies $\tau(L) \neq L$ and hence L cannot be a τ-ideal.

Proposition 6.5. *Let θ be an involution of X^*. If not empty, the (right, left) θ-residue $R_\theta(L)$ of a language $L \subseteq X^*$ is a (right, left) θ-ideal of X^*.*

Proof. Let $u \in R_\theta(L)$ and suppose that, for some $x, y \in X^*$, $x\theta(u)y \notin R_\theta(L)$. This implies $X^* x\theta(u)yX^* \cap L \neq \emptyset$ and hence $X^*\theta(u)X^* \cap L \neq \emptyset$, a contradiction. ♣

Proposition 6.6. *Let θ be an involution of X^*. A language $L \subseteq X^*$ is an ideal if and only if $\theta(L)$ is an ideal of X^*.*

Proof. ($\Rightarrow$) Let $u \in \theta(L)$ and $x, y \in X^*$. Since θ is bijective, there exist $v \in L$, $x', y' \in X^*$ such that $\theta(v) = u$, $\theta(x') = x$ and $\theta(y') = y$. Since L is an ideal, $x'vy' \in L$ and $y'vx' \in L$.
If θ is a morphism, then:

$$xuy = \theta(x')\theta(v)\theta(y') = \theta(x'vy') \in \theta(L).$$

If θ is an anti-morphism, then:

$$xuy = \theta(x')\theta(v)\theta(y') = \theta(y'vx') \in \theta(L).$$

($\Leftarrow$) Let $u \in L$, $x, y \in X^*$ and let x', y' such that $\theta(x') = x$, $\theta(y') = y$. Then $x'\theta(u)y' \in \theta(L)$ and $y'\theta(u)x' \in \theta(L)$. If θ is a morphism, we have:

$$xuy = \theta(x')\theta^2(u)\theta(y') = \theta(x'\theta(u)y') \in \theta(\theta(L)) = L$$

and if it is an anti-morphism, we have:

$$xuy = \theta(x')\theta^2(u)\theta(y') = \theta(y'\theta(u)x') \in \theta(\theta(L)) = L.$$

Hence L is an ideal. ♣

We now consider relations between density and maximality. The next result shows that if θ is an involution of X^*, then right density of a language L is equivalent to right θ-density of L.

Proposition 6.7. *Let θ be an involution of X^*. A language $L \subseteq X^*$ is right θ-dense (θ-dense) if and only if it is right dense (dense).*

Proof. Suppose L is right θ-dense and let $u \in X^*$. Since an involution is a bijective mapping, there exists $v \in X^*$ such that $u = \theta(v)$. The right θ-density of L implies the existence of $x \in X^*$ such that $\theta(v)x \in L$ and hence $ux \in L$.

Suppose L is right dense and let $u \in X^*$. Since $\theta(u) \in X^*$, then there is $x \in X^*$ such that $\theta(u)x \in L$ and thus L is right θ-dense.

The proof for θ-density is similar to the proof for right θ-density. ♣

If the involution θ is the identity, then a θ-p-compliant language L is a prefix code and we obtain the known result that if L^* is right dense, the prefix code L is maximal. The converse is true for prefix codes, but not in general as shown in the following example.

Example. Let $X = \{a, b\}$ and let θ be defined as $\theta(a) = b$, $\theta(b) = a$. This involution of X^* is also a morphism of X^*.

Let $L = aX^*$. This language L is a maximal strictly θ-p-compliant language. Indeed, suppose L is not maximal. Then L is contained in a strictly $\theta - p$-compliant language T with $L \subset T$. Let $u \in T \setminus L$. Then $u = by$ for some $y \in X^*$ and:

$$u = \theta(a)\theta(y) \in T,$$

a contradiction with the fact that T is strictly θ-p-compliant. It follows then that $L = aX^*$ is a maximal strictly θ-p-compliant language.

The language L^* is not right θ-dense. This follows from the fact that $(aX^*)^* \cap bX^* = \emptyset$. This example shows that, contrary to the case of maximal prefix codes, a maximal strictly θ-p-compliant language is not necessarily right θ-dense.

7   Conclusions

This paper is a preliminary study in the formalization and algebraic treatment of problems that arise when encoding data on a DNA substrate, where each word corresponds to a single DNA strand. We define and study the algebraic structure of DNA compliant languages, i.e. languages displaying several "good encoding properties". Moreover, viewing words and languages from this biological perspective leads to generalizations of several well-known notions such as infix code, prefix code, suffix code, density, residue and ideals.

References

1. L. Adleman. Molecular Computation of Solutions to Combinatorial Problems. *Science*, 266, 1994, 1021-1024.
2. E.B. Baum. DNA Sequences Useful for Computation. Proceedings of *DNA-based Computers II*, Princeton. In AMS DIMACS Series, vol.44, L.F.Landweber, E.Baum Eds., 1998, 235-241.
3. R. Deaton, R. Murphy, M. Garzon, D.R. Franceschetti, S.E. Stevens. Good Encodings for DNA-based Solutions to Combinatorial Problems. Proceedings of *DNA-based Computers II*, Princeton. In AMS DIMACS Series, vol.44, L.F.Landweber, E.Baum Eds., 1998, 247-258.

4. R. Deaton, M. Garzon, R. Murphy, D.R. Franceschetti, S.E. Stevens. Genetic Search of Reliable Encodings for DNA Based Computation, *First Conference on Genetic Programming GP-96*, Stanford U., 1996, 9-15.

5. R. Deaton, R.E. Murphy, J.A. Rose, M. Garzon, D.R. Franceschetti, S.E. Stevens Jr. A DNA Based Implementation of an Evolutionary Search for Good Encodings for DNA Computation. Proc. *IEEE Conference on Evolutionary Computation ICEC-97*, 267-271.

6. U. Feldkamp, S. Saghafi, H.Rauhe. DNASequenceGenerator - A Program for the Construction of DNA Sequences. In [16], 179-189.

7. A.G. Frutos, Q. Liu, A.J. Thiel, A.M.W. Sanner, A.E. Condon, L.M. Smith, R.M. Corn. Demonstration of a Word Design Strategy for DNA Computing on Surfaces. *Nucleic Acids Research*, 25(23), 1997, 4748-4757.

8. M. Garzon, P.Neathery, R. Deaton, R.C. Murphy, D.R. Franceschetti, S.E. Stevens Jr., A New Metric for DNA Computing. In J.R. Koza, K.Deb, M. Dorigo, D.B. Vogel, M. Garzon, H.Iba, R.L. Riolo, Eds., Proc. *2nd Annual Genetic Programming Conference*, Stanford, CA, 1997, Morgan-Kaufmann, 472-478.

9. M. Garzon, R. Deaton, L.F. Nino, S.E. Stevens Jr., M. Wittner. Genome Encoding for DNA Computing *Proc. 3rd Genetic Programming Conference*, Madison, WI, 1998, Morgan Kaufmann, 684-690.

10. M. Garzon, C. Oehmen. Biomolecular Computation in Virtual Test Tubes. In [16], 75-83.

11. Handbook of Formal Languages. G. Rozenberg, A. Salomaa Eds., Springer Verlag, Berlin, 1997.

12. A.J. Hartemink, D.K. Gifford, J. Khodor. Automatic Constraint-Based Nucleotide Sequence Selection for DNA Computations. Proceedings of *DNA-based Computers IV*, Philadelphia. In *Biosystems* vol.52, nr.1-3, L.Kari, H.Rubin, D.H.Wood Guest Eds., 1999, 227-235.

13. H. Jürgensen, S. Konstantinidis. Codes. In [11] vol.3, 511-600.

14. L. Kari. DNA Computing: Arrival of Biological Mathematics. *The Mathematical Intelligencer*, vol.19, nr.2, Spring 1997, 9–22.

15. A. Marathe, A. Condon, R. Corn. On Combinatorial DNA Word Design. Proceedings of *DNA-based Computers V*, June 14-15, 1999, E. Winfree, D. Gifford Eds., 75-89.

16. *Pre-Proceedings of DNA-based Computers VII*, Tampa, Florida, June 10-13, 2001, N. Jonoska, N.C. Seeman Eds.

17. J.H. Reif, T.H. LaBean, M. Pirrung, V.S. Rana, B. Guo, C. Kingsford, G.S. Wickham. Experimental Construction of Very Large Scale DNA Databases with Associative Search Capability. In [16], 241-250.

18. H.J.Shyr, *Free Monoids and Languages*, Hon Min Book Company, Taichung, Taiwan, R.O.C., 1991.

DNA Manipulations in Ciliates

David M. Prescott

University of Colorado
Molecular, Cellular and Developmental Biology
Boulder, CO 80309-0347, USA

During the last several years Professor Rozenberg and I have been working closely together to try to unravel the secrets of complex DNA manipulations in ciliates. His creative and incisive analysis has given us a fresh perspective on the remarkable acrobatics that ciliates perform with their DNA gene sequences. I am pleased to contribute this paper on the structure of germline genes, which ciliates process in phenomenal ways, as an expression of my appreciation and admiration for his intelligence and energy in the quest to explain the extraordinary DNA gymnastics that the tiny ciliates perform.

Ciliates are unicellular organisms that contain two kinds of nuclei in the same cell - a micronucleus and a macronucleus (Fig. 1). This paper deals with a particular group of ciliates called hypotrichs, and most hypotrichs have two or more micronuclei and two or more macronuclei. The multiple micronuclei are genetically and structurally identical to each other, and the multiple macronuclei are genetically and structurally identical to each other; therefore, for issues presented in this paper the multiplicity of nuclei is need not concern us.

The micronucleus is a germline nucleus and is used for cell mating. It has no known function in the growth and division of the cell, and during cell proliferation its genes are silent. The macronucleus provides all the genetic information needed for cell growth and division through the transcription of its genes. The two types of nuclei are nevertheless interrelated; after mating between two cells, a copy of the micronucleus develops into a new macronucleus. As long as food organisms, usually algae, are available, the ciliates continue to proliferate. In the absence of food organisms they may undergo mating. During mating, cells adhere in pairs, forming a cytoplasmic channel between them (Fig. 2). A micronucleus in each cell undergoes meiosis, forming four haploid micronuclei (Fig. 3a and 3b). The cells exchange haploid micronuclei through the cytoplasmic channel, and an exchanged micronucleus fuses with a resident haploid micronucleus in each cell, forming a new diploid micronucleus in each cell (Fig. 3c). The new diploid micronucleus divides by mitosis without cell division (Fig. 3d), and one of the daughter diploid micronuclei develops into a new macronucleus during the next three days (Fig. 3e), a process that involves massive and intricate processing of DNA. Simultaneously, the unused micronuclei that are left and the old macronuclei are destroyed by the cell (Fig. 3d). The new macronucleus and the new micronucleus divide to reconstitute the appropriate nuclear numbers (Fig. 3f).

W. Brauer et al. (Eds.): Formal and Natural Computing, LNCS 2300, pp. 394–417, 2002.

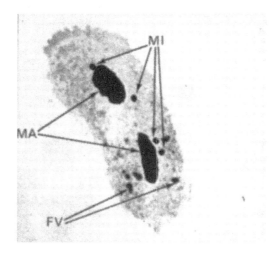

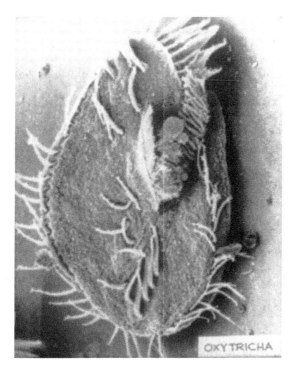

Fig. 1. (Top). A light micrograph of a hypotrichous ciliate (*Sterkiella nova*) stained to show its four micronuclei (mi) and two macronuclei (ma). FV = food vacuole. (Bottom) A scanning electron micrograph of *Sterkiella nova* showing cilia and an oral apparatus (mouth) just below its upper end. Courtesy of Gopal Murti.

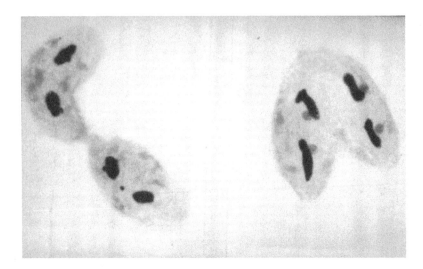

Fig. 2. Left panel: An early stage in mating in which two organisms (*Sterkiella histri-omuscorum*) are connected by a cytoplasmic channel. Right panel: A tightly joined pair of mating organisms (a later stage than the left panel), in which the two micronuclei in each cell have entered meiosis preparatory to exchanging haploid micronuclei.

During eons of evolution some ciliated protozoa have engineered bizarre and intriguing rearrangements in the DNA sequences in their micronuclear (germline) genes. These puzzling modifications disable the micronuclear genes, and they cannot contribute to the functions of the cell. However, the disabling of micronuclear genes is of no consequence because micronuclear genes have been silenced by an independent mechanism of an unknown nature. The structural modifications of germline genes are precisely reversed during conversion of a micronucleus to a new macronucleus after two cells have mated, returning the genes to functional competence as the macronucleus is formed. These reversals in the structure of micronuclear genes are achieved by the cell in a few hours through many thousands of precise and remarkable manipulations of DNA sequences. The magnitude and complexity of the DNA manipulations occurring during macronuclear development can be appreciated in the following comparison between micronuclear and the macronuclear gene structure.

1   Micronuclear and Macronuclear DNA Molecules

The micronucleus of a ciliate like *Sterkiella nova* (formerly known as *Oxytricha nova*; Foissner and Berger, 1999) contains over 100 chromosomes. Each chromosome contains a single, continuous DNA molecule that is many millions of base pairs (bp) in length (Fig. 4). Genes are encoded at irregular intervals along the

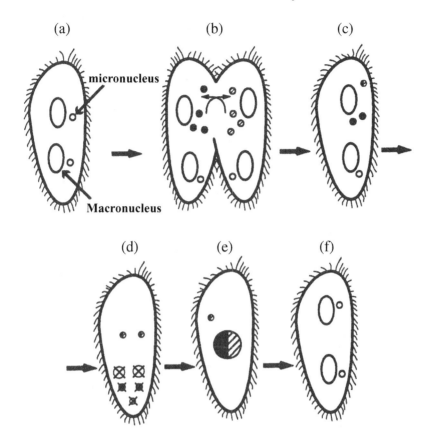

Fig. 3. The mating scheme in hypotrichs. (a) A vegetative cell prior to mating. (b) A mating pair connected by a cytoplasmic channel and about to exchange haploid micronuclei. The micronucleus at the bottom of each cell has not undergone meiosis. (c) A cell just after separation from its mating partner. A new diploid micronucleus formed by fusion of two haploid micronuclei is at the top. Two unused haploid micronuclei are in the middle, and an old diploid micronucleus is at the bottom. (d) The new diploid micronucleus has divided. The two unused haploid micronuclei, two old macronuclei and an old diploid micronucleus are being destroyed. (e) A new macronucleus has developed from one of the new, diploid micronuclei. (f) The micronucleus and new macronucleus have divided to yield two micronuclei and two macronuclei, marking completion of the mating process.

DNA (Fig. 5). The gene density in the DNA is very low; less than 5% of the DNA sequences are genes, and more than 95% of a DNA molecule forms long, nongene spacer segments between successive genes. In sharp contrast, macronuclear DNA is present as short molecules ranging from ~200 bp to 20,000 bp in length (Fig. 6),

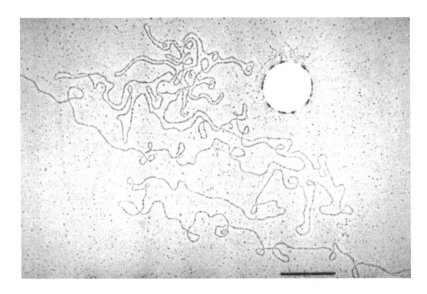

Fig. 4. Electron micrograph of a portion of a micronuclear DNA molecule from *Sterkiella nova*. Bar = 1 μm. Courtesy of Gopal Murti.

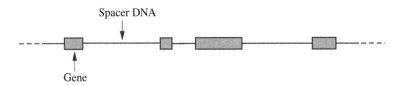

Fig. 5. The arrangement of genes and spacer DNA in micronuclear chromosomes. More than 95% of the DNA forms nongenetic spacers between genes.

and most of each molecule is taken up by a gene(s). Most macronuclear molecules contain a single gene; a few may contain two (Seegmiller et al., 1997) or possibly even three genes (Prescott et al., 2001a). From these and other studies we know that during conversion of micronuclear DNA to macronuclear DNA all the spacer DNA between genes is destroyed, leaving only gene-sized molecules. In the last stage of macronuclear development the gene-sized molecules are replicated many times to yield $\tilde{1}$,000 copies of each molecule, creating the DNA rich macronucleus. There are $\tilde{2}$5,000 different DNA molecules; thus, the mature macronucleus contains $\tilde{2}$.5 x 107 DNA molecules (in *Sterkiella nova*).

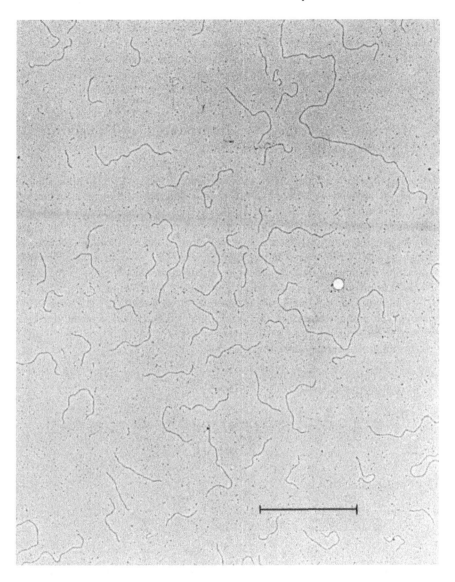

Fig. 6. Electron micrograph of macronuclear DNA molecules from *Sterkiella nova.* Bar = 1 μm. Courtesy of Gopal Murti.

We do not know how the organism identifies gene DNA for retention and non-gene DNA for destruction, but the result is an enormously streamlined macronucleus designed for economy in DNA content and for great efficiency of gene expression through RNA transcription. These events represent DNA processing of unprecedented magnitude, producing the shortest DNA molecules known in Nature - shorter than the DNA molecules in the simplest virus. As dramatic as it is, elimination of nongenetic DNA and formation of gene-sized molecules is not the most intricate event in the processing of micronuclear DNA molecules into macronuclear DNA molecules, as described in the next sections.

2   Micronuclear Genes Are Interrupted by Noncoding DNA Segments Called IESs

Genes in eukaryotic organisms commonly contain introns–noncoding segments that are transcribed as part of the full RNA transcript of the gene. Intron segments are spliced out of RNA transcripts to yield a messenger RNA molecule that can be translated into a protein. Although most micronuclear genes in hypotrichs do not contain introns, they are interrupted by multiple, noncoding segments called internal eliminated segments, or IESs, that superficially resemble introns. Figure 7 shows the structure of the micronuclear gene in the ciliate *Sterkiella histriomuscorum* encoding the protein, β telomere protein (βTP). The gene is interrupted by six IESs of various sizes. In aggregate, in all the genes in a micronuclear genome there are well over 100,000 IESs. Because of the disabling effect of IESs, transcription of micronuclear genes would produce useless RNA transcripts, but no transcription takes place.

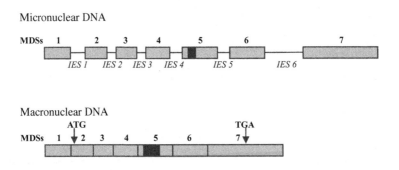

Fig. 7. The structure of the micronuclear gene encoding βTP in *Sterkiella histriomuscorum* . MDSs are blocks and IESs are lines connecting blocks. Removal of IESs and splicing of MDSs creates the macronuclear βTP gene. The ATG is the start codon marking the start of translation of the coding region, and the TGA is the stop codon. The dark block in MDS 5 is an intron. From Prescott and DuBois, 1996.

Interruption of a micronuclear gene by IESs divides the gene into segments called macronuclear destined segments, or MDSs. In the developing macronucleus the 100,000+ IESs are excised from micronuclear genes, and 100,000+ MDSs are ligated together to form a full set of functional genes, as illustrated for the βTP gene in Fig. 7. IES excision occurs before destruction of spacer DNA and release of genes from chromosomes. The organism is able in some manner to identify IESs, to cut the DNA at junctions between IESs and MDSs, and then to ligate MDSs precisely to the base pair so that mutations are not created. An important clue about how these events are accomplished is found in the nucleotide sequence in the ends of the two MDSs that flank an IES. An example is the first IES in the βTP gene in Fig. 7. MDS 1 ends with the sequence CAGTA, at its junction with IES 1. An identical sequence is present at the other end of IES 1 in the beginning of MDS 2. All IESs are flanked by such pairs of repeat nucleotide sequences in the flanking MDSs. The sequence of the repeat can be of any length from three to 20 bp and consist of any combination of A, T, C, and G. In a model of IES excision, the molecule makes a loop so that the two copies of the repeat sequence can align in parallel with each other, and an enzyme(s) cuts the DNA in both repeats. Switching and rejoining of the cut ends (recombination) excises the IES and one complete copy of the repeat sequence, and ligates the two MDSs (Fig. 8).

This model for IES excision has a major shortcoming: the repeat sequences are too short to specify MDS-IES junctions unambiguously, that is, to bring about appropriate alignment of the two copies of the repeat. The repeat sequences that flank IESs are on average four bp long; a sequence of four bp will occur by random chance once every 256 bp. Thus, the sequence of the repeat sometimes occurs one or more times within the IES itself or in the flanking MDSs upstream or downstream from the MDS-IES junctions. The organism must have available some additional information to allow it to identify the appropriate copies of the repeat sequence to be aligned, possibly using a copy of the gene from the old macronucleus to guide alignment of repeat sequence pairs as illustrated in Fig. 9. It may be that the primary role of the repeat sequence pairs is not to guide alignment, but rather to facilitate recombination between the repeats after they have become aligned through some other process such as guidance in template fashion by DNA molecules from the old macronucleus.

Whatever the mechanism of IES recognition and excision, it is a spectacular exercise in DNA processing by the cell. More than 200,000 MDS-IES junctions must be correctly identified and >100,000 MDSs must be spliced precisely to the bp, and all within a few hours, to create a functional macronuclear genome.

3   IESs Are Progressively Added to Genes during Evolution

The arrangement of MDSs and IESs in micronuclear genes observed in several different hypotrichs is shown in Fig. 10. Four genes, encoding the proteins EF1α, histone H4, telomerase, and heat shock protein 70 each contain a single IES and, therefore, two MDSs each. The other genes in Fig. 10 contain two or more IESs. The structure of the gene encoding βTP is different in three different organisms; it contains two IESs in *Stylonychia mytilus*, three in *Sterkiella nova*, and six in *Sterkiella histriomuscorum* (formerly named *Oxytricha trifallax*; Foissner and

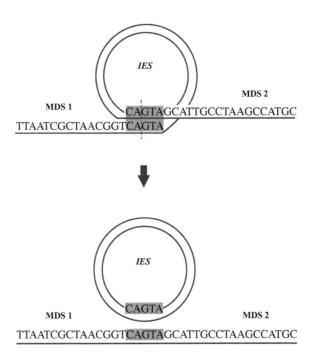

Fig. 8. A model to explain excision of an IES from a micronuclear gene during macronuclear development. The pair of repeat sequences (CAGTA) is aligned in parallel by looping out of the IES. Only nucleotides in one chain of the DNA double helix are shown. The complementary chain is shown as a line. Cutting (dashed vertical line) and switching ends between the two repeats (recombination) excises the IES and joins the two MDSs.

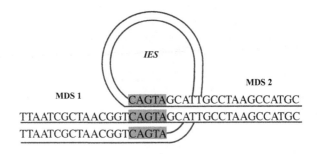

Fig. 9. A model to explain how the short repeats flanking an IES are brought into parallel alignment. A template DNA molecule from the old macronucleus, which lacks the IES, acts as a template to align the two MDSs, forcing the alignment of the repeats. Recombination between the repeats completes the process as shown in Figure 8.

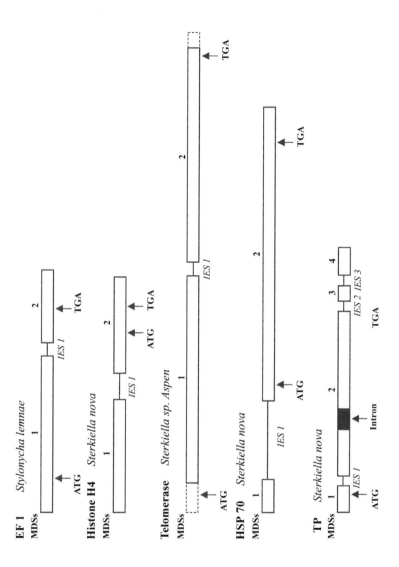

Fig. 10. (Continued) The structure of some micronuclear genes. Genes encoding proteins EF1α (Bierbaum et al., 1991), histone H4 (Kelminson, Hewitt, Kneeland, DuBois and Prescott, in preparation), telomerase (Marandi and Prescott, unpublished), and hsp70 (Lindauer and Prescott, unpublished) each contain one IES and two MDSs. The remaining six genes (three genes for βTP in three different organisms) are interrupted by multiple IESs. MDSs are blocks and the IESs are lines between the blocks. Dark blocks inside MDSs are introns.

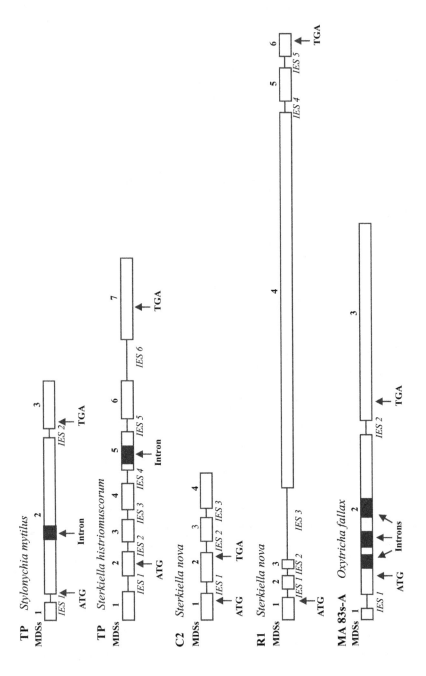

Fig. 10. (Continuation) Start (ATG) and stop (TGA) codons mark the coding region of a gene. The dotted lines for the telomerase molecule indicate regions not sequenced.

Berger, 1999). Our current hypothesis to explain the different numbers of IESs in the βTP gene is that additional IESs are inserted into a gene during evolution. Two primary hypotheses deal with the evolutionary schedule of IES insertions. The first hypothesis proposes that the βTP gene in a common ancestor of the three organisms contained no IESs, and two, three, and six IESs were inserted independently in the three organisms, respectively, during their separate evolutions. In the second hypothesis, a common ancestor of the organisms contained two IESs. During evolution of the three organisms the IES count remained at two in *Stylonychia mytilus*, one more IES was added to the βTP gene in *Sterkiella nova*, and four more added in *Sterkiella histriomuscorum*. Various combinations of these two hypotheses are also possible. However, from one organism to another none of the IESs correspond in position, length, or nucleotide sequence. For example, IES 1 interrupts the βTP gene in three different places in the three organisms: just down from the beginning of the coding region in *Sterkiella nova*, marked by the translation start codon ATG in Fig. 10, immediately before the ATG start codon of the coding region in *Stylonychia mytilus*, and farther upstream of the ATG start in *Sterkiella histriomuscorum*. Moreover, IES 1 is 10 bp, 32 bp, and 82 bp long in the three organisms, respectively, and is totally different in nucleotide sequence among the three. This might mean that IES 1 originated independently in each organism rather than in a common ancestor to the three. However, we know from other extensive evidence that an IES can change rapidly in length and sequence through mutations during evolution. This is permissible because IESs have no coding function. IESs can also migrate pro-

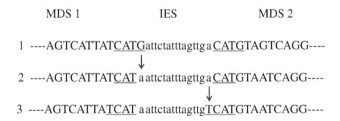

Fig. 11. Migration of an IES along a DNA molecule. The mutation (arrow) of G to a (1) (arrow) lengthens the IES by one base and shortens MDS 1 and the repeat by one base (2) (CAT). Mutation (arrow) of a to T (2) (arrow) shortens the IES by one base and lengthens MDS 2 and the repeat by one base (3) (TCAT). The nucleotides in the IES are indicated by lower case letters. Repeats are underlined.

gressively along a DNA molecule (DuBois and Prescott, 1995). Thus, IES 1 could have been inserted into the βTP gene in a common ancestor and then mutated and migrated as the three organisms evolved.

IES migration occurs by a mutational mechanism, as described in the following example. An IES and its two flanking MDSs containing the repeat sequence

CATG are shown in Fig. 11(1). A mutation of the last base of MDS 1 changes G to a, which adds the a to the beginning of the IES and shortens the repeat to CAT (Fig. 11[2]). Thus, the first MDS is shortened by one base, and the IES is correspondingly lengthened by one base. A second mutation changes the last base in the IES from a to T (Fig. 11[2]). This shortens the IES by one base, lengthens MDS 2 by one base, and lengthens the repeat to TCAT (Fig. 11[3]). Through a series of such mutations the IES can migrate many bases along the DNA. As a result the sequence of the IES progressively changes, and the sequence of the repeats changes. Also, some MDS sequence is shifted from one MDS to another, in this case from the first to the second MDS. None of these changes affect the coding sequence. When the IES is excised, the coding sequence is the same even though the flanking MDSs may have changed in size.

Thus, IES 1 in the βTP gene may have originally been inserted into an ancestor of the three species, and its position, size, and sequence changed during evolution of the three species.

In summary, although we cannot follow a particular IES in the βTP gene through the evolution of a series of organisms, we can nevertheless assert confidently that new IESs may be added in the course of evolution of an organism.

4   Scrambling of MDSs in Some Micronuclear Genes

The seven MDSs in the micronuclear βTP gene of *Sterkiella histriomuscorum* (Figs. 7 and 10) are in the orthodox order, i.e. 1-2-3-4-5-6-7. However, the MDSs in three of the 12 different micronuclear genes sequenced so far are in a nonorthodox order, i.e. they are scrambled, at least in some hypotrichs. An example is the gene encoding the actin protein. The structure of this gene in eight organisms is shown in Fig. 12. The actin I gene in *Urostyla grandis* contains two IESs, creating three MDSs, which are in the orthodox order 1-2-3, and in *Engelmanniella mobilis* three IESs create four MDSs, which are in the orthodox order, 1-2-3-4 (Hogan et al., submitted). Other evidence shows that these two organisms diverged early in evolution from the other six organisms in the order shown in Fig. 12. Divergence of *U. grandis* and *E. mobilis* left a common ancestor for the other six organisms. IESs were probably inserted into this proposed common ancestor to give a total of seven IESs (step 3 in Fig. 12). Recombination among these IESs created a scrambled arrangement of eight MDSs in the order, 3-4-5-7-2-1-6-8 (steps 4, 5, and 6 in Fig. 12). This scrambled pattern has been retained in contemporary *Stylonychia lemnae*. A salient feature of the pattern is the inversion of MDS 2 by recombination between the IESs that flank MDS 2. The basic pattern, including inversion of MDS 2, is also still quite evident in the remaining five organisms but has been elaborated by further evolution consisting of the insertion of more IESs and additional recombinations among IESs (steps 7, 8, 9, and 10 in Fig. 12), producing the gene structures shown in Fig. 12. The pattern reaches its greatest complexity in *Oxytricha sp?* (Misty), whose micronuclear actin I gene contains 11 IESs and 12 MDSs in the partially scrambled disorder, 3-4-5-6-7-9-8-10-12-2-1-11.

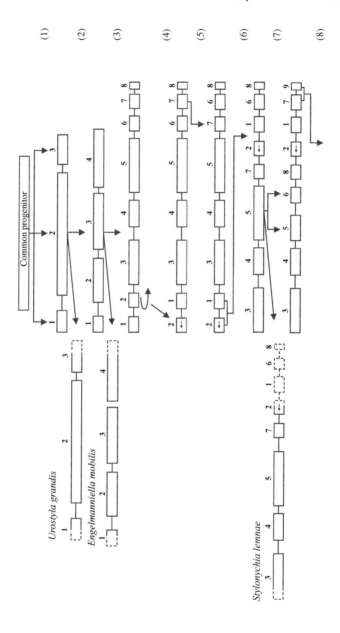

Fig. 12. (Continued) Model to explain the evolution of structure of the micronuclear actin gene in eight organisms. During evolution from *U. grandis* (top) to *O. sp*? (Misty) (bottom) IESs have been added and recombinations between IESs have scrambled MDSs. MDSs are blocks and IESs are lines between blocks. Dashed lines represent segments not sequenced.

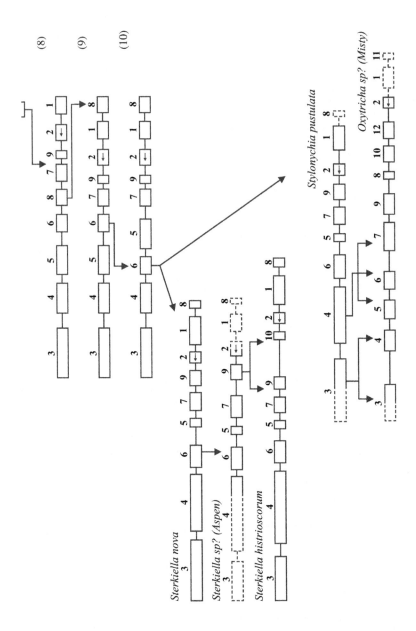

Fig. 12. (Continuation) Numbers in a vertical column on the right indicate evolutionary events: (1) insertion of two IESs, (2) insertion of a third IES, (3) insertion of four more IESs, (4)(5)(6) various recombinations among IESs progressively scramble the MDSs, including inversion of MDS 2, (7) addition of an IES, (8)(9)(10) recombination events changing scrambling patterns of MDSs. From Hogan et al. 2001, submitted.

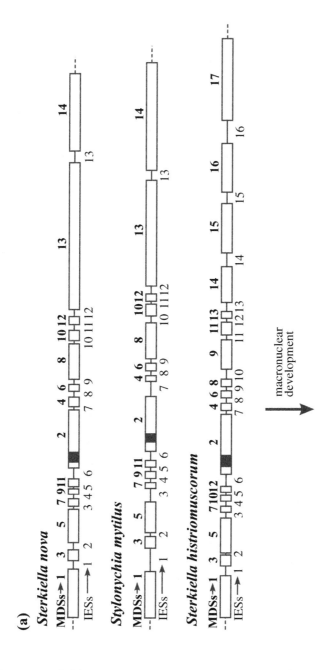

Fig. 13. (Continued) (a) The scrambled micronuclear gene encoding αTP in three organisms. MDSs are blocks. IESs are lines between blocks. Dark boxes inside MDSs are introns.

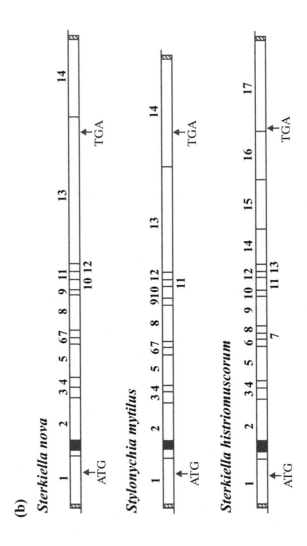

Fig. 13. (Continuation) (b) Removal of IESs and reordering of MDSs during macronuclear development yields the macronuclear molecules. ATG marks the start of the coding region and TGA marks the end. From Prescott et al., 1998.

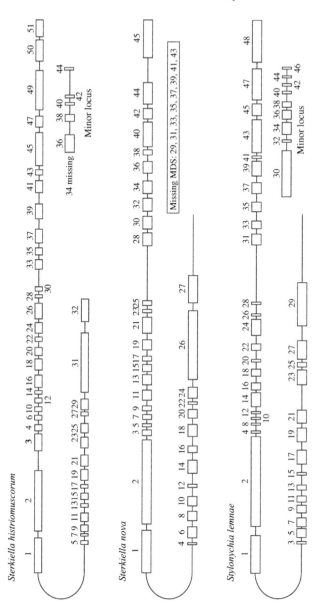

Fig. 14. The scrambled micronuclear gene encoding DNA pol α in three organisms. The gene has separated into a major and a minor locus. MDSs are blocks, and IESs are lines between blocks (*Sterkiella nova* and *Sterkiella histriomuscorum* from Hoffman and Prescott, 1997 and *Stylonychia lemnae* from Landweber et al., 2000). The molecules are drawn as hairpins because an inversion has occurred at the bend of the hairpin, i.e. the upper and lower portions in each molecule are in opposite orientations for reading the sequence of the gene.

It is clear that MDS scrambling arises by recombination among IESs, that new IESs can be added even after a gene has become scrambled, and that new scrambling events may be imposed on genes that have already undergone scrambling.

The MDSs in the actin I gene are scrambled more or less randomly. In the micronuclear gene that encodes α telomere protein (αTP), the 14 MDSs are scrambled in the mostly nonrandom, odd/even series 1-3-5-7-9-11-2-4-6-8-10-12-14 in *Sterkiella nova* and *Stylonychia mytilus* (Fig. 13). The positions, lengths, and sequences of IESs have changed significantly although, unlike in the βTP gene, it is still possible to identify corresponding IESs in the αTP gene from one organism to the other because the overall pattern of IESs and scrambled MDSs has been substantially retained. However, the MDS pattern has evolved somewhat in *Sterkiella histriomuscorum* by the insertion of three more IESs. MDS 8 of *Sterkiella nova* and *Stylonychia mytilus* has been split into MDSs 8 and 9 in *Sterkiella histriomuscorum* by insertion of an IES. This changes the numbering scheme of MDSs 9 and above in *Sterkiella histriomuscorum*, i.e. 9 becomes 10, 10 becomes 11, 11 becomes 12 and 12 becomes 13. Also, MDS 13 in

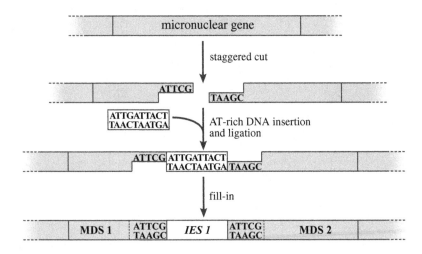

Fig. 15. A model to explain how an IES might be introduced into a micronuclear gene. A staggered cut in the micronuclear gene creates short, single-stranded overhangs. A piece of AT-rich, nongenetic DNA is inserted into the micronuclear gene. Following ligation of the inserted piece the single-stranded gaps are filled in by the cell, creating a pair of repeats. From Prescott and DuBois, 1996.

Sterkiella nova and *Stylonychia mytilus* has been split into MDSs 14, 15, 16 in *Sterkiella histriomuscorum* by insertion of two IESs. Finally, superimposed on the MDS patterns in the three organisms are changes in MDS lengths produced by migration of IESs along the DNA.

The scrambled pattern of the large gene encoding DNA polymerase α (DNA pol α) is the most complex of the three scrambled genes found so far. The overall pattern of MDSs and IESs in the DNA pol α gene is known in three organisms: *Sterkiella nova*, *Sterkiella histriomuscorum*, and *Stylonychia lemnae*. First, the DNA polymerase α gene is interrupted by many IESs throughout its $\bar{5},000$ bp: 44, 50, and 47 IESs in the three organisms, respectively (Fig. 14). Second, in all three genes approximately one-third of the MDSs at one end are inverted relative to the rest of the MDSs. Third, eight, six, and nine MDSs are present as a group elsewhere in an unknown location in the genome, referred to as a minor locus. As in the scrambled genes encoding actin I and αTP, IESs have changed completely in nucleotide sequence and changed in length, reflecting the high rate of accumulation of mutations in these noncoding segments. IESs have also migrated modestly along the DNA during evolution of the three organisms, resulting in shortening of some MDSs and lengthening of others. Finally, new IESs have been added during the evolution of the three species from a common ancestor. For example, the large MDS 2 in *Sterkiella nova* (Fig. 14) is split into MDSs 2 and 3 in *Sterkiella histriomuscorum* by a new IES that was inserted after these two organisms diverged from one another in evolution.

The discovery of IESs and of scrambling of MDSs raises a series of obvious, crucial questions. How and why were IESs inserted into genes, and how and why did MDSs become scrambled? And why did MDSs become scrambled only in some genes and not in others. IESs, which are short segments of DNA rich in A's and T's, may have been recruited from spacer DNA. Spacer DNA is similarly AT-rich and makes up $\bar{9}5\%$ of total micronuclear DNA. Insertion of IESs into genes may have occurred by recombination between spacer DNA and gene DNA. Opening up gene DNA with staggered cuts in the two nucleotide chains (Fig. 15) followed by insertion of a piece of blunt ended spacer DNA would create two single-stranded gaps in the recombined molecule. Filling in the gaps by a DNA polymerase would create a pair of repeat sequences in the gene DNA, which now have become flanking MDSs. What purpose is served by such insertion of IESs is still a mystery.

Although MDS scrambling is almost certainly the result of recombination among IESs, the significance of MDS scrambling is not understood. If recombination can occur among IESs within a gene, then it may also occur between IESs in different genes, creating combinations of MDSs recruited from different genes, a process that might facilitate the evolution of new genes. If MDS scrambling in a gene simply reflects a propensity for IESs to undergo recombination, why are only some genes scrambled? The probability for a gene to become scrambled may be a function of the number of IESs in the gene (scrambled genes generally contain more IESs than nonscrambled genes), but other unidentified influences may play a role.

Whatever its significance, MDS scrambling adds great complexity to DNA processing during macronuclear development. Like the MDSs arranged in orthodox order in nonscrambled genes, the MDSs in scrambled genes have repeat sequences at their ends that define the orthodox order. Fig. 16 is an example

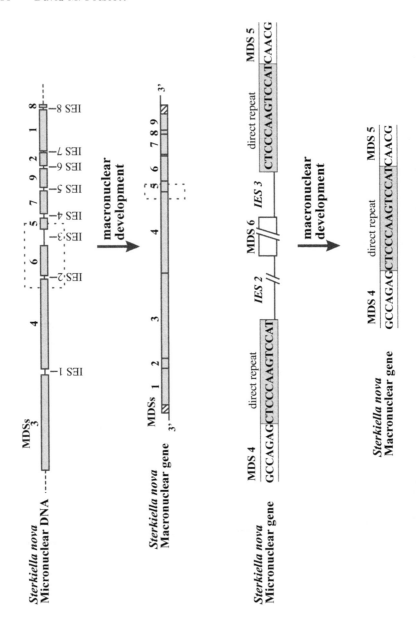

Fig. 16. Diagram of MDSs 4-6-5 in *Sterkiella nova* illustrating repeat sequence pairs for scrambled MDSs. (a) The MDS/IES structure of the micronuclear actin I gene and its resolution into the macronuclear actin I gene. The region from MDS 4 to MDS 5 and IESs 2 and 3 (enclosed by dashed lines) is shown with repeat sequences in (b). Recombination between the repeats removes IES 2–MDS 6–IES 3 and one copy of the repeat and ligates MDS 4 to MDS 5. MDSs are boxes and IESs are lines between boxes.

that shows portions of three MDSs in their scrambled arrangement in the actin I gene of *Sterkiella nova*, i.e., MDSs 4-6-5. The right end of MDS 4 contains the sequence CTCCCAAGTCCAT, which is repeated in the left end of MDS 5. Similarly, the left end of MDS 6 contains a sequence (not shown), that is repeated in the right end of MDS 5 (not shown). Thus, the MDSs appear to contain in their ends addresses in the form of nucleotide sequences that can direct the MDSs to assemble in an orthodox pattern. The delivery of MDSs to their orthodox connections requires that the DNA molecule fold upon itself so as to align the two members of each repeat pair. This is illustrated for the actin I gene of *Sterkiella nova* in Fig. 17. The folding pattern is made more complex

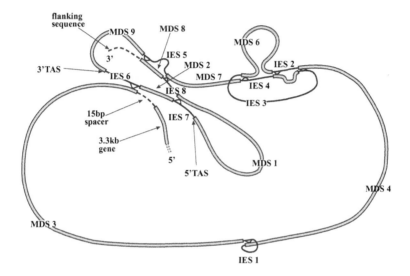

Fig. 17. Model of folding of the micronuclear actin I gene of *Sterkiella nova* to align the eight pairs of repeats during macronuclear development. Recombinations (at ends of the MDSs) between the repeats in a pair eliminate all IESs and join the nine MDSs in the orthodox order, including inversion of MDS 2. 5'TAS and 3'TAS = 5' and 3' telomere addition sites. From Prescott and Greslin, 1992.

because MDS 2 is inverted as a result of recombination during evolution between the two IESs that flank MDS 2. Thus, in the pair of repeats shared by MDSs 1 and 2 the repeats are inverted relative to one another. Similarly, the pair of repeats shared by MDSs 2 and 3 are inverted. In the folded molecule for the actin gene, recombination between the two members of a repeat pair for all eight pairs of repeats eliminates all eight IESs, eliminates one copy of the repeat in each repeat pair, and ligates the nine MDSs in the orthodox order, including reinverting MDS 2. Folding of the actin I molecule may require guidance by a macronuclear copy of the molecule acting as a template, as illustrated in Fig. 9.

In another paper (Prescott, et al., 2001b) we have presented a set of three molecular operations and a formal reasoning system that explain and account for IES excision, unscrambling of MDSs, and MDS ligation in the assembly of macronuclear genes from micronuclear genes. The operations and reasoning system account for all known events of gene assembly in hypotrichous ciliates. The DNA processing by these organisms that reverses evolutionary modifications of micronuclear genes, eliminates spacer DNA, and creates gene-sized molecules is an extraordinary instance of DNA manipulations within an organism. The events demonstrate complex capabilities, including one of the basic data structures of computer science known as linked lists, that evolved in hypotrichs many millions of years ago. Professor Rozenberg is fascinated by the DNA magic that ciliates display. His excitement and enthusiasm are inspirational, and we may yet discover the role of these DNA feats in the evolution and function of the tiny hypotrichs.

Acknowledgements

This work is supported by NIGMS research grant #R01 GM 56161 and NSF research grant MCB-9974680 to D.M. Prescott.

References

[BDK]   Bierbaum, P., Dönhoff, T. and Klein, A. 1991. Macronuclear and Micronuclear Configurations of a Gene Encoding the Protein Synthesis Elongation Factor EF1α in *Stylonychia lemnae*. Mol. Microbiol. **5**: 1567–1575.

[DP]   DuBois, M.L. and Prescott, D.M. 1995. Scrambling of the Actin I Gene in Two *Oxytricha* Species. Proc. Natl. Acad. Sci. USA **92**: 3888–3892.

[FB]   Foissner, W. and Berger, H. 1999. Identification and Ontogenesis of the *nomen nudum* Ypotrichs (Protozoa: Ciliophora) *Oxytricha nova* (= *Sterkiella nova* sp. n.) and *O. trifallax* (= *S. histriomuscorum*). Acta Protozool. **38**: 215–248.

[HP]   Hoffman, D.C., and Prescott, D.M. 1997. Evolution of Internal Eliminated Segments and Scrambling in the Micronuclear Gene Encoding DNA Polymerase α in Two *Oxytricha* Species. Nucl. Acids Res. **25**: 1883–1889.

[HHOP]   Hogan, D., Hewitt, E., Orr, K. and Prescott, D.M. 2001. Evolution of IESs and Scrambling of the Actin I Gene in Hypotrichous Ciliates. Proc. Natl. Acad. Sci. USA, submitted.

[LKC]   Landweber, L.F., Kuo, T-C. and Curtis, E.A. 2000. Evolution and Assembly of an Extremely Scrambled Gene. Proc. Natl. Acad. Sci. USA **97**: 3298–3303.

[PPP]   Prescott, D.M., Prescott, J.D. and Prescott, R.M. 2001a. Coding Properties of Macronuclear DNA Molecules in *Sterkiella nova* (*Oxytricha nova*). Gene, submitted.

[PER]   Prescott, D.M., Ehrenfeucht, A. and Rozenberg, G. 2001b. Molecular Operations for DNA Processing in Hypotrichous Ciliates. Eur. J. Protistol. **37**, in press.

[PDP]   Prescott, J.D., DuBois M.L. and Prescott, D.M. 1998. Evolution of the Scrambled Germline Gene Encoding α-telomere Binding Protein in Three Hypotrichous Ciliates. Chromosoma **107**: 293–303.

[PD]   Prescott, D.M. and DuBois, M.L. 1996. Internal Eliminated Segments (IESs) of Oxytrichidae. J. Euk. Microbiol. **43**: 432–441.

[PG]   Prescott, D.M. and Greslin, A.F. 1992. Scrambled Actin I Gene in the Micronucleus of *Oxytricha nova*. Dev. Genet. **13**: 66–74.

[SWH]   Seegmiller, A., Williams, K.R. and Herrick, G. 1997. Two Two-Gene Macronuclear Chromosomes of the Hypotrichous Ciliates *Oxytricha fallax* and *O. trifallax* Generated by Alternative Processing of the 81 Locus. Dev. Genet. **20**: 348–357.

A *Magic Pot*: Self-assembly Computation Revisited

Takashi Yokomori[1], Yasubumi Sakakibara[2], and Satoshi Kobayashi[3]

[1] Department of Mathematics, School of Education
Waseda University, 1-6-1 Nishi-waseda, Shinjuku-ku,
Tokyo 169-8050, Japan
yokomori@mn.waseda.ac.jp
[2] Department of Information Sciences, Tokyo Denki University,
Hiki-gun, Saitama 350-0394, Japan
yasu@j.dendai.ac.jp
[3] Department of Computer Science and Information Mathematics,
University of Electro-Communications, 1-5-1 Chofugaoka, Chofu,
Tokyo 182, Japan
satoshi@cs.uec.ac.jp

Abstract. Molecular computing is a novel computing paradigm recently emerged from groundbreaking wet lab experiments by Adleman in 1994. His experimental work marks a potential capability and feasibility of "one pot" computing with molecules for solving hard problems of practical size.

This paper concerns a molecular computing paradigm based on "self-assembly" and "screening mechanism". After a brief getting back to and reviewing Adleman's original work, we propose a new molecular implementation method based on *length-only encoding*, which leads us to much simpler molecular implementation techniques to solve graph problems.

With two examples, we demonstrate the effectiveness of the molecular implementation method for *one pot computing based on self-assembly*: one is Nondeterministic Finite Automaton Pot and the other is Hamiltonian Path Problem Pot.

1 One-Pot Computation as a Magic Hat

It was three and a half years ago (as of the time of writing this article) when the first author of this paper was deeply moved by beautiful magic performed by *Bolgani*, a famous computer-science-minded great magician, at Ginza in Tokyo January 1998.

We all (two families) visited Ginza, one of the most thriving and bustling downtowns in Tokyo, to visit tourist spots including, in particular, the place called *Magicland* (a small magic goods shop ... of course, reflecting Bolgani's request). Finally our strolling around Ginza ended up with a trip to the big department store to refresh ourselves with some food and shopping. As soon as we arrived at the side entrance of the department store, all of a sudden,

W. Brauer et al. (Eds.): Formal and Natural Computing, LNCS 2300, pp. 418–429, 2002.

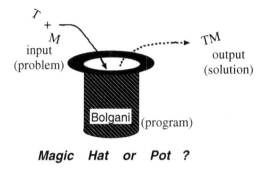

Fig. 1. A *Magic Pot* computation based on self-assembly

Bolgani started shouting *something* to both me (the first author) and his wife. In fact, he urged and compelled both of us, saying, "Oh! You both, stand here! Why don't we take a photo of two of you together !" This urgent request from Bolgani sounded very strange and even queer to everyone standing there, because anybody could easily recongnize that we are at a place (outside floor of the side entrance) that *never* deserves the taking of a picture in any sense, even though the department store was one of the best known in Japan.

However, since there was no firm reason for us to reject Bolgani's request, we simply followed his instructions. Bolgani guided his wife and me to a spot near a big pillar, and he took a photo of us anyway with a "name plate" of the department store as a background. Then, he proudly pointed to the name plate and smiled at us. It was not until the moment we looked back at the name plate behind us that we could realize what had happened to him and us: The name plate illuminated by Bolgani's magic was gently staring at me (*Takashi*) and his wife (*Maya*), fascinating all of us, saying "Welcome to *Takashimaya!* "

In fact, this "Takashimaya magic" stimulated the first author and led him to produce a couple of papers on molecular computing models based on the *self-assembly principle*.

2   Self-assembly Computation Paradigms

In the theory of molecular computing, a variety of computation models have been proposed and investigated, and among others the models of computation based on *self-assembly* are well recognized to be of great importance in that they can provide one of the most basic frameworks for molecular computing paradigms. In fact, Adleman's ground-breaking experimental work ([1]) that solved a small instance of the Hamiltonian Path Problem (HPP) is a typical example of molecular computation based on the self-assembly principle. Winfree ([13]) has proposed his *DNA tiling models* and showed with a great success that the self-assembly of a certain type of high dimensional structural molecules achieves Turing universal computability, that is, generates all recursively enumerable languages. Further

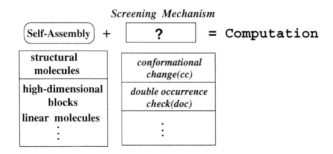

Fig. 2. Computation models based on self-assembly

investigation along this line by Winfree, Eng and Rozenberg ([14]) refines their theory and shows that linear self-assembly models of string tiles can provide alternative characterizations of subfamilies of ET0L languages. Thus, one may claim that *computation = self-assembly + structural molecules*. On the other hand, Yokomori ([17]) proposes a self-assembly computation model called *YAC* and discusses a new computation schema: *computation = self-assembly + conformational change*, where due to the use of comformational change, the structural complexity of molecules used is much simpler than that of Winfree's models in [13]. It is shown that *YAC* has a power of Turing universal computability.

Thus, generally one may also claim the following schema that

(Computation)=(Self-Assembly)+(Screening Mechanisim)

where "self-assembly" is due to hybridization of either uncoded or coded molecular components, while "screening mechanism" is regulated by either natural or artificial constraint. Related discussion on conformation-driven computation can be found in several references [3,4,9].

We observe that there are trade-off relations on computational powers between the structural complexity of self-assembly components and the screening mechanism, while there also seems to be a clear distinction in computation power between uncoded and coded components within the framework of *self-assembly computation paradigms*.

Figure 2 illustrates the overall outlook of computation models based on self-assembly.

2.1 Back to Adleman's Paradigm

In order to learn the lessons from the self-assemble computation paradigm, let us make a brief revisit to Adleman's original work from 1994.

Adleman gave a biochemical algorithm for solving an instance of the HPP where (1) a problem instance of size n was encoded with a set of *linear coded* molecules, and (2) the extraction operations were used $O(n)$ times. Thus, Adleman's algorithm can be formulated into the schema where component structures are sophisticatedly *encoded* into *linear* molecules.

The table below summarizes some of the models based on self-assembly computation paradigm.

Models	Component Structures	Coded/ Uncoded	Screening Mechanism
Adleman([1])	linear	coded	$O(n)$ times
Winfree([13])	high-dimensional	coded	constant time
Yokomori([17])	two-dimensional	coded	constant time
Sakamoto et al.([11])	hairpin	coded	constant time
Sakakibara & Kobayashi([10])	two-dimensional	coded	constant time
this paper	*linear*	*uncoded*	*constant time*

From these observations, a general schema of "one pot" self-assembly computation model is outlined as follows:

1. design a finite set of basic units for assembly computation (one may take this finite set as a program),
2. put all those basic units with sufficiently high concentration into one pot, to create a random pool of a single pot (that is, leave the pot for a certain time period, resulting in producing all possible assembly of basic units),
3. (if necessary) perform screening mechanism to extract only necessary (or unnecessary) assembly of basic units,
4. detect whether or not there is an assembly with desired constraints, and
5. answer *yes* if there is, and *no* otherwise.

2.2   FA Pot – Simplest Implementation of NFA

A finite automaton (FA) is one of the most popular concepts in theoretical computer science, and hence, it is of great use to establish a simple implementation method for realizing an FA in the formulation of molecular computing. Therefore, we consider the problem of how simply one can construct a molecular FA using DNAs in the framework of *self-assembly computation*.

A nondeterministic FA (NFA) is a construct $M = (Q, \Sigma, \delta, p_0, F)$, where Q is a set of states, Σ is the input alphabet, $p_0(\in Q)$ is the initial state, $F(\subseteq Q)$ is a set of final states, and δ is defined as a function from $Q \times \Sigma$ to 2^Q (the power set of Q). If δ is restricted as a function from $Q \times \Sigma$ to Q, then M is said to be *deterministic* and is denoted by DFA. Two NFAs are equivalent iff they exactly accept the same regular language (i.e., set of strings) over the input alphabet.

In the sequel, we focus on ε-free regular langauges, that is, regular languages not containing the empty string ε. Therefore, in any NFA M we consider here, the initial state p_0 is not a final state in F of M.

The following result is easily shown, but is of crucial importance to attain our ends here.

Proposition 1 *Given any DFA, there effectively exists an equivalent NFA M such that (1) M has the unique final state q_f, and (2) there is neither a transition into the initial state q_0 nor a transition from the final state q_f.*

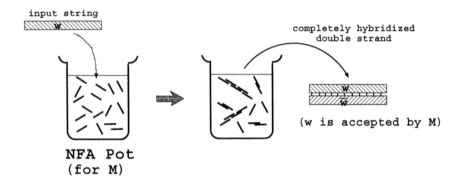

Fig. 3. Finite automaton pot

Thus, in what follows *we may assume that a finite automaton M is an NFA satisfying the properties (1) and (2) in the above.*

Now, we want to present a molecular implementation for NFA that behaves like a "*magic pot* " illustrated in Figure 3. From the viewpoint of self-assembly computation paradigm, such a one-pot implementation of NFA is desirable and one may call it *NFA Pot*.

The molecular implementation of NFA Pot that will be given below has the following advantages:

1. In order to encode with DNAs each state transition of M, no essential design technique of encoding is required. Only the *length* of each DNA sequence involved is important.
2. Self-assembly due to hybridization of complementary DNAs is the only mechanism of carring out the computation process.
3. An input w is accepted by M if and only if a completely hybridized double strand $[c(w)/\overline{c(w)}]$ is detected from the pot, where $c(w)$ is a DNA sequence representing w and the "overline" version denotes its complementary sequence.

Without loss of generality, we may assume that the state set Q of M is represented as $\{0, 1, 2, \cdots, m\}$ (for some $m \geq 1$) and in particular, "0" and "m" denote the initial and the final states, respectively.

Using an example, we show that given an NFA M how one can implement an NFA Pot for M.

Let us consider an NFA M (in fact, M is a DFA) in Figure 4, where an input string $w = abba$ is a string to be accepted by $M=(\ \{0, 1, 2, 3\}, \{a, b\}, \delta, 0, \{3\})$, where $\delta(0, a) = 1$, $\delta(1, b) = 2$, $\delta(2, b) = 1$, $\delta(1, a) = 3$. (Note that M satisfies the properties (1) and (2) in Proposition 1 and that the state 3 is the unique final state.)

In order to encode each symbol a_k from $\Sigma = \{a_1, \cdots, a_n\}$, we associate it with an oligo GGG$\cdots$ G of length k. Further, each transition $\delta(i, a_k) = j$ is encoded as follows:

$$5'\text{-}\overbrace{AAA\cdots A}^{m-i}\overbrace{GGG\cdots G}^{k}\overbrace{AAA\cdots A}^{j}\text{-}3'.$$

The idea is the following. Two consecutive valid transitions $\delta(i, a_k) = j$ and $\delta(j, a_{k'}) = j'$ are implemented by concatenating two corresponding encoded molecules, that is,

$$5'\text{-}\overbrace{AAA\cdots A}^{m-i}\overbrace{GGG\cdots G}^{k}\overbrace{AAA\cdots A}^{j}\text{-}3',$$

and

$$5'\text{-}\overbrace{AAA\cdots A}^{m-j}\overbrace{GGG\cdots G}^{k'}\overbrace{AAA\cdots A}^{j'}\text{-}3'$$

together make

$$5'\text{-}\overbrace{AAA\cdots A}^{m-i}\overbrace{GGG\cdots G}^{k}\overbrace{AAA\cdots A}^{m}\overbrace{GGG\cdots G}^{k'}\overbrace{AAA\cdots A}^{j'}\text{-}3'.$$

Thus, an oligo $\overbrace{AAA\cdots A}^{m}$ plays a role of "joint" between two transitions and it guarantees for the two to be valid in M.

In order to get the result of the recognition task of an input w, one application of "**Detect**" operation is used to the pot, that is, the input w is accepted by M iff the operation *detects* a completely hybridized double strand $[c(w)/\overline{c(w)}]$, where $c(w)$ is a DNA sequence encoding w and the "overline" version denotes its complementary sequence. Specifically, for an input string $w = a_{i_1} \cdots a_{i_n}$, $c(w)$ is encoded as:

$$3'\text{-}\overbrace{TTT\cdots T}^{m}\overbrace{CCC\cdots C}^{i_1}\overbrace{TTT\cdots T}^{m}\overbrace{CCC\cdots C}^{i_2}\cdots\overbrace{TTT\cdots T}^{m}\overbrace{CCC\cdots C}^{i_n}\overbrace{TTT\cdots T}^{m}\text{-}5'.$$

Figure 4 also illustrates the self-assembly process of computing $w = abba$ in the NFA Pot for M (although M is actually a DFA).

2.3   HPP Pot – Simpler Implementation for HPP

We now propose a simpler method for molecular implementation to solve the Hamiltonian Path Problem (HPP) than any others ever proposed. Since this implementation is also based on the "self-assembly in a one-pot computation" paradigm, we may call it *HPP Pot*.

The HPP Pot we will show below has several advantages that are common with and similar to the implementation of NFA Pot given before. That is,

1. In order to encode each directed edge of a problem instance of HPP, no essential design technique of encoding is required. Only the *length* of each DNA sequence involved is important.
2. Self-assembly due to hybridization of complementary DNAs is the only mechanism of carring out the computation process.
3. An instance of HPP has a solution path p if and only if a completely hybridized double strand $[c(p)/\overline{c(p)}]$ of a certain fixed length is detected from the pot, where $c(p)$ is a DNA sequence representing p and the "overline" version denotes its complementary sequence.

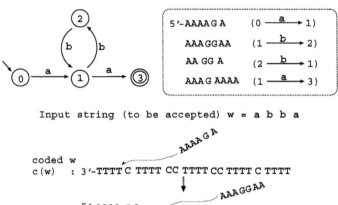

Fig. 4. FA and its DNA implementation

We may assume that the node set of G is represented as $\Sigma = \{0, 1, 2, \cdots, m\}$ (for some $m \geq 1$), where "0" and "m" denote the start and the goal nodes, respectively.

Now define a set of positive integers $\Gamma = \{p_1, \cdots, p_m\}$ (where $1 \leq \forall i \leq m-1$, $p_i < p_{i+1}$) as follows:

$$\begin{cases} p_1 = 1 \\ p_k = ka_{k-1} + 1 - \sum_{i=1}^{k-1} p_i \quad (2 \leq \forall k \leq m). \end{cases}$$

Lemma 1. *The set Γ defined above satisfies the property that for each $p_{i_j} \in \Gamma$, $p_1 + \cdots + p_m = p_{i_1} + \cdots + p_{i_m}$ implies that $i_1 = 1, \cdots, i_m = m$.*

Proof. (By induction on m.) It obviously holds for $m = 1$. Suppose that the claim holds true for $m = k$, that is, $p_1 + \cdots + p_k = p_{i_1} + \cdots + p_{i_k}$ implies that $i_1 = 1, \cdots, i_k = k$. Consider the case when $m = k + 1$: $p_1 + \cdots + p_{k+1} = p_{i_1} + \cdots + p_{i_{k+1}}$. Suppose that $p_{k+1} \neq p_{i_{k+1}}$. Since for all $1 \leq j \leq k+1$, $p_{i_j} \leq p_k$, we have:

$$p_{i_1} + \cdots + p_{i_{k+1}} \leq (k+1)p_k$$
$$= p_{k+1} + (p_k + \cdots + p_1) - 1$$
$$< p_1 + \cdots + p_{k+1}(\text{ a contradiction }).$$

Thus, $p_{k+1} = p_{i_{k+1}}$ and $i_{k+1} = k+1$ are obtained. Further, it holds that $p_1 + \cdots + p_k = p_{i_1} + \cdots + p_{i_k}$. By induction hypothesis, we finally obtain that $i_1 = 1, \cdots, i_k = k$ and $i_{k+1} = k+1$. $\qquad\square$

Now, for a given $\Gamma = \{p_1, \cdots, p_m\}$, let K be a constant such that $K > p_m$. In order to proceed our argument, we need the following lemma.

Lemma 2. *For $p_{j_i} \in \Gamma (1 \leq i \leq d)$,*

$$\sum_{i=1}^{d} p_{j_i} + Km(d+1) = \sum_{i=1}^{m} p_i + Km(m+1)$$

implies that $d = m$.

Proof. Suppose that $d > m$. Then,

$$\sum_{i=1}^{d} p_{j_i} + Km(d+1) > Km(m+2)$$
$$= Km + Km(m+1)$$
$$> \sum_{i=1}^{m} p_i + Km(m+1).$$

Similarly, supposing $d < m$ we have that

$$\sum_{i=1}^{d} p_{j_i} + Km(d+1) \leq p_m \times (m-1) + Km(d+1)$$
$$< Km + Kmm$$
$$= Km(m+1)$$
$$< \sum_{i=1}^{m} p_i + Km(m+1).$$

$\qquad\square$

Now, for each i from $\Sigma - \{0\}$, we associate it with an oligo GGG$\cdots$ G of length p_i, where p_i is an element from the set $\Gamma = \{p_1, \cdots, p_m\}$ introduced above.

Using the Adleman's graph G as an example, we show how to implement an HPP Pot for G. That is, let us consider the graph given in Figure 5, where $\Sigma = \{0, \cdots, 6\}$ and each edge is labeled with the number of its destination node. Thus, for example, since there are three directed edges with the destination node

1: $0 \rightarrow 1$, $3 \rightarrow 1$ and $4 \rightarrow 1$ in the graph, each of those edges is labeled with "1". (Note that 0 is the starting node, and 6 is the goal node.)

Suppose that $\Gamma = \{p_1, p_2, \cdots, p_m\}$ and a constant K have already been fixed. Note that m is the goal node.

Now, an edge $i \rightarrow^j j$ (where $j \neq m$) is encoded as follows:

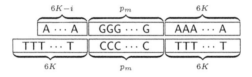

For an edge $i \rightarrow^m m$, we encode

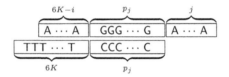

The idea is the following. A path of length 2 consisting of two edges $i \rightarrow^j j$ and $j \rightarrow^h h$ is implemented by concatenating two corresponding encoded molecules, that is,

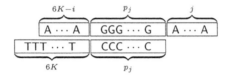

and

together make

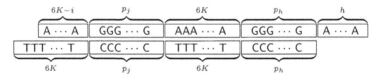

Thus, a double strand

plays a role of "joint" between two edges and it guarantees for the two to be valid in G.

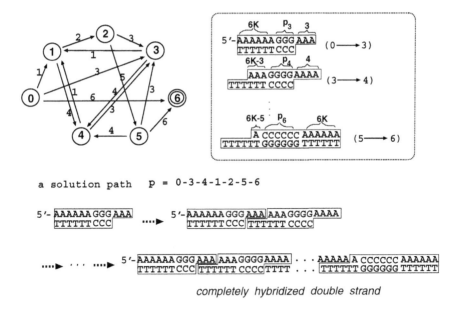

a solution path   p = 0-3-4-1-2-5-6

Fig. 5. Simple implementation of HPP pot

Figure 5 illustrates the self-assembly process of searching for a solution path p in the graph G, where $m = 6$ and $\Gamma = \{p_1, \cdots, p_6\}$.

In order to finish the computation process, all we have to proceed is to detect whether or not there exists a complete double strand of length $L = p_1 + \cdots + p_m + Km(m + 1)$.

To see the validity of the procedure above, we have only check that

1. if there is a solution path p in G, then the corresponding complete double strand $c(p)$ of length L is formed and detected,
2. if there are two complete double strands $c(p)$ and $c(p')$ of length L detected, then by Lemma 2, both must contain the same number of m blocks representing elements p_i from Γ. Further, from Lemma 1, each of those m elements in $c(p)$ exactly corresponds to that in $c(p')$ and vice versa. Thus, both $c(p)$ and $c(p')$ represent correct solution paths in G.

3 Discussion

As we have seen in the previous sections, the implementation methods we have discussed have a common distinguished feature in molecular encoding, that is, *no essential design technique is necessary* in that only the length of DNA sequences involved in the encoding is important.

It should be remarked that the aspect of this non-coding implementation could apply to a large class of problems that are formulated in terms of graph structures. (In fact, one would easily list up a numerous number of problems associated with graphs.)

One can also propose a general schema for solving graph problems in the framework of self-assembly molecular computing paradigm where the *length-only-encoding* technique may be readily applied. In fact, some of the graph-related optimization problems such as the Traveling Salesman Problems can be handled in the schema mentioned above.

Many subjects still remain open to be explored in the direction suggested in this paper. First, it is of clear interest to investigate the manner of molecular implementation of *PDA Pot* for Pushdown Automaton, in the same framework as NFA Pot. Besides self-assembly and Detect operation, how complicated molecular structures or screening mechanisim are necessary to construct a PDA Pot?

In the framework of self-assembly molecular computing, it is of great use to explore the computing capability of the self-assembly schema with "double occurrence checking (doc)" as a screening mechanism, because many of the important NP-complete problems can be formulated into this computing schema. We have shown by constructing HPP Pot that at the sacrifice of *non-linear* length increase of strands, "doc" function can be replaced with length-only encoding technique. It is, however, strongly encouraged to develop more practical methods for dealing with doc function.

References

1. L. Adleman: Molecular Computation of Solutions to Combinatorial Problems. *Science* **266**, pp.1021–1024, 1994.
2. L. Adleman: On Constructing a Molecular Computer. *DNA Based Computers* (Selected Papers from Proc. of DIMACS Workshop on DNA Based Computers'95), DIMACS Series in Discrete Mathematics and Theoretical Computer Science, **27**, pp.1–21, 1996.
3. M. Conrad: On Design Principles for a Molecular Computer. *CACM*, Vol.28, No.5, pp.464–480, 1985.
4. M. Conrad: Molecular Computing Paradigms. *IEEE Computer*, Vol.25, No.11, pp.6–9, 1992.
5. N. Morimoto, M. Arita and A. Suyama: Stepwise Generation of Hamiltonian Path with Molecules. In *Biocomputing and Emergent Computation*, pp.184–192, 1997.
6. Gh. Paun, G. Rozenberg and A. Salomaa: *DNA Computing: New Computing Paradigms*, Springer-Verlag, 1998.
7. J.H. Reif: Parallel Molecular Computation: Models and Simulations. *Proc. of Seventh Annual ACM Symposium on Parallel Algorithms and Architectures*(SPAA'95), pp.213–223, 1995.
8. K. Saitou: Self-assembling Automata: A Model of Conformational Self-assembly, *Proc. of Pacific Symposium on Biocomputing'98* (Eds, R.B. Altman, et al.), pp.609–620, 1998.
9. K. Saitou and M.J. Jakiela: On Classes of One-Dimensional Self-assembling Automata, *Complex Systems*, **10 (6)**, pp.391–416, 1996.

10. Y. Sakakibara and S. Kobayashi: Sticker Systems with Complex Structures, *Soft Computing*, **5** (**2**), pp.114-120, 2001.

11. K. Sakamoto, H. Gouzu, K. Komiya, D. Kiga, S. Yokoyama, T. Yokomori, and M. Hagiya: Molecular Computation by DNA Hairpin Formation, *Science* **288**, pp.1223–1226, (19 May 2000).

12. E. Winfree, X. Yang and N.C. Seeman: Universal Computation via Self-assembly of DNA: Some Theory and Experiments. *DNA Based Computers II* (Papers from Proc. of 2nd DIMACS Workshop on DNA Based Computers, 1996), DIMACS Series in Discrete Mathematics and Theoretical Computer Science, **44**, pp.191–213, 1999.

13. E. Winfree: *Algorithmic Self-assembly of DNA*. Ph.D Dissertation, submitted to Californial Institute of Technology, May 1998.

14. E. Winfree, T. Eng, and G. Rozenberg: String Tile Models for DNA Computing by Self-assembly, In *Proc. of the 6th International Meeting on DNA Based Computers*, Leiden University, June 13-17, pp.65–84, 2000.

15. E. Winfree and P.W.K. Rothemund: The Program-size Complexity of Self-assembly Squares, In *Proc. of 32nd Annual ACM Symposium on Theory of Computing*, pp.459–468, 2000.

16. D.H. Wood: A DNA Computing Algorithm for Directed Hamiltonian Paths. *Genetic Programming 1998*: *Proc. of 3rd Annual Conference* (J.R. Koza, et al. Eds.), Morgan Kaufmann, pp.731–734, 1998.

17. T. Yokomori: YAC: Yet Another Computation Model of Self-assembly, *Preliminary Proc. of 5th DIMACS Workshop on DNA Based Computers*, pp.153–167, 1999.

18. T. Yokomori: Computation = Self-assembly + Conformational Change: Toward New Computing Paradigm, *Preproceedings of DLT 99* (Invited Lecture), Aachen, pp.21–30, 1999.

Author Index

Lecture Notes in Computer Science

For information about Vols. 1–2189
please contact your bookseller or Springer-Verlag